Anthony Downey
EDITOR'S PREFACE

I first experienced Illingworth's immersive video and sound installation *The Watch Man* in 2007. This relatively short film introduced me to a number of abiding themes in her practice, not least how it engages with the relationship of time and trauma to personal, collective, and historical memory. I was struck then, as I am now by Illingworth's *Lesions in the Landscape* (2015) and *Topologies of Air* (2021), with how the immersive context of *The Watch Man* (2007) ensured that the narrative trajectory of one man's trauma gave way to a sensory experience that relates to broader communal and geopolitical realities. It is with these concepts in mind, alongside others, that this volume presents visual and textual material relating to *Lesions in the Landscape* and *Topologies of Air*, while examining how they represent the relationships that exist between trauma, landscapes, and, increasingly, air- and outer-space. How, these projects ask, do we visualize and engage with the political, social, cultural, and historical realities of communities and environments being subjected to unremitting patterns of resource extraction and aerial surveillance?

Upon first previewing *Lesions in the Landscape* and *Topologies of Air* (in 2016 and 2020, respectively), it occurred to me that Illingworth's practice—drawing as it does upon scientific, geographic, cognitive, and mnemotechnic fields of expertise—is clearly involved in effecting its own epistemological reference points. Investigating how we can productively elucidate legislative and feminist discourses through creative and collaborative practices in the arts, the research methods employed by Illingworth in these works bring to the fore imminent concerns with processes of amnesia, cultural erasure, technological automation, hyper-surveillance, military threat, environmental collapse, and the profound transformations in how we understand air- and outer-space today. Reflected in the variety of contributors to this volume, these enquiries were developed in conjunction with ongoing engagements with and discussions about Illingworth's practice that involved a collective effort on behalf of numerous colleagues. Furthering the communal and communicative intent of the work and the volume presented here, these contributions are, in turn, based on a variety of inter- and multidisciplinary research that draws upon theoretical, political, neuropsychological, legal, and ecological discourses. To this end, Illingworth's expanded, practice-based research methodology, grounded as it is in the moving image, sound, digital technologies, and archive materials, not only produces its own forms of knowledge but also propagates a community of practice from which to discuss and debate the import of such processes.

This ambition is evident in *Amnesia Museum* (2012–ongoing), an evolving work that, according to the artist, is a "living archive of forgetting." Drawing together film, photographs, drawings, objects, artifacts, and documents to map both landscapes of forgetting and the future of memory in a (post)digital age, *Amnesia Museum* also holds extensive recordings of the Memory and Amnesia Forums that Illingworth established in 2006. These took the shape of conferences, roundtable discussions, debates, performance, and seminars and underwrote the formal development of works such as *Lesions in the Landscape*. More recently, Illingworth's establishment of the

Airspace Tribunal, with legal expert Nick Grief, has produced a framework to examine—through a series of open public hearings—the case for and against a proposed human right that would afford greater protection from the expanding threats of aerial hyper-surveillance, weapons systems, pollution, and environmental crises. Instrumental in the development of *Topologies of Air*, the Airspace Tribunal is a pioneering project that draws upon a wide range of expertise and lived experience. This returns me to my first impressions of Illingworth's work and its capacity to think both beyond and, crucially, from *within* definitions of memory, time, and space and how they relate to the realities of lived experience.

This volume began as an idea in late 2019 before the global event of a pandemic overtook us, and I am, on a personal level, profoundly grateful to all those involved in its development. We have published acknowledgments and thanks elsewhere to those who have worked with us on this volume and for those who have supported the historical development of *Lesions in the Landscape* and *Topologies of Air*. However, it would be remiss of me not to add my own appreciation of Elisa Adami's tireless and energetic support and Wayne Daly's inspiring approach to the overall design. This volume would not be what it is now without their unfailing assistance, steadfast participation, and timely observations. I would also like to personally thank Caroline Schneider for continued support with this and other projects, Tatjana Günthner for ensuring the volume came together as a viable project, and Sarah Stephenson for her immeasurable attention to detail. A special word of appreciation is likewise due to Gaëtane Verna and all the staff at The Power Plant in Toronto for their indispensable encouragement and unreserved enthusiasm for this volume and the accompanying show.

We have likewise thanked the many authors who contributed to this volume elsewhere, but, again on a personal note, I am indebted to each of them for their involvement and how, during the last two years or so of a global pandemic, they managed to generously find the time and wherewithal to produce engaging and inspiring texts. I have learned a significant amount from their work, and this learning process will no doubt continue into the future as *Topologies of Air* and the Airspace Tribunal evolve further. We have, in accordance with some of our authors' wishes, maintained their preferred variations of place names, spellings, and other phrases, alongside the original punctuation included in legal documents quoted here.

Finally, I want to express my heartfelt thanks to Shona, who, apart from producing extraordinarily capacious, timely, and engrossing work that informs the basis of this project (and no doubt more projects to come), has been a most gracious interlocutor during an extended gestation period that saw the world as we knew it change dramatically. I would also like to thank my old friend Mark Sealy for having introduced Shona and myself—in an all-too-distant, it now seems, time and place—and for fostering our many conversations over the years. I trust and hope they will continue as these projects progress and the discussions develop in the years to come.

SHONA ILLINGWORTH

TOPOLOGIES OF AIR

Edited by Anthony Downey

The Power Plant
Sternberg Press

For Alina and Sonny

Gaëtane Verna

FOREWORD

While Shona Illingworth is known for her works in film, which often take the form of major immersive sensorial installations, her practice encompasses a variety of media, including photography, sound, drawing, and painting. Based on interdisciplinary research and often in dialogue with collaborators who explore a wide array of subjects—from neuropsychology and memory studies to human rights law and environmental degradation—her socially engaged practice brings a much-needed critical voice to contemporary art.

In her first major solo exhibition in Canada and in North America, The Power Plant Contemporary Art Gallery is presenting an exhibition that brings together two film-based installations alongside a new body of work, shedding light on Illingworth's long-term commitment to exploring the lingering effects of modernity, particularly the impact of modern governance, climate change, and contemporary warfare on the body, memory, and environment. More specifically, this exhibition examines the complex ways in which we occupy space today. Through her investigation of science, politics, and the human condition, Illingworth raises critical questions about the territorialization of both earth and sky while examining gaps in our collective consciousness. She probes how current modes of governance, surveillance, and weaponization are invading our interior worlds and transcending the borders of nation-states to create new frameworks of dominance and colonization.

Her inquiry reveals emerging power relations and knowledge structures, as well as visible and invisible architectures that determine how we inhabit the world, contemplating their potentially catastrophic impact on our coexistence and survival on this planet. The global relevance of Illingworth's work is self-evident, but it is especially resonant here in Canada, where urgent, too-often-silenced questions of state appropriation of indigenous land, pollution of waterways, and the imperialism of hydro-electric complexes, fossil fuel companies, as well as the many industries of extraction and mass agriculture complexes plague the country's flora and fauna. They also affect the livelihood and traditional way of life of the many Indigenous communities, leaving long-lasting ecological damage to the air above our heads, unbeknownst to the majority of the country's citizens.

Illingworth's exhibition at The Power Plant comprises three zones. The first is dedicated to the immersive video and sound installation *Lesions in the Landscape* (2015), in which the artist interrogates the manifold individual and societal impacts of memory loss and cultural erasure. By revealing striking parallels between the devastating effects of amnesia on a woman, Claire, and the 1930 evacuation of the inhabitants of the archipelago of St Kilda in the North Atlantic, which brought a sudden end to four thousand years of continuous habitation, the work considers the profound implications of memory loss on identity and space. In both cases, the past is constructed by others—friends and family for Claire, and for St Kilda, almost the entire historical record is written by visitors to the islands, layering myth upon myth, excluding the inhabitants from telling their narratives about that landscape—resulting in the marginalization of the subjects. This loss of agency reflected in an inability to form narratives of the past consequently impacts the capacity to envision the future. Illingworth examines the politics and hierarchies of knowledge production, particularly the insidious methods of cultural censorship exercised by dominant powers. In addition to the installation, this work is accompanied by artworks and objects that form part of Illingworth's *Amnesia Museum* (2012–ongoing), commenting on intersections between human memory, archaeology, militarization, and the ways in which the past might be accessed, commemorated, or erased.

The second and third zones feature interrelated bodies of work. *Topologies of Air* (2021), a new video installation surveying the impact of accelerating political and technological change on the composition and nature of airspace, examines how humans have radically transformed the sky since the advent of modernity, turning it into a complex and multilayered space. In addition to addressing environmental degradation, the project challenges perceptions of airspace as free and limitless, and stresses the need to safeguard our right to live without military and psychological menace from above. The work also demonstrates how previous utopian visions have been displaced by the realities of contemporary economic disparities and climate change.

Through this exhibition, visitors will discover that *Topologies of Air* is connected to *Lesions in the Landscape* in various ways. Illingworth studies the spatial and temporal dimensions of the atmosphere in relation to memory and forgetting, particularly the question of the dynamic construction of memory and its role in imagining the future, as well as the simultaneous influence of forgetting. This is informed by research the artist conducted while creating *Lesions in the Landscape*, but is expanded further, or upward, in *Topologies of Air*. Additionally, working with multiple voices and diverse perspectives has been central to her practice for many years. Early ideas for *Topologies of Air* emerged from her film *Balnakiel* (2009), which focused on the area where she grew up—a remote part of the Highlands of Scotland, and the edge of one of NATO's largest live bombing ranges. These ideas, including the impact of warfare on the environment, are also worked through *Lesions in the Landscape*. Moreover, experientially, both works are approached as installations: sound palpably seeps through the display zone, with a dynamic tonal range that changes the sense, atmosphere, and density of the space, and is aligned to moments when distinct color shifts occur in the films. This works particularly well at The Power Plant, where the pieces inhabit their spaces and create a seamless, all-encompassing experience.

Topologies of Air is informed by extensive travels to afflicted sites around the world and a series of staged international Airspace Tribunal hearings, during which leading experts and community members discuss the future of airspace with recordings forming the drafting history of a new proposed human right. The third zone in the exhibition elaborates on *Topologies of Air* and the Airspace Tribunal in a constellation of new works commissioned by The Power Plant. These probe the accelerating transformations in airspace, outer space, and the planet's atmosphere across a wide range of disciplines, expertise, and lived experiences. These works document Illingworth's understanding of the history of airspace, and the intricate drawings look at intersecting phenomena, such as technology, militarization, artificial intelligence, surveillance, and outer space.

In short, the exhibition underlines Illingworth's interest in probing the realities of how we create, inhabit, and tell narratives about the spaces around us, whether on the ground that we have traditionally traversed or in the sky above, increasingly congested with an ever-accelerating race to control its potentials. The challenging questions she raises through her work have to do with not only how we will live together in years to come but also, indeed, our ability to even exist as a species in this world. She is not looking into some esoteric or otherworldly phenomena—instead, she is pointing out what is right there in front of us, the conditions in which we are all implicated, and yet to which we remain blissfully, and potentially devastatingly, oblivious. The work is both urgent and necessary, and it brilliantly marries Illingworth's mesmerizing aesthetics with some of the most pressing issues of our time.

We were honored at The Power Plant, in partnership with the Master of Visual Studies program at the John H. Daniels Faculty of Architecture, Landscape, and Design, University of Toronto, to have organized the Toronto hearing of the Airspace Tribunal. Like previous hearings, held in cities such as London, Sydney, and subsequently Berlin, the aim was to examine the impact of accelerating geopolitical, technological, and environmental change on the composition, nature, and use of airspace, considering the case for and against a proposed new human right to protect the freedom to live without physical or psychological threats from above. The Toronto hearing was composed of three sessions, and we are truly grateful for the thought-provoking contributions by: Shona Illingworth, Nick Grief, Derek Gregory, Gbenga Oduntan, Andrew Hoskins, Jairus Grove, Jack Penashue, Gabriele Schwab, Anthony Downey, Abrar Mechmechia, and Renata Salecl. I learned so much by chairing these sessions and interacting with these brilliant minds. I cannot wait to see the final outcome of these hearings, and I am thrilled that the artist is integrating highlights from the Toronto hearings in her video installation as well.

I am thankful for Amin Alsaden, our (2019–21) Nancy McCain & Bill Morneau Curatorial Fellow, who curated Illingworth's exhibition at The Power Plant with much care and attention and invested two years of research and careful elaboration of this project in close dialogue with Illingworth. I would also like to acknowledge the dedicated teams at The Power Plant who have helped in making this complex exhibition a reality. We are deeply grateful to Presenting Sponsor, the TD Ready Commitment, and to International Arts Partner, Nordic Bridges, for their generous support of this exhibition and publication. Various individuals and organizations have supported our institution by recognizing the critical importance of the work produced by the artists we engage and have helped share their voices with diverse audiences in Toronto and beyond. The Power Plant also receives significant support from its Board of Directors, the Canada Council for the Arts, the Ontario Arts Council, the Toronto Arts Council, and Harbourfront Centre.

We would also be remiss not to mention the many supporters of Illingworth's work featured at The Power Plant. For supporting *Lesions in the Landscape*, we thank: The Wellcome Trust; FACT; Taigh Chearsabhagh Museum and Arts Centre; Southwark Park Galleries; UNSW Galleries; National Trust for Scotland; and the University of Kent. Illingworth's collaborators on this project included: Claire, Martin A. Conway, and Catherine Loveday. We also thank the supporters of *Topologies of Air*: The Wapping Project, which commissioned *Topologies of Air*; the British Council UK-GULF Award; Bahrain National Museum; Sharjah Art Foundation; Centre for Peace, Hiroshima University; Arts Council England, and the many people that have individually contributed to the work. For supporting the Airspace Tribunal, we thank: Doughty Street Chambers; the Big Anxiety Festival; Ethics Centre, Sydney; Master of Visual Studies program at the Daniels Faculty, University of Toronto; European Center for Constitutional and Human Rights; University of Kent; Counsel to the Tribunal Kirsty Brimelow QC in London, Toronto, and Berlin; Andrew Byrnes in Sydney, and all of the speakers. And to Nick Grief, who collaborates with Illingworth on the Airspace Tribunal, which they established in 2018. I would like to convey, on behalf of the artist, my deep gratitude to everyone mentioned above for their trust and eagerness to share her important work with us, and with the world.

My sincere thanks go to the writers, whose insightful contributions have not only enriched this publication but also elaborated on various aspects of Illingworth's practice, pointing to the expanded field activated by her work. These include: Caterina Albano, Amin Alsaden, Jill Bennett, Giuliana Bruno, Martin A. Conway, Conor Gearty, Derek Gregory, Nick Grief, Andrew Hoskins, Catherine Loveday, William Merrin, Issie MacPhail, Renata Salecl, Gabriele Schwab, and, of course, the book's resourceful editor Anthony Downey, managing editor Elisa Adami, and graphic designer Wayne Daly. My conversation with the artist explored the very personal genesis of her artistic practice, her longstanding interest in the effect of global geopolitics, the complexities of life in seemingly poetic rural areas of the world that are also too often plagued by military complexes, the effect on local populations and their quality of life, and, in the end, the human element that is at the core of all her preoccupations.

My last profound thanks and admiration must go to Shona Illingworth, for her generosity of spirit, for the meaningful dialogue she establishes with so many different voices, and for the strength of her work—all of which show a deep commitment to the important issues she tackles as well as to the diverse audiences who engage with her brilliant human investigations. Her work and ethos and empathy toward her fellow humans reflect our mission and our values at The Power Plant and manifest something I have always believed: art is where we have critical conversations, confront uncomfortable truths, and advocate for a better, shared future.

Gaëtane Verna
Director and Artistic Director
The Power Plant Contemporary Art Gallery

Anthony Downey
INTRODUCTION

"Everyone has the right to life, liberty and security of person."
—Article 3, Universal Declaration of Human Rights, 1948[1]

"Every human being has the inherent right to life. This right shall be protected by law. No one shall be arbitrarily deprived of his life."
—Article 6, International Covenant on Civil and Political Rights (ICCPR), 1966[2]

"We kill people based on metadata."
—General Michael Hayden (former director of the NSA and the CIA), *New York Review*, 2014[3]

I

From the opening shots of *Topologies of Air* (2021), Shona Illingworth's three-screen video and sound installation, we are presented with a restricted view of the sky. Broadly associated with expansiveness, if not freedom, this distilled vista suggests an overdetermined environment that is subject to competing interests—be they national, military-industrial, or economic—that often remain impenetrable to observers. This is a vision of a claustrophobic firmament, a partitioned dome of airspace that is endlessly quartered through the interventions of all-consuming, mercenary systems of power and control. Under these conditions, and to ensure that national, military-industrial, and commercial interests are preserved, the apparent immateriality of airspace needs to be rendered both material and calculable. Fought over, allocated, and reserved, the substance of air must be not only quantifiable but also an instrumental element in the production of data, the maintenance of hegemony, and the projection of power.

The systems that calculate the substance of air are increasingly autonomous apparatuses, as in the case of drone technologies and Lethal Autonomous Weapons (LAWs). Through satellite surveillance systems, their command is evident in the effect they have on the communities that are subject to their disciplinary practices. The unprecedented development and application of aerial surveillance technologies and LAWs, aided by advances in Artificial Intelligence (AI), effectively constitute an evolving regime of power and domination that further establishes the realities of neocolonial forms of subjugation. This process not only amplifies already existing disparities in the application of disciplinary forms of power—based on the extraction and repurposing of data—but renders entire communities susceptible to the invariably devastating, if not catastrophic, impact of an unchecked military-industrial takeover of extraterrestrial space. Whereas occupation was once largely achieved through actual invasion, it is now realized through the application of advanced surveillance systems and drone-led infractions of international law.

All of which leaves us with a pressing question: How do we effectively understand the real-world applications and implications of these air-bound technologies in an age where we appear to be increasingly devolving our responsibility for the decisions that determine the difference between life and death?[4] Furthermore, how do we understand the colonization of airspace and outer space in the context of the diverse

1 The Universal Declaration of Human Rights was proclaimed by the United Nations General Assembly in Paris on December 10, 1948 (General Assembly resolution 217 A).

2 This was adopted and opened for signature, ratification, and accession by General Assembly resolution 2200A (XXI) of December 16, 1966, for entry into force March 23, 1976, in accordance with Article 49.

3 Quoted in David Cole, "We Kill People Based on Metadata," *New York Review*, May 10, 2014, https://www.nybooks.com/daily/2014/05/10/we-kill-people-based-metadata/.

4 A recent United Nations Security Council Report, published on March 8, 2021, observed that a Turkish-made Kargu-2 drone may have acted autonomously in selecting, targeting, and possibly killing militia fighters in Libya's civil war. If this is proven to be the case, it would be the first acknowledged use of a weapons system with AI capability operating autonomously to find, attack, and kill humans. See "Final Report of the Panel of Experts on Libya Established Pursuant to Security Council Resolution 1973 (2011)," March 8, 2021, https://documents-dds-ny.un.org/doc/UNDOC/GEN/N21/037/72/PDF/N2103772.pdf?OpenElement. For a fuller discussion of semi- and fully autonomous lethal weapons, see Paul Scharre, *Army of None: Autonomous Weapons and the Future of War* (New York: W. W. Norton and Company, 2019).

cosmologies and cultural histories that shape our relationship to the sky, not to mention the existential threats of climate change, catastrophic loss of biodiversity, and extractive capitalism? It is toward these complex entanglements that Illingworth directs her practice, nowhere more so than in the consideration of how creative, interdisciplinary platforms can expand and support the development of a new legal argument—effectively, a proposal for a new human right—that critically engages with the accelerating military, chemical, territorial, ecological, and psychological transformations of airspace and outer space.[5]

In foregrounding the escalating threat of actual physical harm for individuals and communities who are subject to satellite surveillance and LAWs, *Topologies of Air* is supported by extended forms of research, the input of legal experts, and a wide range of specialists in subjects including trauma and memory studies. This project, in sum, forms the basis for not only articulating a response to the many questions raised above but also a platform for ensuring future research—based on both lived experience and expert testimony—into the multiple concerns that such interventions raise.

II

Across the three screens of *Topologies of Air*, which produce a series of contrapuntal effects amidst the images and commentary, a plurality of voices speaks of the vast toxic dust storms caused by war, devastating ecological degradation, the aftermath of nuclear bombing, the annihilation of chemical warfare, the deployment of drone swarms, the territorialization of the electromagnetic spectrum, the expansion of hostile surveillance, and the global governance issues of imminent, but yet-to-be realized, geo-engineering projects. These are interwoven with references to early fantasies about the liberatory context of flight and the diverse cultural understandings of the sky as a pluriversal, if not ominous, space. Once a source of imaginative projection and wonder, the sky is scrutinized in *Topologies of Air* in terms of how it is rapidly transforming into a source of ontological insecurity and perpetual threat that pervades all aspects of planetary life and the traditional narratives that were once ascribed to its expanse.

Given the hypothetical inscrutability of these aerial-bound systems, *Topologies of Air* proposes a "blueprint" of sorts for detailing what is at stake in the application of advanced technologies to airspace and outer space. Insofar as Illingworth originally employed such methods to map historical land-rights struggles (in the Scottish Highlands), forced migration, weather patterns, commercial wind farms, and the first transatlantic flight of an Unmanned Aerial Vehicle (a journey that began on Bell Island in Newfoundland and finished on Benbecula in the Outer Hebrides in 1998), the formal concept of a "blueprint" emerged as an idea in 2012 and subsequently determined, in part, the initial development stages of *Topologies of Air*.[6] The diagrammatic concentration of multiple contingencies in "Blueprints" (2012–ongoing) promotes an accessible overview of how a complex matrix of extraterrestrial devices structures the intersections of day-to-day terrestrial operations. Through surveying airspace as an apparatus, a framing device within which military, industrial, commercial, and other proprietary interests coalesce, we can see how aerial surveillance regulates the movement of people on the ground, including migratory patterns and troop movements. To observe as much is to further underline the predictive functioning of aerial surveillance: it seeks to not only document but also anticipate (if not produce) future realities.

5 For a discussion of how autonomous systems of surveillance expansion necessitate new interdisciplinary means to address their complexity, see Tom Holert, "Sensorship: The Seen Unseen of Drone Warfare," in *Image Operations: Visual Media and Political Conflict*, ed. Jens Eder and Charlotte Klonk (Manchester: Manchester University Press, 2016), 101–17, specifically 101–2. See also Roger Stahl, "What the Drone Saw: The Cultural Optics of the Unmanned War," *Australian Journal of International Affairs* 67, no. 5 (2013): 659–74.

6 The project was first conceived, in full, as *Topologies of Air/Ruith na Gaoithe* (the latter title being the Gaelic translation of the work in question) during a residency that the artist undertook, over the summer of 2012, at Taigh Chearsabhagh Museum and Art Centre in the Outer Hebrides of Scotland. The formal three-screen video and sound installation that now comprises the project was in planning since 2016 (commissioned by The Wapping Project in September 2017).

Focused on the opacity of military-industrial interests and the operative logic of surveillance and other aerial technologies, *Topologies of Air* is indelibly informed by the international Airspace Tribunal, which was established by Illingworth and Nick Grief in 2018.[7] A pioneering research project investigating the potential of a new human right to address accelerating threats from airspace and outer space, the Airspace Tribunal hearings brought together contributors with a wide range of expertise and lived experience to consider the case for and against the recognition of a new human right proposed by Illingworth and Grief. This human right would protect a person's freedom to live without physical or psychological threat from above.[8] If airspace is essentially an area-based concept where states exercise juridical control, in relation to both aviation and defense, we need to account for—as Illingworth and Grief have argued—the complex, diverse ways in which the sky is used, impacted upon, and exploited. Crucially, we need to examine how the sky is valued, understood, and experienced across different cultures now and, as we move forward with a new human right, in the future.[9]

Emphasizing how military technologies are imbricated within present-day and future developments in airpower, the over-arching imperative here is to consider the degree to which emerging technologies evoke, if not promote, forms of radical forgetting—or active forgetting—to legitimize their functioning. Through increasing levels of abstraction, to what extent do these technologies distance us from the realities of trauma, injury, despoliation, and death? It is with such points in mind that *Topologies of Air* and the Airspace Tribunal enquire into whether the moment of visualizing and formally articulating—through public hearings—the impact of air-bound technologies can not only reconceptualize the military-industrial-corporate entanglements of airspace, outer space, and environment but also, in so doing, hold them to account?

Drawing upon innovative interactions between art practices, across the fields of the moving image, sound, digital technologies, archive materials, and interdisciplinary dialogues, both *Topologies of Air* and the Airspace Tribunal consider human rights as a "living instrument."[10] As technologies evolve, so too does their threat, and human rights discourse needs to actively anticipate the future of such threats. When the legal debates surrounding the establishment of Article 3 of the Universal Declaration of Human Rights (1948) and Article 6 of the International Covenant on Civil and Political Rights (1966) were being formulated, they most likely did not foresee, to paraphrase General Michael Hayden's utterance in 2014, that the US military would one day kill people based on "metadata." To address these historical lacunae and the imminence of aerial threat, the proposed new human right that the Airspace Tribunal hearings are considering would be formulated and adopted through international and domestic political processes with, crucially, the active involvement of diverse expertise and the lived experience of those subjected to threat from above.

We need, Illingworth and Grief further propose, to not only advocate for and instantiate a new human right to address these transformations of airspace and outer space, but to also determine how airborne threat—manifest in the hazards of nuclear power, exposure to climate change, and lethal aerial weapons—evolved out of multi-domain warfare policies in global military strategies. Throughout these hearings, this spectrum of threat is understood and discussed—from within, as noted, actual lived experiences and diverse knowledge systems—in a process that challenges the traditional state-centric view of how international law is created. To these

7 The Airspace Tribunal was established by Illingworth and Nick Grief, a specialist in public international law and human rights law, in 2018. To date, there have been hearings in London (2018), Sydney (2019), and Toronto (2020), and a recent one took place in June 2021 in partnership with the European Center for Constitutional and Human Rights (ECCHR), Berlin—the latter being an independent, nonprofit, nongovernmental organization with the aim of enforcing human rights through legal means. In 2022, a hearing will take place in partnership with the AM Qattan Foundation in Ramallah and, in conjunction with evidence gathering and interviews with survivors of conflict, bombing, and chemical warfare, a further "people's tribunal" will take place in Hiroshima in 2022. All hearings to date have been recorded and transcribed to form the drafting history of the proposed right that is under consideration. See http://airspacetribunal.org.

8 For a full discussion of its evolution, see Nick Grief, "The Airspace Tribunal and the Case for a New Human Right to Protect the Freedom to Live Without Physical or Psychological Threat from Above," *Journal of Digital War* 1 (2020): 58–64. For fuller details of the process and legislative efficacy of a "people's tribunal," see Andrew Byrnes and Gabrielle Simm, eds., *Peoples' Tribunals and International Law* (Cambridge, UK: Cambridge University Press, 2016).

9 See Nick Grief and Shona Illingworth, "We Need a New Human Right to Protect Our Freedom to Live without Threat from the Skies," The Conversation, October 15, 2018, https://theconversation.com/we-need-a-new-human-right-to-protect-our-freedom-to-live-without-threat-from-the-skies-104495.

ends, *Topologies of Air* and the Airspace Tribunal jointly inquire into how qualitative (or creative) practices and epistemologies, alongside the quantitative (data-led) methods of evidence gathering, could expand upon, if not redefine, the measures needed to address the existential threat posed by air-bound technologies.

This ambition, if we frame it *avant la lettre* as a form of judgment, is, likewise, a monitory warning: we have entered into a new and potentially ruinous era of technological automation, military menace, environmental collapse, and routines of digital rationalization that augurs nothing less than an existential crisis in how we understand the very nature of our existence. Do the affordances of the technologies under debate here, we might want to add, place them beyond the purview and oversight of political and ethical considerations regarding the human right to life and, indeed, what "life" means in a post-digital age? We could rephrase this into another related question: What forms of *being* are brought forth—and, inevitably, disavowed, denied, and destroyed—when the act of "perceiving" and defining life is devolved to the utilitarian and autonomous functioning of air-bound surveillance systems?

III

The study of trauma, in its incipient and manifest forms, and questions of agency remain central here, as we will see throughout this volume. In *Lesions in the Landscape* (2015), an earlier work that draws attention to mnemo-technologies, airspace, and amnesia, Illingworth grounded multifarious debates in the non-virtual and all-too-real landscape of St Kilda, an isolated archipelago situated forty miles west-northwest of the Outer Hebrides of Scotland in the North Atlantic Ocean. Examining the shockwaves of individual and societal amnesia, as they register on the cultural, historical, and geopolitical construction of landscape and place, *Lesions in the Landscape* explores the complex interaction between memory and forgetting. Foregrounding how aesthetic, neuropsychological, and historical discourses relate to the dynamics of spatial politics, this project details how the process of cultural erasure "dis-locates" our capacity to imagine the future. The investigative process that propels this work began with a survey of the depopulated islands of St Kilda and the experience of Claire, a woman living with amnesia. Claire's incapacity to imagine the future due to her inability to access her past, as *Lesions in the Landscape* stresses, embodies the phenomenon of a lost connection. The discombobulation of time effectively evokes a series of parallels between Claire's experience of amnesia and the historical lesions in the physical and cultural landscape of St Kilda.

The tension throughout *Lesions in the Landscape* between the calculation of space and environment is closely associated with martial endeavors, specifically the militarization of airspace in the Outer Hebrides. Operating within, to quote Illingworth, an "affective ecology of ideas and perceptions, and emotional, conceptual, and critical registers," *Lesions in the Landscape* strives to impart a sense of the phenomenology of amnesia and the actual experience of aerial-bound technology and the mnemo-technics of forgetting. This is, in part, a reflection of Illingworth's familiarity with growing up in the Balnakeil Craft Village, which is situated on the edge of a major live bombing range, one mile west of the village of Durness in the Scottish Highlands.[11] Composed of regimented concrete buildings constructed in the mid-1950s for a Ministry of Defense early warning station (which was never fully commissioned and eventually became semi-derelict), this landscape is a historical index of military-industrial interests.

10 The term "living instrument" has long been used to describe human rights treaties such as the European Convention on Human Rights. It was used by Conor Gearty in his representation to the Airspace Tribunal hearing at Doughty Street, London, in 2018. It has since been utilized by Illingworth to describe the performative element of a human right drawn from the lived experiences of those subjected to threat from above.

11 In the context of the historical precedents to the colonization of airspace, it is important to observe here that the colonial project was, in part, perfected through the Highland Clearances in Scotland in the 1700s and 1800s. For an extended discussion of the impact of this on air-bound cartographic practices and technologies, see Caren Kaplan, *Aerial Aftermaths: Wartime from Above* (Durham, NC: Duke University Press, 2018), 34–67.

For Illingworth, who graphically describes the experience of the sonic rupture of low-flying fighter jets and thousand-pound live bombs exploding off-shore (in conjunction with how these eruptions reverberate through bodies and buildings alike), living in such an environment provided an all too intimate understanding of the spatiotemporal context of militarization and the soundscape it produces. There was also, she has remarked, a pervading sense that such armaments were going to be deployed elsewhere, their practice auguring future death and injury. To observe as much is to recall the predictive functioning of these technologies: the martial impetus toward conflict is a proleptic impulse insofar as it collapses chronology and potentially defines the future—in which death will be administered from the sky above—as having, if not already happened, then always about to happen.

IV

The methodologies employed throughout Illingworth's practice actively promote a connection between qualitative, aesthetic forms of inquiry (visual and aural analysis) and quantitative, material, and evidentiary investigation.[12] These interdisciplinary practices prompt us to think from *within* and *through* technological discourses and apparatuses rather than merely reflect upon them. To suggest as much is to return to one of our foundational questions: How do we envisage the real-world applications and implications of aerial-bound technologies in an age where we have devolved responsibility for, and our responsiveness to, their devastating repercussions? How, in short, can we deploy creative practices and their interdisciplinary processes to critically address the fatal global interlocking of surveillance technologies, territorial plotting, imperialist expansionism, environmental degradation, the military debasement of environments and airspace, and the lethal threat of drone warfare? To fully answer these questions, we need to highlight how technologies of erasure and legibility are consistently allied to (neo)imperial ambitions, which not only detail the present materiality of the everyday but also occupy future realities.

The operational future of these systems is largely reliant upon the legislative, political, ethical, cultural, and technical frameworks that are put in place to effect their usage and deployment. In respect of aerial surveillance and drone technologies, for example, it is notable that the short-term, often brutal interests of nation-states vying for increasingly scarce resources invariably take precedence. And yet, despite our waning capacity to control their end results, there still remains the means to determine their design and legislate for their usage. To be clear: if legislation is to keep abreast of the technologies that now control, often autonomously, the realm of airspace, then we need to expand upon how we effectively, rather than theoretically, engage the operative logic of such systems

It is with these and other concerns in mind that the following volume has been organized through a series of extended critical engagements with both *Lesions in the Landscape* and *Topologies of Air*, and how these projects provoke and promote the questions and debates that need to be had in respect of the deliberations and anxieties raised above. The initial section focuses on *Lesions in the Landscape*, and the associated *Amnesia Museum*, the latter being an expanding collection of artworks and objects that examine the dynamics of forgetting. Following an extended interview with Illingworth, subsequent essays consider questions around cultural erasure, trauma, memory, and forgetting, and how they relate to the development of later works such as *Topologies of Air*. In particular, contributors to this section

12 For a fuller discussion of how contemporary digital methodologies in the visual arts relate to qualitative and quantitative research methods, see Anthony Downey, "'Where Is the Knowledge We Have Lost in Information': Speculative Research and Digital Methodologies," in *Institution as Praxis: New Curatorial Directions for Collaborative Research*, ed. Bill Balaskas and Carolina Rito (Berlin: Sternberg Press, 2020), 246–49.

concentrate on how we creatively rearticulate these debates around concepts such as embodiment and affect, ontological (in)security, concepts such as "atmosphere," and the formulation of a practical aesthetics. Taking its cue from the Airspace Tribunal, the penultimate section of this volume explores the productive relationship between *Topologies of Air* and the public hearings that have been convened to date; in particular, how they examine, albeit through a variety of different means, the need for a new human right that offers protection from aerial threat. The final contributions amplify many of the issues raised in Illingworth's work as they relate to the weaponization of airspace, the trauma associated with the state of being hyper-vigilant, information-based methods of on- and off-line totalitarianism, ecological catastrophe, drone warfare, and how the deployment of algorithms in autonomous surveillance systems furthers the colonial ambition to discipline subjects and extract (data) resources.

Can, finally, the process of developing and instituting a new human right, supported through creative practices, debate, and legal discourse, contribute to the decolonization of airspace and outer space? If we have indeed devolved responsibility, consciously or otherwise, for decisions related to the realities of life and death and the future of our planet, is this, we need to ask, a politically, ethically, socially, and historically sustainable stratagem? And if so, is it sustainable only by virtue of the fact that it temporarily (rather than indefinitely) releases us from addressing the trauma and destruction associated with the operative logic of air-bound technologies? To the degree that the opacity and remoteness of the technologies under consideration enable, if not encourage, our active forgetting and self-serving denials of accountability, if not liability, then who do we hold to account for the destruction of people, communities, and environments? It is these questions, alongside others, that this volume pursues and offers, in part at least, a means to develop creative resistance to the post-digital, neocolonial reconfiguration of what it means to exist under present-day and future threats from the sky above.

Anthony Downey is Professor of Visual Culture in the Middle East and North Africa at Birmingham City University. He sits on the editorial boards of *Third Text*, *Journal of Digital War*, and *Memory, Mind and Media*, and is the series editor for *Research/Practice* (Sternberg Press, 2019–ongoing). Recent publications include *Heba Y. Amin: The General's Stork* (2020); *Michael Rakowitz: I'm good at love, I'm good at hate, it's in between I freeze* (2019); *Critique in Practice* (2019); and *Future Imperfect: Contemporary Art Practices and Cultural Institutions in the Middle East* (2016). In his capacity as the Cultural and Commissioning Lead, he is a co-investigator on a four-year Arts Humanities Research Council project that focuses on education, visual culture, and digital methodologies in Palestine, Lebanon, and Jordan (2020–24). Downey is currently researching his forthcoming volume *Unbearable States: Digital Media and Cultural Activism in a Post-Digital Age* (2022).

Lesio

in t

Land

ns

ne

scape

Shona Illingworth, *Stac Lee*, 2014. Archival pigment print.

LESIONS IN THE LANDSCAPE
2015

Three-screen video and multichannel sound installation
35 mins

Lesions in the Landscape explores the complex individual and societal impact of amnesia. Interweaving parallels with historical lesions in the physical and cultural landscape of St Kilda, a remote archipelago located in the North Atlantic, the project reflects on the experience of Claire, a woman living with amnesia and processes of cultural erasure.

Lesions in the Landscape was made by Shona Illingworth over a four-year period through creative dialogue with Claire and neuropsychologists Martin A. Conway and Catherine Loveday.

The full transcript of the work is included on pages 23–43.

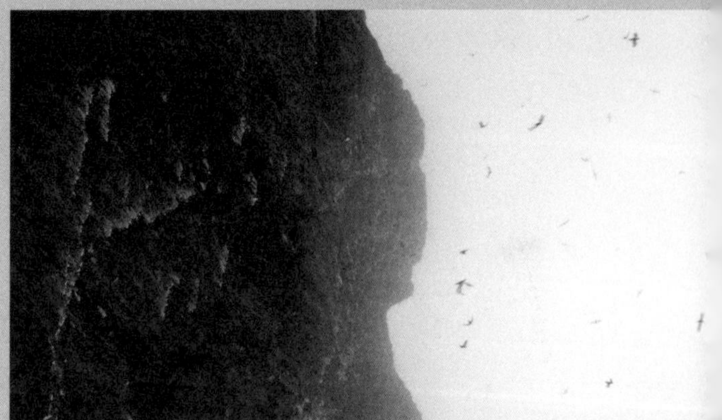

57.8167° degrees north, 8.5833° degrees west

If you turned the map the other way round, you would be south

A way station on the sea route

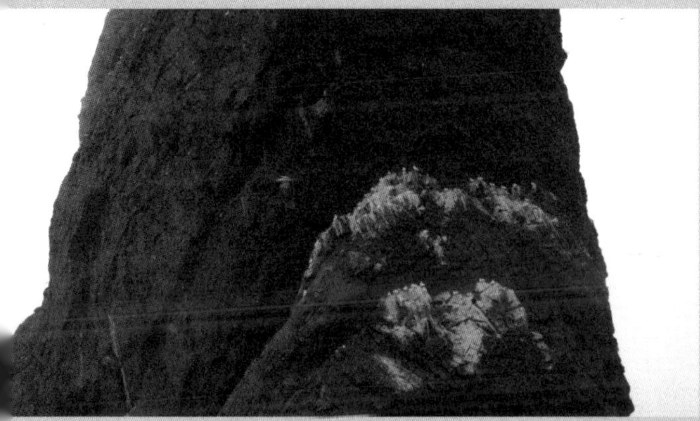

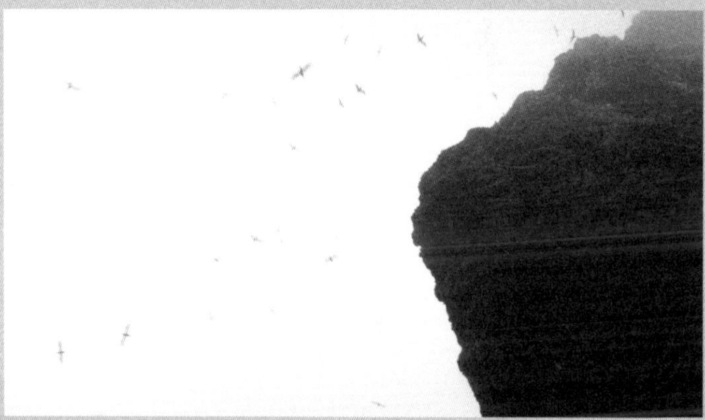

Dark Grey Gabros

Cut through with southwesterly dipping sheets
of fine Cambir Dolerite
Slowly slowly
Light pink granite
Slow-cooling magma
making crystalline rock
along that new old continental edge
Formed in the Paleocene
out of the old new
in a chain of fire
A new volcano
which would become Hirte, Levanish, Soay, Boreray

A clutch of raggedy islands
inhabited for over four thousand years,
Its birds, the spring and summer harvest
a hundred thousand caught each year
by hand, rod, snare,
Its people, the subject of intense fascination
for wealthy summer tourists

Until August 29, 1930
when its story petrified
around the moment of its final evacuation

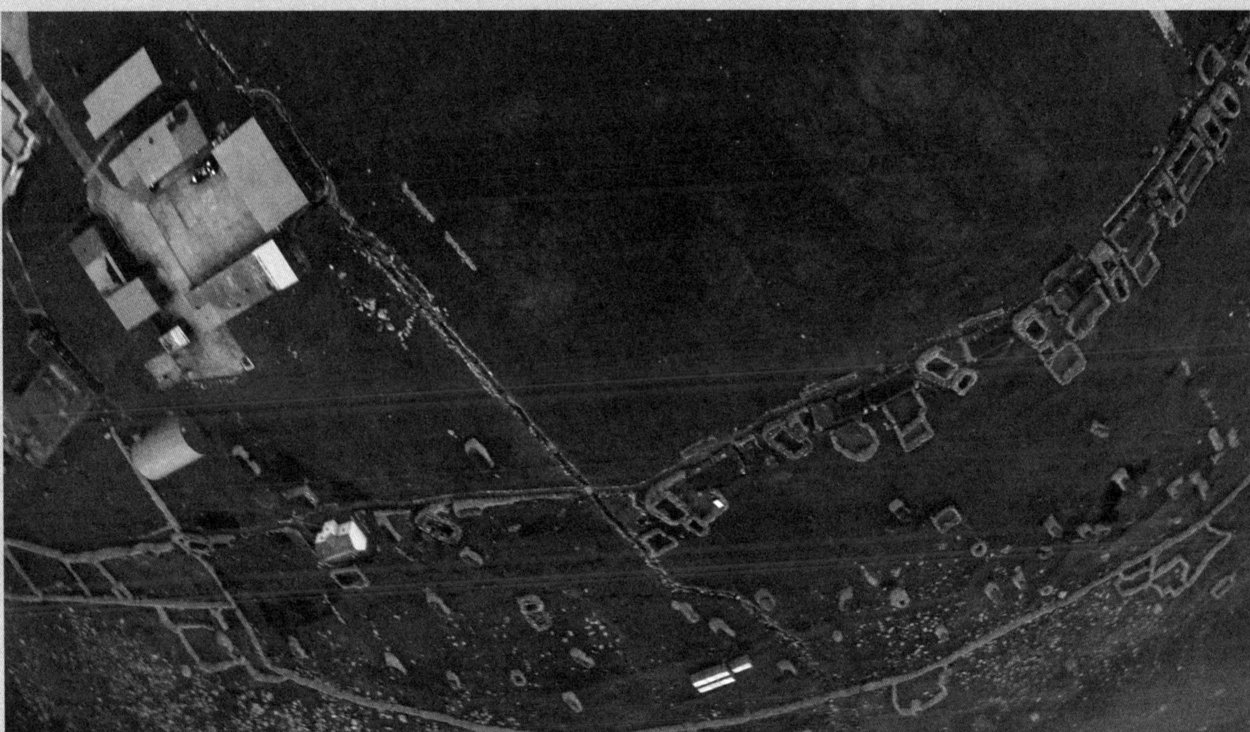

This is now the EGD 701 Danger Area Complex
A sanitized airspace with unlimited altitude
A fully instrumented controlled environment
Redesigned to accommodate safety traces
for modern weapons systems testing

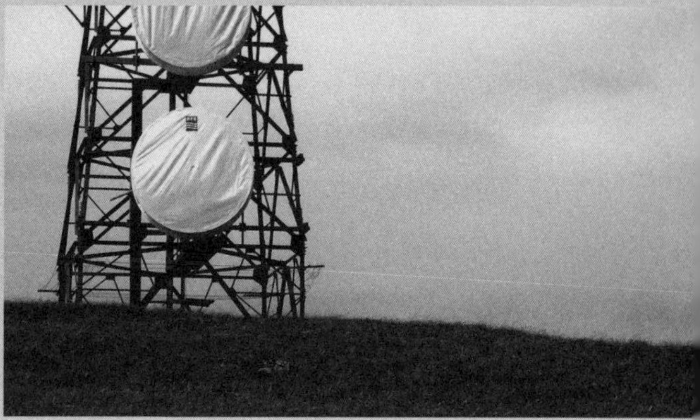

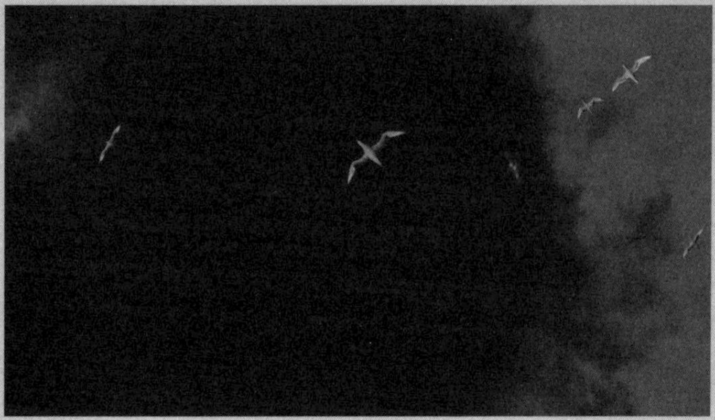

I know that I had really bad frightening dreams
And I presume that that's perhaps when I was first coming round
And I was underground in tunnels
And I was very frightened
But I don't have any of my own memory of coming round at any time
and suddenly thinking about
But I know when I did wake that I was very conscious that I remembered the dreams
Because they were still frightening
And I still didn't know what they'd all
What on earth had been happening
And you know I can't remember the last minute, or ten minutes or quarter of an hour ago
And I forget yesterday

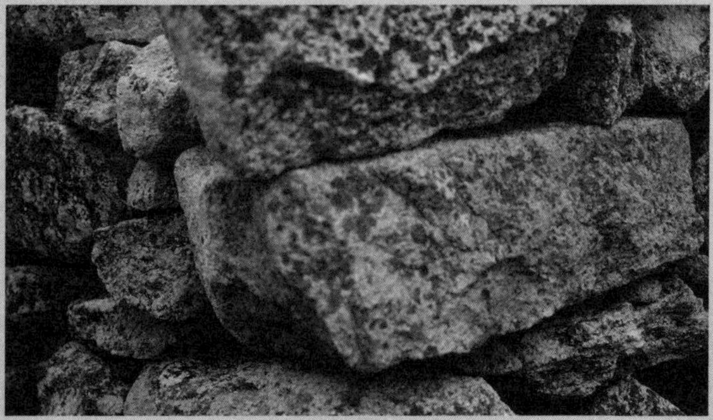

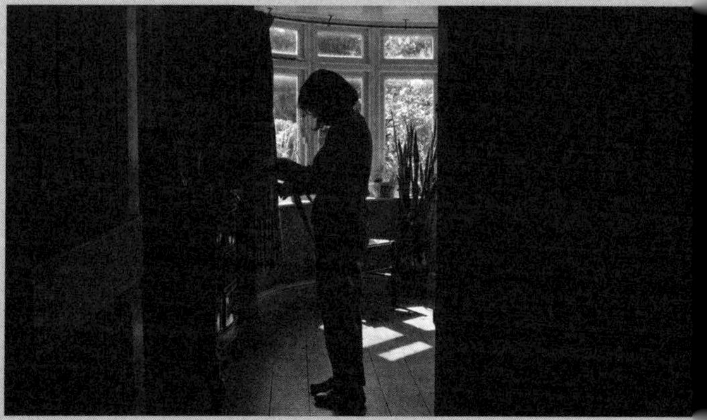

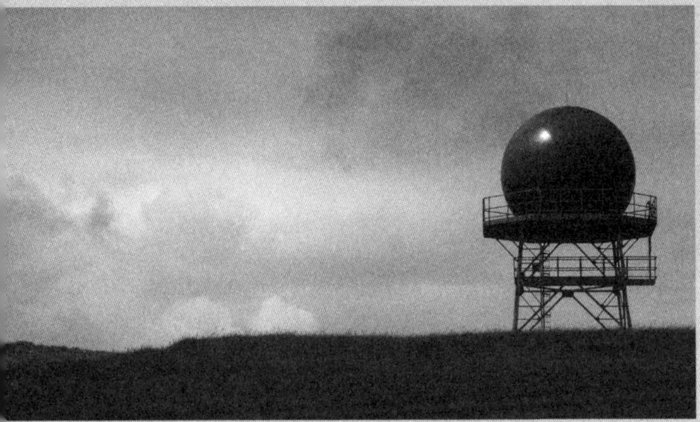

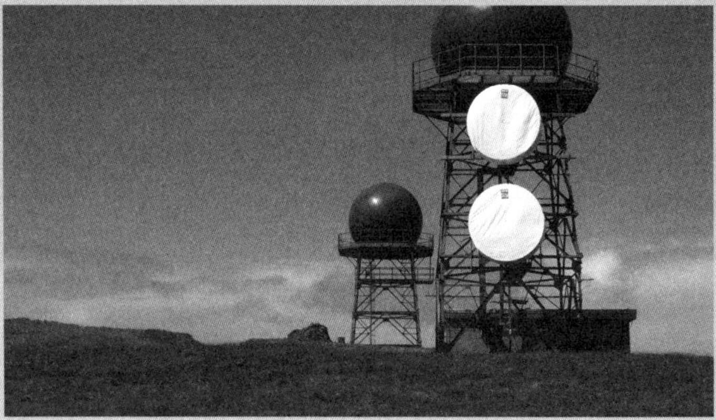

e inhabitants live contentedly together, in a little
lage on the east side of St Kilda, which they commonly
ll the country.
d the Isle Boreray, which is little more than two
agues distant from them, they call the northern country.
e distance between their houses is, by them, called
e High Street;
eir houses are low-built, of stone and a cement of
y earth
ey have couples and ribs of wood covered with thin
rthen turf, thatched over these with straw, and the roof
cured on each side with double ropes of straw or heath,
ised at the end with many stones

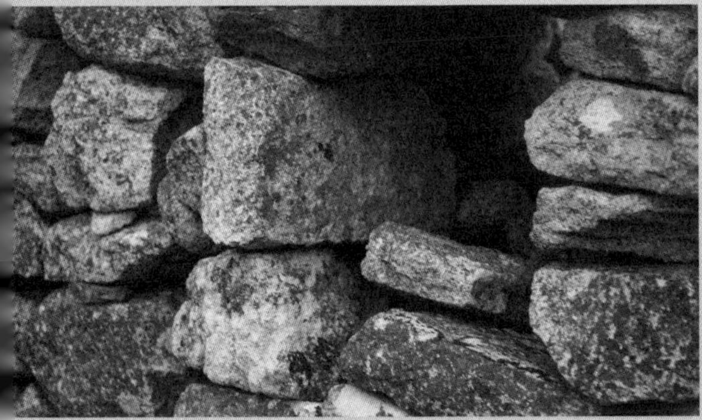

That weight of words
The loops the curls and dots and spatters
The text of the visitors enthralled condescension
or revulsion
That entanglement wrote you into the world
As odd and other
And in need of fixing
A paper artifice
Positioned as a people, who ought not to trouble themselves
Too much about the material circumstances of their
own everyday lives

All memories are time compressed
Your brain selects moments it is going to retain, and
that is what is retained
Those moments are fragments of the experience
We have a feeling now that we're doing something
We actually feel ourselves present here in this moment
If you don't have any boundaries in your cognition
then having a now is quite a difficult thing to have

I came home to a house that I was told was home
That I didn't know anything about
I didn't, I couldn't find my way round
I didn't know were anything was kept
or how to use things
I think I had allowed myself to believe
what had been told me about what had happened
and that the children were mine, ours
with I think, I've always thought, a strong maternal instinct

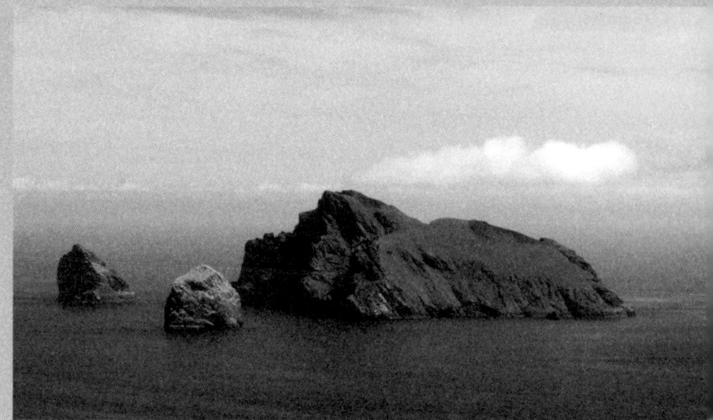

*If you get people in a big room with some objects
they have to remember
and then you get them to walk to one end of the room
they remember them quite well
If you get them to go out of the door into another room
the memory is much poorer
even though they've walked the same distance
When we went through the door that event was over
and so we no longer need to keep it in consciousness
we can turn it into a memory
In turning it into a memory
you lose information
If you're somebody who can't do that
then it probably means you can't have a now
You're always in the same room*

*When Pantagruel and his companions
in mid banquet, unwittingly approached the arctic
seas they begin to hear invisible people talking in
the air about the ship
Then voices of all kinds of men, women, and children
and horses
Then the noise of canon is heard
Although nothing is visible around the ship
Pantagruel speculates that perhaps
they are hearing the voices from a triangular reservoir
of words, ideas, and examples
that lies in the middle of a triangular universe
whence falls occasionally to earth
words or ideas*

Then he hits on the idea that they must be hearing
words frozen in hard winter
The pilot calmly assures the company that Pantagruel is right
and that they are hearing the thawing noises of a great battle
fought on the ice the previous winter
The words are all the colors of heraldic blazons
and melt in the hand
As Pantagruel cast handfuls of the frozen words down
on the deck
the cacophony of the various thawing of the words
is rendered as
boo boo boo boo hin hin hin hin tric trac hiss hiss brb brb
brbbrbbrb
tic toc tac brederan brederan frr frr frrf bou bou bou bou...

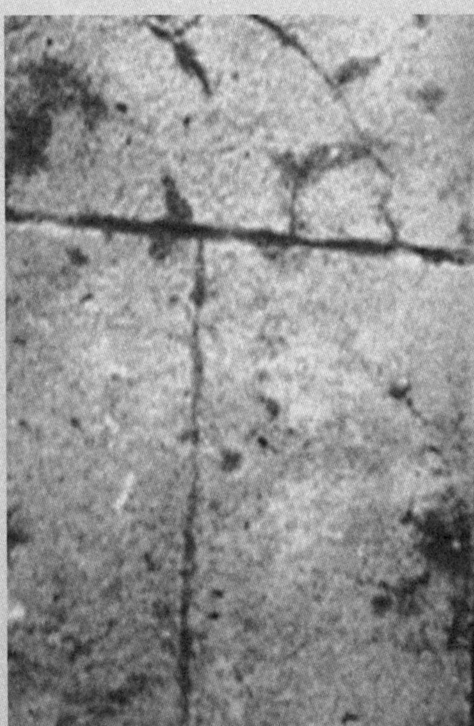

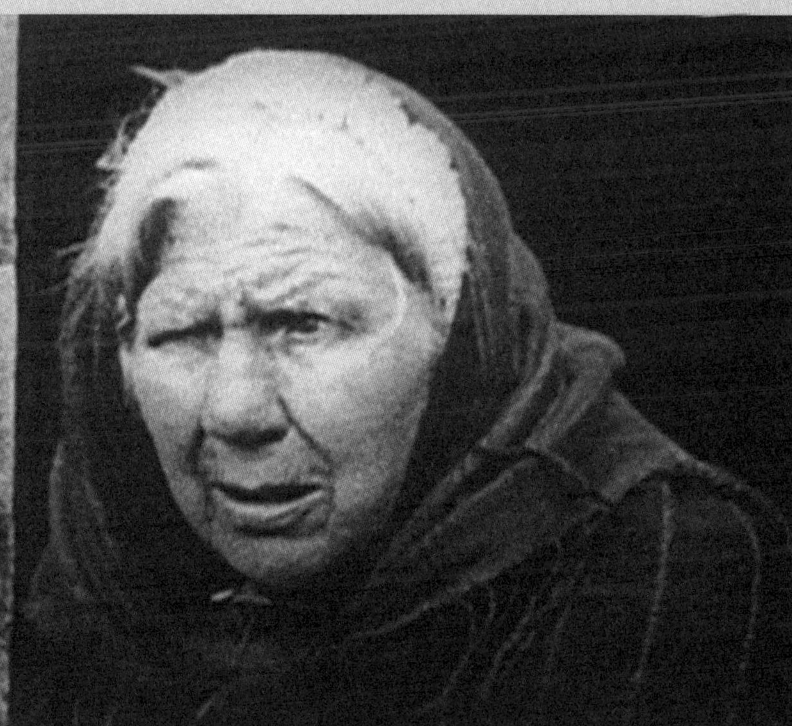

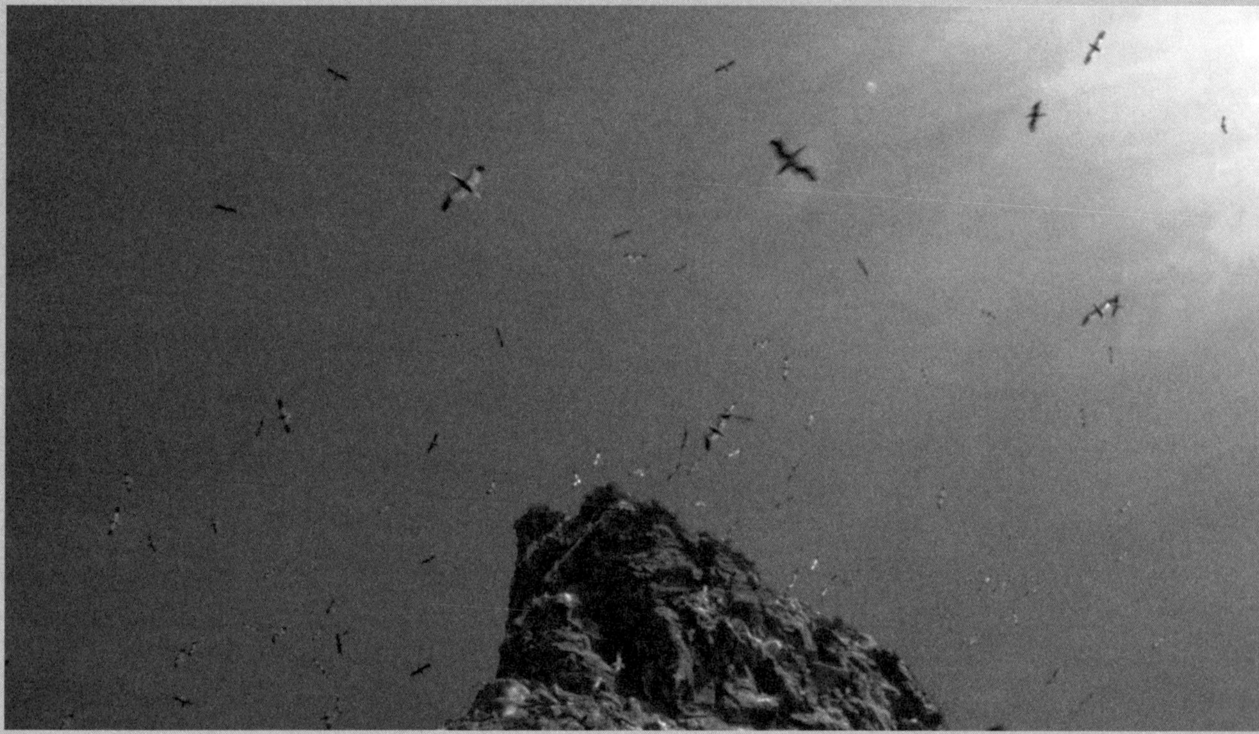

You were cast as living outside of time
Your connections to the wider world
to which you had always belonged, ignored

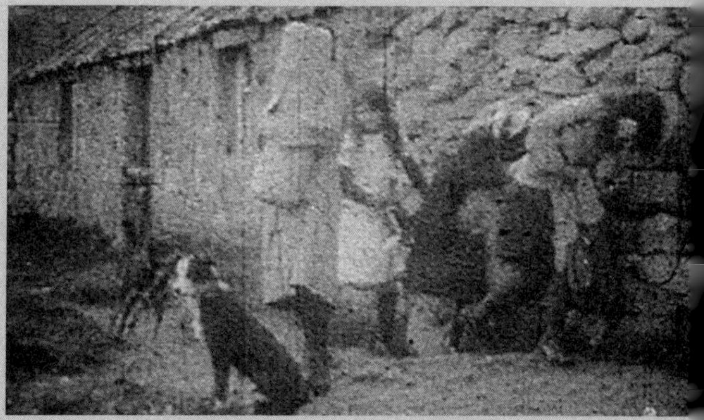

Your history was written by others
They said you had no words for trees,
war, writing, mirror, money
and that on your leaving, you left a bible
open at the page of Exodus
and a handful of oatmeal on every table

Your preparations for evacuation
filmed on August 27, 1930

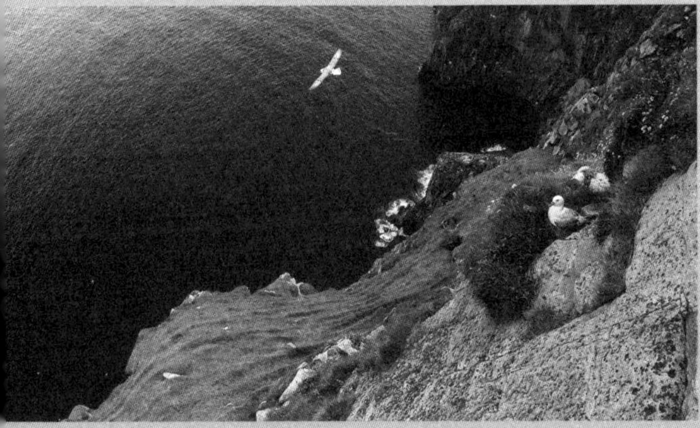

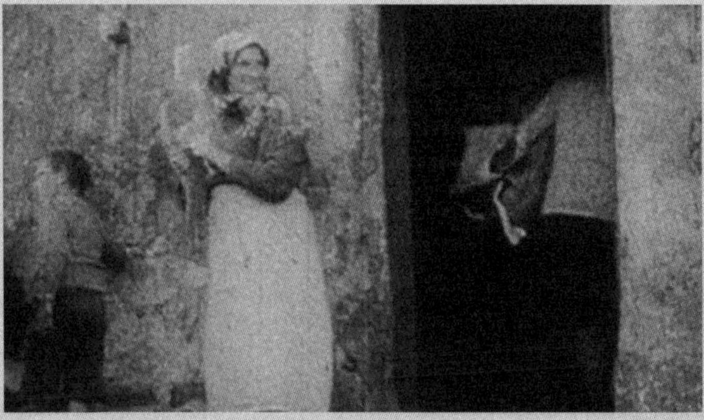

You run from the camera
These images suppressed by the State
until 1979

Already the north is reported as a place of extremes
and ambiguities,
Two opposing ideas of north repeat, and contradict
each other
from European antiquity to the time of the nineteenth-
century arctic explorers, that the north is a place of
darkness and dearth, the seat of evil,
or conversely that it is a place of austere felicity
where virtuous peoples live behind the north wind,
and are happy

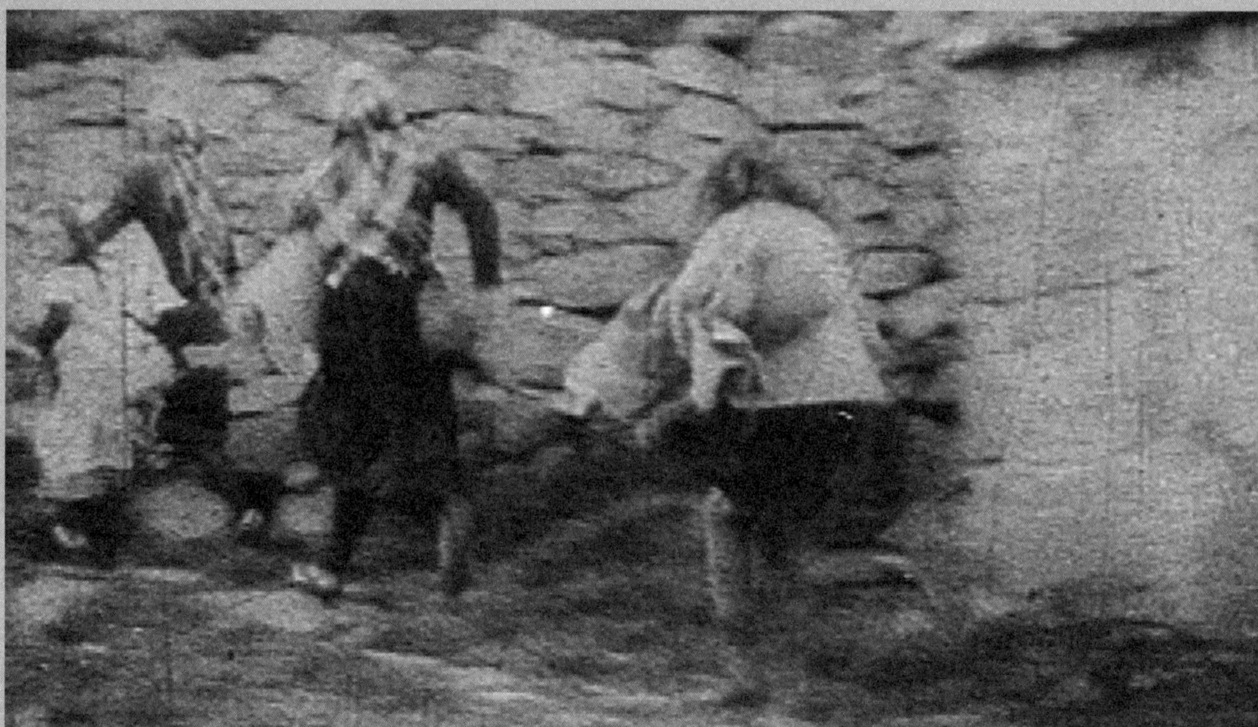

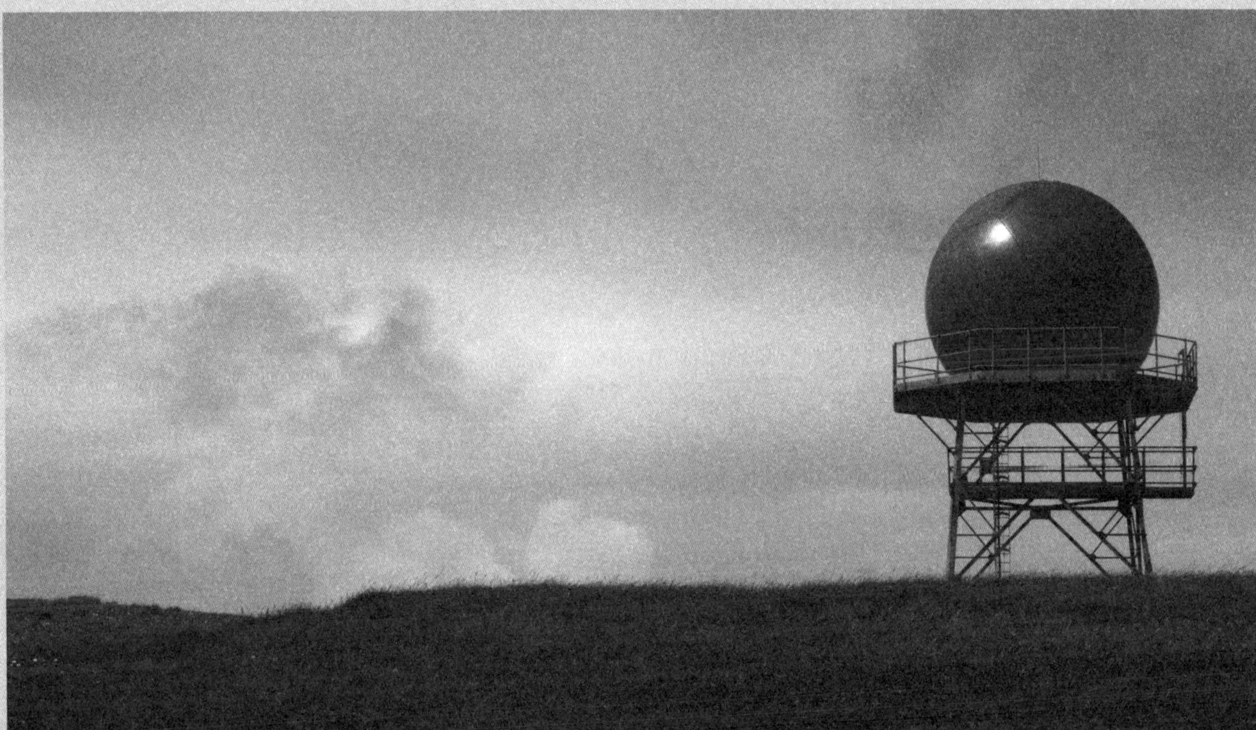

One sub station on HF1 how do you read it
We have you loud and clear Alexander, okay
Then let's go over to region HF1
It's inaudible on HF1

There is subtle swelling and high signal intensity seen on the T2 and FLAIR images in the medial temporal lobe on the right side. This appears of hypo-intensity on T1. These changes are extending into the adjacent basal ganglia, insula, and to some extent, the adjacent inferior frontal lobe. There is minor effacement of the adjacent temporal horn. Subtle high signal changes are seen in the left temporal lobe, best demonstrated on the FLAIR sequence.

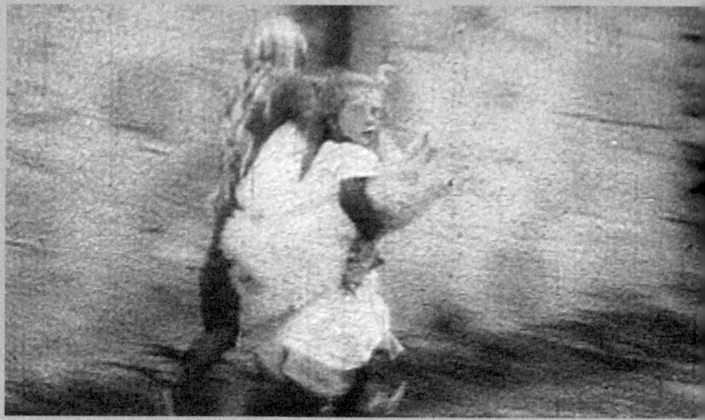

It feels like a world
Well it's a world I've lost all information about
so I can't share it anymore
It feels like I've got no connections to the past
and more frightening than not knowing it myself
seems that everybody else knows it
I feel completely left out of
lives which happened

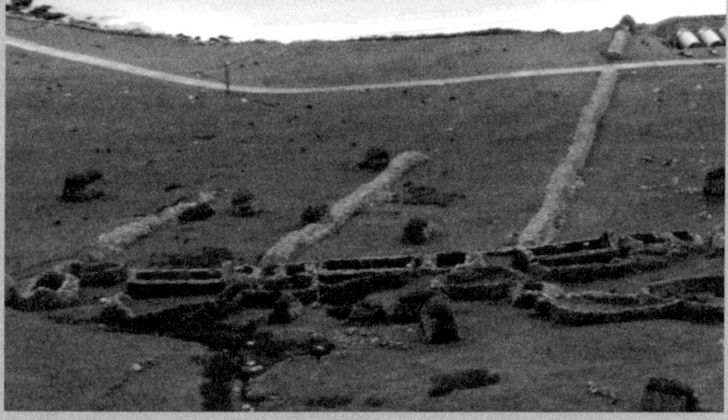

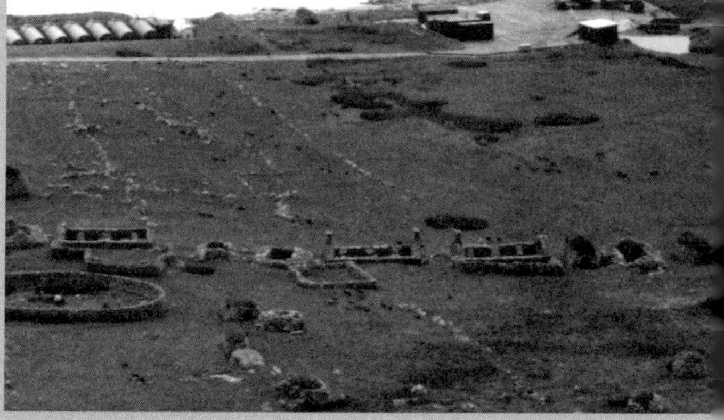

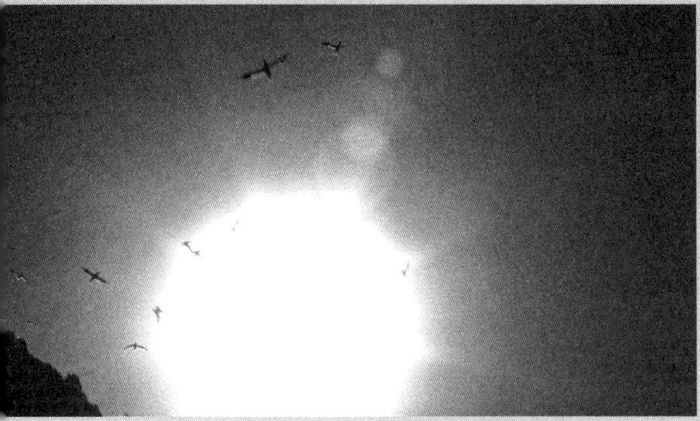
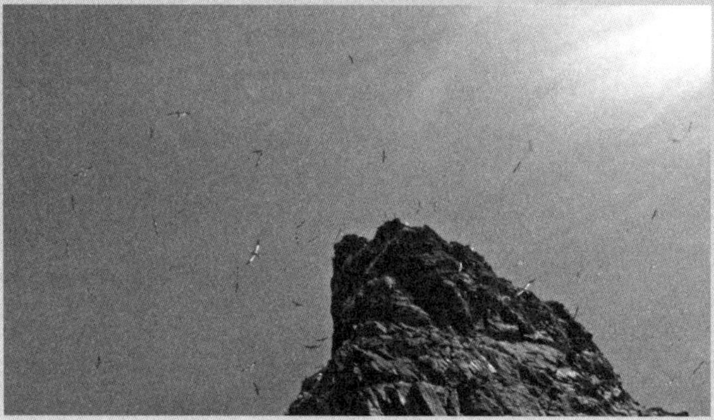
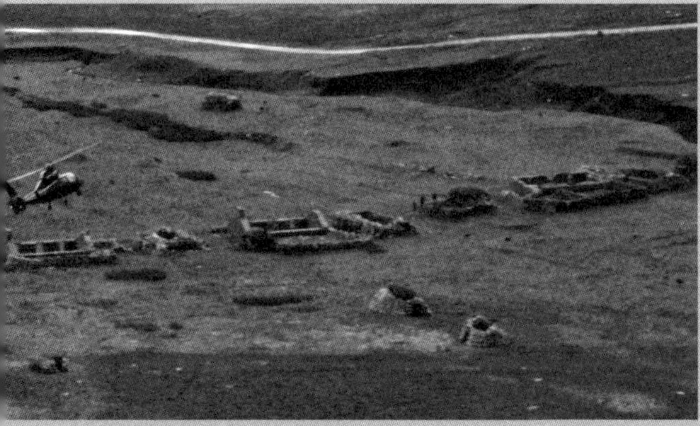

Six runs at each level
within an arc
between radials 160 degrees T clockwise to 025 degrees T
ranges from overhead St Kilda
to 80 NM and reciprocal

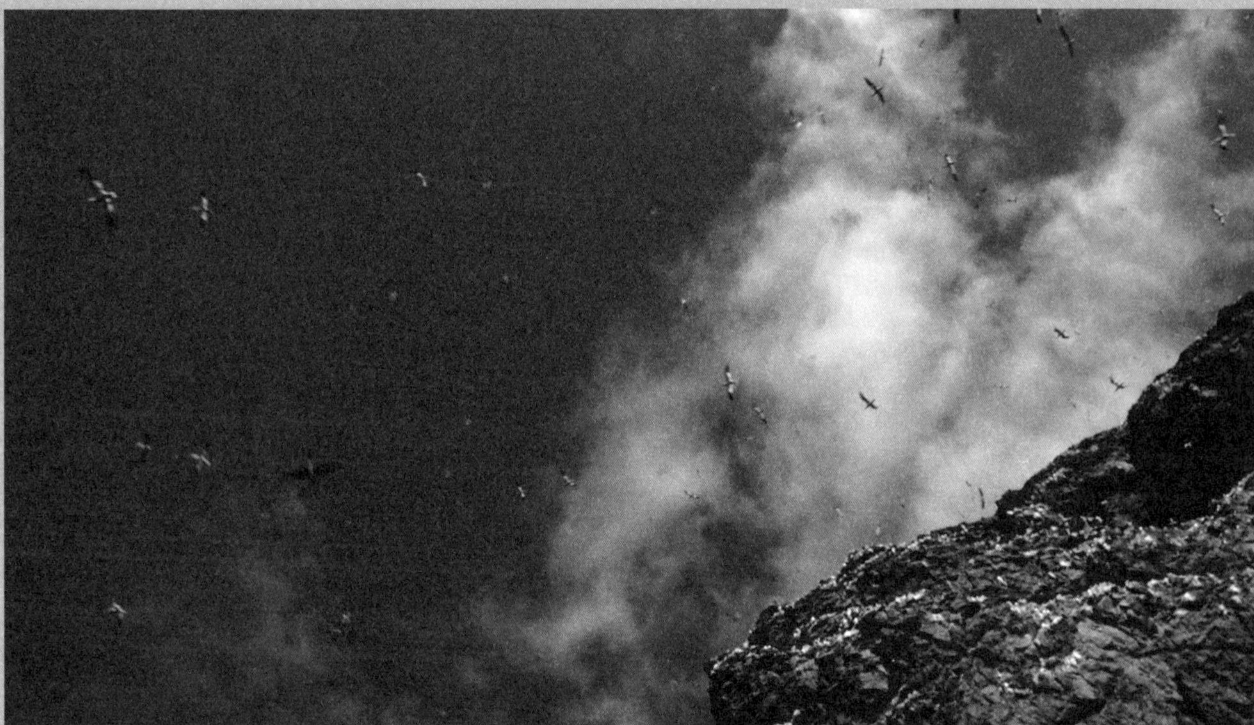

The range including the Danger area
covers more than thirty-thousand square-kilometers
and is so large
that activities go on beyond the line of sight

No airplane trails above
The sky is quiet
A sanitized airspace
The range constantly alert

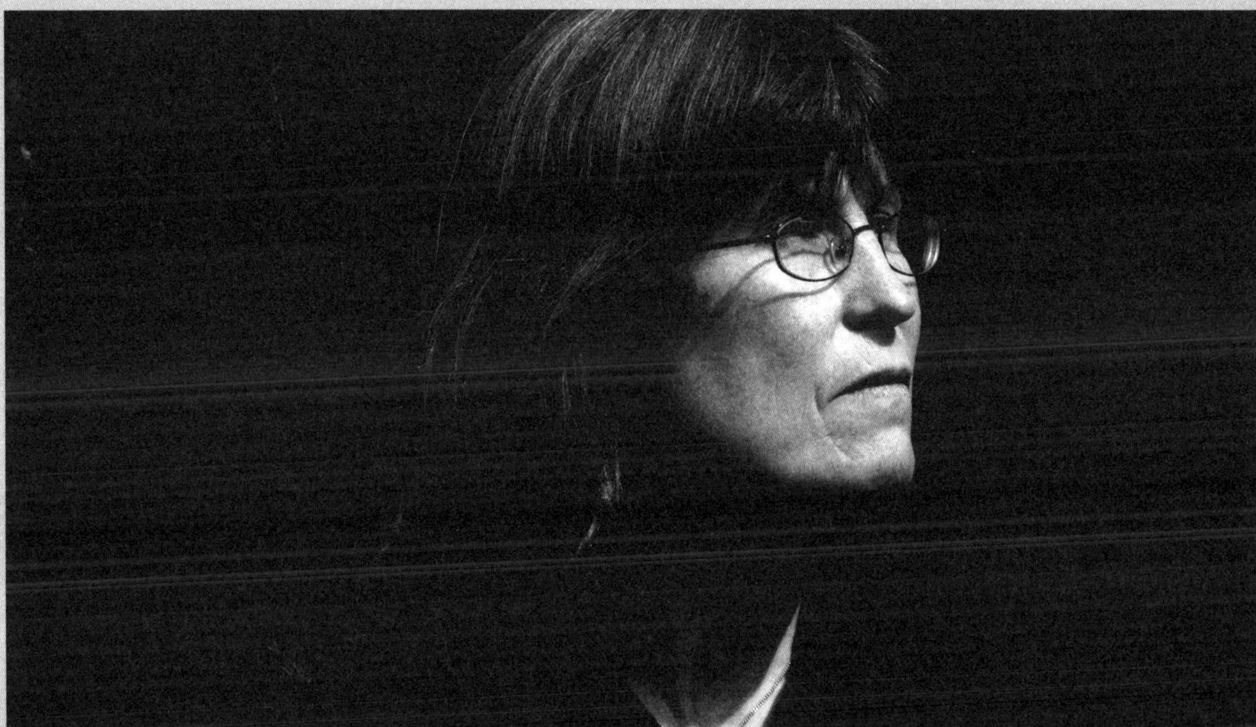

Iron-Age sheep now inhabit your homes and outfields
tagged, genotyped, blood-mapped
to track population dynamics, evolution, and changes
in climate

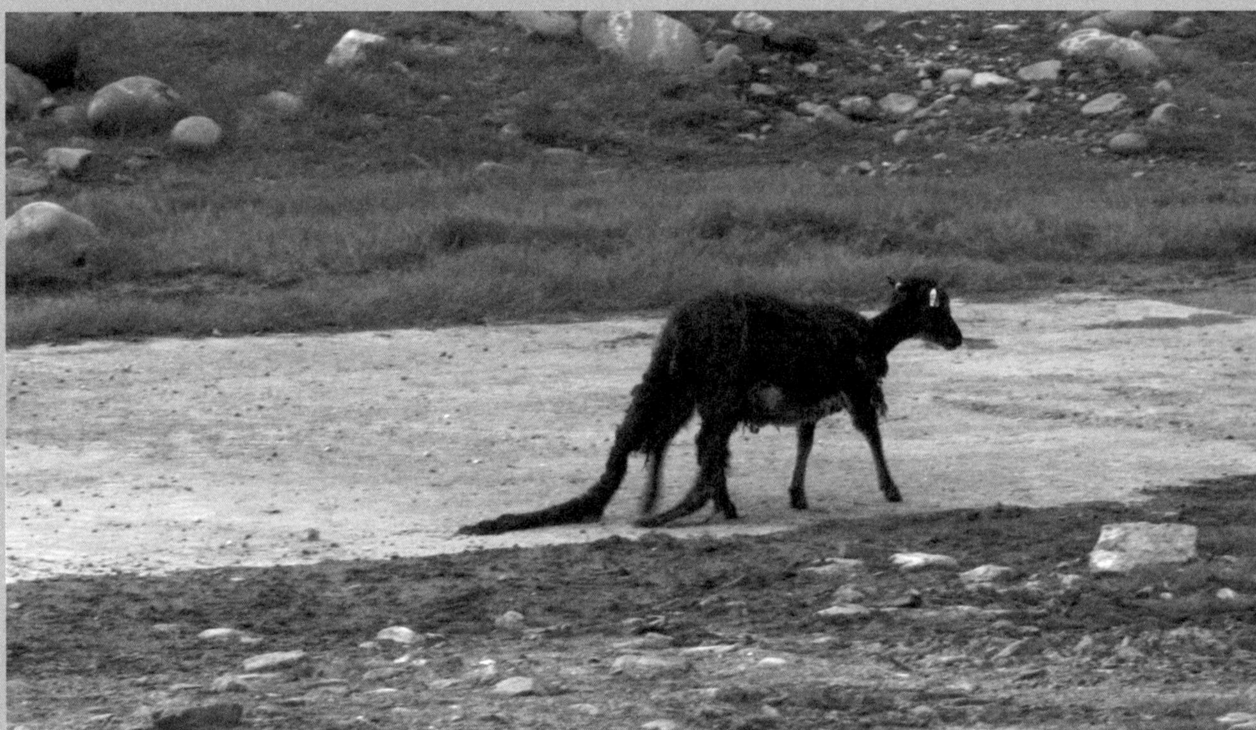

Young Light Blue – Dark Self – Scurred – 24
Beta Yellow – Dark Wild – Polled – 34
Alpha Red – Light Self – Scurred – 68
Beta Red – Dark Self – Normal Horned – 203
Alpha Orange – Dark Self – Polled – 53
Alpha Green – Light Wild – Normal Horned – 42

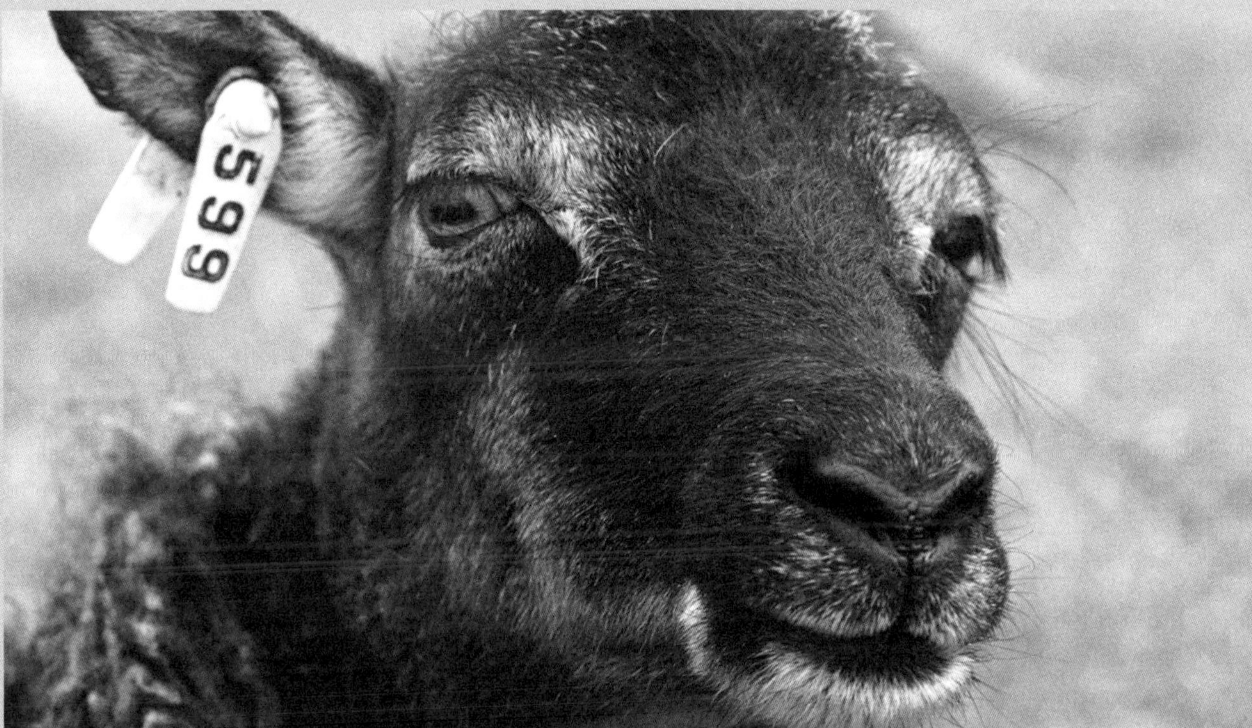

Beta White – Dark Self – 28
Alpha White – Light Wild – 86
Beta Red – Dark Wild – 72
Alpha Green – Light Wild – 3
Alpha Yellow – Dark Wild – 27
Beta Yellow – Dark Self – 22
Beta Light Blue – Light Self – 6

For thousands of years these islands thrived
And its people were successful
Yet its history is dominated by its last gasp

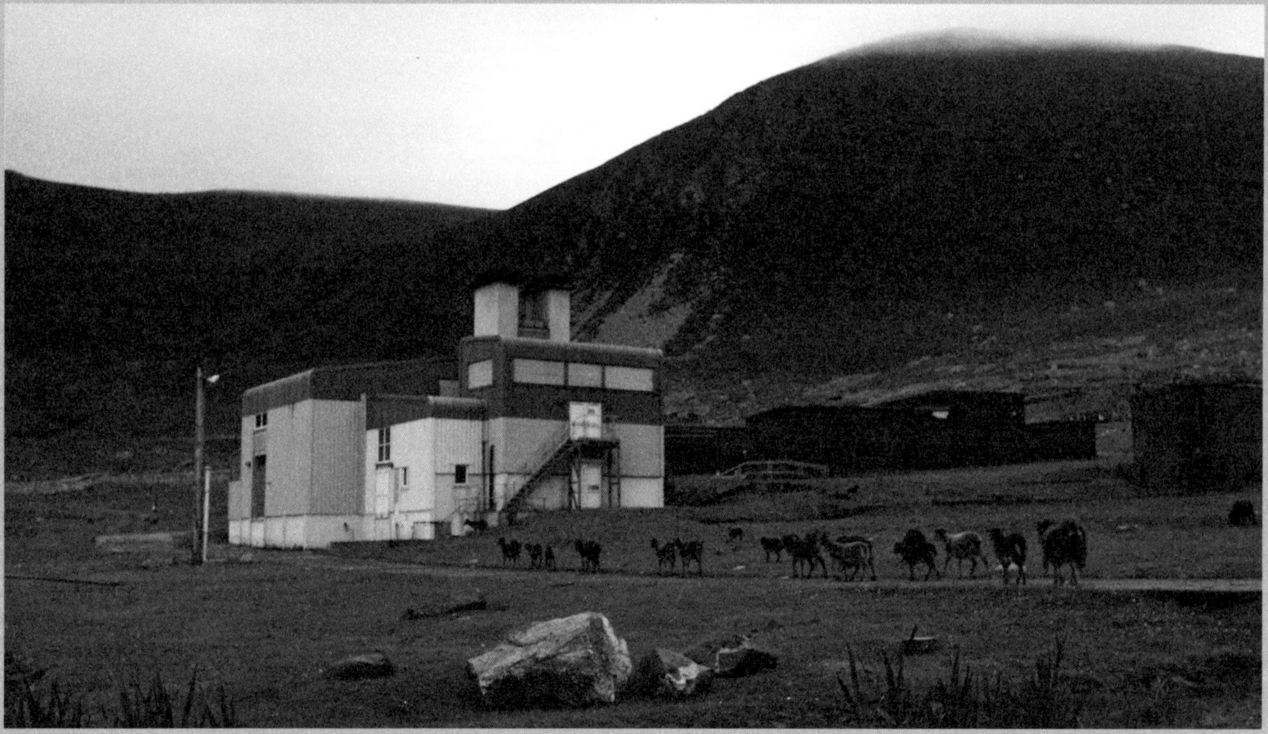

Satellites click overhead
Your surfaces mapped to a four-centimeter accuracy
A finger's length
Seen from space

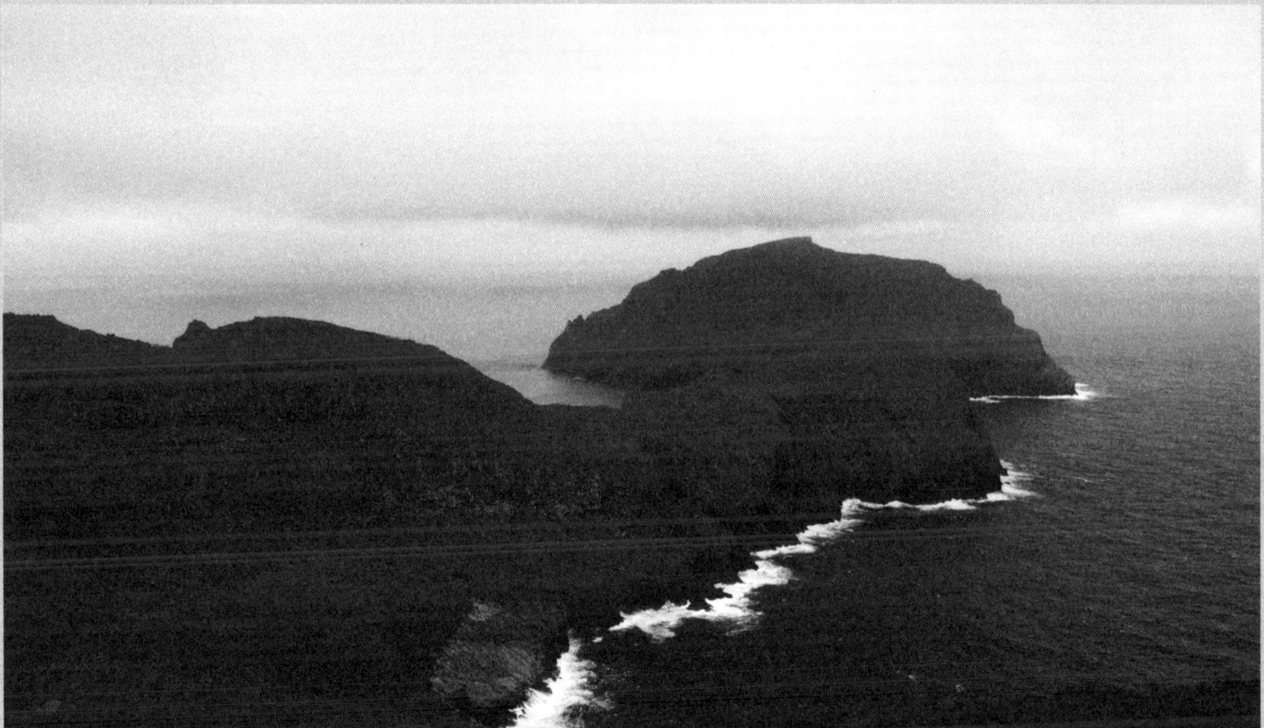

All systems are nominal, copy
And we're back on FM

A Soyuz supply ship docks
At the International Space Station
Satellites pass overhead
In the uncertain territory
Between sovereign airspace and outer space
Mapping complex weapons testing in the rocket range
Plotting the archaeological remains

06 digits remain, target is fairly visible, copy

There is so much that happens non-consciously
As individuals
All we ever experience are the outputs of non-conscious processes

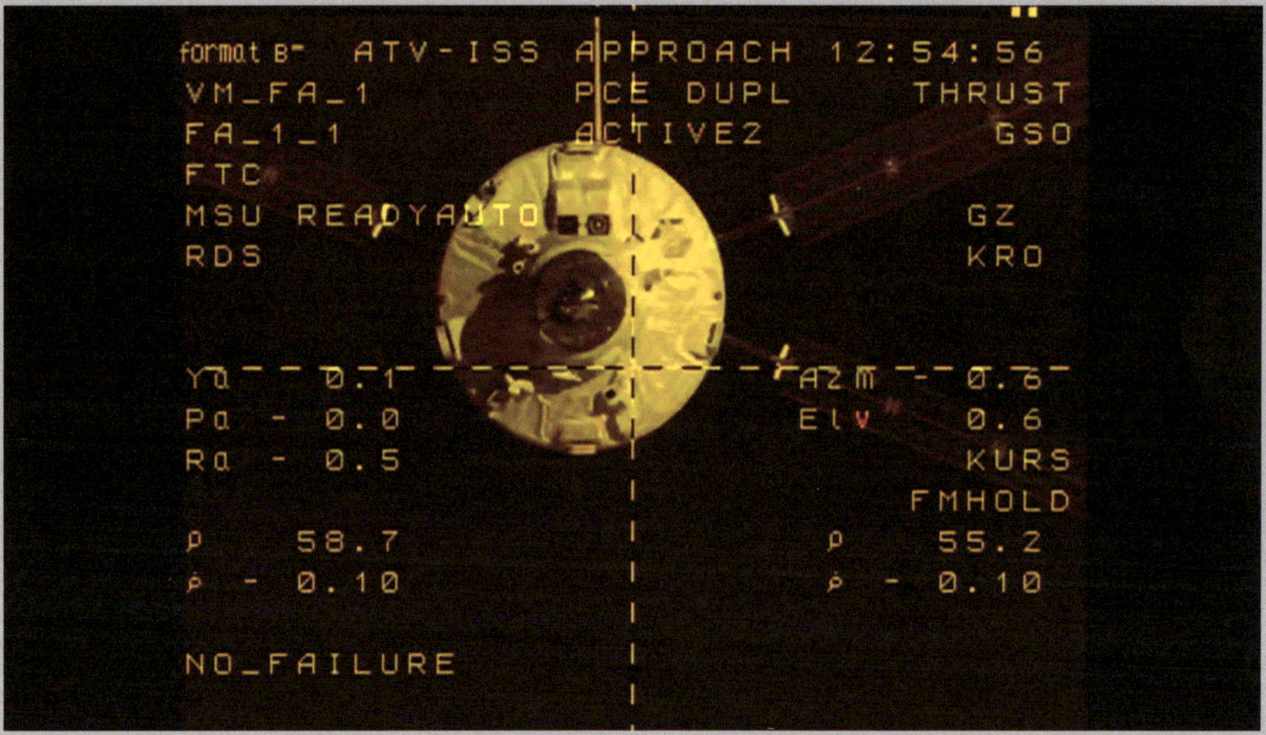

I think our knowledge of ourselves and our past lives
Enable us to have some kind of vision of the future
We know what things we like what direction we want to go in
And who we want to share it with
But I think, life's just become a very rush of the minute at the moment

There are lots of things we do in life that are
driven by memories
that do not come to mind consciously
The things that get into long-term memory
are probably there forevermore
The real problem is how do you access them

Real forgetting occurs when and only when
there's damage to the brain itself
where the actual biological material in which
the knowledge is represented
or which is used to build up patterns of activation
across different networks in order to allow you
to have the knowledge
it's not until that is destroyed that you have real
forgetting

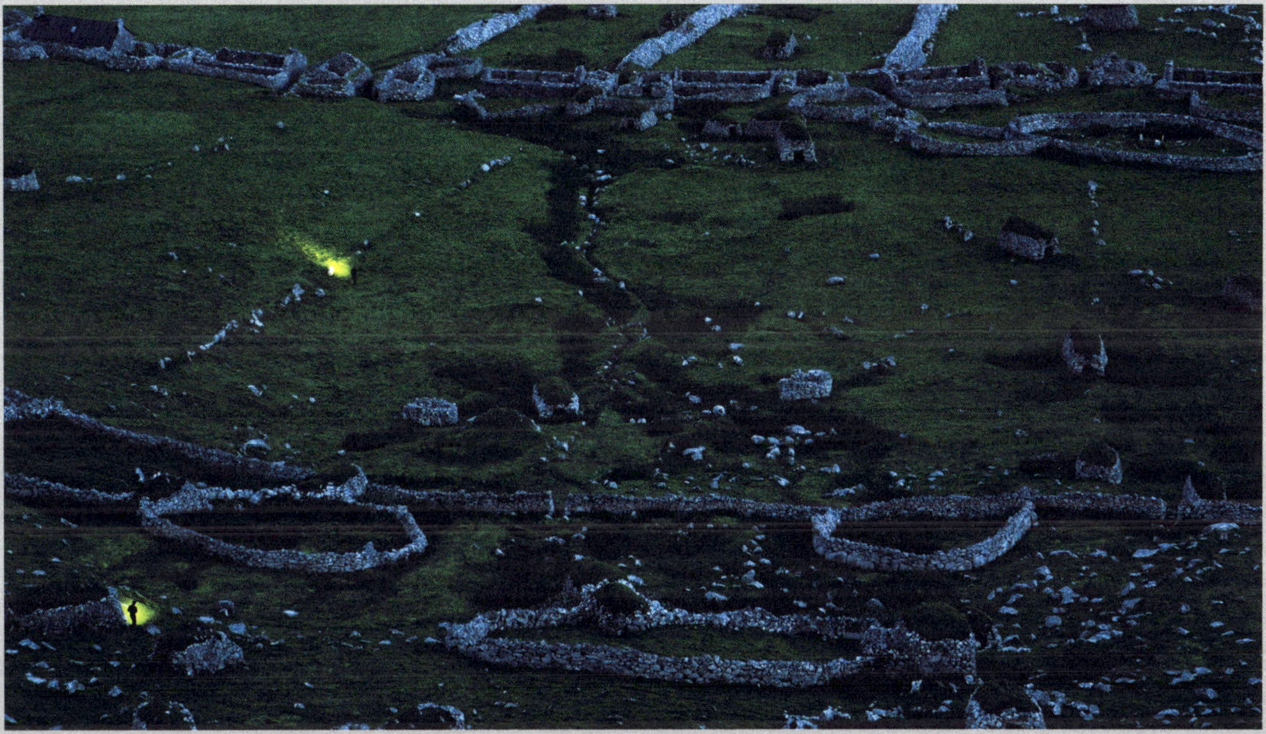

Because everything is time compressed
and memory is quite selective
it's quite possible to have thousands upon
thousands of memories
from your life
However, only a small number of those memories
are accessible

As activation rises in different networks
that activation might be thought of as a sort of signal
to whatever it is that underlies consciousness

Activation in the brain never stops
Activation of knowledge structures
which either are fragments of memories
or contain other memory information are being
activated all the time
and so locate us in the world

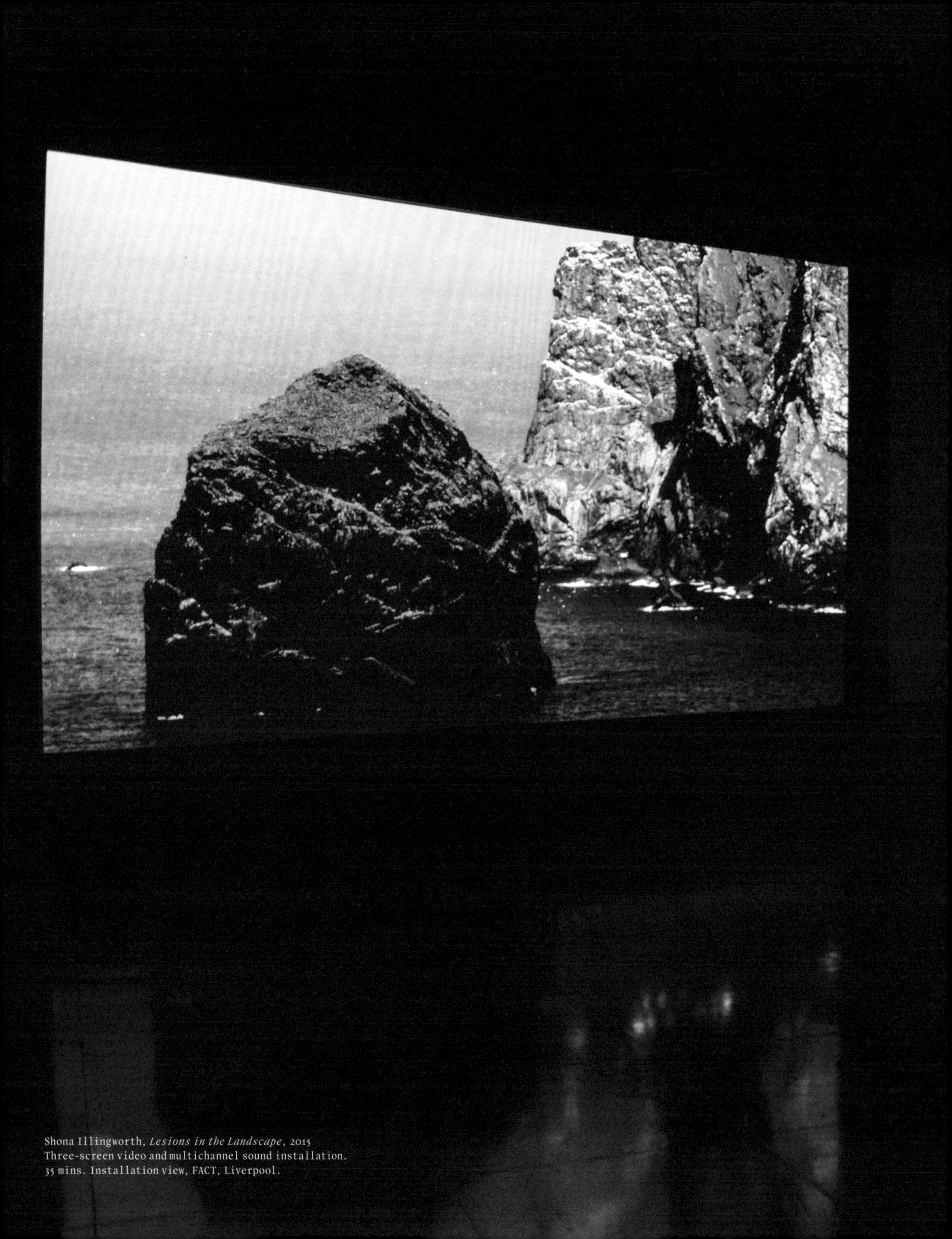

Shona Illingworth, *Lesions in the Landscape*, 2015
Three-screen video and multichannel sound installation.
35 mins. Installation view, FACT, Liverpool.

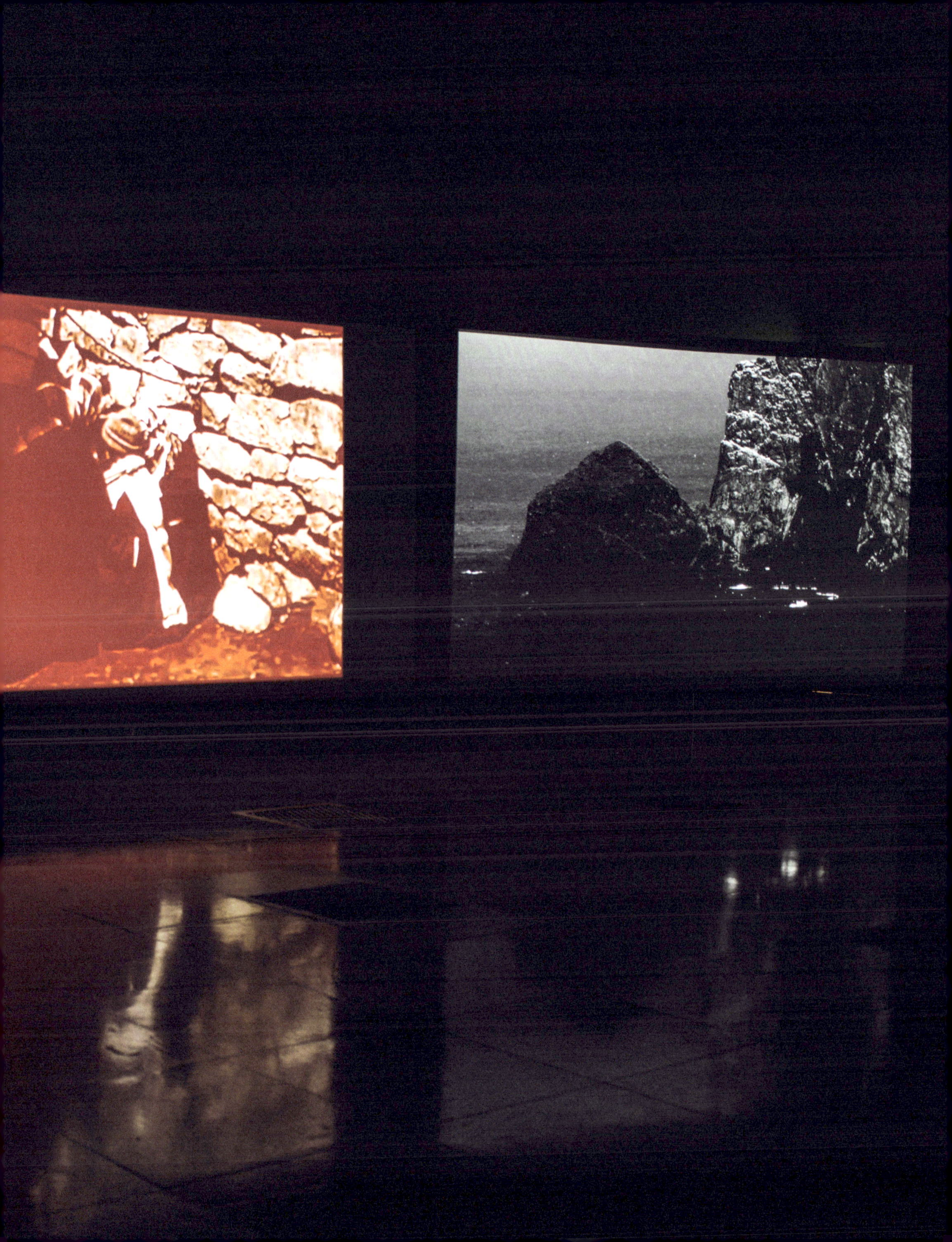

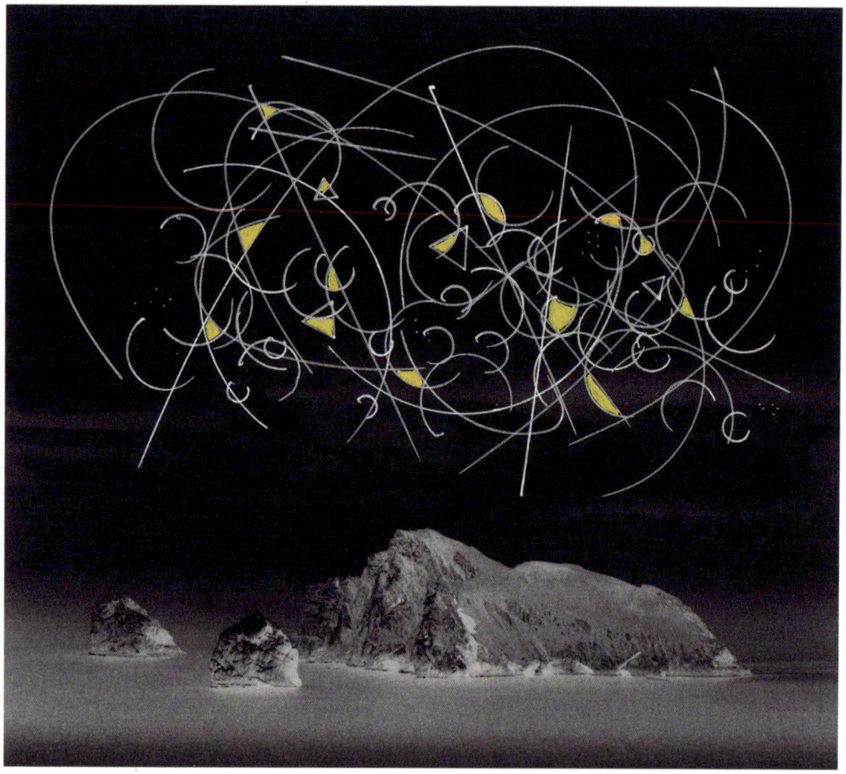

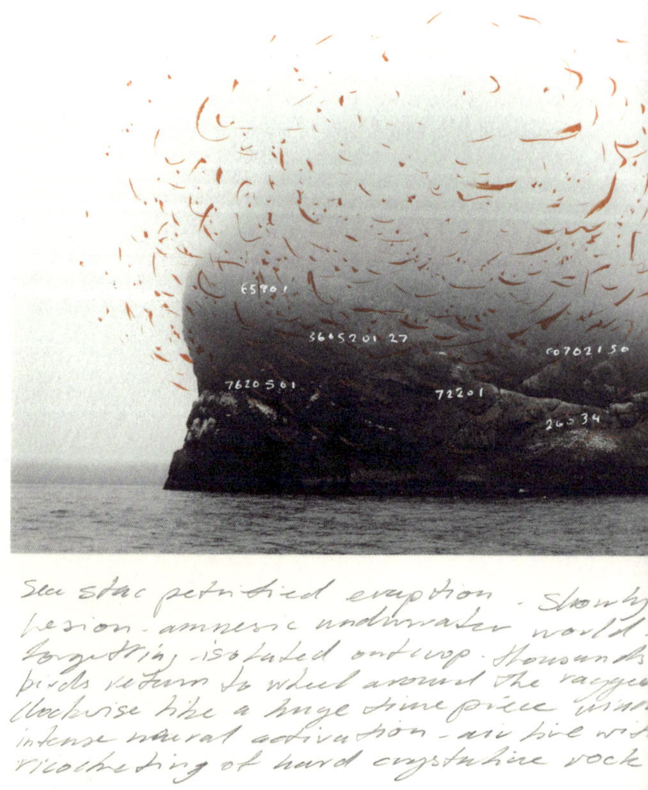

Above: Shona Illingworth, *Telemetry, Cloud, Boreray*, 2015. Archival pigment print, ink, and gouache. 210 × 210 mm.
Right: Shona Illingworth, *Petrified Sea Stac and Birds—Activation Rising in Neural Networks*, 2014. Archival pigment print, ink, and gouache. 210 × 210 mm.

Jill Bennett
LANDSCAPE WITHOUT MEMORY

There is a scene in *Lesions in the Landscape* (2015) that pinpoints the moment in which an event is transformed into a memory. In the central frame of the three-screen video installation, bordered on each side by shots of dry-stone walls, Claire—a woman with amnesia who is the work's main subject—stands alone in her living room, folding a piece of cloth and placing it in a drawer. In a voiceover, psychologist Martin Conway talks about the significance of the room: "If you get people to walk to the end of a room and then test their recall for objects, they remember quite well," he says, "but if they walk through a door, their memory for the same objects is much poorer, even if they've walked the same distance." The door functions as a boundary to a memory event. As soon as one is no longer "in" the event, it is turned into memory—and in that process, information is lost.

In this scenario, the edge of the present is marked not only by the passage of time but also by a physical transition through a boundary. Psychologists have reasoned that such event boundaries enable us to parse ongoing action by segmenting it into episodic chunks. As a result of this segmentation, our memories tend to feel more like discrete time-slices than a seamless film-like reel. Event boundaries in this sense are conceptual rather than natural edges, but they make use of physical divisions. Material structure, in other words, serves to organize and contain memory.

The question of how we engage with representations of space in memory is an issue for aesthetics as much as for psychology, insofar as it concerns experience: an embodied, sensory encounter with the external world as well as with internal sensation, or "the feeling of what happens," in the words of neuroscientist Antonio Damasio.

This sense of a dynamic, experiential relationship between the material environment and memory distinguishes Shona Illingworth's *Lesions in the Landscape* from the kind of memory project that focuses on past events. The landscape posited in *Lesions in the Landscape* does not presuppose an accessible past but an experientially dislocated space. The cinematic sweep of the Hebridean landscape, like the trope of journeying across a treacherous stretch of the North Atlantic, gestures toward an epic, unfolding narrative. But against this expansive backdrop, *Lesions in the Landscape* evokes the feeling of what happens in the moment as we move across the terrain, insecurely, from one event to another, one space to another.

In Claire's case, there is no way through, no memory event. She will not remember the room once she leaves it because, in addition to the retrograde amnesia that leaves her with no memory of entire phases of her life, she has anterograde amnesia, affecting her ability to form new memories. Much of what happens to her in a given day will be forgotten. Without the ability to pass through a boundary and hold information in memory, the distinction between past, present, and future is moot: "You can't have a now," as Conway's narrative concludes, "you are always in the same room." "Life's just a rush of the minute," says Claire.

The incongruously contained shot of Claire in her room, as if in a perpetual present, cuts away to an open expanse of sea, from which emerges the remote Scottish archipelago of St Kilda. In the companion piece, *Time Present* (2016), we see Claire herself standing alone on the bow of a yacht approaching these same islands. The St Kilda presented in *Lesions in the Landscape* is, in one respect, a cipher for anterograde amnesia. The archipelago's depopulation on August 29, 1930, brought to an end two millennia of continuous inhabitation. The final evacuation on that day is the point at which endogenous memory production ceases. Thereafter, St Kilda does not hold or generate its own memory from within, its story perpetuated only by custodians beyond its shores. Claire, likewise, has a history of shared memories that are no longer hers in any meaningful sense: "I came home to a house that I was told was home. [...] I allowed myself to believe what I had been told, that the children were mine."

If St Kilda nevertheless has an abundant, visible history, Illingworth's project draws a careful distinction between this and the activation of memory, envisaging a landscape that is preserved but does not yield to memory. In this sense, *Lesions in the Landscape* is an aesthetic exploration of the felt experience of amnesia: of possessing a past and a body of memories that are, if not erased, beyond reach, even as one inhabits the spaces of their creation.

Memories may persist in biological matter in the brain, even when not accessed, Conway suggests. In a more poetic register, the capture of episodic information is imagined to reside in disembodied matter in the landscape: a passage recited in *Lesions in the Landscape* from Rabelais's *Gargantua and Pantagruel* describes how noises of a bloody sea battle become frozen in the air, trapped for years in ice. When the ice thaws, the battle noises are reheard by passing sailors, long after the action has ended. Claire and her family envisage her memory as similarly frozen or locked-in, as if in an impenetrable vault.

Most of us take for granted the unbidden return of moments from the past: the experience of involuntary memory, irrupting into consciousness. Such memory is often triggered by a sensory cue, like the tea-soaked madeleine that gives rise to sights and sounds from Proust's childhood in *Remembrance of Things Past*. In a study of involuntary memory, the Russian writer and physicist Esther Salaman describes the disciplined process of reconstructing her own autobiographical memory.[1] Involuntary memories, she proposes, are always of events, not of backgrounds or settings. Memory of background, however, can itself function as a cue. Salaman recommends fixing discrete event memories to a background location in order to prompt spatial connections or relations to emerge. Four separate memories of her school days are thus deliberately placed into a generically remembered classroom; once these "islands" of memory are located, she finds she can more easily see the space between them.

For Claire, the "locked vault" of memory may occasionally be opened with the right trigger.[2] Unable to conjure such background memory at will, she uses a sensor-equipped automatic camera to record events in the hope of consolidating and cueing memory. Worn around her neck, the camera takes photographs at roughly thirty-second intervals. The images, viewed on screen, play in a rapid serial presentation like a time-lapse movie, but from a very distinctive, first-person or "field" perspective. The camera's wide-angle, 136-degree lens captures an abundance of peripheral detail of the kind routinely excluded from deliberately framed shots, often picking up the wearer's hands, limbs, clothing, or hair, with the effect that the images convey a sense of our own embodied presence in the field. They are "experience-near" representations, eradicating the distance between observer and action. Conway and Catherine Loveday have inferred that these distinctive images are cognitively compatible with human memory, by virtue of representing short, bounded, time-slices of experience, formed outside intentional awareness—

1 See Esther Salaman, *A Collection of Moments: A Study of Involuntary Memories* (New York: St. Martin's Press, 1971).

2 See Jill Bennett, "New Subjects and Subjectivities," in *Companion to Feminist Art Practice and Theory*, ed. Hilary Robinson and Maria Elena Buszek (Hoboken, NJ: Wiley-Blackwell, 2019).

unlike deliberately framed photographs, which imply an observer perspective.[3]

For Claire, these photographs also facilitate the kind of backgrounding that Salaman advocates as beneficial to memory retrieval. In reviewing her image sequences, Claire appears to engage in a process of feeling into the action, moving methodically through them as if to locate herself in the flow of events. She proceeds slowly, poring over each image, including those obscured by a hand or arm in front of the lens. Whereas someone able to recall and recognize images in a sequence can easily jump ahead, confidently discarding blurred or obscured images in favor of something with salience, for Claire, it is necessary to trace a route, reconstructing her movement frame-by-frame through the landscape.

One of these sequences is from the shoot for *Lesions in the Landscape*, when Illingworth filmed her walking around the abandoned settlement of Village Bay on Hirta, the main island of St Kilda. Looking at the images, some months after the trip, Claire tries to reimagine the walk, focusing on the sensorimotor experience of moving through the landscape. Through this process, she remembers the feeling of talking aloud. She does not know why she was speaking or to whom—speculating that she may have been musing aloud about the inhabitants of the houses or talking to someone encountered along the way, although this is not apparent in the images.[4]

This careful, on-the-ground reconstruction of a field perspective—the basis for recapturing the feeling of what happens in a place—serves as a counterpoint to the technological remapping of the St Kilda landscape in the military airspace operations, which also permeate the soundscape of *Lesions in the Landscape*.

Several image sequences taken with Claire's automatic camera are included in the *Amnesia Museum* archive (2012–ongoing). These capture Claire's walk around Village Bay and a trip by boat around the smaller island of Boreray and surrounding sea stacks. The images are of particular significance as Claire viewed them during an experiment, in which the electrical activity in her brain was monitored by electroencephalogram (EEG). In *Amnesia Museum*, data from the EEG is represented in a sonified form, enabling visitors to hear the waveforms of neural firing in an installation that effectively re-embodies these signals.

This confluence of neurobiological data and experiential knowing is an aesthetic enactment of what the Chilean neurobiologist Francisco Varela called neurophenomenology: a radical approach to science that enmeshes bottom-up subjective understandings of experience with the data of neurobiology. Neurophenomenology (which Varela saw as especially pertinent to understanding time-consciousness[5]) brings these divergent spheres of knowledge together, proposing that the experiential account of neurological activity may give meaning to a signal (a measure of brain activity) that is otherwise just noise.[6]

Illingworth's sonification is a spatialized, immersive experience. Thirty-two channels of sound, corresponding to the sixty-four electrodes placed on key parts of the scalp during the EEG, are output to individual hanging speakers, distributed in a form corresponding to that of an enlarged human skull. The visitor enters this cranial space and is thereby located within the soundscape of Claire's brain, hearing the surrounding patterns of activation and non-activation. This aesthetic experience of data is nonetheless a bleak one. It is hard to find Claire herself in this topographical distribution of signals, which, in essence, embodies a gap—a lesion. The museum does not look to fill this gap with information so much as to map and realize it as a feature within a landscape.

Amnesia Museum is somewhat reminiscent of an archeological collection,

3 See Catherine Loveday and Martin A. Conway, "Using SenseCam with an Amnesic Patient: Accessing Inaccessible Everyday Memories," *Memory* 19, no. 7 (2011): 697–704.

4 See Jill Bennett, "Visual Episodic Memory and the Neurophenomenology of Digital Photography," in *The Routledge Companion to Photography Theory*, ed. Jane Tormey and Mark Durden (New York: Routledge, 2020).

5 See Francisco Varela, "A Dimly Perceived Horizon: The Complex Meeting Ground between Lived and Physical Time," *Ann. N.Y. Acad. Sciences* 879 (1999): 143–54.

6 See Evan Thompson, *Mind in Life: Biology, Phenomenology, and the Sciences of Mind* (Cambridge, MA: Harvard University Press, 2010).

though its specimens are a mix of found and fabricated, objects and anti-objects, marking the negative space of a gap. Vitrines of archaeological remains sit alongside prints and video, incorporating archival film of the final evacuation of St Kilda. One such display case contains a clay object from St Kilda, the label explaining that it is imprinted with Iron Age fingerprints. In another vitrine sits a rocklike form, which turns out to be a contemporary 3-D powder print. Printed from a brain scan, it is a 1:1 scale model of the large lesion in the right hemisphere of Claire's brain, the mass of dead tissue that prevents her from remembering the past and imagining the future. In another, what appear to be remnants turn out to be ceramic casts of the negative spaces between the stones of a cleit (Cleit 1003, Hirta)—the name for the dry stone "bothies" built by St Kildans.

There is a particular scene in *Lesions in the Landscape* that echoes this excavation of negative space: an oblique aerial shot of the houses and stone cleits set against the lush green hillside as darkness falls on Hirta. Pools of light move across the stone structures, emanating from torchbearers on the ground, their figures too small to make out. These are interpreted as searchlights "looking for signs of life" by a group in a facilitated discussion during the work's exhibition in Liverpool.[7] The group sees in this landscape an image of brain activity, evoking "synaptic gaps and little missing bits," and "impulses rather than memories." The sporadic blips of light poignantly suggest that the search yields little; there is no one left, the lights are fading. The people in the discussion are living with dementia. Claire's experience of amnesia is, for them, moving and resonant.

For this audience, *Lesions in the Landscape* promotes a meaningful expression of the grief accompanying dementia. The landscape is immediately associated with "desolation," but in the course of a shared reflection, the experience of the work is described as "amazing and exhilarating." Such an engagement is instructive. If *Lesions in the Landscape* is about amnesia, then its capacity to connect to those who live with forms of memory loss is integral to its purpose. The way in which it is taken up by this audience tells us something about the meaning of the work. It also speaks to the function of art more generally, implicitly challenging the limitations of those arts programs for people with dementia that restrict their focus to in-the-moment pleasure rather than self-reflection.

If art's purpose is to elaborate experience—in fact, to proffer an aesthetic engagement that shifts feeling and perception—the function of its dialogue with neuroscience is never simply to communicate science. Art transforms scientific understanding of memory loss at the point at which a signal is mapped to a felt experience. To that end, aesthetic expression arises from a direct relationship to experience, whether elaborating self-experience or a shared sensibility, as in this case, where Claire is a key collaborator along with the artist and scientists.

An aesthetic transaction is a dynamic engagement rather than a message. The challenge for art is never simply to tell a story of someone else's condition but to realize, in an external form, a connection to internal experience. Art is rarely needed to deliver information in a normalized format that conforms to expectation. It is, however, vital to registering the information that is lost in conventional communications, which struggle to accommodate and even to recognize neurodivergent experience.

Memory-traces are less traces of things than of past interactions, scenically envisaged, suggests the German psychoanalyst Alfred Lorenzer.[8] Those who work with memory loss and its psychosocial impact have long argued that

7 Jill Bennett, Lynn Froggett, et al., "Memory Loss and Scenic Experience: An Arts Based Investigation," *Forum Qualitative Sozialforschung/Forum: Qualitative Social Research* 20, no. 1 (2019), https://doi.org/10.17169/fqs-20.1.3126.

8 See Alfred Lorenzer, "Language, Life Praxis and Scenic Understanding in Psychoanalytic Therapy, Translated" (1983), *International Journal of Psychoanalysis* 97, no. 5 (2016): 1399–414, 1402.

9 See Steven Sabat, "Implicit Memory and People with Alzheimer's Disease: Implications for Caregiving," *American Journal of Alzheimer's Disease and Other Dementias* 21, no. 1 (2006): 11–14.

10 See Steven Sabat, "Capacity for Decision-Making in Alzheimer's Disease: Selfhood, Positioning and Semiotic People," *Australian and New Zealand Journal of Psychiatry* 39, no. 11 (2005): 1030–35.

we need to value different forms of memory and interaction, supporting reflection as much as recall.[9] A memory of experience may be implicit, reflected in actions and behaviors regardless of the ability to recall it.[10] In dementia, for example, emotions and traces of experiences persist after explicit memory has faded. And for Claire, emotions and traces of experiences may be regenerated in viewing her photographs, even where recall of the detail of an event is limited.

If Illingworth's work is about the lesion that compromises memory, it is also, in a profound sense, an open-ended exploration of adaptation—of the way in which the structure of a landscape might, for some, contain experience or ground free-floating memories of events. *Lesions in the Landscape* attends to interactions and the potential for using landscape to orient, remember, and envisage loss. This is not a memory aesthetics that indulges a commemorative poetics, nor a sentimental cleaving to the past; instead, it proposes an investigation of memory as a step-by-step, moment-by-moment encounter that begins and ends with an embodied feeling. Landscape, as it is configured in this work, is not an accumulation of memory traces but the site of a search.

Jill Bennett is a Scientia Professor and Australian Research Council Laureate Fellow at the University of New South Wales Sydney, where she leads fEEL (feltExperience and Empathy Lab), a transdisciplinary lab studying subjective experiences of mental/emotional health, dementia, and trauma. She is Founding Director of The Big Anxiety, a festival of people, art, and science (thebiganxiety.org). As a writer, curator, and immersive media producer, she creates work that includes arts, science, and community collaborations and design of engagement relating to mental health. Through fEEL, she has codeveloped innovative, immersive environments and virtual-reality tools designed to cultivate empathy and/or play a direct role in mental-health support or suicide prevention. Bennett has worked extensively in the areas of trauma and memory. Her books include *Empathic Vision* (Stanford University Press, 2005) and *Practical Aesthetics* (Bloomsbury Academic, 2012), as well as monographs on art, creative technology, and its social impact. She is currently writing a book on The Big Anxiety (Bloomsbury Academic, forthcoming).

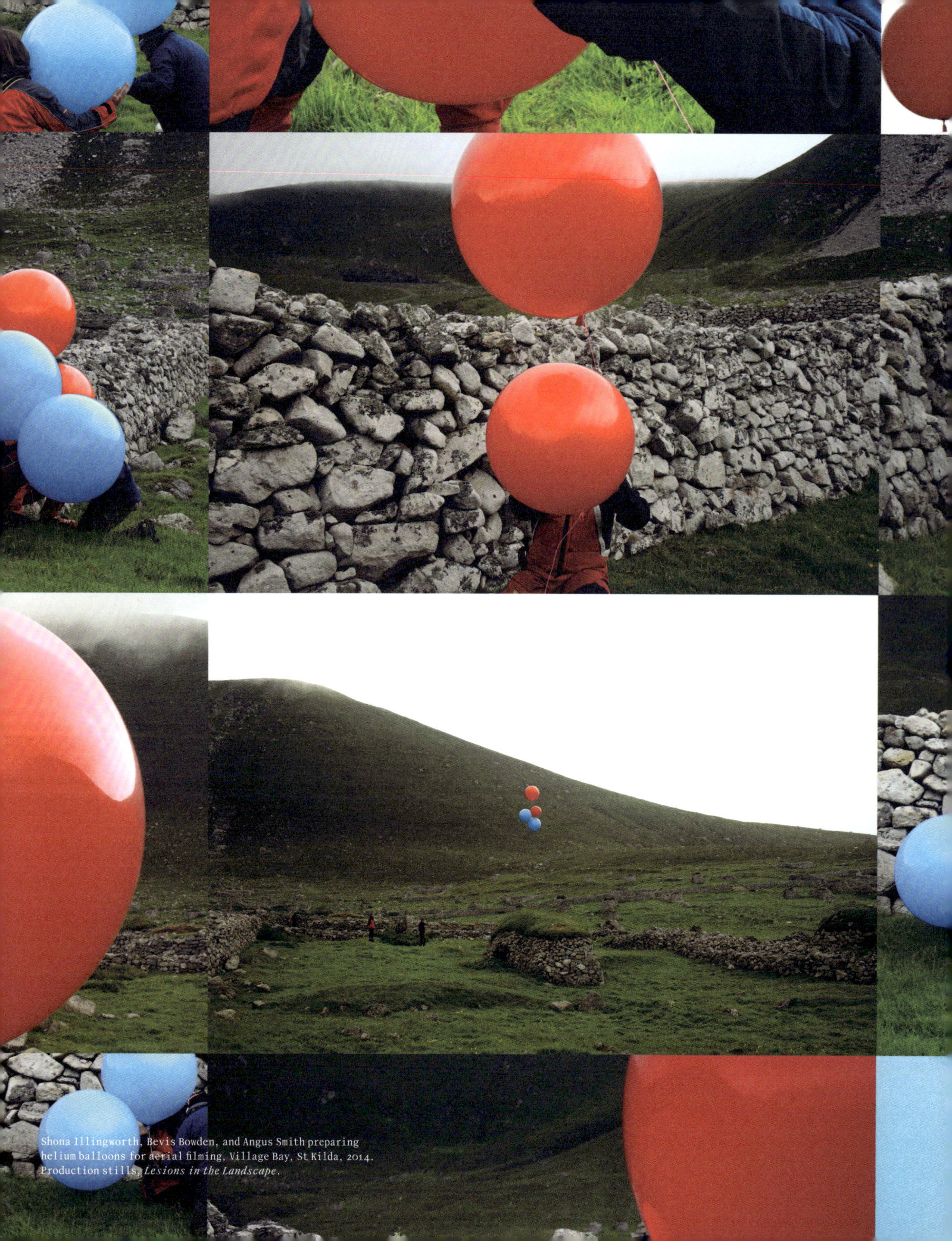

Shona Illingworth, Bevis Bowden, and Angus Smith preparing helium balloons for aerial filming, Village Bay, St Kilda, 2014. Production stills, *Lesions in the Landscape*.

Issie MacPhail
FIELD NOTES

Fragments and moments from the learning, making and dwelling practices used over three journeys to St Kilda, in the making of Shona Illingworth's *Lesions in the Landscape* (2015).

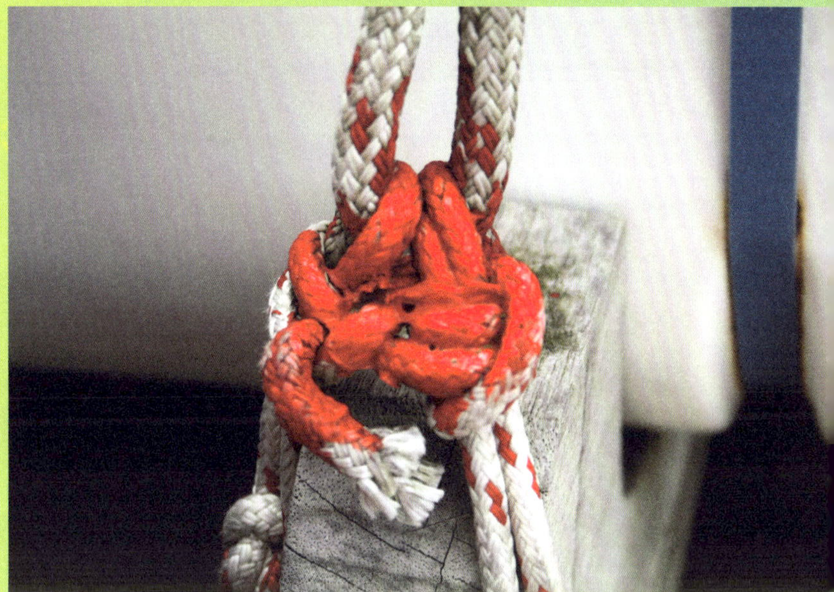

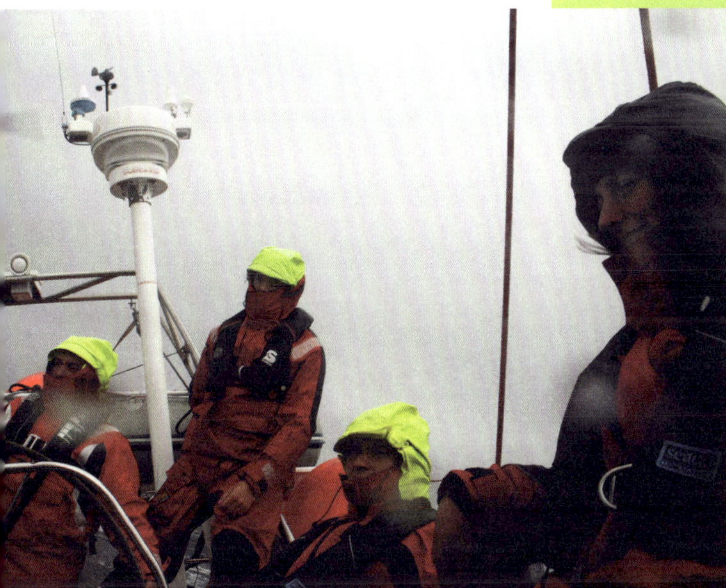

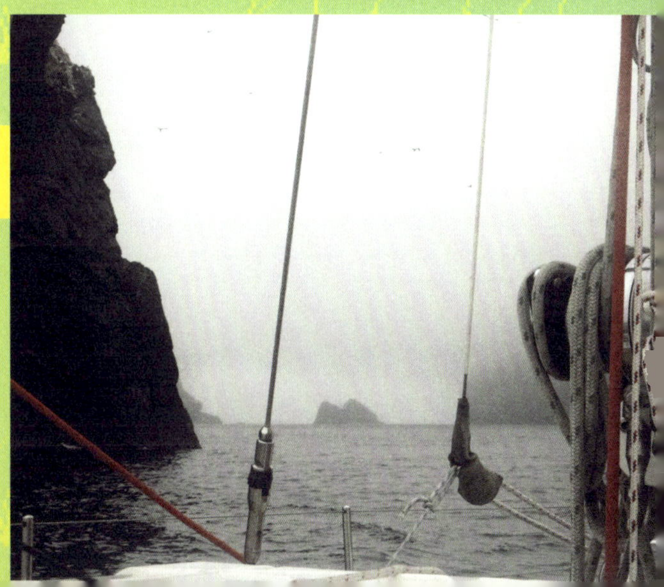

Stormy weather, filming in the *Elinca*, St Kilda, 2014.
Production stills, *Lesions in the Landscape*.

Finding our Way

"Peripheral" places are not beyond the reach of late capitalism, nor historic mercantilism. The pivot of sustained colonial relations is to change people's cultural, legal, and economic relationship with their natural resources, and with each other.[1] Historically, Scottish island and Highland people were both colonised and coloniser. Such global flows are local, peopled and personal. The moppings and wipings and clerkings. The sweatings and swearings. The mundane daily minutiae through which practices of colonial administration become naturalised and embedded into personal and statist moral economies.[2]

Visual and Technical Cultures

"Maps are powerful cognitive instruments that control your imaginary and your feelings."
—Walter D. Mignolo, "On Pluriversality and Multipolar World Order," *Constructing the Pluriverse*[3]

The orientation of J. W. Norie's 1816 *New Improved Chart of the Hebrides or Lewis Isles* reminds us of the peculiarly strong impact on ideas of remoteness or peripherality affected by cartographic conventions.[4] This maritime chart positions the sea as an enabler of connection and commerce.[5] West is bottom of the page. By opening with an observation on the effects of turning "the map" upside down, Shona Illingworth's video installation engages firmly with the conceptual work of decolonisation. To us, St Kilda is south. Shona grew up in northwest Sutherland, on the Scottish mainland. I spent my childhood summers in northwest Sutherland and my adult life on a croft there. For us, St Kilda is part of that wider cultural imaginary. Decoloniality restores radical import to our local histories.

1 See Issie MacPhail, "Land, Crofting and The Assynt Crofters Trust: A Post-Colonial Geography?" (PhD diss., University of Wales, Lampeter, 2002).

2 See Issie MacPhail, *A Sprinkling of Salt; A Sprinkling of Pride*, my theatre piece commissioned for Scottish Trade Union Congress AGM, 2012.

3 Walter D. Mignolo, "On Pluriversality and Multipolar World Order: Decoloniality after Decolonization; Dewesternization after the Cold War," in *Constructing the Pluriverse: The Geopolitics of Knowledge*, ed. Bernd Reiter (Durham, NC: Duke University Press, 2018), 90–116.

4 J. W. Norie, *New and Improved Chart of the Hebrides or Lewis Islands and Adjacent Coast of Scotland from the Mull of Cantire to Cape Wrath/ Drawn from the Latest Surveys* (London: J. W. Norie & Co., 1816).

5 Kevin James Grant, "Hebridean Gaels and the Sea in the Early 19th Century," *Proceedings of the Society of Antiquaries of Scotland* 147 (November 2018): 261–84.

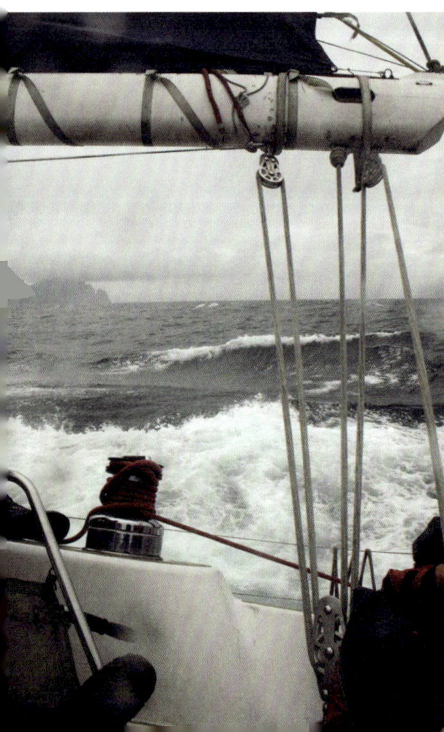

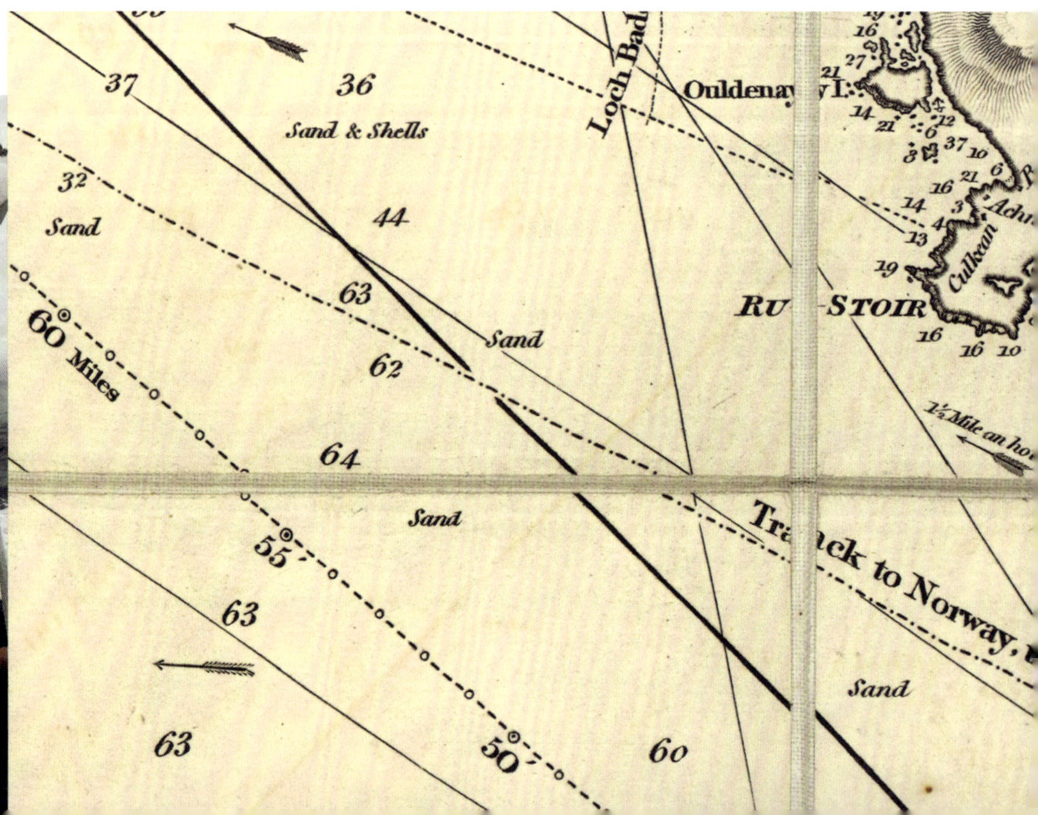

Wave-world

"… light, sound and feeling tear at our moorings […] In the words of the environmental philosopher David Macauley (2005:307), 'we breathe, think and dream in the regions of the air': not on the fixed surface of the landscape but in the swirling midst of the weather-world."
—Tim Ingold, *Being Alive*[6]

I was with Shona and cinematographer Bevis Bowden in St Kilda, and created an ethnography using cameras, audio recording, fieldwork diaries and GPS tracking. I drew upon Tim Ingold's concepts of dwelling and "weather-world" as a means of interrogating our mutual, emplaced praxis. Ingold's theory of dwelling focuses "upon embodied practices of dwelling and being-in-the-world."[7] He recommends sea-ing the land because academic convention has privileged "land-ing the sea."[8] This scape-focused convention renders land and sea as surfaces instead of material mobilities and flows. Our St Kilda work revealed that this weather-world is a wave-world.

6 Tim Ingold, *Being Alive: Essays on Movement, Knowledge and Description* (London: Routledge, 2011), 135.

7 John Wylie, "landscape," in *The Dictionary of Human Geography*, ed. Derek Gregory (London: Blackwell Publishers, 2009), https://nls.idm.oclc.org/login?url=https://search.credoreference.com/content/entry/bkhumgeo/landscape/0?institutionId=238; Tim Ingold, *The Perception of the Environment: Essays on Livelihood, Dwelling and Skill* (London: Routledge, 2011).

8 Ingold, *Being Alive*, 131–35.

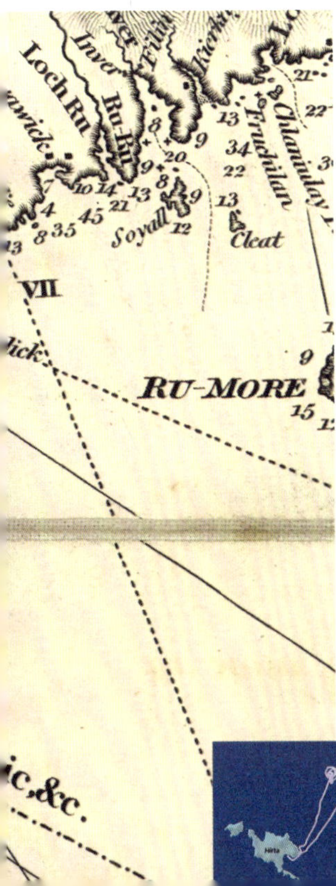

Issie MacPhail, *How Space Hides Time: GPS Journeys in the St Kildan Archipelago*, 2014. Fragments from GPS tracks made during fieldwork and filming in and around St Kilda, in the course of the *Lesions in the Landscape* project

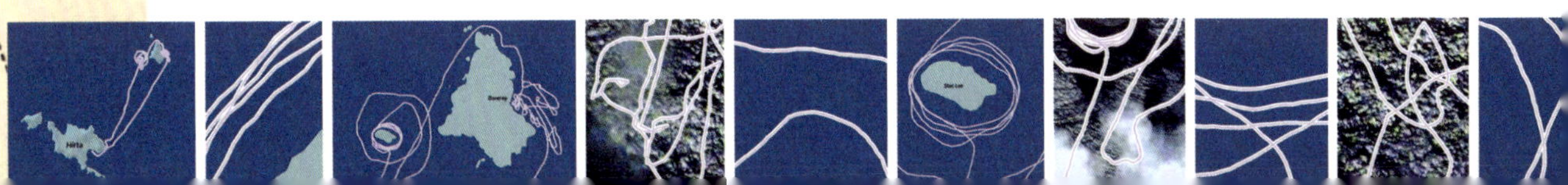

Approaching St Kilda

Ten years ago, Donald Meek stated:

> Out of the tsunami of 700-plus books and articles which has all but overwhelmed the archipelago, less than (perhaps) ten books can be justly regarded as properly authoritative, in the sense that they are founded firmly on a detailed examination of the St Kilda islands, coupled with residency and overall familiarity, as well as an exhaustive interaction with relevant sources, oral and literary, Gaelic and English.[9]

This paper artifice is inhibiting. St Kilda is a place made in the minds of outsiders. The lesion in this landscape enabled that tsunami. Now, only spectral traces of the old *Hiortaichs'* lives are etched into that place. Past National Trust for Scotland archaeologist Kevin Grant explains:

> "St Kilda" is something which outsiders bring with them to the islands. [...] When, at 4pm, they motor off over the horizon, they take St Kilda with them and the islands revert to Hiort, a working Hebridean landscape which is home to one of the world's most unusual present-day communities.[10]

Amnesia is not a historic force of forgetting. Its' most frightening power of erasure is its' momentum within the topologies of the present. Learning from Chakrabarty's thoughts on the task of "provincializing" Europe, our work in St Kilda makes it clear to us that this cannot be achieved without writing back into notice, and power, the erased cosmologies of the peripheral other.[11]

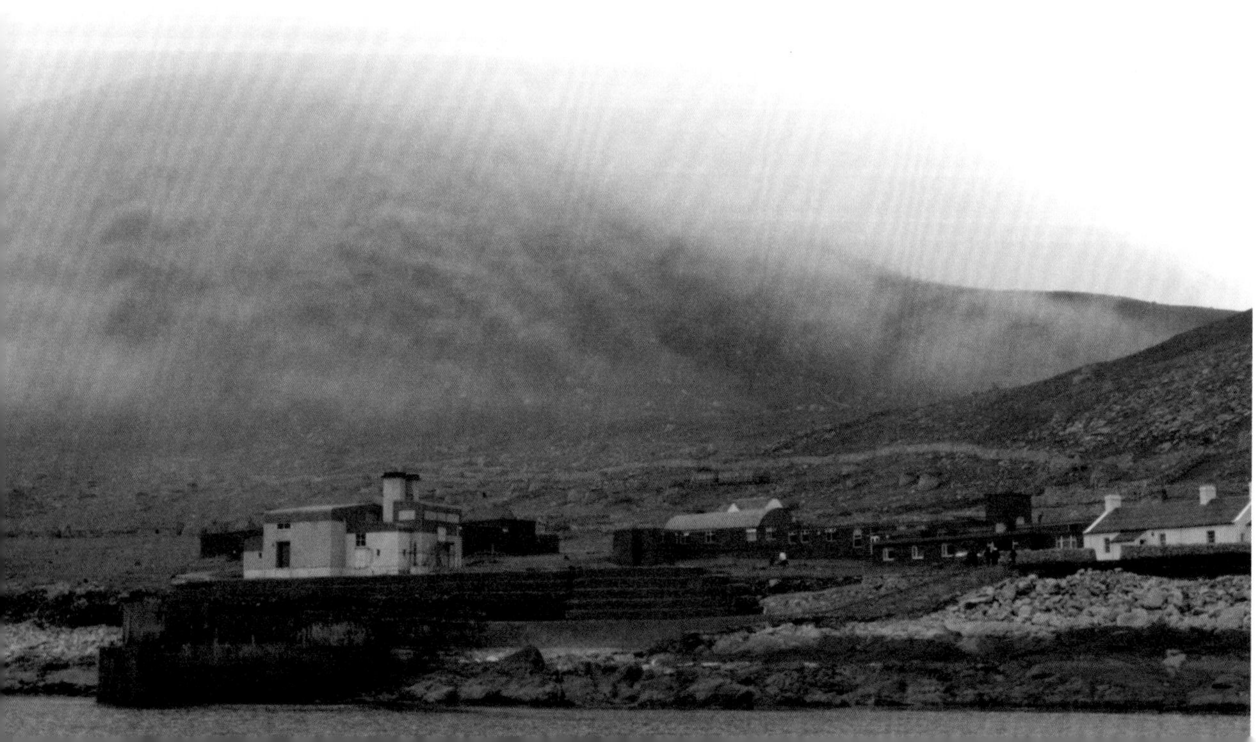

9 Donald E. Meek, "Eileanaich Cian a' Chuain'/ 'The Remote Islanders of the Sea?' Towards a Re-Examination of the Role of Church and Faith in St Kilda," in *Rewriting St Kilda: New Views on Old Ideas* (Isle of Lewis: Islands Book Trust, 2011), 90.

10 Alex Boyd and Kevin James Grant, *St Kilda: The Silent Islands* (Edinburgh: Luath Press Ltd., 2018), 32. *Hiort* (Gaelic) is Hirta, the principal island in the St Kilda archipelago. *Hiortaich* (Gaelic) means the inhabitants of St Kilda (St Kildans) or pertaining to St Kilda.

11 See Dipesh Chakrabarty, *Provincializing Europe: Postcolonial Thought and Historical Difference* (Princeton, NJ: Princeton University Press, 2000).

Faith, Hope, Charity

The sound of a Lewis church choir, singing Psalm 133, creates a sensory crescendo in the video installation. This braided vocal flow streams around the sea stacs, punctuated by gannets in flight. The delicacy of this sequence quietly reveals the ways in which *Gàidhealtachd* histories are part of our being-in-the-world.[12] One of the distinctive beauties of this culture is Gaelic psalm singing. Ornamentation of the voice, and of the mind, is historically important in the *Gàidhealtachd*.[13]

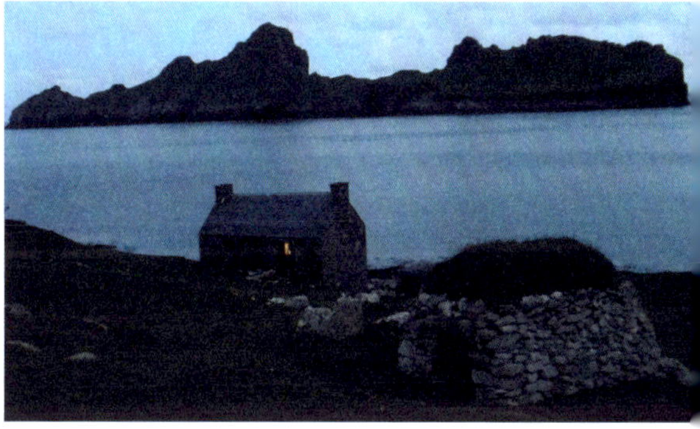

The Empire at Home

"Your joint letter of this date [8 November 1811] offering me, the Estates and Property left to Marion Macleod alias Maclean one of you, and Spouse of the other by the last will and testament of her deceased brother Alexander MacLean of the Bahama Islands, with all the Produce of Said Estate, and slaves therein or belonging to the said Alexander at the time of his death, with Buildings etc."
—Neil Macleod, Letter to Lachlan Macleod, 1811[14]

This letter is to the St Kilda minister, Lachlan Macleod, from his cousin, Neil Macleod of Gesto, Isle of Skye. Neil Macleod agreed to pay £200 sterling for the Bahamian estate, produce and slaves. From Pretoria, in the following century, attunement to colonial violence and entanglement are voiced by the Gaelic poet Duncan Livingstone:

Do chorp donn an-sin 'na laighe,	Your brown body lying before me,
Toll air tholl a ' sileadh fala.	Blood pouring out from wound on wound.
Baba Inkòsi Sikelele, Baba Inkòsi Sikelele.	Baba Inkòsi Sikelele, Baba Inkòsi Sikelele.[15]

12 *Gàidhealtachd* (Gaelic) is the Gaelic-speaking cultural region, or the Scottish Highlands and western islands.

13 See Fraser MacDonald, "St Kilda and the Sublime," *Ecumene* 8, no. 2 (2001): 151–74, 163; Murdo Macdonald, Lesley Lindsay, Lorna J. Waite, and Meg Bateman, *Sealladh às ùr air Ealain na Gàidhealthachd: brìgh lèirsinn ann an dualchas nan gàidheal = Rethinking Highland Art: The Visual Significance of Gaelic Culture* (Edinburgh: Royal Scottish Academy, 2013).

14 Michael Robson, *St Kilda: Church, Visitors and "Natives"* (Isle of Lewis: Islands Book Trust, 2005), 248.

15 Extract from Donnchadh MacDhunléibhe (Duncan Livingstone), "Bean Dubh a ' Caoidh a Fir a Chaidh a Mharbhadh leis a ' Phoileas (A Black Woman Mourns Her Husband Killed by the Police)," in *An Tuil: Anthology of 20th Century Scottish Gaelic Verse*, ed. Ronald Black (Edinburgh: Polygon, 1999), 77.

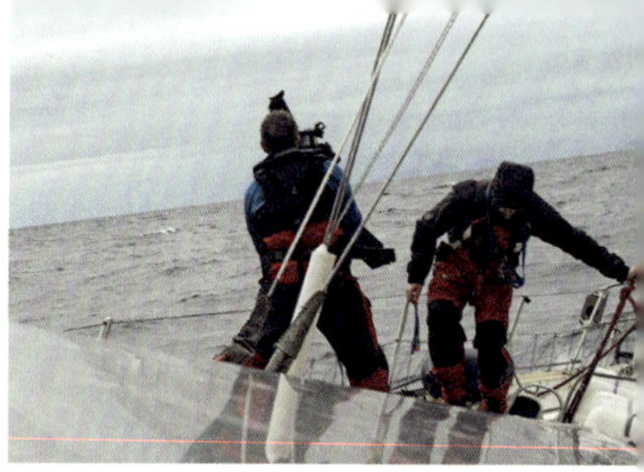

Sea Tracks

Our journeys to St Kilda and our work there were enabled by a boat. The *Elinca* is a sixty-seven-foot Atlantic Challenge yacht, built to go round the world "the wrong way"—against the trade winds. Today, the trade winds are associated with colonisation and the triangular trade. The older meaning of "trade" is a path. This notion of sensory corridors of sea travel, along known tracks and enabled by geographically located types of wind, only later came to mean winds that facilitated historically specific forms of exploitative commerce.[16] These tracks are formed and fuelled by air currents and the birling of the earth—the Coriolis effect.[17] Local seas and channels are also governed by streams, flows, and eddies, in the air and in the sea.

16 See Issie MacPhail, *How Space Hides Time: GPS Journeys in the St Kilda Archipelago*, the visual art I created for *Lesions in the Landscape* Amnesia Museum (2015).

17 *Birl* (Scots) means "to revolve with a whirring sound; to twirl round; to spin." Alexander Warrack, ed., *Chambers Scots Dictionary* (Edinburgh: W. & R. Chambers, Ltd, 1975).

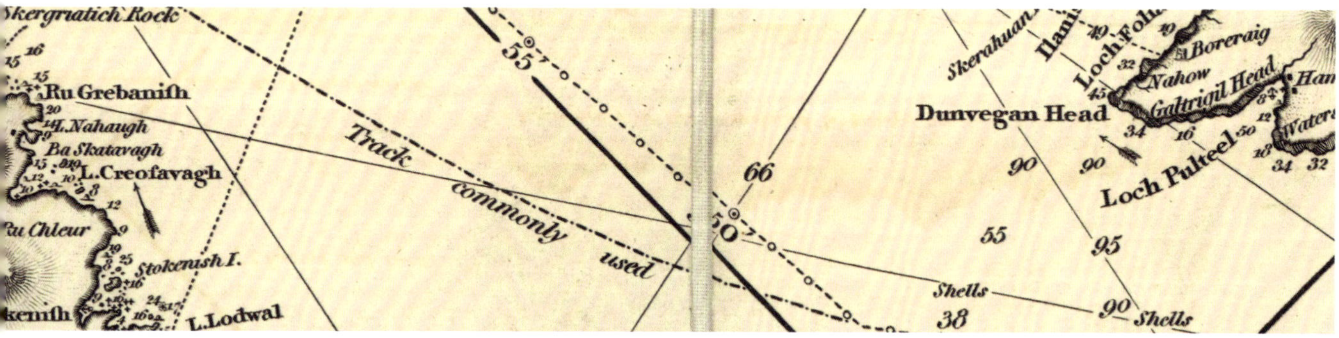

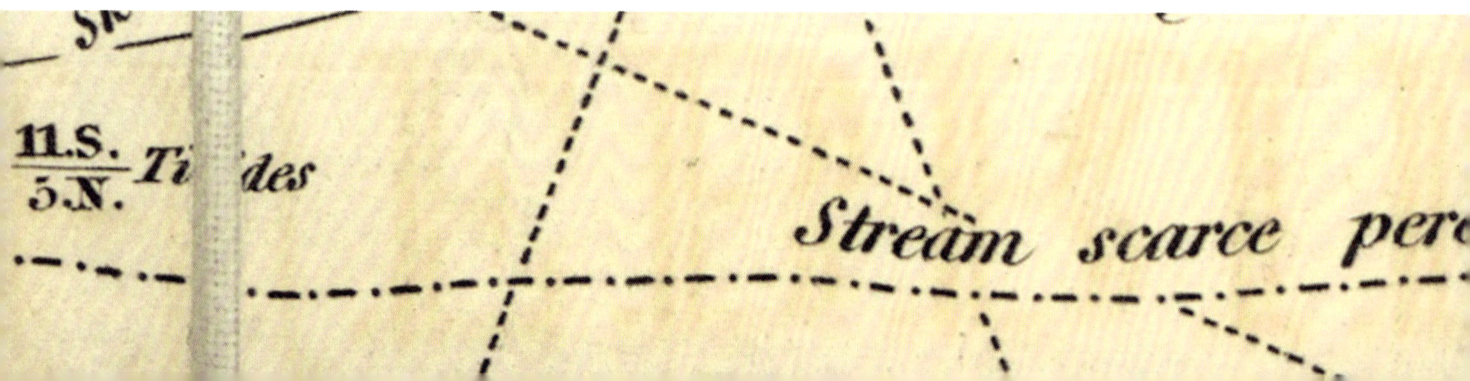

Technologies of Empire Past: Water

During the eighteenth and nineteenth centuries, pilot books and marine charts began to replace the human pilots who knew particular waters. Charts began to transpose, from pilot books and captains' logs, pen and ink sketches of strategically important horizons.[18] The micro-histories of literate Europe, collating diverse but particular maritime and coastal knowledges into systemised written and visual forms, is a critical enabler of empire.[19]

Technologies of Empire Present: Air

Mathematical means of navigation and positionality slice the air, sketching invisible geometries. Danger Area EG D701, the Hebrides Range, "occupies 115,000 km^2 of sanitised airspace with unlimited altitude."[20] Unlimited altitude signals an assertion of volumetric sovereignty.[21] Fraser MacDonald reminds us that the colonisation of outer space, "rather than being a decisive and transcendent break from the past, is merely an extension of long-standing regimes of power."[22]

In Uist, Angus Peter Campbell bears witness:

Eadar Beinn Sheaval is mullach na Urals
Tha mìltean de ràdars a ' feitheamh ri sprùilleadh
Air cliathaichean mòintich ar leisg 's ar ciùineis –
Air sléibhtean ar coingeis tha freumhan a phuinnsein.

Between Beinn Sheaval and the tops of the Urals
Are thousands of radars waiting for crumbs
On the mountainsides of our sloth and docility –
On the hills of our apathy are the roots of its poison.[23]

18 See Christopher Fleet, Margaret Wilkes, and Charles W. J. Withers, *Scotland: Mapping the Nation* (Edinburgh: Birlinn Ltd., 2012), 173–98.

19 See Domhnall Uilleam Stiùbhart, "The Making of the Minch: French Pirates, British Herring, and Vernacular Knowledges at an Eighteenth-Century Maritime Crossroads," in *The New Coastal History: Cultural and Environmental Perspectives from Scotland and Beyond* (London: Palgrave Macmillan, 2017).

20 QinetiQ, "MOD Hebrides," MOD LTPA, 2021.

21 See Franck Billé, "Volumetric Sovereignty Part 1: Cartography vs. Volumes," *Society and Space* (March 2019).

22 Fraser MacDonald, "Anti-Astropolitik: Outer Space and the Orbit of Geography," *Progress in Human Geography*, no. 31 (2007): 610.

23 Extract from Aonghas Padraig Caimbeul (Angus Peter Campbell, South Uist), "Ràdar Beinn Sheaval (The Radar of Beinn Sheaval)," in *An Tuil*, 672.

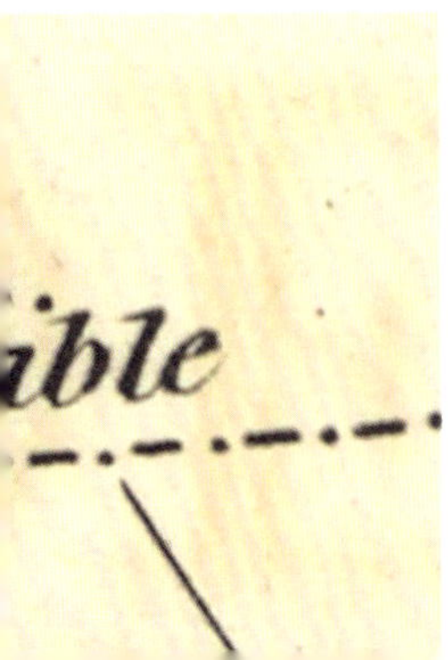

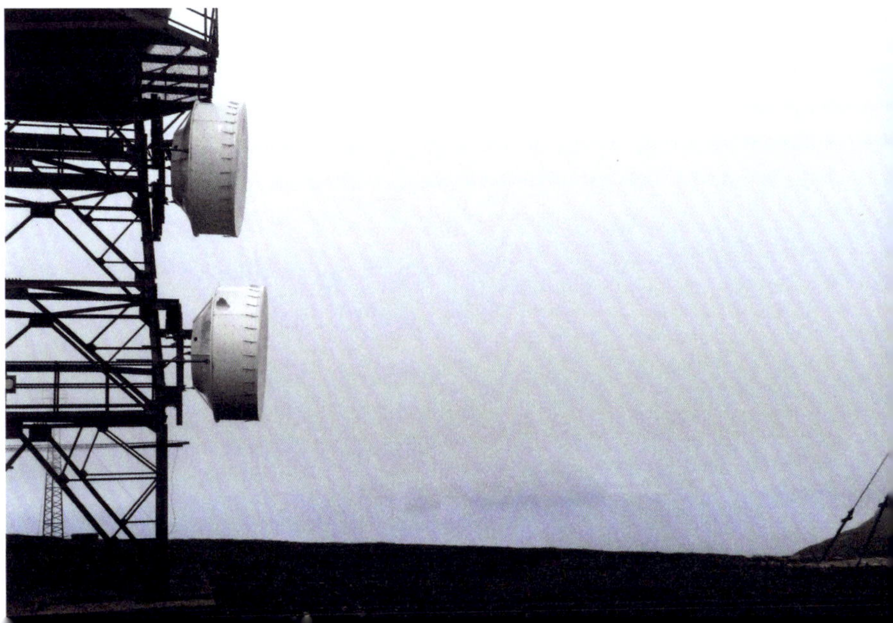

24 Extract from Donnchadh MacDhunléibhe (Duncan Livingstone), "Feasgar an Duine Ghil (The Evening of the White Man)," in *An Tuil*, 72.

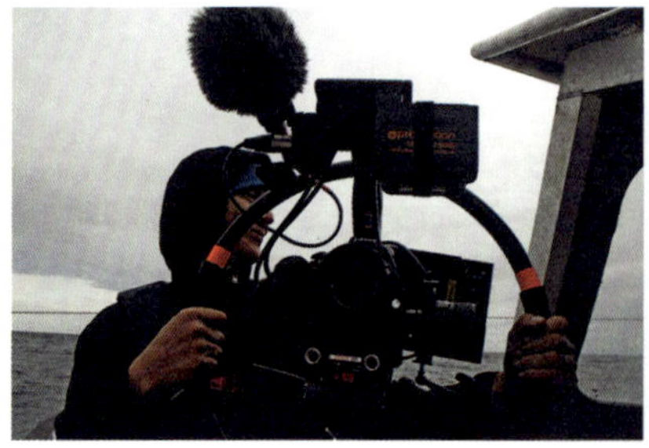

Shona Illingworth, on location, St Kilda, 2014. Production still, *Lesions in the Landscape*.

Rockets Galore

In *Lesions in the Landscape*, we observe Russian and American operatives guiding a Soyuz supply ship into dock at the International Space Station. Below, in Danger Area DG701, British and NATO operatives have been keeping careful watch for incoming missiles or aircraft ever since the old Cold War.

> *Is a-nis sgéith san iarmailt, a ' seòladh fànas tha gun chrìoch*
> *Le cumhachdan pleasgach, reubach, stiallach, le rocaidean fiadhaich udroighne.*
> *Is shìos san aigeann, air tighinn fìor, tha an sgeul a dh ' adhbharaich caochladh snuadh*
> *Aig oimadh céilidh, a ' toirt oirnn grìs: fomhairean ag éirigh ás a ' chuan.*
>
> And now flying in the sky, penetrating outer space
> With cracking, tearing, ripping forces, with wild exotic rockets.
> And down in the deep, come true is the tale that turned faces pale
> At many a ceilidh, making us shudder: monsters rising from the ocean.[24]

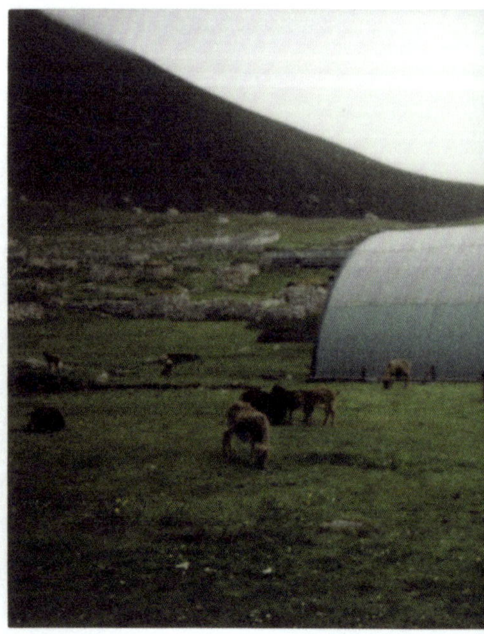

Making Art and Making Home

Humans and non-human animals have a remarkable tendency to create "home" wherever they find themselves. This individual and collective arranging of spaces and rapid creation of "tradition," or collective habits, is a fascinating counterpoint to social constructions of homemaking as settled, slow, and fixed in place. Working somewhere strange is achieved through the mutual rituals we create in our makeshift homing.

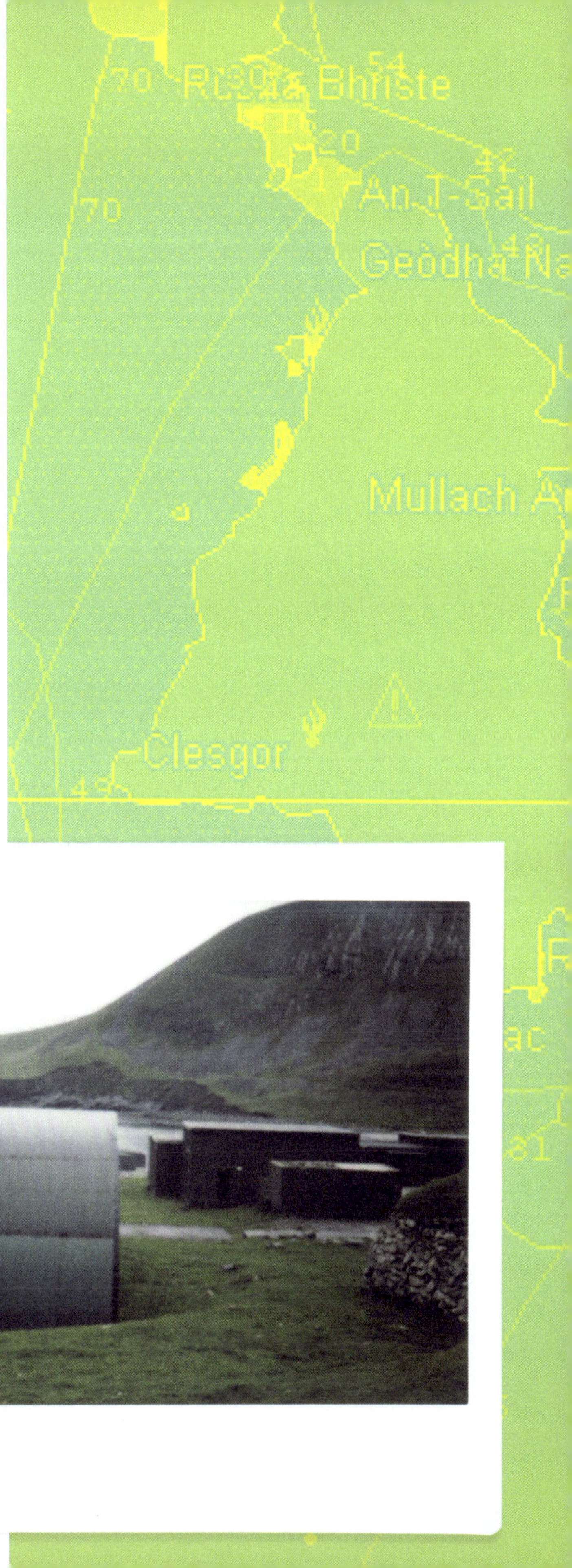

Shona Illingworth, *Soay Sheep and Nissan Shed*, 2014. Polaroids.

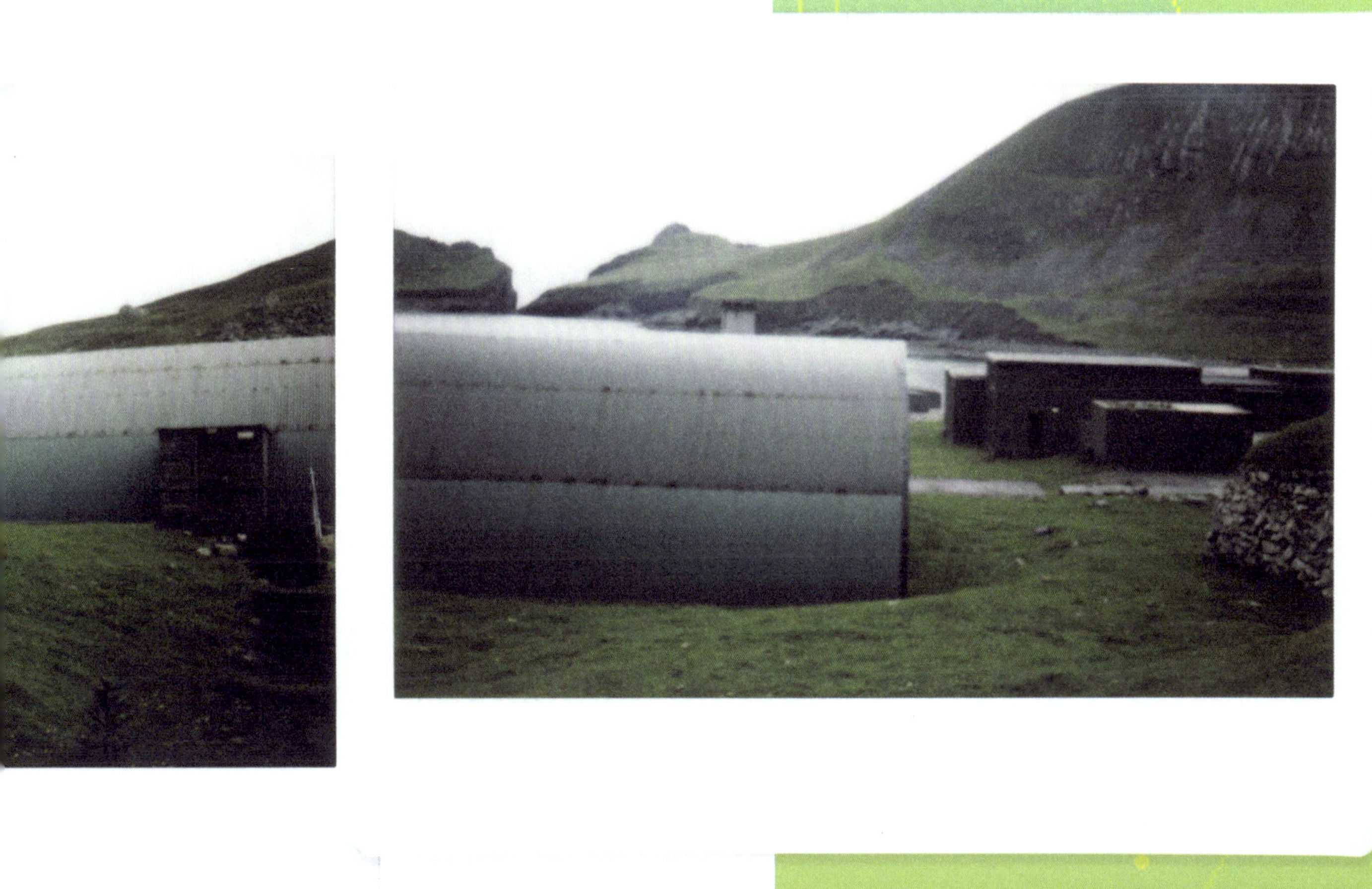

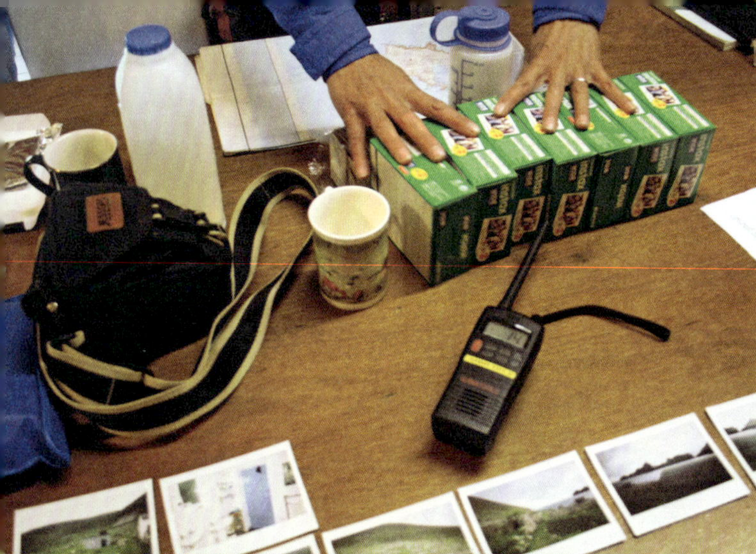

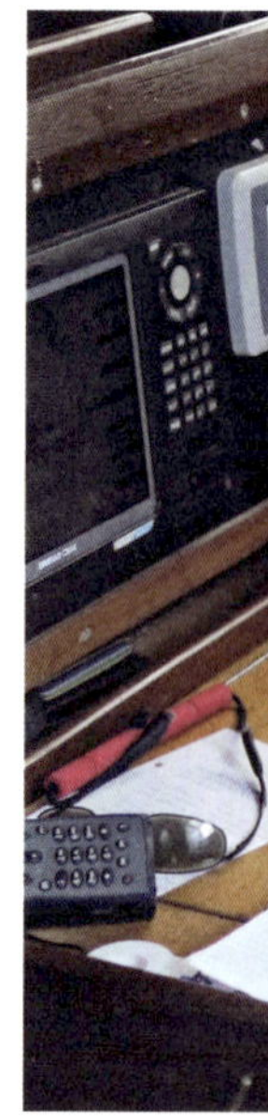

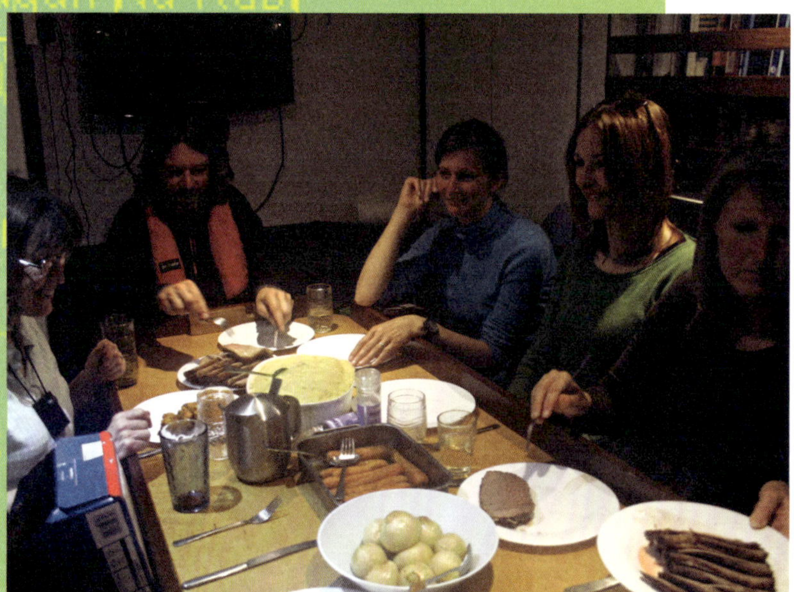

Claire, Charlie Fleming, Shona Illingworth, Jill Bennett, and Catherine Loveday on the *Elinca*, St Kilda. Production still, *Lesions in the Landscape*.

At Home in Hirta

What I mind most is the laughing—great, wild belly laughs, till we wept.[25] About something and nothing. The exhaustion. Minds whirring, bodies walking. Walking, walking, walking. Is making art in place a peculiar form of shared and shifting harmonisation?

Sweating in waterproofs. Surprising sunshine. Scratchy heather on the hill. Ripping waterproofs.

Bevis keeping and making order in every space we used. Cleaning, sweeping, unpacking, arranging. Order and disorder, creating the whole. Charging, backing up, copying. Applying his place-sensitive ingenuity to our intricate artistic turbulence.

Neighbours for dinner. Post delivered. Chats in the street. Minding to empty the wastewater container from under the sink. Walking for showers at The Ablutions Block. Not bothering to walk for a shower.

Night filming. Dawn filming. Daylight filming. Land filming. Boat filming. Cliff filming. Scribbling. Thinking. Sometimes sleeping. Fear. Elation. Listening. Laughter.

Dinners on the *Elinca*.
Hot food. Pudding. Wine and chocolate.
Doing the dishes.

Talk and thought beautifully entangled amongst us.

25 *Mind* (Scots): to remember, remind, notice, take care of. Warrack, *Chambers Scots Dictionary*.

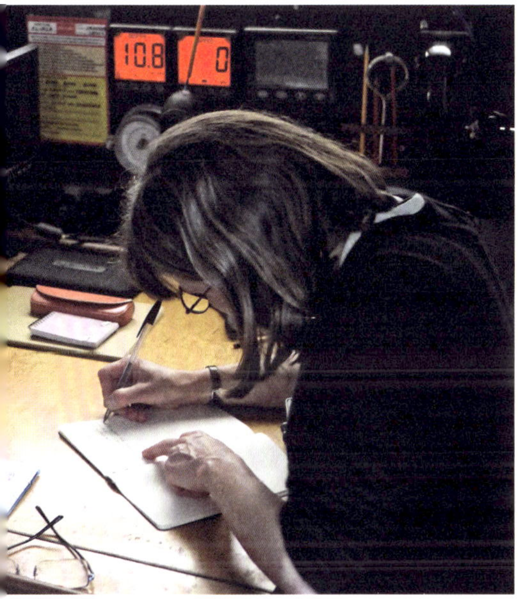

Above: Claire on the *Elinca*, St Kilda, 2014. Production still, *Lesions in the Landscape*. Below: Shona Illingworth and Bevis Bowden, the Feather Store, St Kilda, 2014. Production still, *Lesions in the Landscape*.

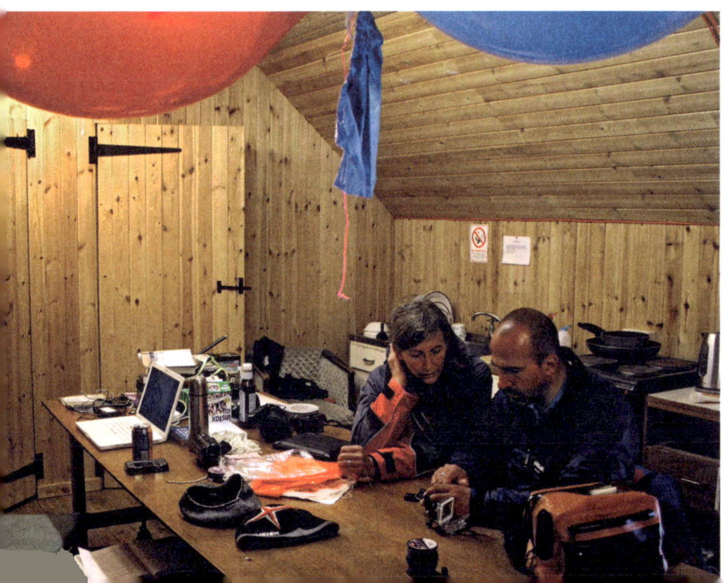

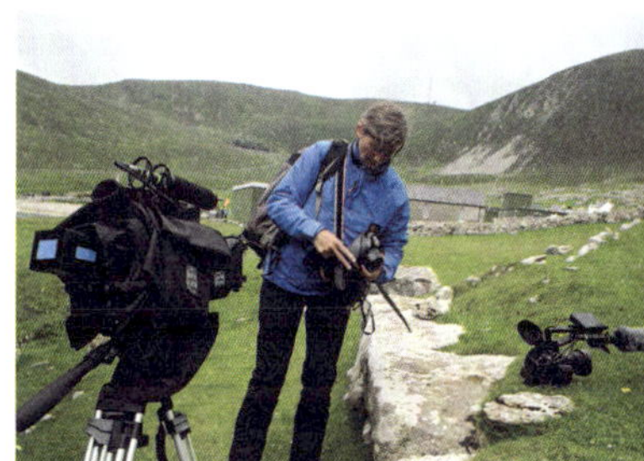

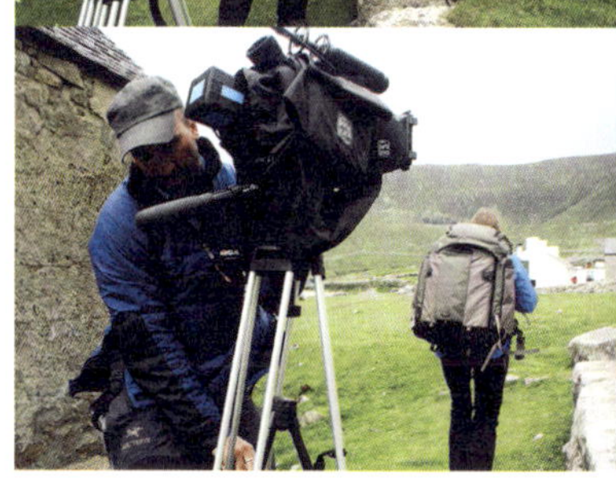

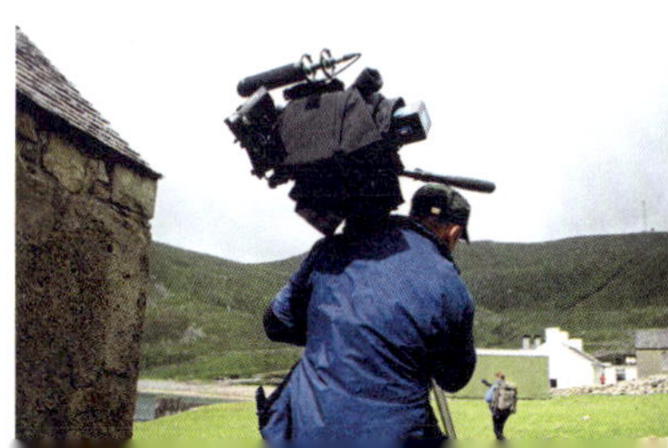

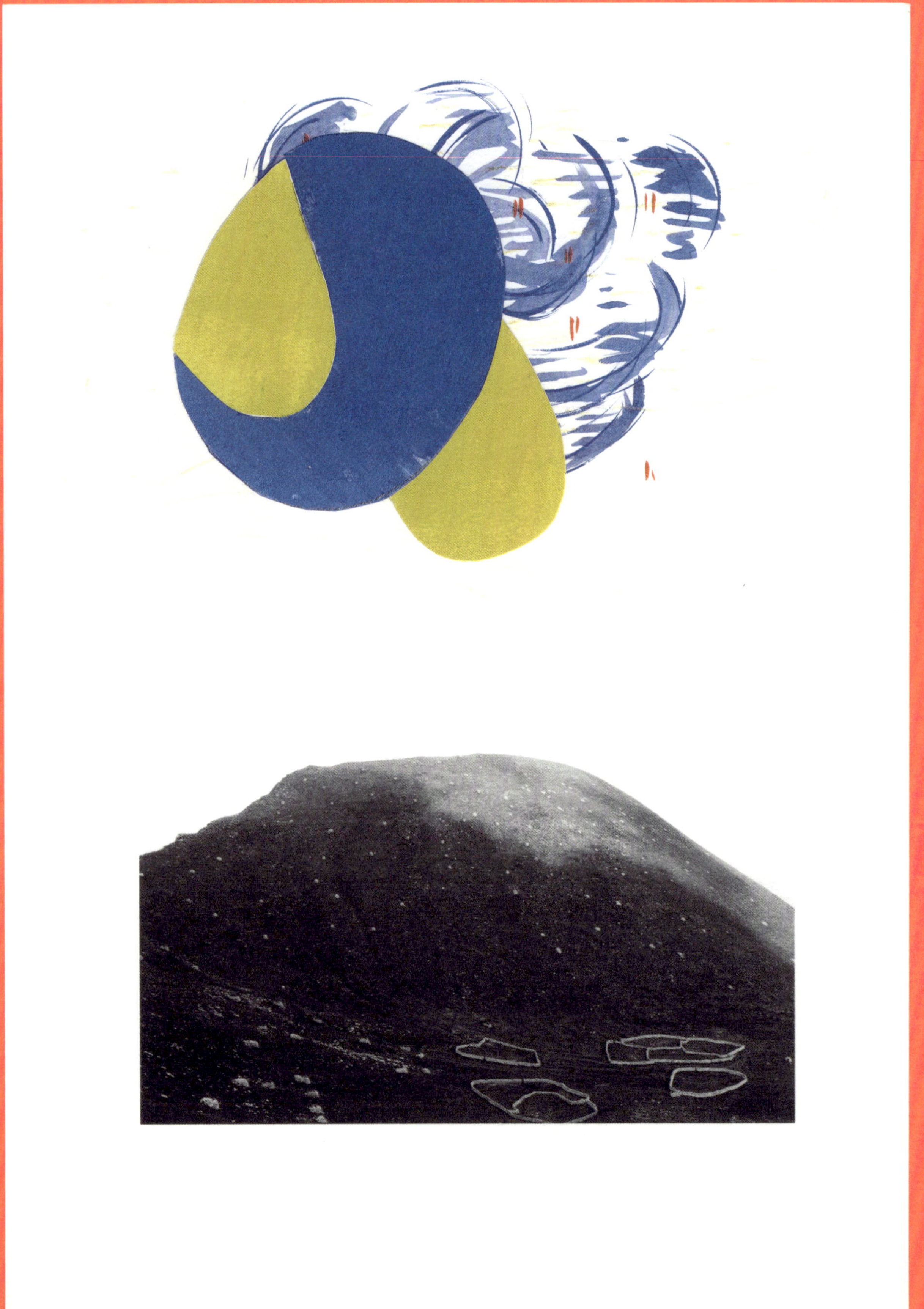

Shona Illingworth, *Aerial Spinning Camera and Cleits*, 2014. Archival pigment print, ink, and gouache, 210 × 297 mm.

26 Shona Illingworth, in conversation with the author, March 2021.

27 See Karen Michelle Barad, *Meeting the Universe Halfway: Quantum Physics and the Entanglement of Matter and Meaning* (Durham, NC: Duke University Press, 2007).

28 *Jabbled* (Scots): ripples, waves, and agitations in fluids. Warrack, *Chambers Scots Dictionary*.

Wave Forms: Light, Sound, Air, Water

Illingworth's artistic praxis emerges from her situated knowledge, allied to an intense attention to "ways of thinking different materialities." In conversation, she explains that "the camera is not just a framing device. Being with the camera is an embodied engagement in a turbulent topology of surfaces, diffracted light, refracted sound, and shifting temporalities."[26] The camera caresses, hurries, ponders, lingers, touches, trails fingers and startles, through considered entanglement with the physics and chemistry of seeing and hearing. The pinhole cameras create multiple fragments of "now", through changes in duration, light frequencies, interferences, and emulsions. The elemental, Baradian intra-actions in the St Kilda weather-world make wave theory, chemical energies, and quantum physics an acutely embodied encounter.[27] The microphones and video cameras turn to, move with, or focus upon, small moments of refraction, diffraction and interference patterns, within our wave-world.

Tracing the Air

An important puzzle was how to avoid simply repeating the slicing, geometric interrogation of the wave-world, constantly carried out by radar and satellite. How might one create a "different eye"? An eye that turns an "embodied" gaze back upon the military space? Shona and Bevis used clusters of helium-filled weather balloons with a GoPro attached. Once cast off, the balloon assemblage etched out the air flows, in its easterly, elliptical drift. When the balloon cluster met the updrafts and gusts rushing around the steep slopes of Oiseval, the turbulence made the balloons dance. The footage swoops and swirls, birdlike.

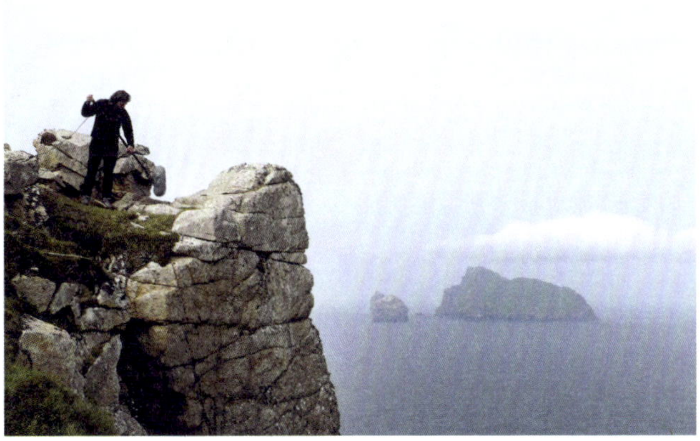

Jabbled Praxis[28]

Making and doing are shaped by the wave-world. The sea forms a sound boundary, aurally distinct from land-bound reverberations. Bevis and Shona send cameras over the Hirta cliffs on ropes, to sense the eddies diffusing at the cliff face. The visceral aspects of sound waves vibrate through our bodies like the shudder that animates a boat, thumping off the top of the swell.
The sea stacs' topography generates perpetual interference patterns in all the waveforms present: sea, sound, air, light, radar, brain. The stacs themselves are the eroded remnants of landforms created by the unruly action of waves of magma and lava.

A triptych birthing
crystalline rocks
in arctic shores,
chains of extinguished fire.
The air a home still
for vibrant life,
thousands and thousands
of birds,
their song a voiceover.

Villagers flee
aerial and tidal threats,
beholding vanishing
gasps of history.
The eye of a satellite
swallows memories
of the future
as things defy gravity,
falling upwards

forever

—Gabriele Schwab, 2021

Gabriele Schwab

WORDS FROZEN IN AIR: SHONA ILLINGWORTH'S VIDEOSCAPES

1 For this and the following, see the supplemental catalogue to the exhibition.

"We are the memories we don't remember."
—Tommy Orange, *There There*, 2018

Catastrophic Abandonment: The Invisible Life of Amnesia

When I first watched *Lesions in the Landscape* (2015), I took in the images in the triptych and the surrounding sounds like signposts from an alien world. At first, I didn't even identify the mysterious dark objects as rocks. By the time a background voice identified them, I was already captivated by the mood, the ethereal beauty of images, sounds, voices, and rhythms. Slowly, a narrative aggregated around fragmented impressions of the haunting life of Claire, a woman suffering from amnesia. Like all of Shona Illingworth's work, *Lesions in the Landscape* is of astounding complexity, both in its historical references and its formal composition. To emphasize the entanglement of the personal and the political, the artist enfolds two layers of an individual and a collective story. Viewers receive the necessary information about both through fragments they have to assemble gradually, like pieces of a puzzle.

On first view, Claire appears in the middle panel of the three-screen video and multichannel immersive sound installation. Not knowing Claire's history, we are guided by her mournful voice as we begin to assemble the fragments that never quite congeal into a full story. But we are made to experience Claire's sense of being lost in a place she cannot recognize as home with children she does not remember raising. As she conveys the feeling of living like an alien on her own planet, we are viscerally affected by her catastrophic loneliness. Encountering Claire in her evacuated here and now, we are invited to experience sensorially what it feels like to be dropped into a space, a time, a story we do not know. We cling to bits and pieces, images that emerge from the void, feeling them, not knowing where they come from or where they will lead.

From the texts that supplement the exhibition, we learn that Claire suffers from the loneliness of amnesia.[1] At age forty-four, she came down with a severe case of viral encephalitis, during which a lesion in her brain destroyed key mnemonic functions. She could barely access any memories of her past, including living with her children. She could neither recognize their or other people's faces, nor could she form any new long-term memories. In her video installation, Illingworth interweaves Claire's story with the amnesia that erases the history of St Kilda, a remote depopulated Scottish archipelago in the North Atlantic. Extreme weather fronts made access to the islands difficult and eventually prompted the decision to evacuate the population, despite St Kilda's four-thousand-year history.

On August 29, 1930, the entire population was removed. A state of historical amnesia followed the abrupt ending of cultural life, transforming the place into an abandoned settlement. While the ruins of a ghostly village contain a material archive of the history of its people, there is no one left to witness or remember. The old stone dwellings seem frozen in a vacant here and now, a history without future, a timeless zone of abandonment. A collective form of amnesia—or so it seems, because, as it turns out, the story is more complicated.

While the past history of St Kilda is buried in the archives or no longer accessible, its present history is systematically erased. The role of archives in Illingworth's work can hardly be overstated. It is not only that the artist is driven by a certain archive fever in the production of her work. She herself adds to and disseminates existing archival material in artistic form. Rather than describing the disruption of St Kilda's community or of Claire's memory in historical or scientific terms, the video installation evokes them viscerally, thus transmitting an emotional knowledge to the viewer. Any supplemental textual information is, consequently, never a mere addition of outside knowledge. We might, instead, see it as a discursive translation of something that is already inscribed in the work.

As I learned in conversations with Illingworth, the story of St Kilda as an abandoned archipelago is deceptive and politically contentious. The narrative construction of St Kilda as an abandoned set of islands covers up the presence of a large military establishment with radar towers and technologies for weapons testing. Military armaments companies use the Hebrides Range to test armed drones, and NATO uses it for testing ballistic missiles. Delivering services to the UK Ministry of Defense as well as commercial arms companies, Qinetiq, the company that runs the testing range, defines the airspace in the film's voiceover as a "sanitized airspace with unlimited altitude." It thus portrays the airspace as an empty arena, suitable to be instrumentalized for weapons testing. Covering up the damage caused by aerial weapons, this rhetorical strategy promotes a dangerous large-scale politics of cultural amnesia. In fact, we could add that, even more perniciously, the very rhetoric of the empty islands compounds their militarization with a militarization of amnesia.

Doubling St Kilda's story with Claire's story, *Lesions in the Landscape* uses the archipelago as a highly suggestive analogy for the neurological experience of amnesia. Disconnected from the memory of its past, unable to aggregate new memories, and without a future, St Kilda embodies a condition of cultural amnesia that resonates powerfully with the condition we witness in Claire. In different ways, both have been cast out of time. The carefully preserved material ruins and archeological traces that show over four thousand years of habitation form a stark contrast to the current presence of the military and its ever more complex weapons testing. When Illingworth traveled with Claire to St Kilda in order to explore with her the analogies between the two forms of amnesia, as well as the efforts to address and undo some of its damages, it becomes all the more notable that Claire is effectively cast out of the chronological sense of a lifetime commonly generated by memories.

Illingworth and Claire become powerful collaborators in a joint effort to understand this and express the experience of living with amnesia on both an individual and collective level. They trace its complex entanglements with self, place, culture, society, and politics. Weaving together fragments of the stories of Claire and St Kilda, Illingworth's installation performs a work of repair, if not healing. Restoring, or even creating, a new story of St Kilda also means refashioning parts of the self or the place that are lost in amnesia. This work of repair is framed by a systematic self-reflection on the collaborative process that enables it.

To ground this self-reflection, Illingworth solicits the participation of the cognitive neuropsychologist Martin A. Conway, whose neuroscientific reflections on amnesia we hear throughout the film. Together, Illingworth, Claire, and Conway explore not only the relationship of amnesia to the past but also its agency in the present and its impact on, if not foreclosure of, the future. As Claire said in a conversation with Illingworth: "The past is a space you can't enter or feel—the future a space you can't imagine."[2] The video installation enters the space of the past through the way its loss feels in the present. And while it doesn't imagine a future, it opens memories of the future that are foreclosed in amnesia.

Alongside Conway, Claire also worked with another cognitive neuropsychologist, Catherine Loveday, and used sensory-operated camera technology called SenseCam.[3] The latter visually engages an entangled layering of mnemonic fragments in the brain, hoping they can serve as triggers of recall. With the help of such visual triggers, SenseCam activated encoded memory traces to release forgotten fragments of Claire's life story. One of the existential problems connected to amnesia is linked to the question of access and agency. In order to have a sense of self, people need a story of their lives. Those afflicted with amnesia lose agency in the fashioning of their own life story. Often, it is others who tell their story, which can feel like an intrusion into a damaged self. Similarly, the people of St Kilda lost control over their own story and the story of the islands themselves when it started being told by others, including those serving military and corporate interests.

In collaboration with Conway and Loveday, Illingworth draws on neuropsychology to lend her artistic explorations of forgotten mnemonic landscapes a scientific basis. Conway defines autobiographical memory relationally as an emergent product of interactions between different processing systems in the brain.[4] Illingworth expands this relational approach to memory by including interactions between Claire and her environment. Her artistic process of linking psychic or mnemonic space and landscape or environment also resonates with neuropsychological studies of the distributed mind.

In *Into the Silent Land: Travels in Neuropsychology*,[5] Paul Broks, who works with patients with brain injuries, presents a relational study of the brain, including different forms of amnesia:

> The brain evolved as a means of orchestrating adaptive interaction between the organism and the world. To achieve this, it must maintain both an inward and an outward orientation, monitoring and regulating the state of various internal systems, while at the same time responding to the flow of events in the external world. [...] An emerging theme in neuropsychology is that [...] the brain has evolved systems dedicated to social cognition and action. It constructs a model of the organism of which it is a part and, beyond this, a representation of that organism's place in relation to other, similar organisms: people.[6]

Broks highlights the damages amnesia causes to the sense of selfhood as well as a person's interaction with others and the world. The brain negotiates the social environment and thereby assembles a "self." According to Broks, the mental processes—feelings, thoughts, memories—that contribute to the assemblage of a self "come together in a work of fiction. [...] A human being is a story-telling machine. The self is a story." Rather than us telling the story, however, "the story is telling us."[7]

What if memories can no longer contribute to the assemblage of a self? Claire can no longer tell her own story. Entering this void, *Lesions in the Landscape* assembles Claire's story with fragments provided by her in connection with her experience of the surrounding environment and the story of St Kilda. It is crucial for Illingworth that Claire retains agency in the composition of her story so as not to repeat the trauma of having one's own story disowned and told by others. The result is a highly complex composite narrative, coproduced by Claire, Illingworth, St Kilda, landscape, technology, sound, and light. Unfrozen words emerge in the here and now, leaving us with open questions. How do Claire's

2 The quote is published in the supplementary exhibition text to *Lesions in the Landscape*.

3 See Catherine Loveday and Martin A. Conway, eds., *SenseCam: The Future of Everyday Memory Research?* (London: Taylor & Francis Ltd., 2011).

4 See Martin A. Conway's reflections on his dialogue with Shona Illingworth in Shona Illingworth, *The Watch Man/Balnakiel* (London: Film and Video Umbrella, 2011), 52–57.

5 Paul Broks, *Into the Silent Land: Travels in Neuropsychology* (London: Atlantic Monthly Press, Grove, 2003).

6 Broks, *Into the Silent Land*, 50f.

7 Broks, *Into the Silent Land*, 41.

dreams remember? What stories do they tell? What does Claire feel in the transitional space between the words she finds in the here and now and the stories she can no longer tell?

With her emphasis on the dynamic of haunting, Illingworth insists that, beyond national politics, war is always personal and that its effects extend beyond its official end. At the same time, the image of a haunted airspace also evokes the trans-generational trauma inflicted by aerial violence and the ways it becomes entangled with amnesia. *Topologies of Air* (2021), I propose, is a project driven by a certain archive fever; that is, the desire to record and preserve images and memories of aerial violence as well as its psychic traces. Interestingly, the freezing of images, words, and stories creates a very particular kind of amnesia. Critics ranging from Roland Barthes, Walter Benjamin, and Marguerite Duras, for example, have talked about photography as a medium of forgetting rather than remembering. Freezing the flow of life induces a sensorial, if not existential, forgetting. *Lesions in the Landscape* is, in Illingworth's own words, a project about the individual and collective impact of traumatic amnesia. Amnesia induces distance. The testing range in St Kilda establishes distance not only through its remote location but also through the erasure of its presence from St Kilda's stories.

Freezing and amnesia are also related to psychic numbing. The latter occurs at both the individual and the societal level, undercutting the link between violence and grief for people with stories of suffering and death. Aerial violence effects a chronic state of psychic numbing, a paralysis of emotions, and a traumatic forgetting that freezes not only memories, words, and stories but also the feelings attached to them. It also undercuts the link to the mourning of destroyed places with deep histories. Just as there are no stories of the current aerial violence, there are also no stories of St Kilda's that mourn its people, histories, or landscapes. Telling the story of St Kilda, Illingworth thus also performs an act of mourning.

Establishing links between Claire's amnesia, the erasure of St Kilda's cultural memory, and present aerial violence, interspersed reflections on memory guide the audience through the dense network of images, sounds, and fragmented stories. These artistic reflections unfold on three interconnected layers. Apart from juxtaposing an individual and a collective case of amnesia through Claire's and St Kilda's stories, amnesia is also addressed at a meta-level. Illingworth includes an artistic self-reflection on the media she uses to portray amnesia as a psycho-political phenomenon. At its most general level, *Lesions in the Landscape* is a philosophical reflection on memory: for Claire, the past exists as a space she can't enter or feel and the future a space she can't imagine. In characteristic fashion, Illingworth's installations work with temporal layers that resonate with the entanglement and fluid messiness of past, present, and future in the experience of time. In the case of amnesia, however, time itself is frozen into a perpetual here and now. Like the dream, amnesia has no existential knowledge of either past or future. In waking life, amnesia forms the dark core of the most extreme ontological insecurity.

Children of Fire, Children of Air

Like a companion piece to *Lesions in the Landscape*, *Topologies of Air* is a three-screen video and multichannel sound installation. A triptych of panels exhibits a blue sky and clouds that morph into maps of weather, atmospheric pressure, and airflow that look like psychedelic shapes and colors, followed by aerial shots of trees. A voice tells us how, in today's world, aerial technologies of documentation provide

8 See Sven Lindqvist, *A History of Bombing* (New York: New Press, 2003), np.

9 See Andrew Hoskins, "The Forgetting Conundrum," (lecture, International Summer School of Mnemonics: Network for Memory Studies, Leuven, Belgium, September 4, 2018), https://youtu.be/JzAlTiT4Gh8. See also a more extended discussion of a threatening cultural amnesia about the continuing nuclear danger in Gabriele Schwab, *Radioactive Ghosts* (Minneapolis: University of Minnesota Press, 2020).

us with information about climate change and sea-level rise. Competition among governments and corporations for the domination of aerial perspectives turns airspace into a commodity, creating an asymmetry of power and access. Subject to this logic of domination, airspace is no longer part of a natural environment but politically, militarily, economically, and culturally fashioned.

Like *Lesions in the Landscape*, *Topologies of Air* displays an ethereal beauty disrupted by technological intrusions. Drone noises compete with bird song. Marking the moods of the installation, a pervasive atmosphere of dissonance affects sensorial response. Viewers are induced to viscerally feel the violent intrusiveness of military technologies. But then another voice emerges, returning us to the early history of human conquest of airspace. In a reference to Sven Lindqvist, we hear that, when humans learned to fly, they greeted the aerial age with almost religious ecstasy as a sign of human perfection.[8] The air was heralded as a space of freedom. Storytellers created the utopia of an aerial kingdom with people born and residing in the air. Yet, unbeknownst to many, airspace was soon turned into a tool of empire. New forms of aerial sovereignty emerged and new forms of aerial war. Illingworth's video installation marks this contrast with images and sounds that depict illuminated oil refineries and the launching of space rockets.

Again, scale assumes a central role. Illingworth uses technologies of layering and scaling to orchestrate shifts between local and planetary perspectives, insisting on their intertwinement. Subtly and gradually, these shifts induce an awareness in viewers that the new aerial technologies surpass the limits of our capacity for sensual experience. Satellite views and technologies of surveillance are refined by the day. Aerial weapons dominate modern warfare.

Meanwhile, aerial toxicity has risen to a critical level, and largely invisible agents poison humans and other species on a daily basis. Some of the most lethal threats in today's world, such as radioactive contamination as well as other toxins in air, water, soil, and food, are invisible. *Topologies of Air* illustrates how, in response, a new military and eco-scientific imaginary sponsors bifurcating fantasies of weaponizing asteroids to enhance warfare and of releasing sulfite aerosols into the air to offset climate change by deflecting sunlight. Meanwhile, radionuclides already settle deep into our lungs and into the arctic ice. They create the slow violence of a catastrophe of time. The film's voiceover calls them a "radioactive signature," and they form a hidden archive that registers the radioactive contamination of air and earth.

Shifting to voices of Hiroshima victims, the panels of the triptych change to colors of intense red, alternating with a ghostly blue. We see the raging fires and ruins of Hiroshima as we hear the story of Hirada Hiroshi, a survivor. We see silhouettes of children as we hear of the 140,000 people who died instantly. Another voice speaks of people who believe that the air above Hiroshima is full of the spirits of victims who never left—children of fire, children of air. We are viscerally affected by one survivor's intimate and haunting story, while simultaneously witnessing the global significance of Hiroshima and its role in changing airspace security and planetary safety forever.

Hiroshima's ghostly shadows remain burnt into the collective memory, haunting generations to come. And yet, as Andrew Hoskins demonstrates in his research on memory, we are threatened by a widespread, multifaceted cultural amnesia of the persisting nuclear danger.[9] This forgetting will come to haunt us unless we keep the stories alive, telling them again and again in different ways and contexts. Enfolding the story of one individual Hiroshima

10 The artistic reflections on Hiroshima in *Topologies of Air* resonate deeply with the concerns of my recent book *Radioactive Ghosts* that appeared just a few months before the Airspace Tribunal was launched at The Power Plant Gallery in Toronto. In particular, I include detailed discussions of memory and trauma, ontological insecurity, scale, and the role of literature and the arts in figurations of nuclear politics and trans-generational nuclear trauma.

survivor into the trans-generational expansion of Hiroshima's history, Illingworth's installation participates in this global work to keep the stories alive in order to counter the cultural amnesia that covers the persistent danger of nuclear war and catastrophe.[10]

Later in the video, the voice of an archeologist shifts the focus to the present, speaking of the erasure of the ancient sky by the light pollution of megacities. Image and voice invoke the destruction of old civilizations that gained a sense of ontological security by seeking wisdom from the sky and finding their place in the universe. We see magnified particles floating in the air and hear about air molecules colonizing our bodies with new toxins, a new molecular attack on and colonization of the body. We hear a polyphony of voices, some of them from Illingworth's interviews in various places, including Hiroshima and the Middle East, others recorded from previous Airspace Tribunal hearings. Listing the wide range of new aerial technologies and their perils, the final comments leave us almost breathless, warning of the threat of total destruction through the use of new weaponry in space. A voice invokes the robot bomber as an embodiment of the ideal soldier who kills without compassion, guilt, or mercy.

The distancing effects of technologies such as the robot bomber and drone warfare also emerge as forces that propel forgetting, if not amnesia. Killing at a distance makes it easier to forget you even killed. It makes it easier to forget the pain of those who suffer at a distance, easier to forget compassion. This new form of cultural amnesia affects our humanity, haunting us with what we cannot or do not want to feel. In *Lesions in the Landscape*, we witnessed psychic numbing as an effect of Claire's individual trauma of amnesia. In *Topologies of Air*, psychic numbing is threatening to become a collective psychological condition that sustains warfare at a distance. Images of bomb craters show lesions in the earth. Pointing to images of craters on the moon, the narrator ends by invoking the poetic image of the suffering of the moon.

Creating a discordant mood, Illingworth's poetics of contrasts and dissonances offers an antidote to the numbing against suffering at a distance. Scale determines human relations to suffering at a distance. Unless we can break through the defensive wall that numbs us against suffering at a distance, or indeed, unless we can expand our sensorium to imagine the suffering of the moon, the eclipse of our emotions will come to haunt us. With her poetic invocation of a distant celestial body, Illingworth connects the suffering of people, other beings, and nature on earth with the suffering of the moon. We are the memories we don't remember.

Techniques of scaling are crucial for Illingworth. In today's world, filled with multiple threats from the air, scale takes on new dimensions and challenges the limits of human scalar imagination. Threats of radioactive contamination and climate change unfold at a spatiotemporal scale that by far exceeds what humans can imagine, let alone experience sensorially and emotionally. At the same time, the miniaturization of technologies, including swarm technologies, presents a challenge to think at new levels of scale and complexity. They also summon us, one of the voices in the video suggests, to begin thinking in terms of a decolonial cosmology.

Launched with legal scholar Nick Grief, the Airspace Tribunal (2018–ongoing), a project that pursues the goal of claiming airspace security as a human right, forms a central component throughout *Topologies of Air*, exploring as it does the language of human rights. It is these rights that might be the last remaining resource we have to address the increasingly pervasive threats and attacks from the air. The petition for airspace security as a new human right is a necessary first step toward decolonizing the use of airspace. While technologies

11 See Eyal Weizman, *Forensic Architecture: Violence at the Threshold of Detectability* (Princeton: Princeton University Press, 2019). Weizman also leads Forensic Architecture, a multidisciplinary research group at the University of London that uses aerial technologies and architectural techniques to investigate state violence and human rights violations around the world.

of surveillance still focus mainly on areas outside the body, the installation's final warning echoes as the images fade: "The future is internal … the future is internal … the future is internal." Aerial technologies can support what Eyal Weizman calls "forensic architecture," that is, the use of architectural techniques and technologies to investigate state violence and violations of human rights across the world.[11] We can thus harness available technologies as defenses against the very threat of aerial violence. Illingworth herself harnesses visual and sound technologies to support her struggle for the decolonization of airspace and for airspace security as a human right.

Stories of Ontological Insecurity

In a world threatened by cultural and political amnesia, the right to a safe airspace needs a story. Storytelling, literature, and the arts are crucial to grasping the escalating scale of aerial violence. The arts have always expanded the boundaries and scales of human imagination. We need and already have works that create sensations, experiences, and structures of feeling necessary to relate to damage and suffering at a scale and distance commonly outside of human perception. We also need work that moves, like Illingworth's immersive installations, across and between scales.

Carefully orchestrating juxtapositions of distance and proximity, large and small scales, local settings and global war machines, psychic and physical spaces, mental and natural landscapes, Illingworth uses scaling techniques to increase emotional intensity. Her installations are exemplary in demonstrating that we must train our perceptive sensorium to see and feel the psychological and the political together. Installations such as *Lesions in the Landscape* and *Topologies of Air* provide training grounds for precisely such immersive sensorial experiences. While exploring the psycho-political conditions of local places such as St Kilda, Hiroshima, or, in an earlier work, Balnakeil in the Scottish Highlands, Illingworth insists that the individual stories of these places and the people that inhabit them have a global reach and relevance way beyond the local settings.

Finally, perhaps one of the most far-reaching effects of Illingworth's immersive installations is that they explore the chronic condition of ontological insecurity that people in today's ecologically damaged and war-torn world suffer all over the globe. We are living in a world without airspace security, threatened by nuclear weapons, drone warfare, and military plans to weaponize asteroids. We live in a world poisoned by toxic air, water, soil, and food, a world now also threatened by the onset of a global pandemic and the disenfranchisement and disposability of large populations who already suffer disproportionally from these threats. Under these conditions, nobody can escape the effects of ontological insecurity. Even if this insecurity is not experienced in full awareness, it pervades the political and cultural unconscious. It has become an ontological condition.

To raise to a level of awareness or, even more importantly, to become a public and political issue, ontological insecurity needs local stories embedded in thick descriptions of people who suffer from it in their daily lives on the ground. Illingworth provides such stories. She grasps the affective fallout of an ontological insecurity that is specifically generated by living in today's world with its unsettling feelings and unconscious anxieties. Moreover, Illingworth's installations create a link between this ontological insecurity and a pervasive haunting from both past and future.

Despite their stunning beauty, the landscapes she features are anything but pristine. Eerie and disquieting, they

12 See R. D. Laing, *The Divided Self: An Existential Study in Sanity and Madness* (London: Penguin, 1965).

13 Caterina Albano, "Balnakiel: In the Spaces of Memory," in *The Watch Man/Balnakiel*, 113.

14 Jill Bennett, "Atmospheric Affects: Past Events and Present Feeling," in *The Watch Man/Balnakiel*, 159.

resonate with an ontological insecurity deeply felt without being experienced consciously as such. Figuring landscapes that are both resonating and haunting invokes a past of environmental violence as well as a future of pending destruction through wars and environmental catastrophes. Those who inhabit these landscapes and experience the ontological insecurity they generate are, in R. D. Laing's terms, "divided selves," condemned to perpetually pursue the phantom of the split-off internal other.[12] Chasing figments of a phantom self, the ontologically insecure face a different form of amnesia. They feel the loss of something they might never have had, yet that still feels like a loss, a forgetting. In this sense, too, we are the memories we don't remember.

Choosing paradigmatic local sites, Illingworth illustrates a global condition of ontological insecurity. She tries, as with Claire, to affect her viewers by reacting to a condition that has undermined the very foundations of a secure sense of belonging. The sensorial experience of her installations is designed to open pathways to something we can't remember but feel, something that haunts us unless we can apprehend it. Illingworth gives this experience an artistic form that enables apprehension in the double sense of perturbation and recognition. As Caterina Albano said about the horizontal demarcations and edges in *Balnakiel* (2009), "They intimate the haptic knowledge [...] that affects the subject's nonconscious experience of place, as a memory imbued both in the body of the individual and in the physical texture of the landscape."[13]

In a similar way, the characteristic triptychs in the immersive installations of *Lesions in the Landscape* and *Topologies of Air* hold local and global, even cosmic, perspectives together. In dynamic movements across scales, Illingworth conveys the effects of aerial violence at both a macro- and a micro-level. She traces the effects at the molecular level of bodies on the ground and simultaneously reveals their penetration into psychic and mental space, including their trans-generational transmission.

As Jill Bennett points out in "Atmospheric Affects: Past Events and Present Feeling," Illingworth focuses on something we rarely discuss, namely, "the interdependence of social atmosphere and the biosphere that underpins it."[14] In this process, she also opens the perspective from airspace to outer space, addressing questions of cosmic belonging. Her artistic work of scaling conveys how aerial forms of violence, including the recent phantasms of *Star Wars* and space wars, have refashioned how humans see their place in the order of the planet, the universe, and the cosmos.

Gabriele M. Schwab is Distinguished Professor at the University of California, Irvine. She holds appointments in the departments of Comparative Literature, Anthropology, English, and European Languages and Studies. She received her PhD in Literary Studies and Critical Theory at the University of Constance, Germany, in 1976, and a PhD in Psychoanalysis from the New Center for Psychoanalysis in Los Angeles in 2009. Schwab is a recipient of a Guggenheim Fellowship and a Heisenberg Fellowship, and her research interests range across critical theory, psychoanalysis, trauma studies, literature, anthropology, and twentieth- and twenty-first-century comparative literatures. Monographs in English include: *Subjects without Selves: Transitional Texts in Modern Fiction* (Harvard University Press, 1994); *The Mirror and the Killer-Queen: Otherness in Literary Language* (Indiana University Press, 1996); *Haunting Legacies: Violent Histories and Transgenerational Trauma* (Columbia University Press, 2010); *Imaginary Ethnographies: Literature, Subjectivity, Culture* (Columbia University Press, 2012), winner of the 2014 Choice Award for Best Academic Book; and *Radioactive Ghosts* (Minnesota University Press, 2020). Schwab's edited collections include: *Accelerating Possession: Global Futures of Property and Personhood* (Columbia University Press, 2006; with Bill Mauer); *Derrida, Deleuze, Psychoanalysis* (Columbia University Press, 2007); and *Clones, Fakes and Posthumans: Cultures of Replication* (Rodopi, 2012; with Philomena Essed). She is currently completing a monograph on *Beckett in the End Times* and working on a new book project on trans-species imaginaries.

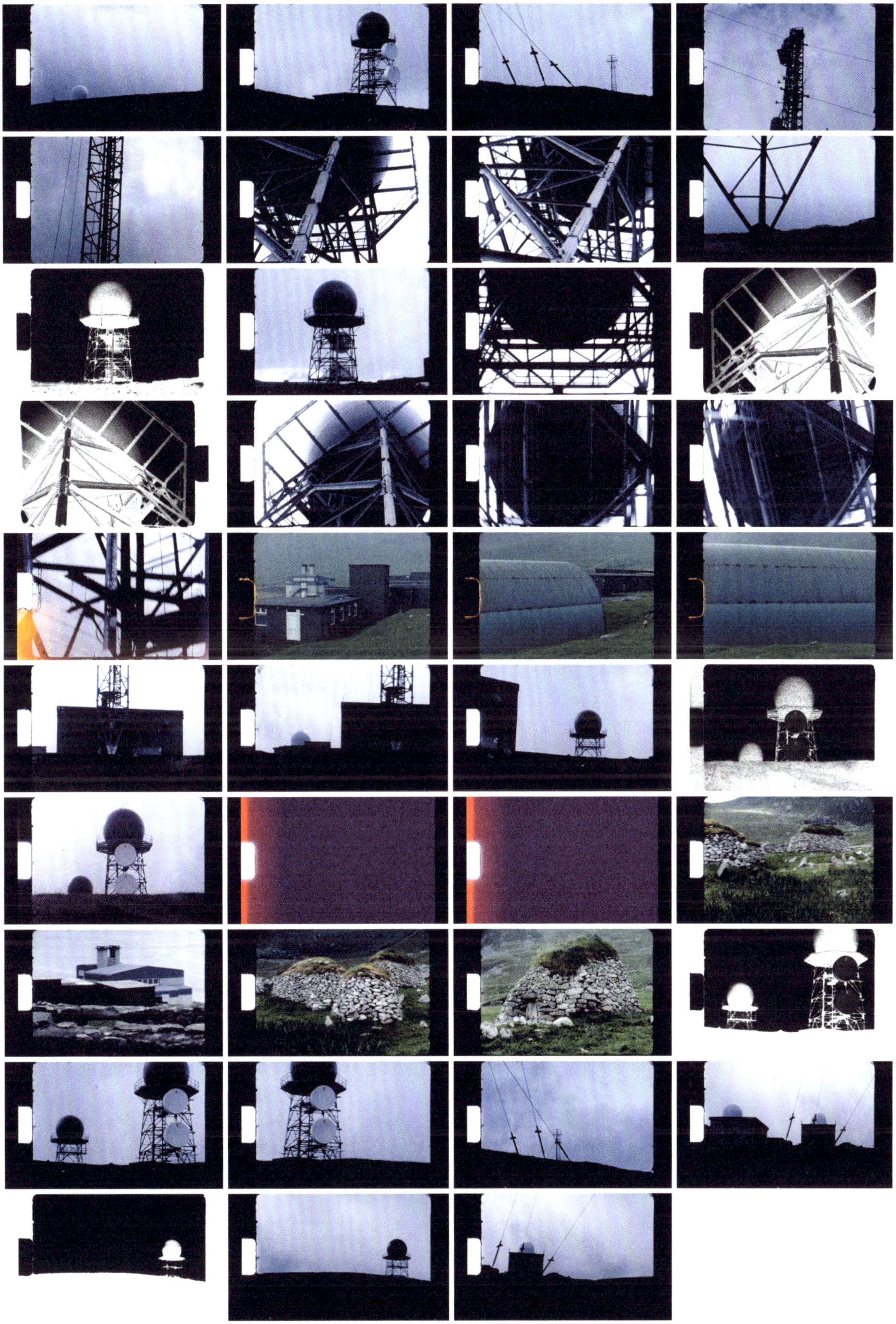

Shona Illingworth, *Super 8, Hirte, Black Domes and Cleits*, 2015. Archival pigment print. 440 × 620 mm.

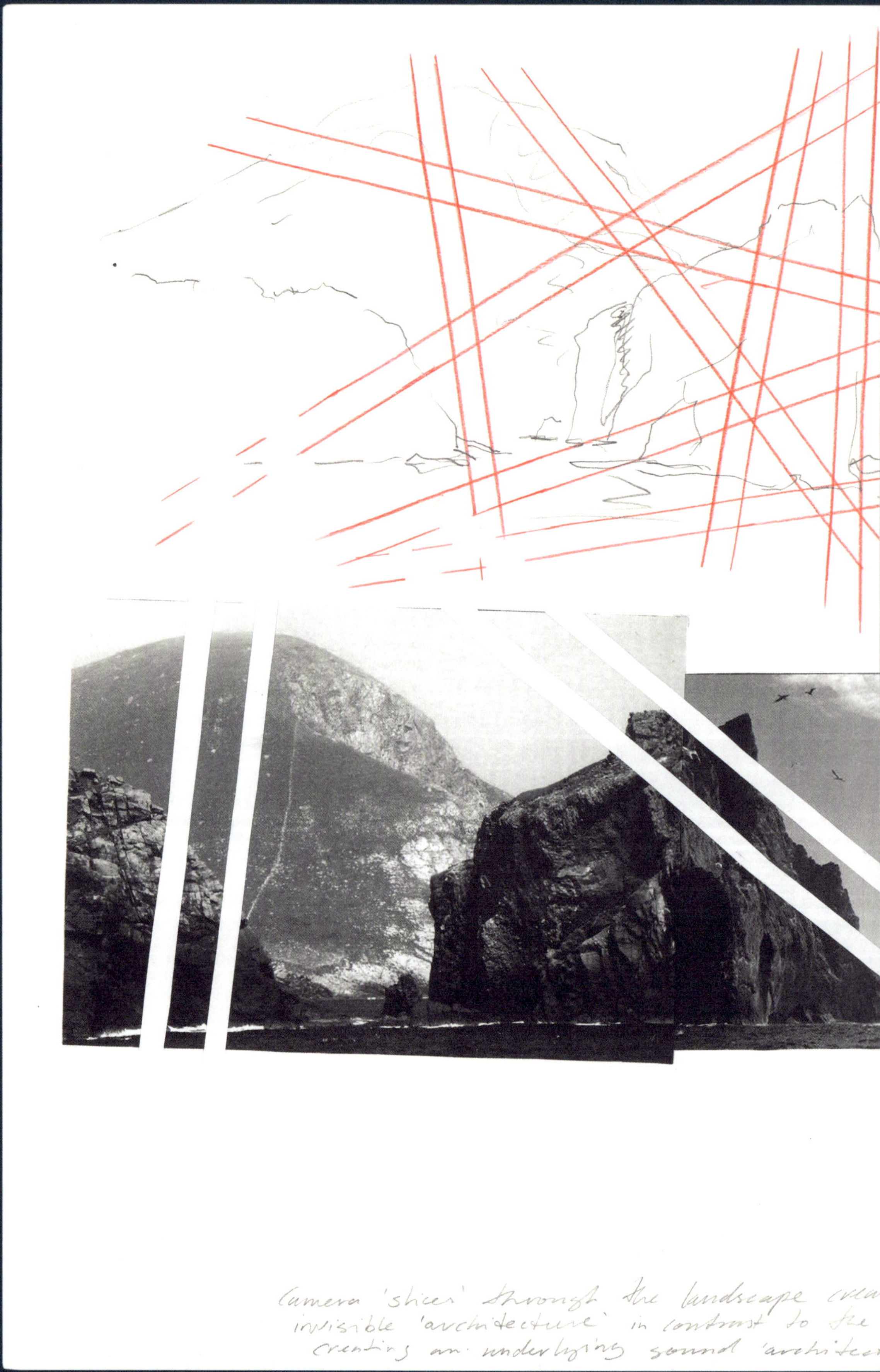
Camera 'slices' through the landscape
invisible 'architecture' in contrast to the
creating an underlying sound

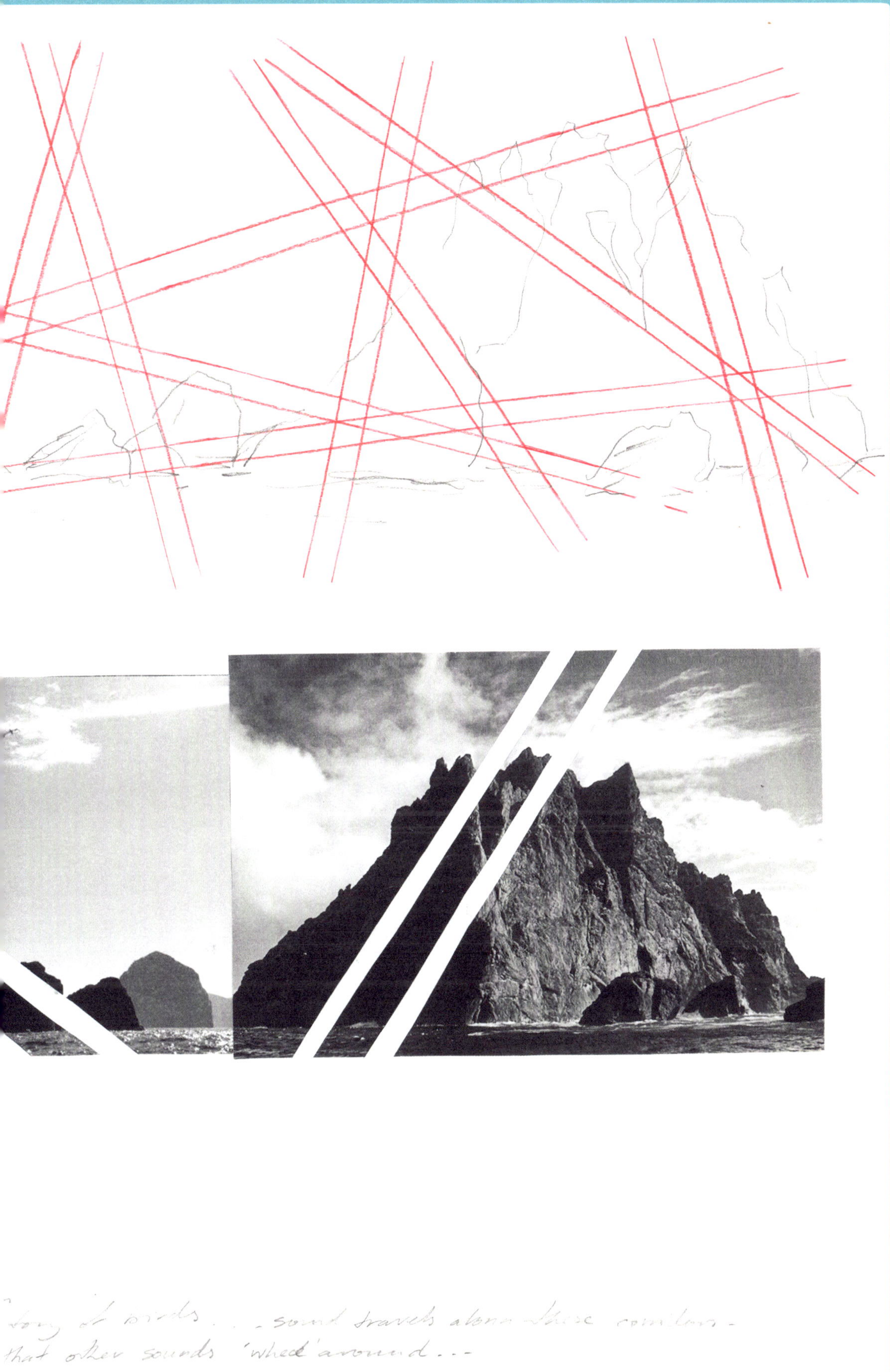

Shona Illingworth, *Sound Drawing 1*, 2012. *Lesions in the Landscape*. 841 × 594 mm.

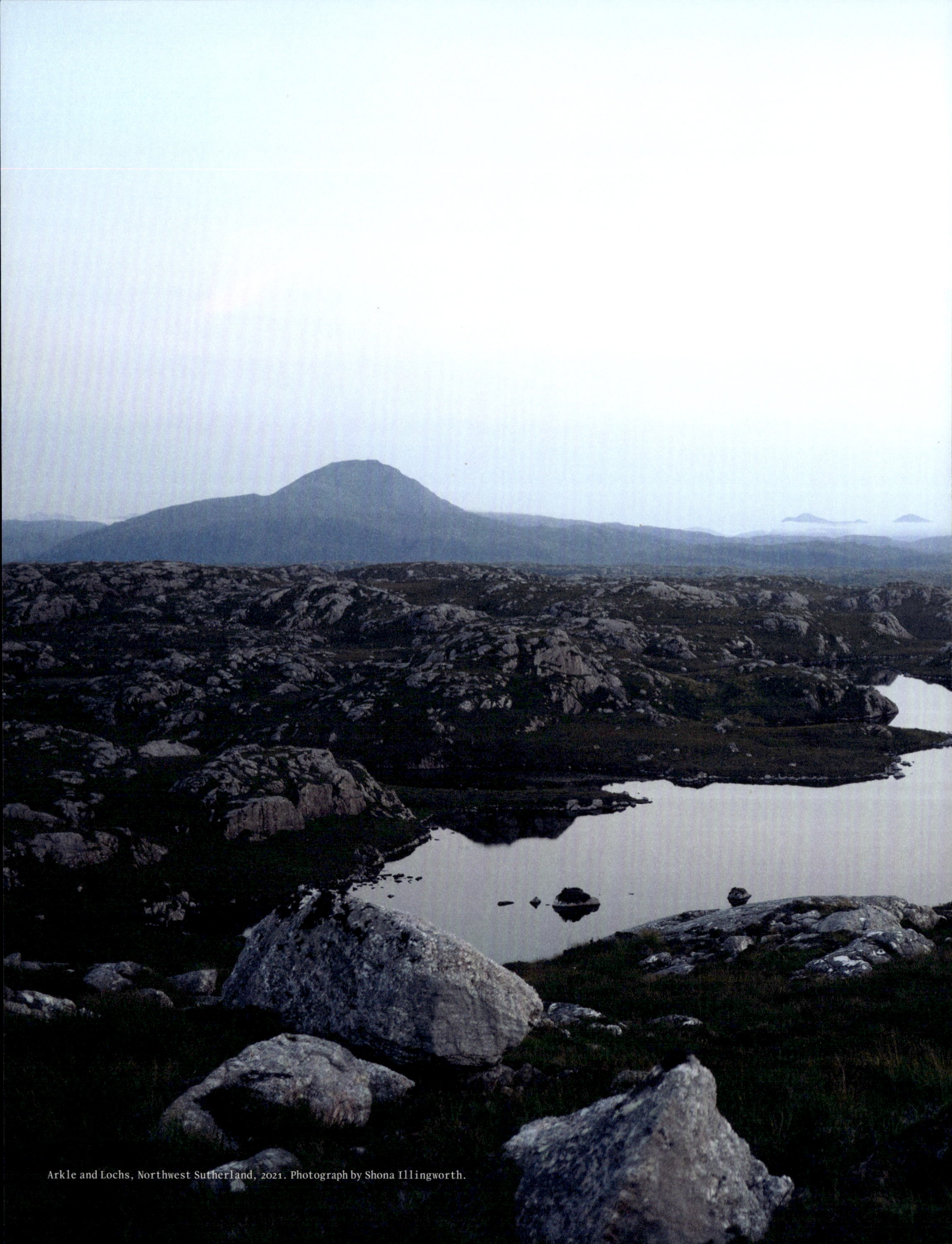

Arkle and Lochs, Northwest Sutherland, 2021. Photograph by Shona Illingworth.

Shona Illingworth and Gaëtane Verna

TOPOLOGIES OF AIR: IN THE MAKING

Gaëtane Verna Throughout your work, there's a constant presence of memory and local stories situated in relation to a global political history. You start with personal narratives and then expand far beyond the autobiographical. There's a persistent thread, which encompasses war, colonization, and vast, remote spaces where the dramatic landscape feels infinite. While there's very little representation of humans, the impact of human beings is ever-present in your work. What is the catalyst for producing work in this manner—works in which the landscape feels infinite, and there are few immediate physical representations of people?

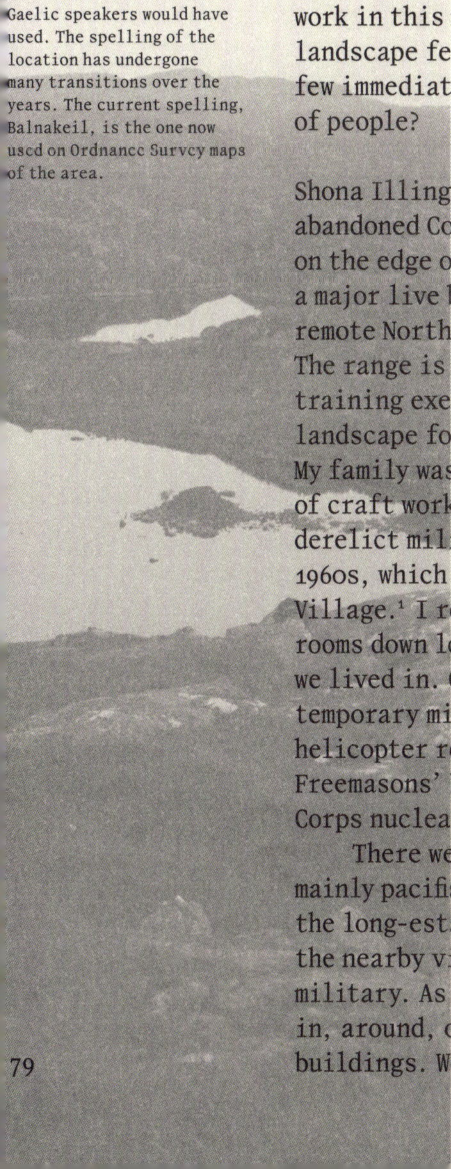

Shona Illingworth I grew up in an abandoned Cold War early-warning station on the edge of the Cape Wrath Firing Range, a major live bombardment range in the remote Northwest Highlands of Scotland. The range is used for extensive military training exercises and as a proxy landscape for war and conflict globally. My family was part of a small community of craft workers who moved into the semi-derelict military buildings in the late 1960s, which became the Balnakeil Craft Village.[1] I remember vandalized, empty rooms down long corridors in the building we lived in. Other buildings were used as temporary military barracks, a Sea King helicopter refueling station, a local Freemasons' hall, and a Royal Observer Corps nuclear bunker.

There were tensions between the mainly pacifist community of craft workers, the long-established local community in the nearby village of Durness, and the military. As children, we roamed freely in, around, over, and through the concrete buildings. We learned how to work with clay, leather, and wood. We navigated intense social and cultural tensions and were absorbed in playing war games. We felt the pervasive fear of imminent nuclear annihilation and the latent presence of my father's unspoken trauma from his harrowing experiences during World War II. It was a complex place to grow up in.

The former military camp was surrounded by a vast glacial and elemental landscape within a highly volatile North Atlantic weather system. Growing up, I had a sense of constantly changing light, atmosphere, air density, sound, and space. From a distance, the landscape looks empty. There are no trees, little grass. A large mountain range runs down to the edge of the sea. But if you look closely, there's an intense layer of life teeming across its surface: small, brightly colored flowers, lichens, mosses, deer grass, and insects. There are dramatic contrasts in scale. You become aware of how shifts in air, space, and materials change this acutely spatial sound-world. At any time, the sonic rupture of low-flying fighter jets and thousand-pound live bombs exploding just offshore could cut through the air, the stress reverberating through bodies and buildings. Limitless space above becomes a delimited, militarized weight above your head. You know that these weapons are destined for people who will have no escape. Your body is momentarily pinned to the ground, and your sense of space is shattered.

The landscape of the Scottish Highlands is marked by a long history of colonial violence, forced eviction, and displacement during the Highland Clearances and the repression of Gaelic culture. It's where, in the mid-1700s, a small group of military commanders developed the Military Survey of Scotland,

1 Balnakeil Craft Village is situated one mile west of the village of Durness in the Scottish Highlands. The village is composed of a collection of regimented concrete buildings constructed in the mid-1950s for a Ministry of Defense early-warning station. The station was never commissioned and became semi-derelict. The craft village was established there in the late 1960s. This publication refers to the location of Balnakiel using a spelling from the Gaelic name for the place—*Baile na Cille*—that most Gaelic speakers would have used. The spelling of the location has undergone many transitions over the years. The current spelling, Balnakeil, is the one now used on Ordnance Survey maps of the area.

a meticulous process of mathematical abstraction that took place on the ground to create a totalizing view as if from above.[2] This mapping process flattens out and erases complex cultural and social life and histories. It was used to subordinate Highland populations and bring contested land under military control. Once established, this cartographic technique was exported as a powerful tool of colonization and Empire. This is now mirrored in the flattening of sensorial space by the overpowering military control of airspace, with accelerating developments in artificial intelligence and technology extending the scale, reach, and impact of militarization into all areas of our lives and occupying our future in critical ways.

In many ways, my explorations of memory, cultural erasure, and how landscapes are experienced, constructed, and militarized stem from these formative experiences. Creating immersive moving image and sound installations that work across multiple scales, atmospheres, critical perspectives, and affective encounters is, for me, a form of creative resistance against the reductive narratives and totalizing views that diminish life and drive dangerous forms of oppression, control, and erasure.

Growing up, we were caught between the ground and air, always looking up. My film *Balnakiel* (2009) explores how military occupation of airspace affects people on the ground. It examines how individual and collective memory, embodied experience, and a sense of landscape evolve for the local community, the incoming community, and the military across the sociopolitical tensions in this area. Military training creates mental schema[3] for complex coordinated sets of actions, which are then transposed to sites of conflict elsewhere, most recently in Iraq, Afghanistan, and Syria. *Balnakiel* explores how this process instrumentalizes memory as a weapon of war.

GV We often try to evaluate the work of artists by looking at it through the lens of art history, but I think individual histories can be magnified and touch different people through the landscape of storytelling and memory, which then brings us back to the body. Because all of it truly starts within the body.

SI I was born in Denmark and arrived in the Highlands as a small child. I was not from this place and yet was completely immersed in the landscape. There was intense hostility from the local community in Durness toward the much smaller incoming community in Balnakiel, who was seen as a cultural threat. This tension becomes internalized, embodied. When I left the relative isolation of the Highlands, I began to understand that belonging is contested in myriad ways in the relentless micro-moments that are part of being enmeshed in larger structures of oppression and constraint. This comes with an acute sensitivity and hyper-vigilance to changing atmospheres, which was part of my experience growing up.

GV From the perspective of being a Black-Caribbean immigrant in Canada, no matter my age, I have always had to be very conscious of how I show my face wherever I walk. I am different. I am perceived as other. And it is quite puzzling to me then to try to reconcile the idea that even if you're white, even if you're European, even if you could pass for these local people, you would never be accepted as one of them.

SI Where I grew up, we were all navigating this complex cultural space and were all constrained by its narratives and history.

GV Then, we can consider the monopolization of media outlets. The information that we receive is dominated by a group that chooses what subjects will be shared with the general public based on advertising sales. There are many layers

2 See Caren Kaplan, *Aerial Aftermaths: Wartime from Above* (Durham, NC: Duke University Press, 2018), 34–67.

3 My conversations with neuropsychologist Martin A. Conway, an expert in human memory, spanning almost twenty years, have been central to developing my thinking. See Shona Illingworth, *The Watch Man/ Balnakiel* (London: Film and Video Umbrella, 2011).

of this imperialist domination of people's psyches, and most people don't even realize this because they're busy just trying to survive. This provides us with an interesting reference point for considering your multichannel works that foreground individual experience by re-creating environments through images, sound, and individuals speaking.

SI Through working on memory, I became increasingly interested in the processes and impacts of forgetting. *Lesions in the Landscape* (2015) is part of a large body of work that explores the complex impact of individual and societal amnesia and cultural erasure. I collaborated with Claire,[4] a woman living with amnesia, and neuropsychologists Martin A. Conway and Catherine Loveday for over five years on this work. Claire was forty-four years old when she awoke from a coma to find she could no longer remember much of her past, recognize faces, or form new memories. Without memory, you cannot imagine the future. You become trapped in the present moment.

Lesions in the Landscape draws parallels between Claire's experience of amnesia and the historical lesions in the physical and cultural landscape of St Kilda, a group of volcanic islands in the North Atlantic. St Kilda has a powerful presence in the cultural imaginary of the Highlands, but it's also highly complex and contested. People thrived there for thousands of years, but life became unsustainable, and at the request of the islanders, St Kilda was evacuated on August 29, 1930,[5] bringing more than four thousand years of successful habitation to a sudden end. The meticulously conserved archaeological remains appear to me like petrified scars in the landscape, echoing Claire's abrupt loss of access to her memories and petrification of the dynamic of self. Claire describes the sense of having crash-landed into someone else's life, a life everyone knows about except her. When the past is constructed by others, the loss of agency is immense.

In the imaginations of wealthy nineteenth-century visitors, St Kilda was a place on the edge of the world, existing outside of time. The islanders were exoticized and viewed with condescending fascination.[6] Far from being remote, St Kilda was part of a wider cultural and economic landscape. However, these constructions and myths persist in the ongoing fixation on the archipelago's evacuation, reducing thousands of years to a moment of irretrievable loss in an endless, enclosing act of cultural erasure. These narratives also omit the presence of a military radar tracking station in St Kilda, which is part of an extensive, complex weapons-testing range—the Hebrides Range—with unlimited altitude for long-range and ballistic missiles, combat drones, and new weapons systems.[7]

In *Lesions in the Landscape*, this instrumentalized airspace is juxtaposed with the immensity of the sky in constructions of the oceanic sublime. Both are commanding but strangely exclusive amnesic spaces. In the work, this sanitized airspace becomes dense with multiple forms of signals and measurement: sonified EEG[8] data of Claire searching for memory; GPS plotting of archaeological sites; scientific tracking of the genealogy of prehistoric Soay sheep, population crash, and climate change; electromagnetic frequencies and telemetry used for testing devastating weapons, which will, in turn, cause catastrophic physical, social, and psychological lesions in other parts of the world.

You hear Gaelic psalm-singing in *Lesions in the Landscape*, collective voices rise and swell, weightless in air dense with the flight of gannets, as the image grazes the geological surface of towering sea stacks. Each voice embellishes the sound in a call and response, a form of release and expression freed from the confines of those leaden narratives of constraint. For me, voice can take multiple forms, evoking a multiplicity

4 My creative collaboration with Claire and her profound reflections on her experience of amnesia were central to the development of this work and dialogue with Conway and Loveday.

5 See Bob Chambers, ed., *Rewriting St Kilda: New Views on Old Ideas* (Isle of Lewis, UK: The Island Book Trust, 2011).

6 See Fraser MacDonald, Rachel Hughes, and Klaus Dodds, eds., *Observant States: Geopolitics and Visual Culture* (London: I. B. Tauris, 2010), 267–89.

7 See "About," MOD Hebrides website, accessed December 23, 2020, https://www.qinetiq.com/en/hebrides/about.

8 An electroencephalogram (EEG) is a recording of brain activity. Small sensors are attached to the head to pick up the electrical signals produced when brain cells send messages to each other. EEG data of Claire looking at photographs taken by a body-worn sensory-activated camera of her journey to St Kilda were transformed into sound and form part of this project.

of registers, affects, and meanings. It can challenge singular constructions of the past that disenfranchise people and environments, releasing them from perpetual narratives of failure and irretrievable loss. This is not only a question of agency in the present. The dynamic between memory and imagination is also critically important to how we imagine, plan for, and act in the future. We need to ask: What histories, archives, and knowledges are we drawing on to imagine the future? How are they being used, and by whom? The many different forms of knowledge, temporalities, and practices that we need to expand our sense of how we live in the world and decenter our understanding of our relationship to planetary life are rapidly becoming disregarded, oppressed, or erased. For me, art and cultural praxis can evoke different kinds of knowledge and expand perception in ways that are powerful and, critically, enable other possible futures to be imagined.

GV It's like a counterculture that subverts the hegemony of the press, the government—all of the players that are dictating the same myopic narrative. As countries too slowly apologize for some of their past wrongs, such as slavery four hundred years ago, you wonder why it is so complicated for them to accept responsibility. Leaders could say sorry even though we know they aren't the only

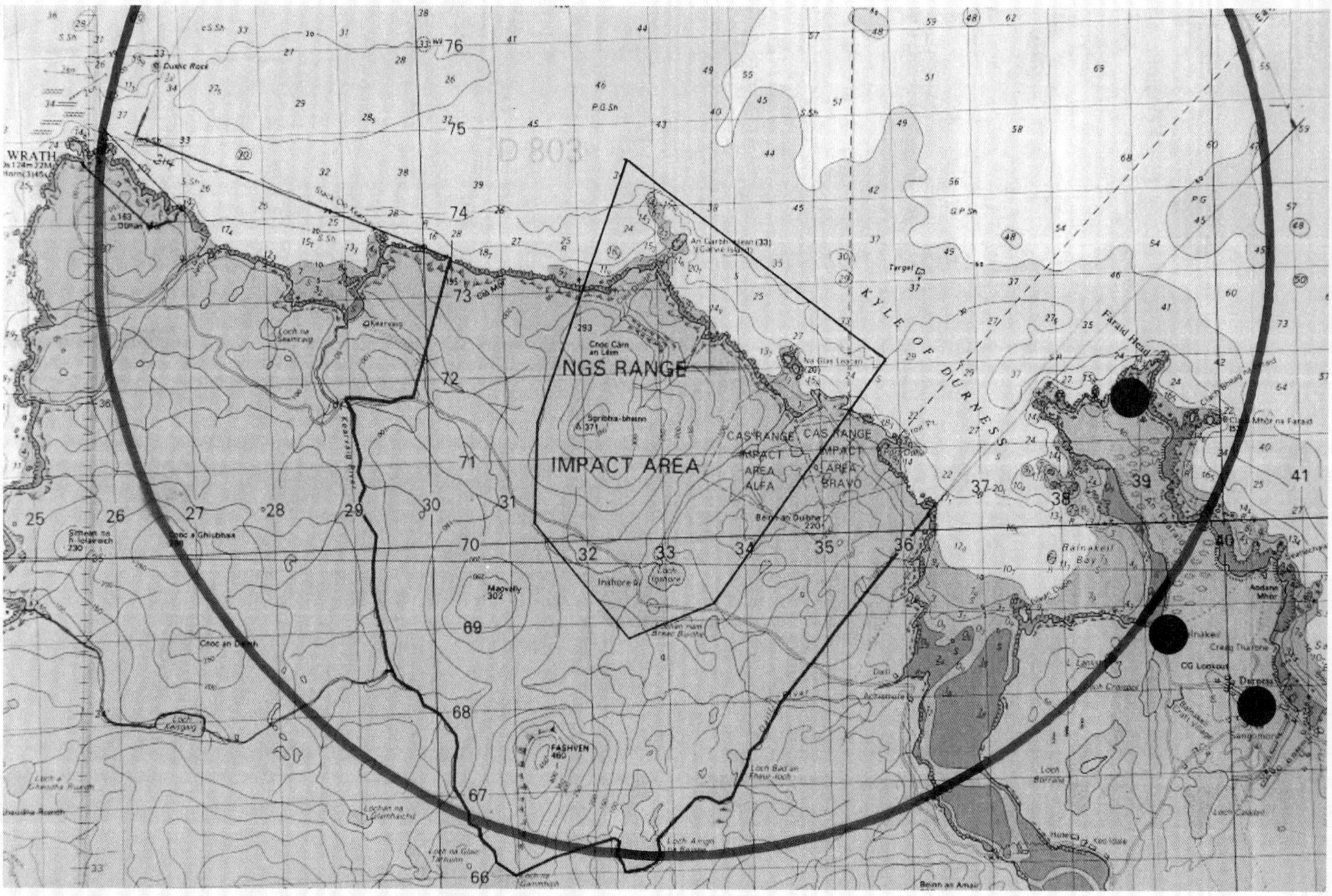

Impact Bravo Alpha, Cape Wrath Bombardment Range, 2009. Chart, pen, and paper. Chart of Cape Wrath Bombardment Range, Northwest Highlands of Scotland detailing the perimeter of the Danger Zone and the location of the Range Control Tower, Balnakeil, and the Clearance village of Durness.

ones to blame. I wonder why it seems so complicated to admit the truth? I have learned much about the history of humanity by listening to contemporary artists and engaging with their work. I'm reminded of conversations I've had with artists from Congo and Belgium who talk about how the Belgian state refused to acknowledge their responsibility for what happened in Congo under King Leopold II's rule. And then suddenly, this year (in 2020), King Philippe of Belgium finally expressed his "deepest regrets" for what he calls the "painful episodes of the colonial era." These are whispers of responsibility but not formal apologies, not calls for reparations.

I feel that non-collecting galleries have much more latitude, are safe spaces where these stories and learnings can be shared with the public. Of course, it's always through the voice of an individual, or a succession of individuals, but at least in galleries such as The Power Plant, we present a different voice than that of the government or the press. I imagine that our audiences, informed through a diversity of channels, come out as better-thinking humans and citizens who can have a greater impact within their communities by understanding what trauma is, what memory is, or, as you said, what the consequences of cultural erasure are. This is why I appreciate practices such as yours. How do you engage in deep conversations with others about important issues and then transfer the lessons learned into an artwork? Can you elaborate on the tension between the themes addressed and how you share them with others by way of a work of art?

SI I've worked for many years with people and communities whose knowledge and life experiences have been marginalized. Their experiences are central to understanding the invisible social, political, and cultural architectures we inhabit. Reclaiming spaces of imagination, creativity, and agency has been central to my development of aesthetic processes in which different conversations, critical thinking, and explorations can become active and produce new cultural meanings. Creating the artworks themselves, particularly immersive video and sound installation, involves an intense process of attunement to a multiplicity of voices, images, and sounds. This includes working with an incredibly fluid aesthetic involving different audio frequencies, dissonances, surfaces, movement, color, density, and compression. This process works toward creating an affective ecology of ideas and perceptions and emotional, conceptual, and critical registers across image, sound, atmosphere, and space to move people toward a sense of the phenomenological experience of others and intimacy with the critical issues that the work explores.

GV At The Power Plant, *Lesions in the Landscape* will be shown with *Topologies of Air* (2021). For this second series of works, you and human rights lawyer Nick Grief established the Airspace Tribunal.[9] Each tribunal hearing—from London to Sydney, Toronto, Berlin, with further venues to be announced—brings together different protagonists who are lawyers, researchers, and experts from various disciplines. How did the Airspace Tribunal originate?

SI I began formulating *Topologies of Air* during an artist residency at Taigh Chearsabhagh Museum and Arts Centre in the Outer Hebrides in 2012.[10] I was developing the first of a series of "Blueprints" (2012–ongoing) that examined the changing relationship to the sky in the context of a history of cultural oppression, depopulation, and land rights struggles on these islands.[11] My research included reading consultation documents for substantial expansion of the Hebrides weapons-testing range. In 2016, I met with Nick Grief, an expert in human rights and international airspace law, to discuss the narrow terms of the consultation documents, which were based on constrained

9 See the Airspace Tribunal website, http://airspacetribunal.org/.

10 The Wapping Project supported the development of *Topologies of Air*, through commissioning the video and sound installation in 2016. See "About," The Wapping Project website, accessed December 23, 2020, https://thewappingproject.org/about/.

11 See Andrew Hoskins and Shona Illingworth, "Inaccessible War: Media, Memory, Trauma and the Blueprint," *Journal of Digital War* 1 (2020): 74–82.

12 See Nick Grief, "The Airspace Tribunal and the Case for a New Human Right to Protect the Freedom to Live without Physical or Psychological Threat from Above," *Journal of Digital War* 1 (2020): 58–64.

13 See Institute for Economics and Peace website, https://www.economicsandpeace.org/.

representations of economic and environmental impact. During this first meeting, Nick and I agreed that there was a need for a new human right and that we would establish a people's tribunal to examine this proposal and work across legal practice and art practice from the beginning.[12]

We established the Airspace Tribunal in 2018 to bring together a wide range of expertise and lived experience in a series of international public hearings to consider the case for and against a proposed human right to protect the freedom to live without physical and psychological threat from above. Kirsty Brimelow QC has been our Counsel to the Tribunal for successive hearings and has played a central part in the development of these discussions. Her role is to question the speakers and then facilitate questions from members of the Tribunal—the public—who are our judges. In this way, the Airspace Tribunal challenges the traditional state-centric view of how international law is usually created. The hearings are recorded and transcribed to form the drafting history of the proposed right. They are also an essential part of the making of *Topologies of Air*. The aim is to create a compelling, people-focused proposal to present to states and institutions such as the United Nations. The development of this work also includes workshops, recorded conversations, and creative cultural praxis. This builds on the interdisciplinary forums that have been part of my practice for many years—where I bring people with different expertise and perspectives together to discuss critical issues through performance, film, sound, presentation, and interactive technologies.

GV It is as if you are creating a new inclusive global narrative, and the temperament of each participant's voice is so different. There's a sense of peace in the work that strongly contrasts with that tension that was also present in the environment in which you were raised. I can just picture walking in this pristine landscape and then… Armageddon! So, there's that tension in the way that governmental structures keep us in a position of not knowing. It's good for them. It serves their purposes to keep citizens outside of those conversations. When I watched a preview of *Topologies of Air*, I was astounded. It just made me realize that we are in really deep trouble, and we don't even know it. So what do citizens who vote, who presume their elected officials will tend to their personal safety, need to know that they don't know?

SI *Topologies of Air* interweaves evidence presented at the Airspace Tribunal hearings with archival film, video that I have filmed in many parts of the world, recorded conversations, and research developed over many years. We hear people speak about their experience of chemical weapons and the long-term affects of atomic bombing. We hear accounts of environmental degradation, the development of autonomous weapons systems, increasing air pollution, global governance risks of geoengineering, military and commercial hardware in space, predictive targeting, and the penetration of surveillance ever more deeply into all aspects of our lives.

Our relationship to the sky is being transformed by developments in technologies, pollution, and global warming at a phenomenal rate. We are all increasingly vulnerable to the commercial and military exploitation of airspace and outer space, and climate change. The physical, psychological, and environmental consequences are immense. There is something fundamental about the ability to be outside, unwatched, and to be able to look up at the sky and feel its immensity as a space of imaginative projection and deep cultural meaning, to wonder at a sense of infinity and the unknown, and not feel threatened. The sky is one of the very last unbounded and shared spaces of our

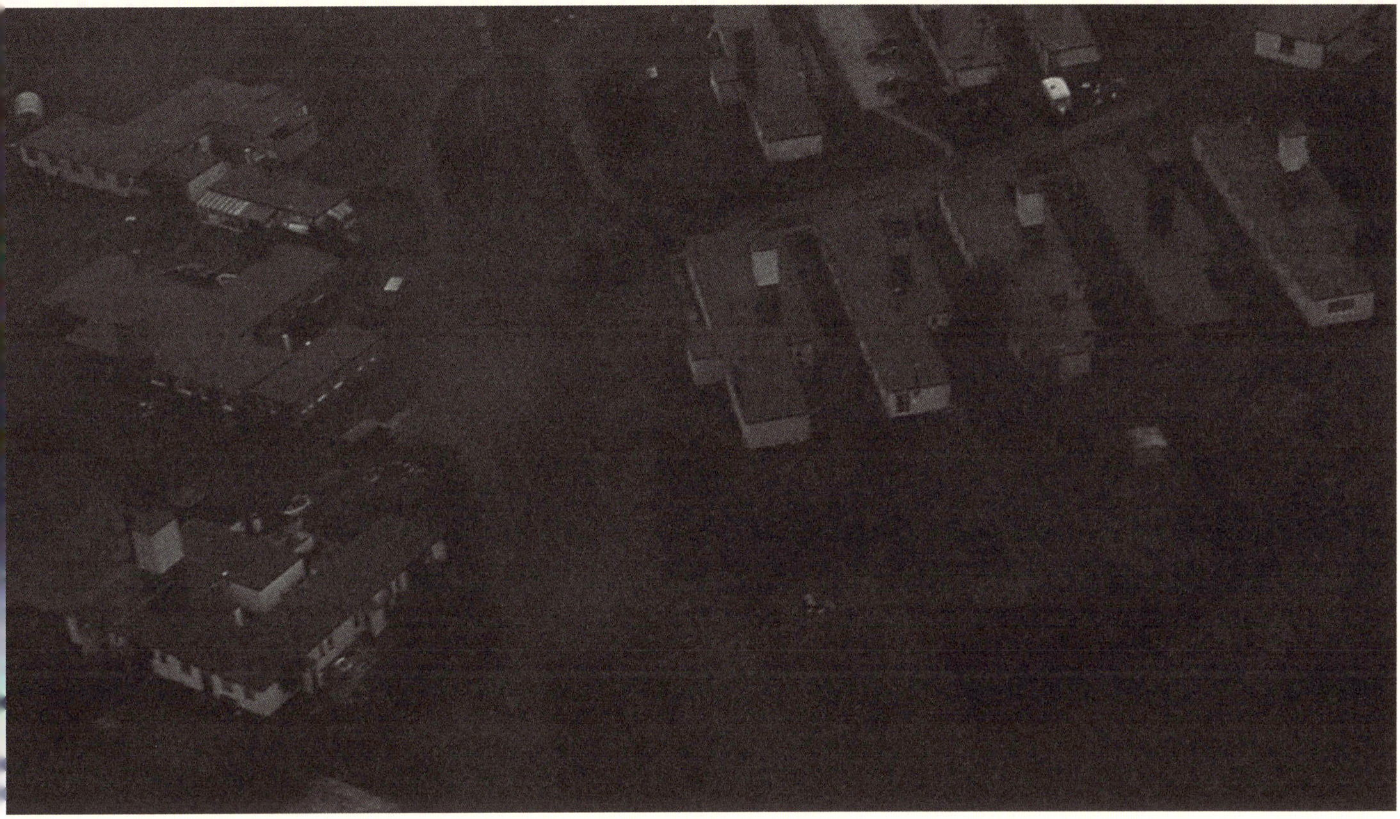

Balnakiel, 2009. Video and sound installation, 30 mins. Video still. Aerial view from a helicopter of Balnakeil Craft Village in the former early-warning station and military barracks.

planet, but every micro-element is becoming corporatized and militarized. The colonization of airspace ignores the very different cosmologies and cultural histories that form a more pluriversal understanding of the sky, and increasingly, these understandings are important modes of resistance. In the context of the proposed new human right, it is vital to bring the long-term psychological impact of these multiple threats into focus, particularly for those growing up and living in perpetual fear of being surveilled and targeted from above.

I want the viewer to see and hear the cultural resonances, atmosphere, and beauty of the sky, its profound place in many cosmologies, in contrast to its devastating history of pollution, war, and exploitation. Intersecting existential threats such as climate change, extractive capitalism, and catastrophic loss of biodiversity are driven by an endless cycle of colonialities, political violence, and constant competition for military and economic advantage, which is radically transforming the sky. I hope *Topologies of Air* will bring into focus the complexity of threats that are transforming our relationship to the sky above us into a space of closure, anxiety, and fear, while challenging the hierarchies and levels of abstraction that devalue some lives, elevate others, and distance us from the immense global challenges we face. For example, the impact of rising global temperatures includes predictions that up to 1.2 billion people will be subject to forced migration due to climate change by 2050.[13] It is hard to comprehend the enormity of what we are facing.

GV We are already in this conversation because of the current global migration and refugee crisis. People are leaving their homes and homelands to escape state-sponsored oppression and wars, ethnic conflict, and drastic climate change.

Some governments choose to do nothing, and refugees perish. Some individuals and organizations say, "No, this is not acceptable; we will rescue them," and they are being prosecuted for going into international waters or countries to rescue those in peril. Once in a refugee camp or resettled in a new land, most of the time, the refugees are condemned: "Who are these outsiders? And why are they coming here?" But at the end of the day, they have no other choice; stay and perish, or leave and risk your life. *Topologies of Air* encompasses so many urgencies on the horizon or already here. You had been researching this for a long time, and then, right at the moment when we planned to present this new work, we were struck by this global pandemic—and this virus is airborne.

SI And, meanwhile, the pandemic is accelerating the tech companies' penetration into all facets of our lives. We need to radically rethink and reorientate the trajectory of technological development, who has access to it, and its relationship to knowledge production, life, and environment. We need greater parity and wider critical access to its development, application, and use, for example, for increasing understanding of planetary life, the connections between geopolitics, conflict, ecocide, and climate change, and for identifying human rights abuses, genocide, and pollution.

GV This brings us back to the necessity of artworks such as *Topologies of Air* to be produced and exhibited, to show audiences what is truly happening, and to prompt them to take action.

SI We are part of a complex living ecology. The language of human rights enables us to develop our understanding of the world through empathy and equality. Through further development of human rights as a living instrument, we can also pursue extending those rights to other beings, communities, and the world itself as a living entity—and perhaps even the universe. The advocacy for this proposed human right is inscribed in *Topologies of Air* and the work the artwork does. In this sense, *Topologies of Air* could also be conceived as a living instrument for thinking, for questioning, for generating different kinds of dialogues, in attempting to address the urgent questions we're now facing.

GV So, *Topologies of Air* is a never-ending process of questioning the status quo and a catalyst for real change, for taking a stand. You are working through multiple layers, using our collective memories and our individual perspectives, in order to bring this very specific history to the surface. Hopefully, this will lead us to an understanding of our personal roles in this shared future and our responsibility to speak out.

SI The Airspace Tribunal needs to develop through the partnerships, local and global networks of conversations and actions, to push the proposed human right forward. That's why it's so fantastic that The Power Plant has supported the Airspace Tribunal at precisely this time. That's why working with organizations such as the European Center for Constitutional and Human Rights is critical. The Airspace Tribunal is focused on bringing about critical change through developing the human rights dimension of airspace and outer space, whether through the eventual recognition of the proposed human right or through creative interpretation of existing rights, and through mobilizing conversations that need to take place across many disciplines, experiences, world views, and forms of activism. Within this, I think art and cultural practice play an essential role.

This conversation between Shona Illingworth and Gaëtane Verna took place on December 23, 2020, via Zoom. It has been edited for clarity and length.

Shona Illingworth is a Danish-Scottish artist. Solo exhibitions of her work have taken place at: The Power Plant, Toronto (forthcoming 2022); Bahrain National Museum (forthcoming 2022); UNSW Galleries, Sydney (2016); FACT, Liverpool (2015); Wolverhampton City Gallery (2010); and John Hansard Gallery, Southampton (2009). Her work has been exhibited at the Wellcome Collection, London (2007 and 2018–19); Imperial War Museum, London (2017–18); Museum of Modern Art, Bologna (2008); and Akbank Sanat, Istanbul (2006). It has been screened at: WORM, Rotterdam (2018); Turner Contemporary, Margate (2016); Nottingham Contemporary (2016); the MAC, Belfast (2016); Whitechapel Gallery, London (2016); Museum of Modern Art Buenos Aires (2014); and Modern Art Oxford (2011). Illingworth's work has been commissioned by The Wapping Project; Film and Video Umbrella; Animate Projects; Hayward Gallery, London; and Channel 4 Television. Illingworth was a recipient of the Stanley Picker Fellowship and shortlisted for the Jarman Award (2016). She is Professor of Art, Film, and Media at the University of Kent, an Imperial War Museum Associate, and on the international editorial boards for *Journal of Digital War* and *Memory, Mind and Media*.

Gaëtane Verna is an art historian and an arts administrator. She is Director and Artistic Director of The Power Plant Contemporary Art Gallery, Toronto. From 2006 to 2012, she was Executive Director and Chief Curator of the Musée d'art de Joliette, Quebec. For more than seven years, Verna also served as Curator of the Foreman Art Gallery at Bishop's University, Sherbrooke, while also teaching in the Art History department of both Bishop's University and the Université du Québec à Montréal. Since 1992, Verna has curated and organized exhibitions by emerging, mid-career, and established artists and has edited and contributed essays to numerous books and catalogues. She serves on the Board of Directors of the Canada Council for the Arts, TV5 Québec Canada, and the Sobey Art Foundation. In 2017, Verna was named Chevalier de l'Ordre des Arts et des Lettres (Order of Arts and Letters) by the French government.

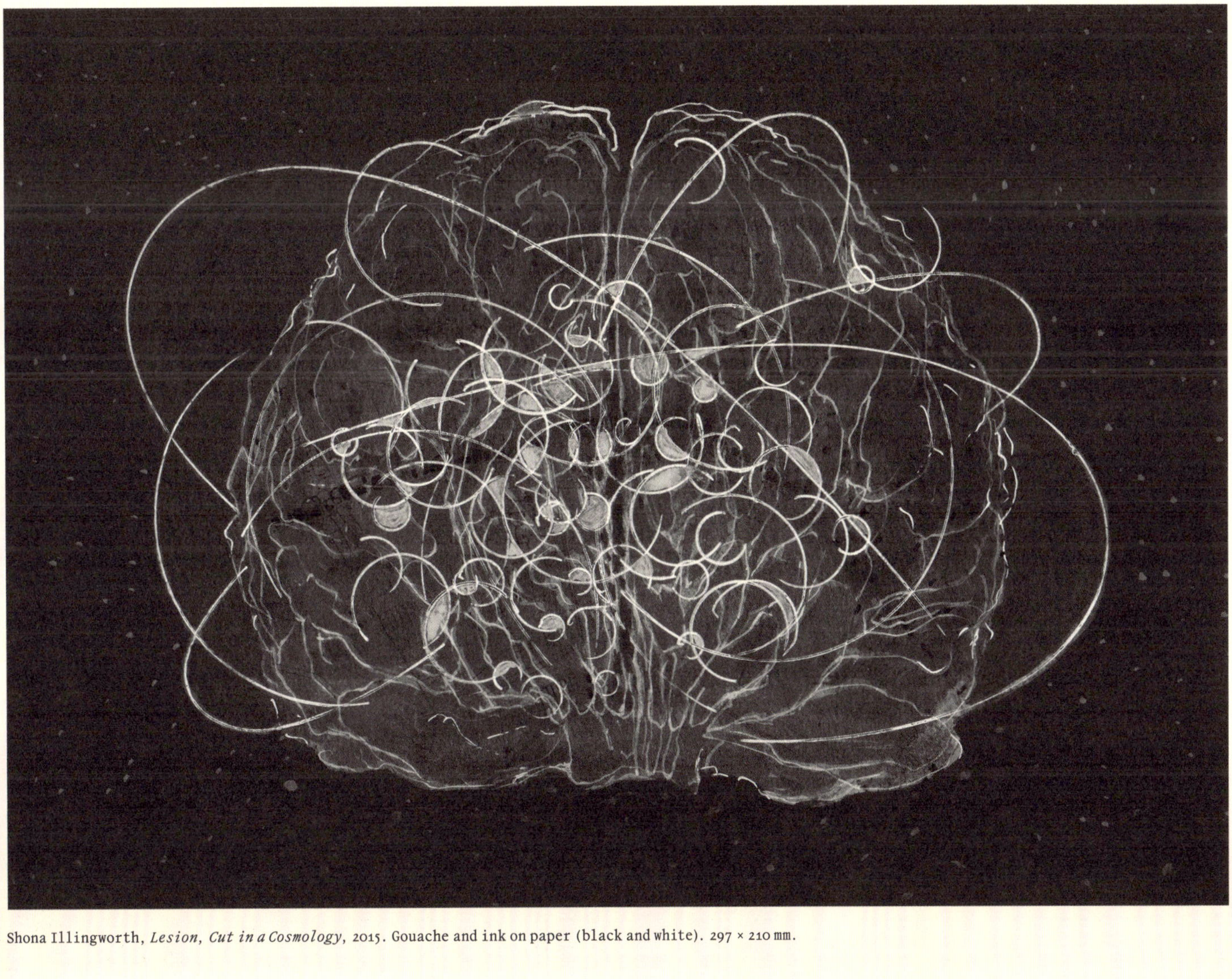

Shona Illingworth, *Lesion, Cut in a Cosmology*, 2015. Gouache and ink on paper (black and white). 297 × 210 mm.

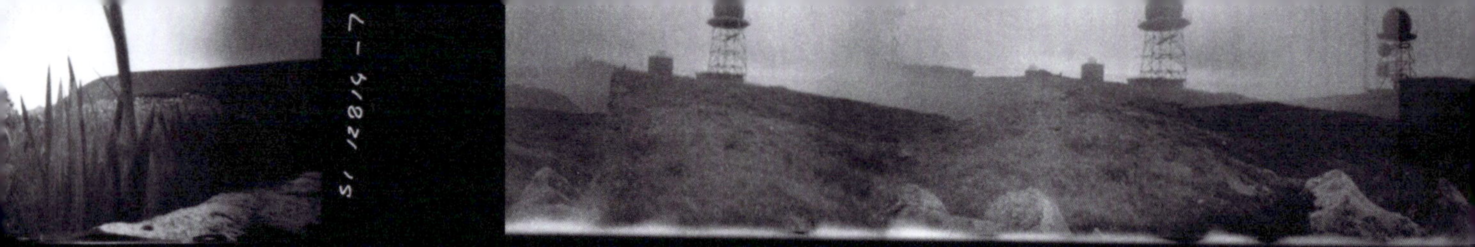

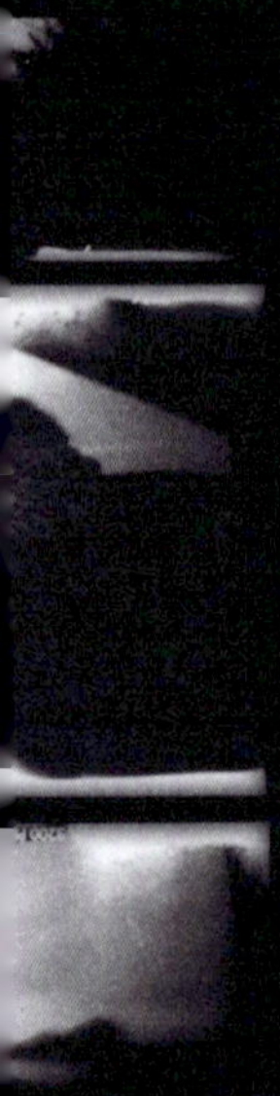

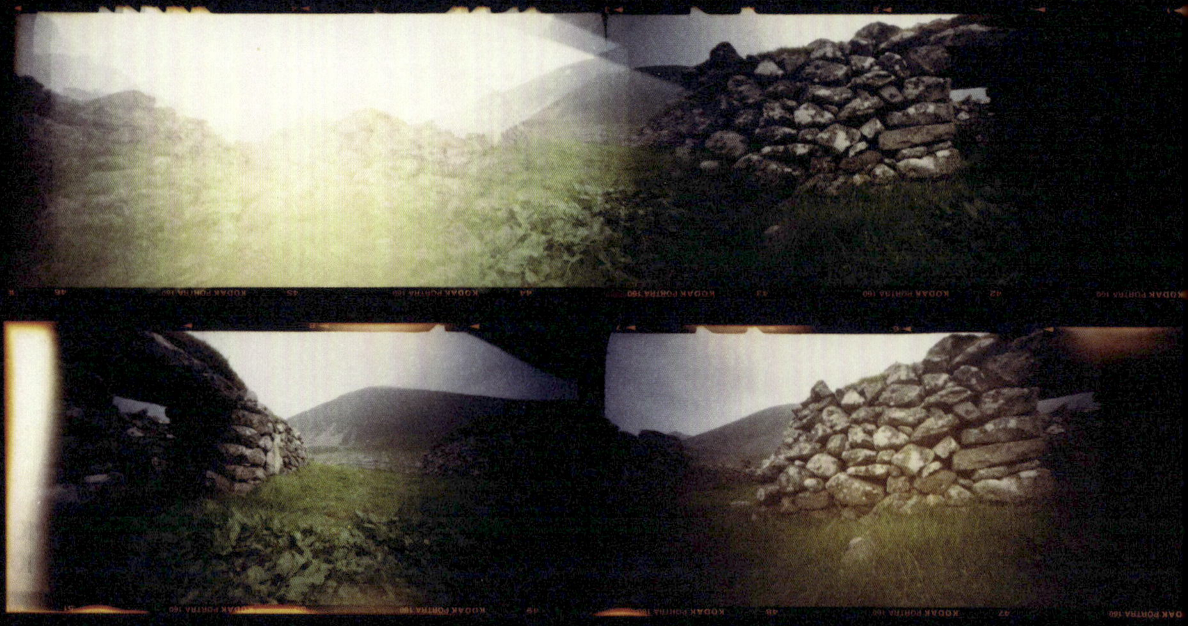

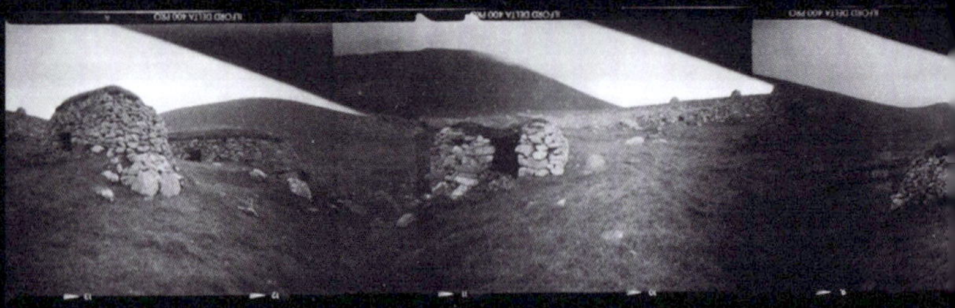

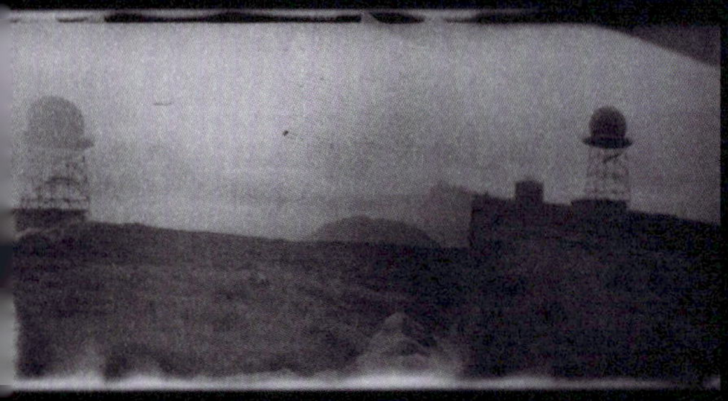

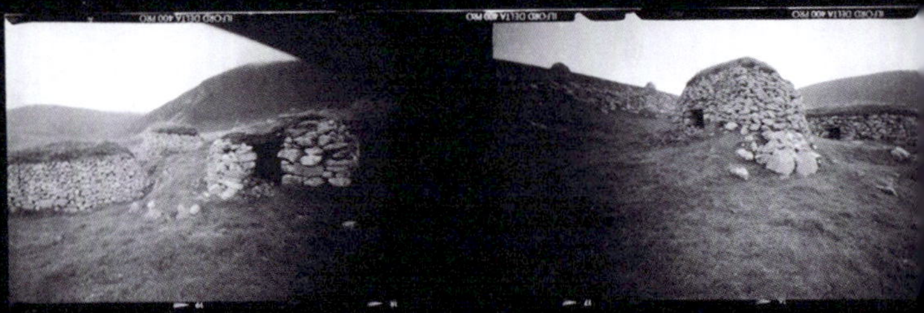

This page: Shona Illingworth, *Military Radar, Conachair, Cleits, Hirte, Hebrides Weapons Testing Range, St Kilda*, 2012. Photograph series made with a pinhole camera (details). Opposite: Shona Illingworth, *Stone Thrown Light in Silver Nitrate, Petrified Ruins, Village Bay, St Kilda*, 2012. Photographs made with a pinhole camera.

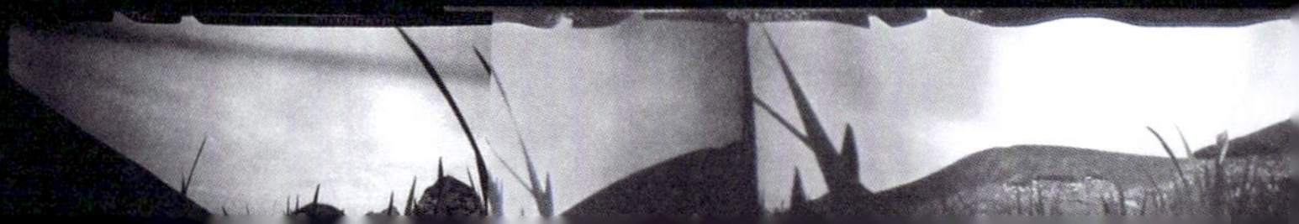

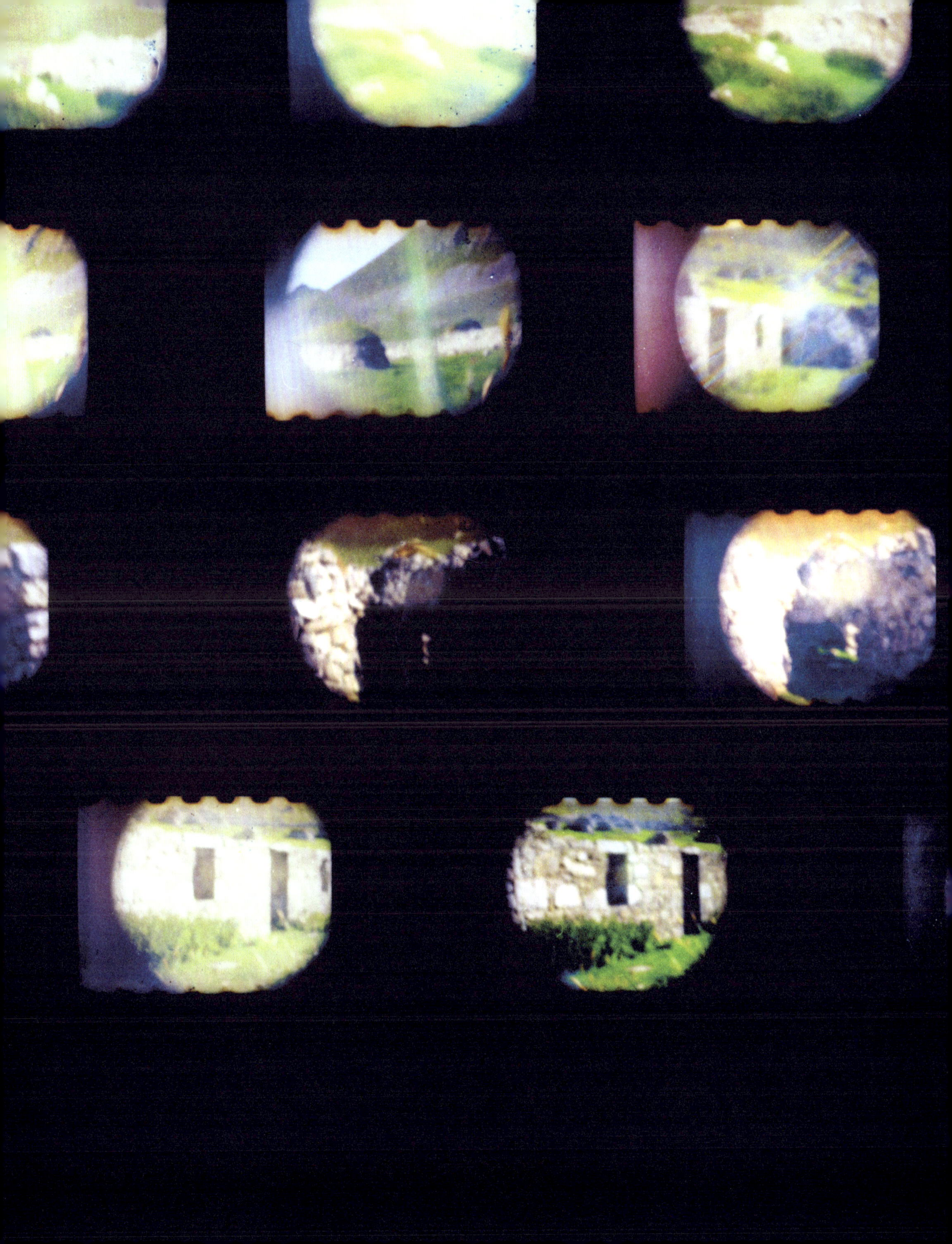

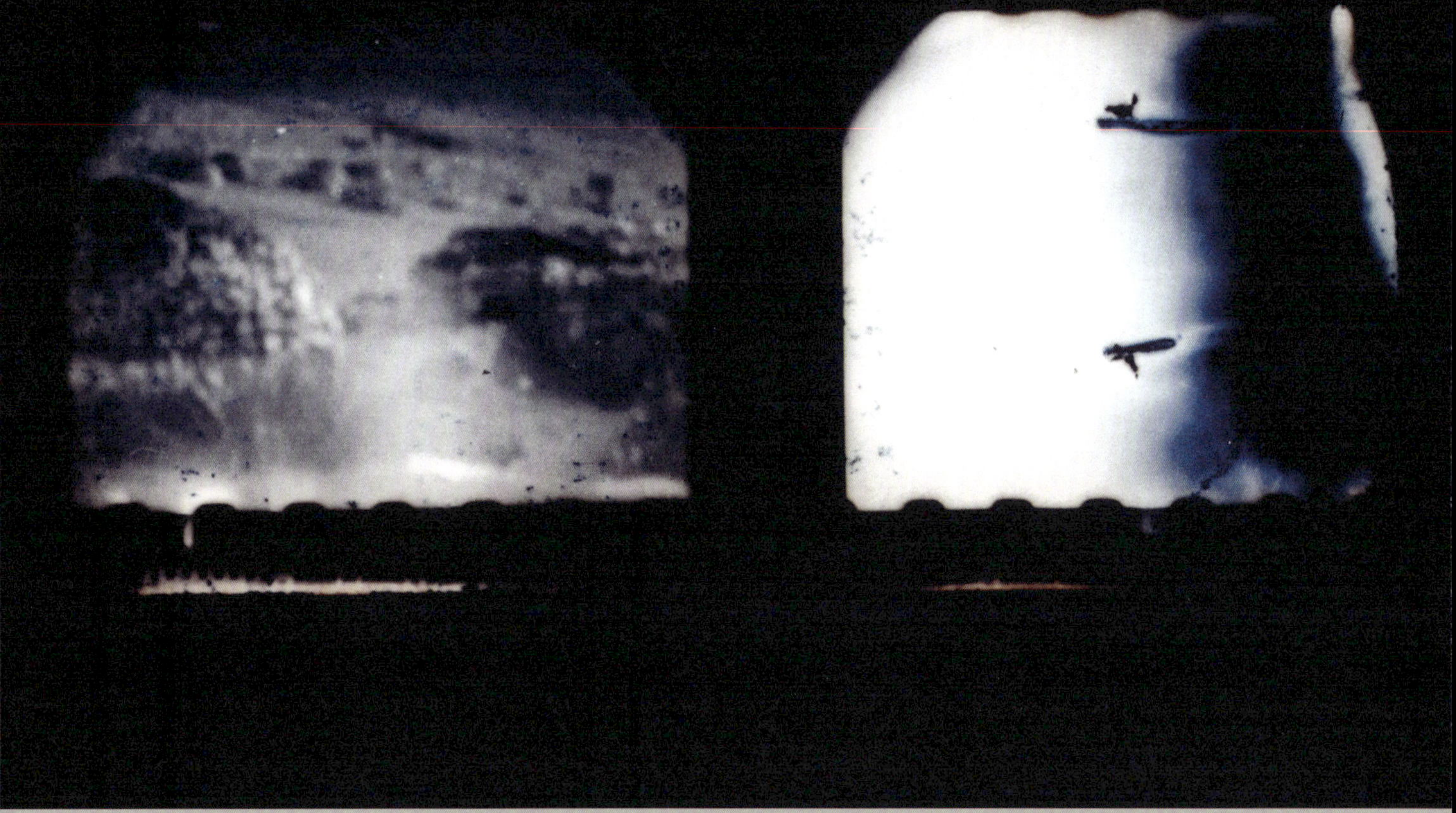

Shona Illingworth, *Stone and light burned edge Village Bay, Hirte*, 2012. Photographs made with a pinhole camera.

TIME PRESENT
2016

Two-screen video installation
35 mins

Time Present explores the dynamic role memory plays in enabling us to move through time and space. Claire can no longer remember much of her past, form new memories, or recognize faces—not even her own. Revealing the daily feat of creativity, determination, and commitment that Claire undertakes in order maintain to connections to her past and future, the work explores the impact of amnesia and the devastating consequences of being trapped in the present moment and, therefore, stranded in time.

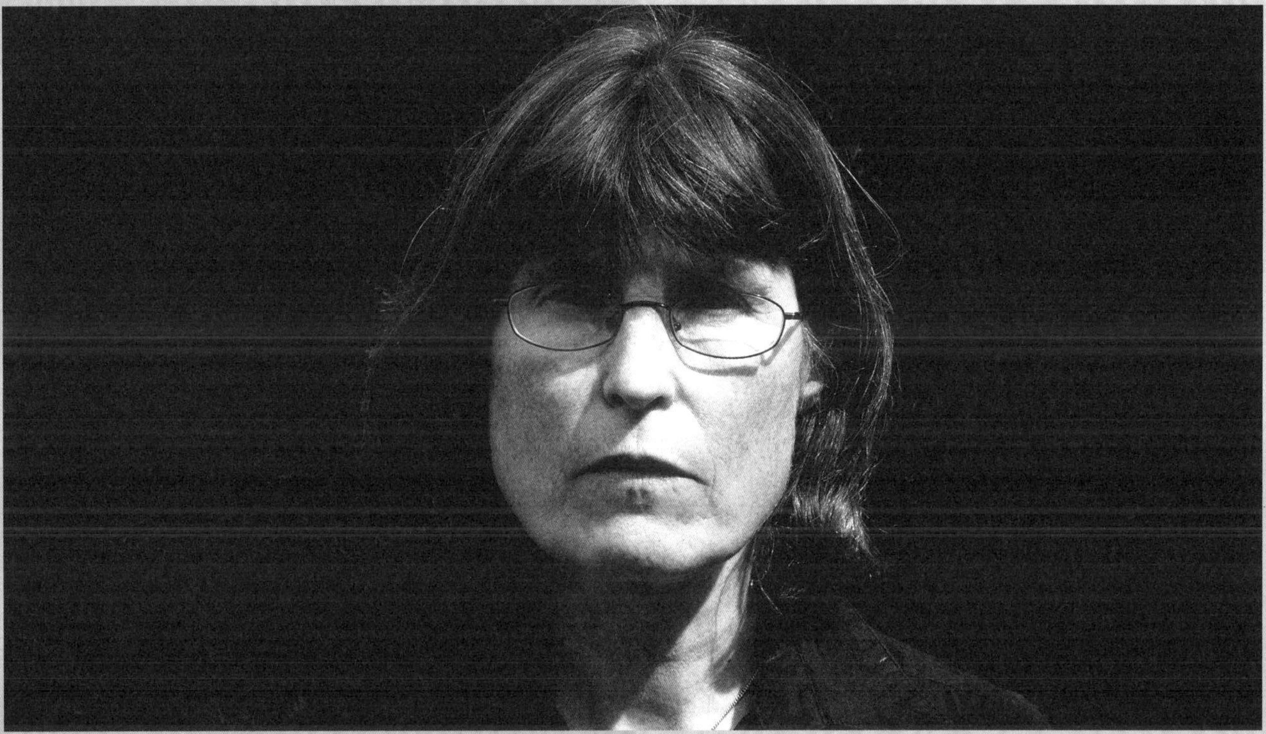

CLAIRE

I was very scared, shaky and running
in a frightening, very scary place underground
and there were tunnels, like stone tunnels,
man-made sort of thing
I was sort of conscious that somebody was nearby,
scraping against the side of the tube or running
but at anytime I didn't know if this scary thing was
behind me or in front of me but there were times
when I kind of sat to the side for a while.

And then it all happened again.

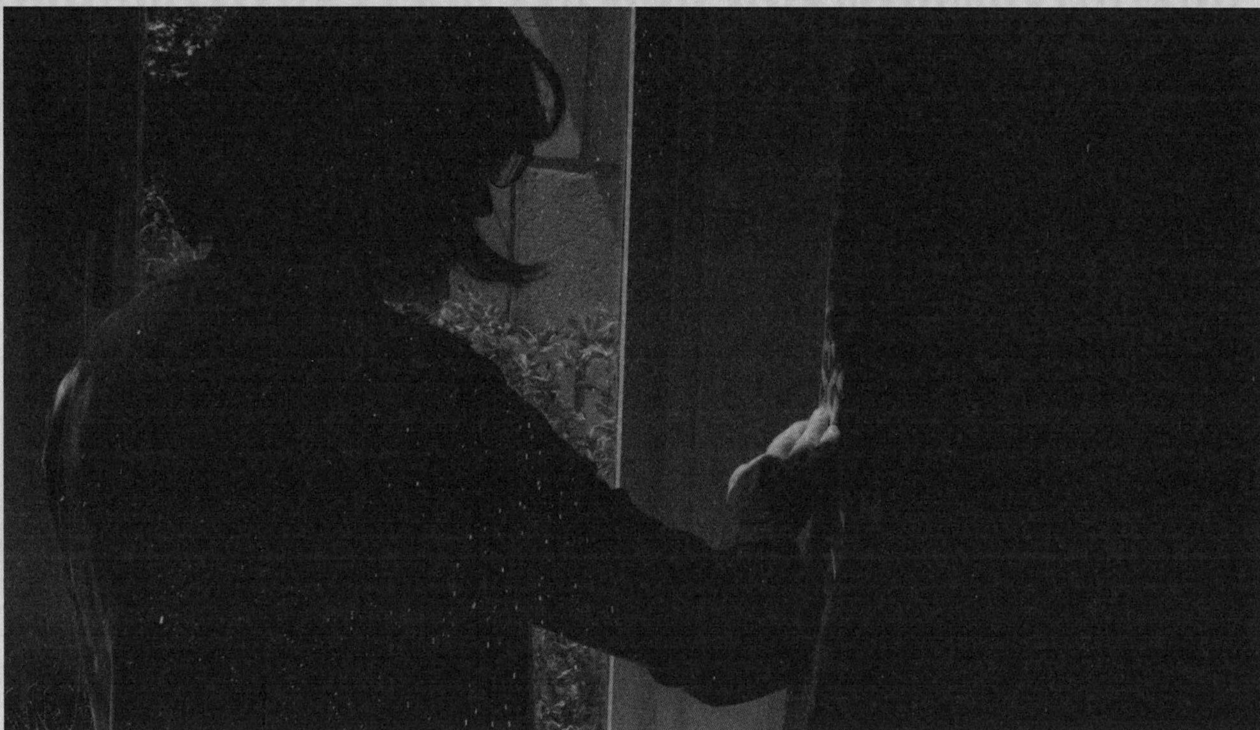

CLAIRE

I came home to a family of four children, ours
and I knew nothing about any of them
A home I didn't know anything about or where
anything was kept
and a family I couldn't recognize
it was just like coming into a complete ... unknown place
and I told myself I have to believe he's my husband
and believe they were our children
and believe that I'd had ... a life here

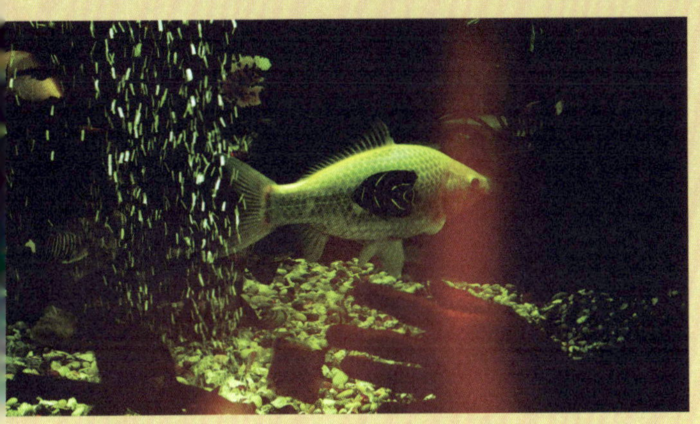

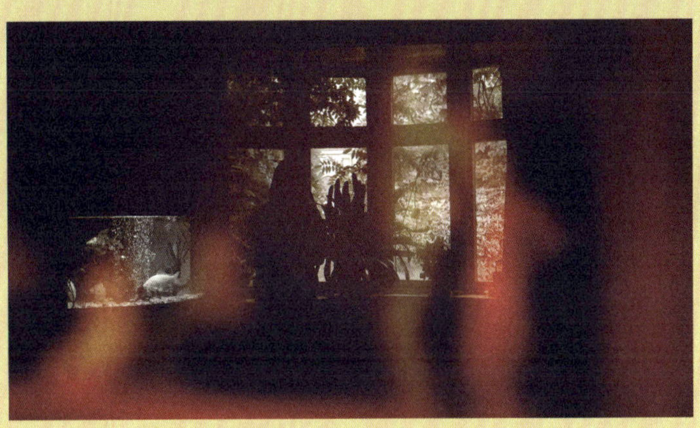

MARTIN

There's a dynamic relationship between memory, self, and the world.
The whole system is being constantly updated by experiences you have, by thoughts that you have, by daydreams that you have.

There's a system called the default network, which is a large brain network that becomes active when we're not task-focused, and that's when we daydream, and that's one of the key moments

when this dynamism begins to occur, in which we update the self, in which we become aware that we're moving forward in time, passing through time.

And one of the consequences of passing through time is change, a person changes

For somebody with amnesia who can no longer create new memories, they can no longer maintain that dynamic relationship between long-term memory and this envelope of conscious awareness of the near past and the near future, and if you can't do that then you're stranded in the present moment, stranded in time.

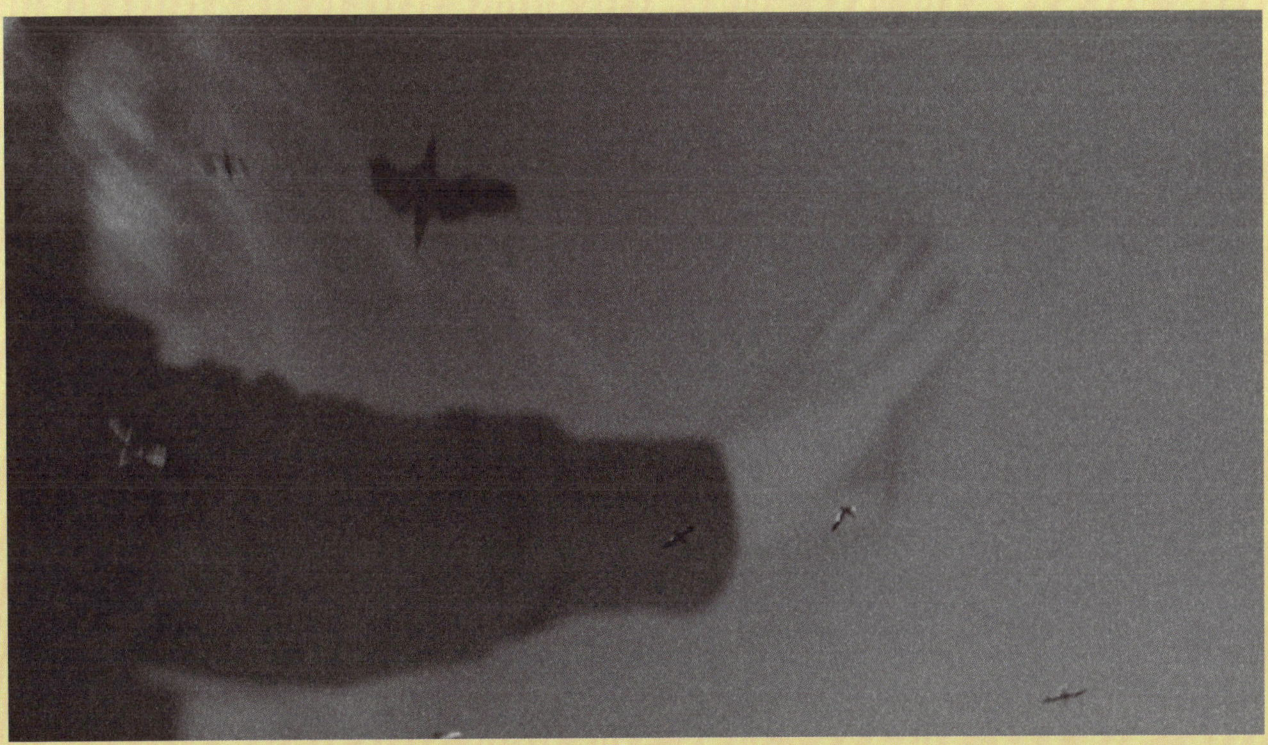

CLAIRE

You know my connections with everybody are completely lost
on top of that I'm unable to store new memories
to make memories very easily
and they are gone very quickly

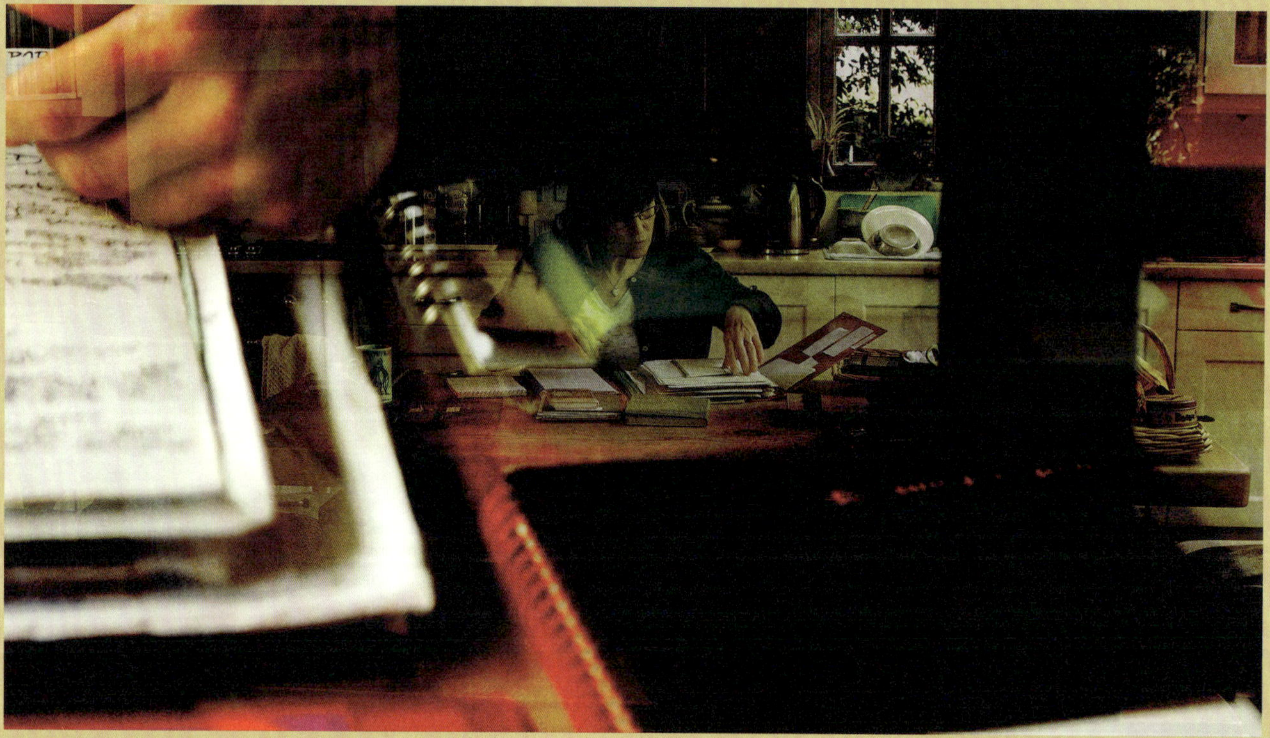

It's difficult to see how we can have a continuous self, and of course some philosophers claim we do not, or to have characteristic emotions, which we experience and others don't or not in the same way.

It's difficult to know how one can have continuity of these things, self, memory, and emotion, given that the body itself is changing physically all the time.

MARTIN

The brain is changing every single millisecond, in fact it's faster than that because the cells in your body are changing and they're changing on an even faster timescale
And the brain is made up of cells, how can you have these cells dying and new ones being created and maintain a memory?

CLAIRE

The minute I wake I want to get up because it all starts spinning through my mind of all the things I've got to-do and trying to remember and the fear of not remembering things and not having any possibility to write things down gets me into a panic and so that I have to get up and get to my to do list and start writing things down before I forget.

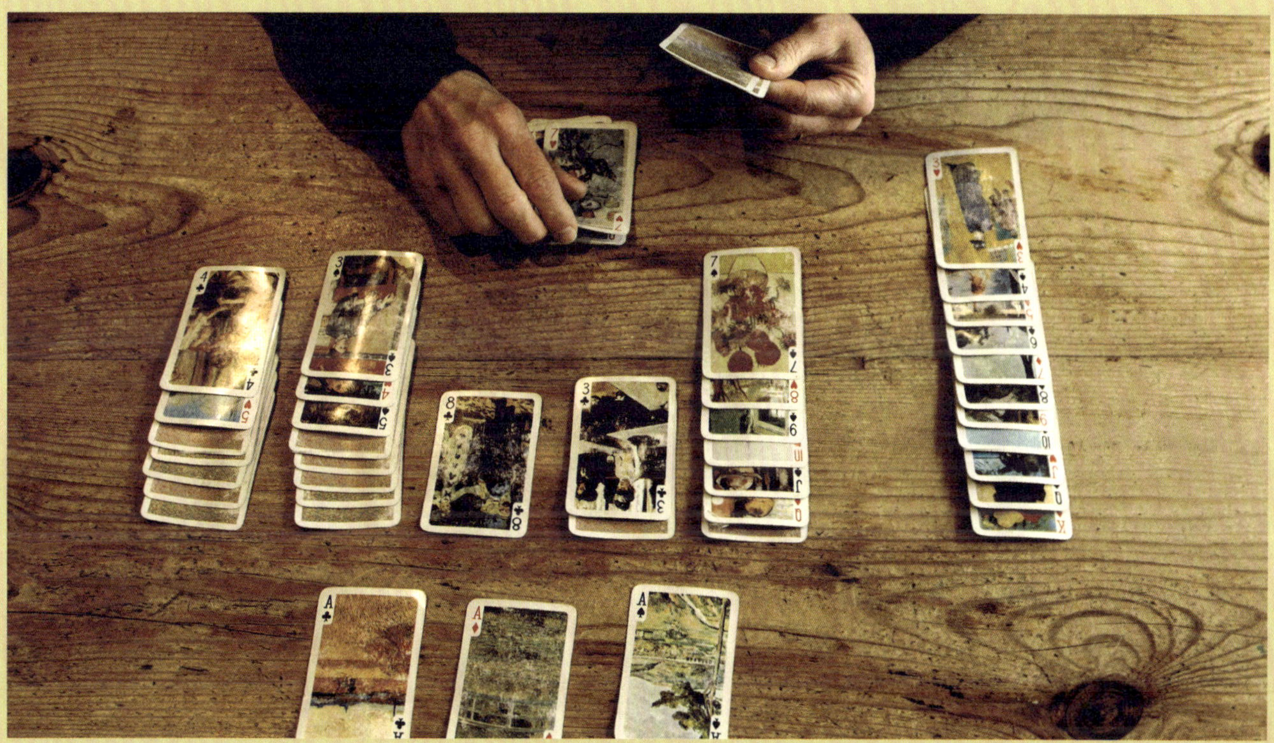

CLAIRE

The to-do list is a good structure
but once I get too tired or emotional to manage it, that's
when I get my pack of cards out

And I think the numbers and the structure of playing a game
of cards just helps my mind relax

I think at times when I can't even play cards
I find that my whole thought processing is just in a real muddle
It's to have some control of thoughts somehow
just having the structure, controlling thinking
red six on a black seven

MARTIN

Memory not only represents facts, episodes, incidents
from the past
but memory can also be used to construct particular histories,
the organization of autobiographical memory is not linear
although linearity can be imposed on it,
autobiographical memory can be used to build different sorts
of histories or different shapes
and giving shape to what you do or do not remember is
perhaps quite an important creative process that allows you
to come to terms with change

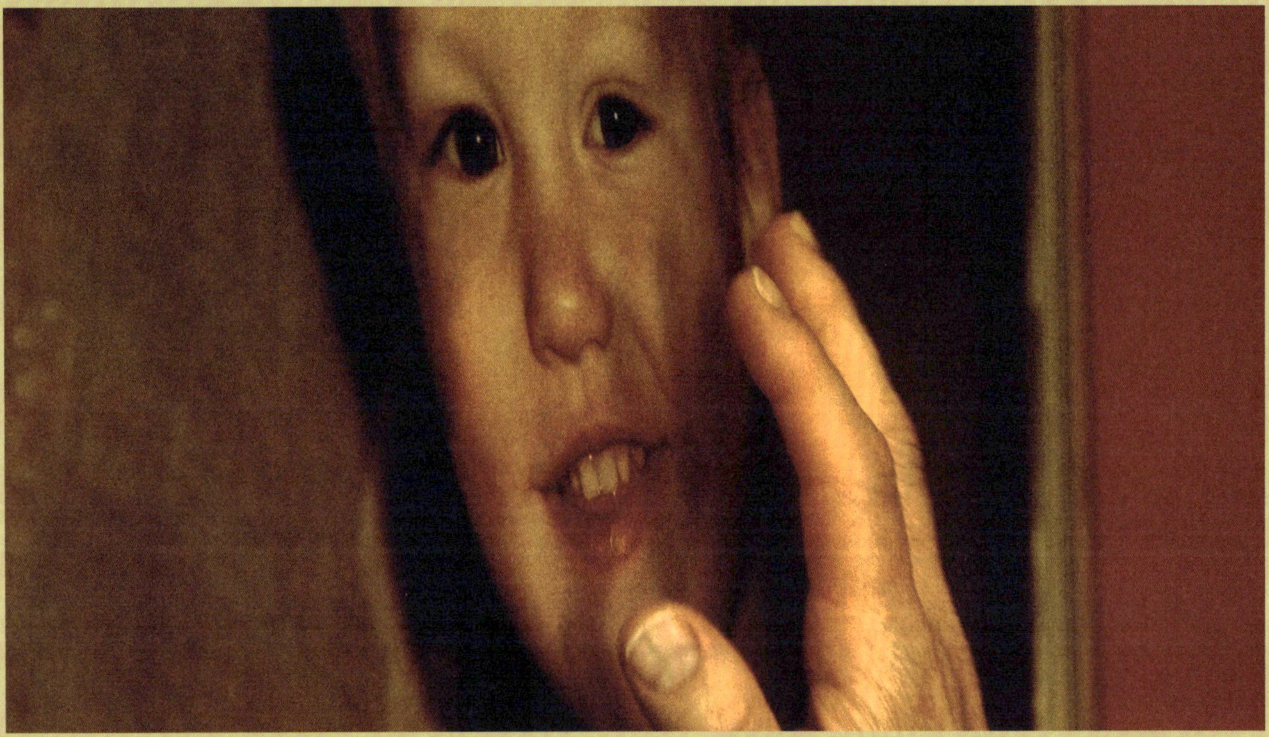

MARTIN

What would happen if you couldn't imagine
could you then have a memory?
It seems to us that quite probably it is the case that if you
lost the ability to imagine
then you would lose the ability to create new memories
and that's because imagining and remembering
are part of the same process

CLAIRE

It's been a bit scary in a way going into rooms that have strange feelings of no sense of belonging to any of it or things I don't understand, I think I used to know about things in the house, who gave us that lovely chair or you know even memories of choosing a carpet or something.

The future is frightening, not knowing how I'm going to fit into a world that once knew this person I have to call me.

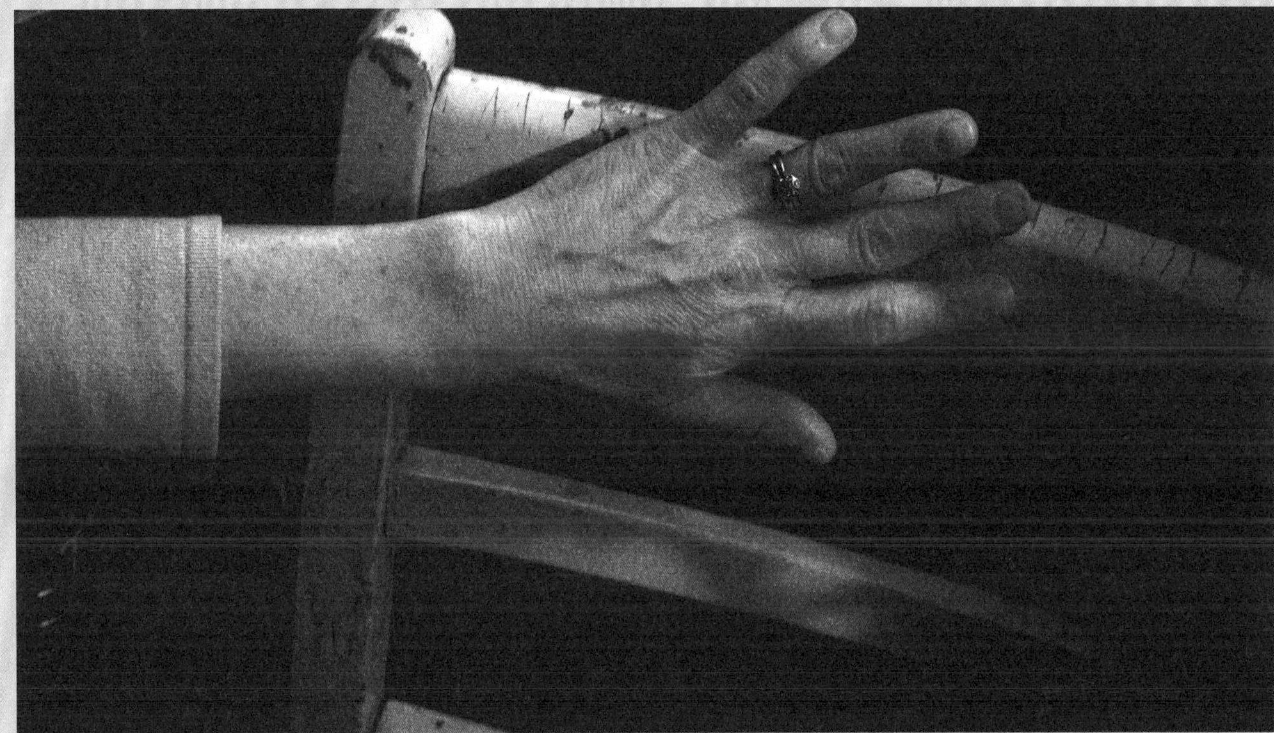

MARTIN

*We all exist in an epoch of remembering and imagining
which forms a system that moves through time in a
window of consciousness
with the past fading and the imagined future manifesting.
Within this remembering-imagining system
it is not possible to imagine the future
without, in some way, remembering the past.*

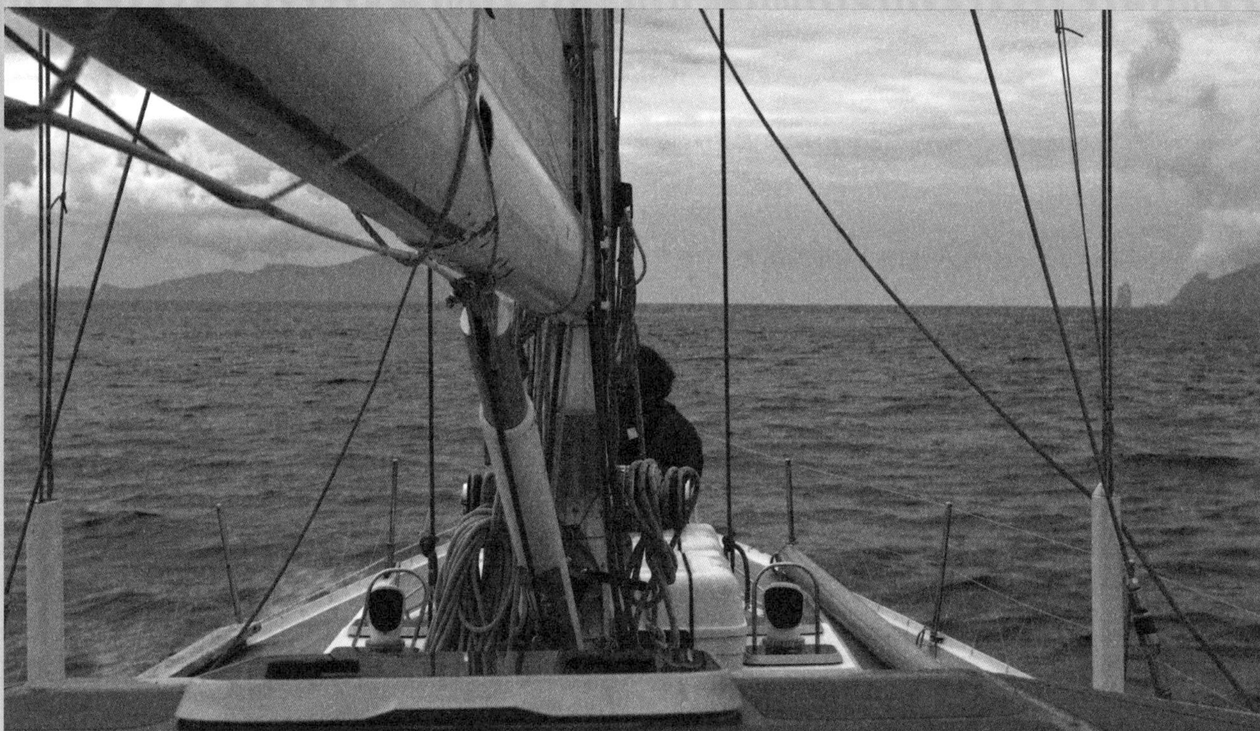

Extracts from the full transcript of *Time Present*.
Parts of this text have been edited for syntax

Martin A. Conway
SELF AND CONSCIOUSNESS

Much has been written about *the* self. I emphasize "the" because its function is to objectify self, to make it into an object to which one can point. For instance, someone might point to an area of the brain and say this is where *the* self is. In this short commentary, I will not review the work on *the* self but rather confine myself to some more general speculations. Let's start with getting rid of *the* self. Replacing it simply with "self." In doing this, we recognize self as a *process* rather than an object, which is not to deny that there are mental representations—knowledge representations—that exist in the mind and that can be, at least to some extent, pointed to in the brain. These knowledge representations may have a long duration and may provide grounding for self. After all, a process that was unconstrained or un-channeled would be unstable and uncontrolled.

What then of consciousness? And I note, in passing, that we do not say "*the* consciousness," "*the* memory," or "*the* vision," implicitly recognizing that it is more like a process than an object. At least as much has been written about consciousness as about self. Whether this body of work has helped in understanding consciousness is a debatable point. I will make no attempt to review this work here but more simply make some points that might be of interest and then mention some related work. This work formed the basis of at least several of the projects conducted by Shona Illingworth and myself.[1]

My suggestion is that consciousness is a process to which self can give rise, sometimes but not always. In other words, the self-process can run without consciousness, but not vice versa—you cannot have consciousness without self. An everyday example is sleep, when the consciousness process is stepped down to varying degrees in different phases of sleep. Of course, as long as there is a functioning brain, no processes can be switched off, but it may be attenuated or weakened. Is the self-process also attenuated in sleep? That is a more difficult question, but it seems unlikely that it is—after all, even dreams involve self.

It has been found that the neural networks that support self, to a large extent, run along the mid-line of the brain from front (anterior) to back (posterior). These are highly complex interlocked neural networks consisting of many millions of neurons—the basic computing unit of the brain at the cellular level—with trillions of interconnections between them, some short, some lengthy. Patterns of activation constantly arise and dissipate in this complex of neural networks, and it is these transitory patterns of activation that may represent self at any one time. In a similar way, there are interconnected complex neural networks throughout the brain that appear to give rise to conscious states. Some of these are emotional, and some have more to do with everyday feelings of being connected with our goals, plans, environment, and the future, especially the near future. When brain damage occurs, it is almost inevitable that these complex processes of self and consciousness will be impacted in some way, if only because the neural substrate that supports these processes is complex and distributed through the neocortex and subcortical areas too.

Consider, for example, someone who has amnesia. Amnesia can arise from damage to a variety of different brain areas, and obviously, people with amnesia have problems in recalling the past but,

1 Illingworth is the artist, and she initiated, led, and realized these projects; I was merely a collaborator, which has been very enjoyable, and I recommend it.

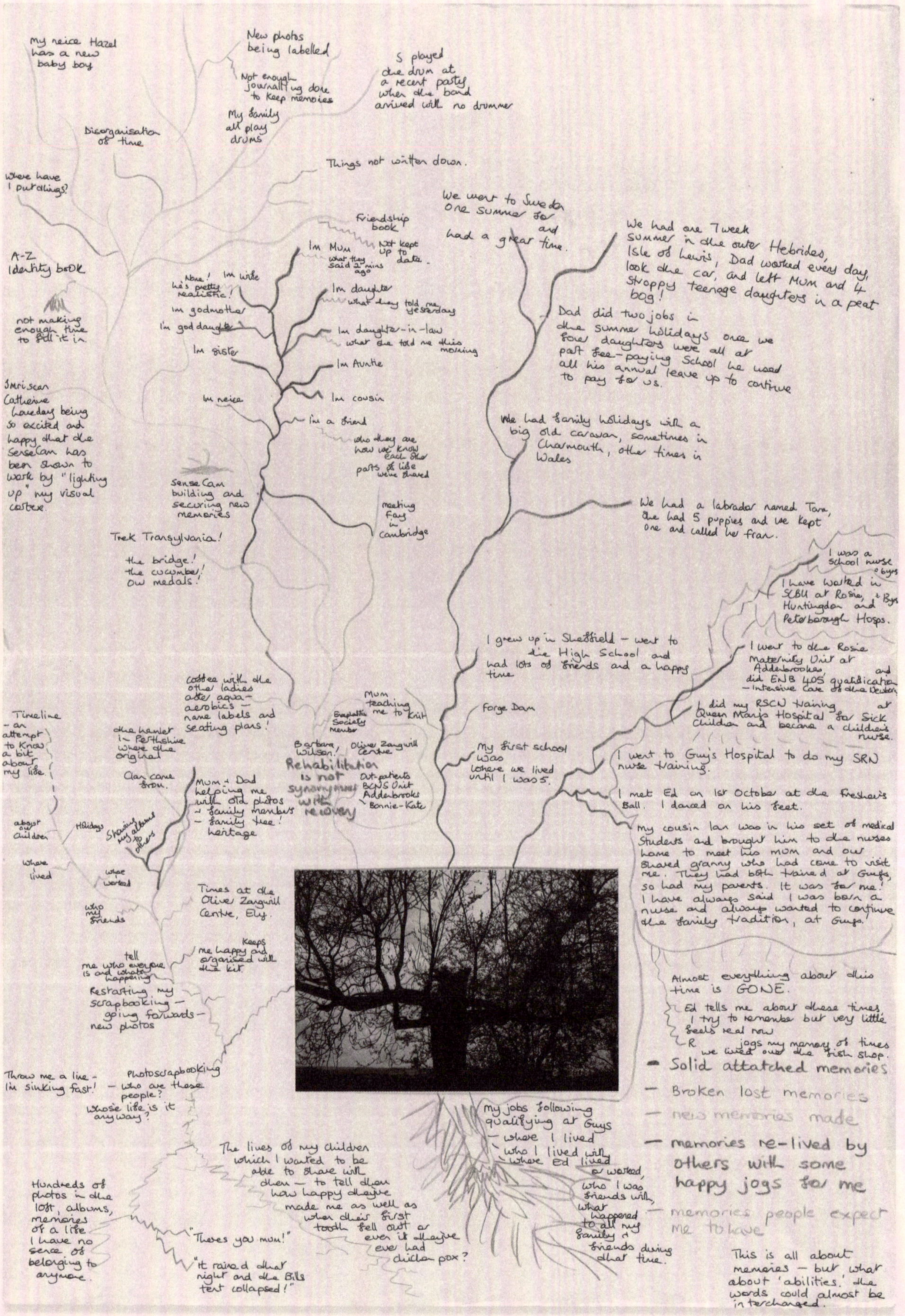

Claire, *Dendritic Map of Amnesia*, 2014. Photograph and ink on paper. 841 × 594 mm. *Amnesia Museum* archive.

more often than not, they also have problems in encoding the present into long-term memory—in other words, they cannot form new memories or, if they can form them, access to them is rapidly lost. We will come back to this in a moment, but let's consider another problem, a particularly interesting one at that: people with amnesia often cannot imagine the future. In other words, self does not extend into the future as it does for most of us. Their self has been truncated by their brain damage, and in those few cases that have been examined, it appears that few, if any, changes or developments to self take place post–brain damage. A clear implication of this is that the ability to encode new experience into long-term memory—i.e., to create new memories—is critical both to planning and self. Thus, a dynamic and ever-changing long-term autobiographical memory—memory for the experiences of our lives—underlies a dynamic self that is able to have new and nuanced conscious states.

With her extensive right-sided lesion (an area of dead neural tissue in the temporal lobe) that extends through the neocortex to subcortical areas toward the base of the brain, Claire also has problems with the future. Although she has been through fairly extensive rehabilitation programs and has learned to keep detailed lists of what needs to be done on certain days, she, nonetheless, frequently consults these lists. A particular problem Claire has is she often does not know how much of the day has passed and chronologically where she is in the day; her orientation for time is strikingly disrupted. By looking back at her lists and checking what has been ticked off, she can infer approximately where she is in the time of a day or, at least, her own subjective sense of the time of the day—a sort of self-time versus clock-time, the latter can always be checked against a clock, and Claire frequently consults one. Those of us without brain damage do the same, but we do so mentally by accessing our memories and bringing to mind visual images of the very recent past and recollections of actions and thoughts that occurred earlier in the day. Interestingly, Claire has lists for both long-term plans as well as specific days. This, too, mirrors our planning for the future that also entails long-term and daily plans. But in the non-amnesic person, these are integrated within self and are consciously brought to mind. For Claire, they are written on lists.

Especially interesting is that Claire can form memories and can often recall what took place several minutes or hours ago. Given that the duration of short-term memory is approximately two minutes, then, by definition, these must be long-term memories. However, if queried about these the following day, or at even longer retention intervals, say seven days, she can rarely remember any of them and usually remembers none. Nonetheless, they must be encoded in long-term memory. What seems to be the case for Claire is that she rapidly loses access to long-term memories that she has, nevertheless, formed and encoded.

In our work, we have found that Claire can gain access to some of these long-term memories if she is given a very specific cue in the form of a photograph taken by a body-worn camera during the event. Her impairment seems to be one of *accelerated loss of access* to her long-term memories. Of course, we all lose access to our long-term memories, but not at the rapid rate Claire does. Moreover, when she looks at a photograph and begins to recall a memory, her recall is different from that of a person who does not have amnesia. For Claire, highly specific details suddenly flood her consciousness in what seems to be an uncontrolled way, suggesting that the original experience was encoded in some nonstandard way.

For most of us, our episodic memories are embedded in layers of self-knowledge. Knowledge about who we have known, places we lived, occupations we have had, our families, and so on—a sort of palimpsest of autobiographical knowledge in which, at the lowest layer, are very specific memories containing information about single unique experiences. In terms of memory research, these are called "episodic memories." It seems that Claire, when given a specific cue such as a photograph or a series of highly specific contiguous photographs, bypasses the layers of knowledge most of us would start working with when recalling an episodic memory and gets there directly. And when she gets there, she gets to many more highly specific details that "flood" her consciousness in an uncontrolled way.

Control systems in the neurologically unimpaired brain may be designed to prevent such hijacking of consciousness by memory and, instead, support a more controlled and orderly access of different levels of self-knowledge, terminating in the access of a specific episodic memory, or set of episodic memories, of which there are only a few details we can ever become conscious. In the neurologically unimpaired brain, memory only occasionally hijacks consciousness and self, for example, in the recall of highly emotionally charged memories, i.e., memories of trauma.

Such uncontrolled access of memory details is maladaptive in that it appears to impair other, ongoing, cognitive processing. Indeed, controlling her thoughts and experience of the world is one of Claire's major difficulties, which she has developed various practices to manage: one is "switching off" her experience of the world (actually, her experience of her mind) by intensively playing the card game "patience." Brain damage, especially when it affects memory, can lead to widespread disturbances of self and consciousness. One of the most marked being a loss of sense of self and a loss of consciousness of time.

Martin A. Conway is Professor of Cognitive Psychology and Director of the Centre for Memory and Law at City University London. Conway has been studying human memory for more than thirty years and is known for his pioneering theoretical work on autobiographical memory, as well as for his studies of the neuropsychology of memory and memory's neurological basis. His research also includes memory impairment and enhancement, and he has recently explored the links between the ability of humans to remember past events and imagine future ones. He was awarded the British Psychology Society's Distinguished Contribution to Psychological Knowledge in 2018.

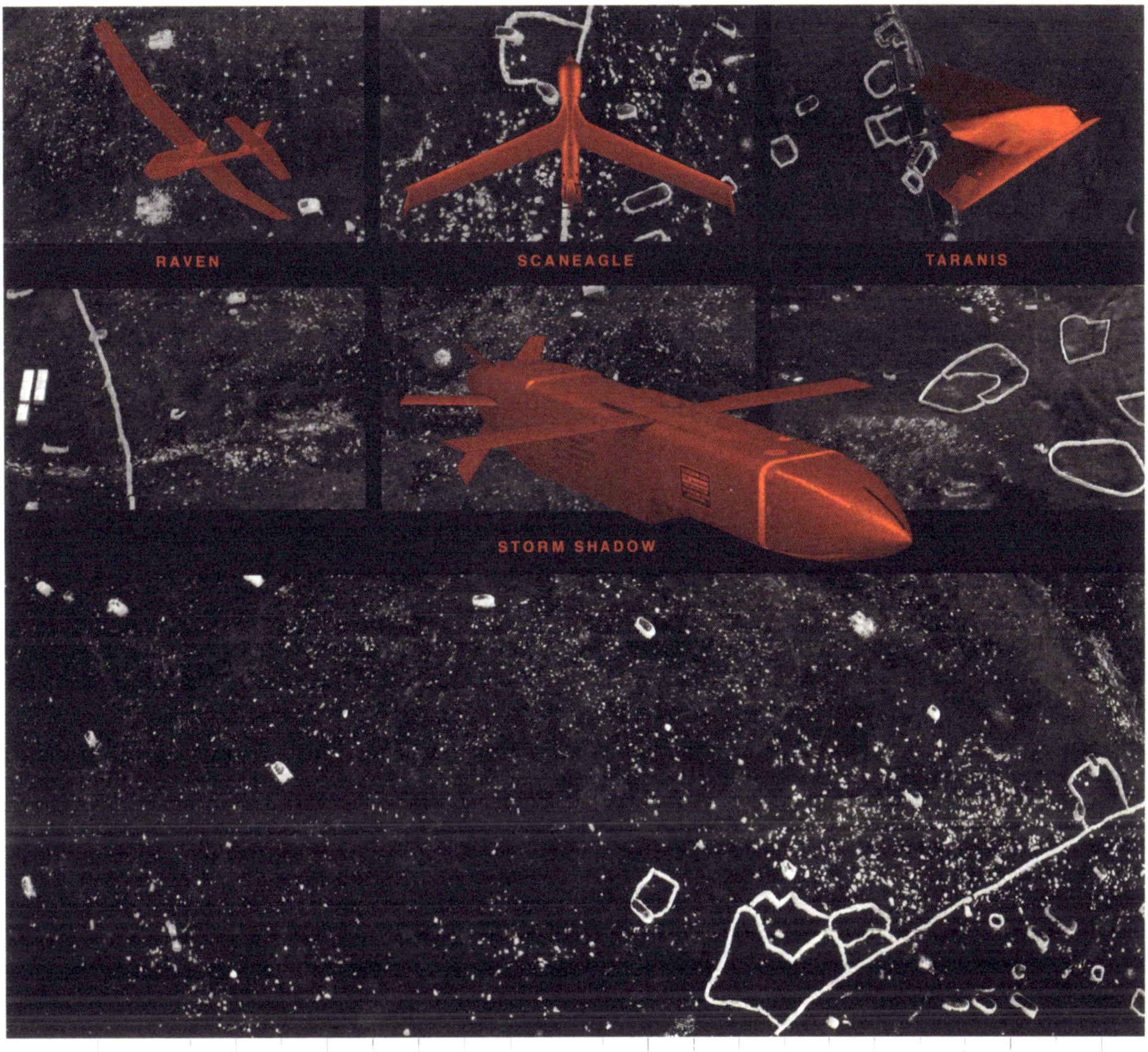
RAVEN
SCANEAGLE
TARANIS
STORM SHADOW

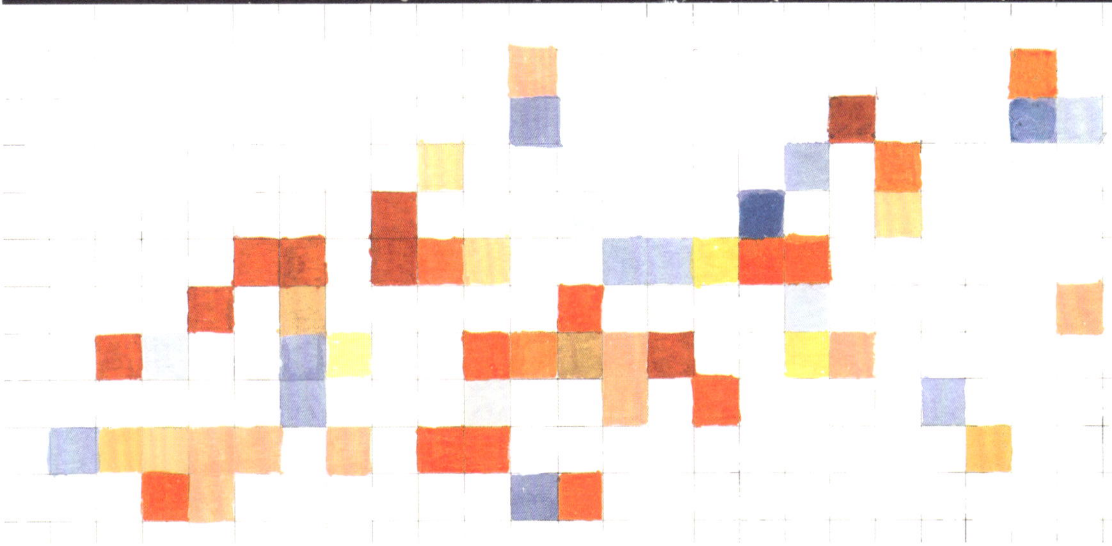

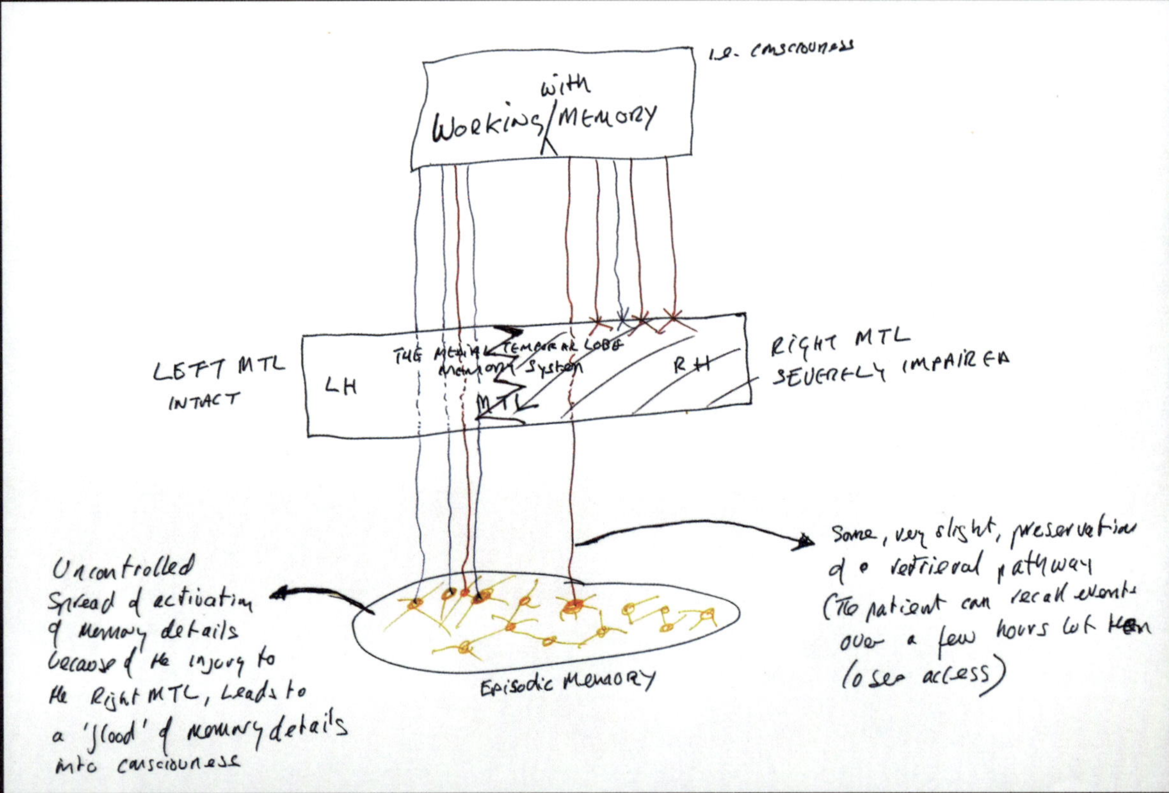

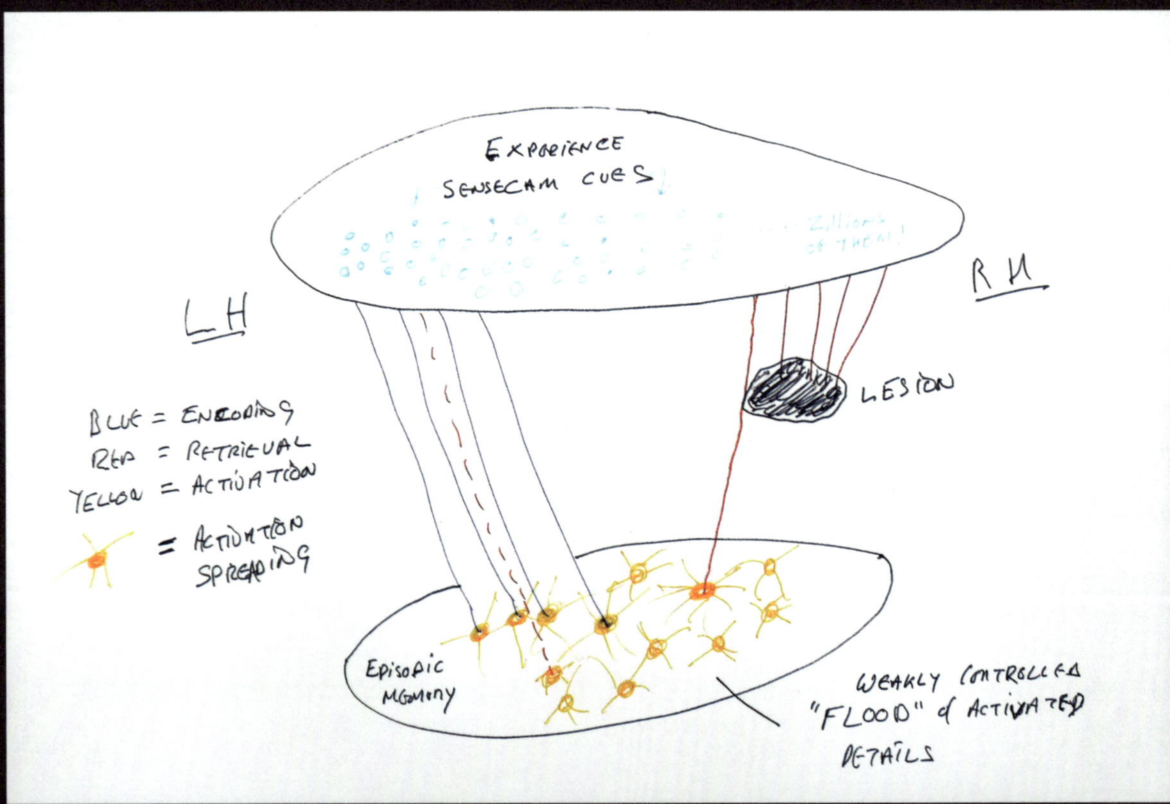

Amnesia Drawings # 2 and # 3, 2014. 841 × 594 mm. From a series of drawings by cognitive neuropsychologist Martin A. Conway made in conversation with artist Shona Illingworth that visualize the impact of a brain lesion on the processes of memory. *Amnesia Museum* archive.

Martin A. Conway
WHEN FAMILIARITY FAILS

Everything is familiar. By which I mean that all conscious moments are accompanied by a feeling of familiarity—a distinct *cognitive feeling*. It is a cognitive feeling that lets us know, in an experiential sense and without further thought, where we are in time and space. Without it, we would be lost. Amnesic patients such as Claire have impaired familiarity—she has a large lesion (dead tissue due to an infection) on the right side of her brain in a region called the temporal lobes, known to be involved in memory. Her feeling of familiarity functions some but not all of the time and often breaks down or vanishes altogether.

What happens when familiarity fails? The two main processes of memory, recognition and recall, fail, too. At that point, one really is lost in time and space—but not quite. Claire, for instance, has good conceptual knowledge of the world; she knows meanings and does not lose these when her familiarity fails. In fact, she has an impressive working memory and understands a wide range of words and concepts. Placing her at the more advanced end of memory abilities, her problems relate mainly to what is termed "episodic memory" (memory for the events of our lives and also memory for environments in which we live). The feeling of familiarity might be considered a *control process*, which helps us attend to what is relevant while still recognizing the context and even recalling relevant memories (sometimes unexpectedly, so-called "remindings" or "spontaneous" remembering). This never, normally, happens for Claire, who can recall a small range of events, mostly very recent (same day), but some (very few) older.

Interestingly, however, if she uses a body-worn camera that takes photographs roughly every minute or so, and then reviews those photographs, usually days later, she does have feelings of familiarity and spontaneous recall of events, with some recognition, too. This shows that her problem does not lie in encoding experience but rather in accessing it from long-term memory. Thus, given a powerful enough cue (i.e., a set of automatically taken photographs of an experience she previously had), representations of the past in her long-term memory can be brought to consciousness. Yet, her recall is not like that seen in an undamaged brain. Instead, it is a flood of highly detailed episodic memories that rush into the mind stimulated by the photographs. It is essentially uncontrolled recall. Indeed, she has crisis moments in which she describes the world "crashing" through her mind in a way she cannot control. She has taught herself to control these moments externally by sitting in her kitchen and playing solitaire for extended periods of time.

Claire's impaired feeling of familiarity has other consequences, too: she suffers from prosopagnosia, a disorder in which a patient cannot recognize familiar faces. Indeed, Claire cannot recognize her own face—there is no feeling of familiarity when looking in the mirror. So extreme is this breakdown in familiarity, she once became highly anxious because of a woman who kept looking at her when she was on a London tube train. In fact, the woman was her own reflection in the window opposite. Another interesting aspect of Claire's impaired familiarity is that when, for example, she moves from one room to another in her house, she becomes disorientated. The only room she really has a feeling of familiarity for is her kitchen (which became highly disrupted when her family reorganized it to make life easier for her). All this is interesting because it is now known that when we move from one room to another, our brain starts forming a memory of what took place in the room we just left. This is something that Claire can only rarely do.

If the feeling of familiarity is so important, then what is it? Unfortunately, we have no good theories of what feelings in general are, and certainly not of what cognitive feelings might be. But one suggestion is that cognitive feelings have evolved to allow the brain to experience what state it is in, i.e., remembering, imaging, in another room, another place, seeing a friend or family member, or just going about one's daily business. Feelings of familiarity embed us in the world, and this "embedding" is something Claire and lots of other neuropsychological patients lose or become impaired in experiencing.

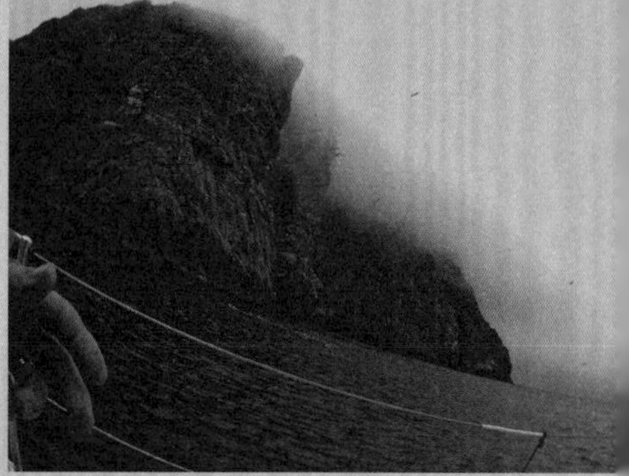

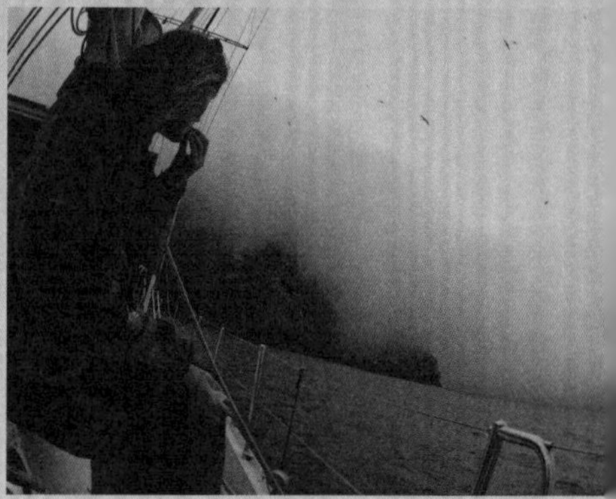

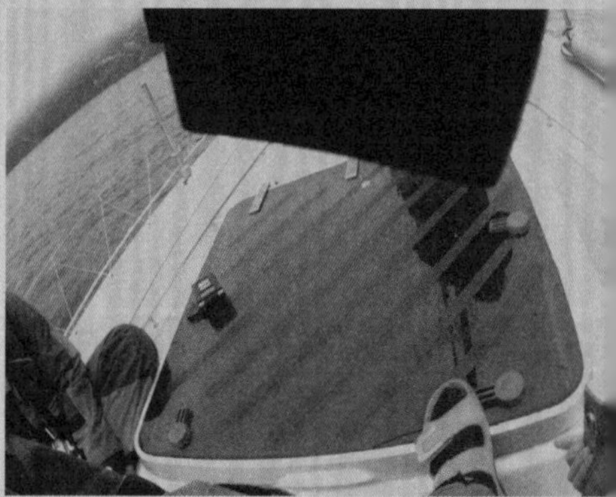

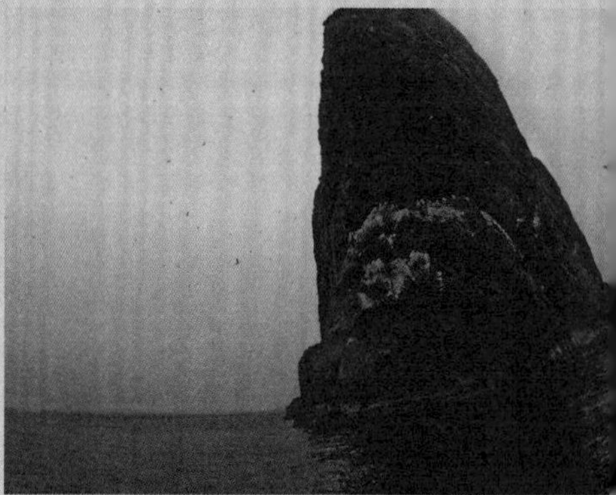

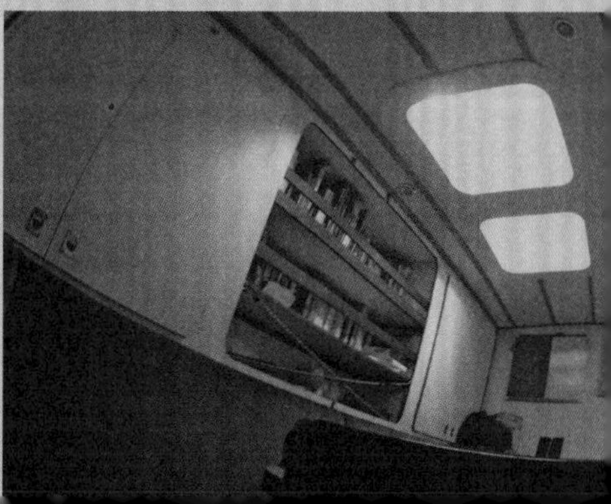

This page and opposite: Stac an Armin and Boreray from the *Elinca*, St Kilda, 2014. *Amnesia Museum* archive. A sensory-operated camera worn around the neck automatically records photographs regularly throughout the day. When reviewed, these photographs can help Claire retrieve memories that are otherwise inaccessible. Functional MRI scans show that when a memory is consolidated by viewing these images, the brain response is significantly stronger than for a typical memory recall. The images were taken by Claire on a journey that she made with Shona Illingworth to St Kilda in 2014.

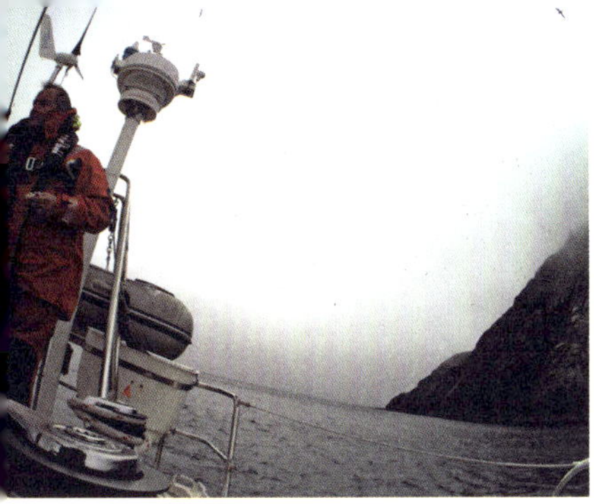
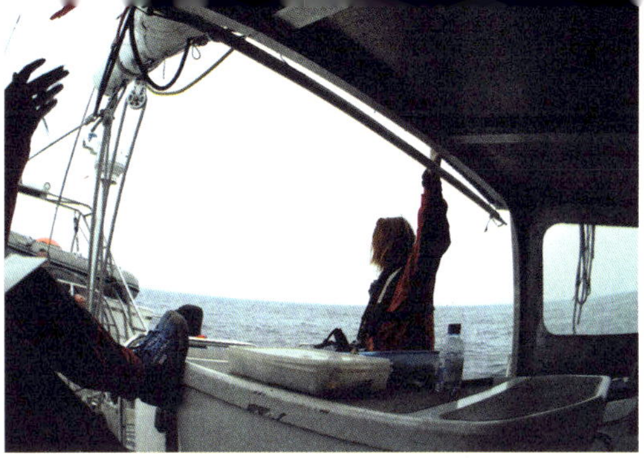
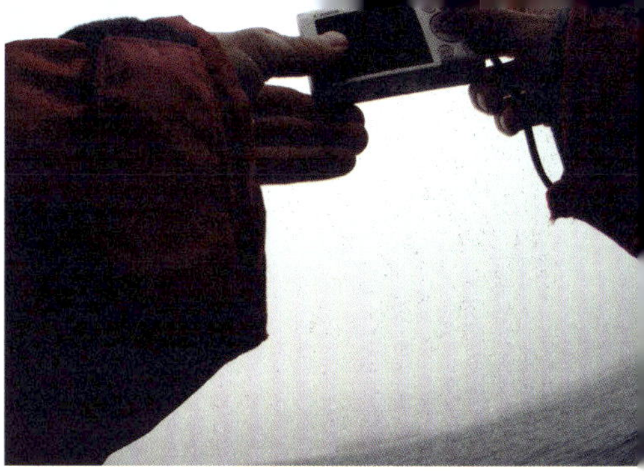
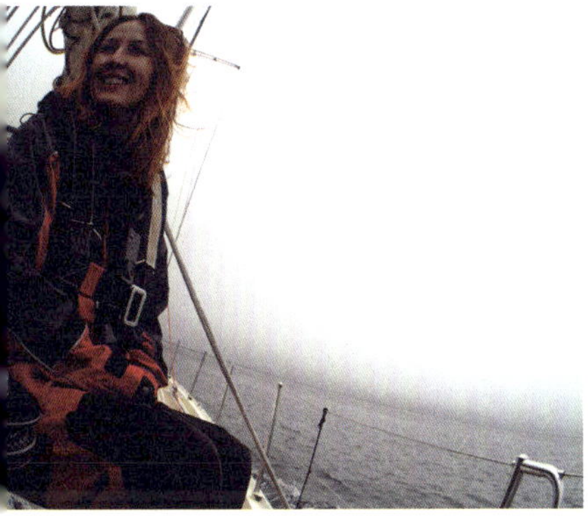
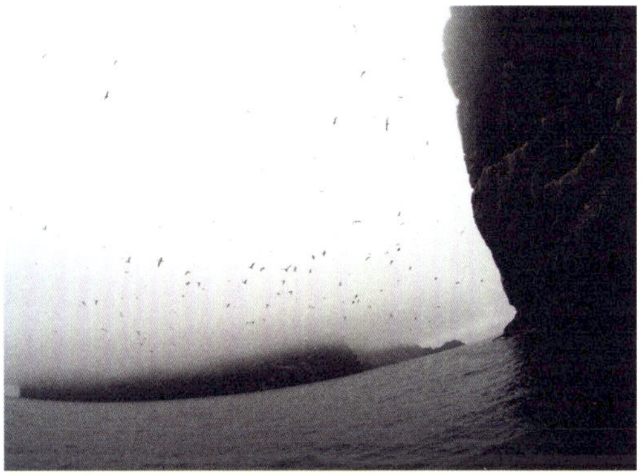
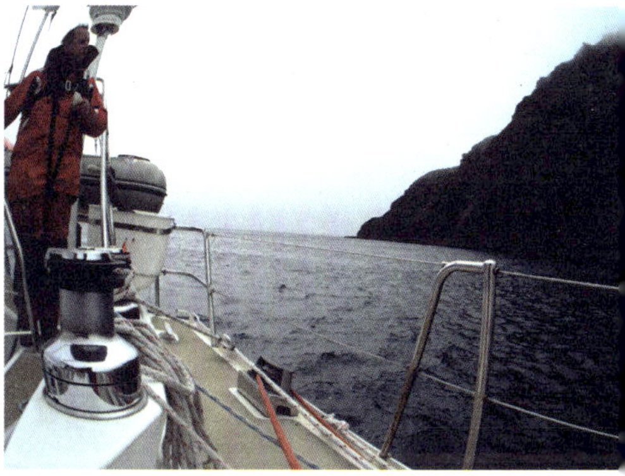
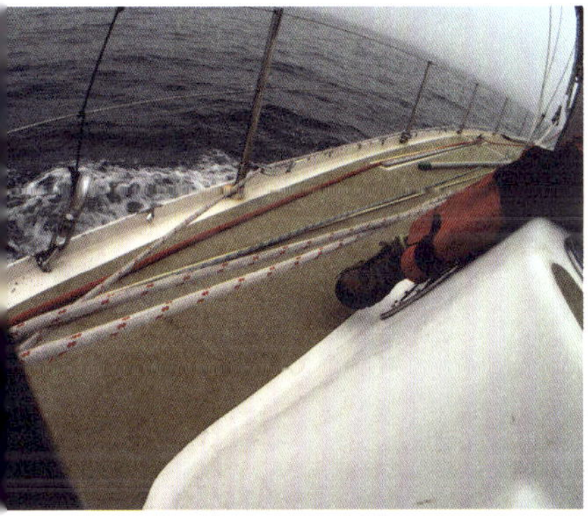
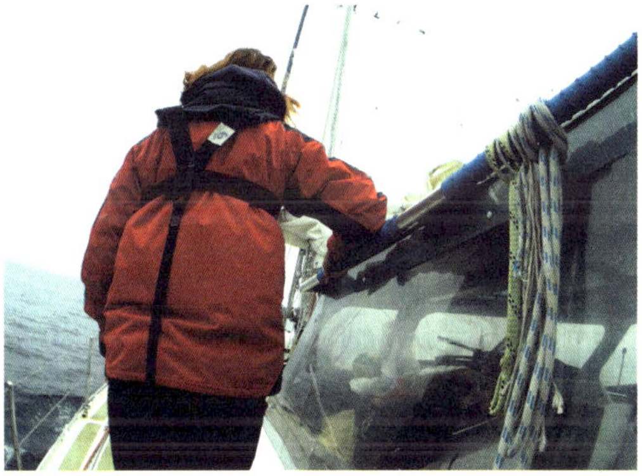
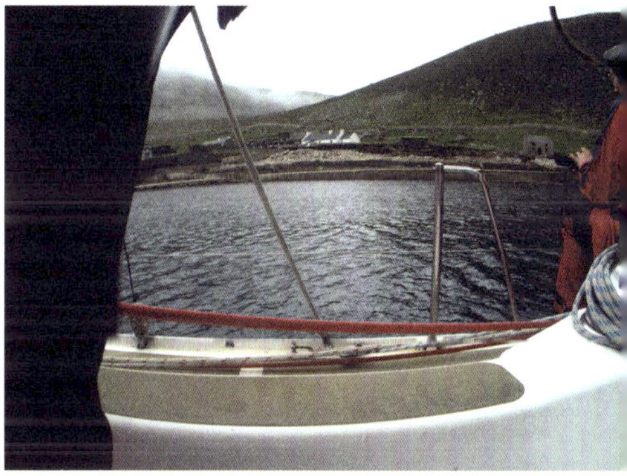
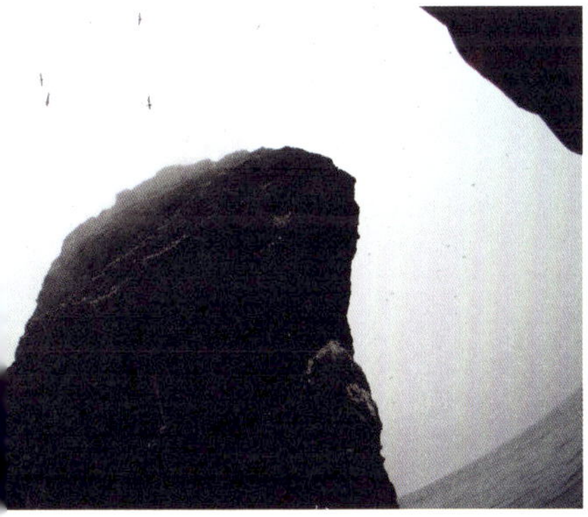
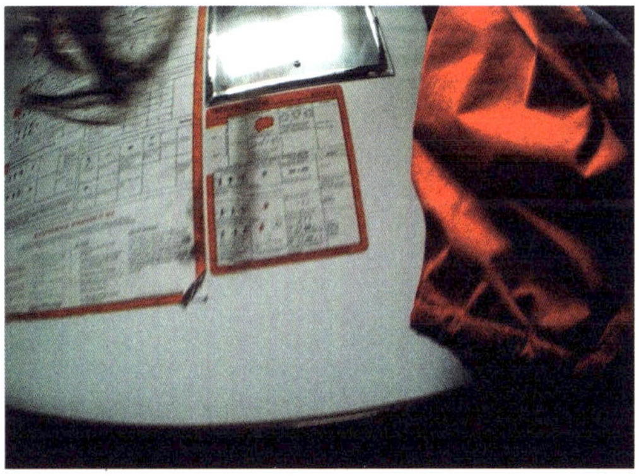
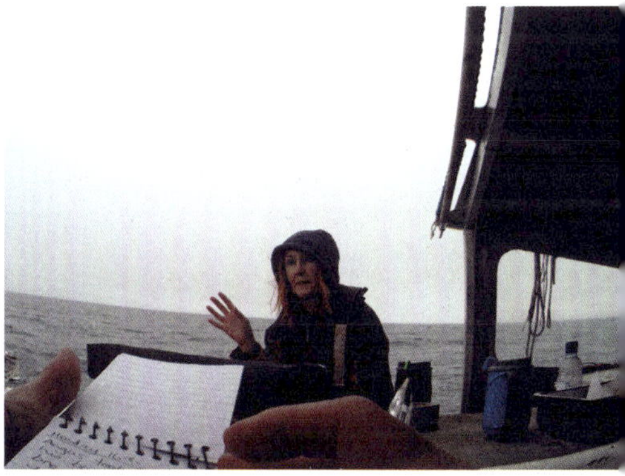
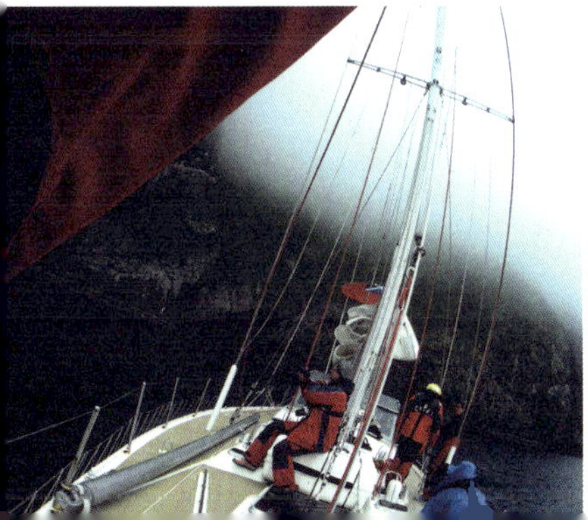
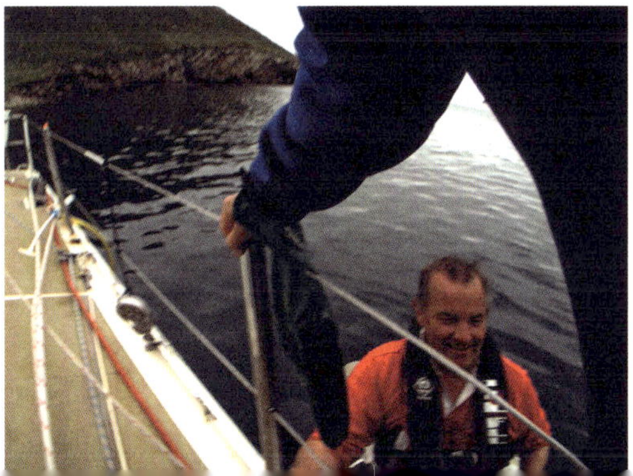
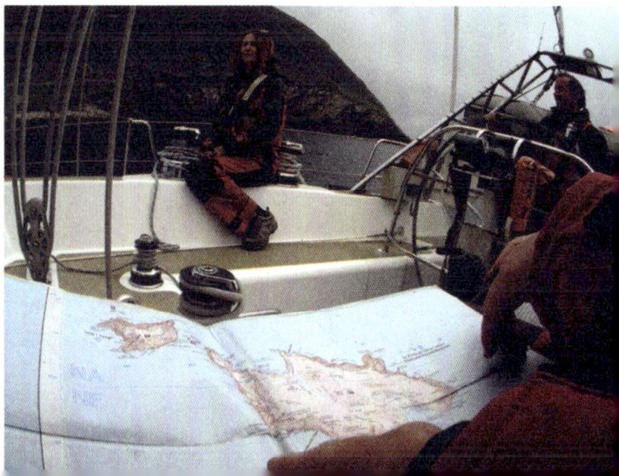

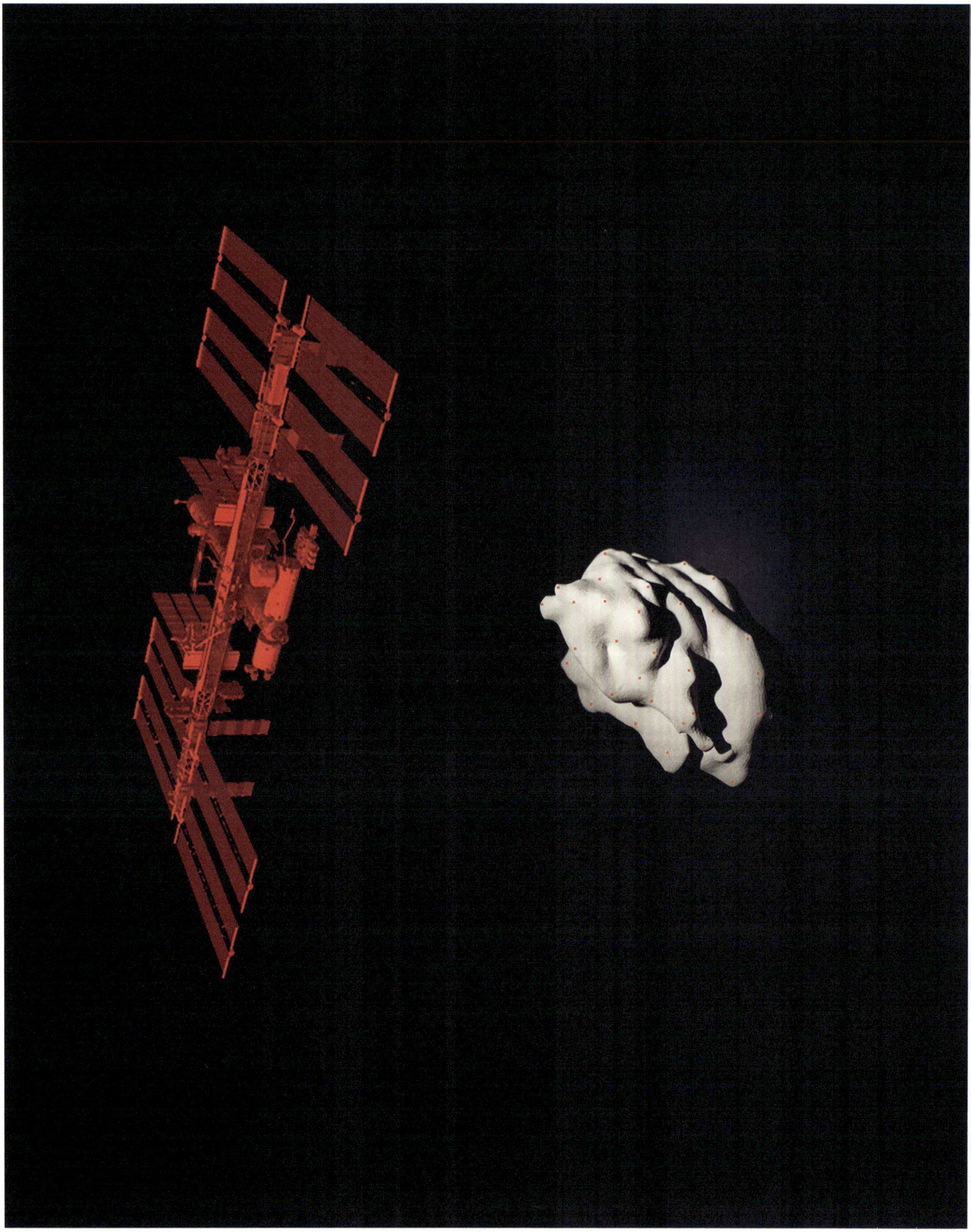

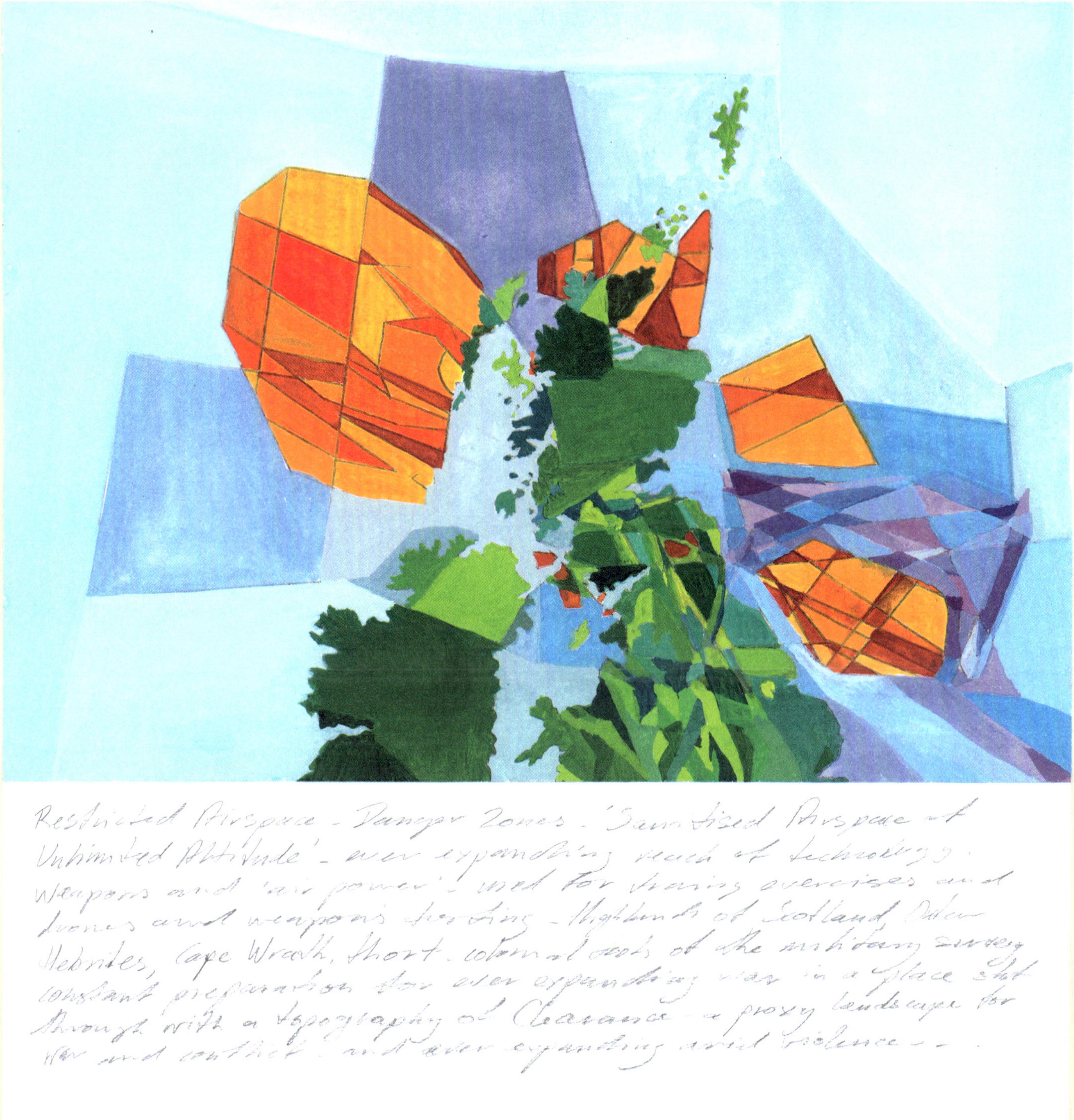

Above: Shona Illingworth, *Restricted Airspace in Oranges and Reds*, 2016. Gouache and ink on paper. 297 × 275 mm. Military airspace restriction zones for weapons testing, military training, and live bombing in Scotland.
Opposite: Shona Illingworth, *International Space Station and Lesion*, 2015. Archival pigment print and ink. 280 × 230 mm.

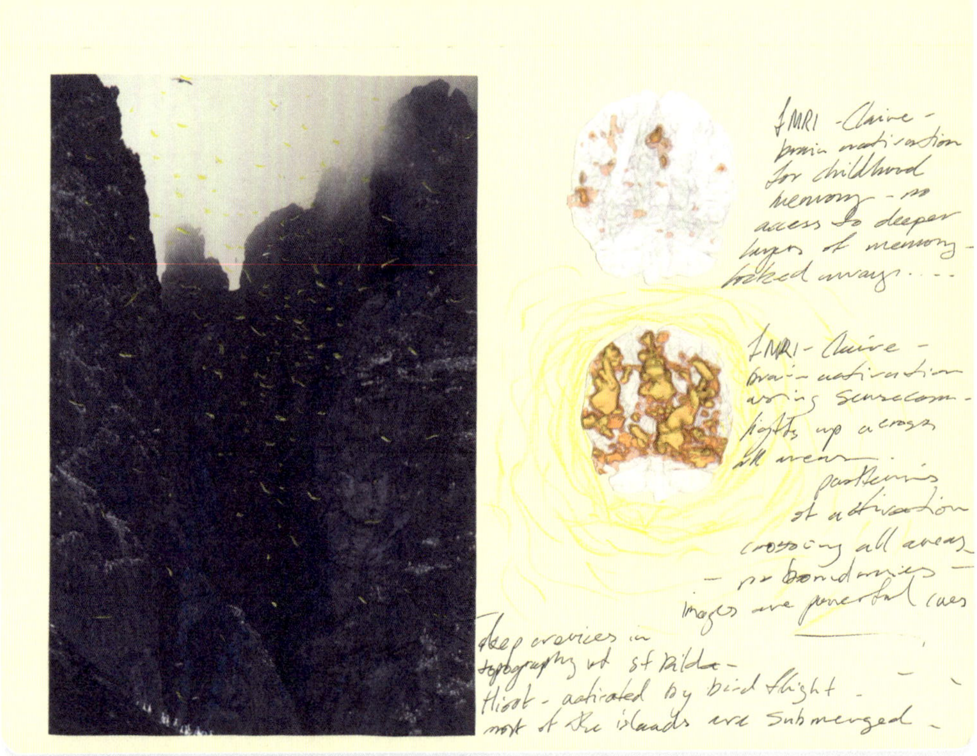

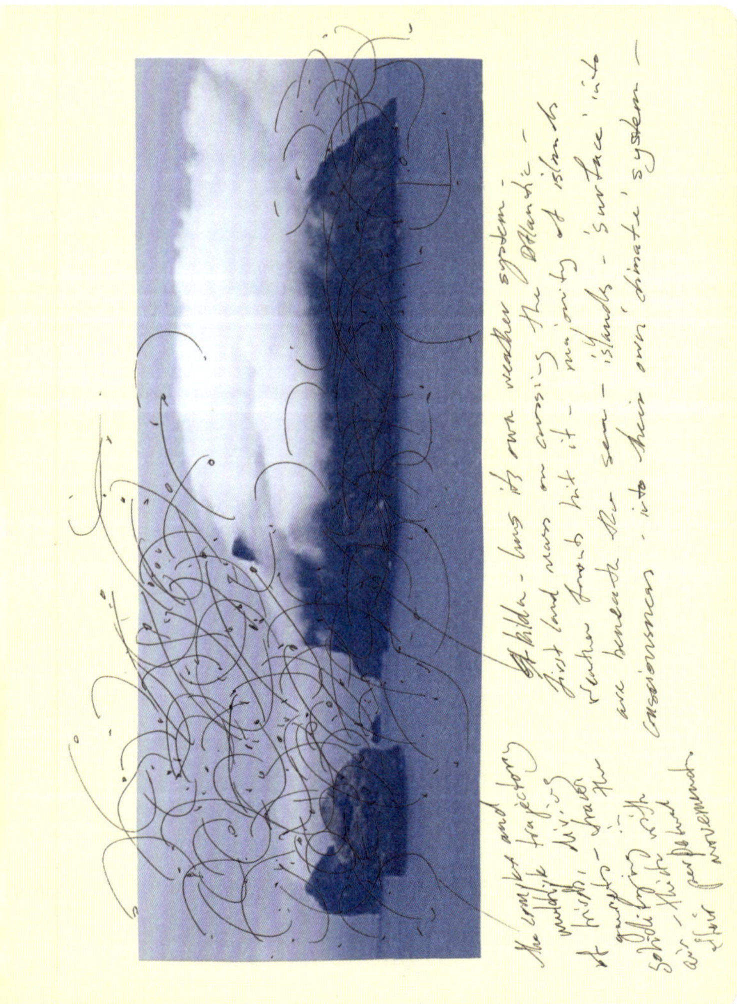

Shona Illingworth, *Notebook for Claire*, 2012. 297 × 210 mm. Above: *St Kilda Weather World, Bird Flight Complex Trace Lines in Air*. Left: *Birds, Cliff/Lesion—Neural Networks* Opposite: Shona Illingworth, *Weapons Testing Zone, Shards in a Triangular Universe*, 2016. Gouache and ink on chart of the Hebrides Range. 210 × 297 mm.

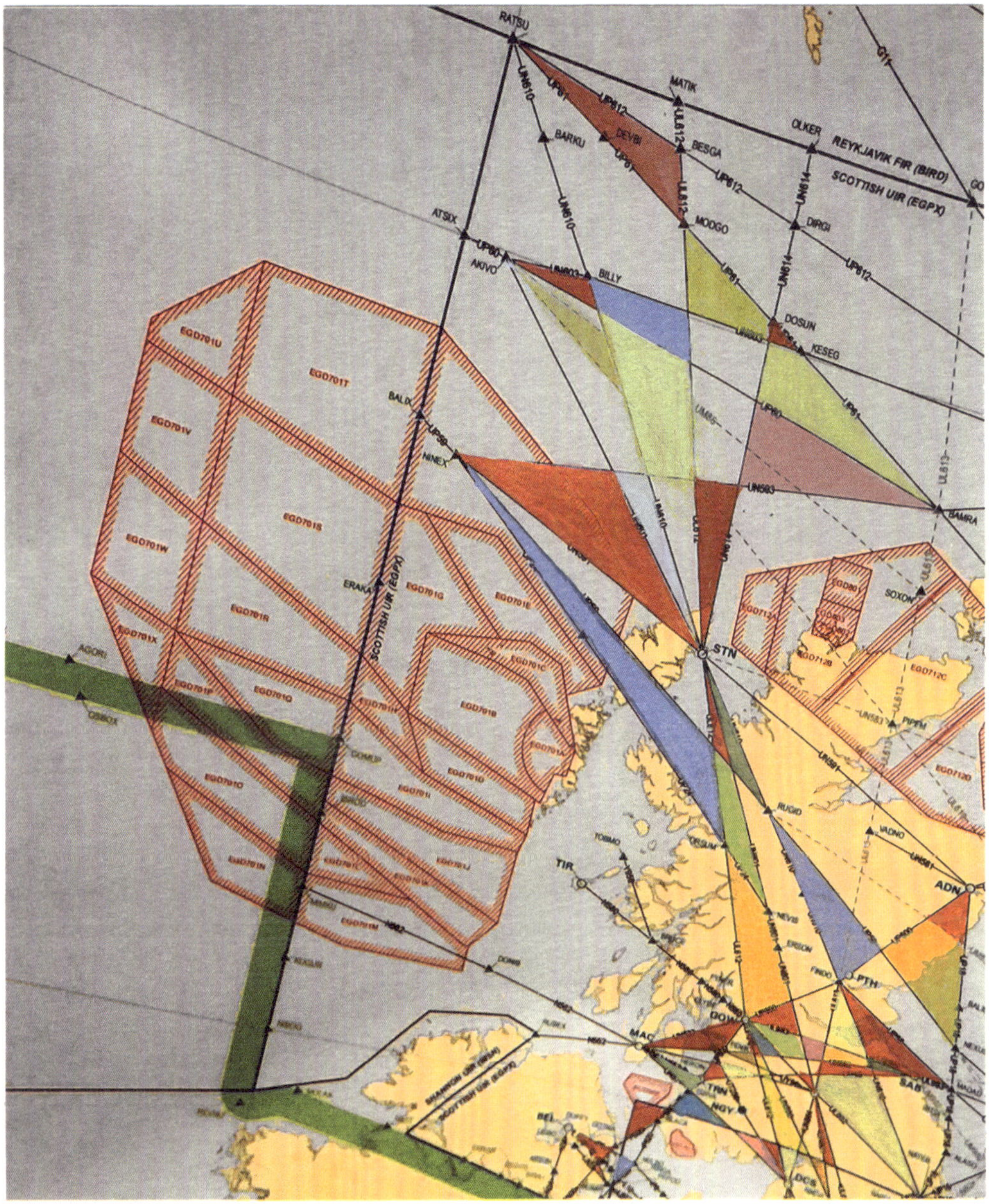

Weapons testing range - flight paths and shards - Pantagruel's words frozen in air - in a triangular universe - previous battles breaking through an amnesic veil - violence spreading outwards and into the future --

AMNESIA MUSEUM 2012–ONGOING

Drawing together film, photographs, drawings, objects, sound installations, recordings, digital material, and documents, Illingworth's *Amnesia Museum* is an expanding archive of forgetting. Investigating how evolving processes of amnesia and cultural erasure shape the past and present and impact our capacity to imagine the future, the *Amnesia Museum* also houses Illingworth's Memory Forum and Amnesia Forum archives.

Opposite: Shona Illingworth, *Lesion*, 2015. 3-D powder print. A 3-D model of Claire's brain lesion (1:1 scale), created using data from a scientific study by Martin A. Conway and Catherine Loveday. The data set was produced by André Gouws, York NeuroImaging Centre, and printed by Lol Baker, FabLab, Liverpool John Moores University. Overleaf: Shona Illingworth, *Connectome*, 2016. Video with sound, 22 mins. Digital video stills.

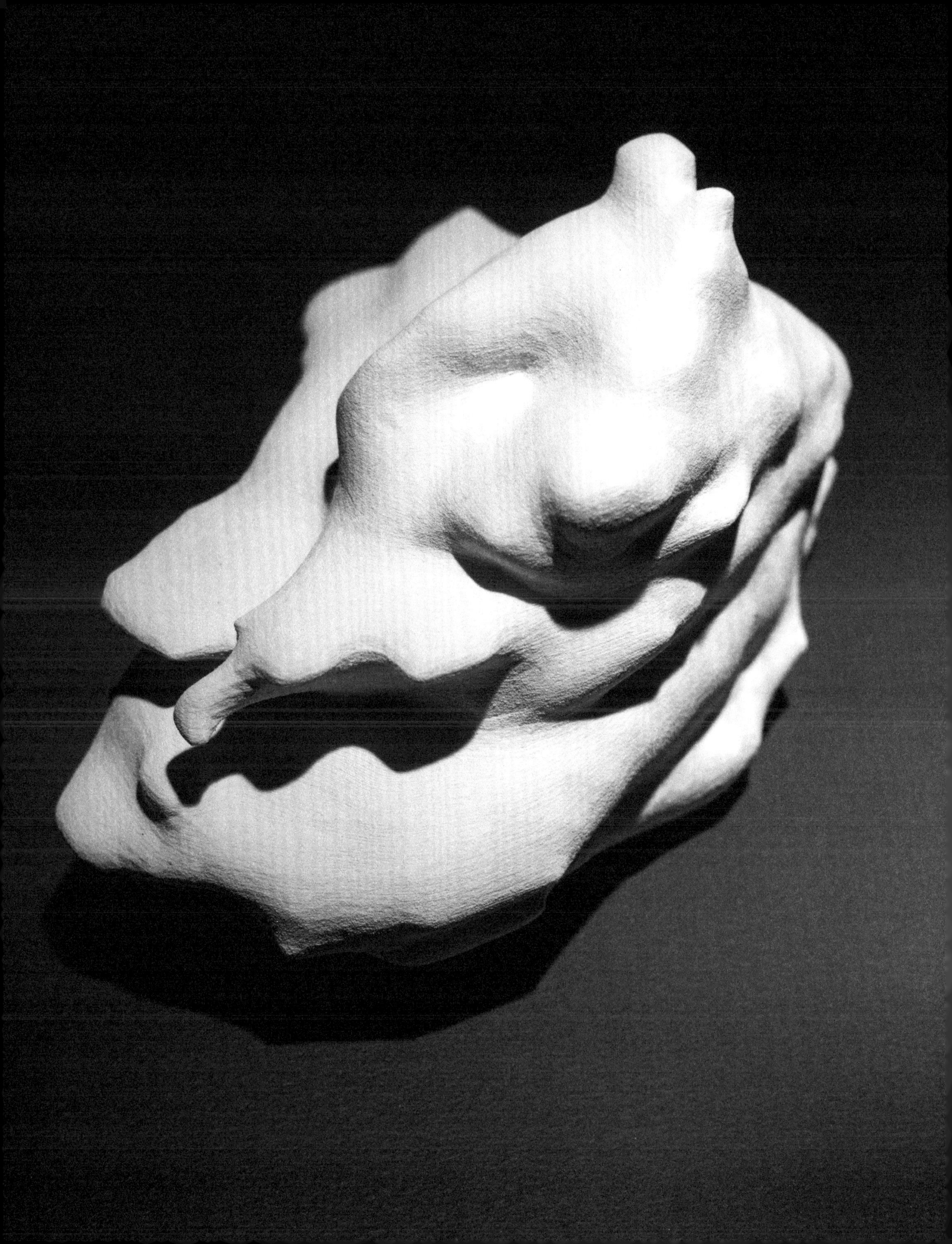

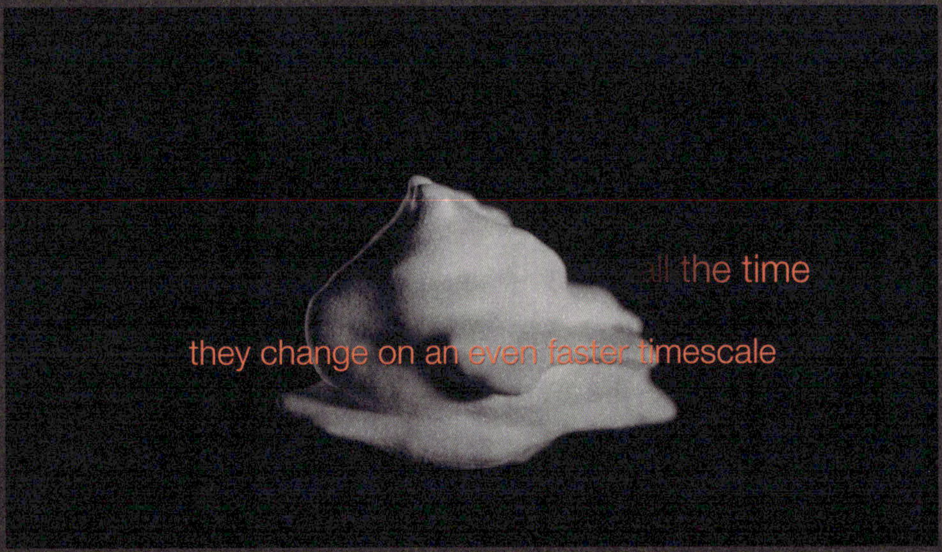

20:21:19

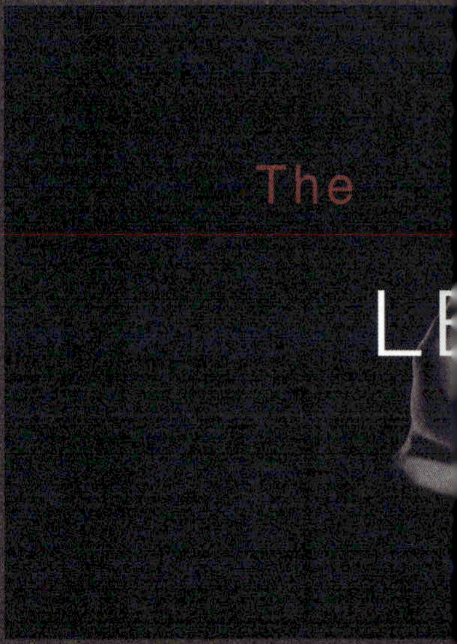

20:28:14

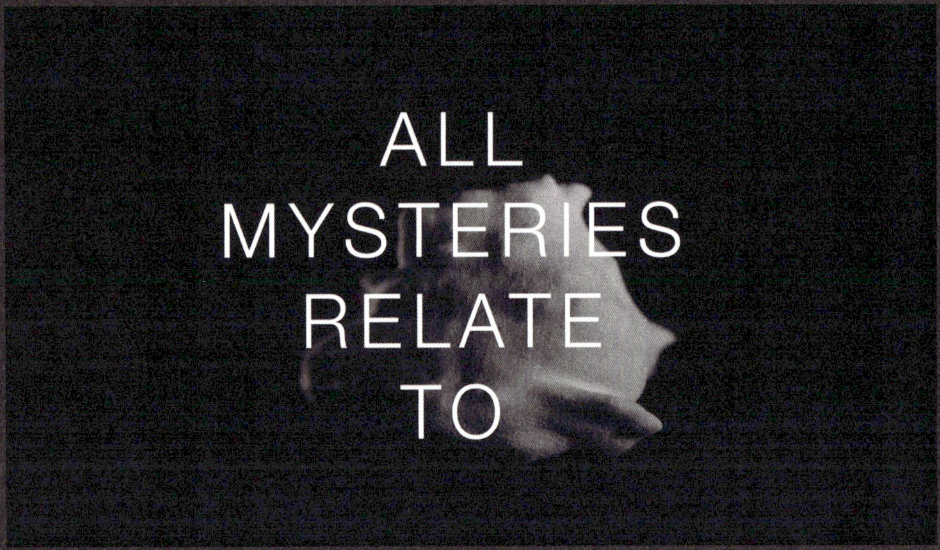

20:47:21

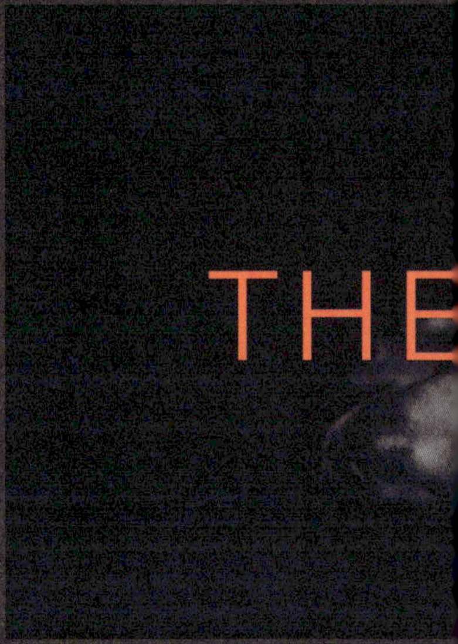

20:54:05

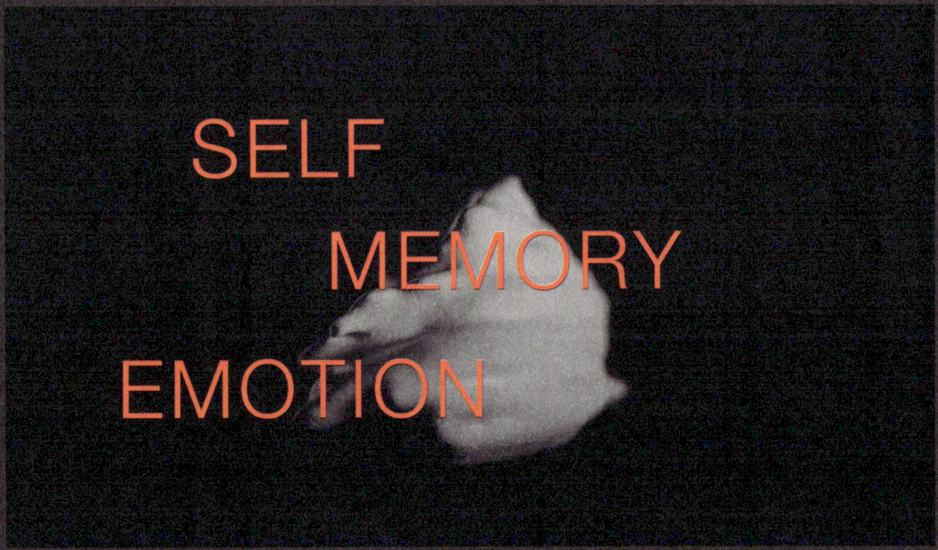

21:11:08

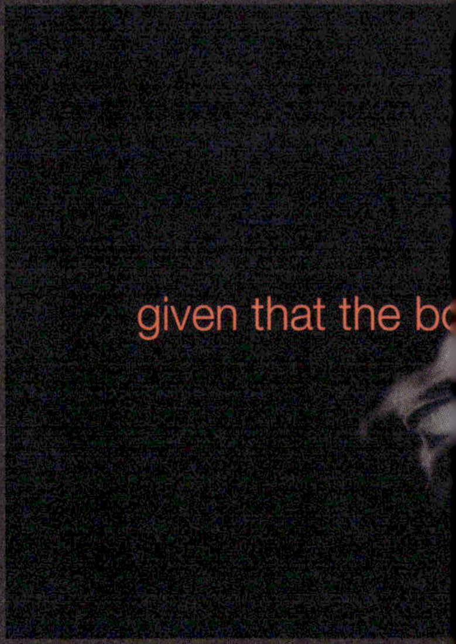

21:18:05

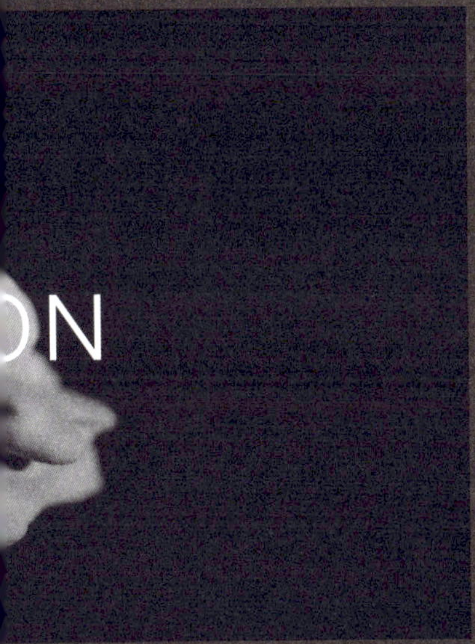

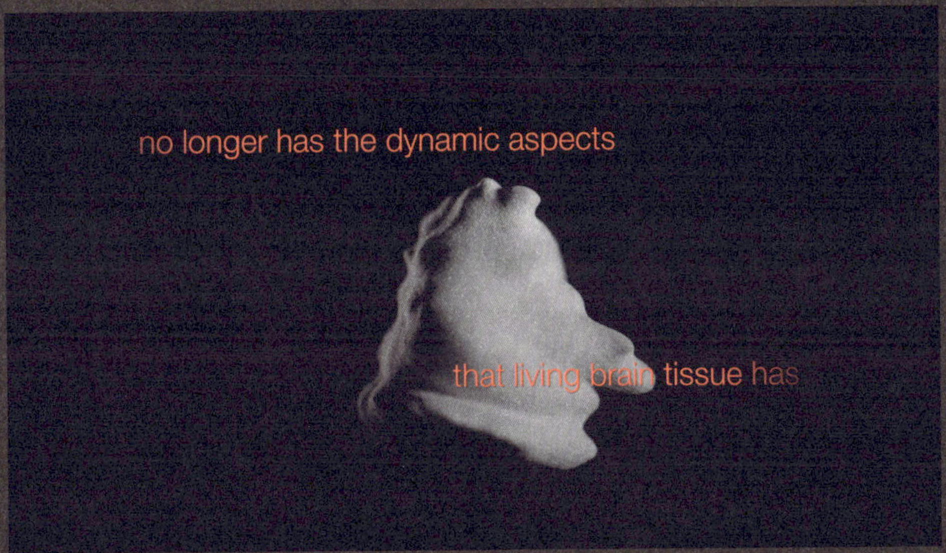

20:34:18

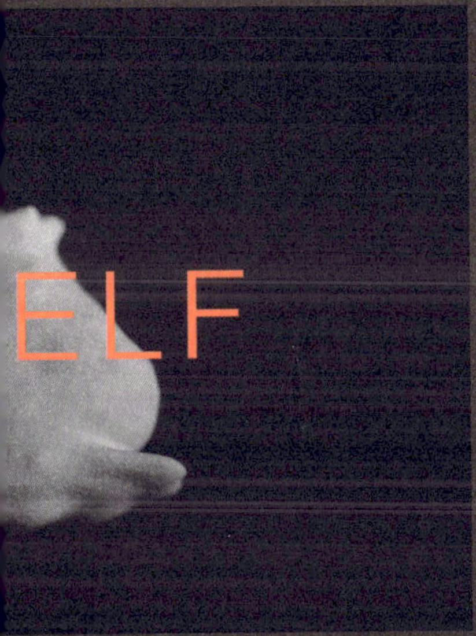

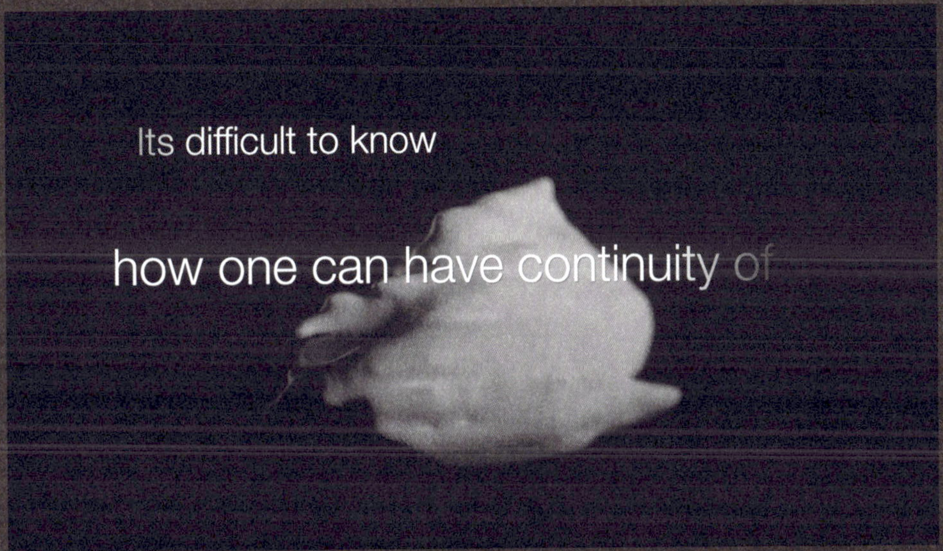

21:04:11

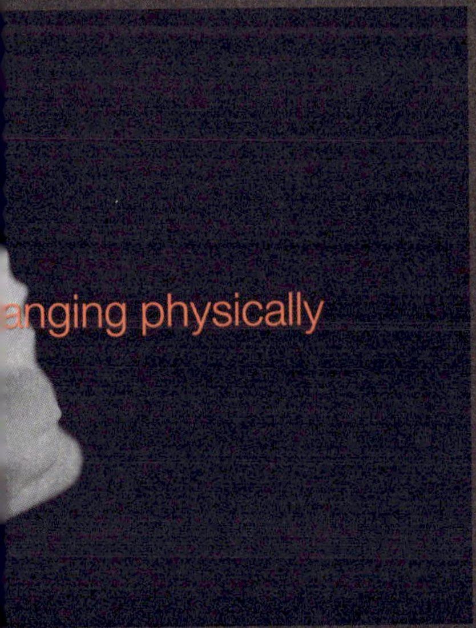

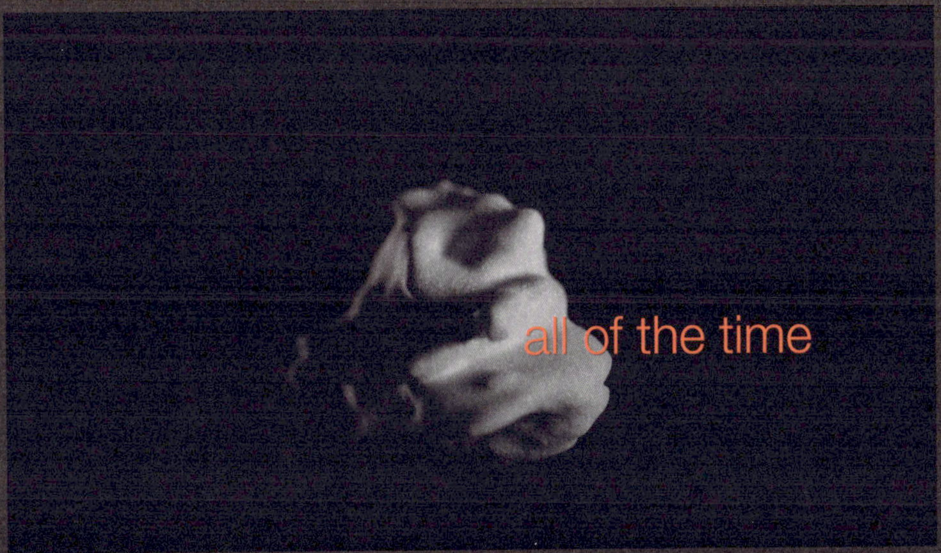

21:23:19

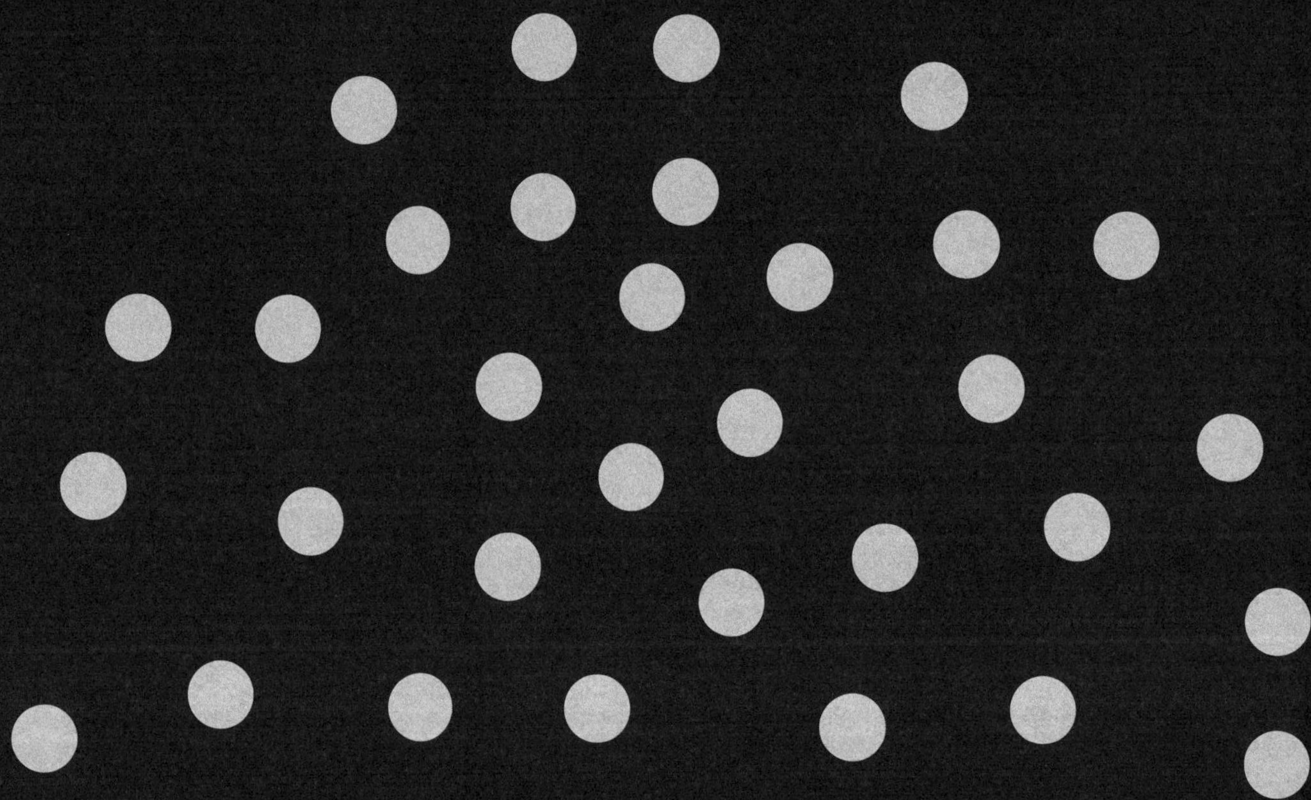

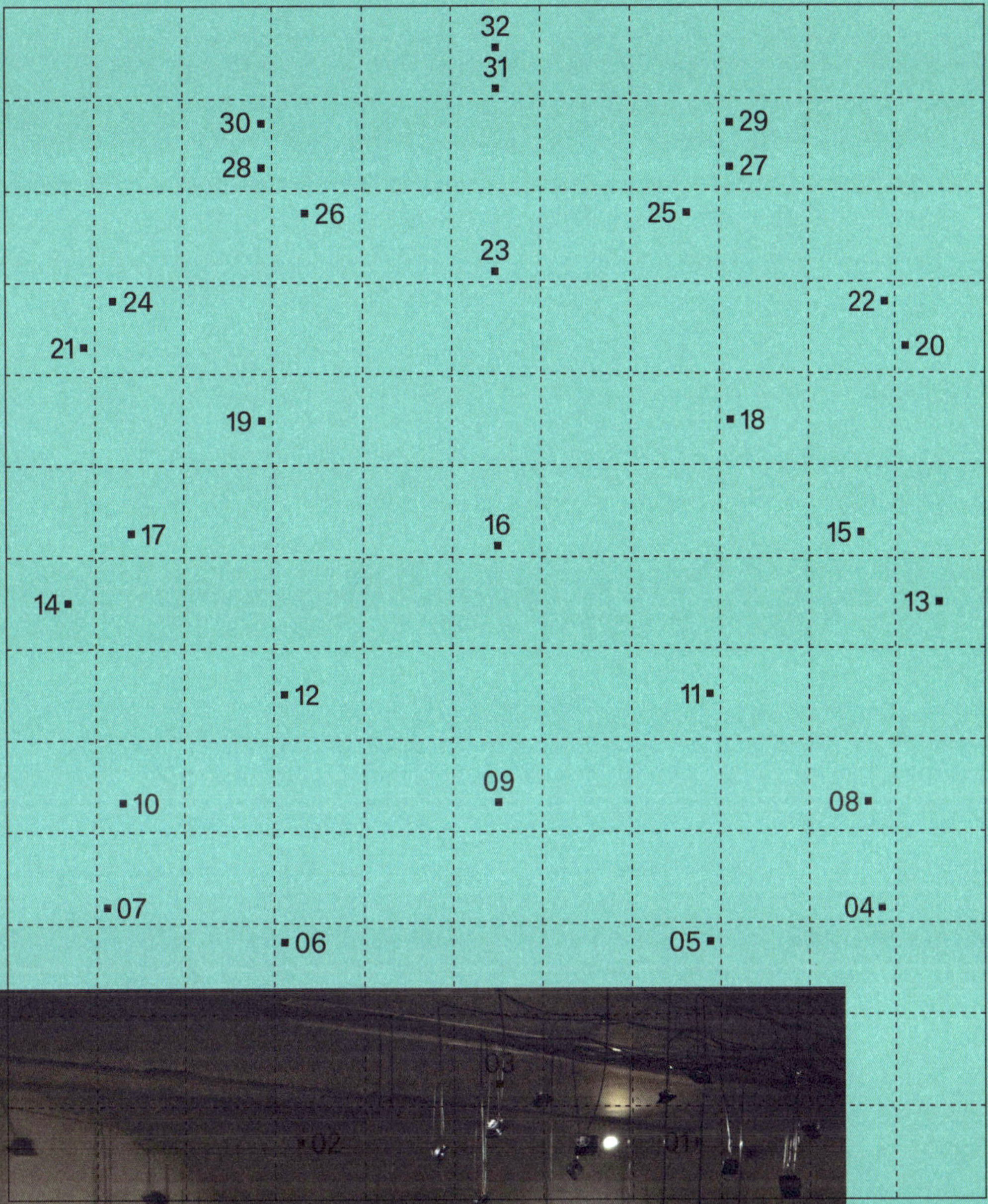
32
31
30
29
28
27
26
25
23
24
22
21
20
19
18
17
16
15
14
13
12
11
10
09
08
07
04
06
05
03
02
01

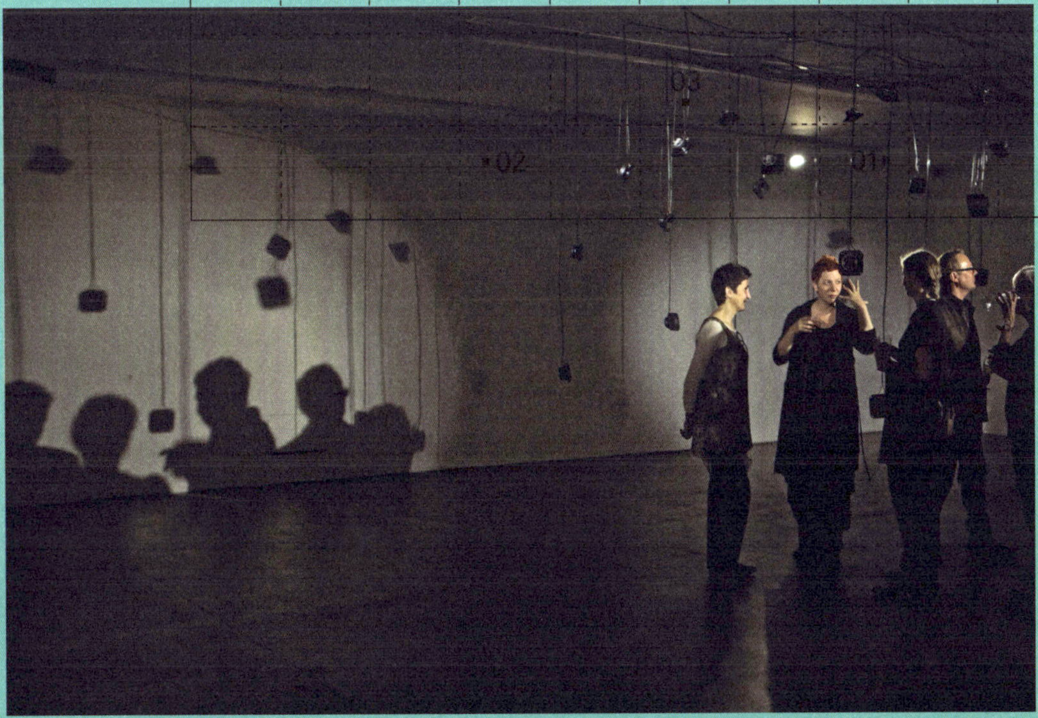

Previous spread: Shona Illingworth, *Sounding Amnesic Memory*, 2014. EEG sonifi cation of Amnesic Memory Data. Installation view, UNSW Galleries, Sydney.

Using data from an electroencephalogram (EEG) study of Claire viewing SenseCam images of her journey to St Kilda, this work depicts the neurological landscape of amnesia and the sudden bursts of activity in the brain during Proustian moments of recollection cued by SenseCam, a sensory-operated camera. The waveforms of neural fi ring output from the EEG have been transformed into sound—the thirty-two channels corresponding to thirty-two electrodes placed on key parts of the scalp. Each sound is played through a separate speaker to form a multichannel sound installation that reconfi gures the shape of the head, so that the listener stands in the sonic space of the search for access to irretrievable memory. EEG study directed by Catherine Loveday with Corinna Haenschel and Maciej Kosilo undertaken at the Cognitive Neuroscience Research Unit, City University, London. Sound design by Charlie Fleming.

Opposite: Shona Illingworth, Drawing for *Solid Gaps of Air*, 2014. Polaroid, archival pigment print of archaeological map of Village Bay, St Kilda, and ink.

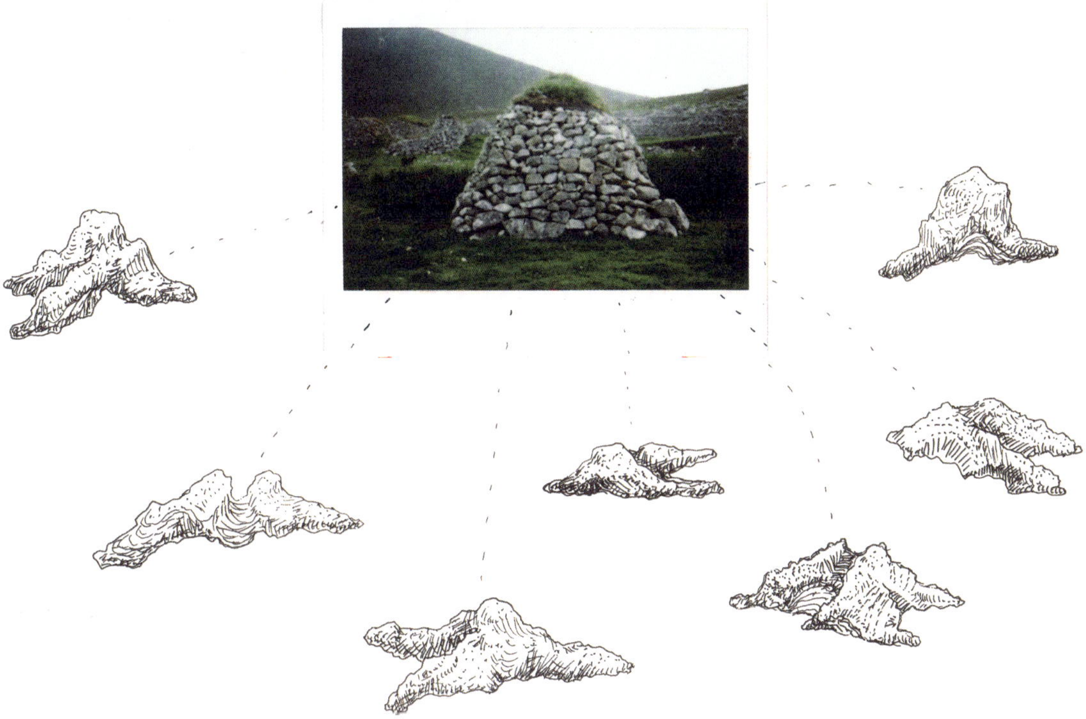

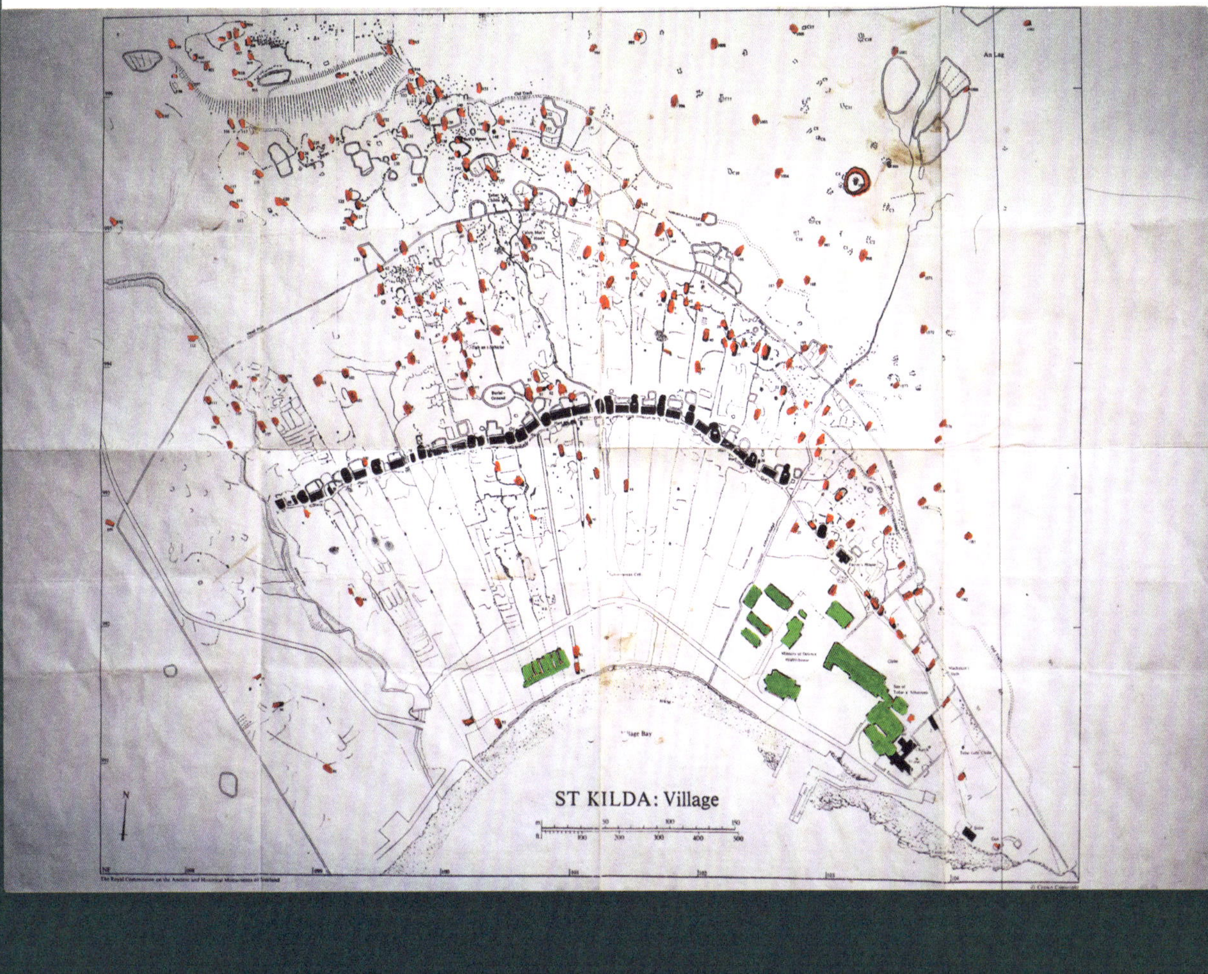
ST KILDA: Village

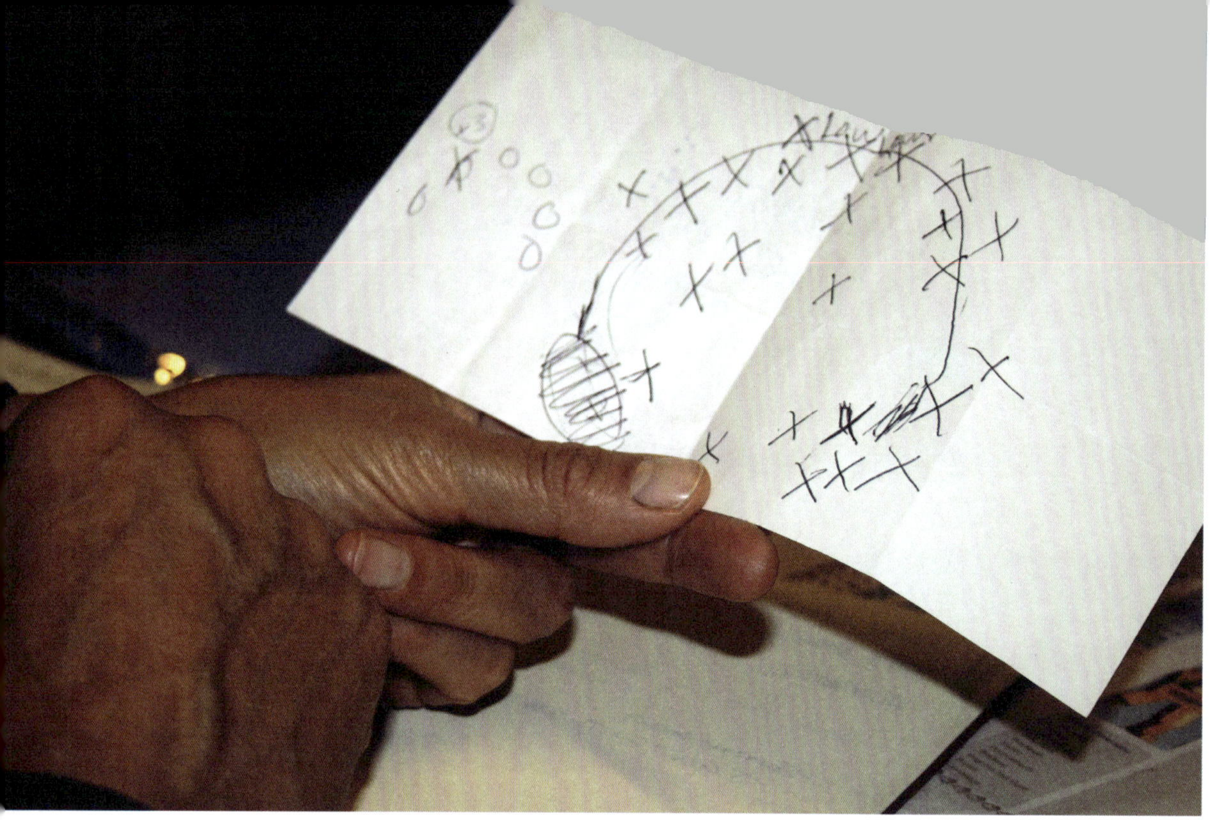

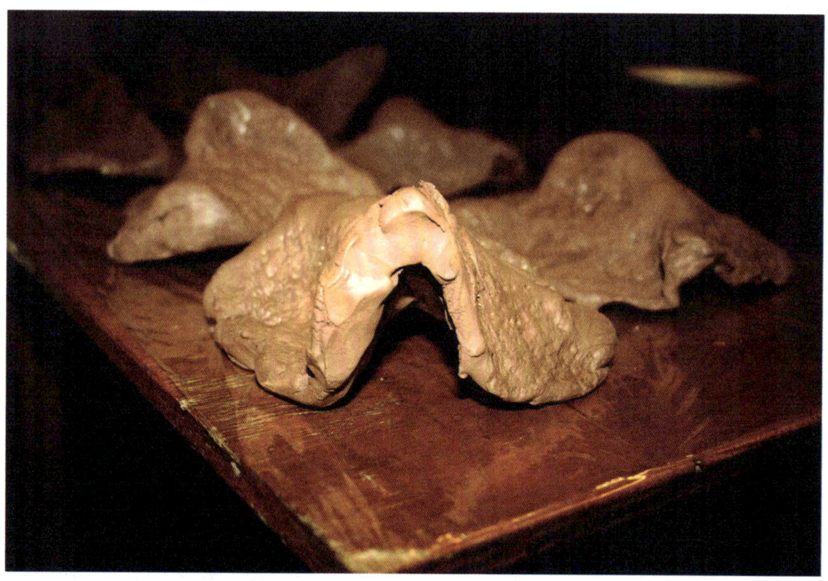

Shona Illingworth, *Solid Gaps of Air*, 2014.
Fired ceramic, single cast details.

Fired ceramic casts of the gaps between the stones of Cleit 1003, Hirta, St Kilda. Cleits are dry stone "bothies" understood to have been built by St Kildans for storing food and other materials. There are mysteriously over one thousand cleits in St Kilda. Skilled cleit builders focused on the immaterial spaces between the stones as much as on the stones themselves, passing this expertise down through many generations. Ceramic fired by Nickolai Globe.

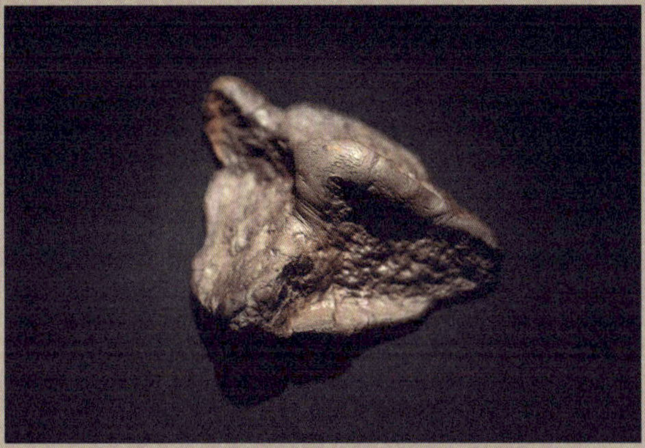

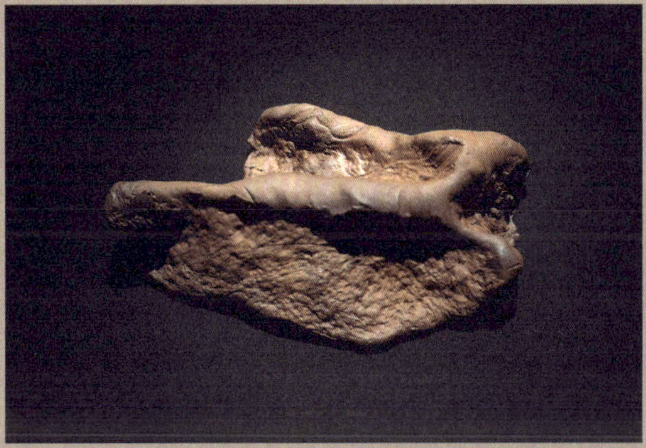

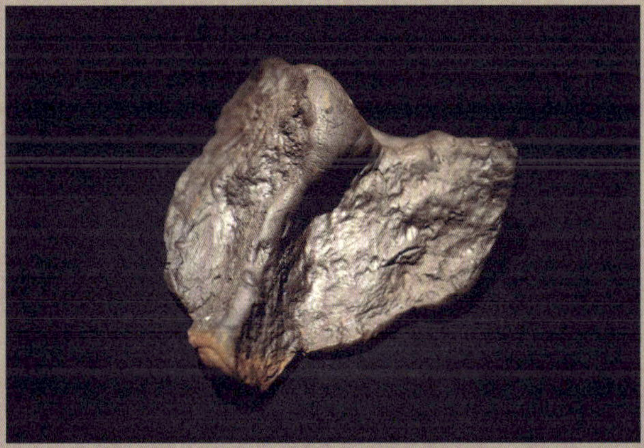

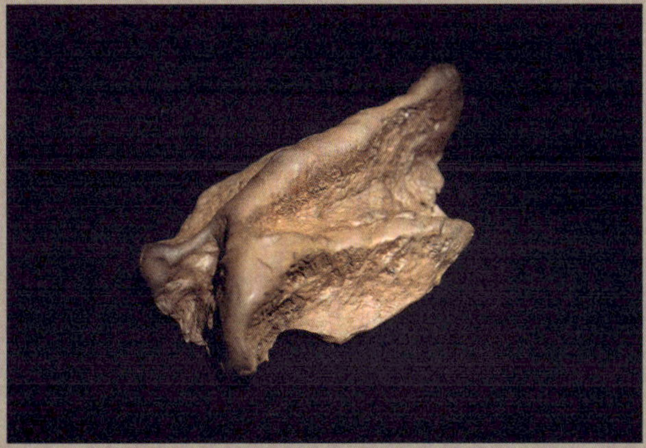

an old woman knitting socks outside her cottage [photographer paid £2 for the privilege of takir

women and girls **take fright and run away** from t

the rowing boat is loaded with sheep at the jetty. Shot of men and furniture on pier

the loaded **rowing boat casts off** and another comes in to take its place (2

shot from jetty of two sheep being pulled on

one rowing boat loaded with sheep is towed by motor boat to the "Dunara

collected at Tarbert, Harris, on the outward journey, to assist with the evacuation as there was nc

women carrying bundles run into house to avoid camera (3.13)

girl appears at the same door but shies off. Group of islanders outside house (3.14

women **hide their faces** from camera (3.16)

old man smoking a pipe outside his house.

A younger man **picks up a stone** to throw at the camera (3.22

Group of visitors outside the post office (3.31)

woman walks toward the camera carrying a large bundle of material possibly tweed, delib

girl walks away calling to a dog (3.44)

group of people outside house. A man from the mainland distributes sv

when the sweets are finished (4.08)

Cockerel on path (4.14)

woman **walks away** to hide behind a

into the doorway of an 1830-style house, comes out again and into an 1860-style house (4.4

another woman **runs away** from the camera (4.45)

two old women sitting outside, one covers her face with her shawl (4

cattle grazing in front of the houses (5.04)

t] (2.06)

a into their cottages (2.16)

4)

ard the loading point, motor boat passes behind (2.57)

ne motor boat seen here and later being **hoisted on board** "Dunara Castle" was

d boat on St Kilda] (3.09)

ies to walk out of shot, row of cottages in the background (3.42)

children and adults. Women turn away from camera and run off quickly

eed. Another collects a **glass of water** from a bucket, walks past gable end of house and

Shona Illingworth, *(2.16); (2.44); (2.56); (2.57); (3.09); (3.13); (3.14); (3.16); (3.22); (3.31); (3.42); (3.44); (4.08); (4.14); (4.42); (4.45); (4.52); (5.04)*, 2015. Archival pigment prints with mono sound (voice).

Images of the preparations and evacuation of the archipelago of St Kilda, filmed on August 27, 1930, by John P. Ritchie, an amateur cine-enthusiast and ornithologist, during an egg-collecting expedition to the islands. The existence of this film was kept secret until 1979 as Scottish Office regulations prohibited any photos or newsreel recordings of the evacuation. Angela Maclean, a native Gaelic speaker from the Outer Hebrides, reads the shot list from the Scottish Screen Archive, National Library of Scotland, recounting details of women and children fleeing from the camera. See previous page for extracts.

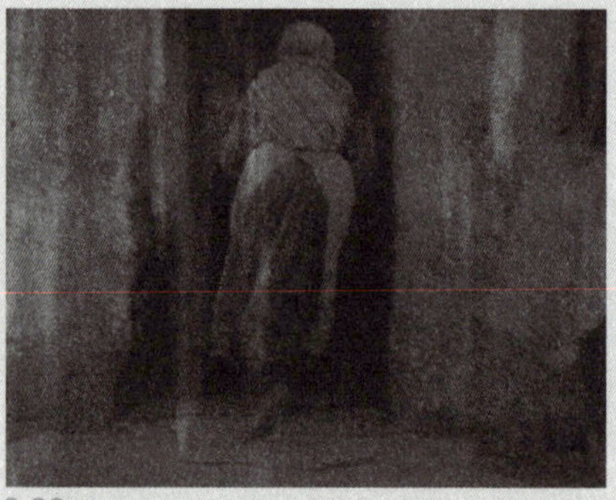

2.29

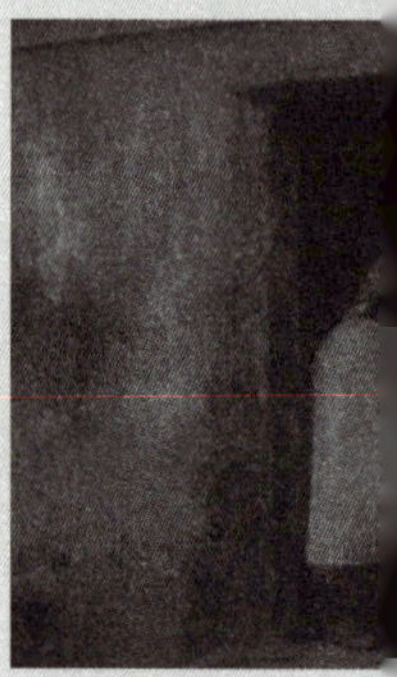

2.42

3.19

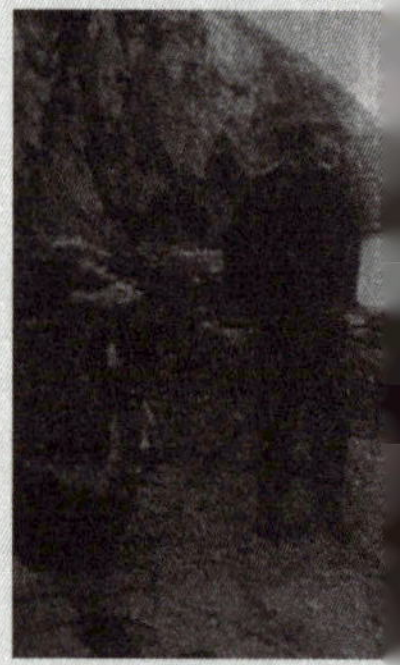

3.45

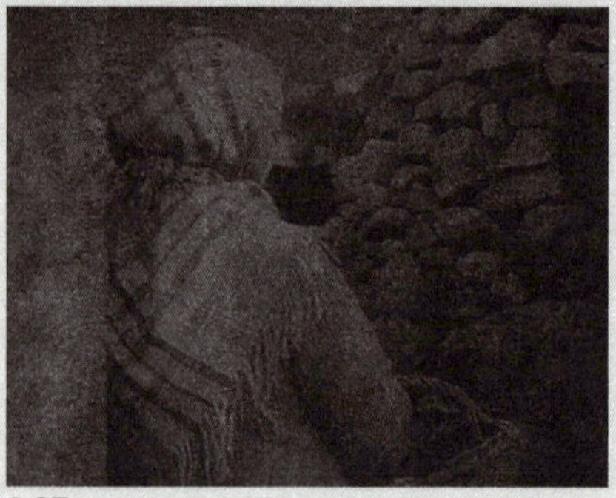

4.07

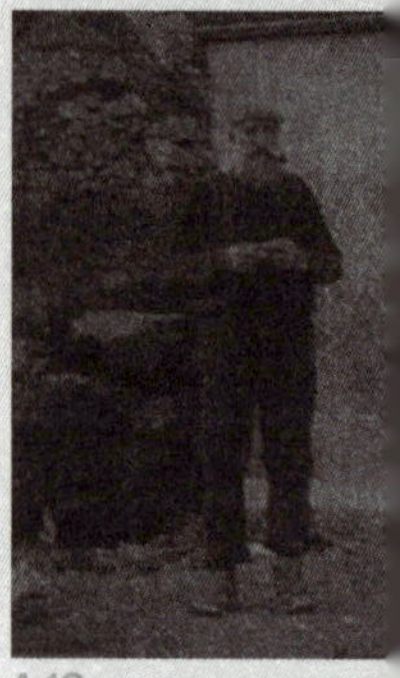

4.13

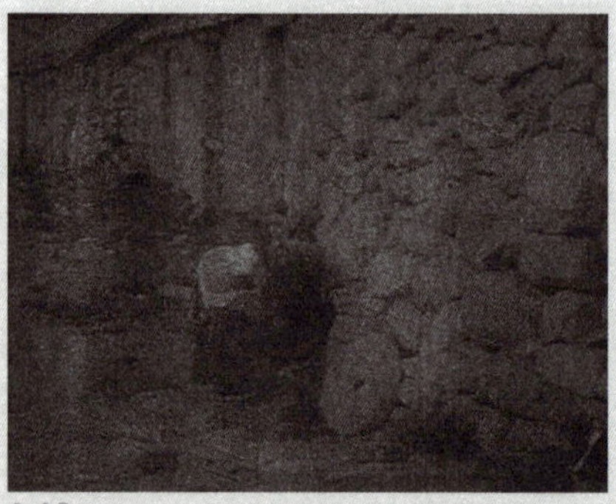

4.49

5.10

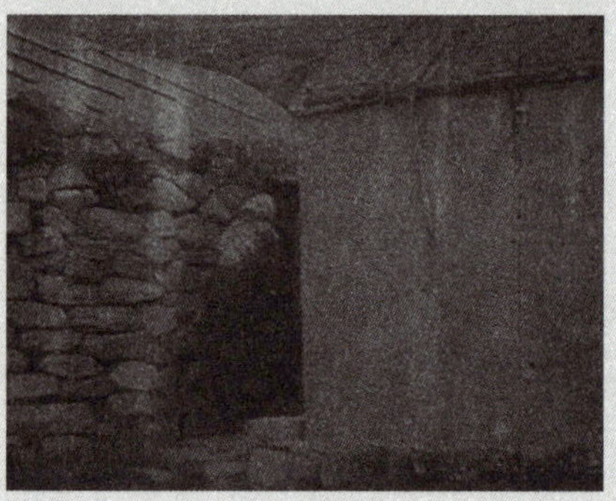

5.50

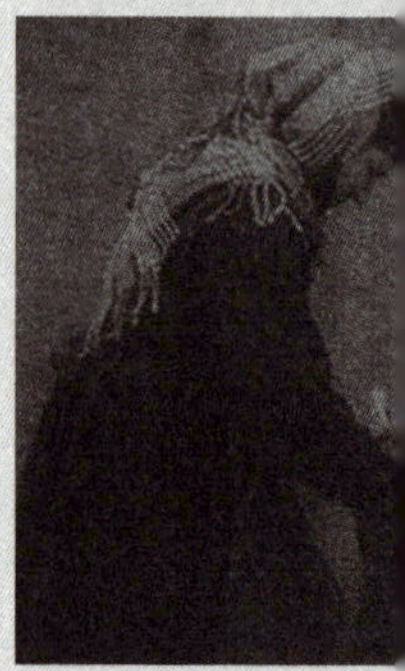

5.57

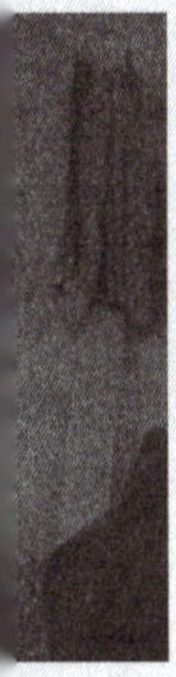

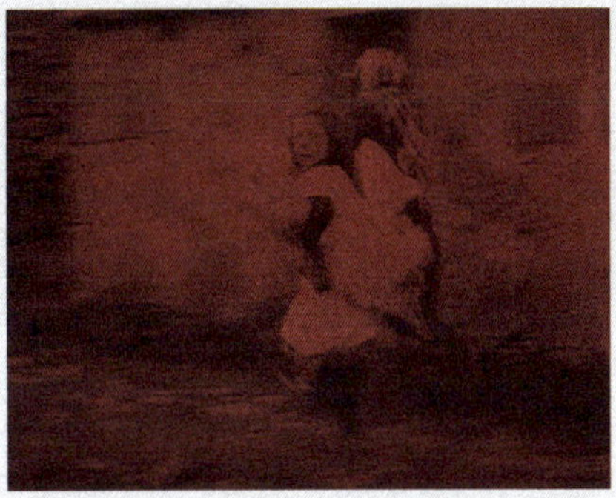

2.44

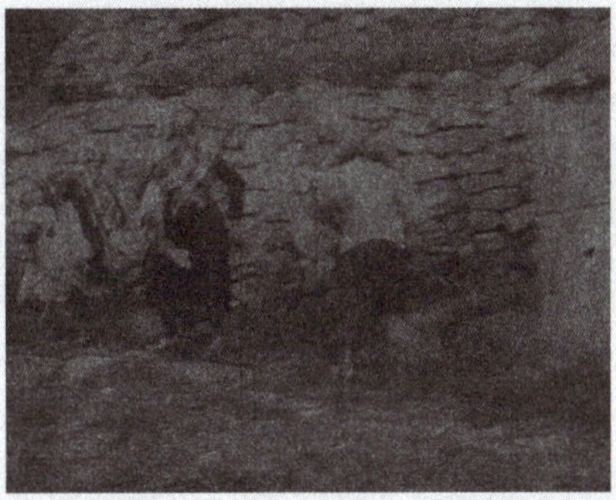

2.46

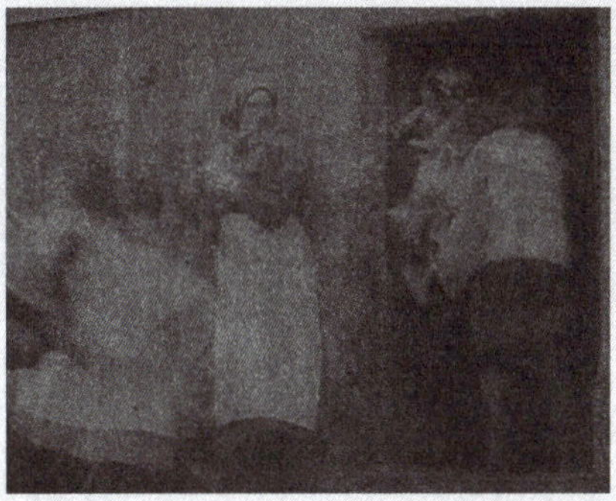

2.49

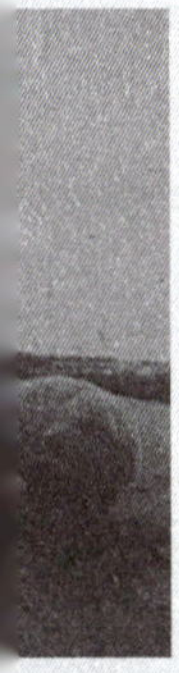

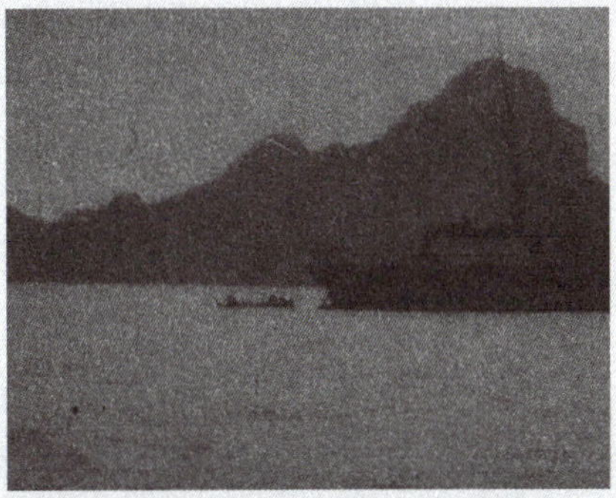

3.59

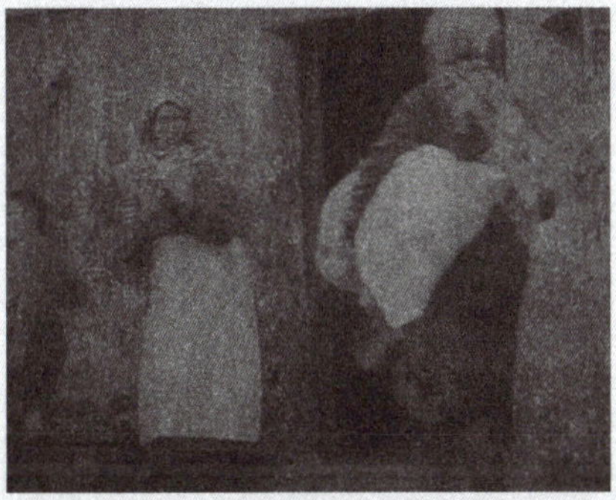

4.00

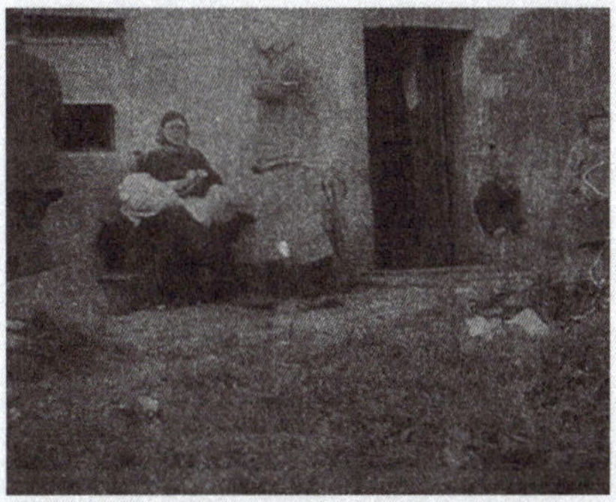

4.04

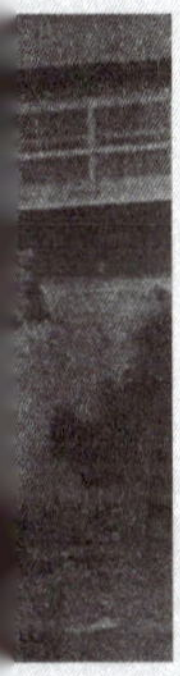

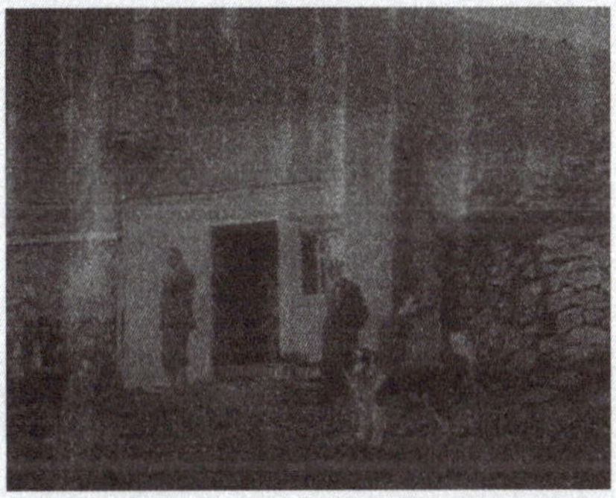

4.19

4.38

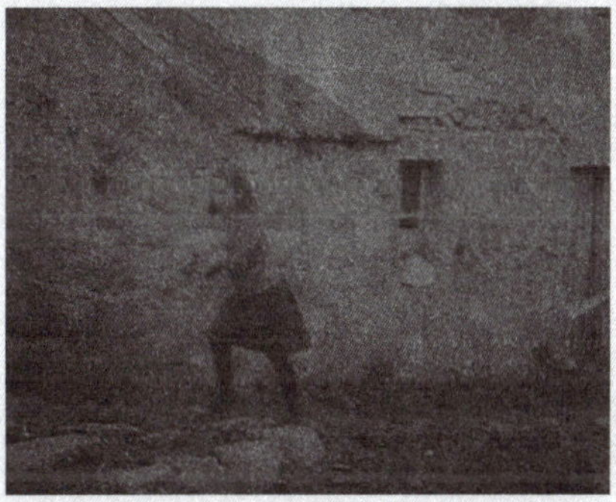

4.45

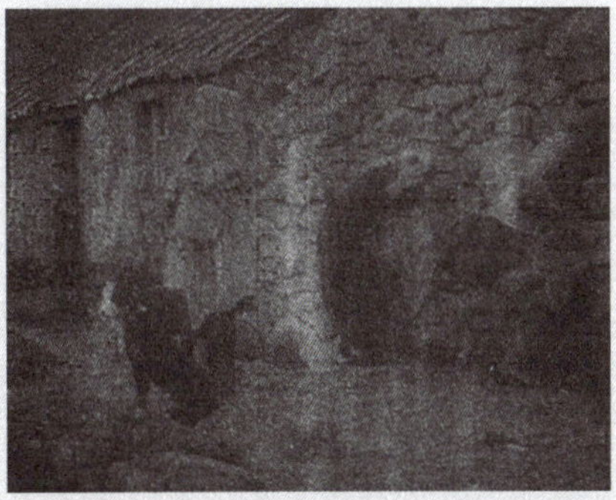

5.13

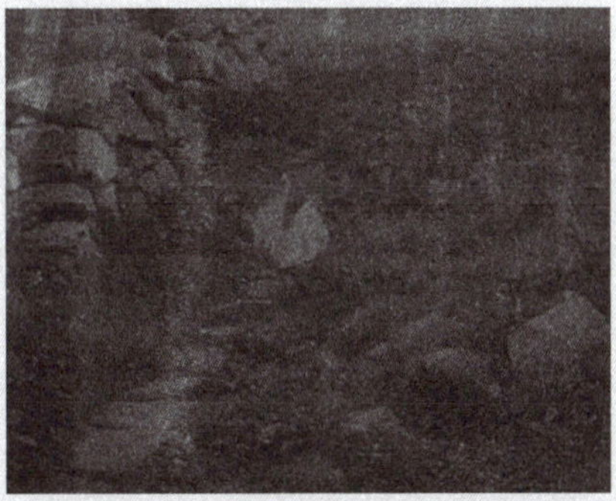

5.19

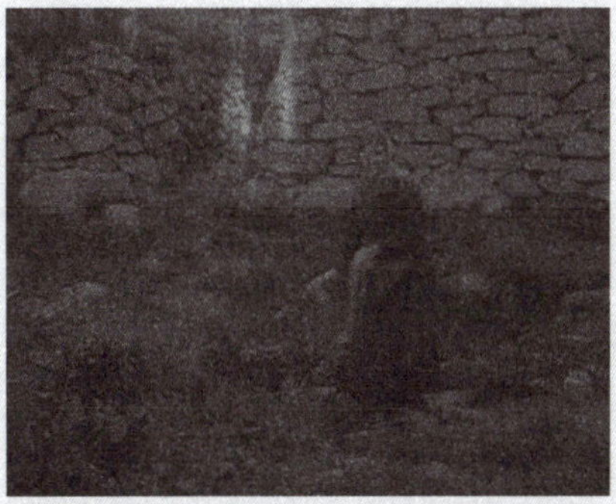

5.33

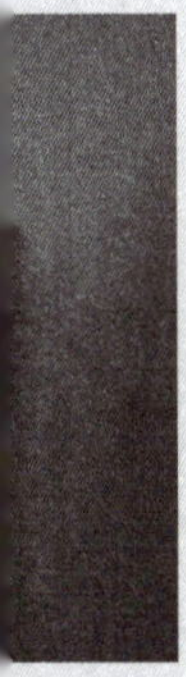

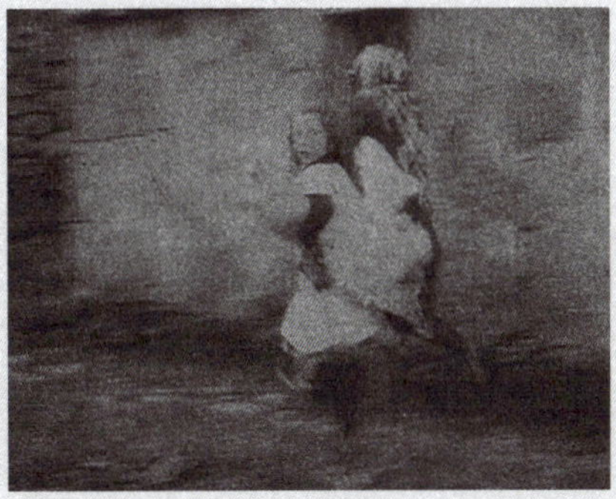

2.44

6.05

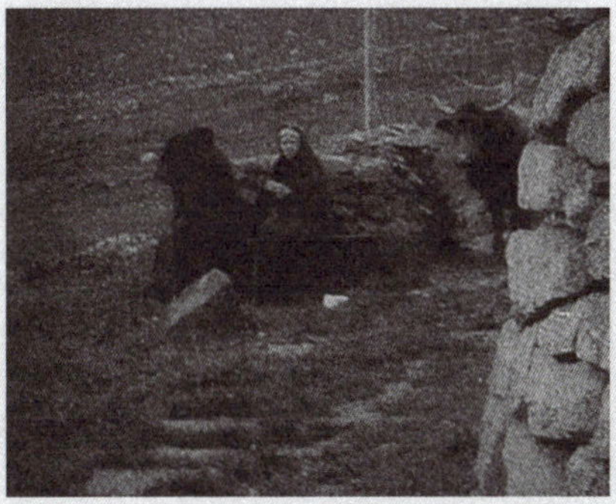

6.12

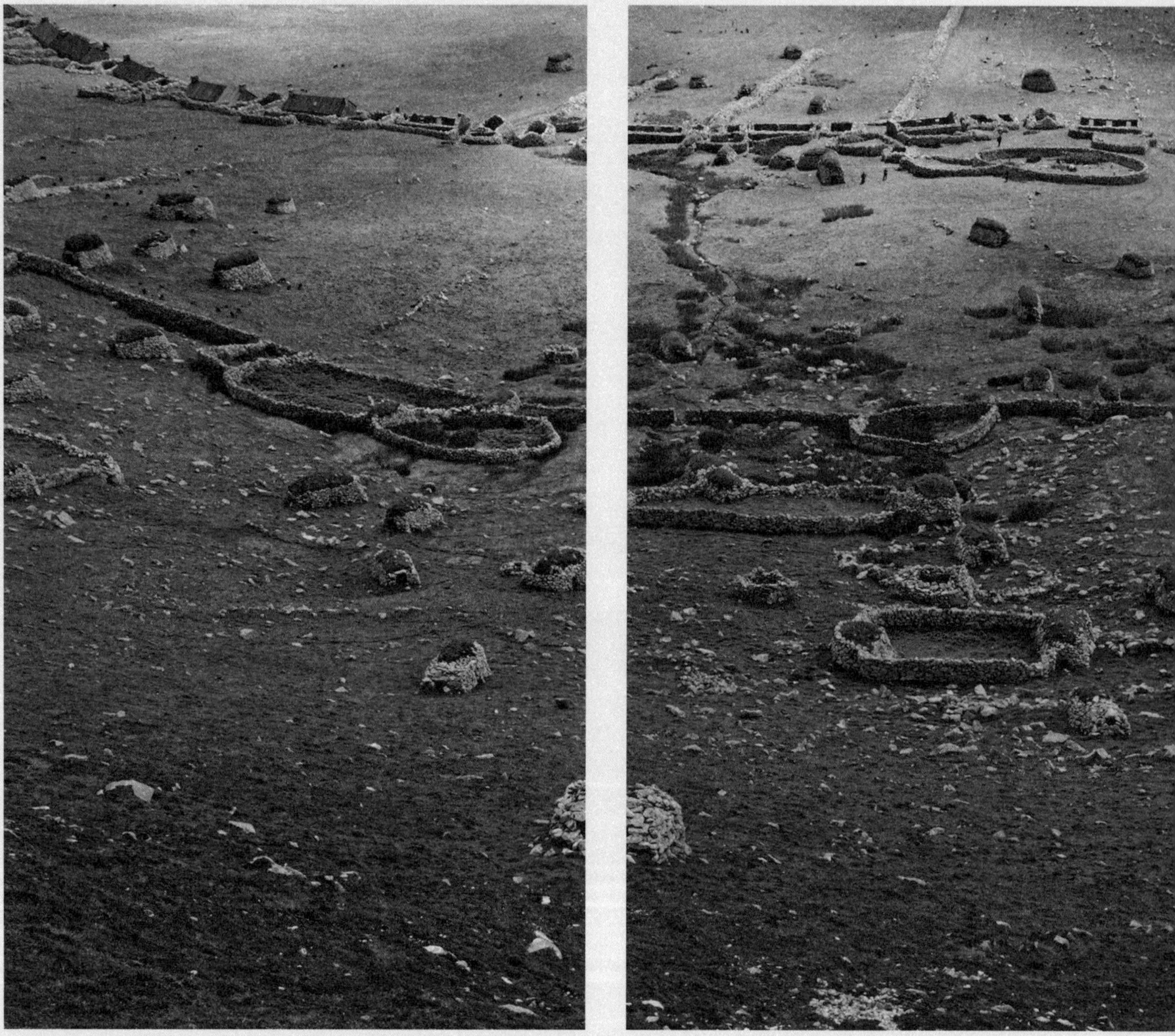

Shona Illingworth, *Searching for Discovery*, 2015. Video installation, 20 mins shown on a seamless loop. Video still.

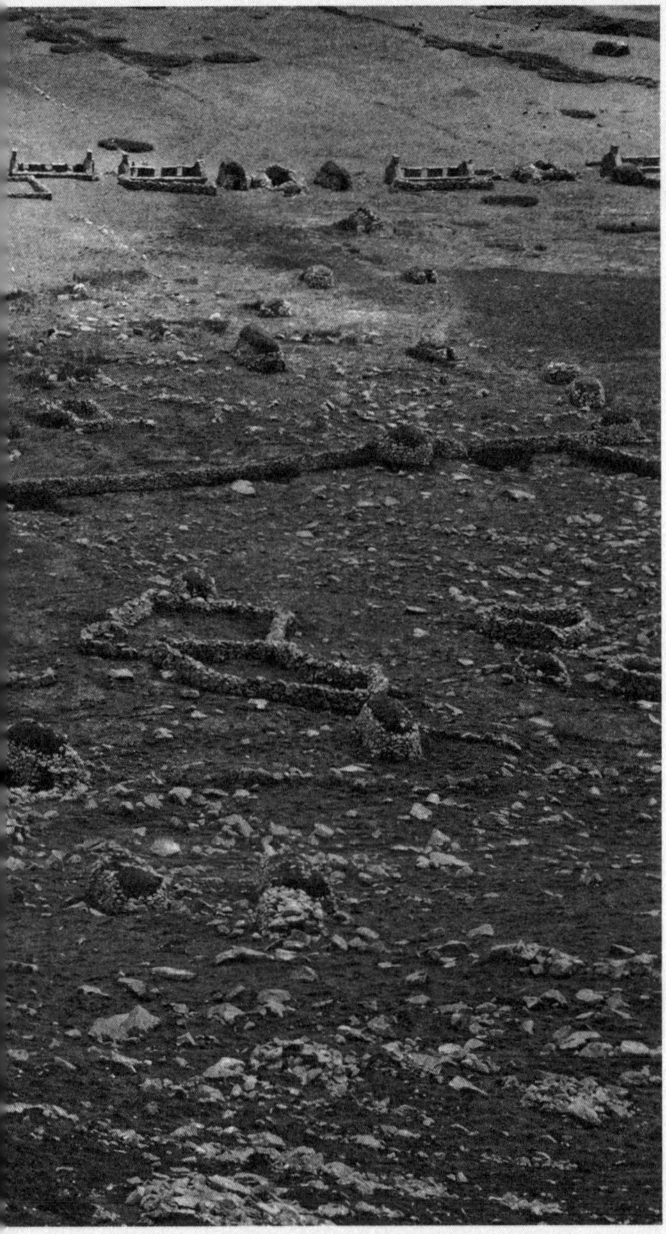

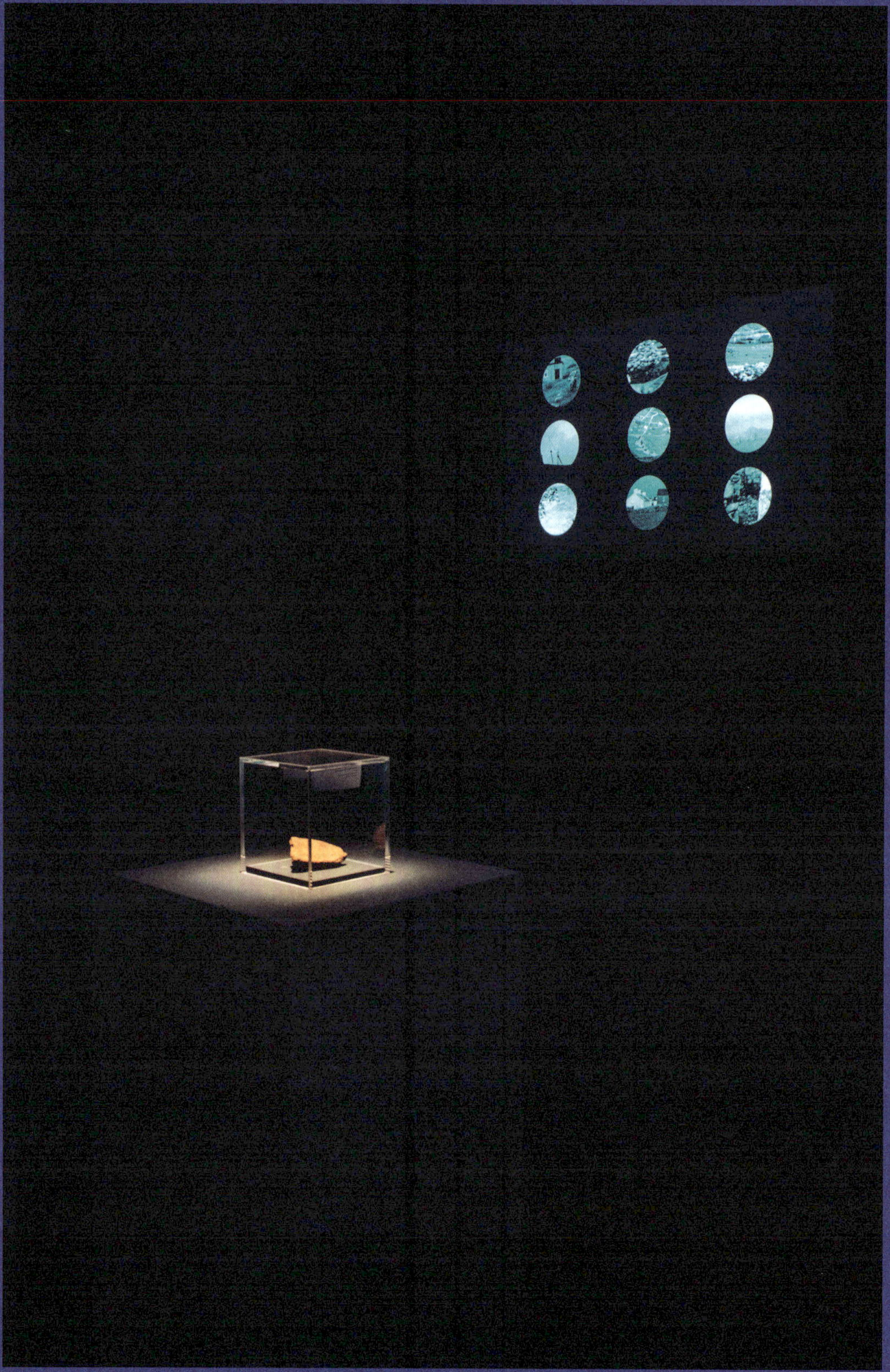

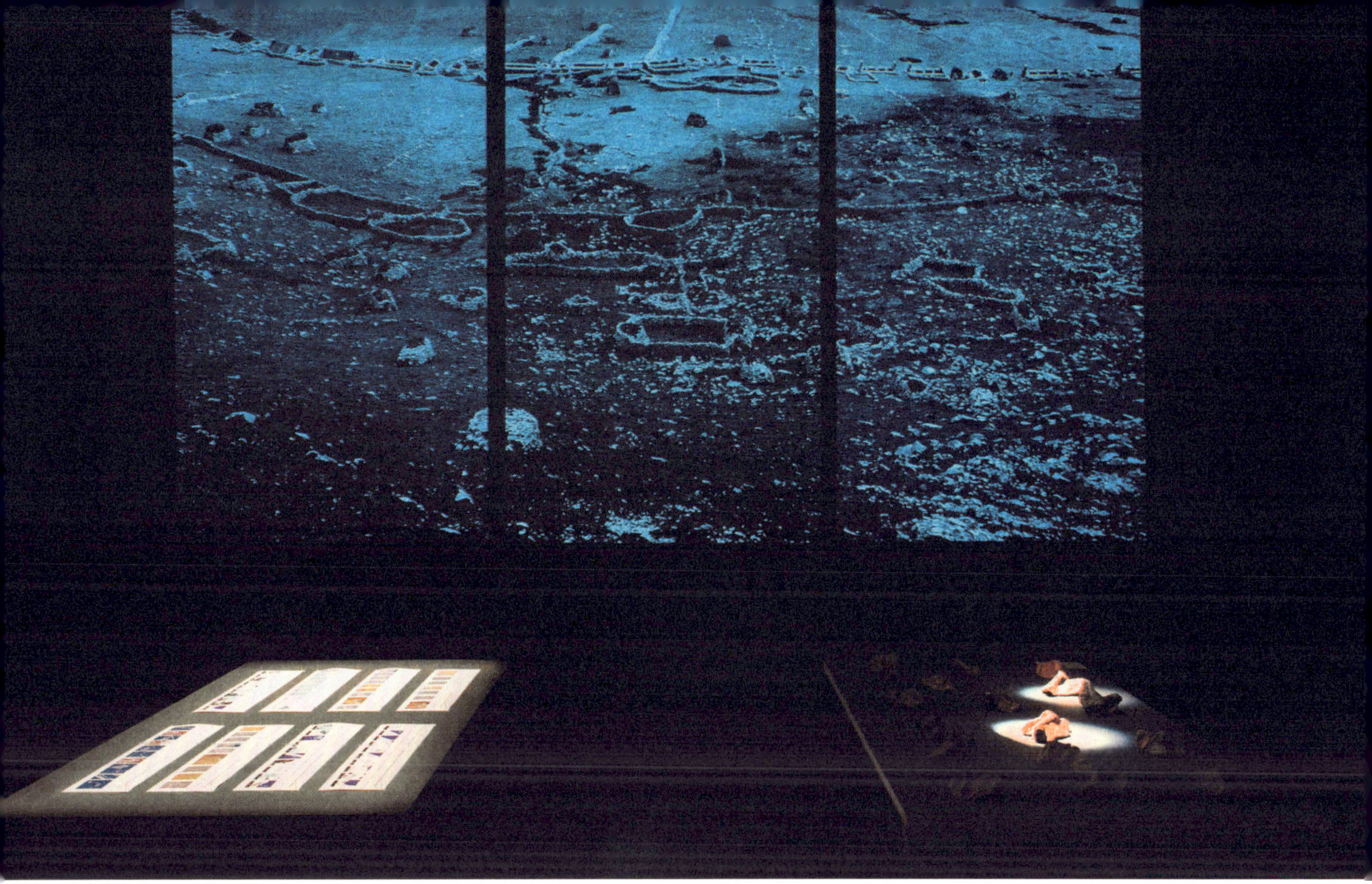

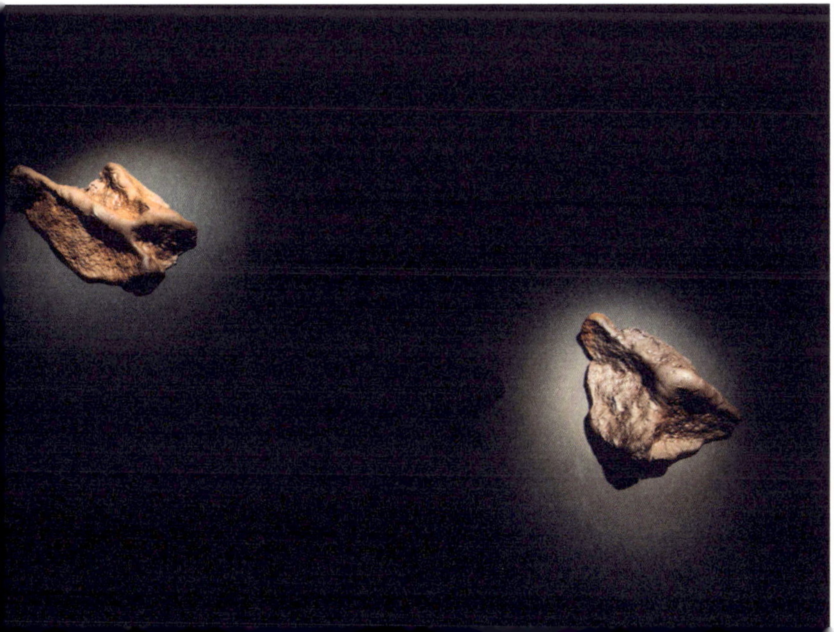

Above and opposite: Shona Illingworth, *Amnesia Museum*, 2012–ongoing. Installation views, FACT, Liverpool. Overleaf: Shona Illingworth, *Sanitised Airspace*, 2015–ongoing. Evolving wall text work, dimensions variable. 2021. Design Daly & Lyon.

R A V E N

F A L C O N

T O R N A D O

S C A N E A G L E

M E R L I N

H A R R I E R

S E A H A W K

G O S H A W K

TYPHOON

NIGHTJAR

KESTREL

TARANIS

PHANTOM

NEURON

STORMSHADOW

TERRIERORION

METEOR

PREDATOR

NIGHTWARDEN

CONDOR

AURA

GRAY

EAGLE

RAPTOR

PERDIX

HUNTER

SKYWARRIOR

LIGHTNINGII

REAPER

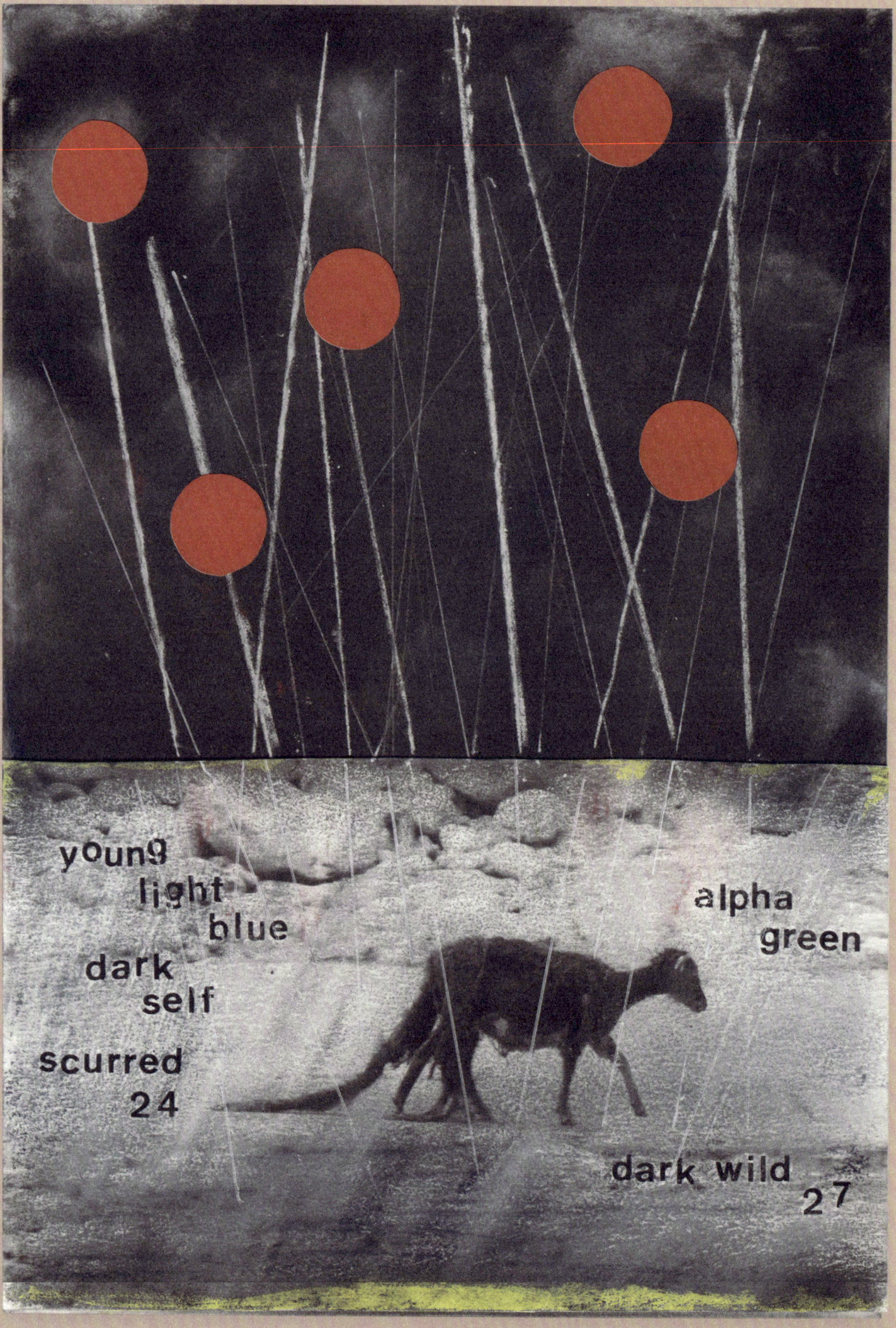

Shona Illingworth, *Prehistoric Sheep, Genome and Satellites*, 2014. Archival pigment print, collage, pastel, and ink.

Renata Salecl
TOPOLOGIES OF MEMORY

One of the most striking photos from 2020 was the satellite image of Yemen's landscape that showed innumerable new graves. This war-torn country has not been reporting on its Covid-19 cases, but the satellite view made the world think that behind the silence might very well lie the terrible truth of numerous people dying from novel coronavirus.

In the early nineties, during the war in Bosnia and Herzegovina, satellite images were also essential in discovering mass graves—and the Serbian army denied their existence until satellite cameras revealed large spots of freshly dug land around the country. In 1999, at the time of the Kosovo war, commercial French SPOT satellites collected data from an altitude of 822 kilometers to show displacement and destruction happening on the ground. Here, too, the public was informed about ethnic cleansing with the help of satellite images, which revealed mass graves, refugees in the mountains, burning mosques and villages, and organized deportations. As Laura Kurgan points out, in this war, satellite photos were released as pictures that "showed less the facts-on-the-ground than the ability of the technology to record, in minute detail, these facts."[1]

The new satellite technology reinterprets the facts on the ground and creates a reality that serves particular purposes, one of them being the creation of cultural memory—which was the case during the wars in Bosnia and Herzegovina, Kosovo, and other war-torn countries. Satellite images have, however, often served less dignified purposes. In the last decades, the military has increasingly relied on airspace and outer space to attack and control presumed enemies. In these operations, fiction also plays an important role. It is not only that computer-generated images of what is happening on the ground can be highly unreliable, but they can also easily be manipulated in such a way that things become invisible.

For example, there are parts of California where streets and houses don't show up on Google maps since wealthy homeowners who live in these areas were able to convince Google not to expose their dwellings to the general public.[2] Furthermore, homes that the US military attacked in Pakistan with the assistance of drones, often working directly from satellite images, look intact—the drone bomb easily creates only a small opening in the roof, which is invisible from afar. The bomb that exploded inside the house and killed its inhabitants, thus, remains hidden and unacknowledged.[3]

In *Topologies of Air* (2021), Shona Illingworth reflects on the current battle in airspace and outer space, where new technologies are often used for surveillance and destruction. This battle, however, is not only about which country will, with the latest technology, use the space high above the ground for economic and political purposes. It is also about interpreting what it means to be a human being and what fantasies and memories are created with the help of new technologies.

There are also dilemmas in regard to the rights of the countries and corporations who create these technologies and the people who suffer from their use. These problems have led Illingworth to initiate the Airspace Tribunal project with Nick Grief (an expert in international law and human rights), which opens up a public discussion on whether the changes

1 Laura Kurgan, "Inadvertent Memory," *Cabinet* (Winter 2000–1), http://cabinetmagazine.org/issues/1/kurgan.php.

2 Kate Allen, "How the Super-Rich Are Making Their Homes 'Invisible,'" *Financial Times*, August 25, 2016, https://www.ft.com/content/7a707048-648d-11e6-8310-ecf0bddad227.

3 For the analysis of such drone attacks, see "Drone Strike in Miranshah," Forensic Architecture website, https://forensic-architecture.org/location/pakistan.

concerning airspace and outer space require legal conceptualization of a new human right.

Battles in the Air

A video and sound installation, *Topologies of Air* juxtaposes images from the sky, where we can see new weapons of mass destruction, and human fragility on the ground. The air is shown as the new battleground and a sublime space full of color. And the interventions happening in this vast arena are often invisible to observers. Soldiers who operate drones on their computer screens look like they are just playing computer games. The results of their actions are, however, death and devastation on the ground—far from where they are based.

In the opening scene of *Topologies of Air*, we see the camera zooming in from above on what looks like a normal city-dwelling, and we hear the sound of an armed drone. However, when the camera closes in, we see a hole that appears to be the result of drone warfare. But when the camera focuses on the opening in the ground, it becomes clear that what we are looking at is not a hole in a house, but an archaeological excavation site of a Dilmun burial mound in Bahrain, dating from between 2200 to 1700 BC. In the next scene, we see a satellite orbiting earth—an object that both aids archaeological surveying and research and supports armed drone systems and attacks on people's homes.

Topologies of Air focuses not only on current devastations due to aerial attacks but also on traumatic episodes from the past. Here, Illingworth reflects on cultural amnesia and individual memory related to the nuclear bomb dropped on Hiroshima in 1945. When visitors to Hiroshima promenade through the well-tended park covering the vast epicenter of the attack today, they can easily ignore the fact that this place used to be densely populated. Only the remnants of the Hiroshima Prefectural Industrial Promotion Hall (now called the Genbaku Dome) and public monuments remind visitors of the terrible hidden truth. Hiroshima schoolchildren sometimes stand near the monuments, asking foreign visitors if they know about the nuclear attack—they are frequently given the assignment by teachers to find out how much the world knows about Hiroshima's past.

Foreigners often have limited knowledge of the nuclear bomb. Survivors' stories, however, also attest to the cultural amnesia at work in Japanese society regarding the Hiroshima attack. For decades, many refused to speak about their experience, and some were afraid the community would learn they had been in the vicinity of the explosion since, after the bombing, it soon became known that radiation could have a lasting impact on survivors' and their offspring's health, as it affected their genes. Marriages were even canceled if it became public knowledge that one of the partners was anywhere near the radiation sites.

Topologies of Air reflects on this cultural amnesia relating to nuclear war. Images of a busy city street are juxtaposed with the shadowy image of a child running toward the camera. At the same time, we hear the voice of Hiroshi Harada, who, in Japanese, shares his memories of the devastation he witnessed after the nuclear attack. This Hiroshima survivor remembers how his father shielded him from the explosion with his own body and how, when they were fleeing the scene, his father's back looked like an open wound. Harada also recalls seeing burned people lying on the ground around him, waiting to die. Later, we see Keisuke Imanaka touching a gravestone, and in the voiceover, he explains how his mother never reconciled with his sister's death since they never found her remains. His mother believed that, one day, her lost daughter would return, so she always left a door to her house open at night.

While survivors of the Hiroshima attack continue to be haunted by traumatic memories, some of the physical remains of the devastation are in danger of being removed. With the threat of an earthquake potentially causing the collapse of the historic ruins, some city planners have proposed removing these war-torn buildings. Hiroshima citizens strongly opposing such proposals point out that, for the memory of Hiroshima's tragic history to survive, it is essential to preserve at least some physical remains of the nuclear attack.[4]

Individual and Cultural Amnesia

In *Lesions in the Landscape*, Illingworth's 2015 video and sound installation, the artist questions what happens when we are unable to form individual memories and when there is an erosion of the physical remains of the past. Illingworth started exploring individual amnesia when she began working with a woman named Claire, who suffers from a particular neurological disorder that prevents her from forming and retrieving memory. At the age of forty-four, Claire developed viral encephalitis, which caused a large lesion in her brain's right hemisphere. As a result, Claire lost access to most of her memories. Among other things, she could not remember the years she spent bringing up her children.

Claire continues to be unable to form new memories from her daily life and suffers from prosopagnosia, a neurological condition that precludes her from distinguishing or recognizing faces. Consequently, Claire relies on what others tell her about her past and lives in the continuous present—which, because nothing is remembered, also prevents her from thinking about the future.

Lesions in the Landscape makes a connection between individual and cultural amnesia when Claire is taken to the depopulated Scottish archipelago of St Kilda. In 1930, all of the inhabitants of St Kilda were evacuated due to population decline after World War I, when the islands lost a large number of men. In addition, people started dying of influenza, and numerous bad harvests prevented the islanders from supporting themselves independently.[5]

Illingworth draws a parallel between Claire's amnesia and the remnants of cultural memory visible on these now-depopulated islands. In the video, viewers can see how mental space is mapped onto external terrain and how individual and cultural amnesia shapes social, cultural, and historical landscapes. The camera moves from Claire, who, with her body-worn camera, records her surroundings so that she stores at least some visual trace of her days, and the abandoned roads of St Kilda, where lesions of time past cover the remains that exist now.

As Claire patches together the tale of her daily life with the help of a camera, notes, and voice recordings, the Hiroshima survivors create a tapestry of cultural memory with their stories. By making her memory, Claire is holding herself together: she holds onto the physical mementos that are remnants of her life. Images, notes, and recordings, thus, counter her amnesia. Hiroshima survivors, with their public recollections of the past, equally fight against their society's cultural amnesia, their testimonies informing younger generations of the country's traumatic history. And, most importantly, the survivors hope that nuclear devastation will never happen again.

Active Forgetting

When psychoanalysts examined the problem of trauma, they observed that after people experience something profoundly traumatic, they have trouble talking about that painful event. And although people might not discuss what happened, the trauma persists in their unconscious. Years later, the event's memory may suddenly resurface and can be experienced brutally. For some dealing with a traumatic past experience, learning something new is also

4 "Hiroshima Buildings That Survived Bombing to Be Razed," *NewsKarnataka*, December 16, 2019, https://www.newskarnataka.com/world/hiroshima-buildings-that-survived-bombing-to-be-razed.

5 Charles MacLean, *Island on the Edge of the World: The Story of St Kilda* (Edinburgh: Canongate Books, 2006).

6 Friedrich Nietzsche, *The Genealogy of Morals* (1887), trans. and ed. Douglas Smith (Oxford: Oxford World's Classics, 1996).

challenging—something psychoanalysts observed in many migrants fleeing violence in their homelands. Some are unable to learn a new language, while others cannot remember anything about their new country—and, as a result, many are unable to pass their citizenship tests. Amnesia about the past and the inability to learn something new are, thus, not only neurological conditions, as in Claire's case.

When we remember things from the past, we are also opening up the possibility to think about the future. As a society, and as individuals, we engage with the memory of what was in the hope that we might not repeat traumatic events, will learn from the mistakes, and be proud of our achievements. We also hope that the future will be different from the past, that pains will be amended, while glorious moments will be remembered. When we lose the possibility to remember, we, sadly, also lose the power to imagine what is to come.

Both *Lesions in the Landscape* and *Topologies of Air* reflect on this need for memory. Both projects show how important it is for society and individuals to remember the past so we might imagine the future. However, while *Lesions in the Landscape* reflects on the physical limits of memory (neurological lesions and the lesions nature grows over remnants of the past), *Topologies of Air* exposes the social and political limitations of memory. Past devastations from the air are forgotten for ever-new ways of exploiting airspace and outer space for surveillance and military interventions.

With the rapid development of science, the internet revolution, and, especially, the emergence of the world of big data, memory and amnesia are rethought in new ways. Geneticists and neuroscientists are engaged in studies thinking through new forms of forgetfulness, where it might be possible to erase specific traumatic memories by manipulating the brain or administering drugs that enable such effects. Alongside the massive, rarely erased collection of data, many crave amnesia for their digital footprints. The popularity of the messaging app Snapchat can be read within this context—Snapchat offers the illusion of amnesia because text and photo messages self-erase a few seconds after being viewed. But behind this illusion of erasure is the collection of data—storage of memory completely outside of our control. We can neither erase it nor control its meaning.

When Friedrich Nietzsche was reflecting on the power of memory, he coined the phrase "active forgetting,"[6] in that sometimes we need to forget to make room for something new. Rather than dismiss the power of memory, Nietzsche cherished archives people built about their past. However, his point was that excessive remembering could prevent people from taking action since not all past forms of knowledge or all experiences are beneficial for present and future life.

Intrinsically connected to active forgetfulness is what might be called "active remembering." When we parse through the past, art often presents a way for memory to be reworked, trauma to be alleviated, and something new to come to the surface. Illingworth's installations allow for such active remembering. Though her work does not have the power to amend physical lesions, it does remove cultural ones. With this, it opens the possibility to imagine a different future.

Renata Salecl is a philosopher and sociologist. She is Professor of Psychology and Psychoanalysis of Law at the School of Law, Birkbeck College, University of London, and a Senior Researcher at the Institute of Criminology at the Faculty of Law in Ljubljana, Slovenia. Her book *Tyranny of Choice* (Profile Books, 2010) has been translated into fifteen languages and was featured at TED Global. Her previous books include *The Spoils of Freedom* (Routledge, 1994), *(Per)versions of Love and Hate* (Verso, 1998), and *On Anxiety* (Routledge, 2004). Salecl's most recent book is *A Passion for Ignorance: What We Choose Not to Know and Why* (Princeton University Press, 2020). She has also written on contemporary art and has contributed essays to the art catalogues of Francis Bacon, Anthony Gormley, Jenny Holzer, and Sarah Sze.

193.100 191.000 190.100 191.600 193.300 188.400 185.000 187.600 188.600 188.600 189.500 187.700 187.500 189.400
179.300 177.800 177.500 178.600 177.600 177.700 173.900 167.700 165.900 166.500 159.300 158.100 159.700 157.300
142.900 138.200 138.400 137.100 137.300 136.700 132.900 124.500 119.200 115.000 115.600 114.000 112.000 111.900
102.200 102.100 100.800 103.100 99.700 101.200 103.300 104.700 102.500 96.700 93.900 92.300 90.200 90.700
85.900 85.700 83.500 80.800 79.800 75.600 74.600 75.100 73.100 69.900 67.200 61.000 55.900 53.200 54.500 55.300
44.600 42.800 44.500 45.200 45.200 44.500 42.800 44.200 45.100 43.900 45.200 48.100 46.800 44.600 45.500 44.800
36.200 36.900 36.500 33.000 33.500 31.600 31.800 32.500 33.500 32.200 34.500 30.900 28.300 29.300 25.800 25.800
17.200 18.200 15.600 18.200 18.500 20.400 18.100 14.000 13.800 10.800 13.000 11.300 12.300 15.100 14.100 9.700
10.200 5.300 5.500 7.700 7.600 8.200 7.700 7.700 5.300 3.800 0.700 -2.100 -2.100 -2.300 -5.900 -4.300 -3.200
-8.100 -5.400 -8.000 -4.500 -2.100 -2.600 -4.000 -3.100 -2.100 -2.300 -6.000 -5.800 -1.600 -0.800 -0.700 0.700
-9.100 -9.800 -9.800 -9.100 -7.300 -7.100 -9.200 -8.500 -4.800 -2.600 -3.500 -9.300 -8.700 -7.200 -5.600 -8.400
-10.200 -9.700 -10.900 -11.900 -12.300 -10.800 -12.700 -10.800 -12.200 -17.200 -17.300 -18.000 -20.200 -19.900
-17.500 -19.700 -22.100 -21.800 -20.200 -21.000 -25.200 -24.800 -21.700 -21.600 -20.900 -21.500 -23.400 -22.900
-17.900 -17.800 -19.300 -20.800 -21.300 -20.300 -21.700 -21.100 -25.700 -26.000 -22.900 -20.500 -20.000 -20.100
-16.800 -17.200 -20.700 -16.300 -13.500 -16.200 -15.700 -12.900 -12.900 -16.100 -14.000 -11.800 -9.700 -12.300
-16.100 -15.800 -13.600 -15.000 -16.700 -13.200 -15.800 -13.700 -15.000 -21.400 -20.500 -17.200 -12.200 -11.100
-20.600 -22.200 -18.600 -15.500 -16.200 -16.100 -14.600 -17.600 -18.800 -16.500 -19.500 -17.600 -16.600 -16.200
-23.800 -24.800 -26.700 -20.600 -19.500 -18.000 -16.900 -13.700 -16.600 -12.700 -13.000 -16.800 -15.500 -17.600
-27.500 -27.200 -26.300 -26.700 -31.000 -35.900 -38.300 -32.800 -28.800 -32.300 -31.700 -30.700 -30.500 -32.200
-29.800 -30.500 -28.400 -30.100 -29.600 -29.900 -29.100 -26.200 -28.500 -30.600 -26.200 -28.700 -28.000 -30.300
-33.600 -32.600 -29.700 -30.400 -33.500 -32.200 -33.800 -32.100 -30.300 -29.000 -31.600 -33.400 -34.400 -35.700
-32.300 -32.500 -33.400 -31.600 -30.500 -30.500 -29.100 -31.300 -30.300 -28.900 -25.800 -25.200 -27.800 -30.500
-20.200 -23.100 -21.200 -21.600 -22.400 -20.700 -19.000 -17.600 -19.000 -17.000 -19.400 -20.500 -21.900 -22.100
-7.100 -10.300 -9.400 -4.800 -7.100 -10.800 -7.700 -6.300 -7.400 -8.000 -6.900 -6.900 -6.600 -6.600 -5.600
.200 6.300 14.100 10.200 16.400 16.100 9.800 8.400 10.000 13.700 13.500 17.200 19.400 21.900 22.200 25.200
15.300 18.900 23.300 27.500 34.600 37.400 42.700 45.900 46.400 49.000 49.900 47.600 46.800 50.100 51.900 53.200
60.400 64.100 62.500 65.000 69.700 70.500 67.100 69.000 69.800 71.200 70.800 69.500 72.100 75.900 78.500 81.100
84.100 91.500 89.800 89.800 88.900 87.400 85.200 87.400 88.500 91.300 93.000 91.900 95.100 95.700 98.300 99.400
100.800 101.200 100.300 98.400 97.700 101.800 108.100 113.700 115.700 113.800 115.800 118.300 117.500 115.800
110.100 109.300 111.100 111.100 112.300 117.600 121.200 124.800 127.500 130.300 133.000 135.600 134.300 130.600
127.300 126.600 122.100 122.400 124.300 125.200 128.900 136.400 141.000 145.600 151.300 153.500 154.500 153.400
140.700 137.500 141.500 142.800 141.800 151.100 153.600 152.700 154.500 160.600 159.600 161.000 159.500 156.100
156.200 163.200 163.400 161.700 160.600 160.400 159.300 161.000 163.900 162.500 159.500 158.600 159.500 160.800
164.200 160.300 158.200 161.600 165.700 169.300 175.000 179.000 178.200 179.800 182.300 181.400 181.400 177.100
166.700 167.600 170.800 172.000 175.100 173.700 172.800 171.900 169.400 175.900 177.200 175.900 180.100 183.100
184.900 186.500 183.500 185.000 184.900 180.200 182.100 187.100 185.300 184.600 186.700 185.400 187.300 188.300
183.700 185.300 186.000 185.700 185.600 185.300 189.700 195.600 195.800 194.700 190.000 192.600 194.300 194.000
185.700 188.300 189.500 187.900 185.900 189.200 190.700 190.600 193.100 197.000 199.500 198.400 199.300 201.600
197.200 198.500 196.400 195.700 192.800 187.800 191.700 193.600 194.900 194.500 193.300 190.800 184.600 182.600
204.100 204.000 205.100 202.000 196.400 198.400 199.000 196.400 197.000 193.000 191.900 193.500 195.900 201.600
207.800 205.400 206.300 206.900 207.600 208.900 207.200 209.200 208.600 205.600 209.400 209.900 211.500 214.400
211.100 209.800 209.600 206.700 210.200 209.700 207.300 211.900 218.500 222.600 222.500 224.800 225.100 224.300
216.800 215.800 215.300 219.300 216.900 212.600 219.500 221.500 221.000 223.000 221.600 219.000 218.600 218.800
220.400 218.700 217.000 215.200 216.900 221.900 224.600 225.900 227.700 233.600 234.800 231.500 232.800 235.600
220.300 220.300 223.500 223.700 220.800 216.400 219.700 217.000 213.400 212.700 212.200 214.600 213.800 221.000
225.800 224.000 225.700 226.200 225.200 223.600 223.000 222.000 221.600 216.600 213.200 216.600 216.800 215.400
224.200 222.800 224.300 225.400 227.500 223.100 223.900 221.900 218.400 217.500 217.400 219.900 219.200 218.200
230.600 228.800 227.200 216.800 217.500 214.500 213.500 215.800 216.500 215.400 220.400 219.200 219.900 222.500
219.500 222.300 225.300 226.800 224.800 227.800 228.100 224.700 222.700 223.300 219.900 221.900 220.200 219.300
227.200 229.400 230.200 227.900 227.500 224.400 226.000 223.000 223.200 222.300 220.900 218.000 219.200 219.000
234.700 233.800 234.000 234.100 233.900 230.300 228.200 227.400 224.800 222.600 217.600 219.800 219.300 219.100
226.600 227.200 225.600 223.200 223.200 219.000 220.000 215.700 217.200 220.300 224.600 224.600 229.800 231.500
226.600 223.900 224.200 224.800 224.000 222.800 224.300 224.700 227.000 230.100 230.700 228.700 227.700 230.400
230.200 232.100 233.200 230.900 231.100 229.000 230.300 232.300 230.400 233.700 235.500 232.300 230.100 229.800
234.800 233.600 238.000 236.400 230.900 229.600 229.300 230.700 230.500 228.900 229.400 234.900 237.300 240.200
245.900 241.700 240.700 237.800 235.000 234.300 233.000 234.500 239.400 241.600 243.800 246.700 249.800 250.300
240.900 241.500 240.900 236.400 237.000 240.400 243.300 248.300 248.300 250.100 249.800 243.700 245.300 247.200
233.300 235.600 236.500 238.400 243.000 241.600 240.200 239.600 239.000 238.300 238.900 236.200 238.400 238.300
237.400 236.400 237.100 241.100 240.900 237.300 236.800 238.400 240.200 241.800 242.000 245.900 248.600 244.400
237.300 238.900 241.400 239.100 238.000 238.700 239.200 238.000 234.500 240.700 241.300 239.200 239.100 241.400
237.200 232.800 231.400 231.200 232.000 230.100 231.600 232.500 235.100 238.800 241.100 242.600 240.700 241.100
239.600 244.300 243.300 239.700 243.300 241.900 240.100 243.200 247.100 253.000 256.200 259.400 259.100 259.200
258.600 261.600 256.800 256.800 263.800 262.100 261.700 260.700 261.800 264.200 261.700 259.000 256.000 255.800
250.600 250.100 250.400 255.400 261.800 258.900 258.300 257.900 262.200 264.300 262.000 263.000 263.900 263.900
265.100 265.600 266.300 265.400 264.600 264.100 266.200 269.200 268.700 268.300 268.300 266.800 265.700 258.300
258.900 261.100 264.500 260.800 265.000 265.400 266.500 267.800 268.200 265.300 267.700 267.100 264.200 260.800
271.400 271.300 273.100 272.500 273.300 272.400 265.700 263.400 261.000 256.500 255.200 255.800 256.700 255.800
270.400 276.500 272.200 268.900 271.100 273.700 269.000 267.400 267.900 263.500 264.600 262.800 263.100 264.800
261.600 261.900 261.400 265.400 261.300 264.000 269.800 271.800 268.000 262.100 260.600 255.500 256.100 256.700
257.700 259.200 258.100 257.500 257.600 260.000 258.300 259.300 259.700 257.200 257.900 259.100 261.900 262.500
262.800 257.600 256.700 257.100 258.000 256.200 255.700 256.700 256.300 257.300 262.800 260.600 262.500 264.900
257.800 262.100 262.400 264.400 264.900 262.000 267.900 270.200 268.900 273.400 276.300 274.300 272.900 271.400
273.900 274.200 273.700 271.900 271.000 276.200 278.900 278.000 277.400 283.400 284.700 280.500 277.100 278.000
274.400 275.100 270.800 266.800 268.100 269.100 268.100 269.300 268.600 270.100 271.500 271.400 271.700 270.300
269.000 268.100 269.900 267.200 262.100 266.600 267.600 264.800 266.700 265.900 260.700 261.100 262.300 261.200
263.300 262.100 262.100 259.200 253.800 252.200 250.800 248.800 248.700 254.100 260.000 258.900 256.300 260.700
262.200 267.300 269.200 266.600 267.300 267.200 270.600 274.000 269.500 262.500 262.100 260.400 259.300 255.800
265.300 264.200 263.700 265.000 266.200 263.100 258.000 255.600 253.500 255.000 255.700 254.200 252.700 252.100
257.300 255.200 258.100 257.100 253.900 252.500 252.500 254.600 254.500 252.100 251.400 250.500 253.100 256.000
266.000 267.200 265.400 264.500 263.400 259.200 260.400 258.600 258.100 259.500 258.000 260.800 260.300 255.600
265.800 269.800 269.900 270.800 272.800 274.500 271.300 268.800 268.100 271.600 276.100 275.900 278.100 282.900
267.300 271.600 271.100 272.300 273.900 272.000 271.500 270.800 270.600 272.400 280.300 277.900 276.400 272.500
263.900 267.700 265.400 263.400 261.100 263.800 269.000 270.000 264.300 263.700 265.300 267.600 267.000 267.400
276.000 281.400 274.200 270.900 273.700 271.700 271.500 274.200 274.400 271.200 266.900 266.400 260.800 255.500
266.500 271.000 272.700 272.500 274.700 274.000 266.600 266.000 263.500 269.100 270.600 269.800 274.200 272.400
266.300 268.700 274.200 269.000 264.500 266.200 267.300 267.000 266.700 260.800 262.000 259.100 260.100 265.700
264.900 266.400 268.000 269.700 269.700 271.600 271.400 269.000 270.100 270.500 266.100 267.500 269.300 270.000
269.800 269.300 272.100 269.800 273.100 275.400 275.600 271.500 270.100 273.600 274.000 276.200 280.700 280.400

Shona Illingworth, *Sounding Amnesic Memory*, 2014. EEG sonification of Amnesic Memory.

FORUMS

Shona Illingworth has organized and collaborated on interdisciplinary forums, which form a vital part of her practice since she launched the Memory Forums series at Coleman Project Space in London in 2006. The Memory Forums brought together a wide range of expertise and experience to discuss memory, spatial politics, and cultural oppression. These were followed by the Amnesia Forums, Amnesia Lab, and a two-day international symposium, "Invisible Architectures: Lesions in the Landscape," which was coorganized by Illingworth and Jill Bennett in 2016 and hosted by Whitechapel Gallery, London.

More recently, the Sky Forums have examined the significance of the sky and cosmos in Bedouin, Arab, and other cultures, the present conditions of human and natural life in a global context, and how geopolitical realities and climate change transcend borders. These forums—which further explore the sustainability of existence on our planet, the impact of artificial intelligence, and the search for life beyond our solar system—directly inform and contribute to Illingworth's recent project *Topologies of Air* (2021).

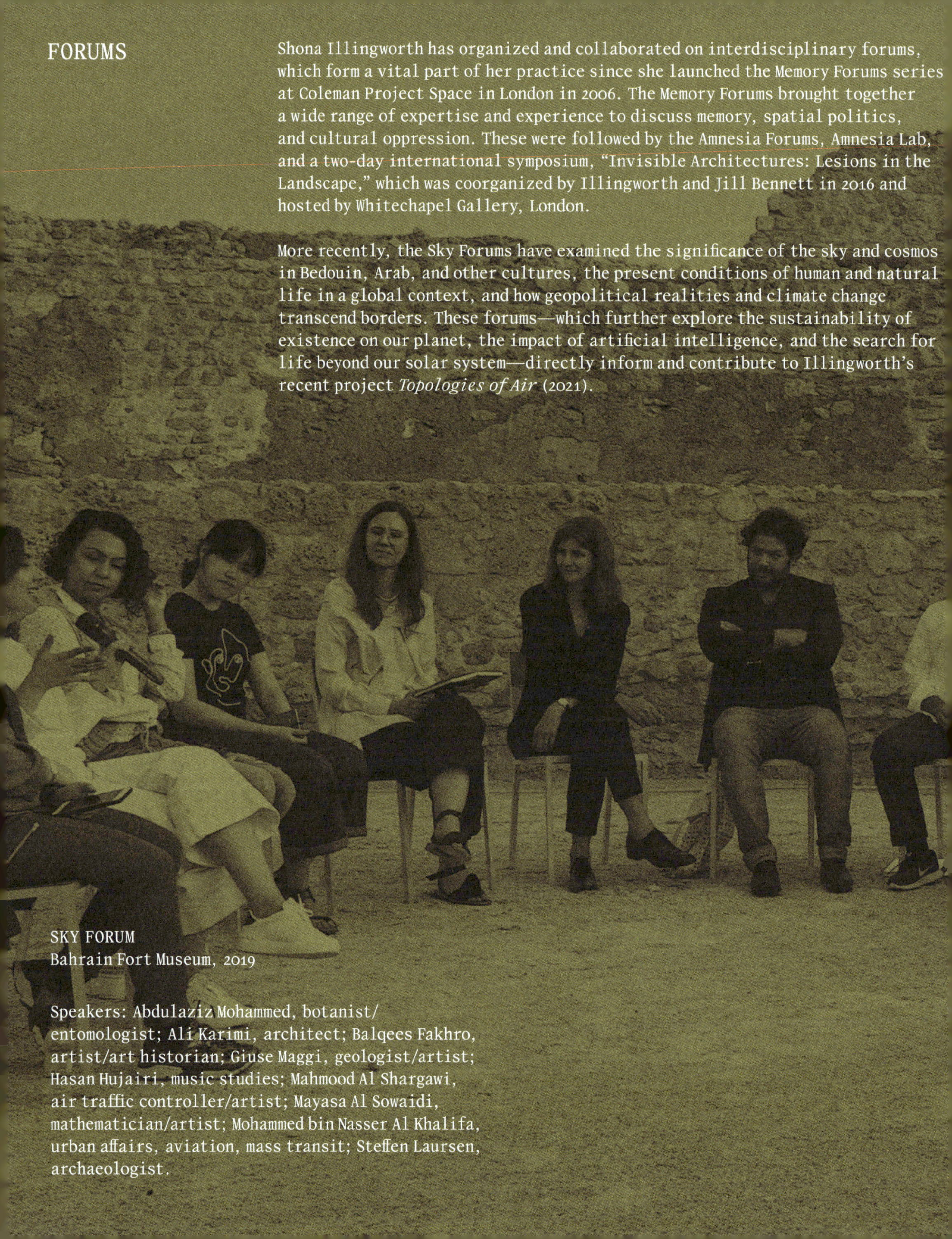

SKY FORUM
Bahrain Fort Museum, 2019

Speakers: Abdulaziz Mohammed, botanist/entomologist; Ali Karimi, architect; Balqees Fakhro, artist/art historian; Giuse Maggi, geologist/artist; Hasan Hujairi, music studies; Mahmood Al Shargawi, air traffic controller/artist; Mayasa Al Sowaidi, mathematician/artist; Mohammed bin Nasser Al Khalifa, urban affairs, aviation, mass transit; Steffen Laursen, archaeologist.

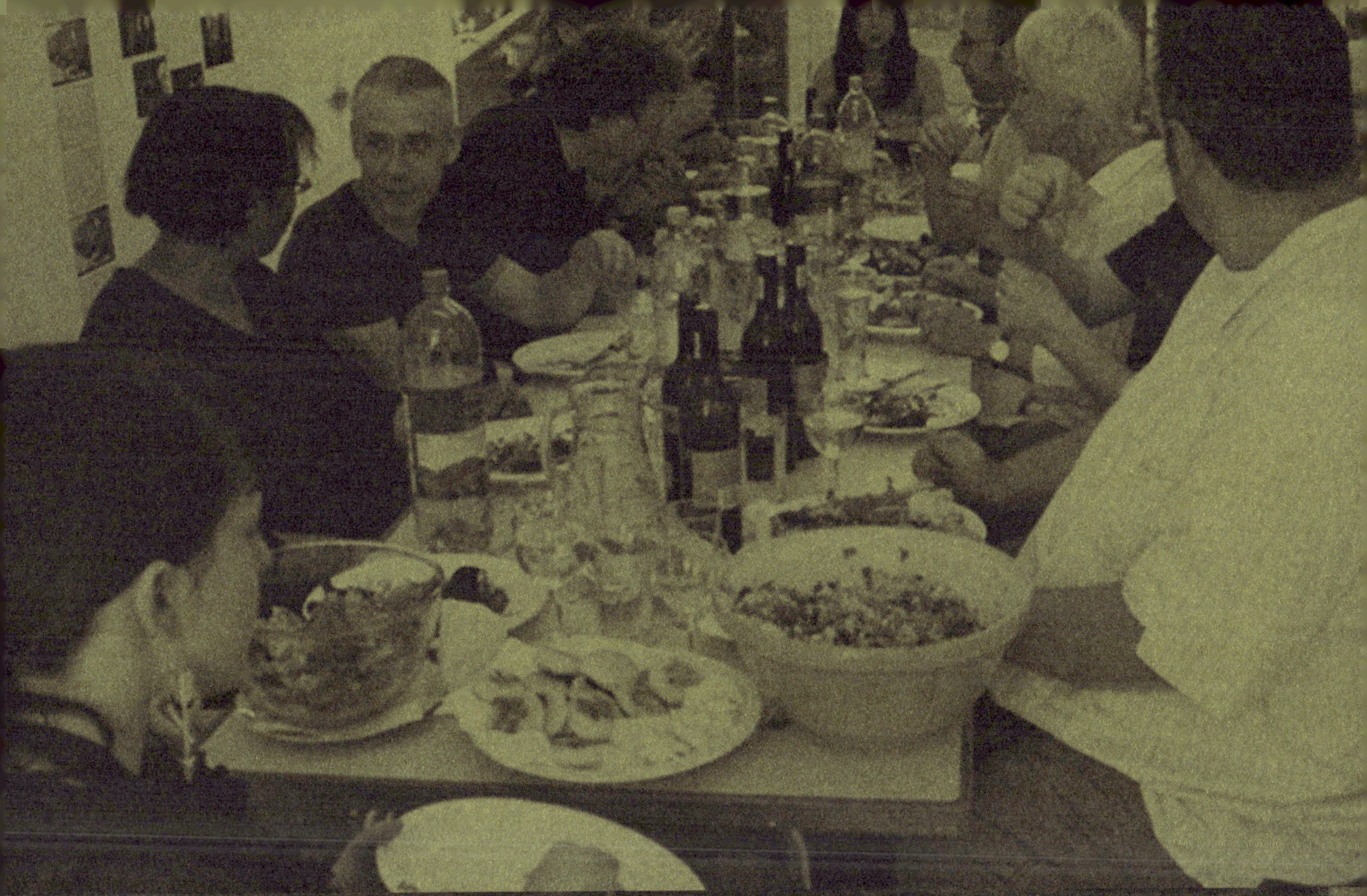

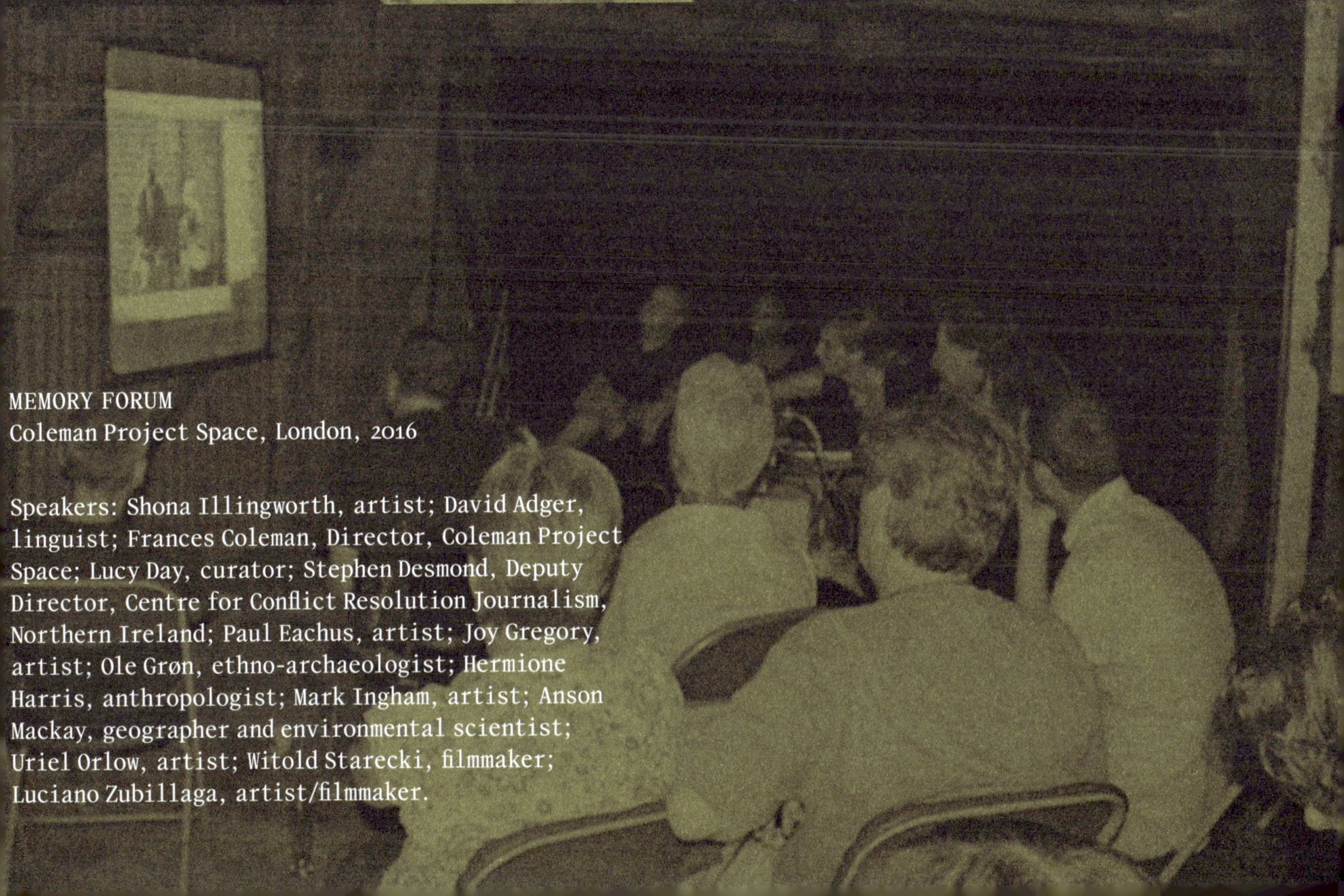

MEMORY FORUM
Coleman Project Space, London, 2016

Speakers: Shona Illingworth, artist; David Adger, linguist; Frances Coleman, Director, Coleman Project Space; Lucy Day, curator; Stephen Desmond, Deputy Director, Centre for Conflict Resolution Journalism, Northern Ireland; Paul Eachus, artist; Joy Gregory, artist; Ole Grøn, ethno-archaeologist; Hermione Harris, anthropologist; Mark Ingham, artist; Anson Mackay, geographer and environmental scientist; Uriel Orlow, artist; Witold Starecki, filmmaker; Luciano Zubillaga, artist/filmmaker.

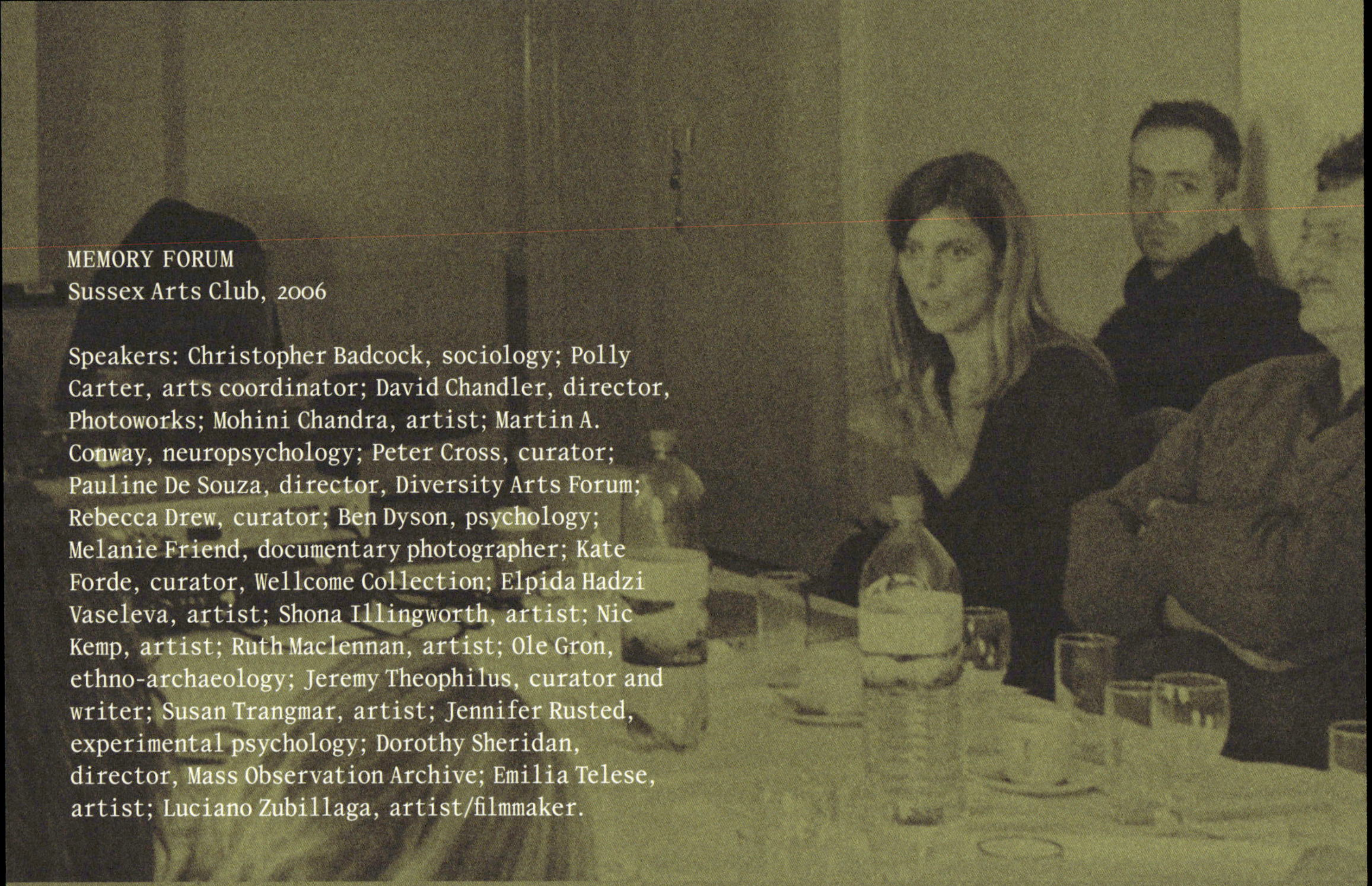

MEMORY FORUM
Sussex Arts Club, 2006

Speakers: Christopher Badcock, sociology; Polly Carter, arts coordinator; David Chandler, director, Photoworks; Mohini Chandra, artist; Martin A. Conway, neuropsychology; Peter Cross, curator; Pauline De Souza, director, Diversity Arts Forum; Rebecca Drew, curator; Ben Dyson, psychology; Melanie Friend, documentary photographer; Kate Forde, curator, Wellcome Collection; Elpida Hadzi Vaseleva, artist; Shona Illingworth, artist; Nic Kemp, artist; Ruth Maclennan, artist; Ole Gron, ethno-archaeology; Jeremy Theophilus, curator and writer; Susan Trangmar, artist; Jennifer Rusted, experimental psychology; Dorothy Sheridan, director, Mass Observation Archive; Emilia Telese, artist; Luciano Zubillaga, artist/filmmaker.

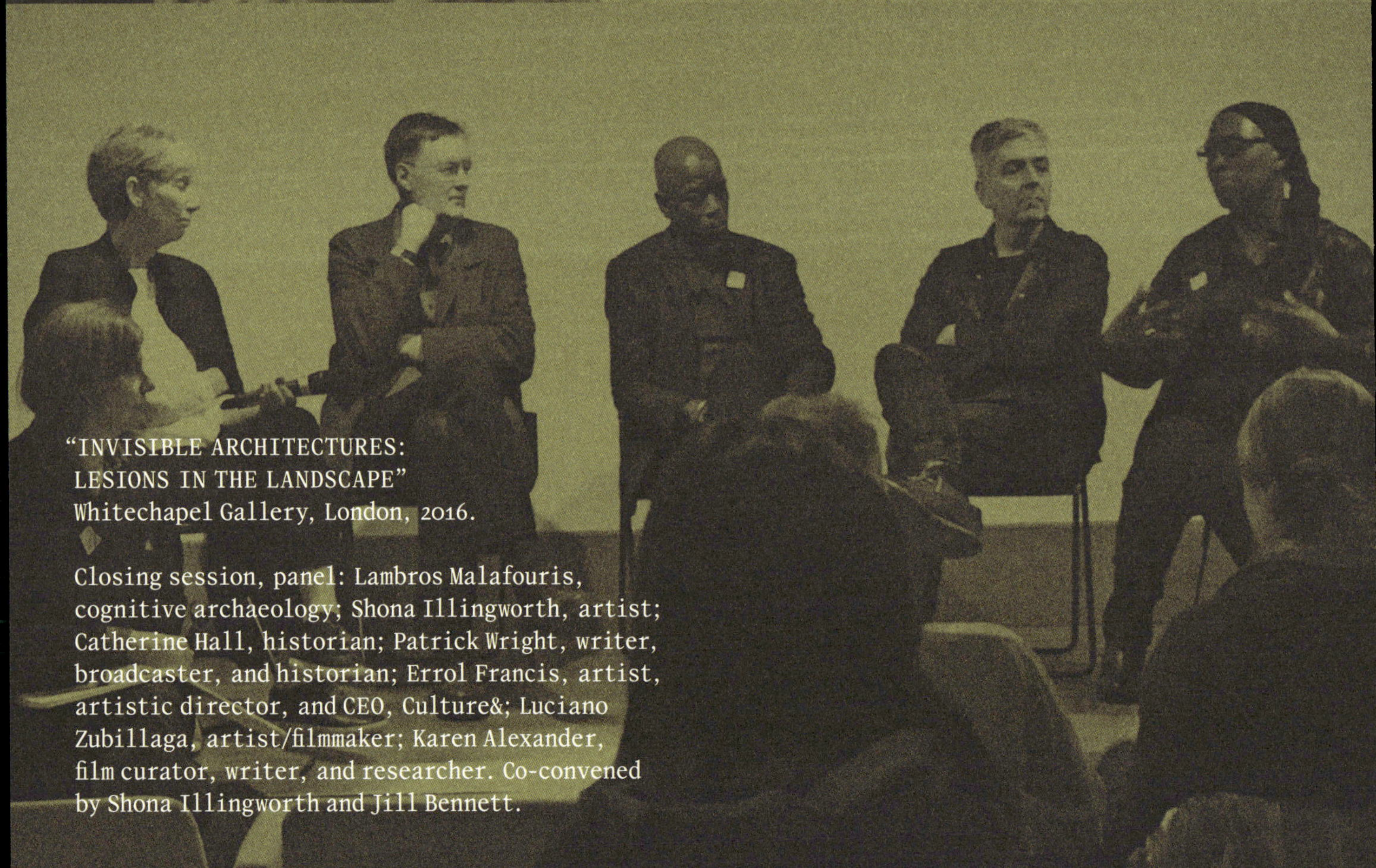

"INVISIBLE ARCHITECTURES:
LESIONS IN THE LANDSCAPE"
Whitechapel Gallery, London, 2016.

Closing session, panel: Lambros Malafouris, cognitive archaeology; Shona Illingworth, artist; Catherine Hall, historian; Patrick Wright, writer, broadcaster, and historian; Errol Francis, artist, artistic director, and CEO, Culture&; Luciano Zubillaga, artist/filmmaker; Karen Alexander, film curator, writer, and researcher. Co-convened by Shona Illingworth and Jill Bennett.

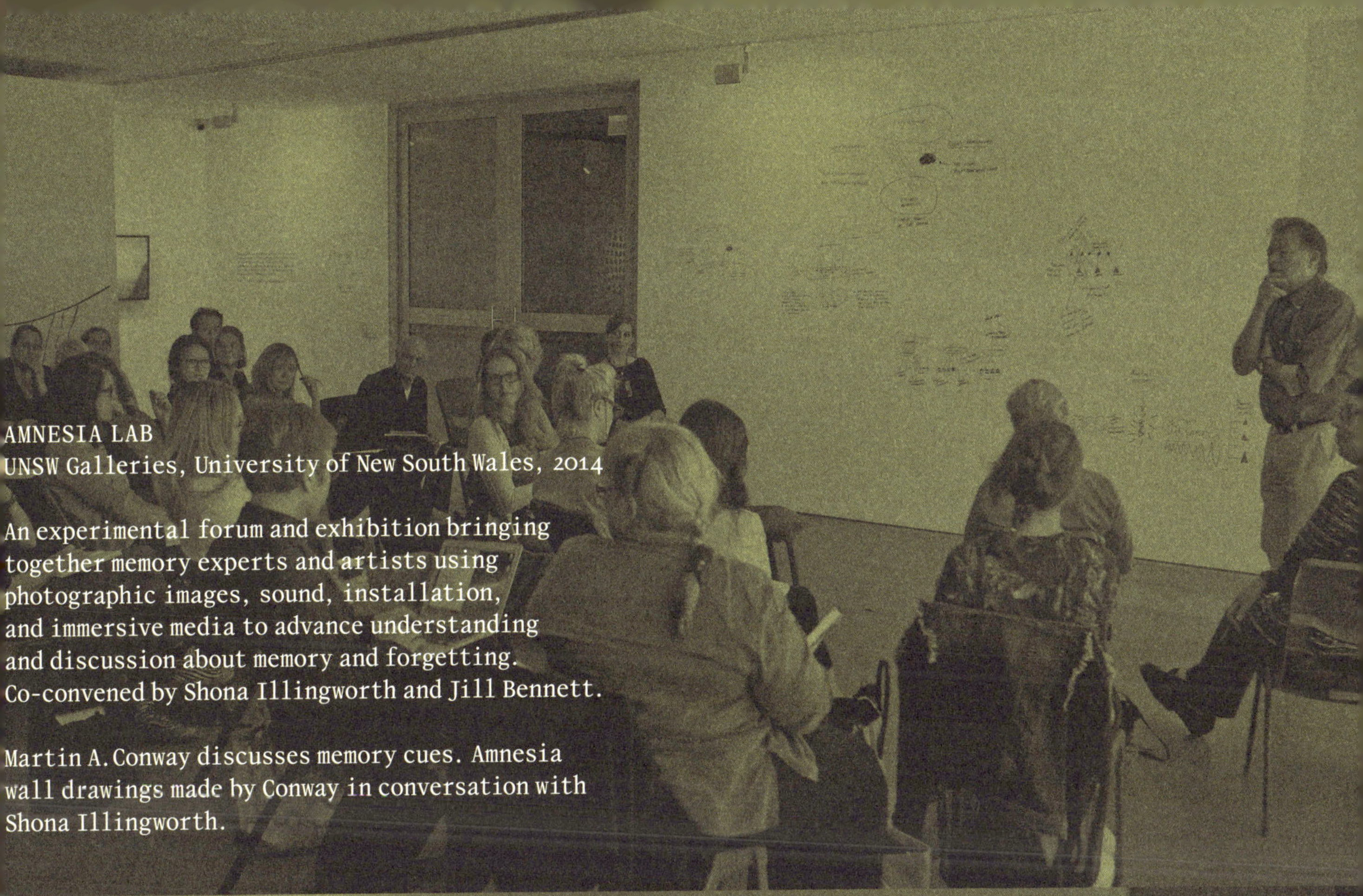

AMNESIA LAB
UNSW Galleries, University of New South Wales, 2014

An experimental forum and exhibition bringing together memory experts and artists using photographic images, sound, installation, and immersive media to advance understanding and discussion about memory and forgetting. Co-convened by Shona Illingworth and Jill Bennett.

Martin A. Conway discusses memory cues. Amnesia wall drawings made by Conway in conversation with Shona Illingworth.

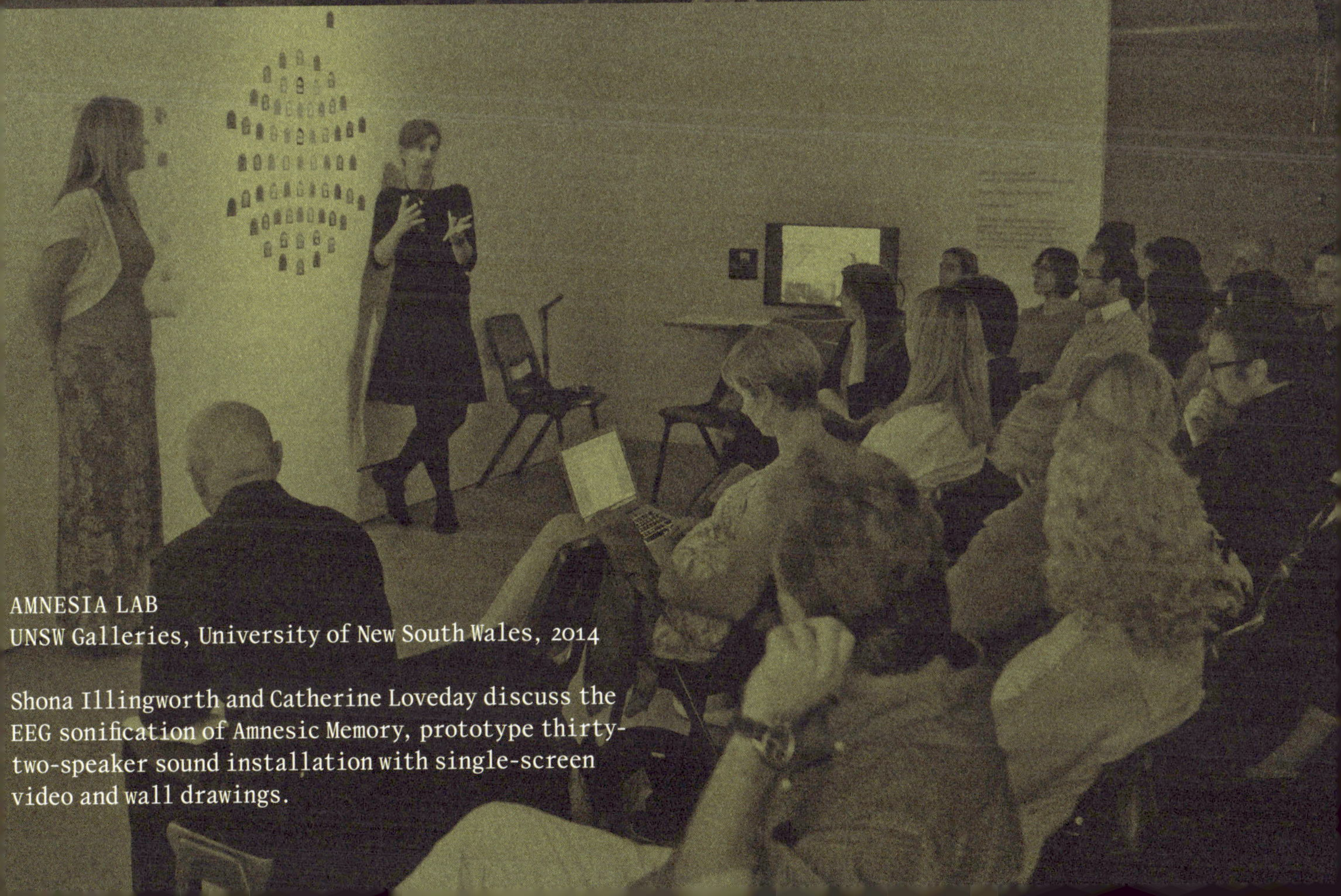

AMNESIA LAB
UNSW Galleries, University of New South Wales, 2014

Shona Illingworth and Catherine Loveday discuss the EEG sonification of Amnesic Memory, prototype thirty-two-speaker sound installation with single-screen video and wall drawings.

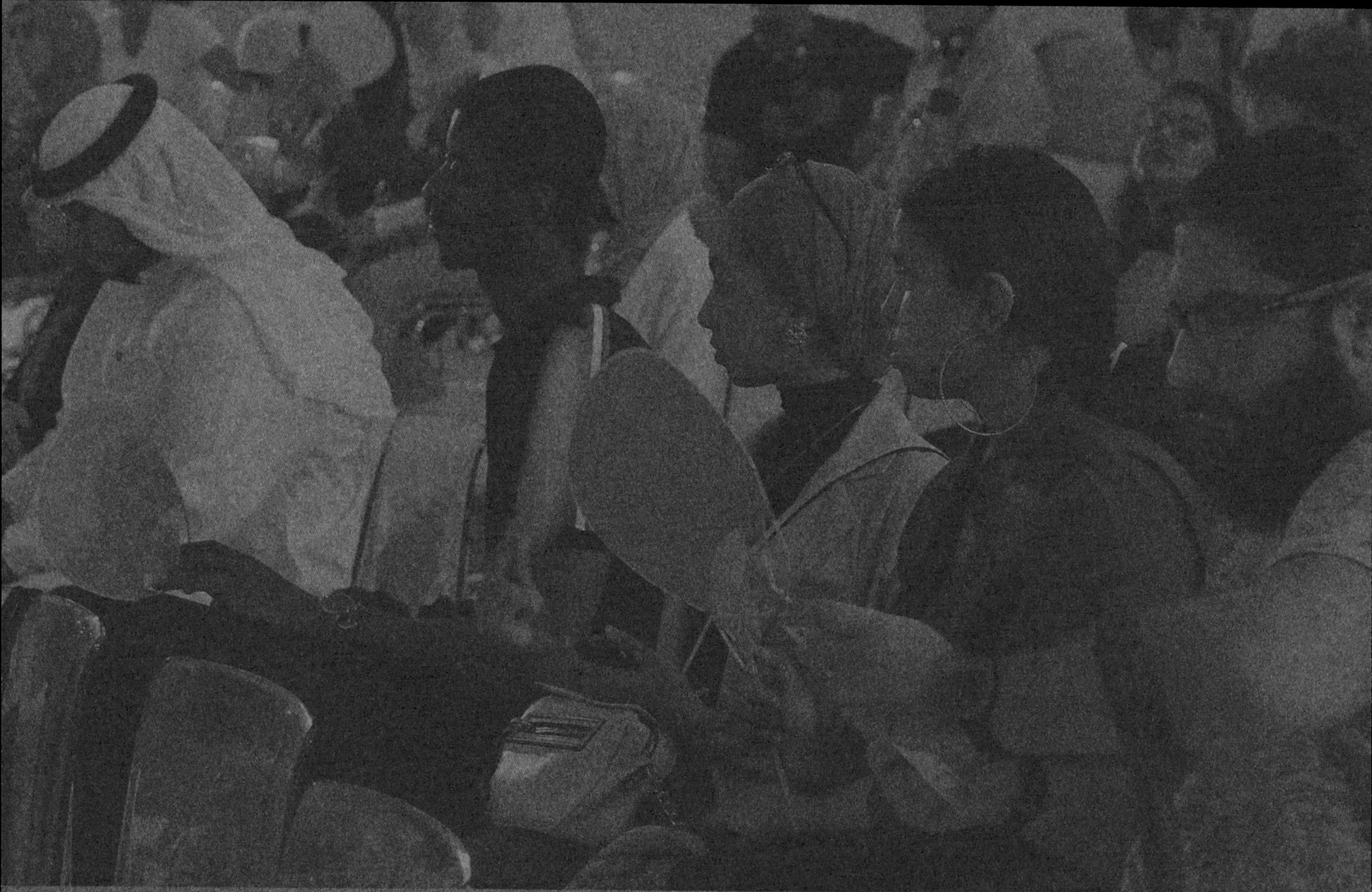

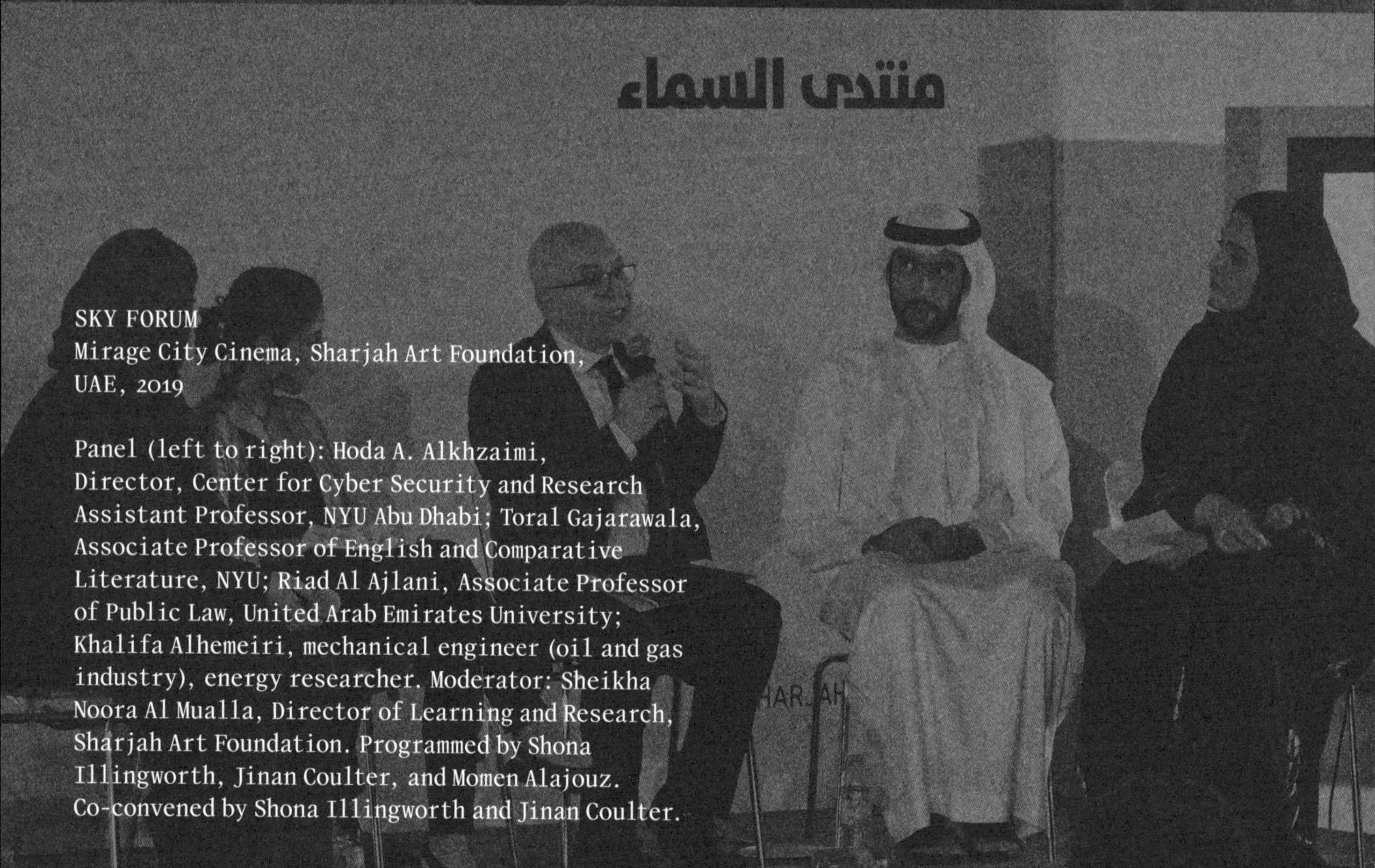

SKY FORUM
Mirage City Cinema, Sharjah Art Foundation, UAE, 2019

Panel (left to right): Hoda A. Alkhzaimi, Director, Center for Cyber Security and Research Assistant Professor, NYU Abu Dhabi; Toral Gajarawala, Associate Professor of English and Comparative Literature, NYU; Riad Al Ajlani, Associate Professor of Public Law, United Arab Emirates University; Khalifa Alhemeiri, mechanical engineer (oil and gas industry), energy researcher. Moderator: Sheikha Noora Al Mualla, Director of Learning and Research, Sharjah Art Foundation. Programmed by Shona Illingworth, Jinan Coulter, and Momen Alajouz. Co-convened by Shona Illingworth and Jinan Coulter.

Topo

ogies

Air

TOPOLOGIES OF AIR
2021

Three-screen video and multichannel sound installation
45 mins

Topologies of Air examines how the rapid colonization of airspace and outer space intersects with the existential threats of climate change, pollution, and planetary destruction. Filmed in different parts of the world, including voices from the Airspace Tribunal hearings, recorded conversations and Sky forums, and utilizing archive film as source material, the project examines the accelerating military and commercial exploitation of airspace and outer space. Investigating how humans have radically transformed the sky into a source of existential planetary threat, *Topologies of Air* maps an ever-more complex, weaponized, and instrumentalized space of surveillance and never-ending war.

Extracts from the transcript of the work are included here on pages 148–207.

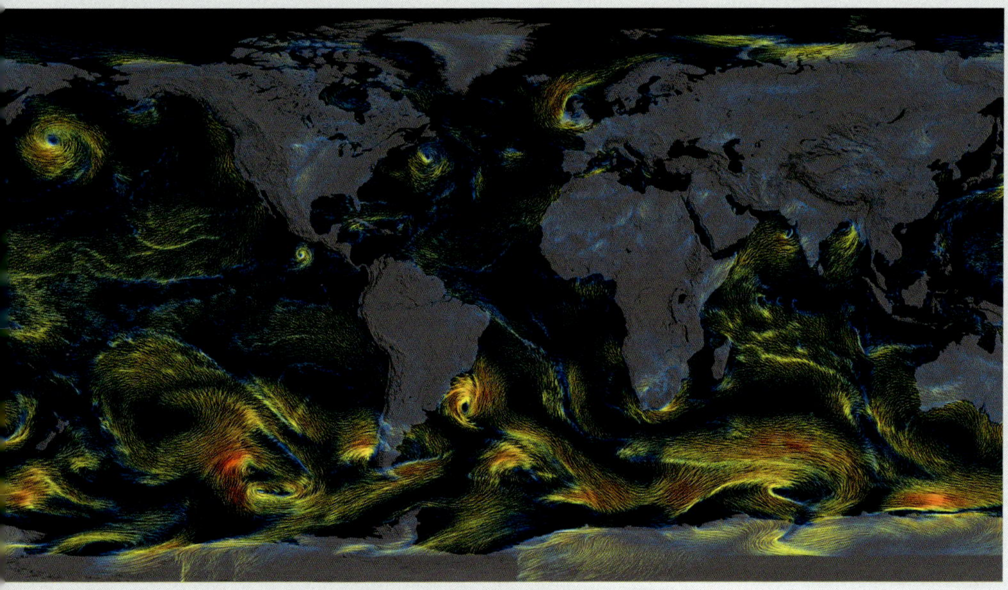

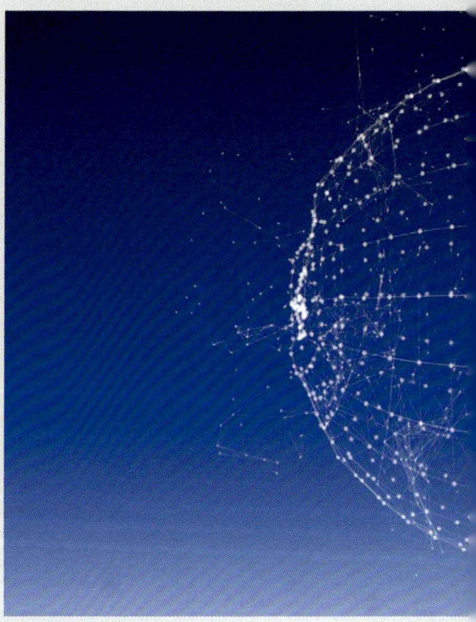

The sun
Sends this solar wind
A huge amount of these highly charged particles

And they may disturb
This upper atmosphere
So if you send a signal through this upper atmosphere
The signals cannot pass through
Or it can be absorbed
Or it can be refracted
That's why our atmosphere
Is not stable

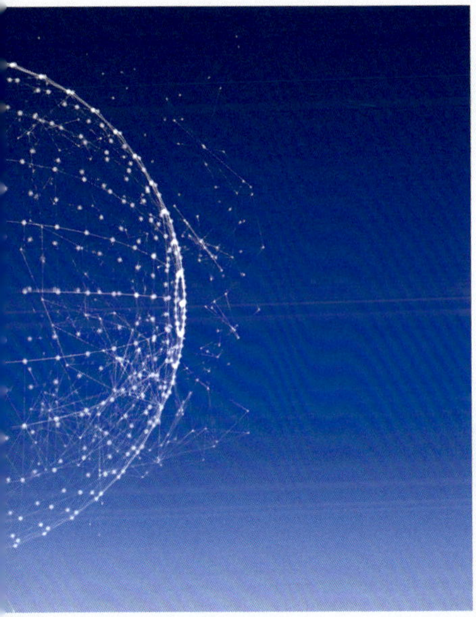

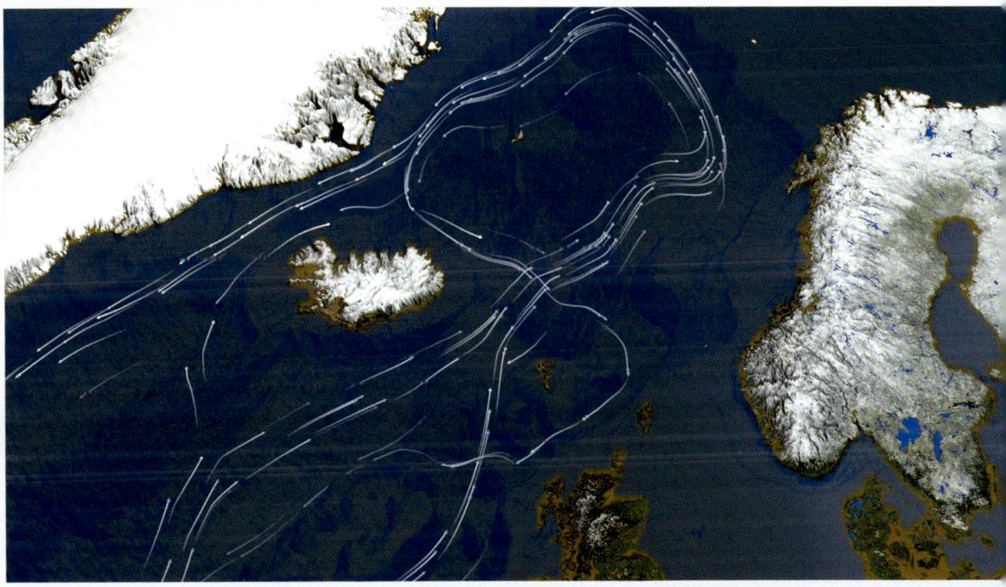

Space is not regulated and does not belong to the country
Above which it sits
As is the airspace
To me it means that it's an open space for information collection

The single ecosystem, which the earth is
And the single population of people
Doing terrible things not only to the environment but to each other
I think we need an examination tool

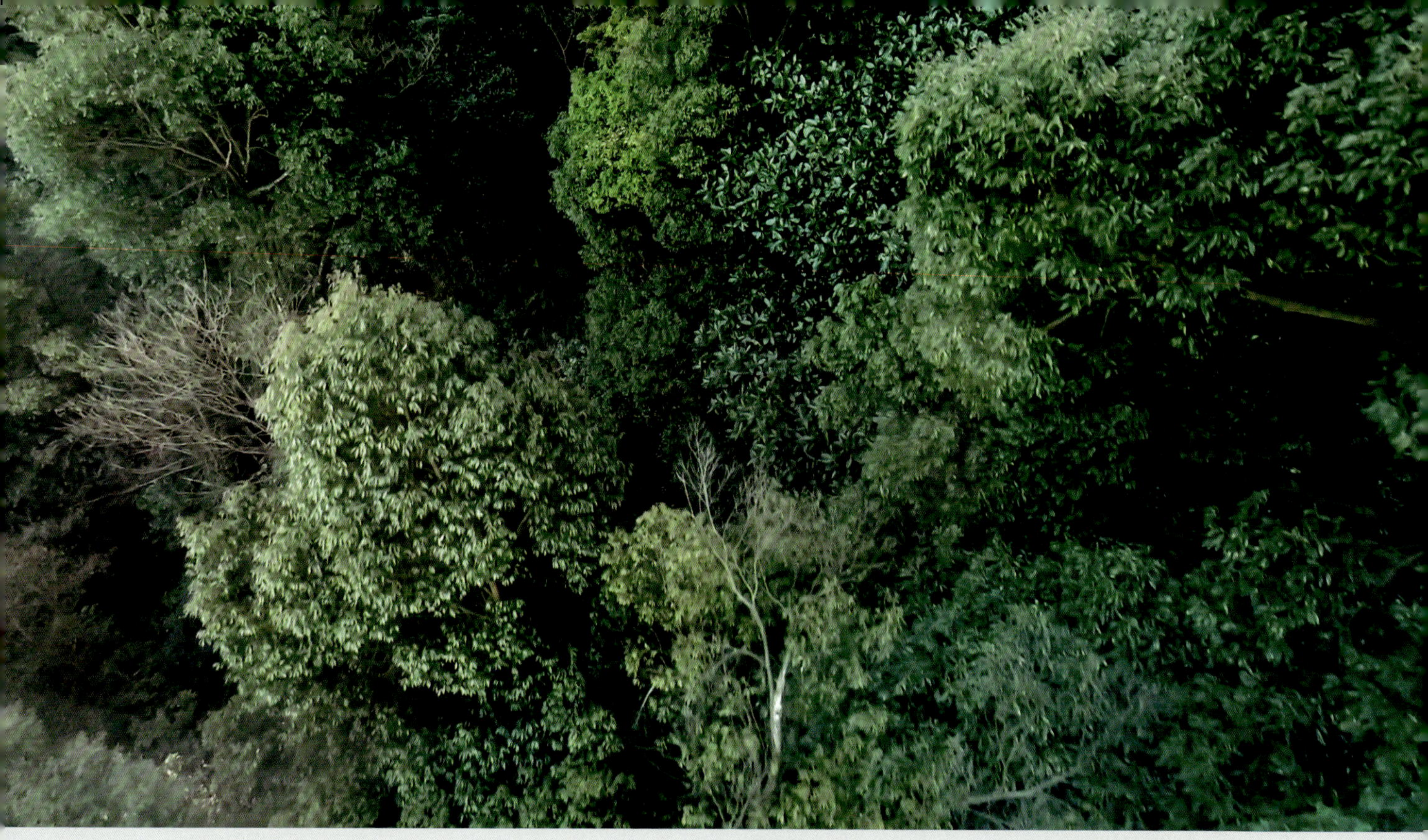

The understanding in progress of human life
For example, the understanding of the earth's system

Climate change, sea-level rise
Absolutely rely on access from above and the view from above

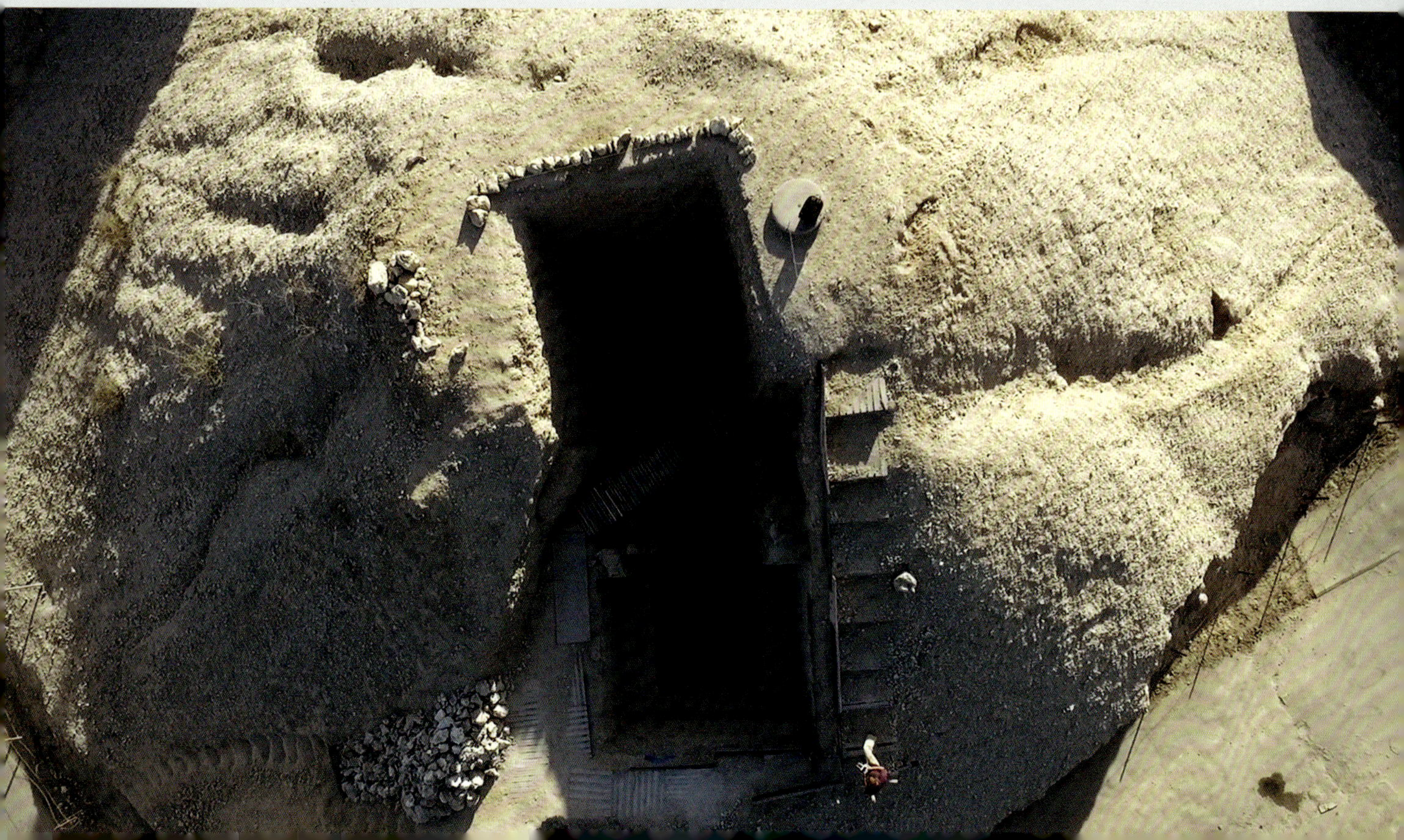

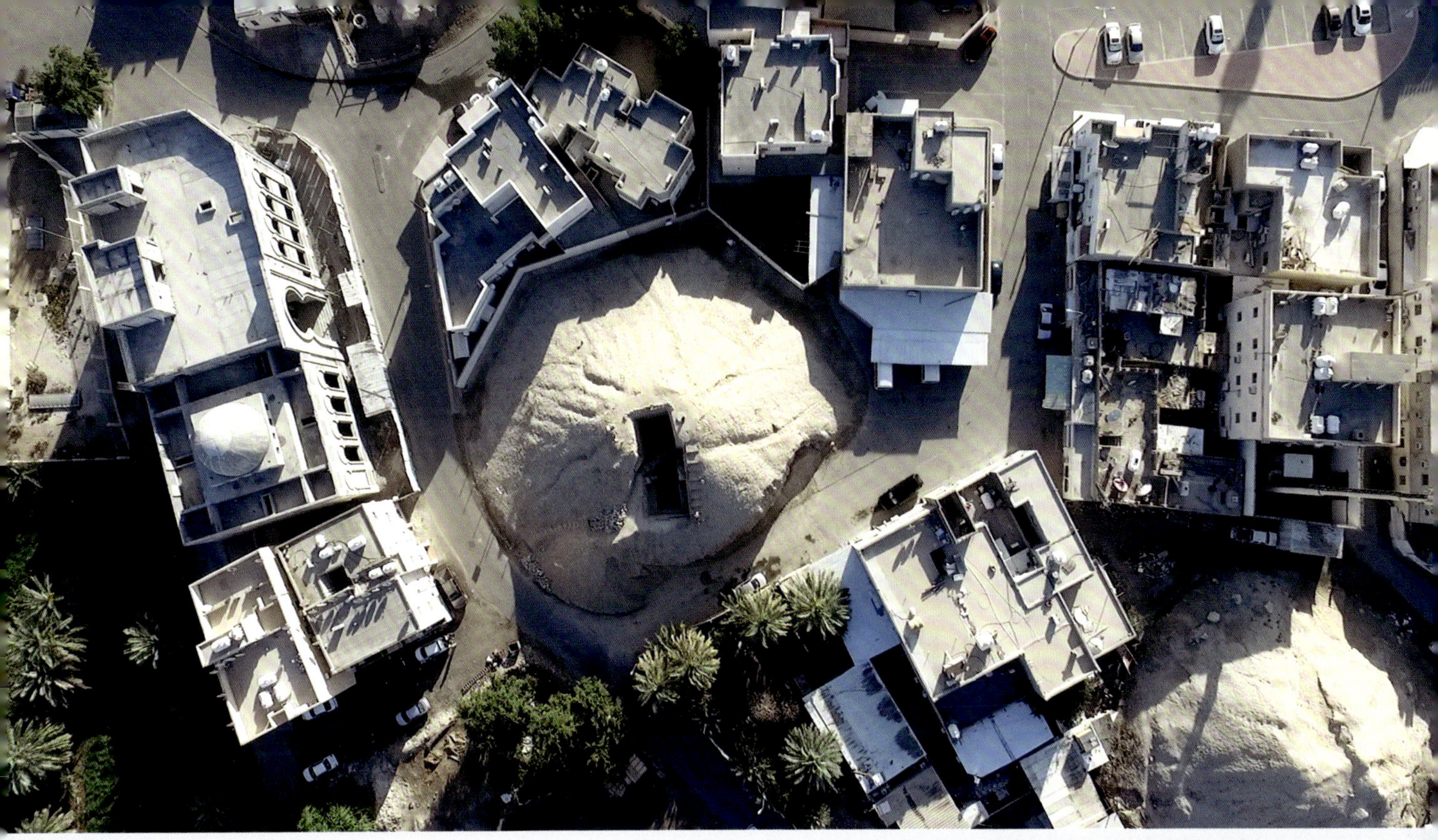

All these processes we are documenting from above
At different spatial and also temporal scales
Related to deforestation, illegal mining, agricultural activities, soil, coastal erosion, human-trafficking

But also urban planning, infrastructure assessments
That we actually use aerial technology now for
Terrestrial mapping of various manmade and natural ecosystems
All rely on access from above

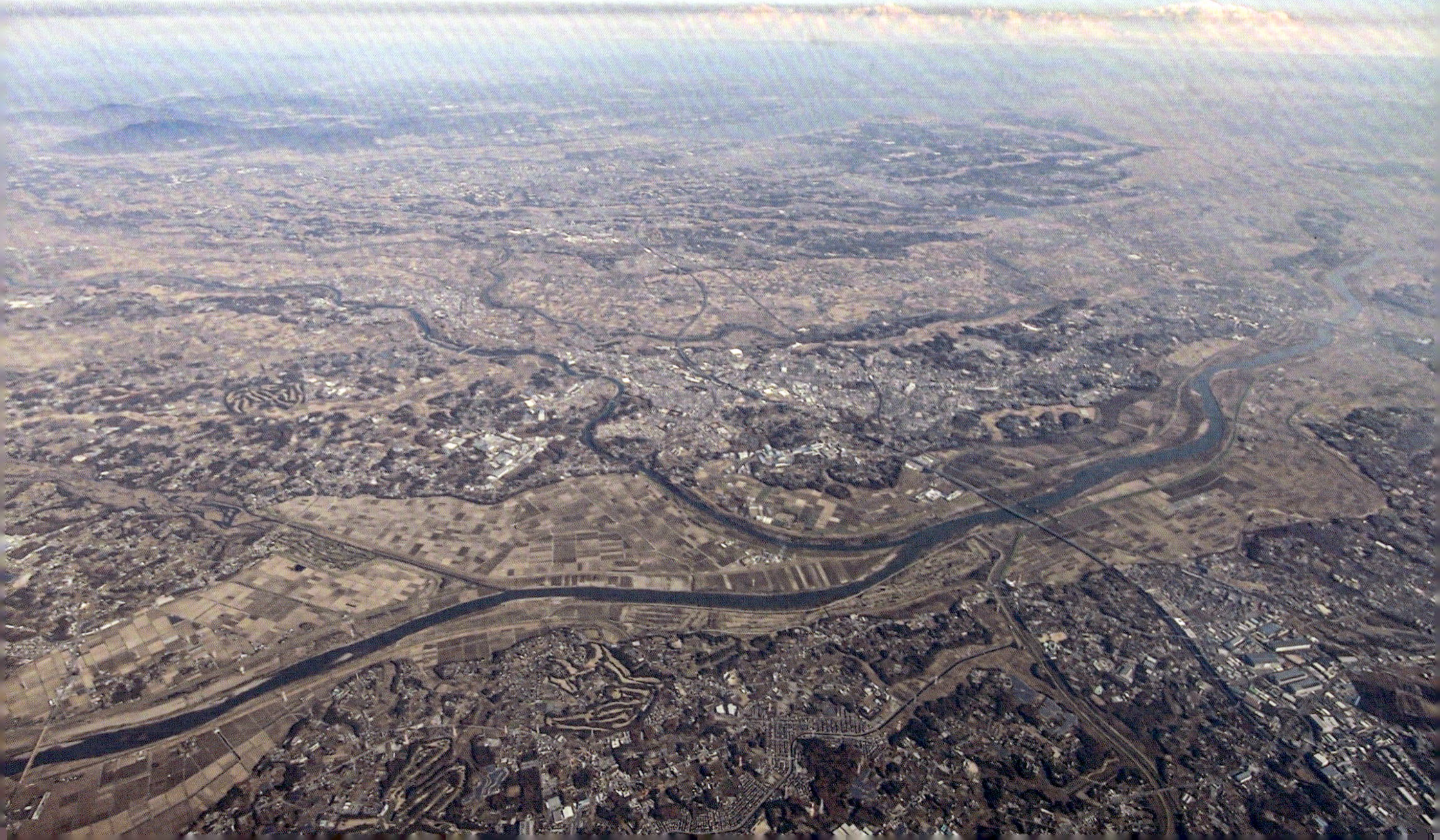

The electromagnetic spectrum
On which satellites most use to function
Is absolutely not a commons

In terms of the kind of optical regime
Where there's a kind of asymmetry of power
And an asymmetry of access to satellite information
That's intelligence, surveillance, and reconnaissance,
Which is absolutely integral
To contemporary air-dominated campaigns

That kind of intelligence
That is gathered through drone feeds and satellite imagery
Is what will then determine
If the strike takes place or not

So that kind of asymmetry of power
Is shifting even further
Toward governments and for-profit companies
Being those who have the commanding aerial perspective

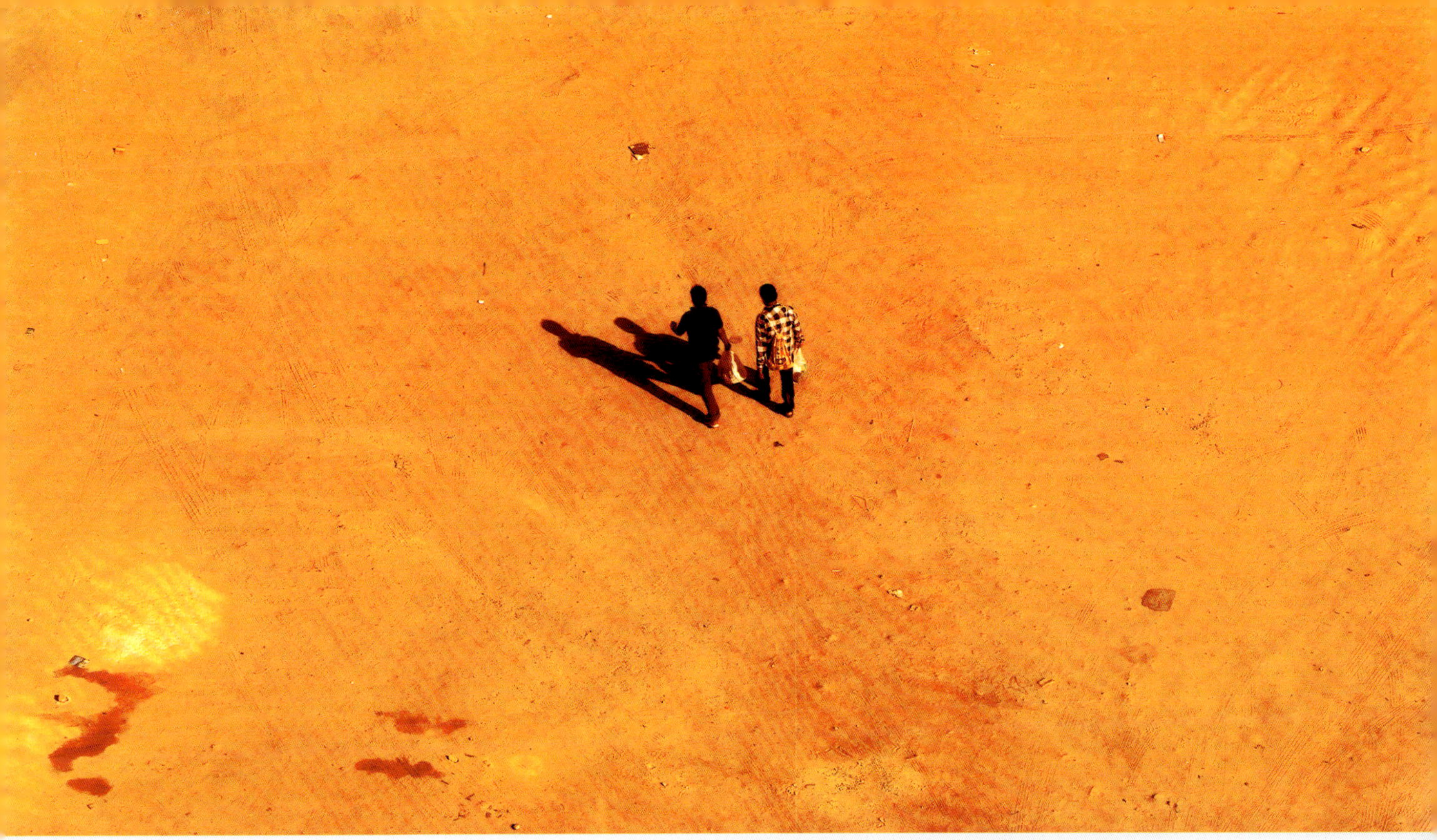

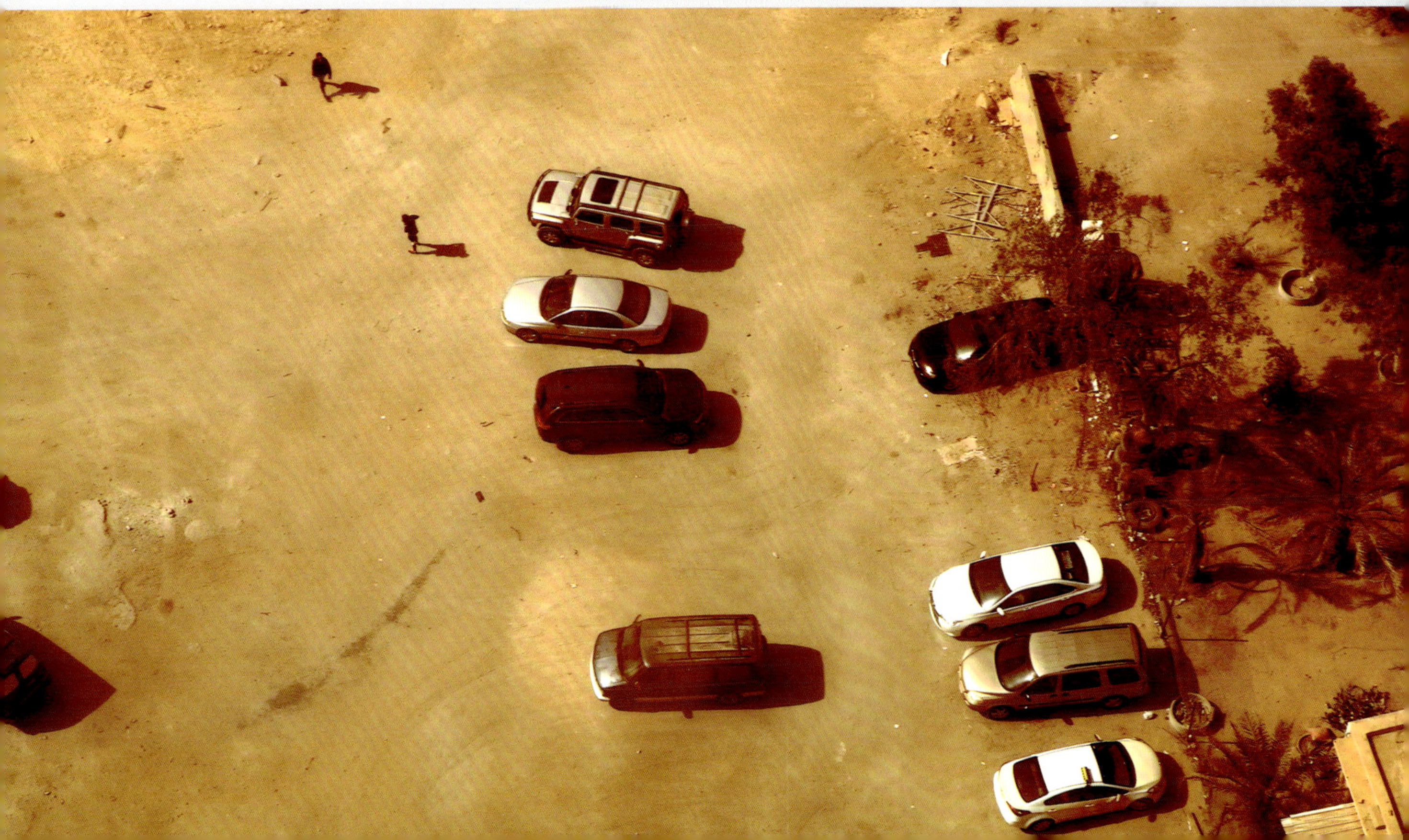

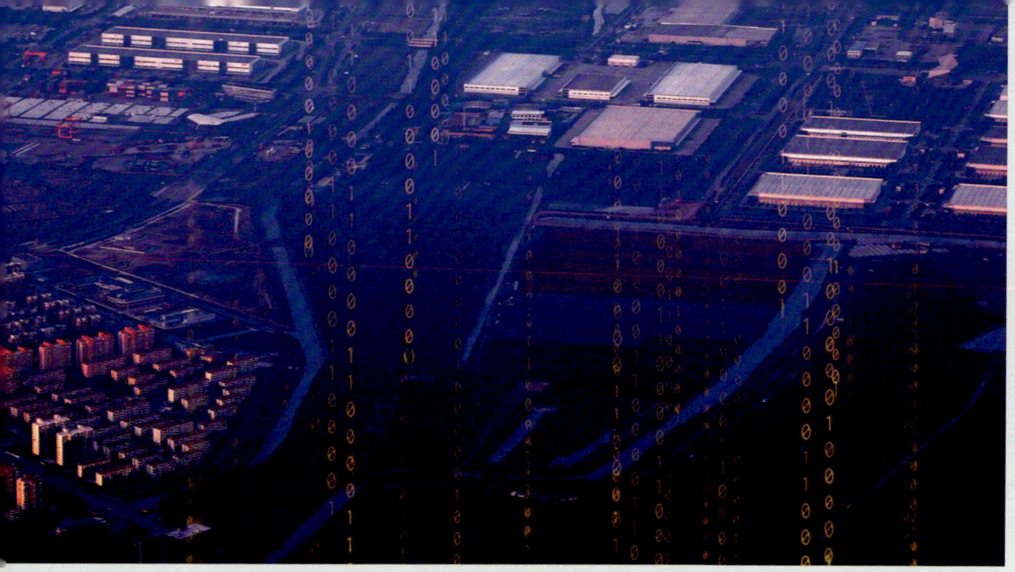

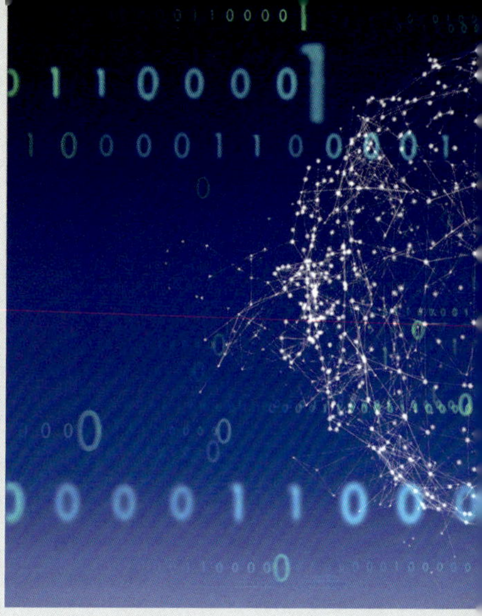

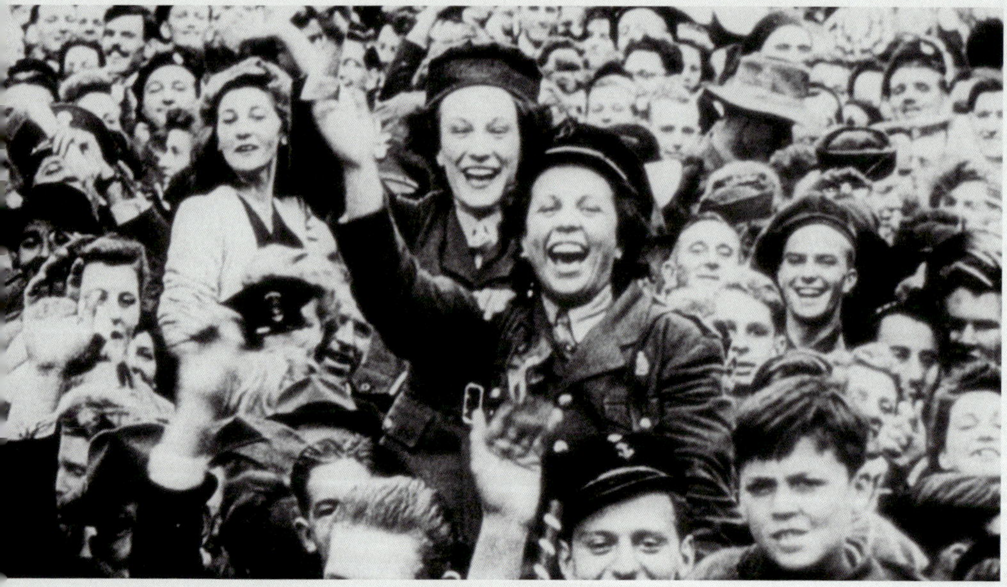

We're in very grave and serious times
Where potentially the destruction
of the planet
Is one of the things now on the list
that are concerns because of
what now is above our heads

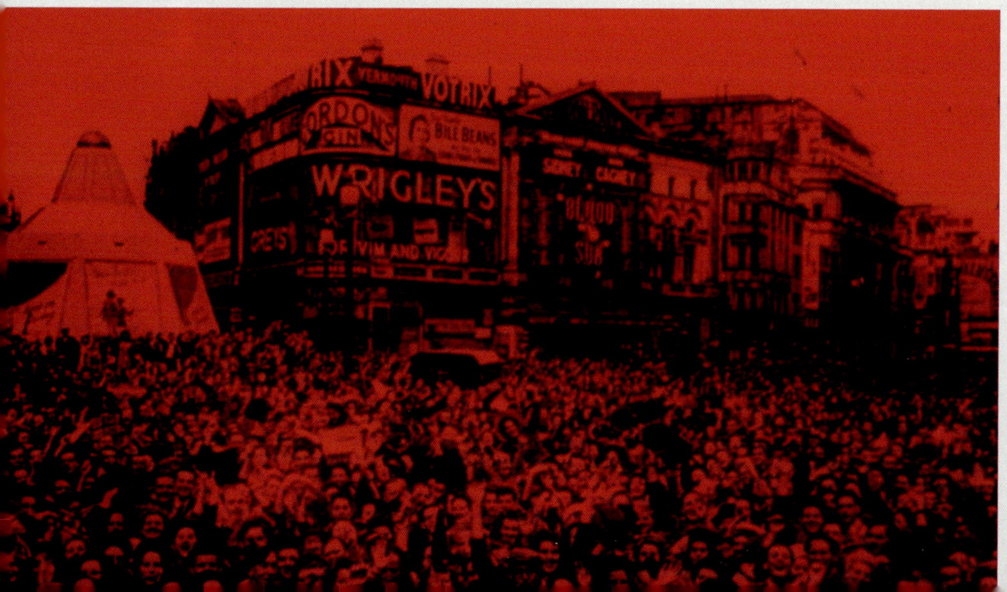

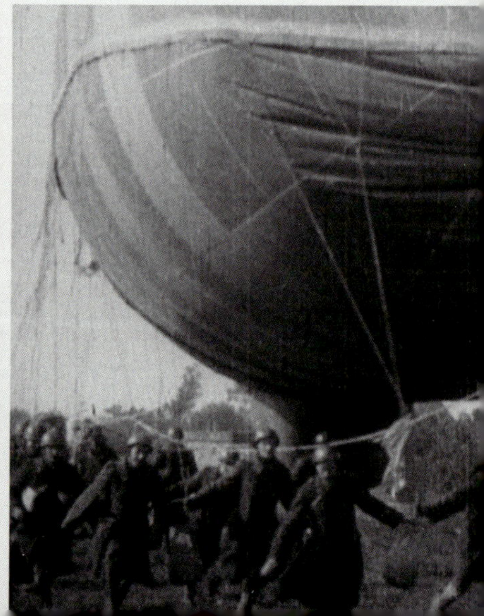

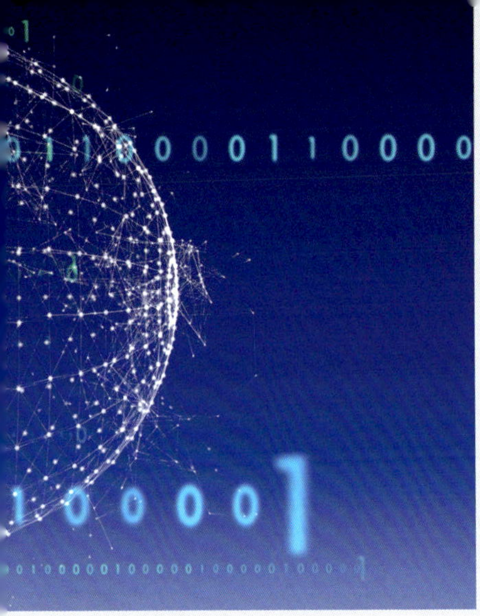

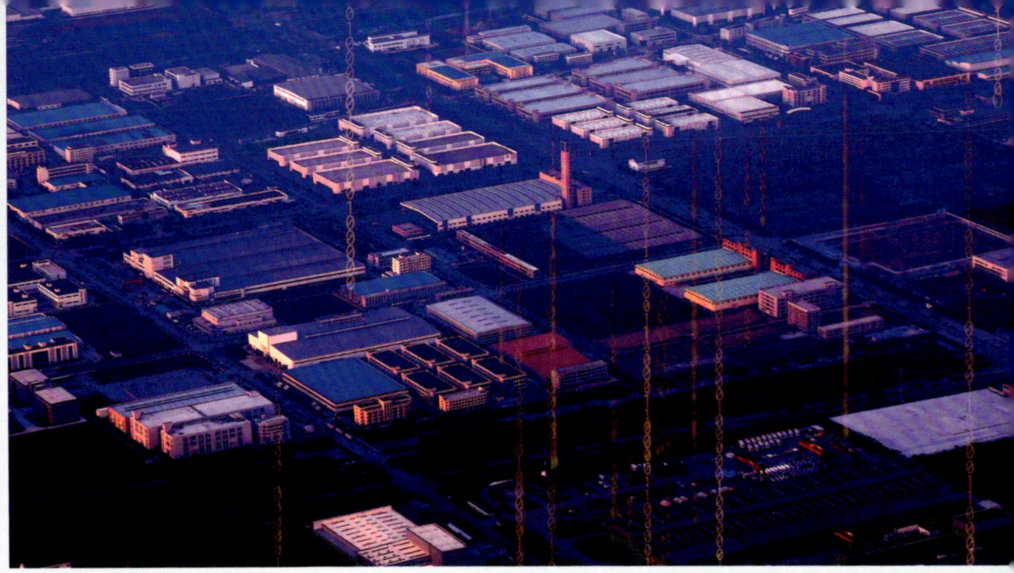

What people saw as they stood there with
upturned faces
Was not merely a new means of transport
In the ability to fly, they saw a sign of human perfection,
And they received it with almost religious ecstasy

Flight seemed to be a step into a new element,
a new world
People spoke of the "aerial age"
And felt that we had now left behind
Our earlier earthbound existence
And were launched into a new way of life.

Soon human beings would be able to move freely
in three dimensions...

All good things would come with flight
Democracy – Equality – Freedom

The air was freedom's realm

Female flyers saw a great future in the air
Where old gender differences would no longer apply

When cars were replaced by planes
Black chauffeurs would train to be pilots
And soon be the leaders of the air

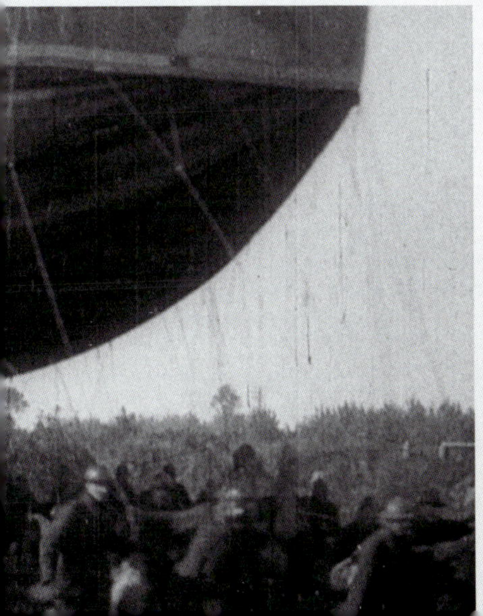

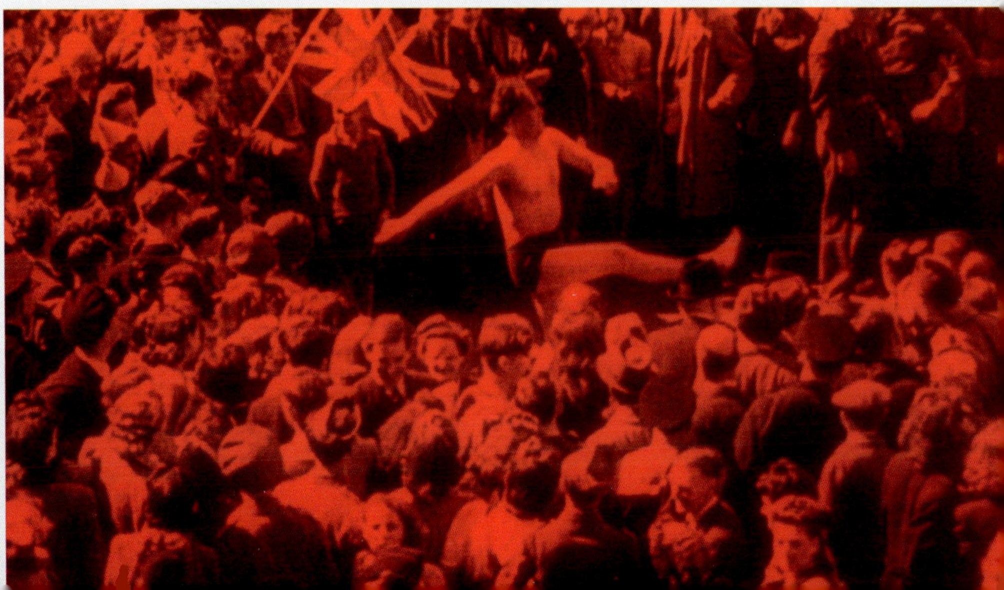

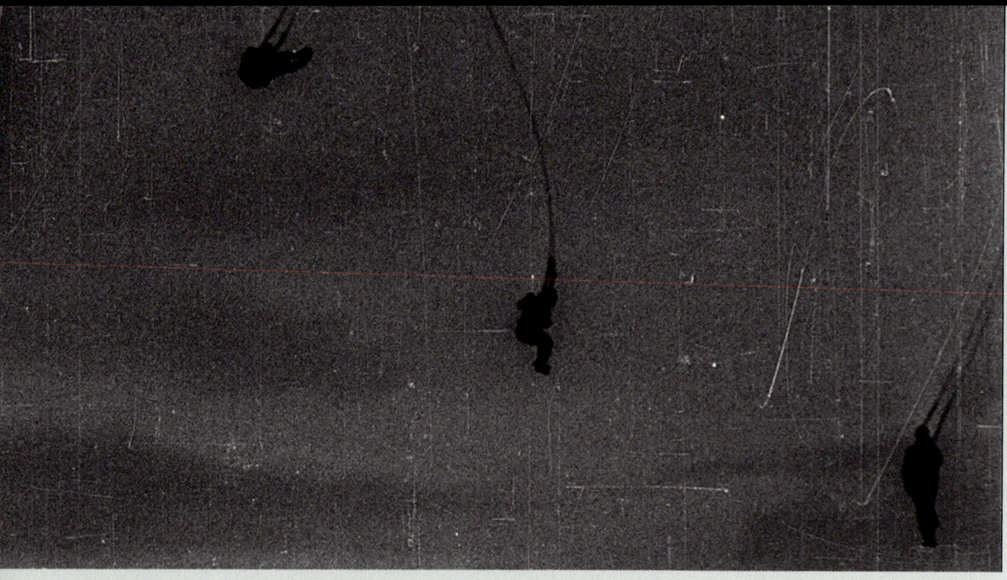

"Up, up into the pure microbe-less air
The sick and the suffering will be carried
And nursed back to health
In private sanatoria
And state and municipal air hospitals"

Flight would lift humankind from the filth of the earth
And create a new life form
The alti-man,
Who would be born in the air
And live his whole life up there

The alti-man
Would conquer all the limitations of the earth
And become an angel
Or a god

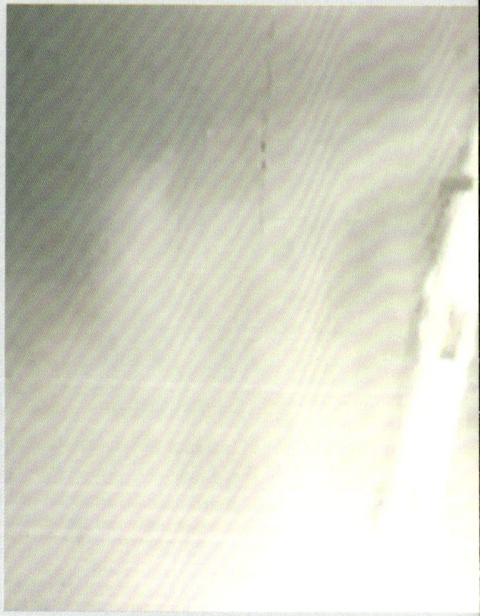

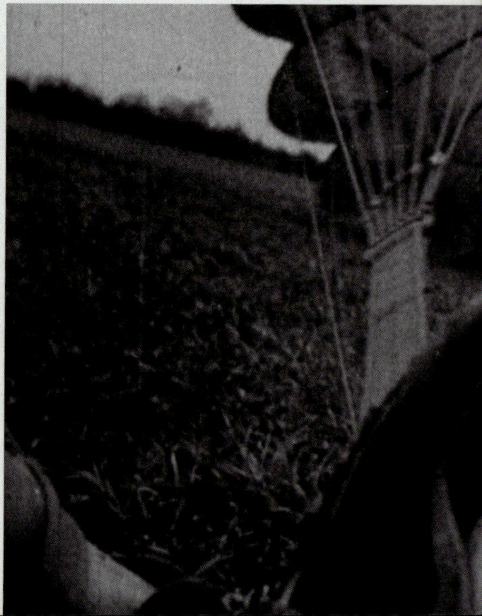

Forty seconds into the flight, Discovery*'s engines are now throttling down to 70 percent of graded frost as it passes through the area of maximum aerodynamic pressure we are already at an altitude of five-and-a-half miles*

10 9 8 7 6

Discovery

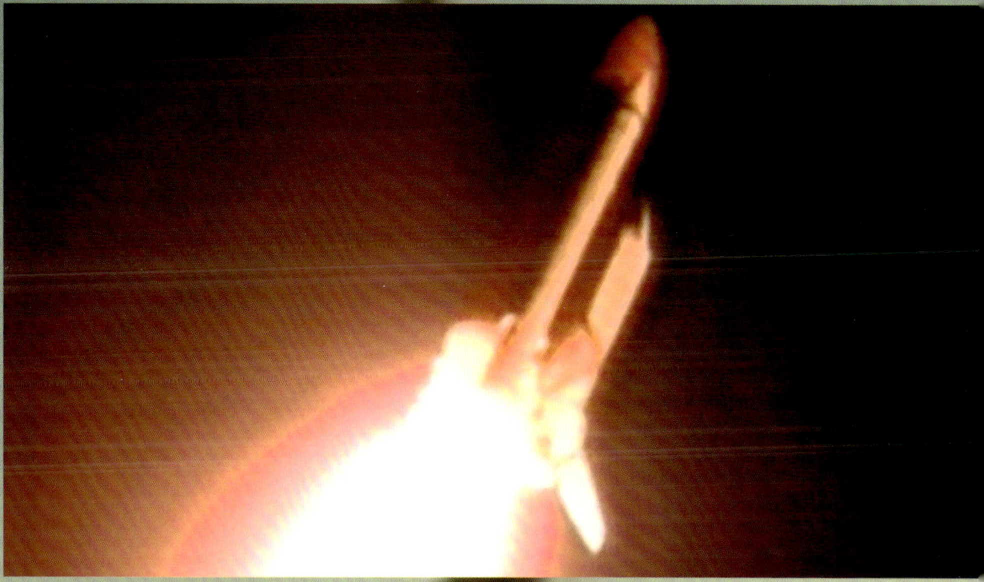

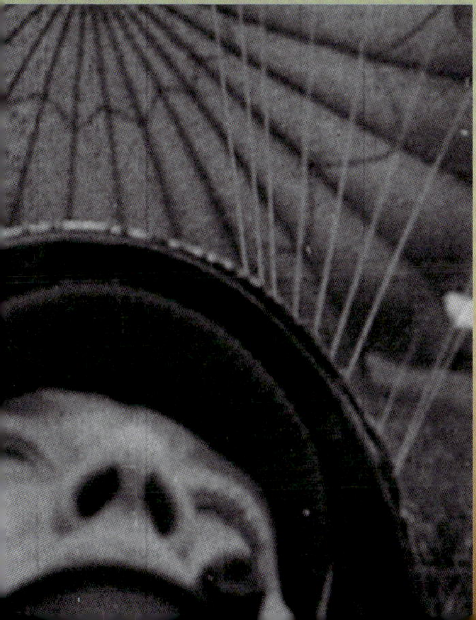

Discovery *has now expended two-and-a-half-million pounds of propellant*
November 22, 1972 0017 GMT Lift Off
Dix Neuf Huit Sept Six Cinq Quatre Trois Deux

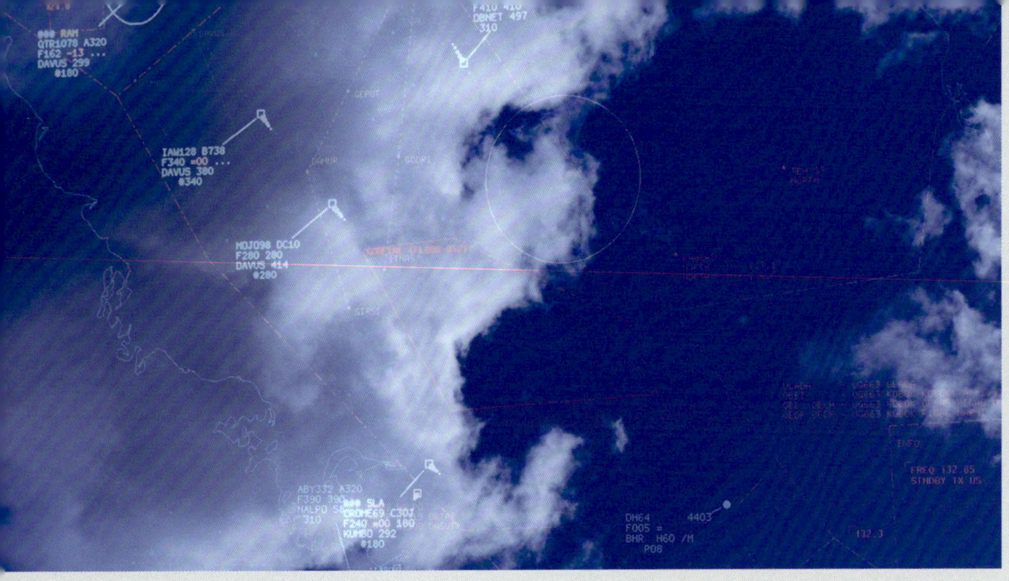

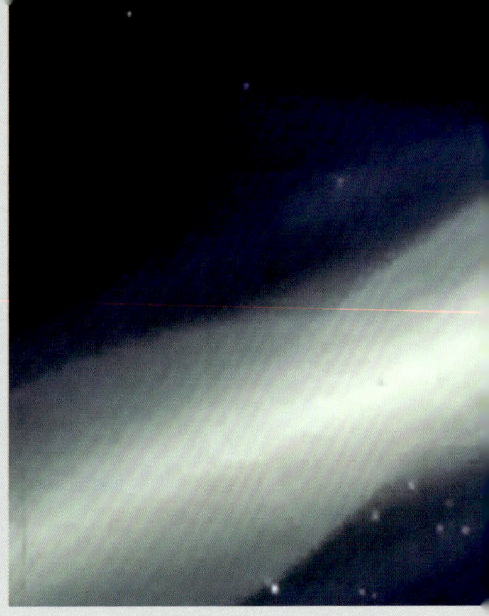

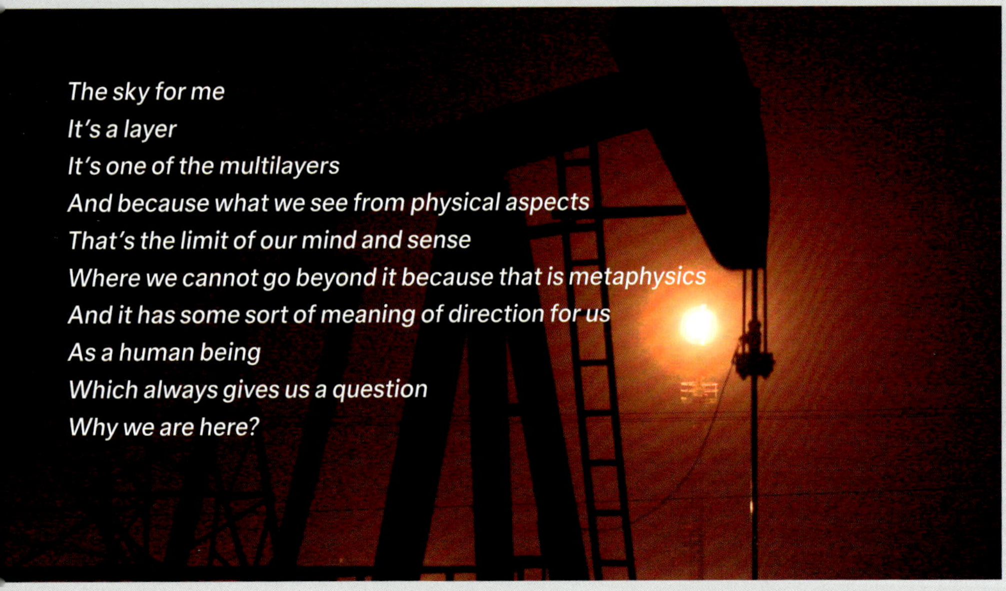

The sky for me
It's a layer
It's one of the multilayers
And because what we see from physical aspects
That's the limit of our mind and sense
Where we cannot go beyond it because that is metaphysics
And it has some sort of meaning of direction for us
As a human being
Which always gives us a question
Why we are here?

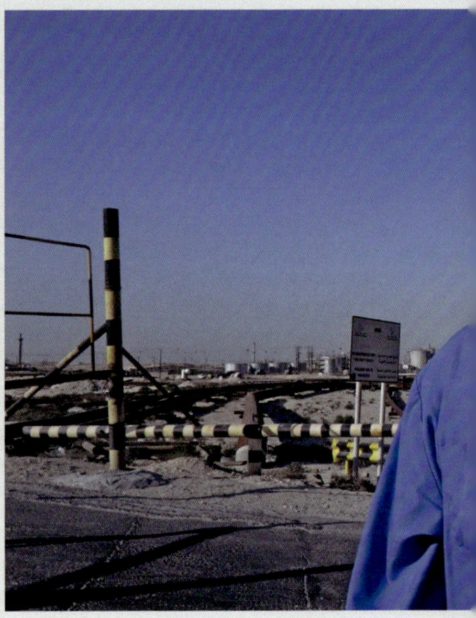

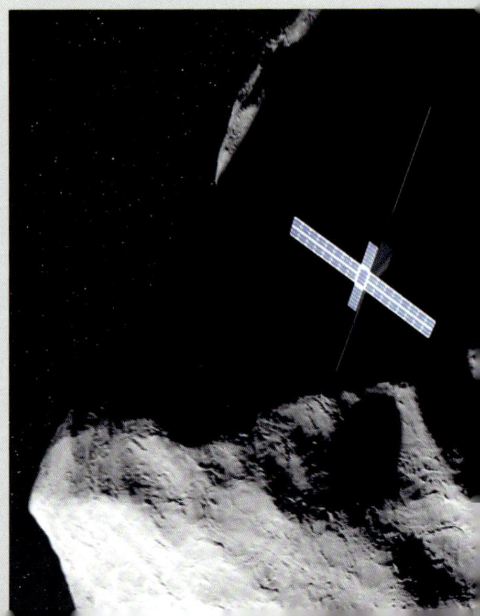

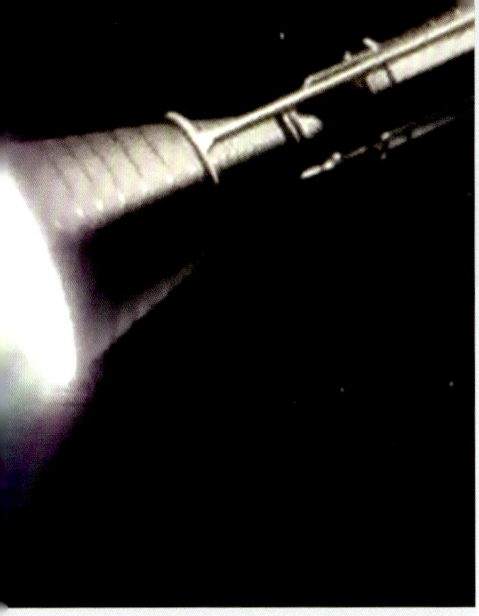

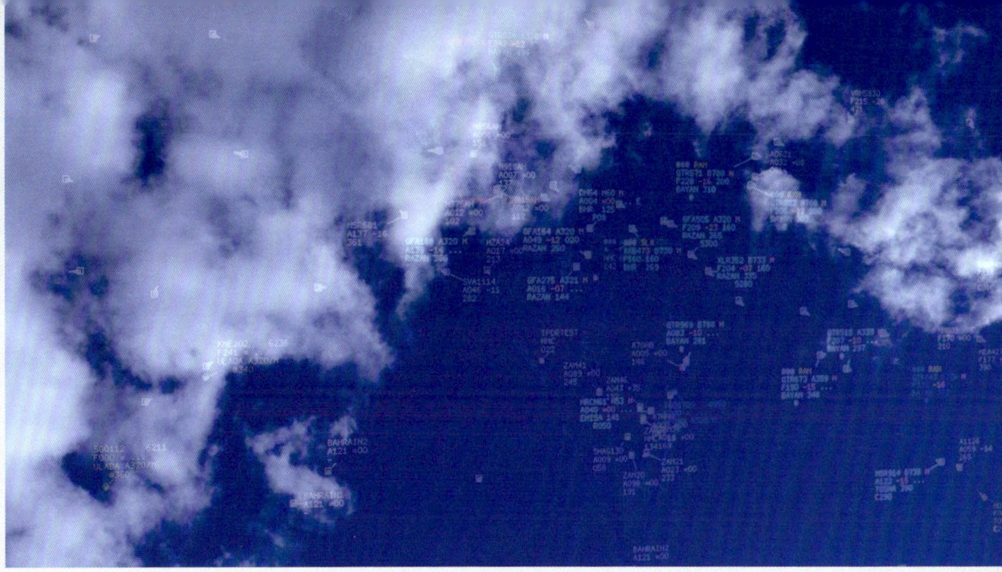

Oscar Romeo 01 77 report your flight plan
Flight level 340 11 Flight level 21...

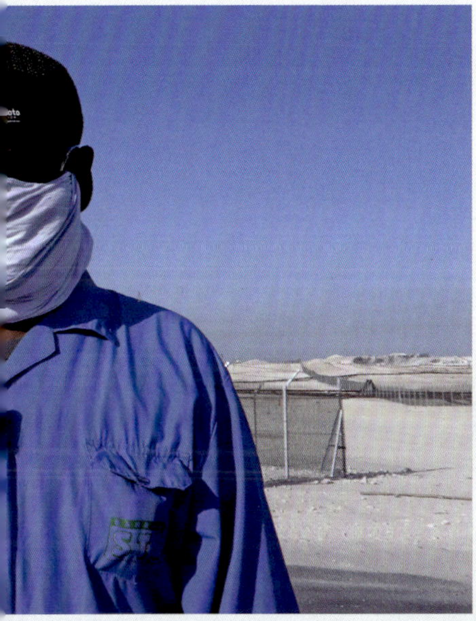

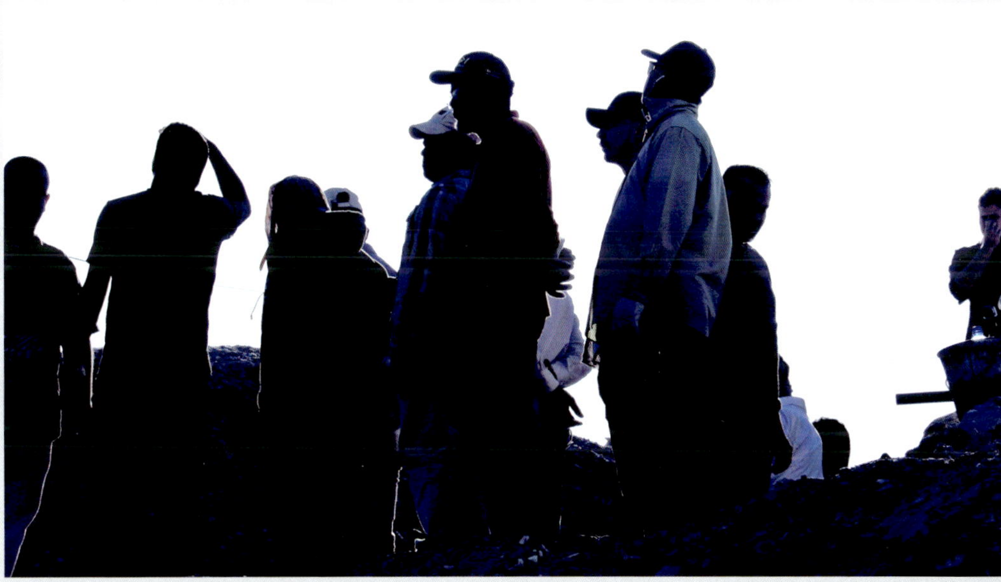

I learned the atmosphere
Had been formed on earth
And I have a great respect of this atmosphere, sky
Because it took billions of years
To give the percentage of oxygen that now we are breathing
So I want to continue to defend this blanket that we have

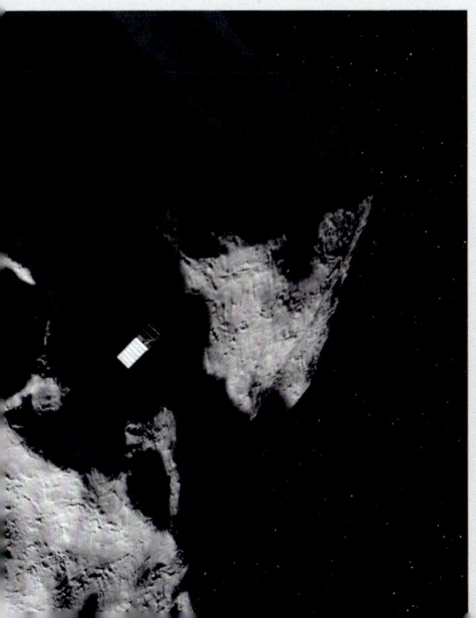

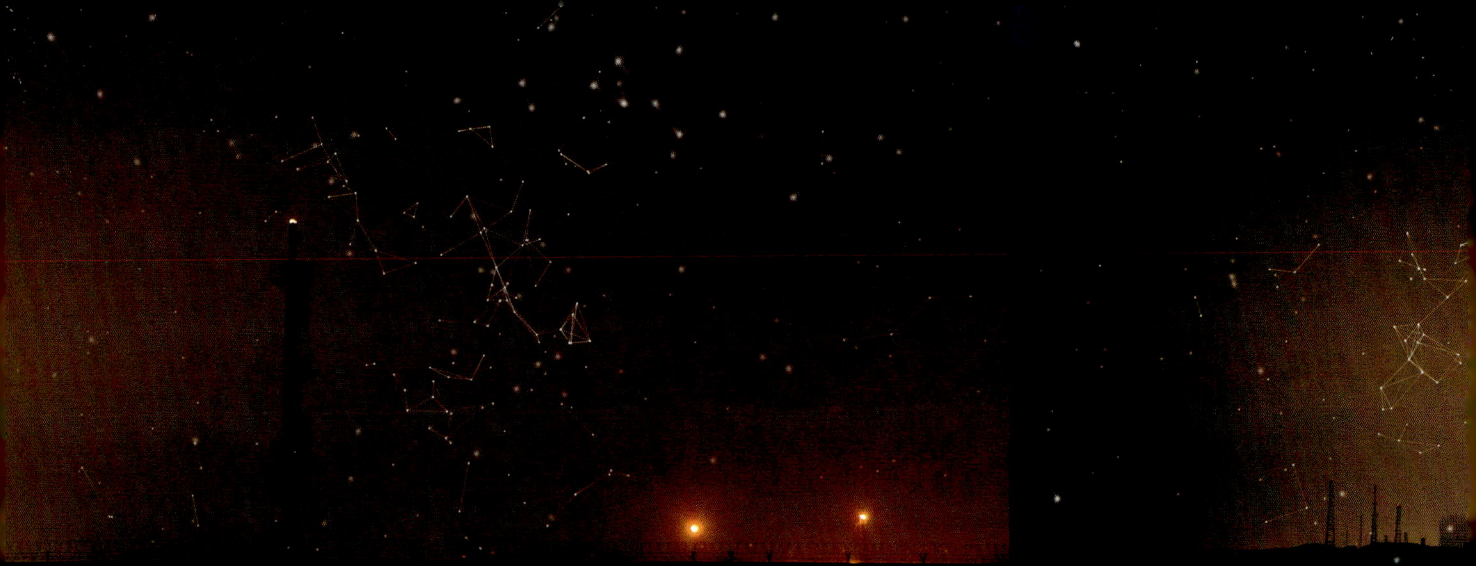

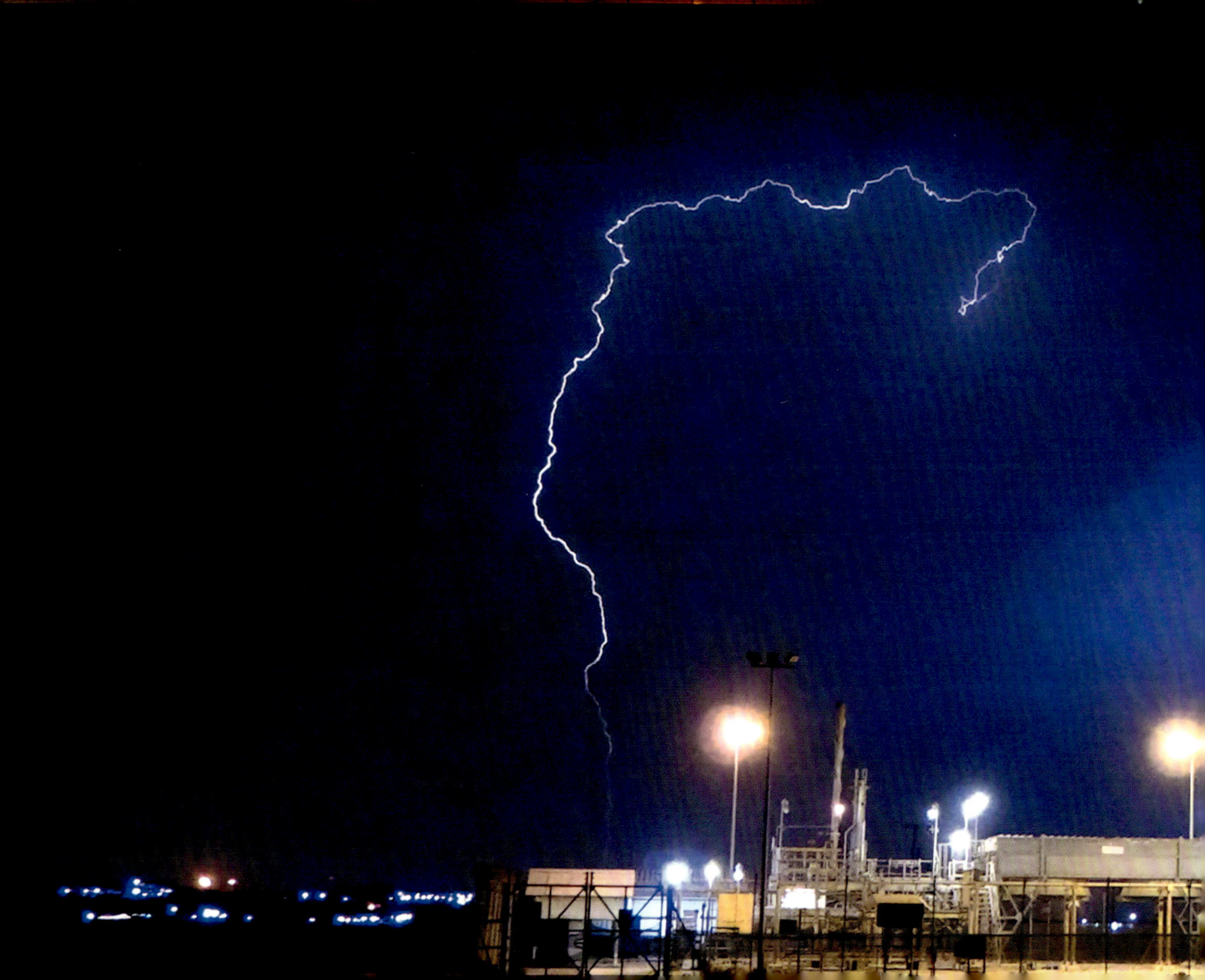

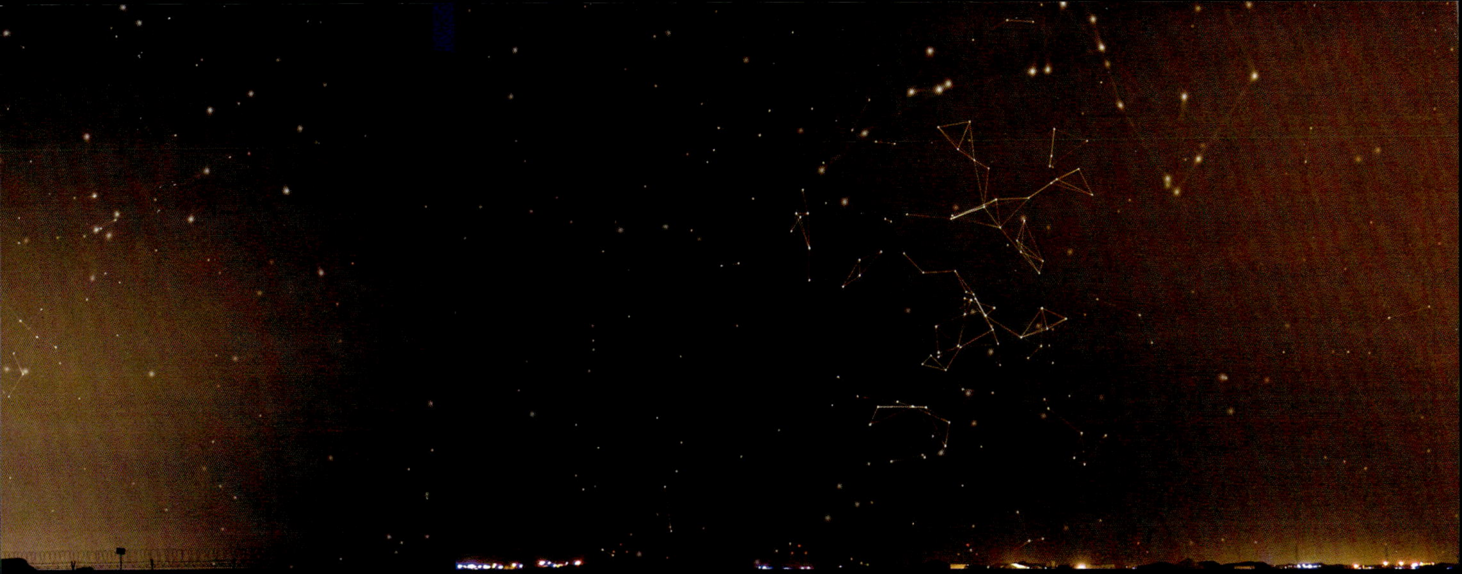

Fine particles fill the air
Radioactive materials, nutrients, and chemicals
In complex interaction across their invisible surfaces

Vast dust storms gather on land broken by war
The horizon disappears in a dense haze
Land disappears from satellite view

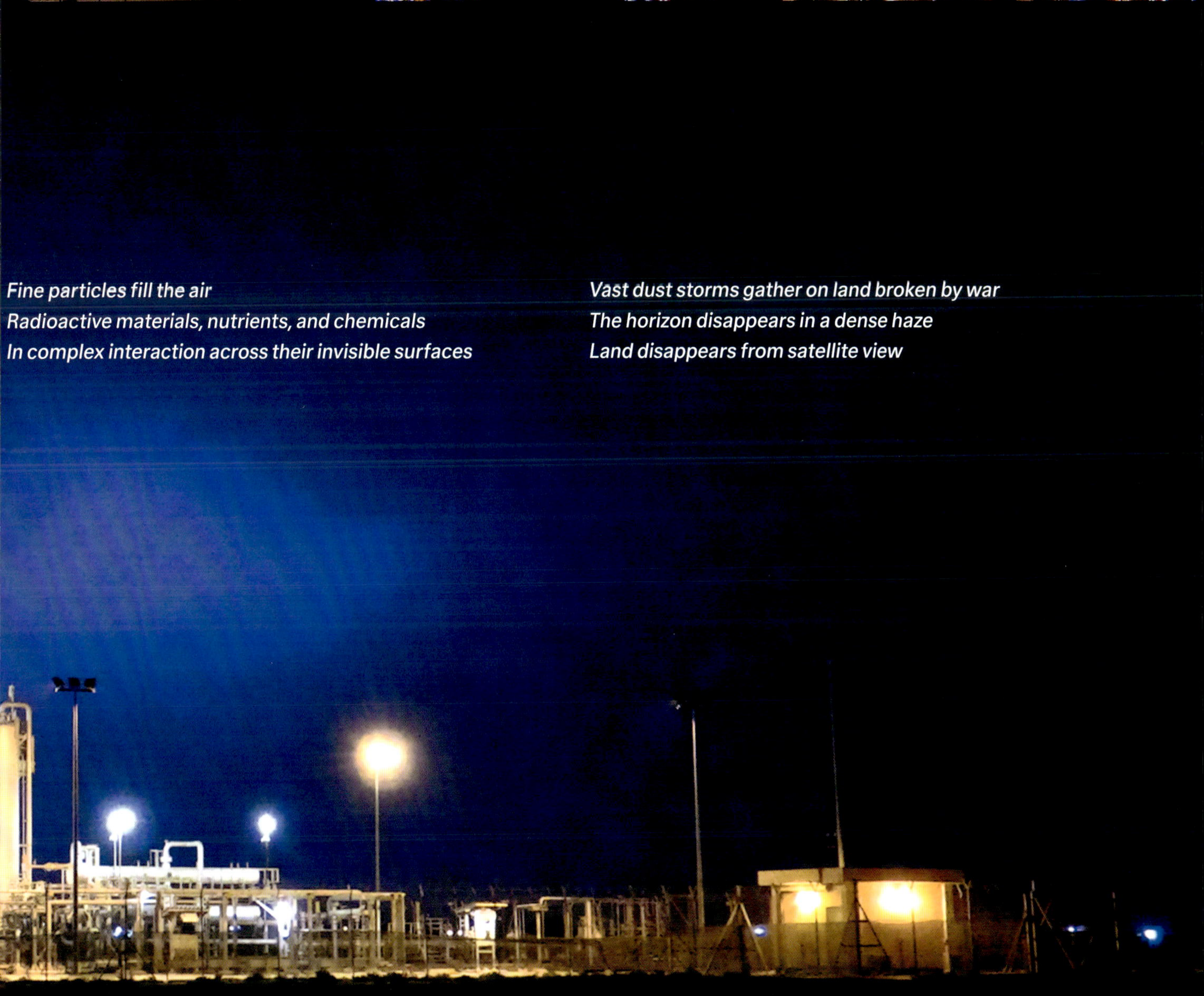

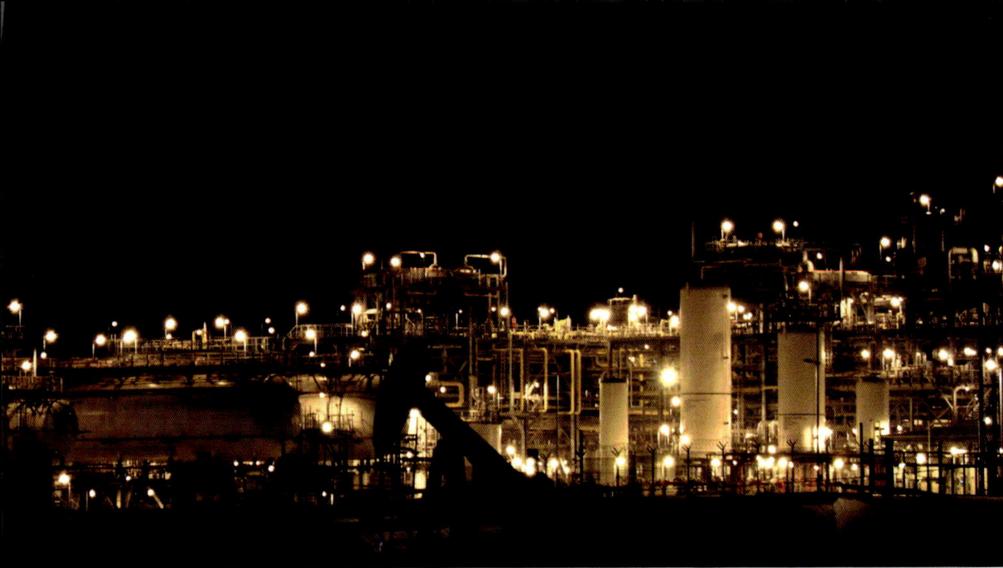

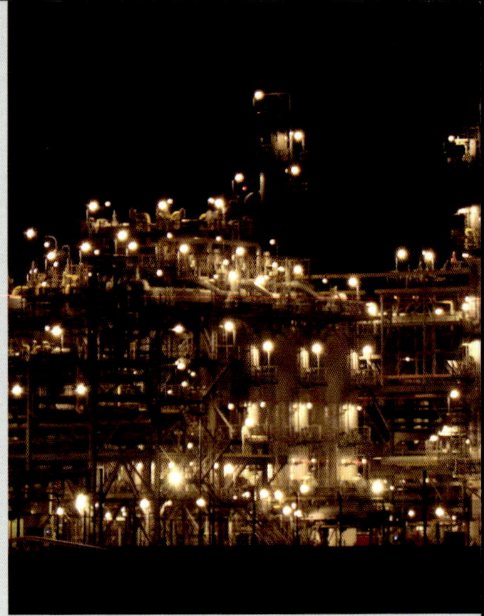

Weapons and bombs it's disturbed the nature
Those wars it's increased the storms

And the
Even some skin sickness coming

It's not usual here
It's not usual

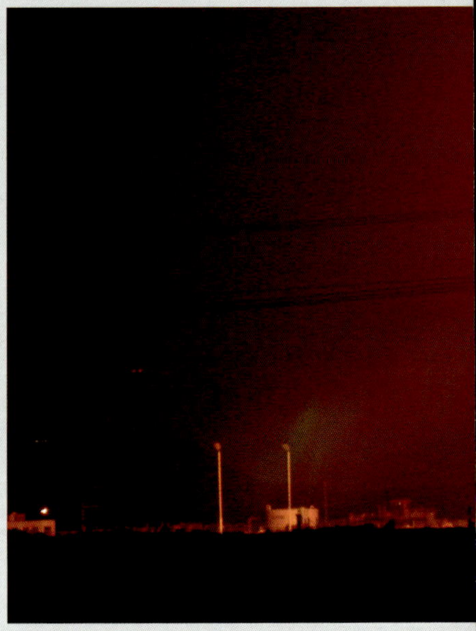

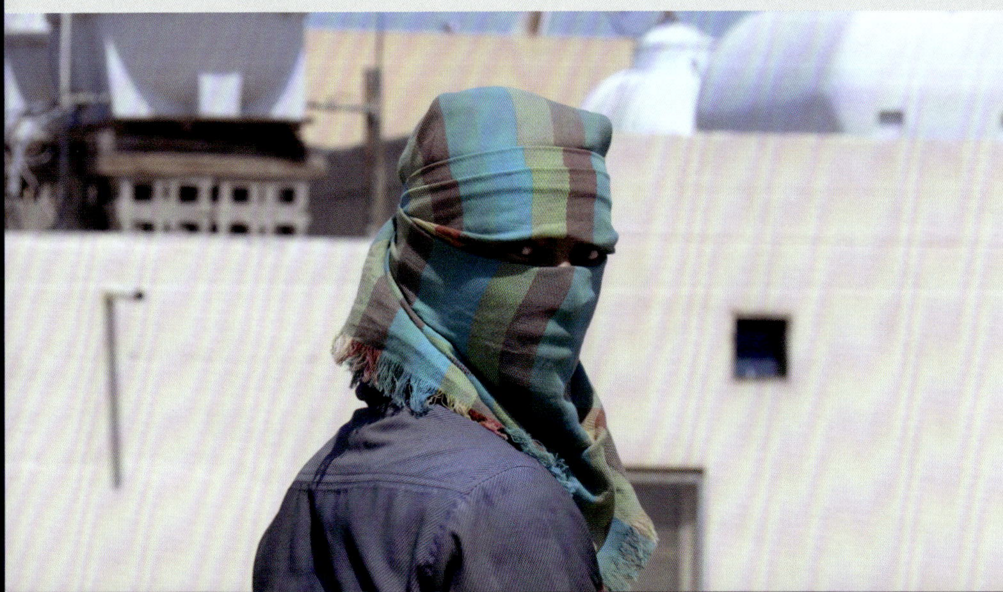

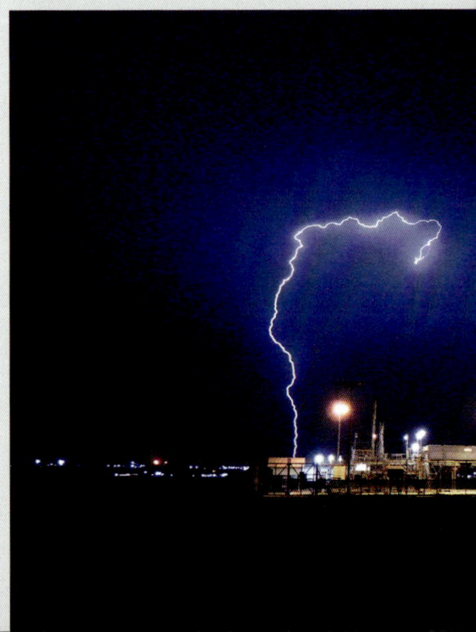

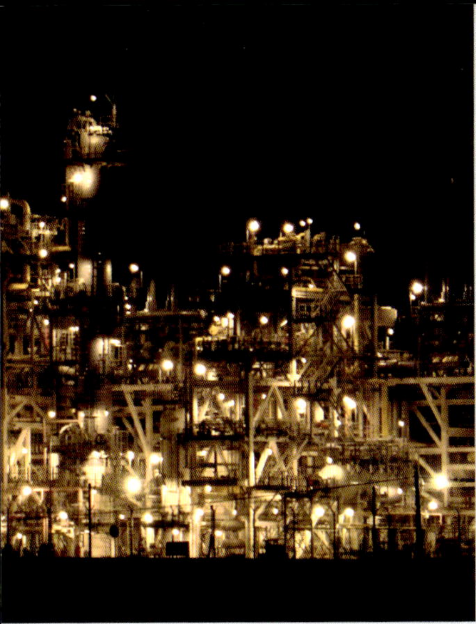
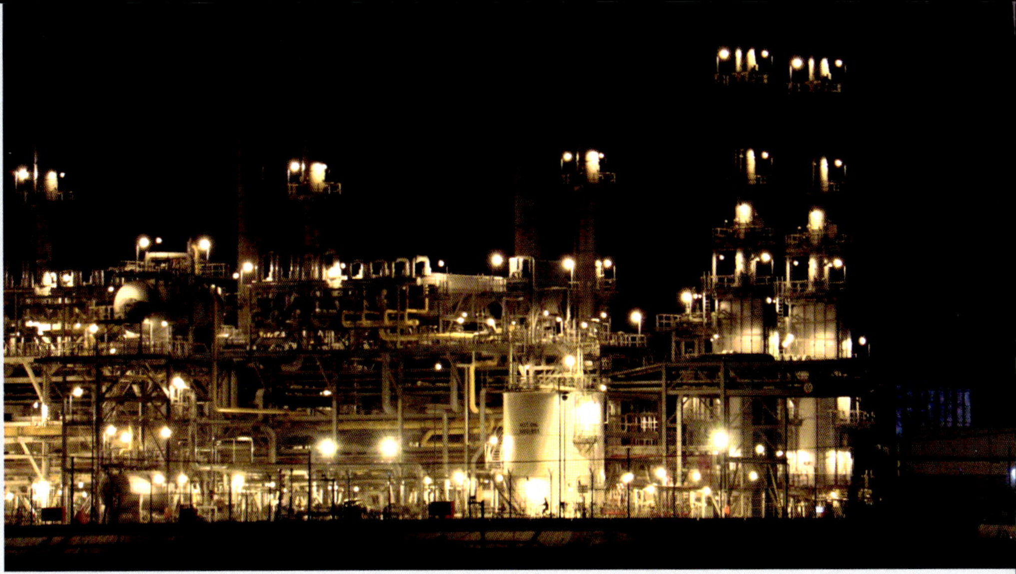
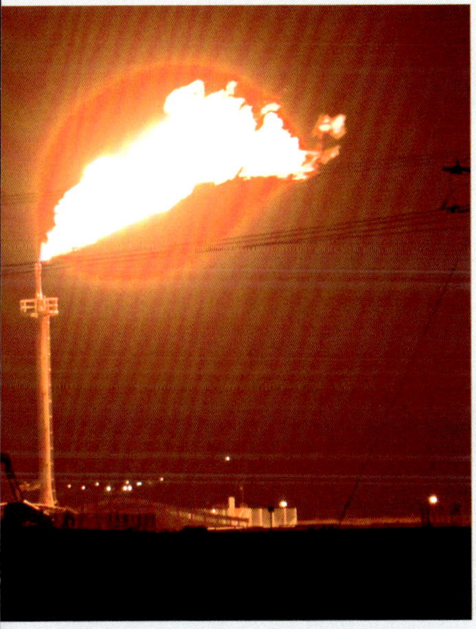

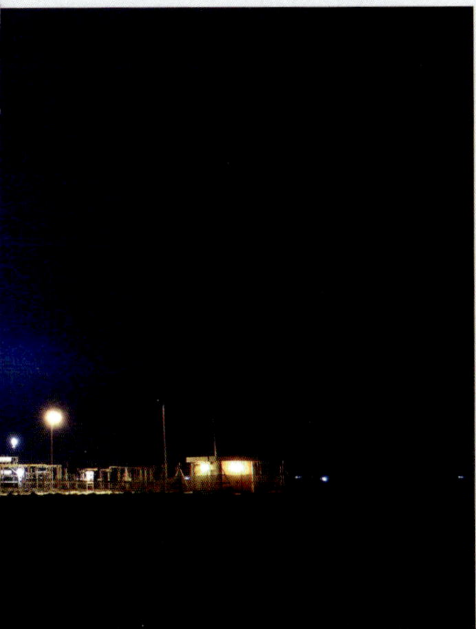
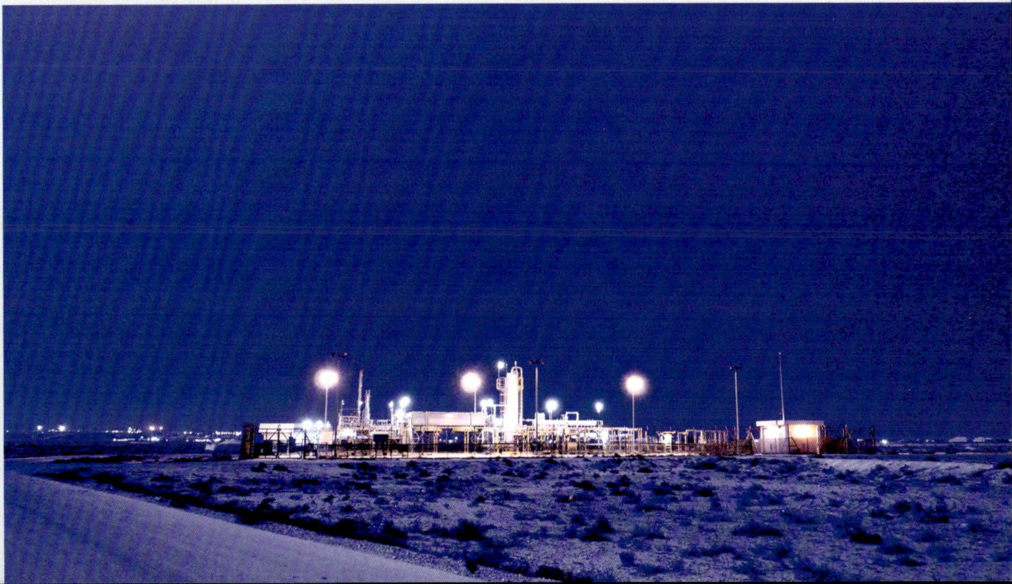

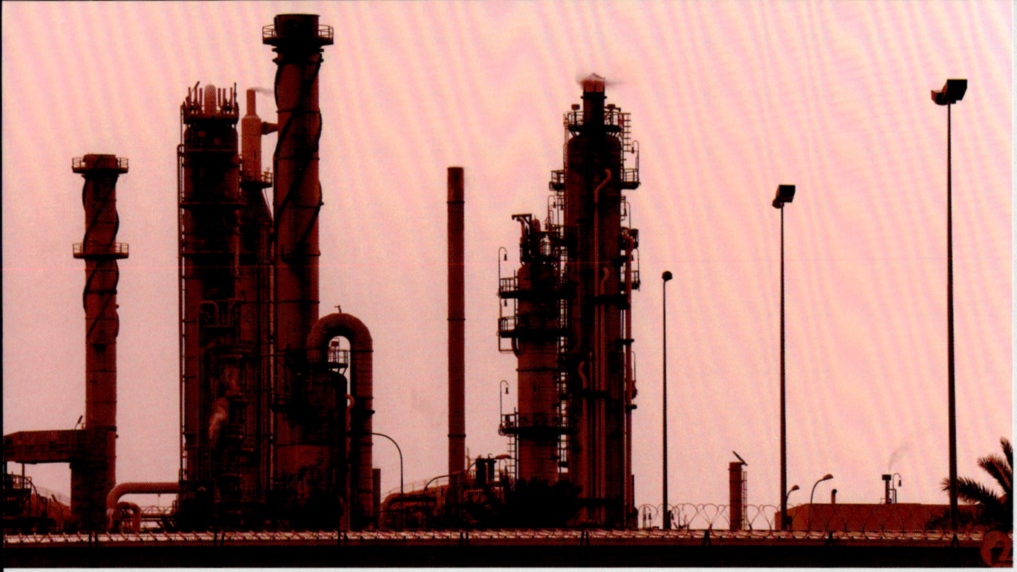

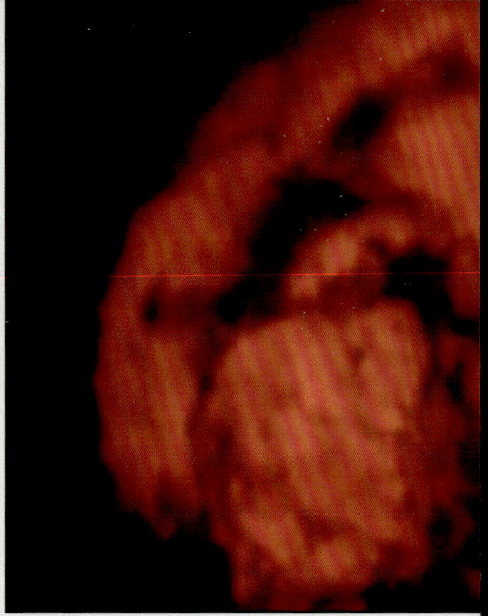

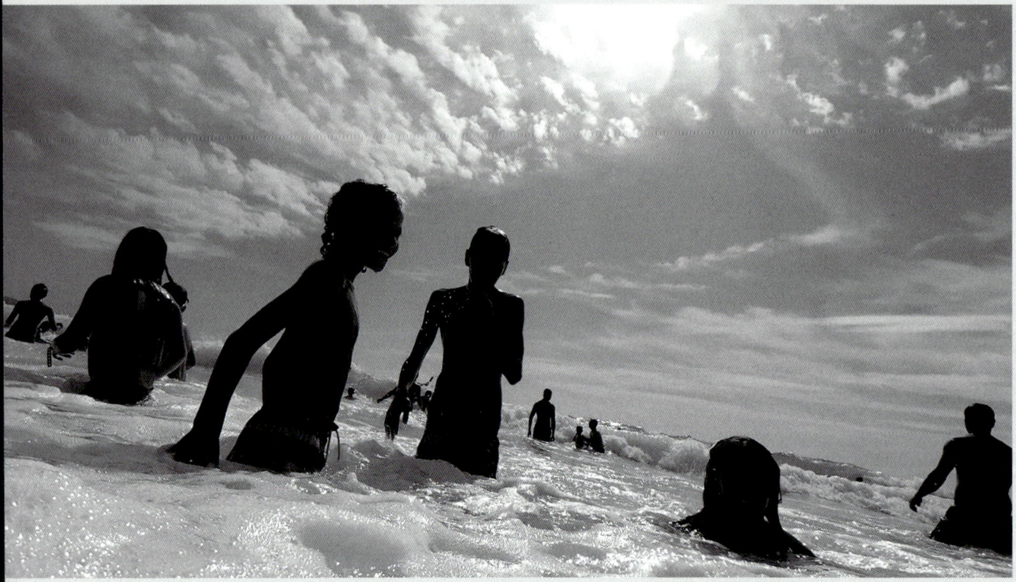

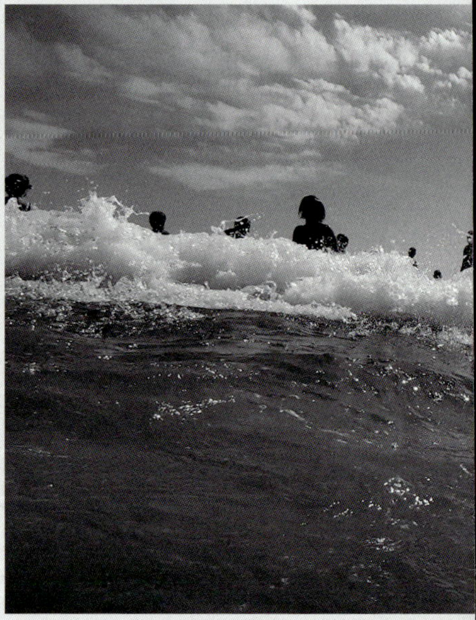

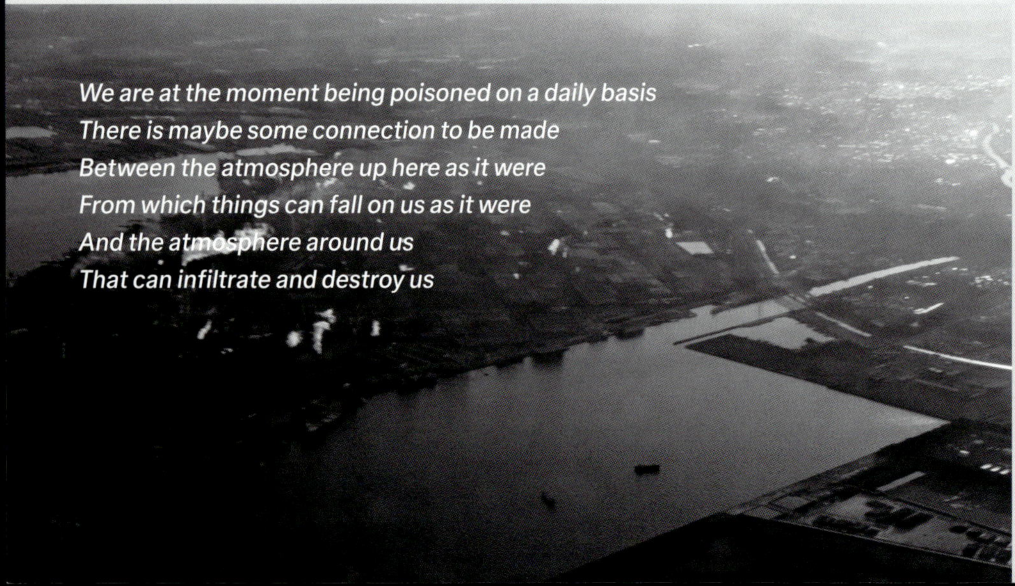

We are at the moment being poisoned on a daily basis
There is maybe some connection to be made
Between the atmosphere up here as it were
From which things can fall on us as it were
And the atmosphere around us
That can infiltrate and destroy us

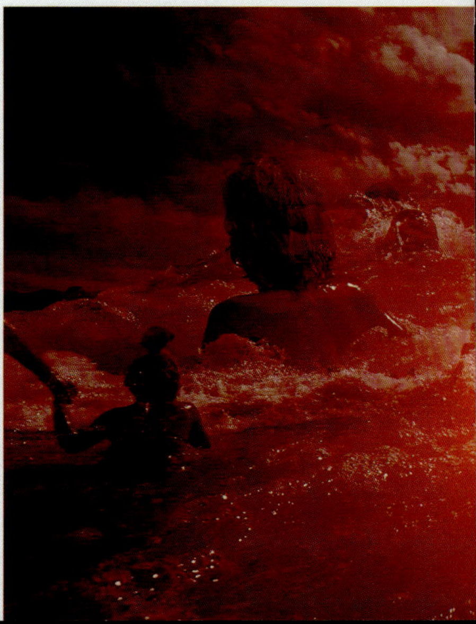

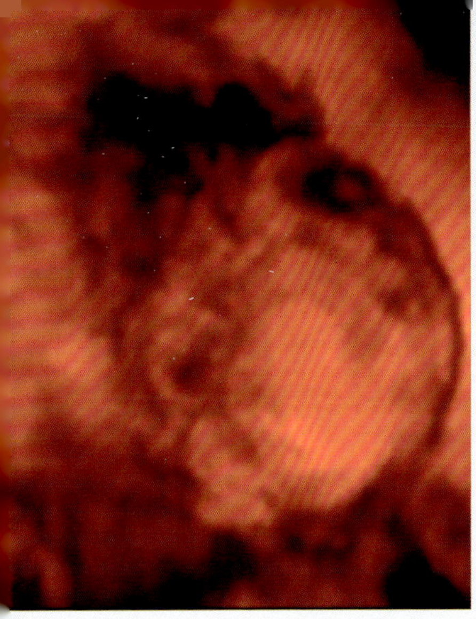

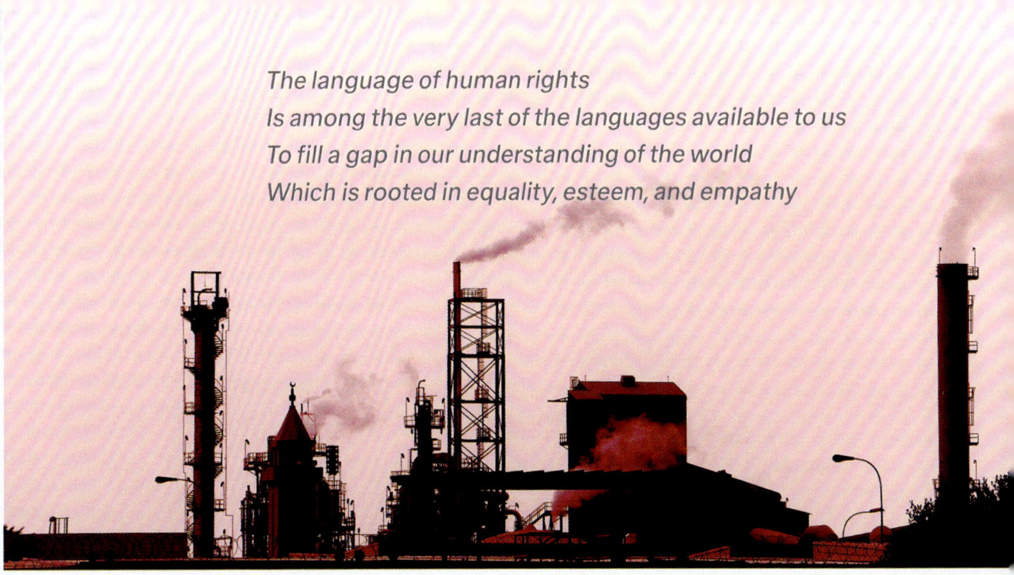

The language of human rights
Is among the very last of the languages available to us
To fill a gap in our understanding of the world
Which is rooted in equality, esteem, and empathy

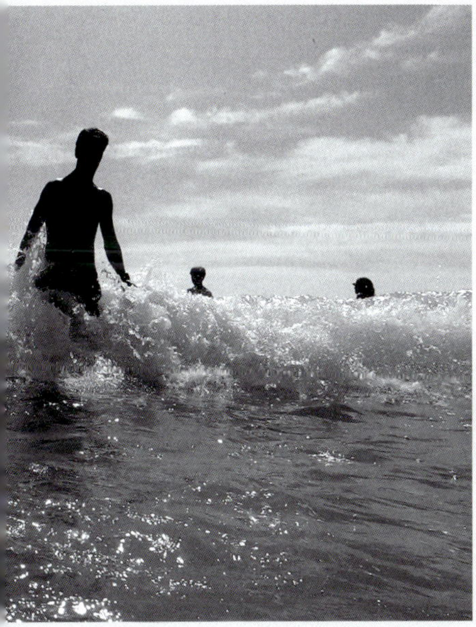

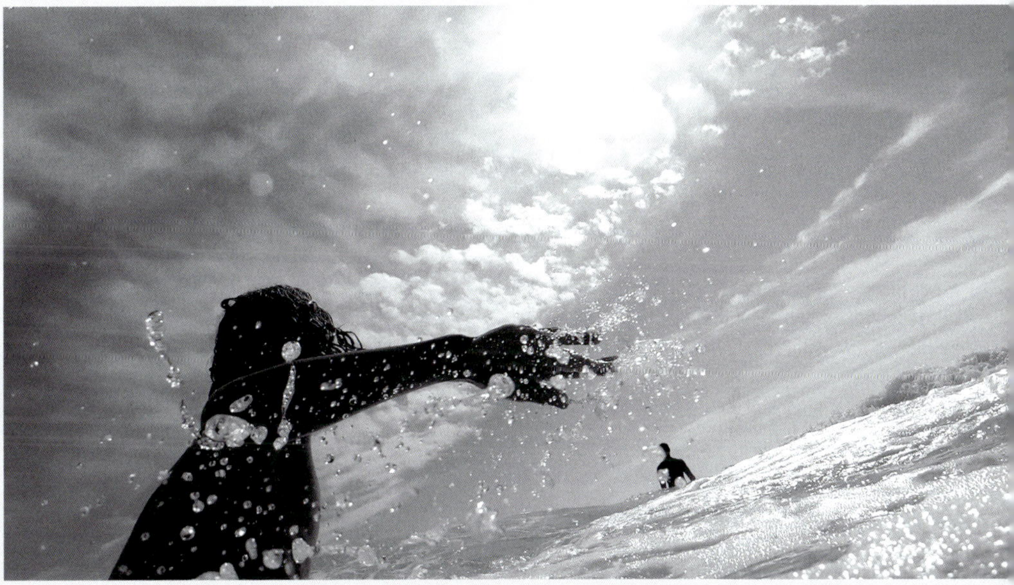

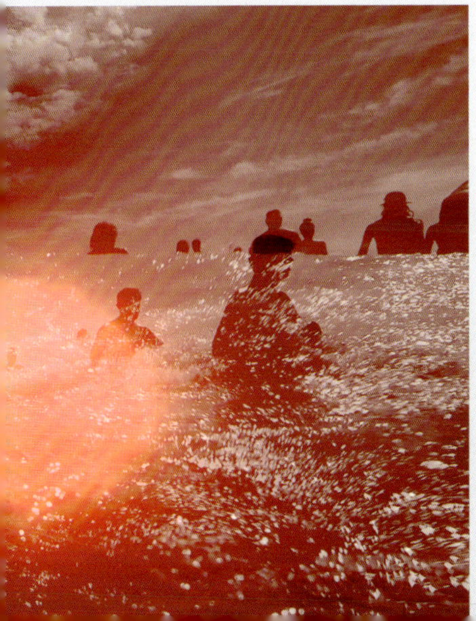

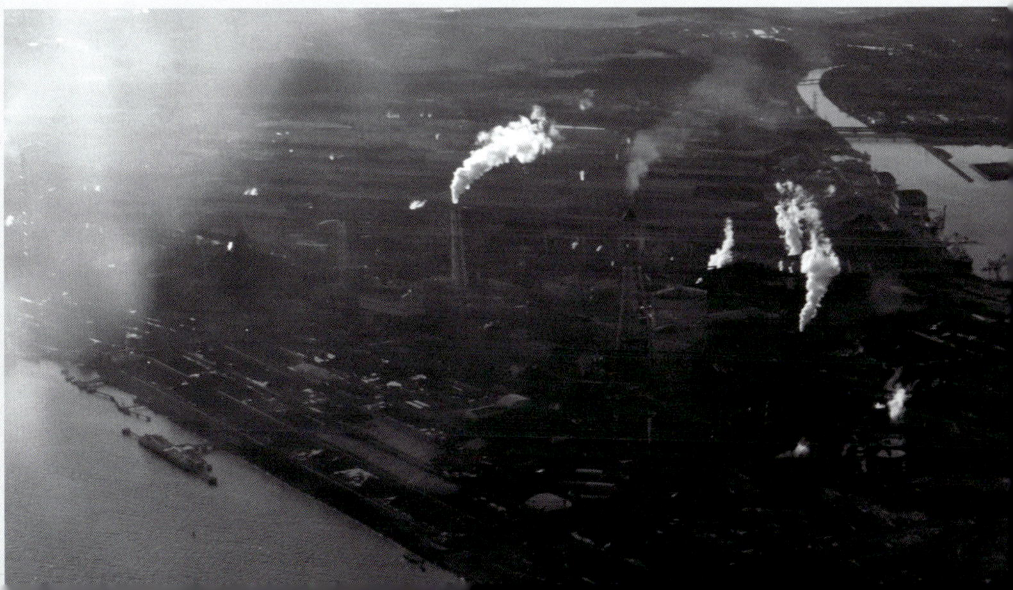

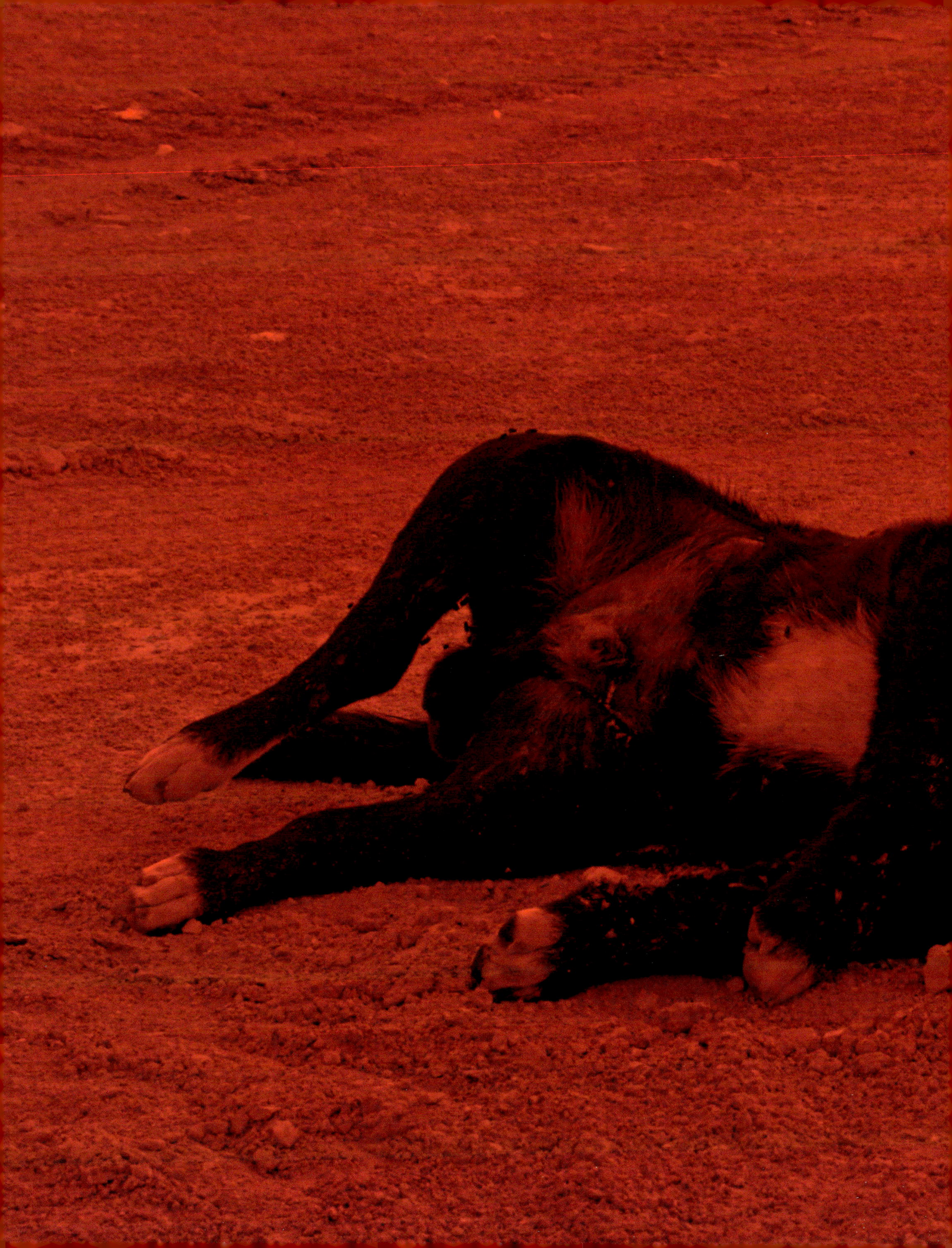

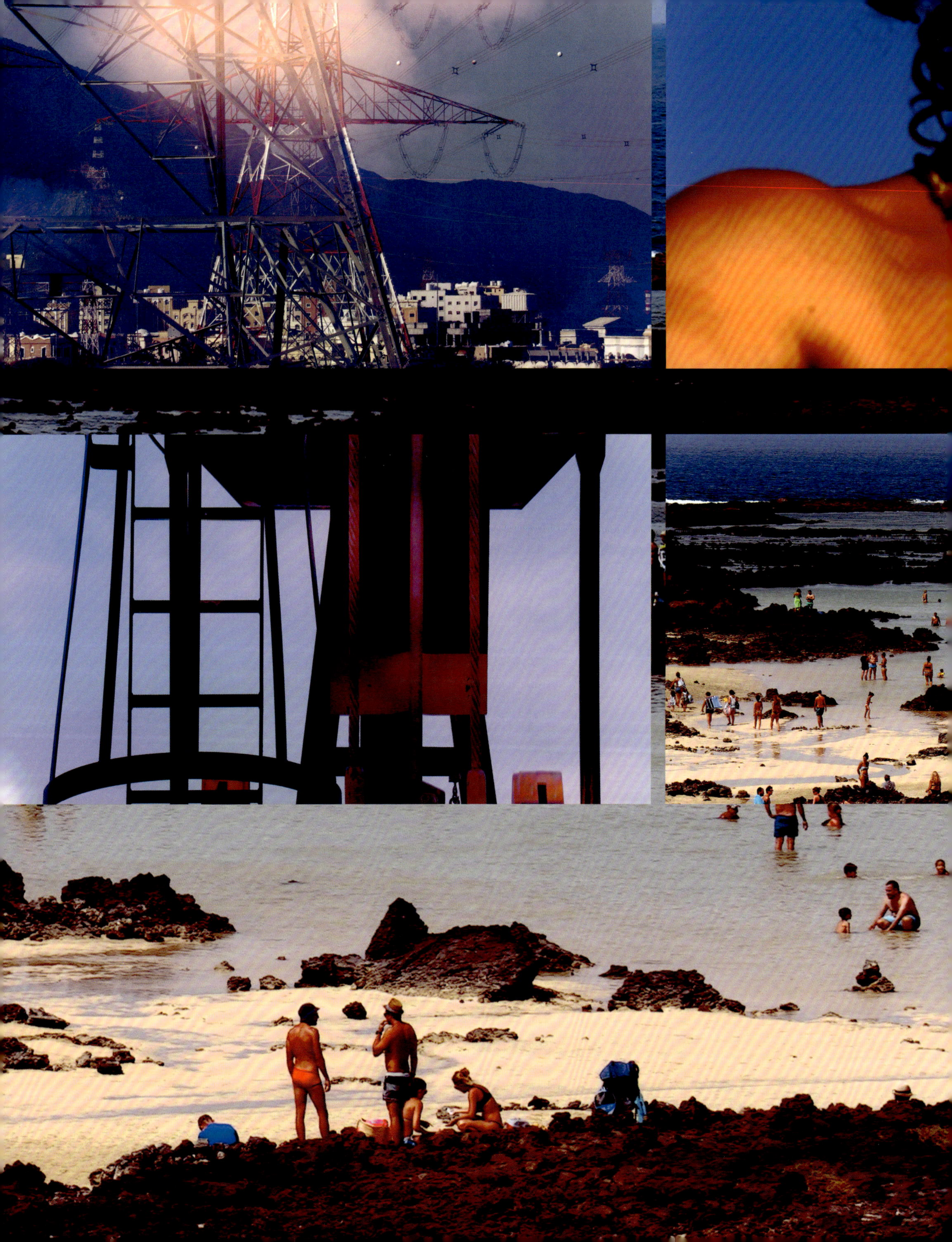

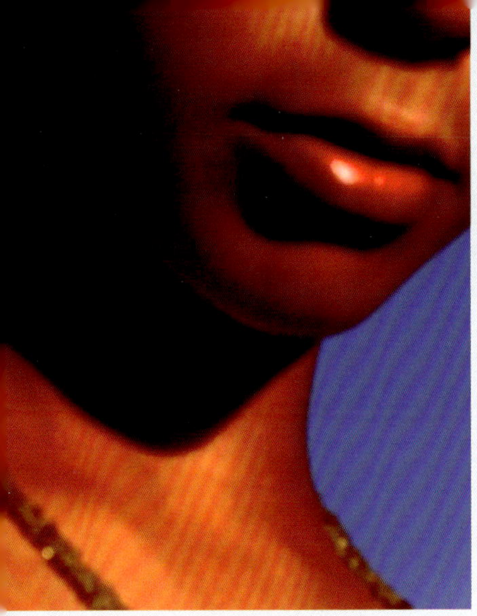

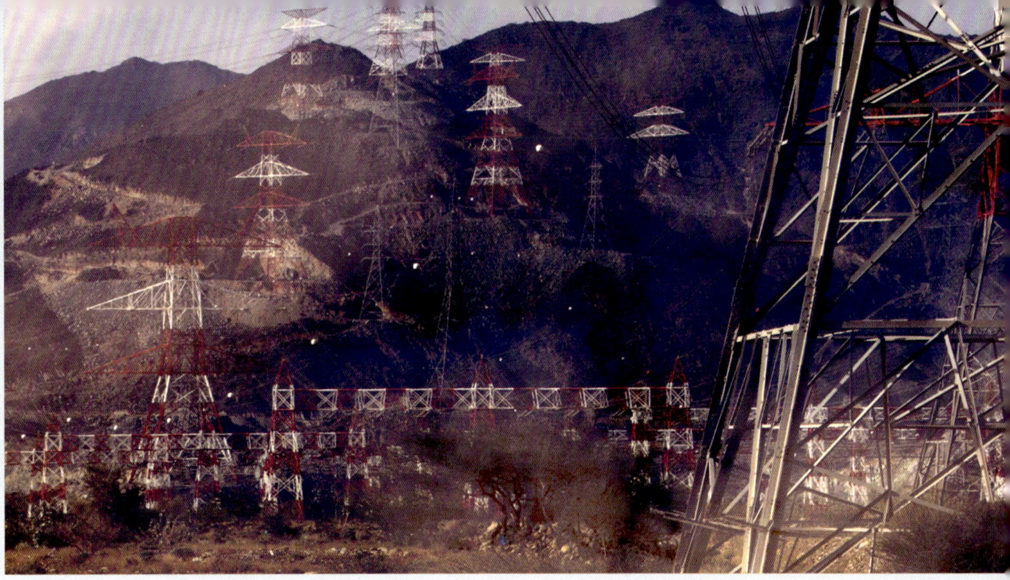

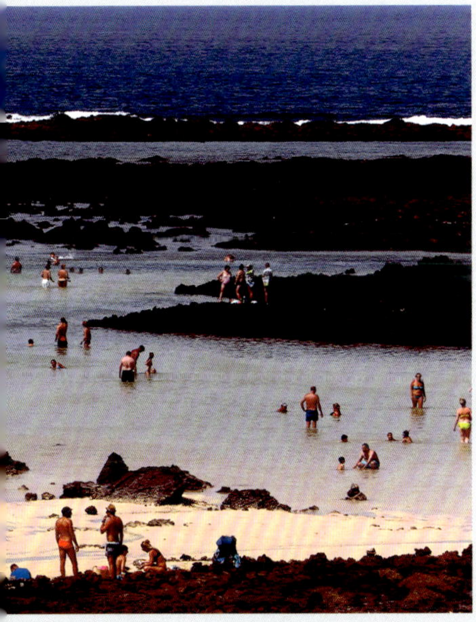

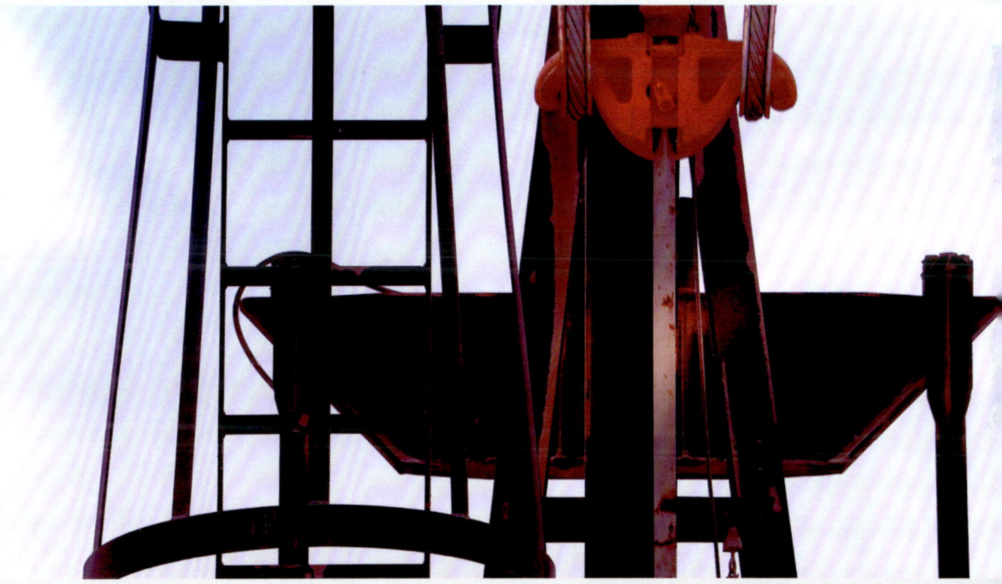

Humanity has been altering the air
The atmosphere
For thousands of years
In the last two hundred years
They have been altering it
To an exponential rate
We're now at a
New geological force of nature

Plans are to release these sulphate aerosols
into the stratosphere
Great big reflectors, mirrors in space
That can reflect sunlight away

If the impact of this fails
It will be absolutely catastrophic

Four million people a year are dying because of pollution
The same pollution that we are suggesting
That if we put higher up
Can then control the climate

Something like mirrors in space
I just think
Are men's egos to be honest

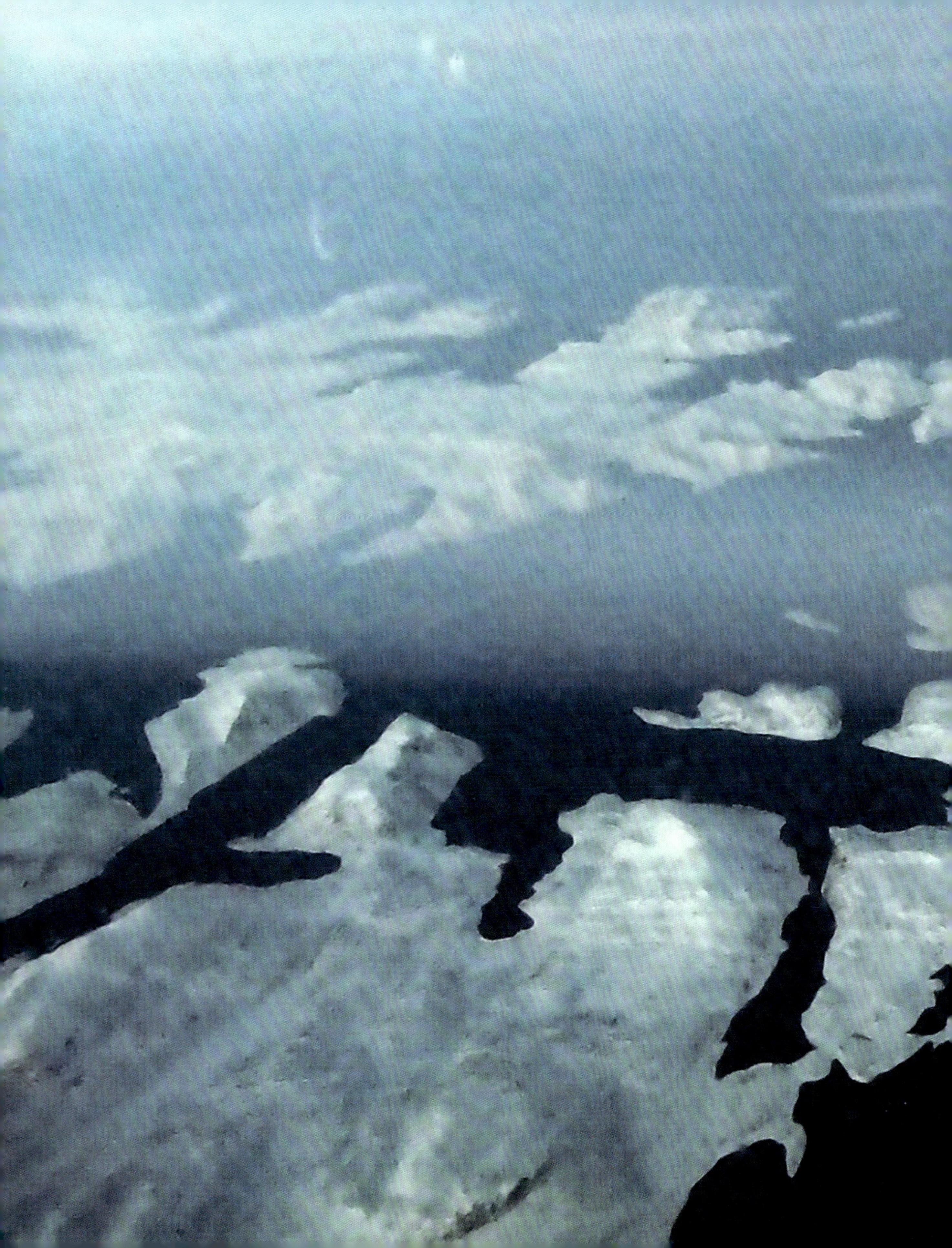

A layer of radionuclides
Settles deep in the Antarctic ice
A radioactive signature
In the geological record

A catastrophe of time

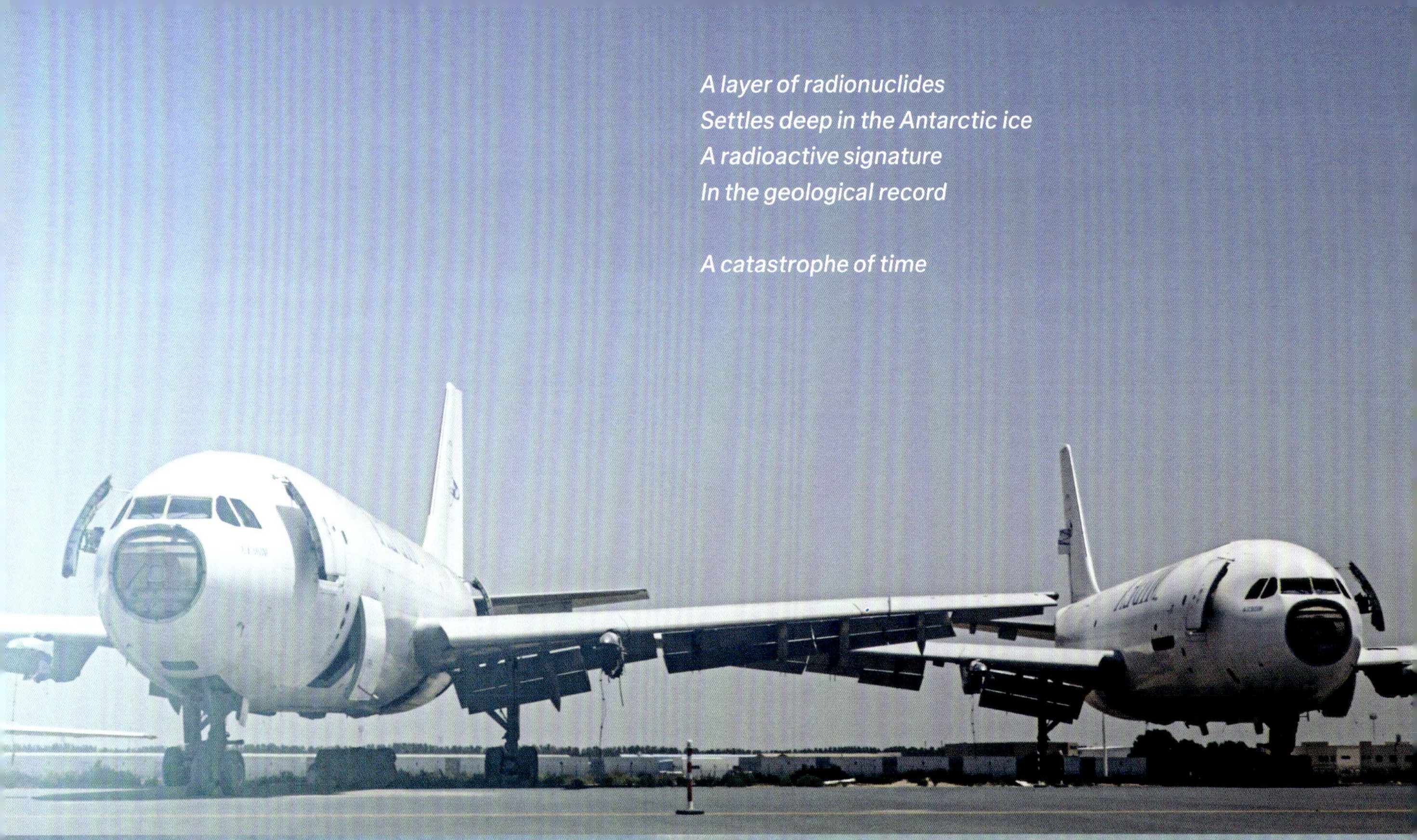

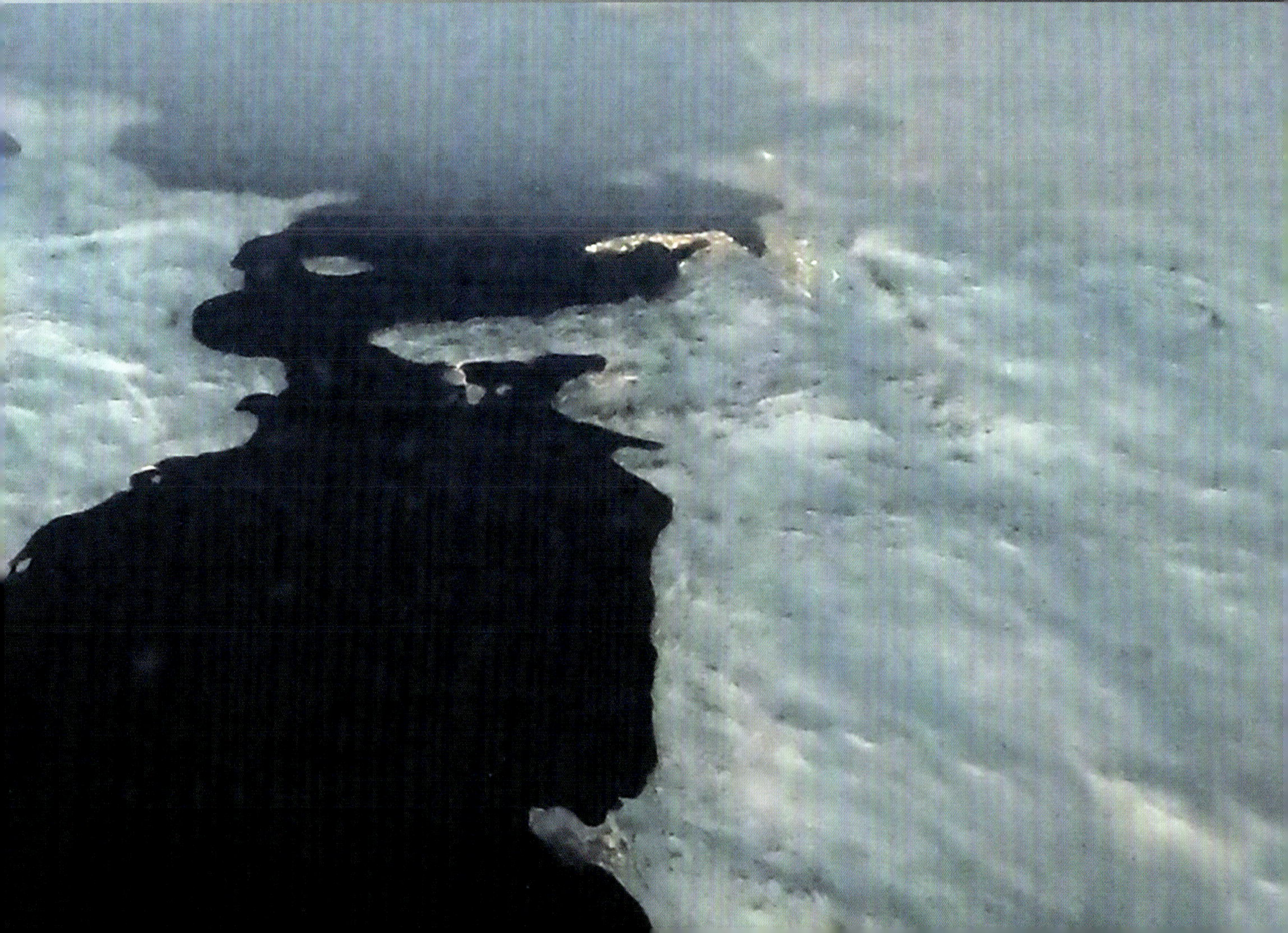

I had a very tiny peach in my hand
And these people who were badly burned
They saw me carrying this peach
And asked for anything
That has water

This was my father
I saw an enormous injury on the back of his body
All we could do was to run and escape
From the flames running after us

His injury was made when the explosion occurred
He put himself in front of me
And covered me with his body
That's why he was injured so badly

The most devastating thing as I remember was though
So many people were burned so badly
And in need of immediate relief
Even the doctors and nurses and health care specialists
were also killed
Or badly injured so nobody was able to help anyone
Which meant that
Those who were half dead just had to lie down
Under this heat of August 6
As long as they had last breath of life
They just lingered on
On the ground

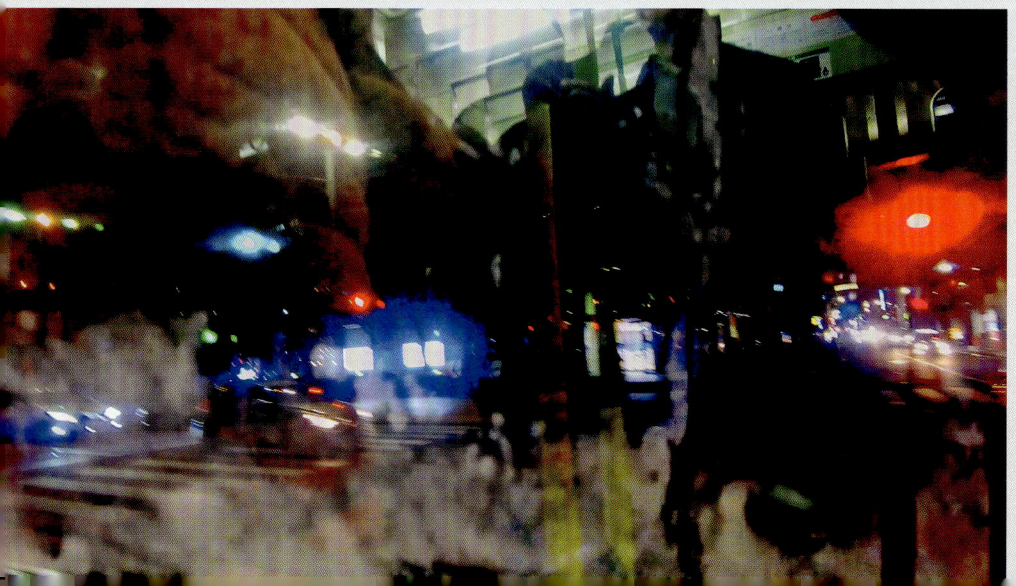

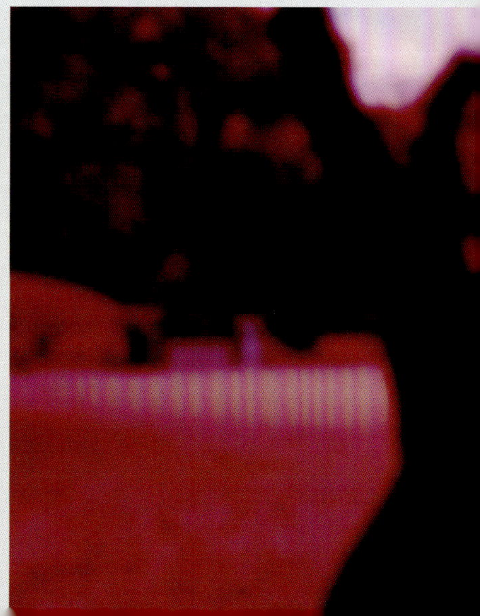

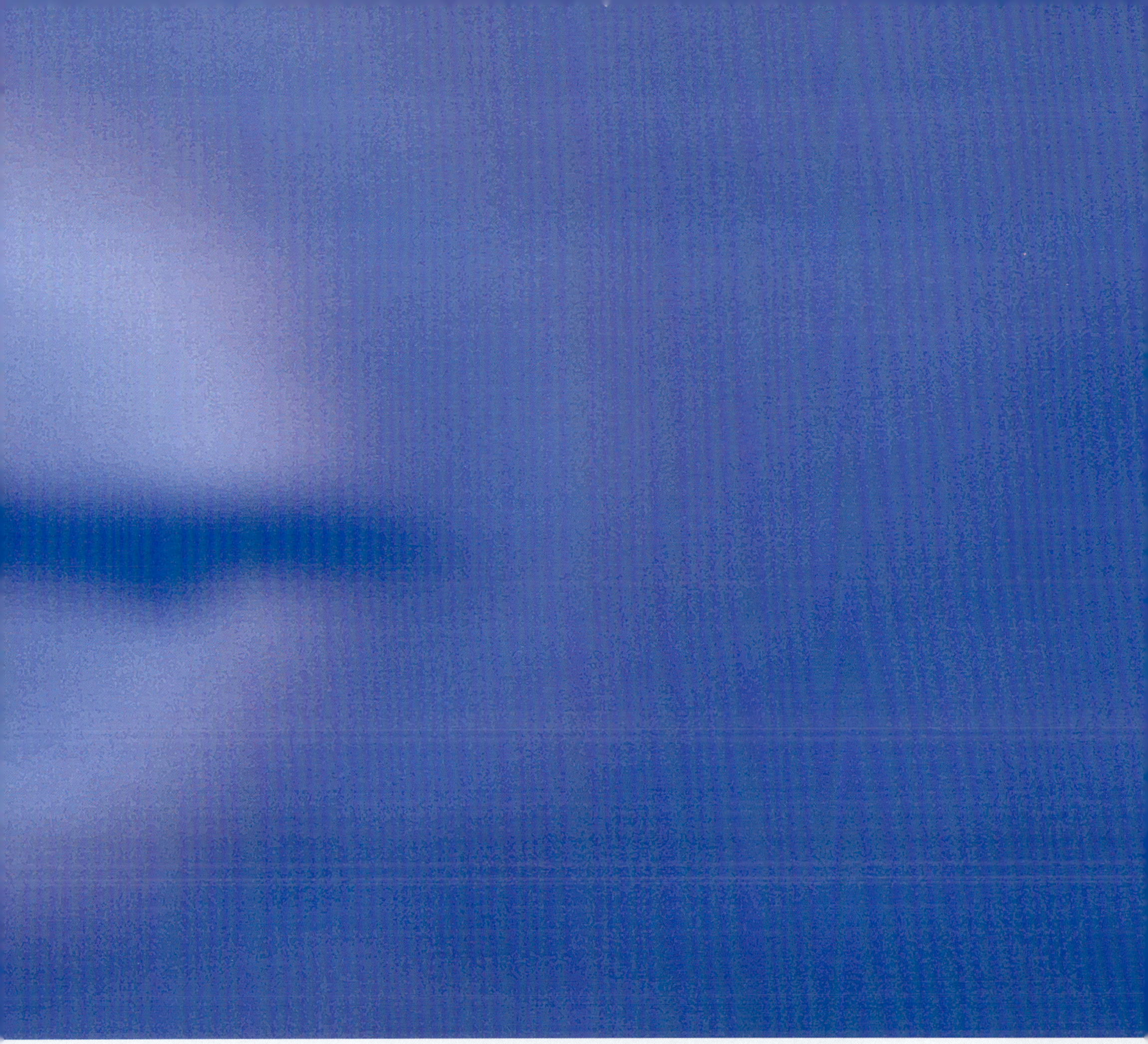
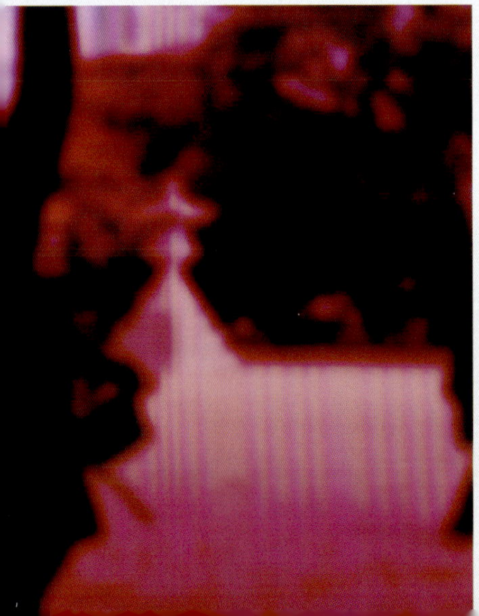
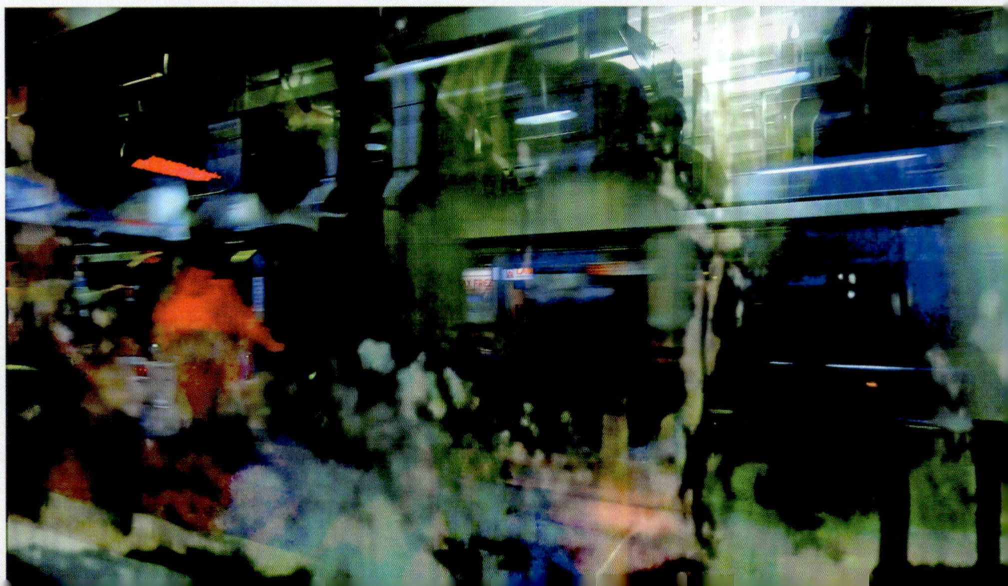

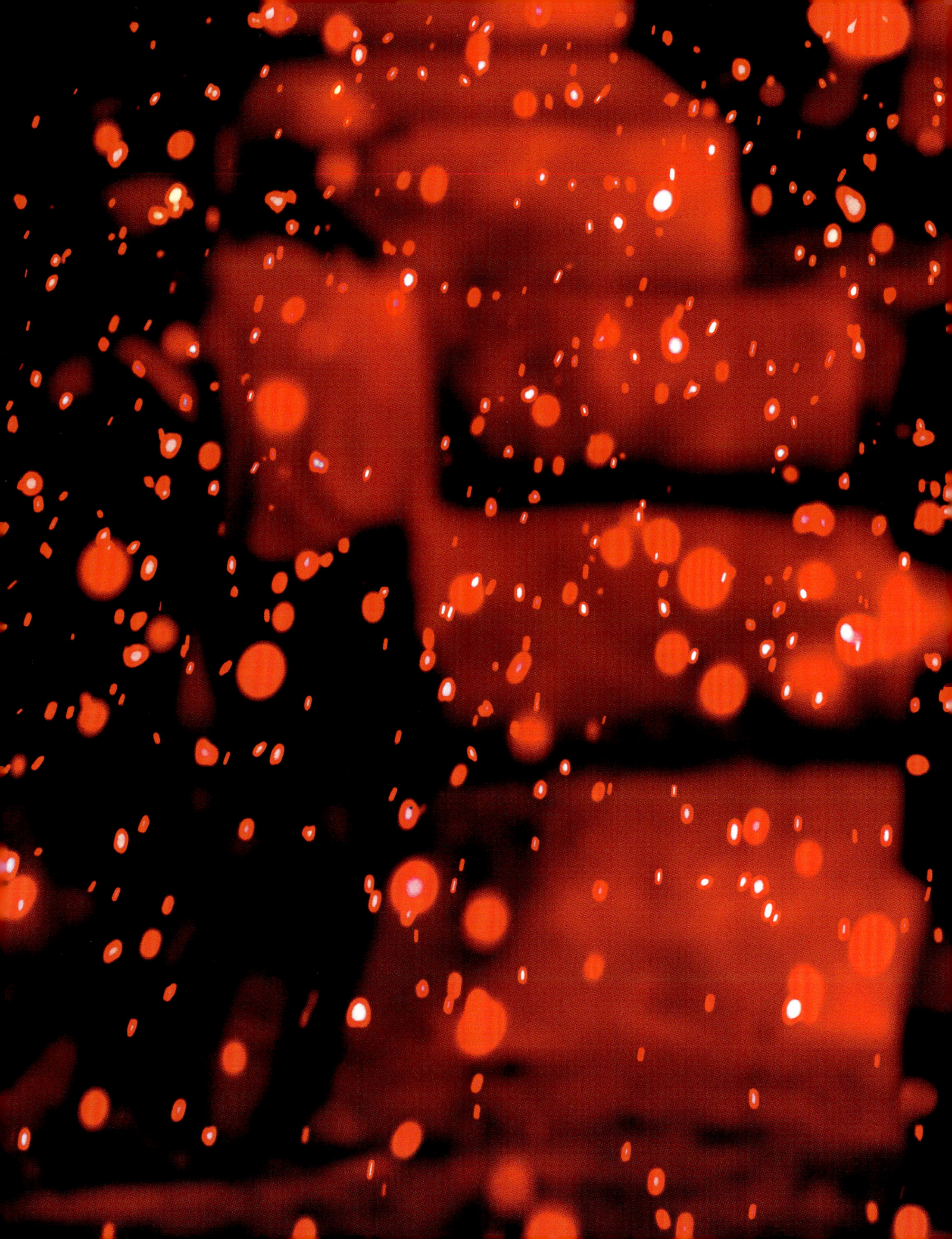

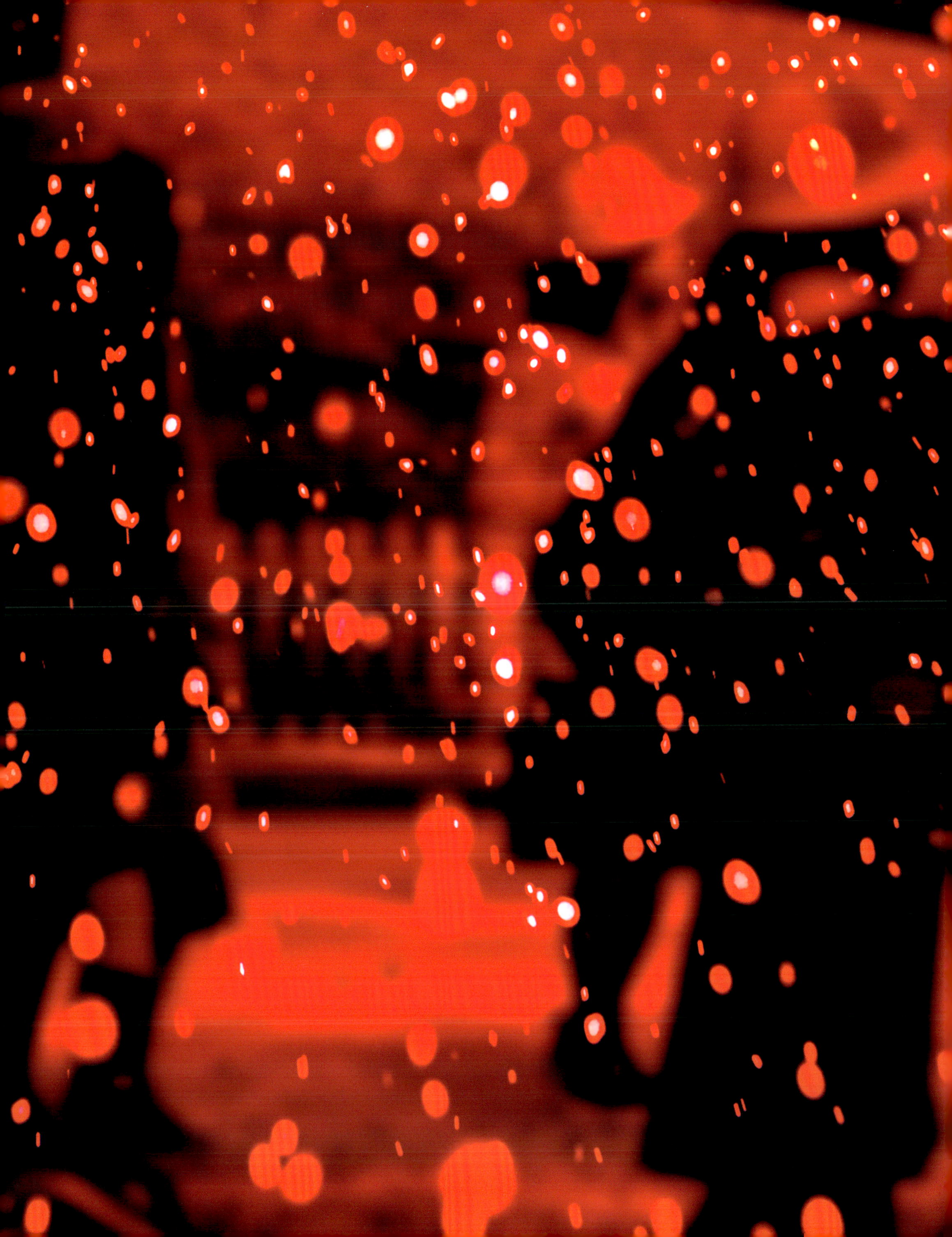

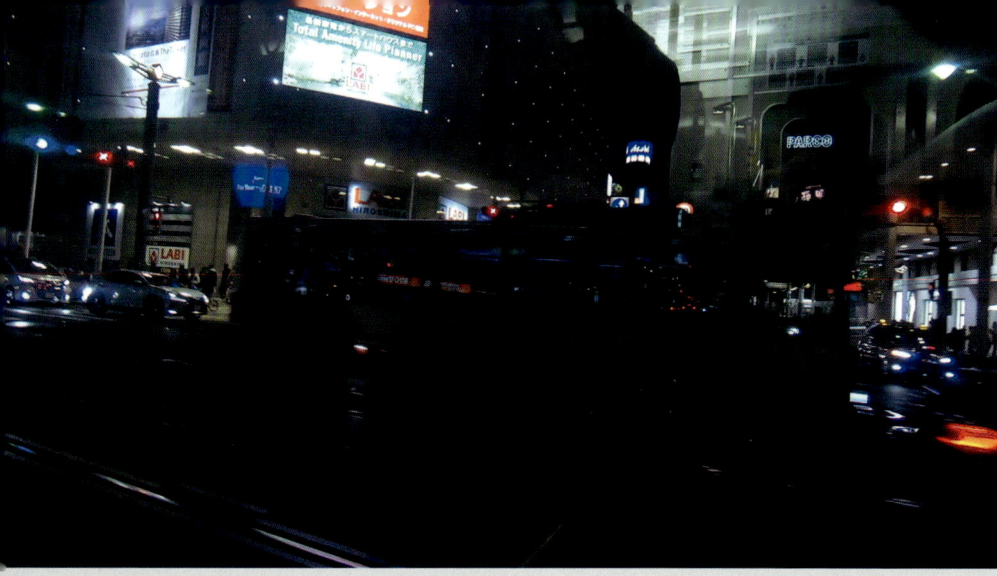
Total Amenity Life Planner
LABI
PARCO
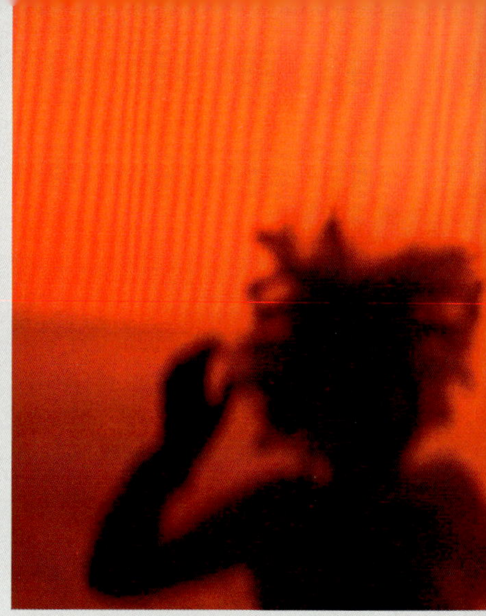
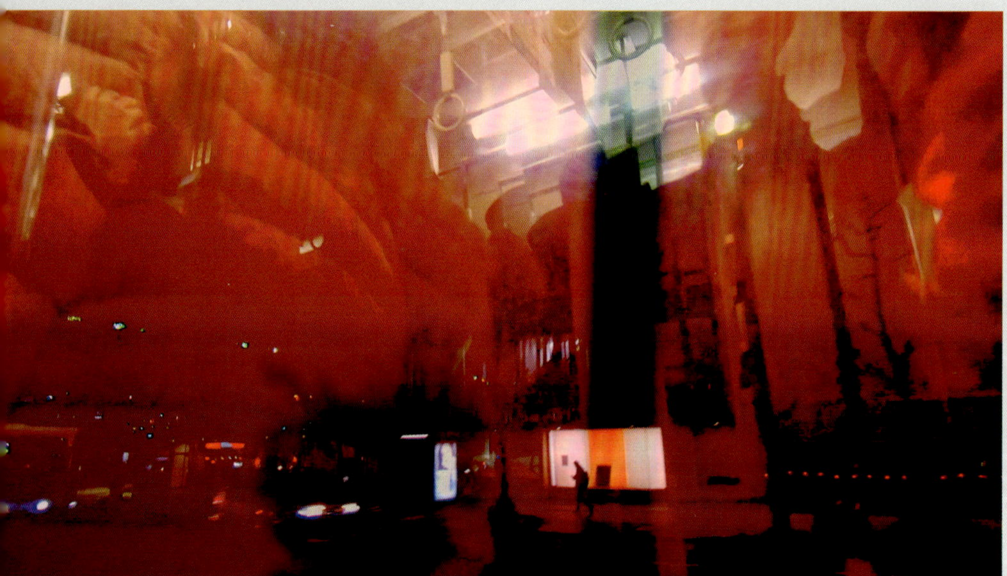
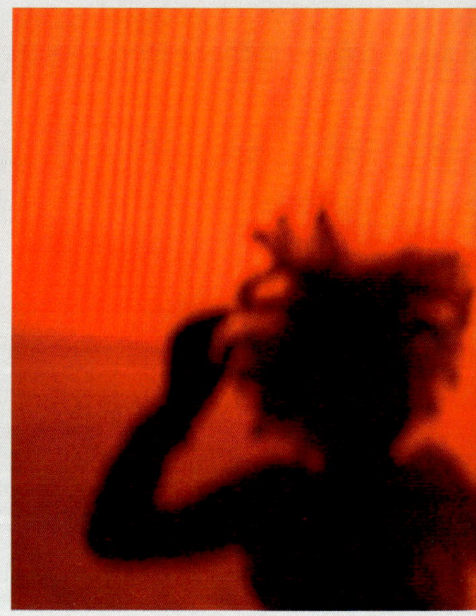
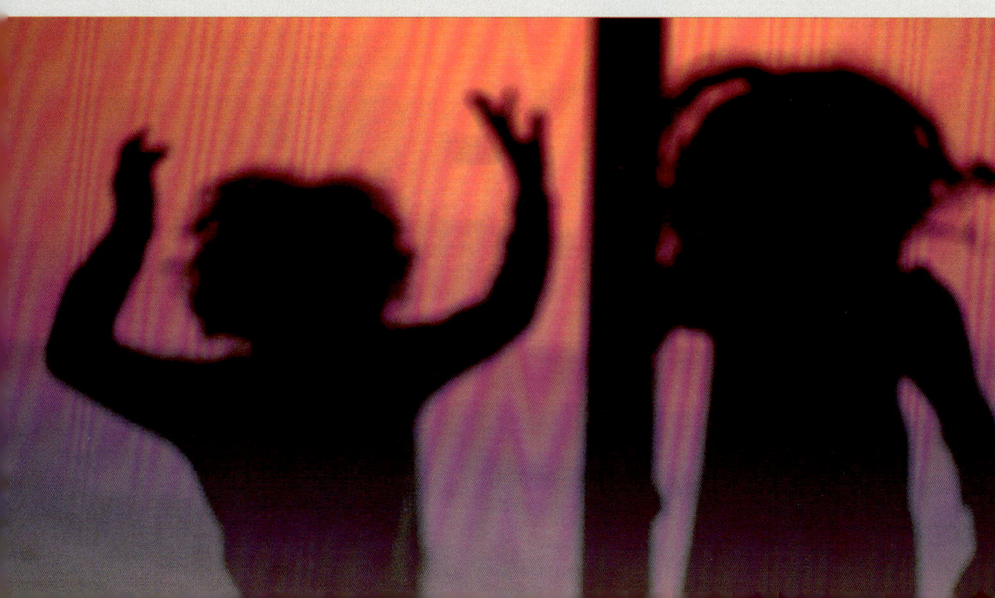

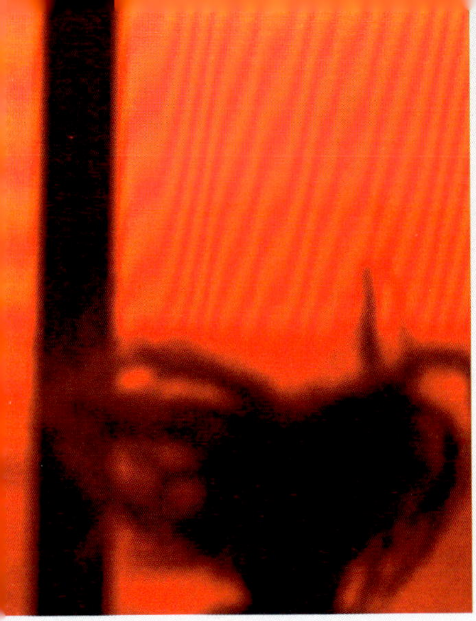
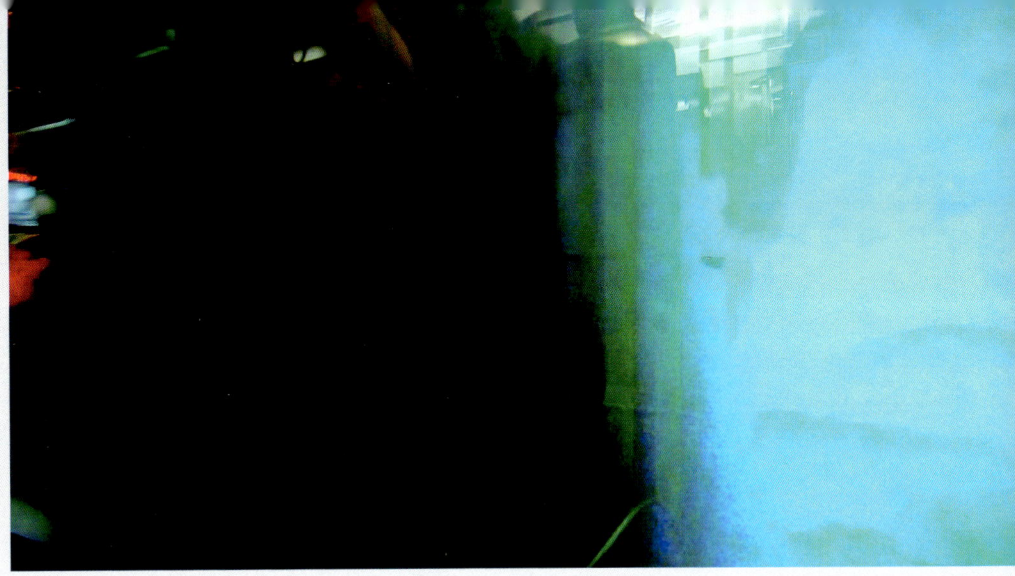
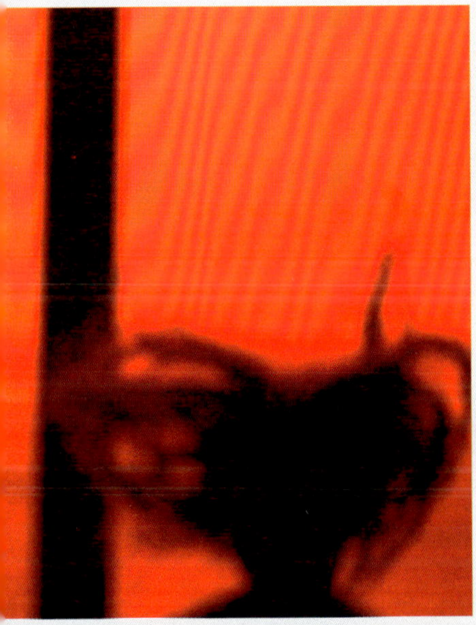

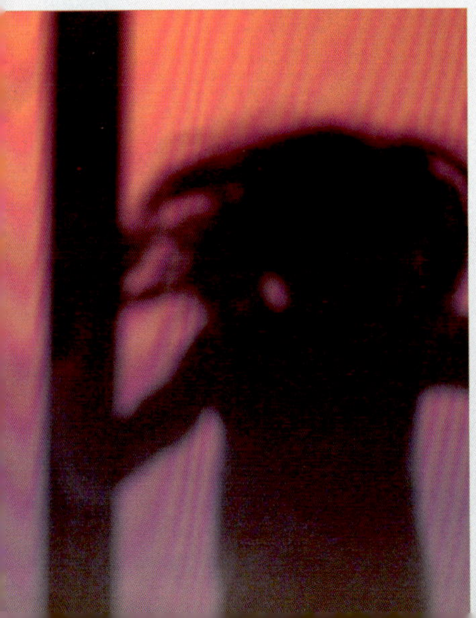
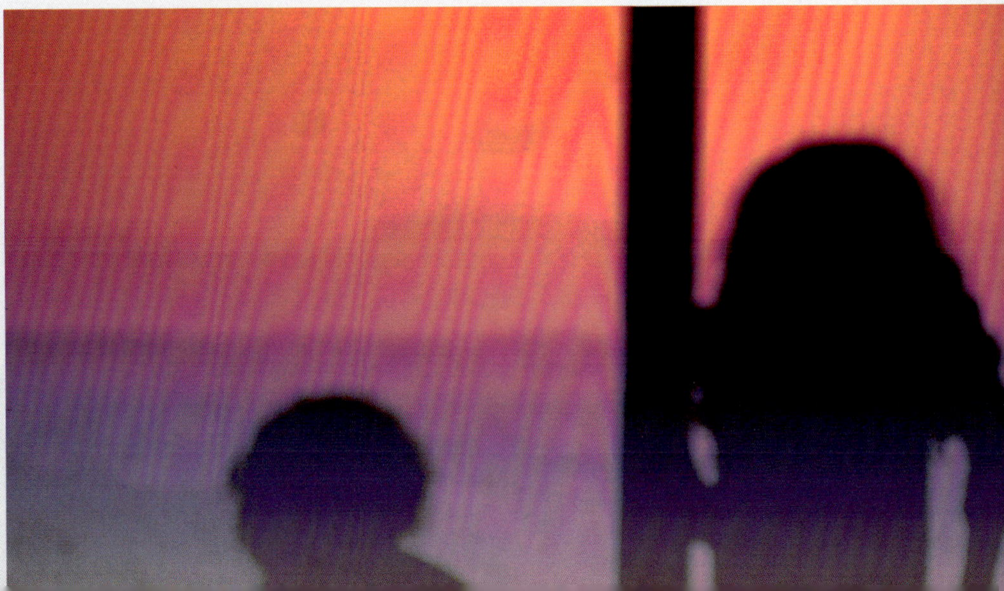

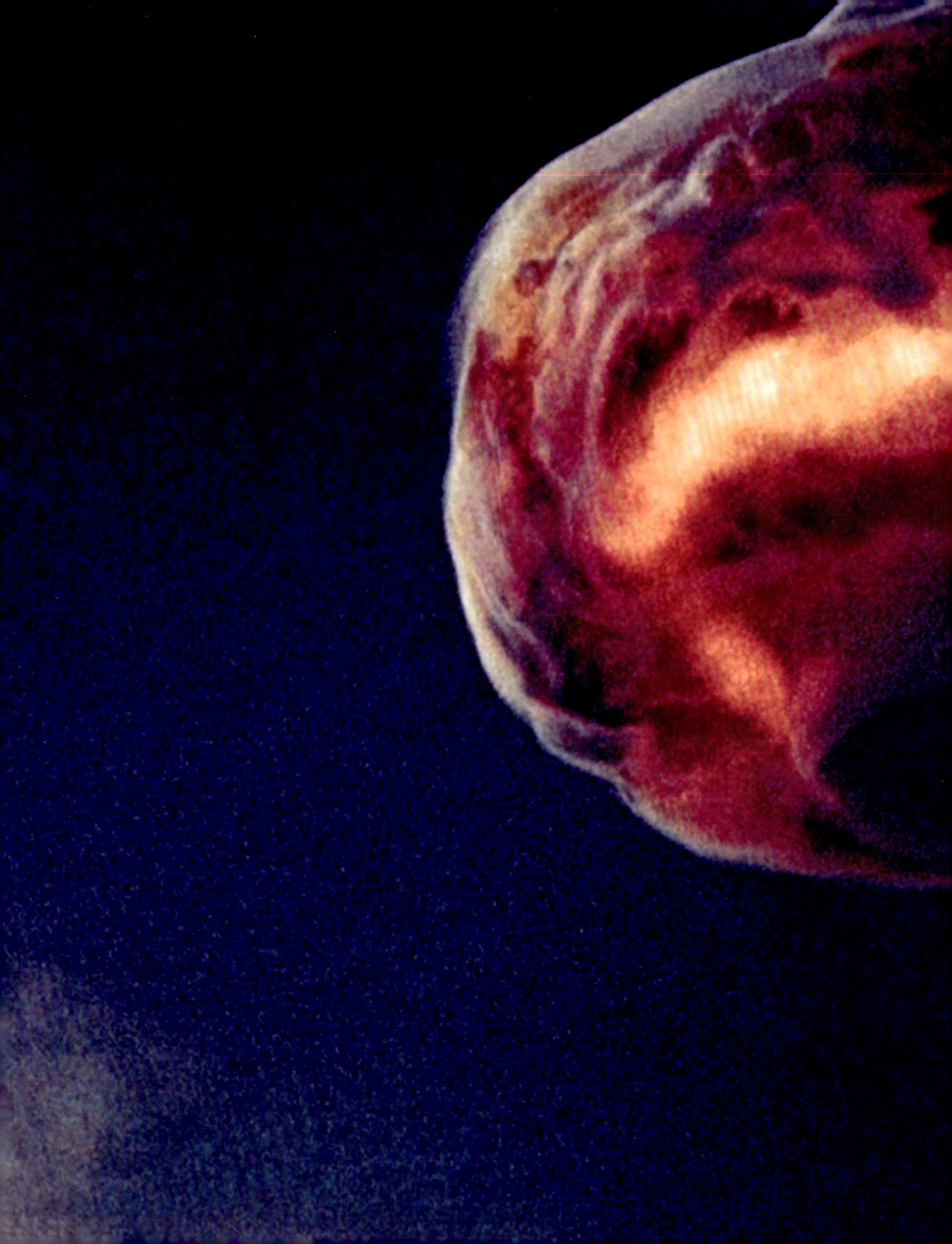

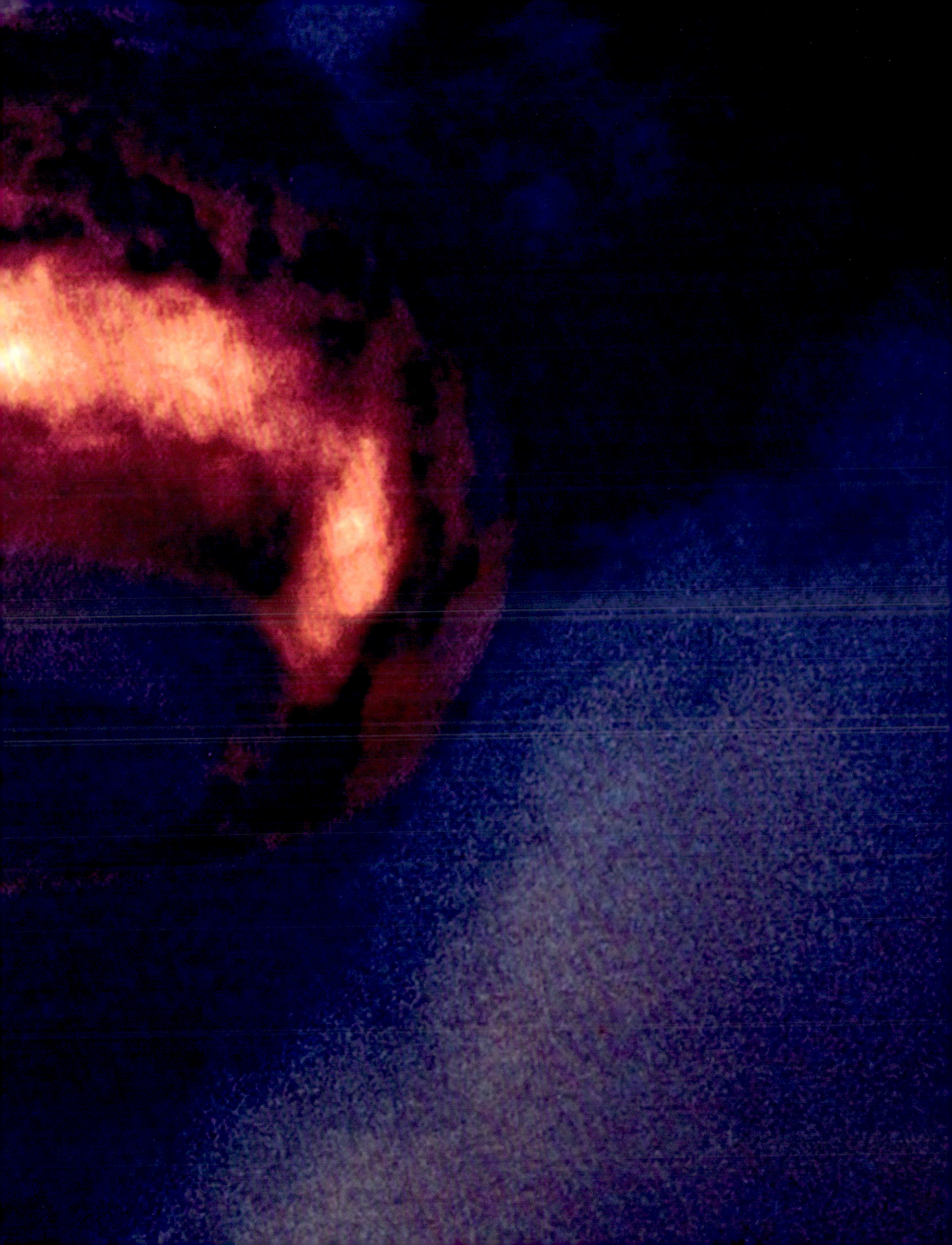

He looked out in the middle of the night
And saw some phosphorous blue lights here and there
Only after many years he learned that those were
Decaying bodies
Remembering these blue lights
He thought that the air was full of spirits

And these dead spirits never left Hiroshima
But they keep floating in the air

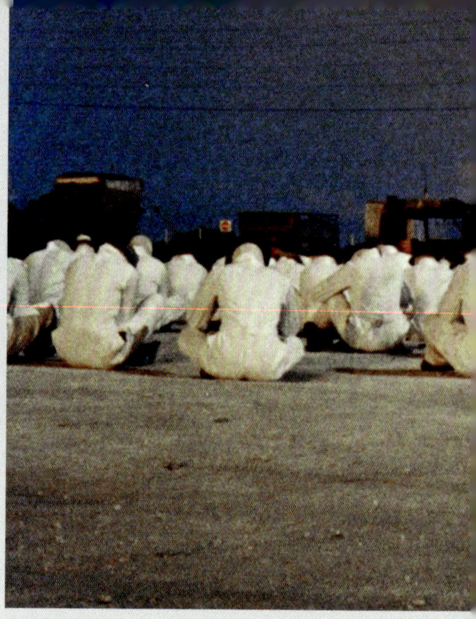

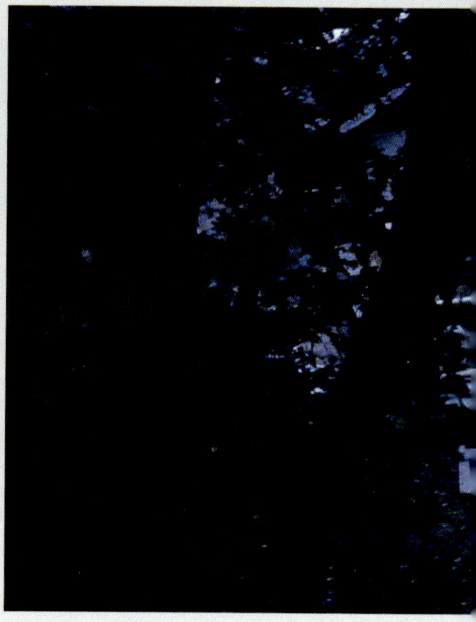

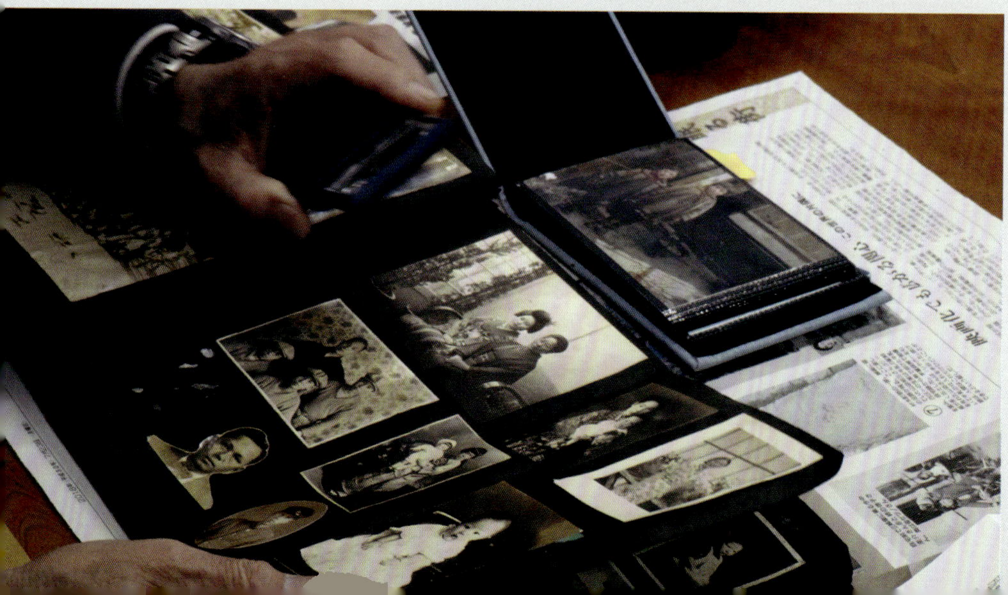

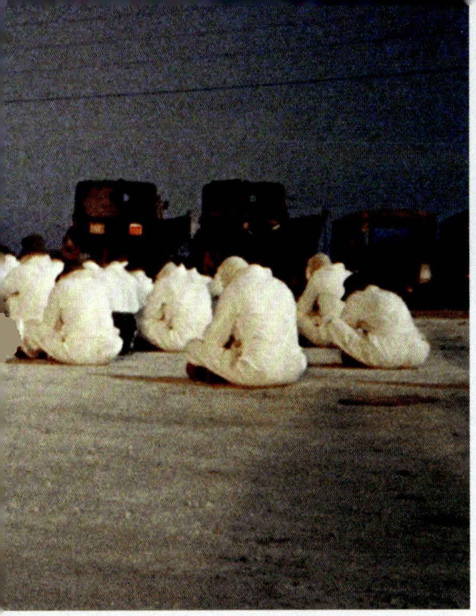

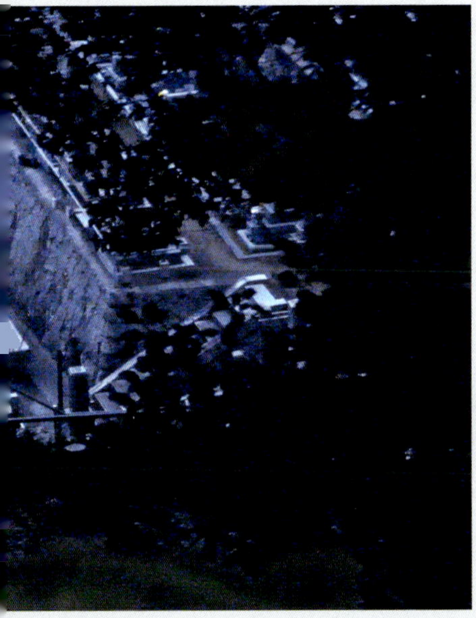

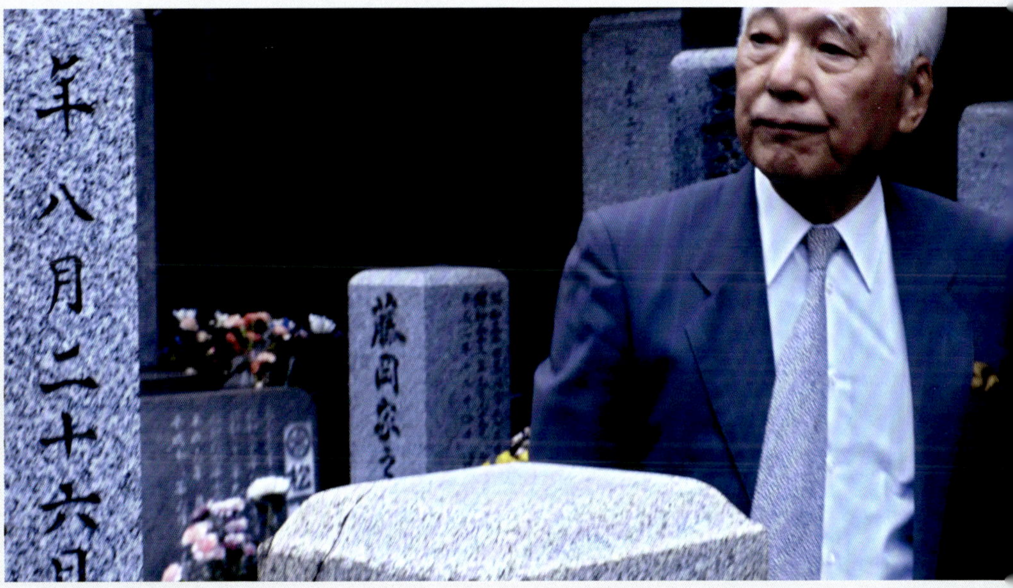

My mother had a very hard life
Because she couldn't find the bones of my elder sister
She kept believing that she would come back one day
She never closed all of the doors of the house

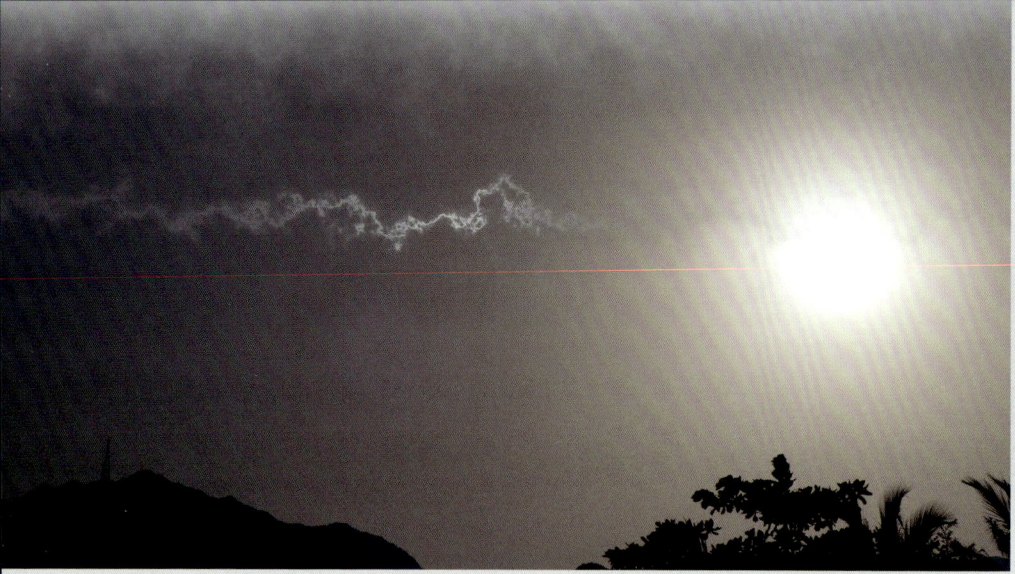
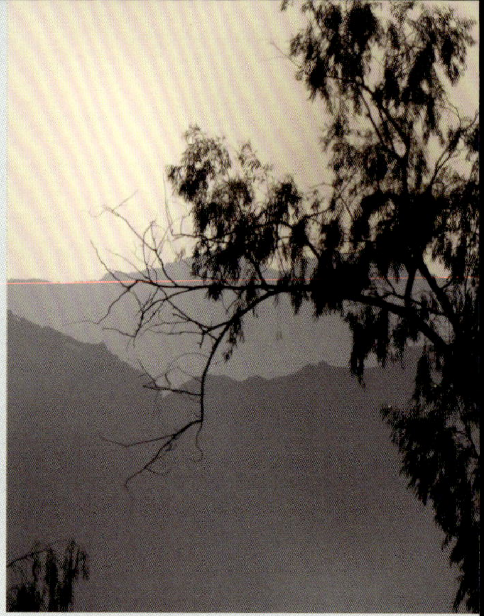

It's out of imagination
Nothing alive
Nothing
Animals, sheeps, cow, kids, women, men
All bleeding from mouth and nose
You can feel how they died
From pain

Our imagination is about the bombing, bullet and

But that was chemical weapons
And that's nothing alive there
Nothing

It's I think stuck in my memory
I never can forget it

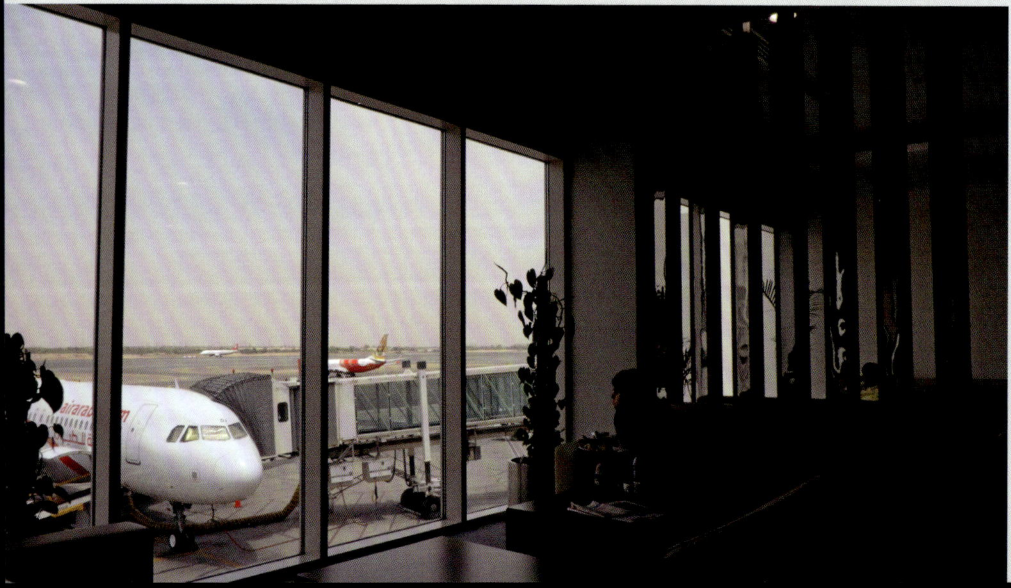
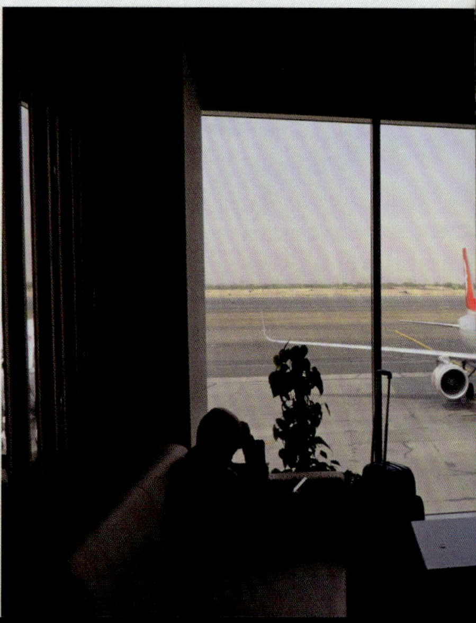

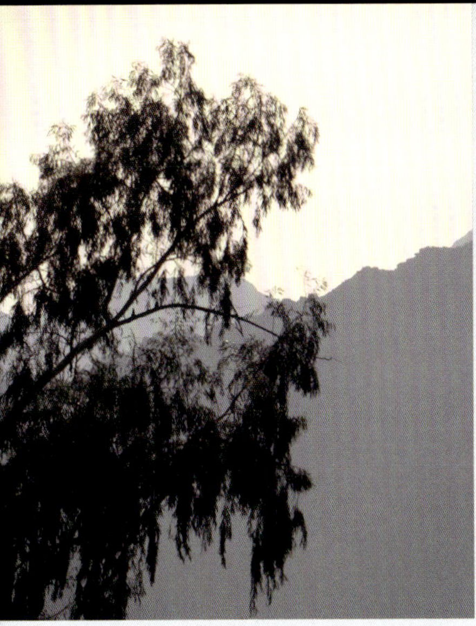

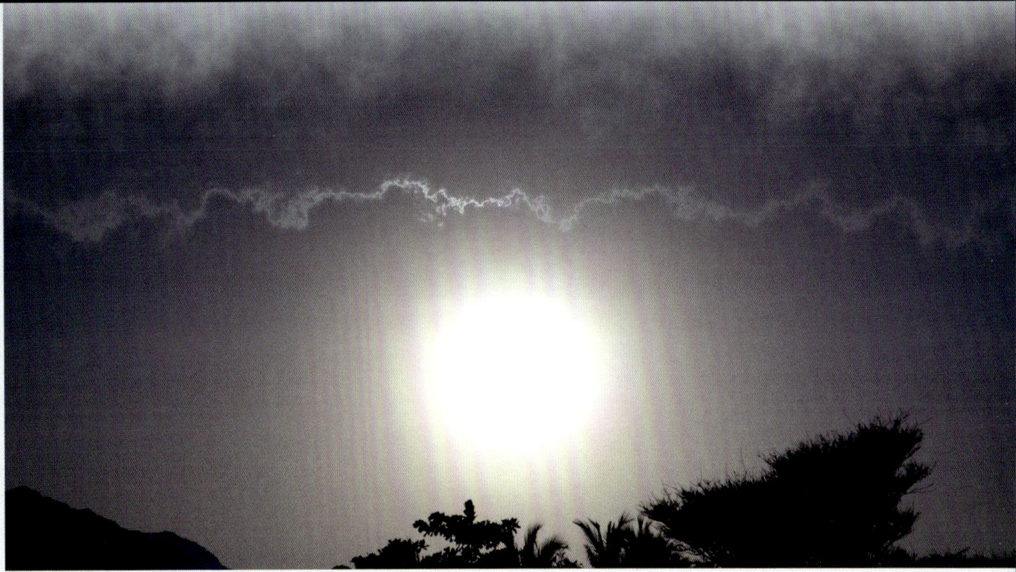

Emirates flight 3862 to Hong Kong via...

There are twenty-five thousand miles of air routes in the British Empire
The safety and comfort of these routes
Depends largely on a network of over eighty airports

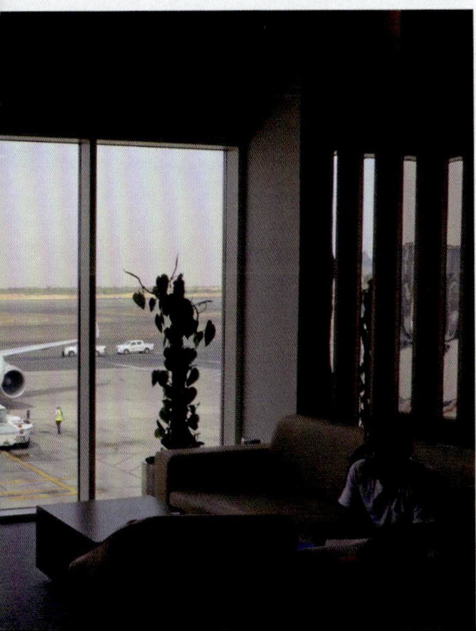

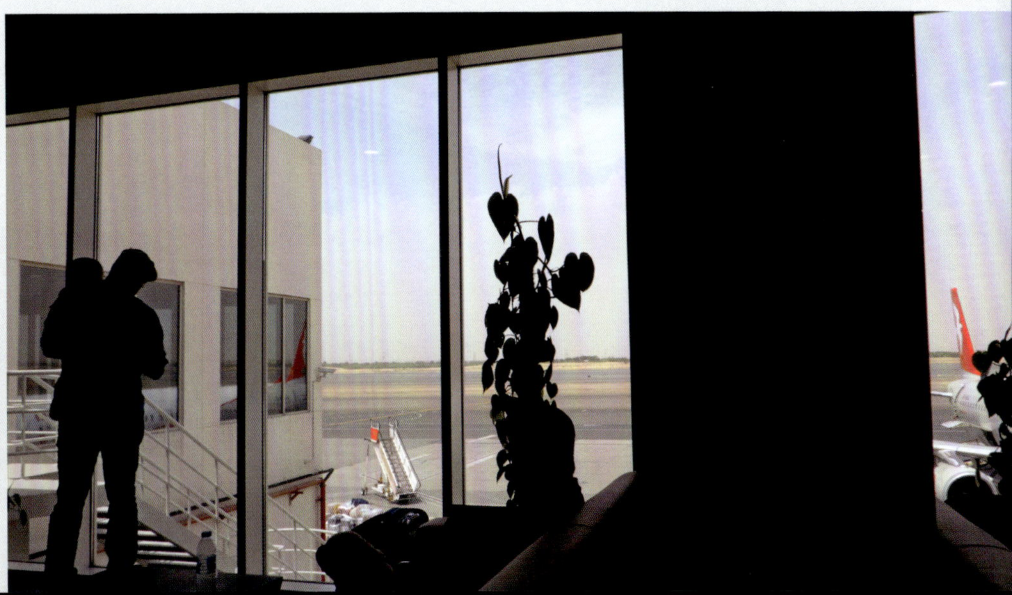

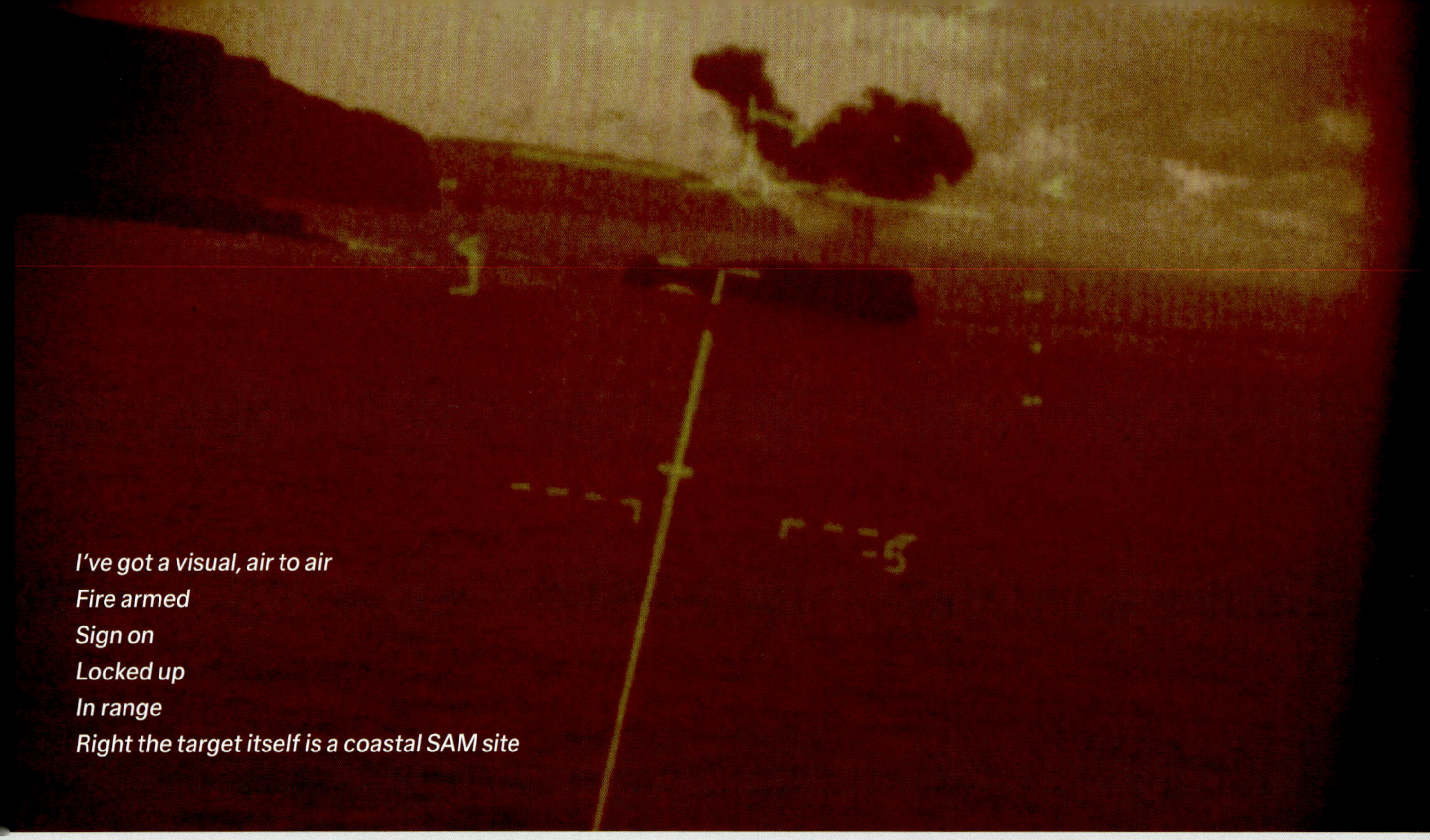

I've got a visual, air to air
Fire armed
Sign on
Locked up
In range
Right the target itself is a coastal SAM site

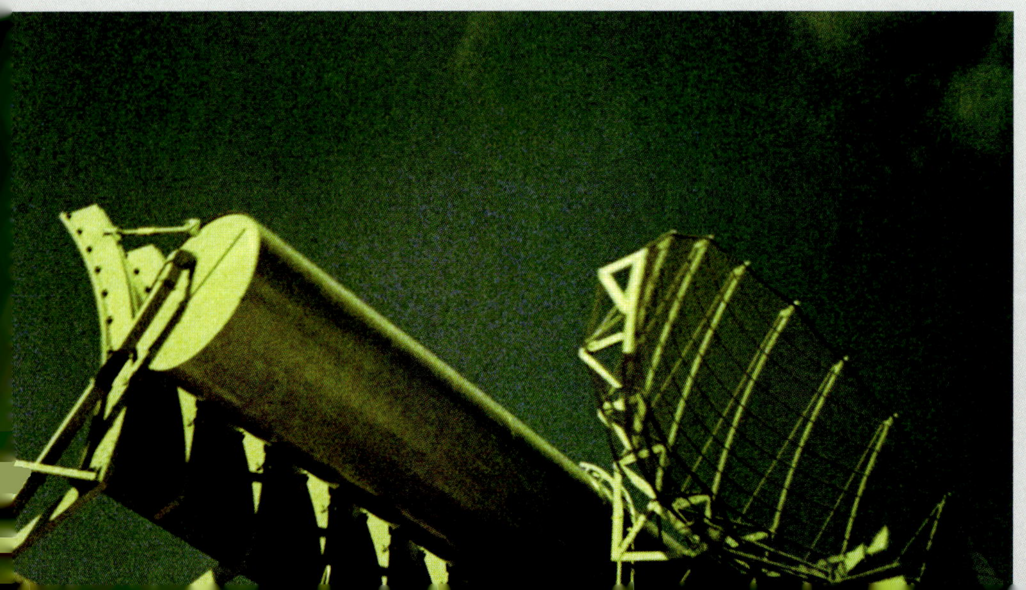

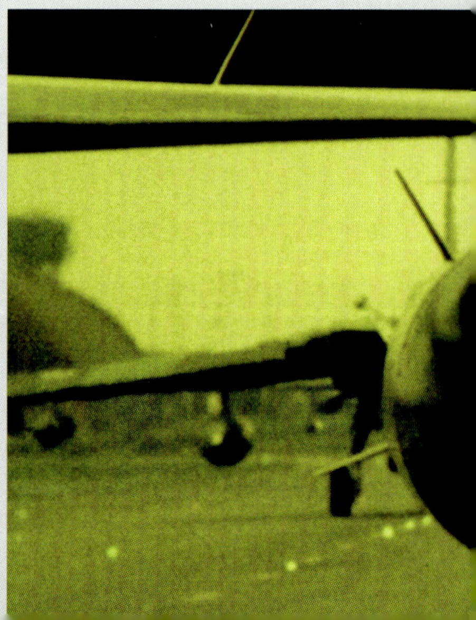

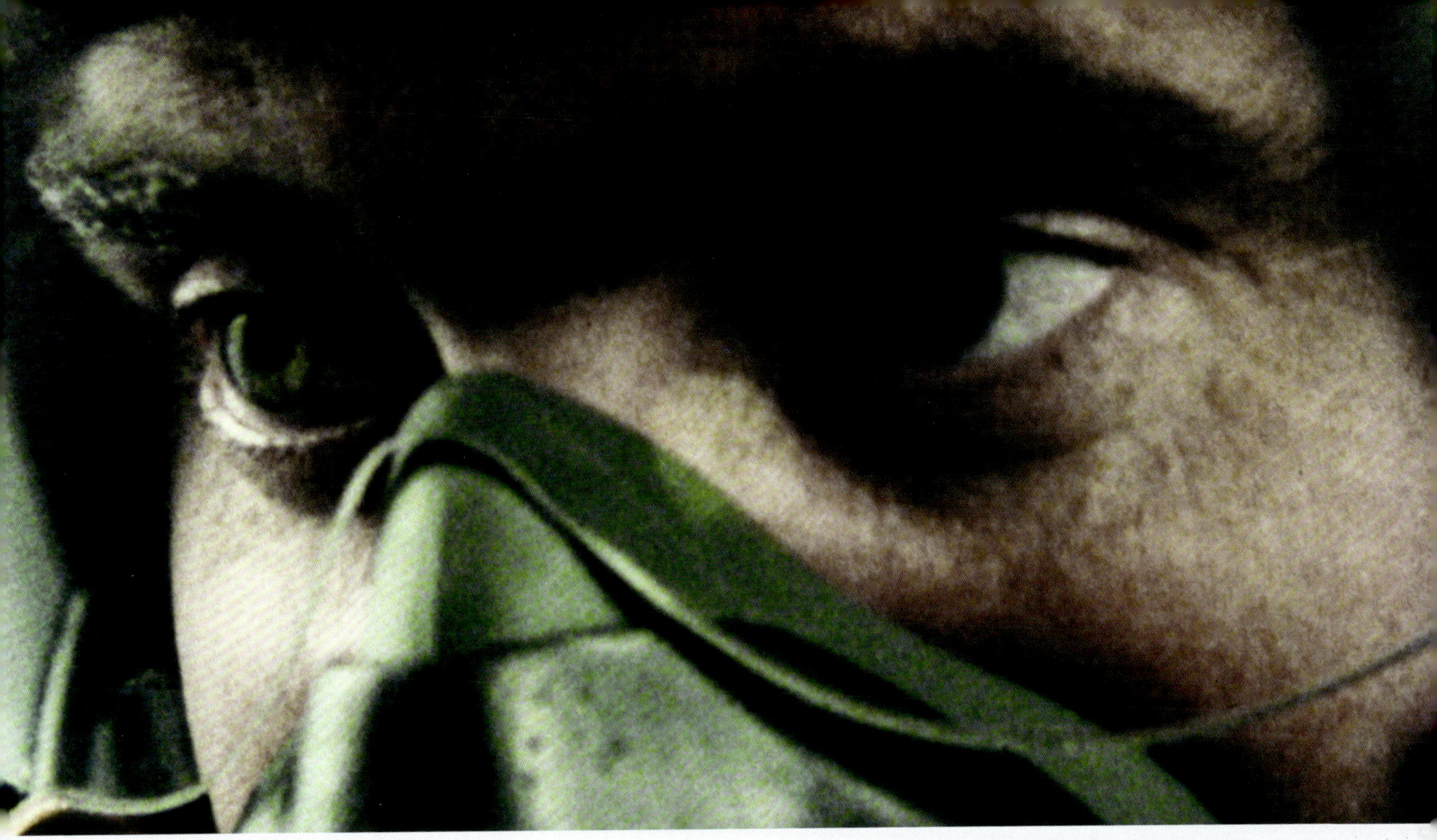

Leader and two are going for the hardened control bunker
On the lefthand side of the island
Three and four for the lay down
Are aiming for the missile complex to the center and right
Of the target area
As your man

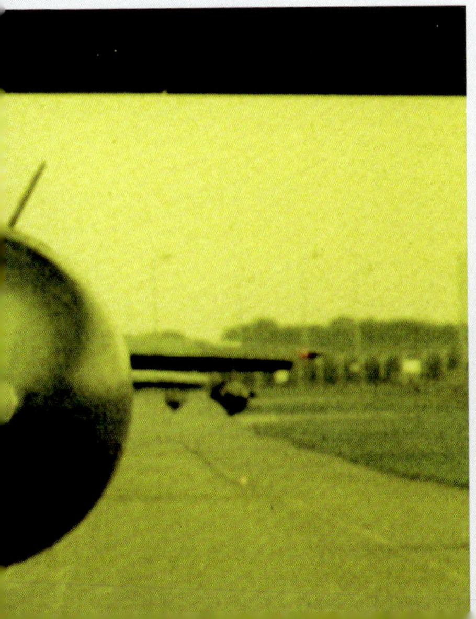

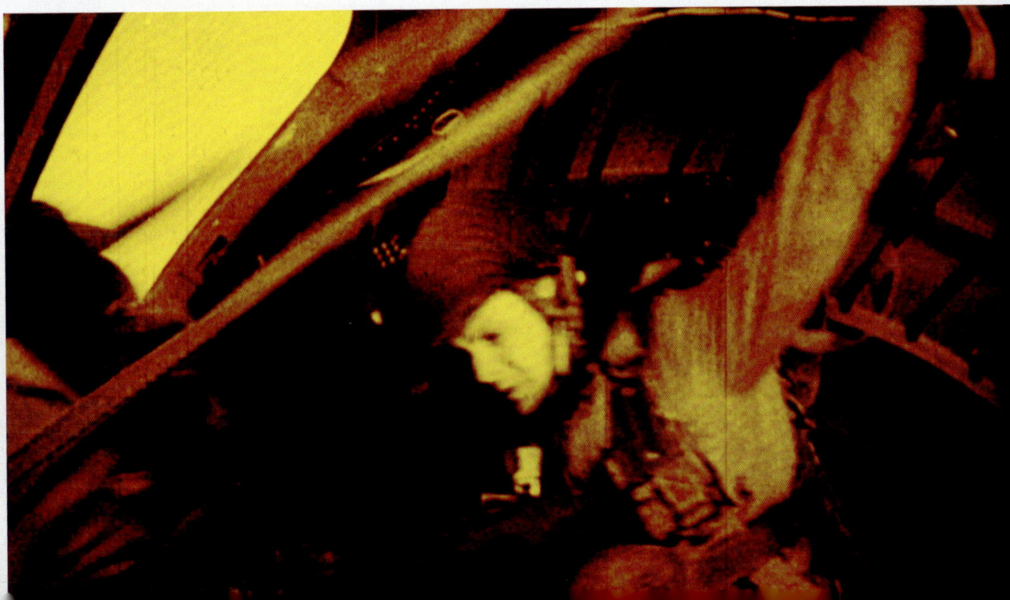

Airspace has always been tethered to the ground
A tool of empire
Its invisible aerial corridors
Forming a matrix of power
That legitimize violence
Exercised exclusively from above
And sanction the emergence of a new form
Of aerial sovereignty and control

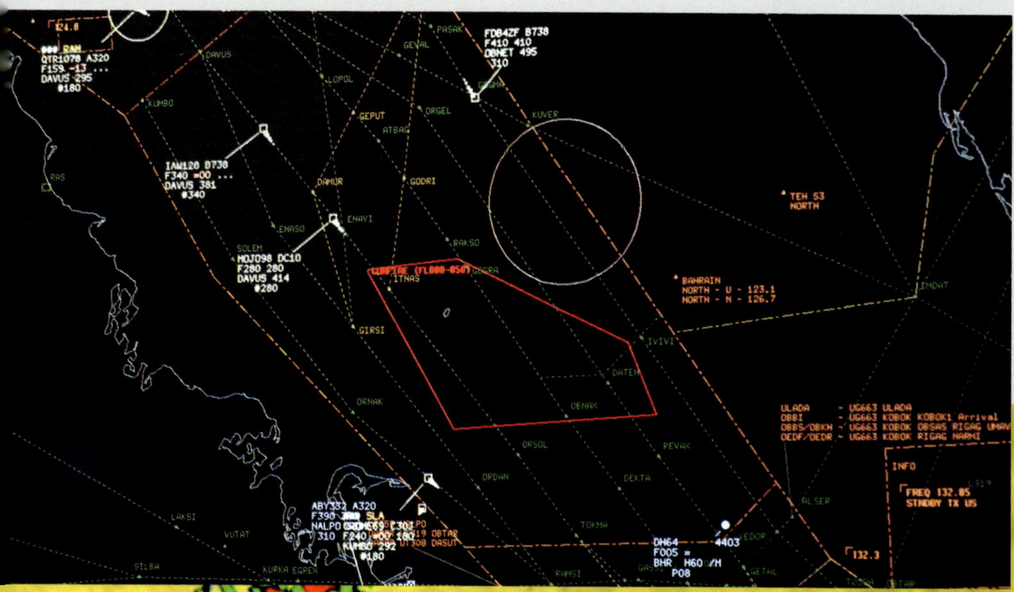

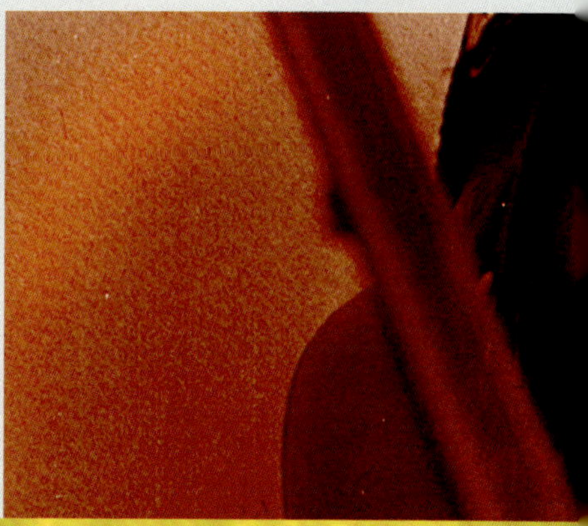

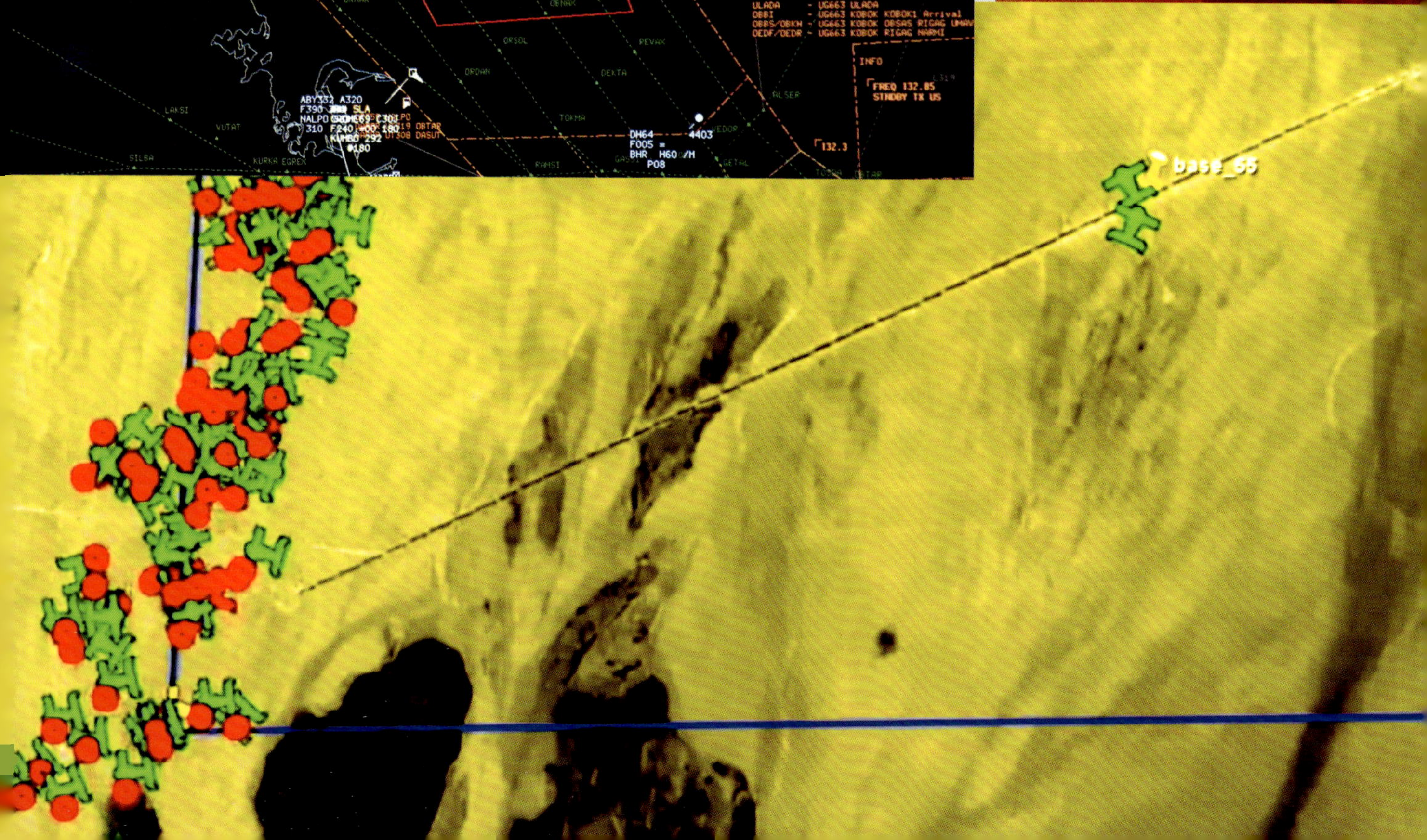

The robot bomber
Is the ideal soldier
Never tired
Never angry
Never afraid
Never hungry
Never forgets its orders
Feeling no compassion and no guilt
The bombing drone acts without intention
And without mercy

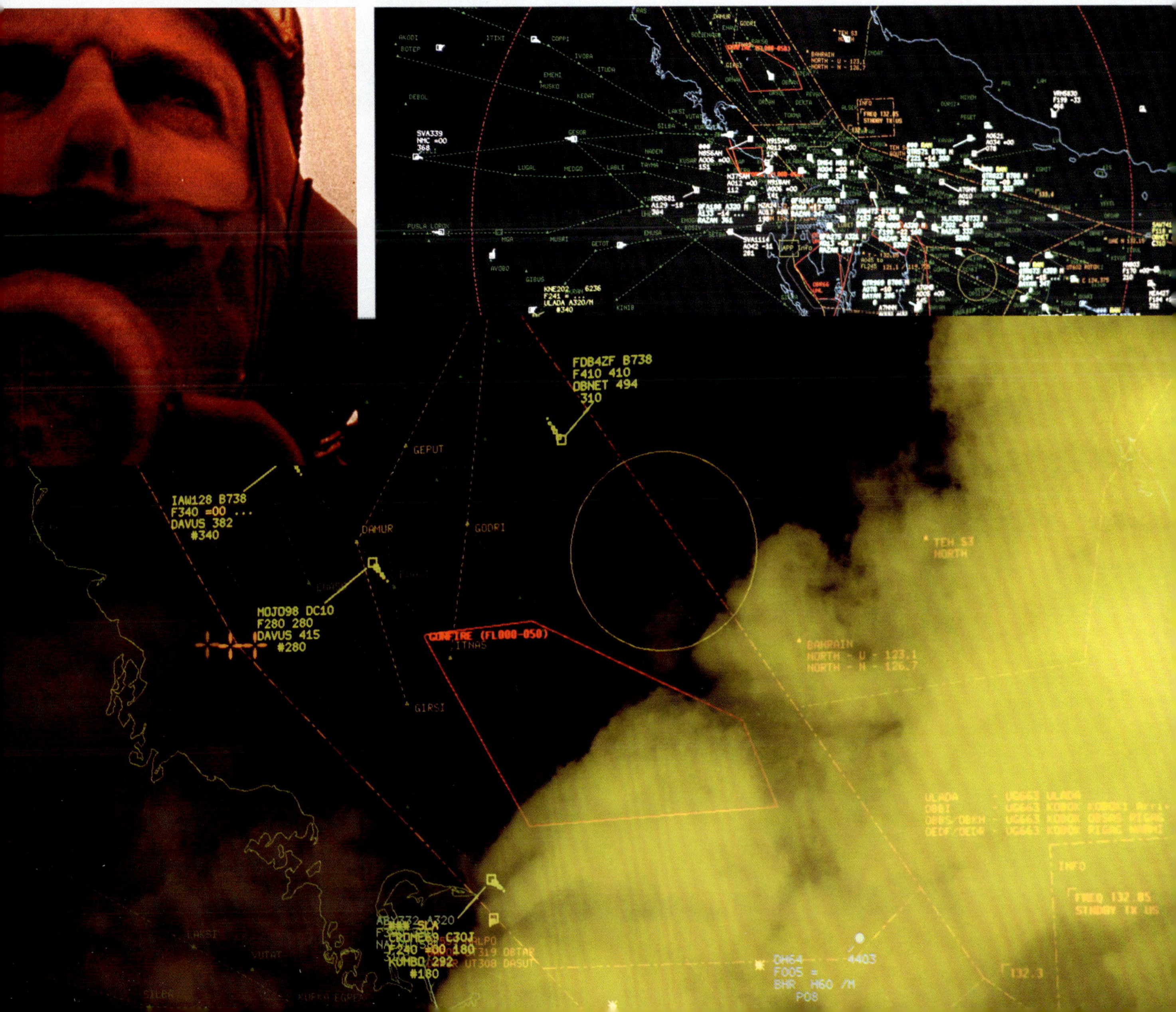

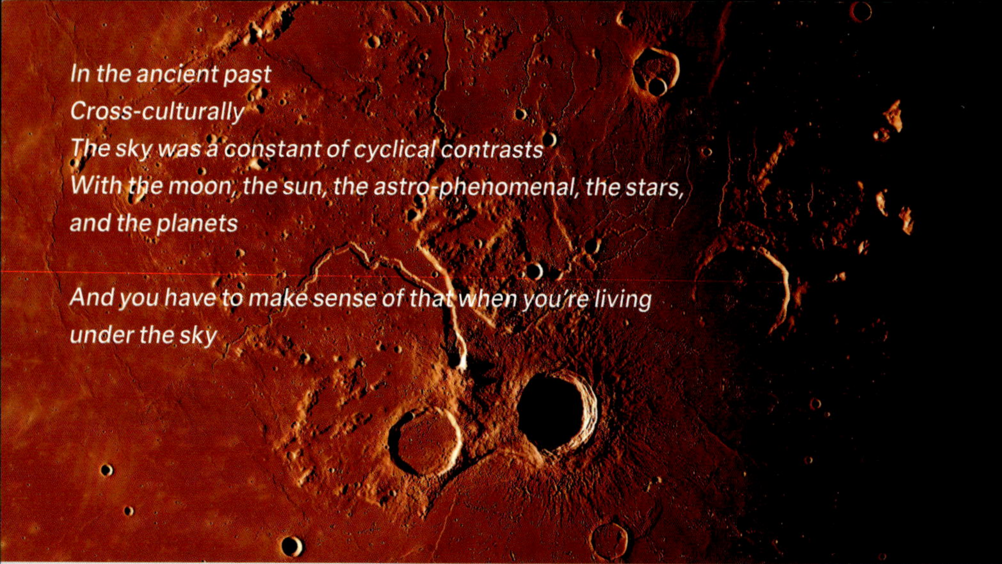

In the ancient past
Cross-culturally
The sky was a constant of cyclical contrasts
With the moon, the sun, the astro-phenomenal, the stars, and the planets

And you have to make sense of that when you're living under the sky

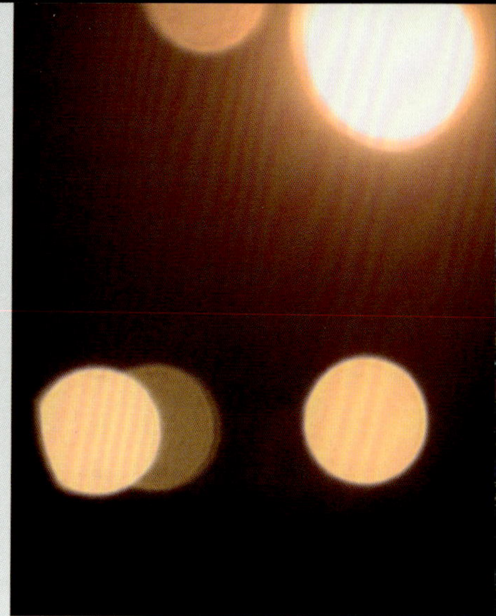

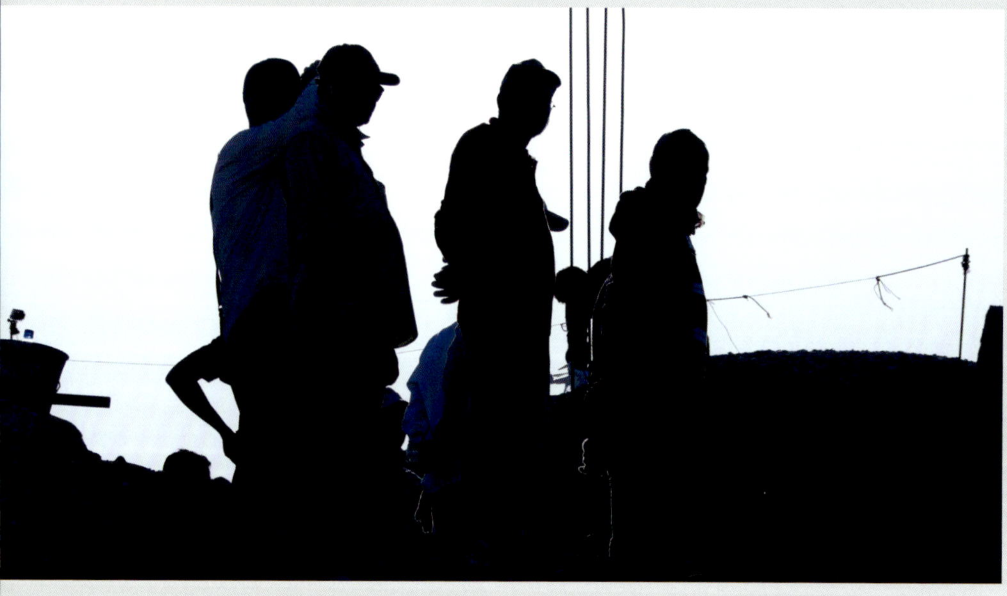

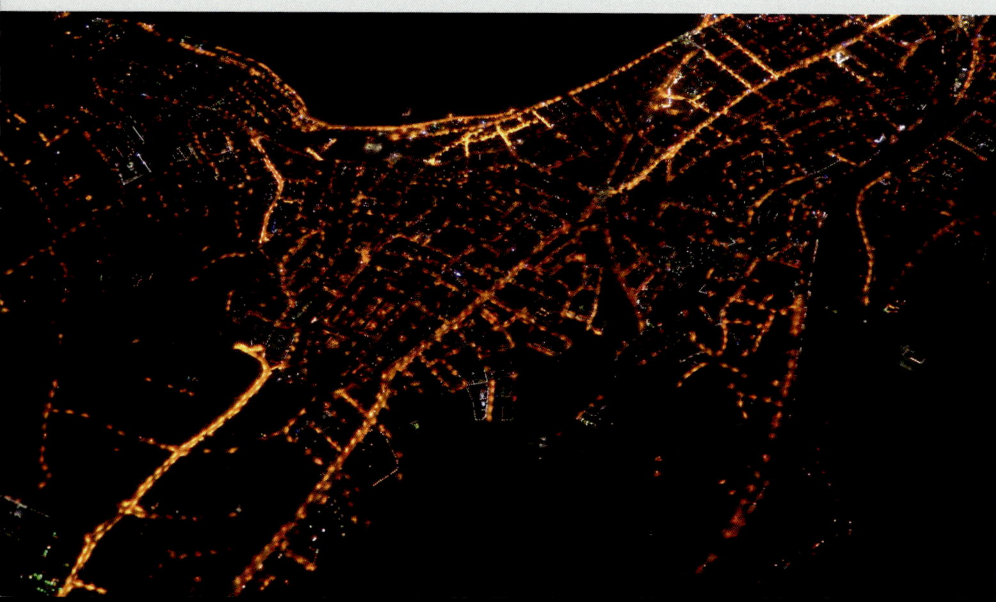

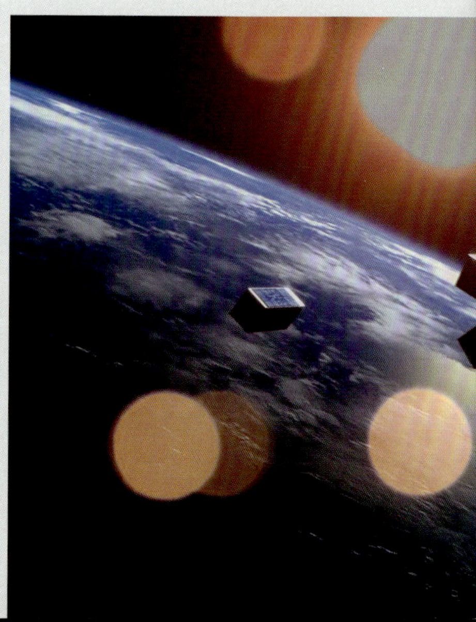

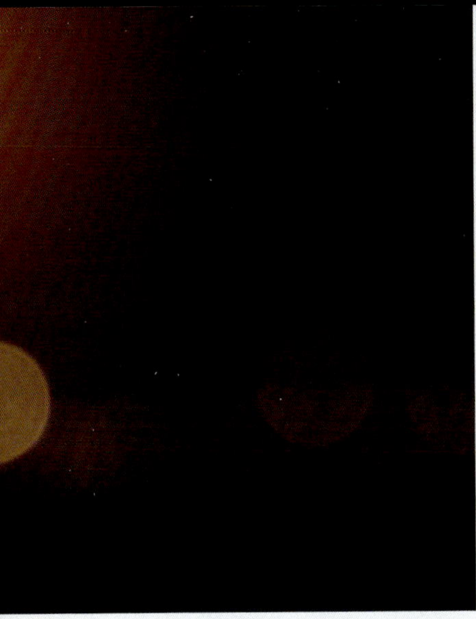

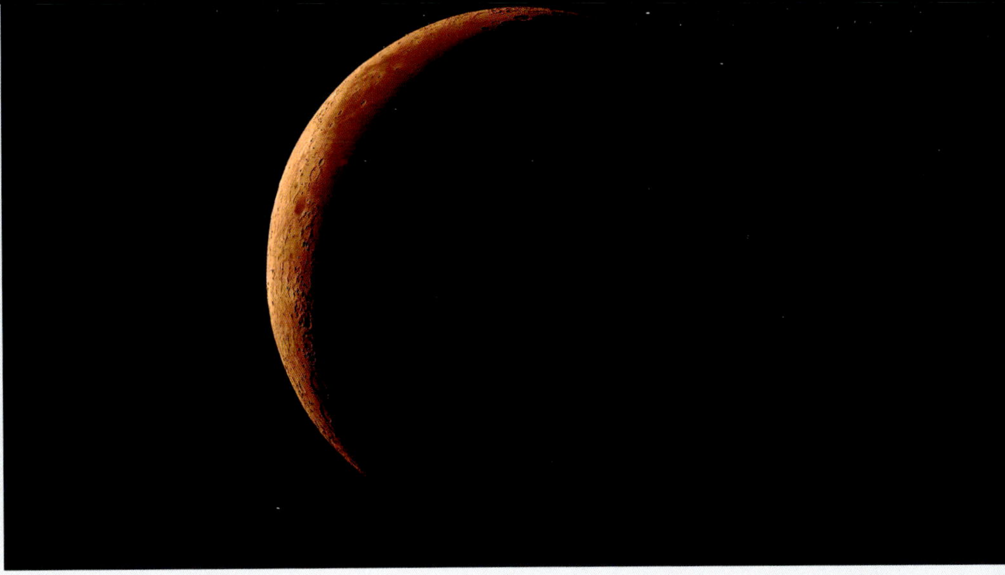

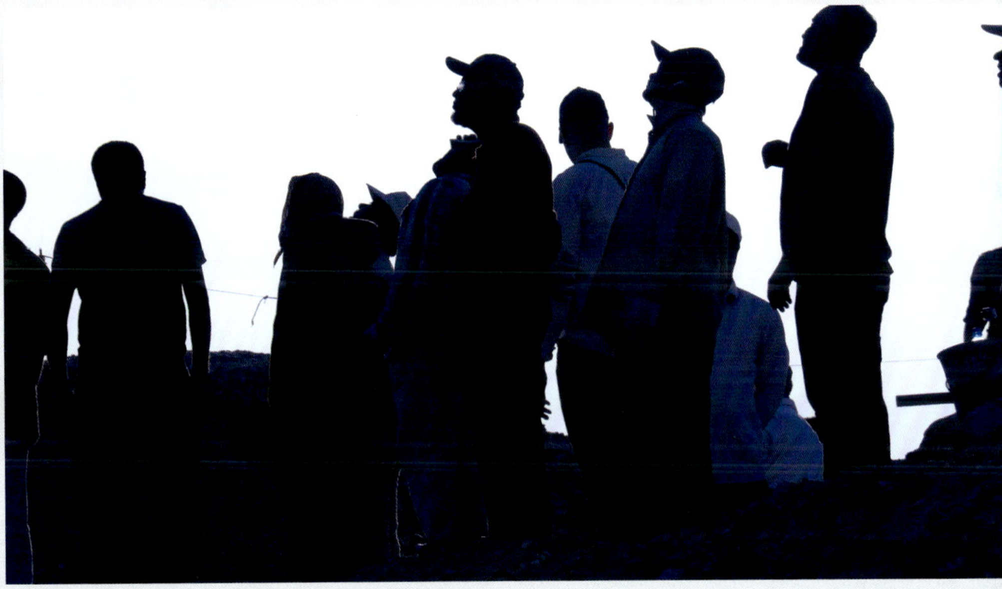

Once you as a society developed a conceptual framework
To explain what happens above you

In the day sky and the night sky
It provides a society with a sort of ontological security

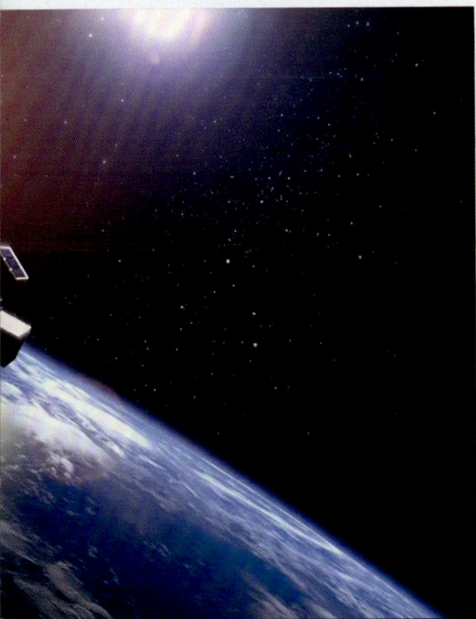

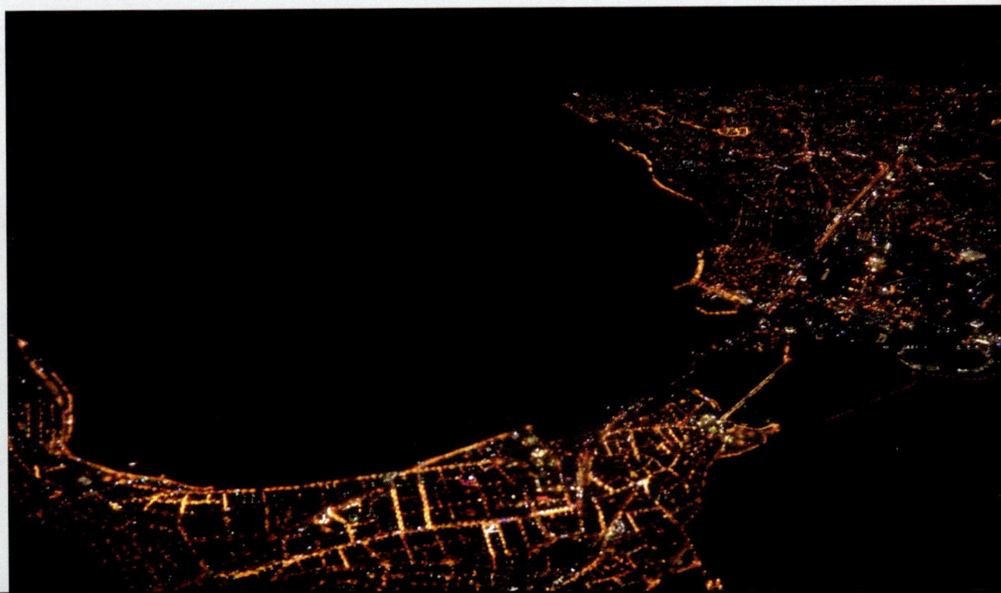

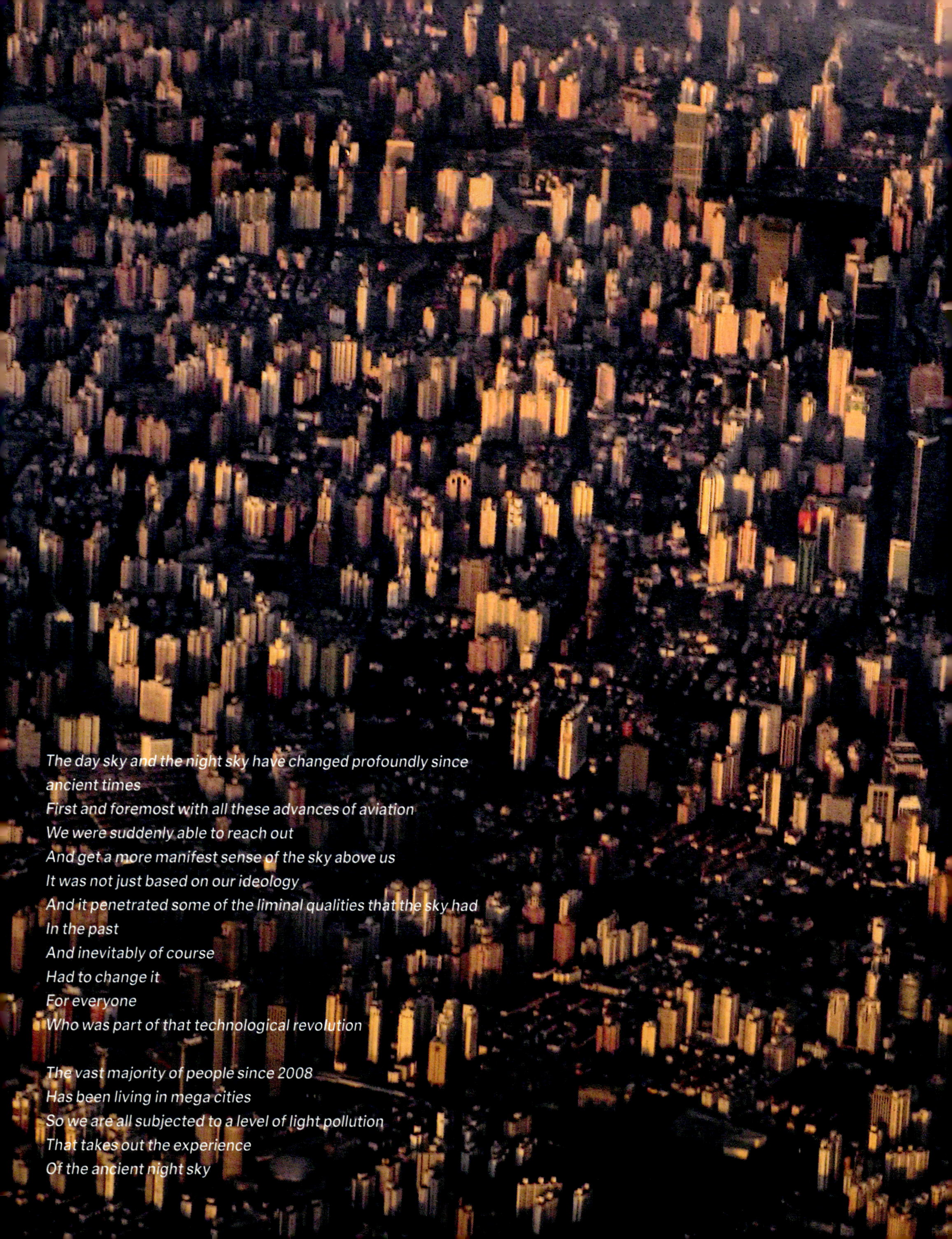

The day sky and the night sky have changed profoundly since
ancient times
First and foremost with all these advances of aviation
We were suddenly able to reach out
And get a more manifest sense of the sky above us
It was not just based on our ideology
And it penetrated some of the liminal qualities that the sky had
In the past
And inevitably of course
Had to change it
For everyone
Who was part of that technological revolution

The vast majority of people since 2008
Has been living in mega cities
So we are all subjected to a level of light pollution
That takes out the experience
Of the ancient night sky

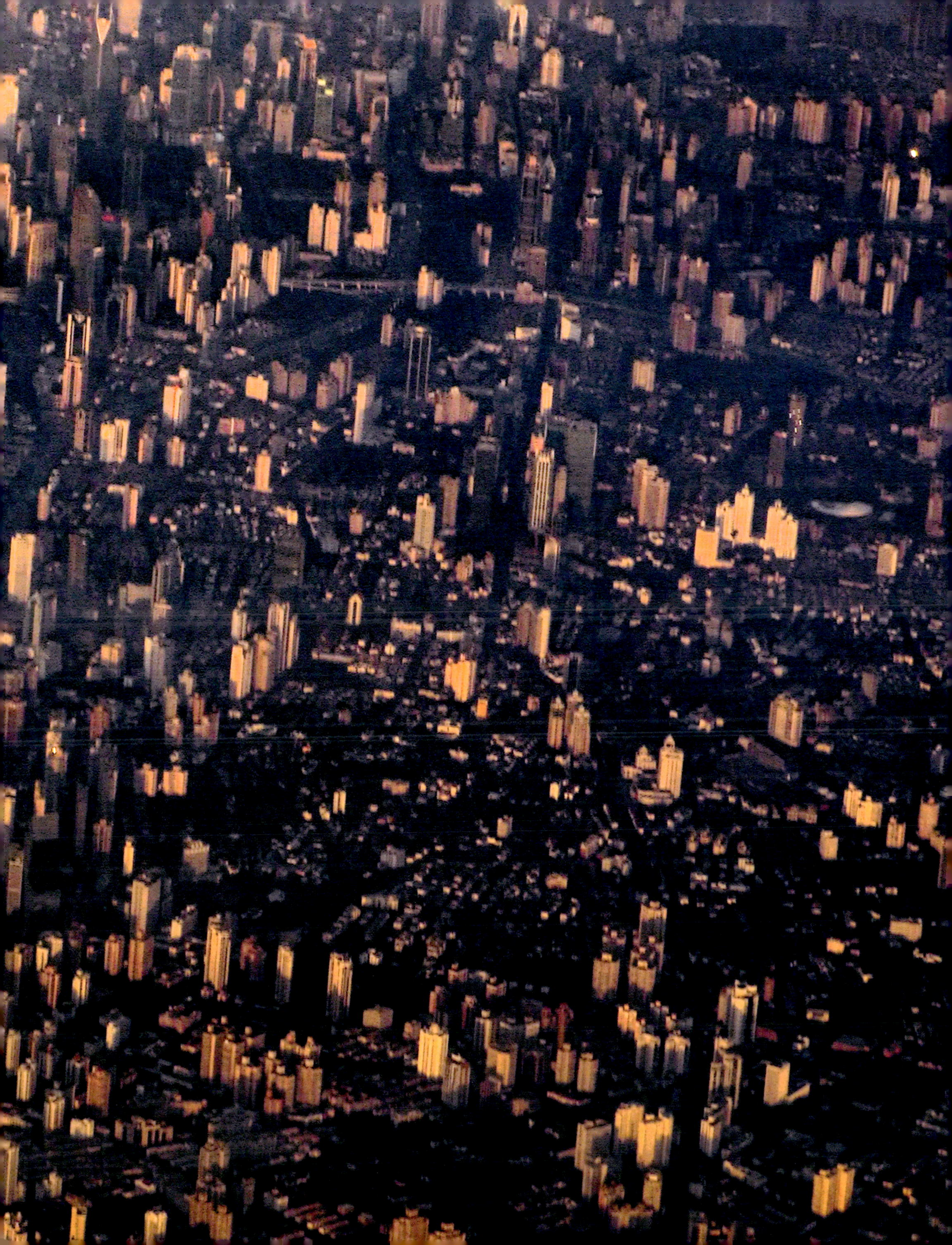

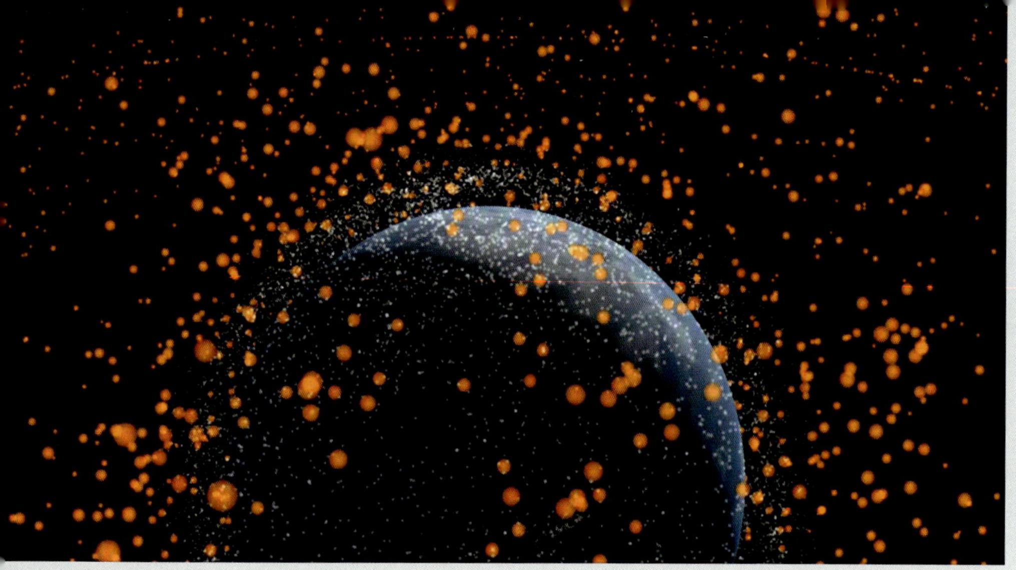

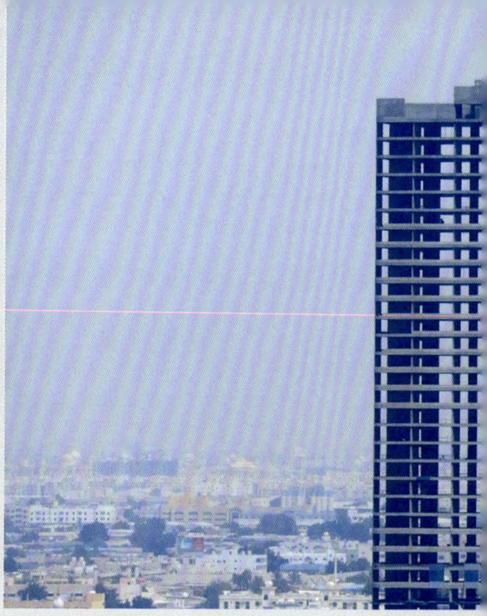

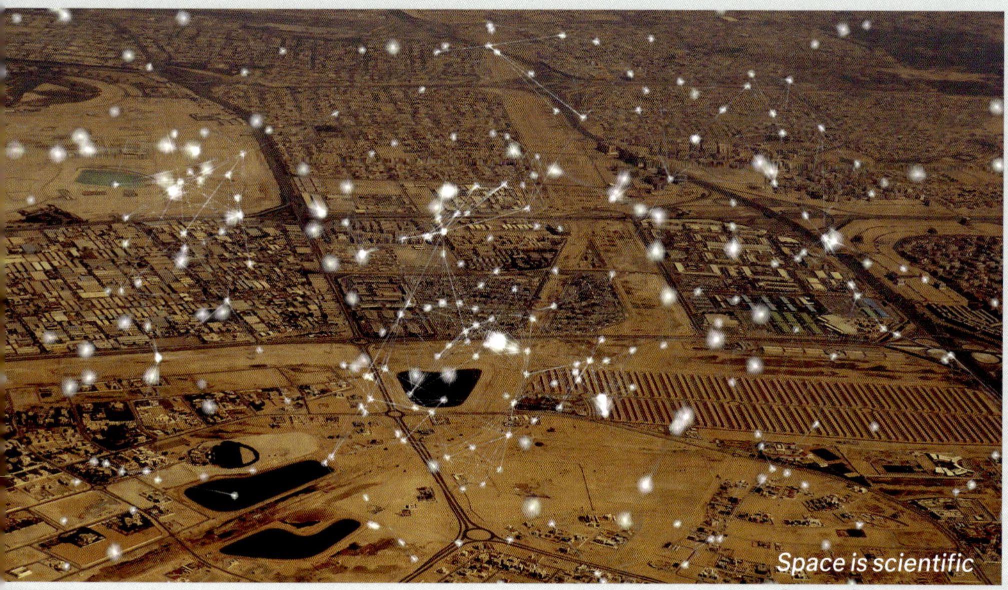

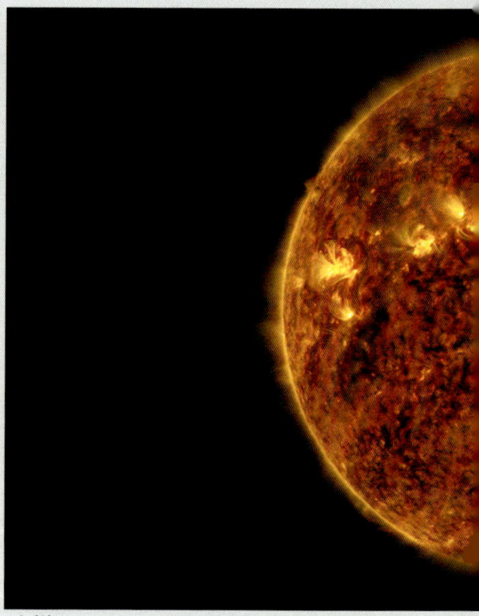

Space is scientific
Space is about sustainability
Space is about humanity
Space is about culture
Space is about memory
Space is also about strategic issues
Commercial issues
About military issues
Who's going to suffer the most with climate change?
It's the small island states
It's the poorer countries
If we screw up in space
Who suffers the most?
The large super powers
Who potentially pose the biggest danger and threat to us
Because their economies are totally dependent
Their total infrastructure is dependent on this

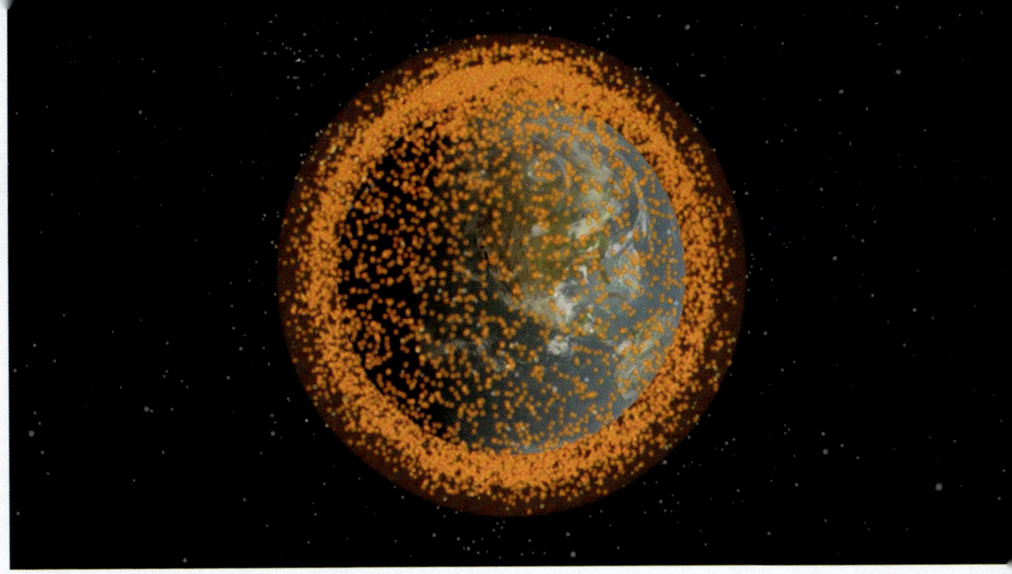
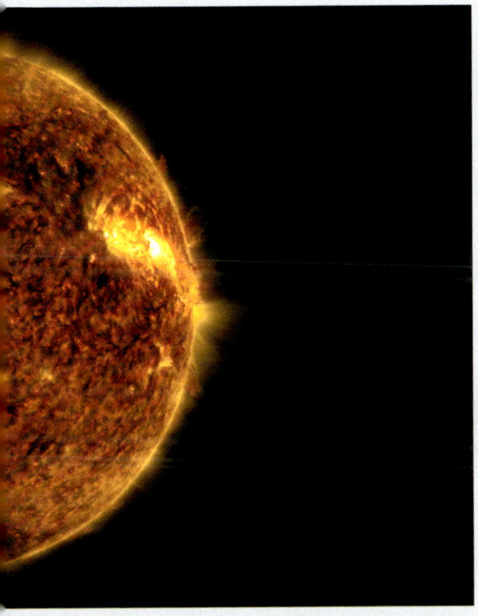
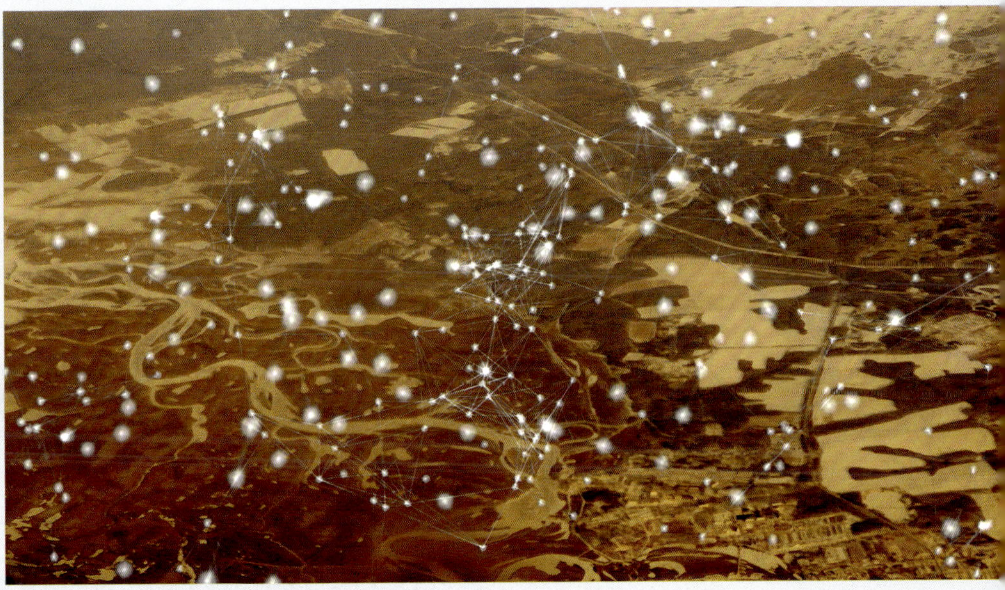

I think most of the civilization
They were seeking the knowledge, the wisdom
From the sky

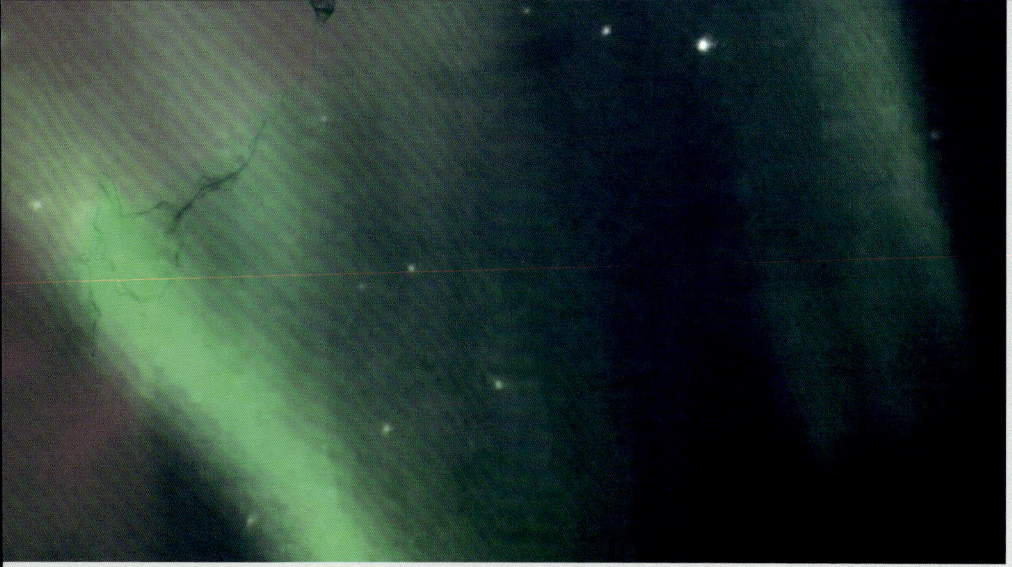

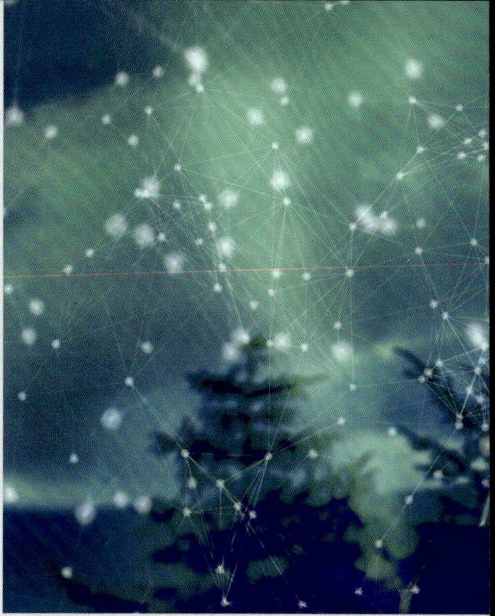

Air molecules scatter sunlight photons in all directions
The earth's shadow falls on the atmosphere itself

We live here in the turbulent troposphere
Warmed by the heat from the ground

Above this the air thins and the temperature falls
As we climb through the stratosphere and warming ozone layer

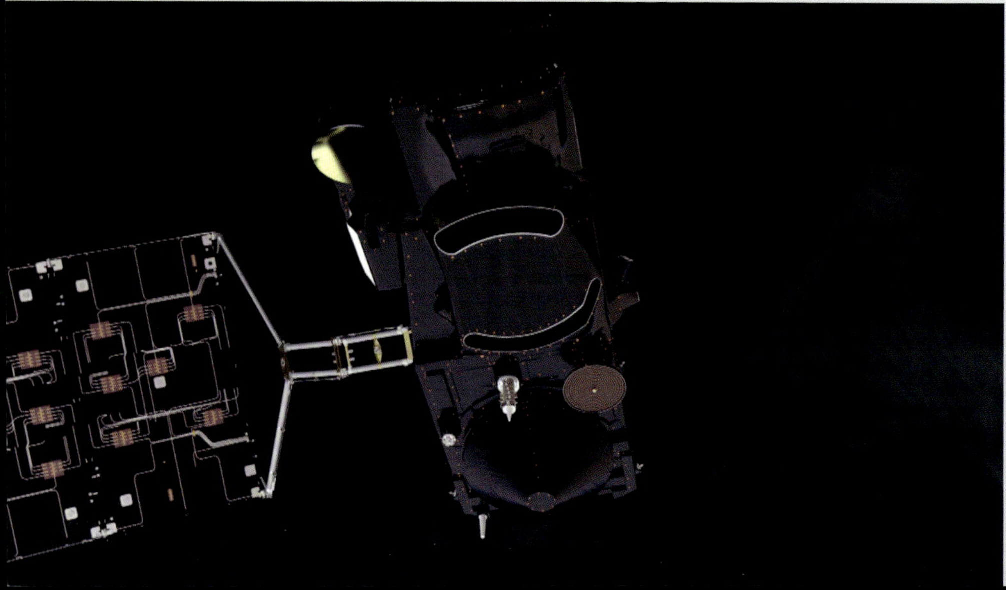

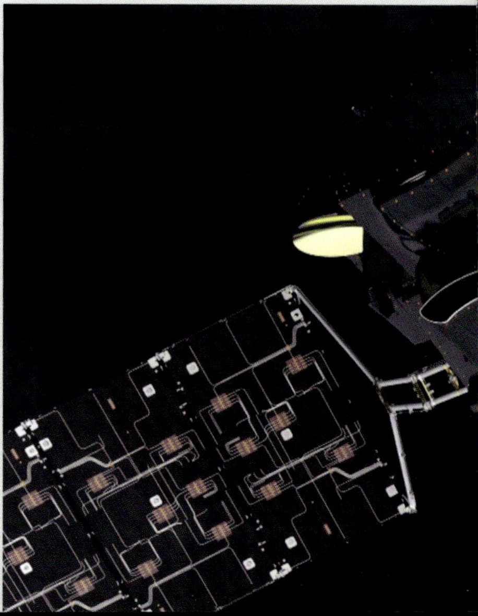

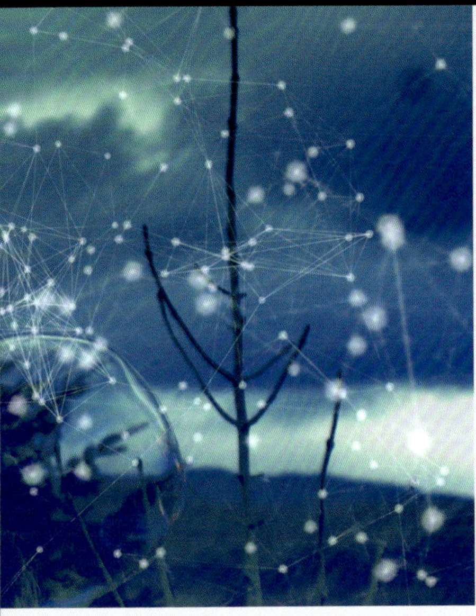
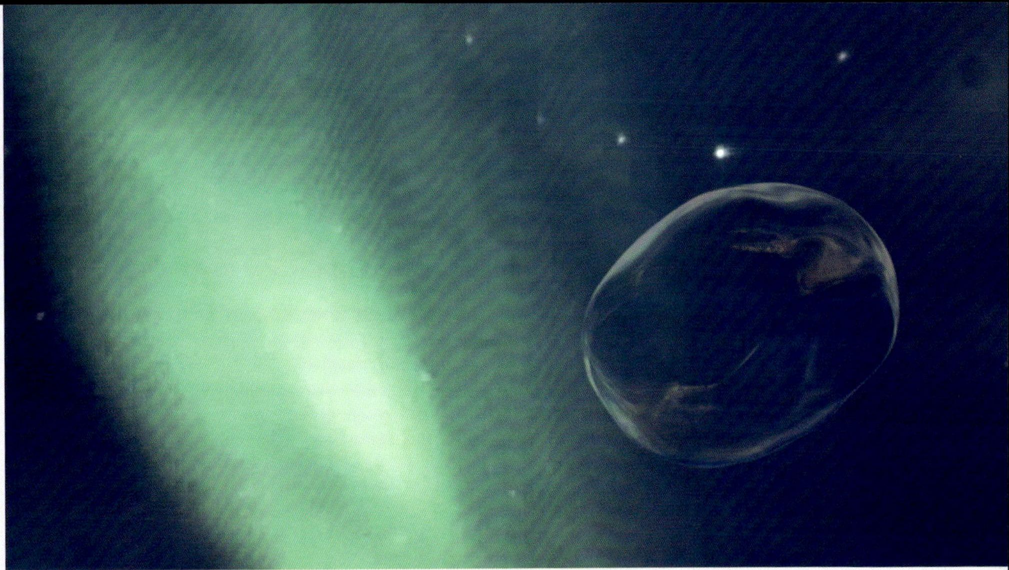

To the realm of the night shining
To the slowly shifting bands
Of the thermosphere's airglow

Winds, violent thunderstorms, jet stream shear, and solar radiation
Cause gravity waves to break over thousands of miles
Transferring energy, momentum, and chemical species
Moving upper atmosphere winds—turbulence, temperature, and chemistry
As the earth tries to stabilize
And breathe

You could absolutely wreak total destruction
Through the use of weaponry in space

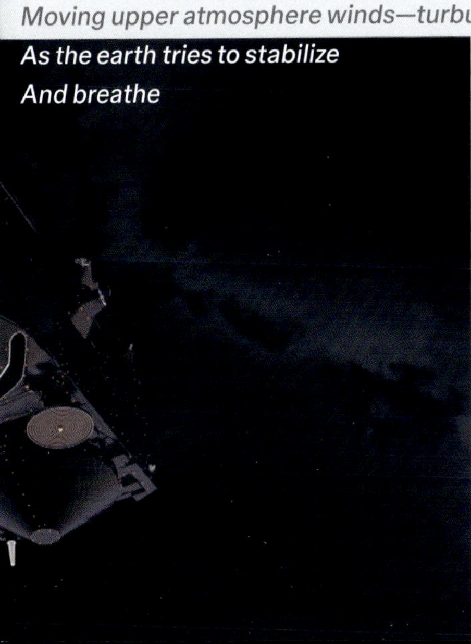
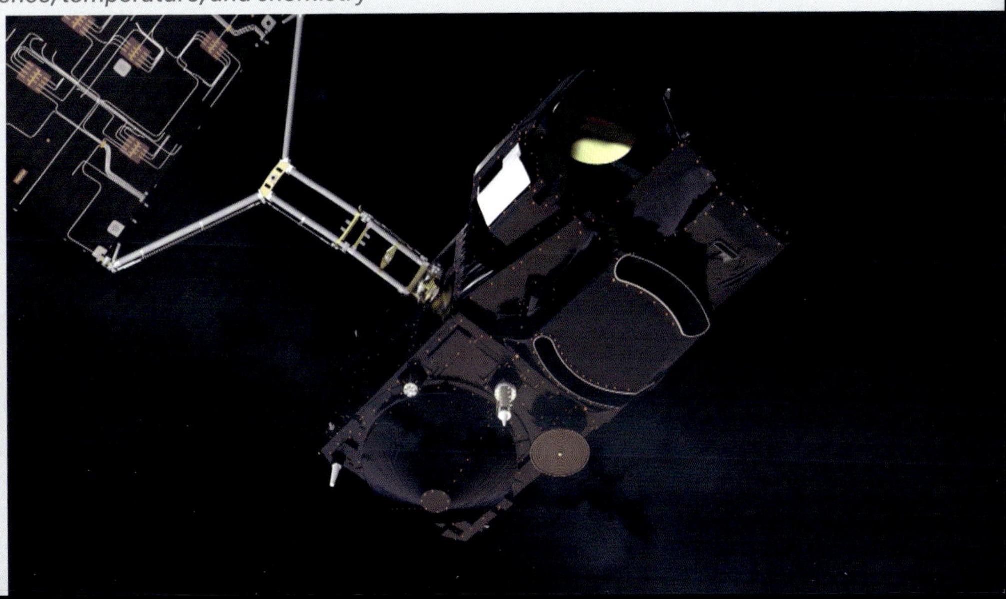

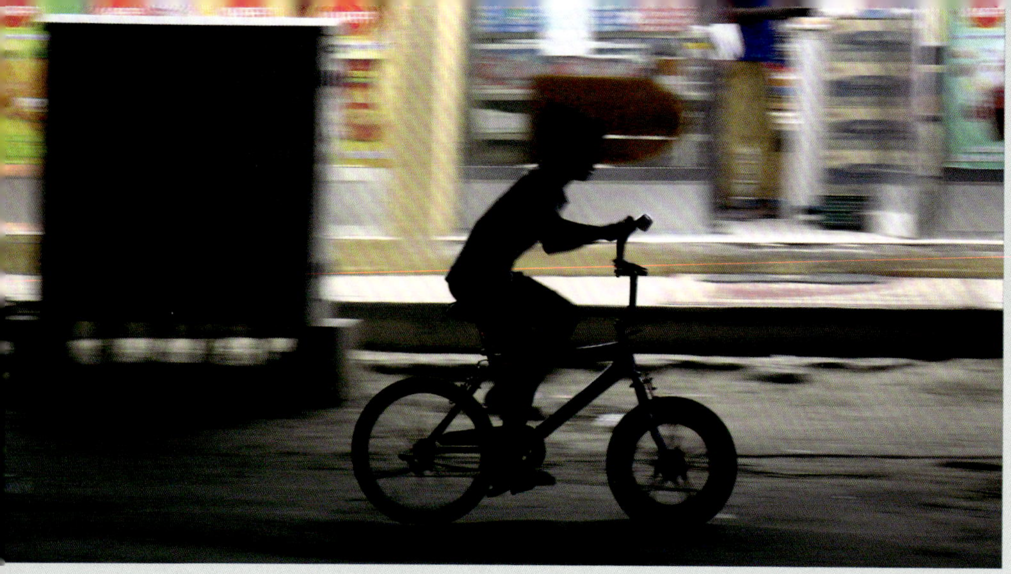

Sometimes you see
There's like a monster shade or something
On the moon
And the moon is like squeezing
We used to feel the suffering of the moon
How the moon suffer from this pressing on him

On the earth
We were just sad
And making this praying
For the moon to be free

What other means do we have
Philosophically or ethically or culturally
To think about the sky?

Decolonial cosmology
Might be the unlearning of a certain hubris
That says one specific version of the cosmos
Is universal

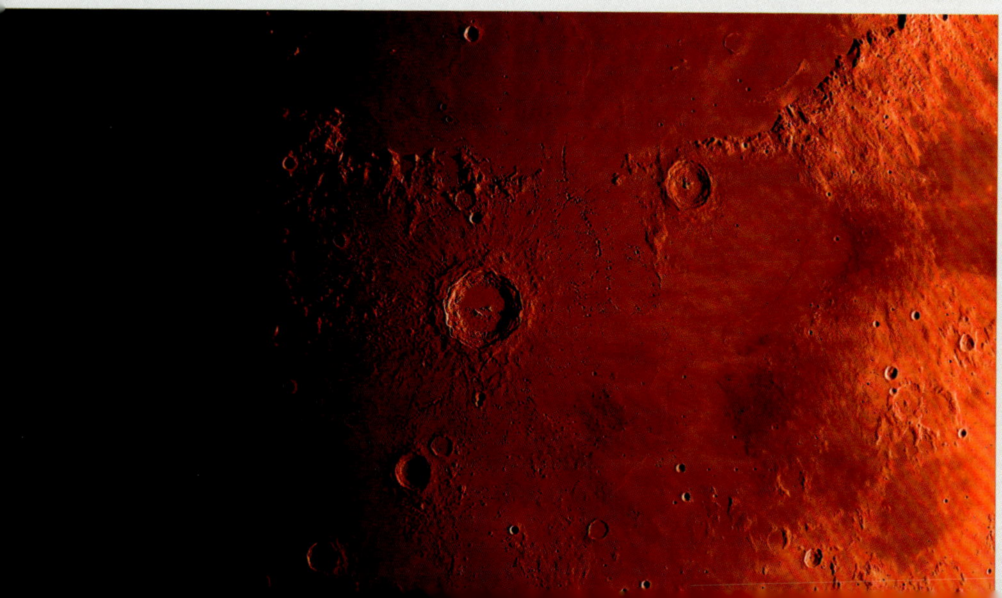

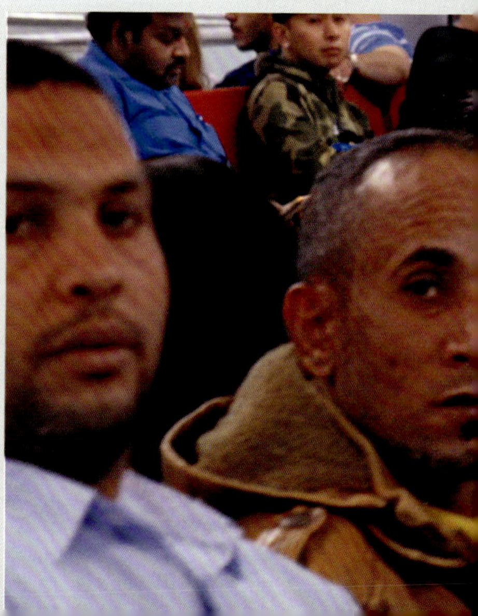

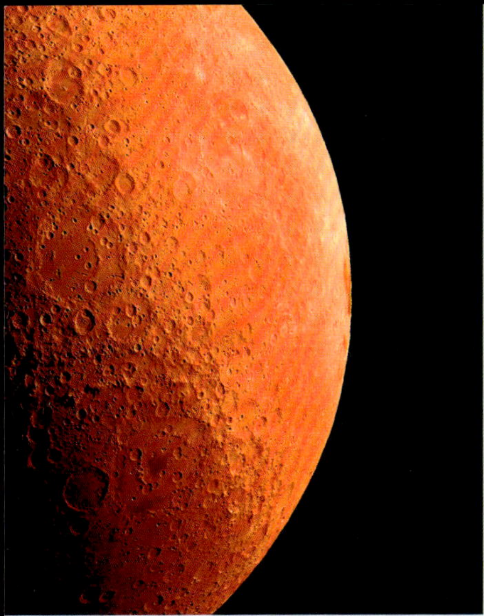
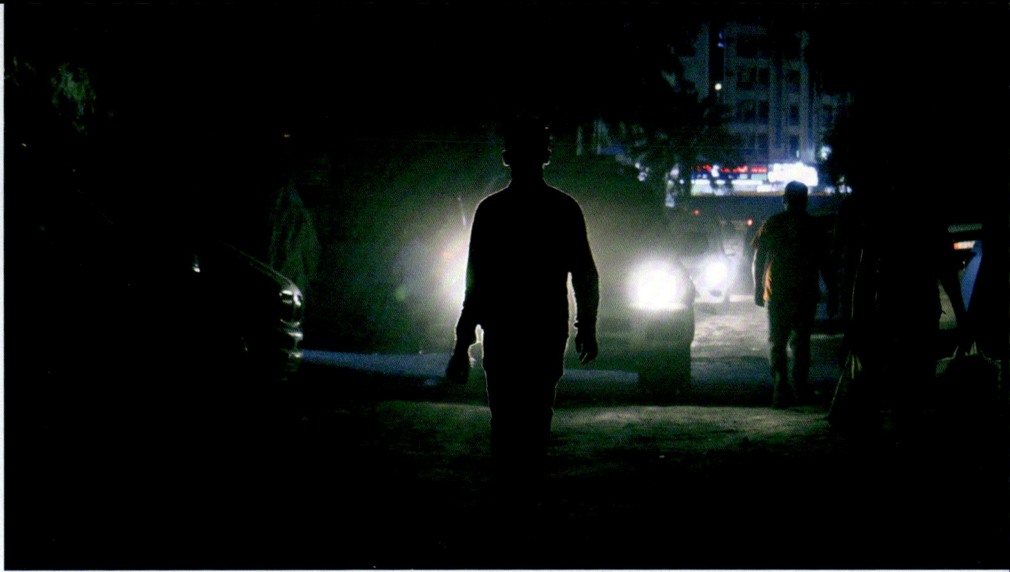
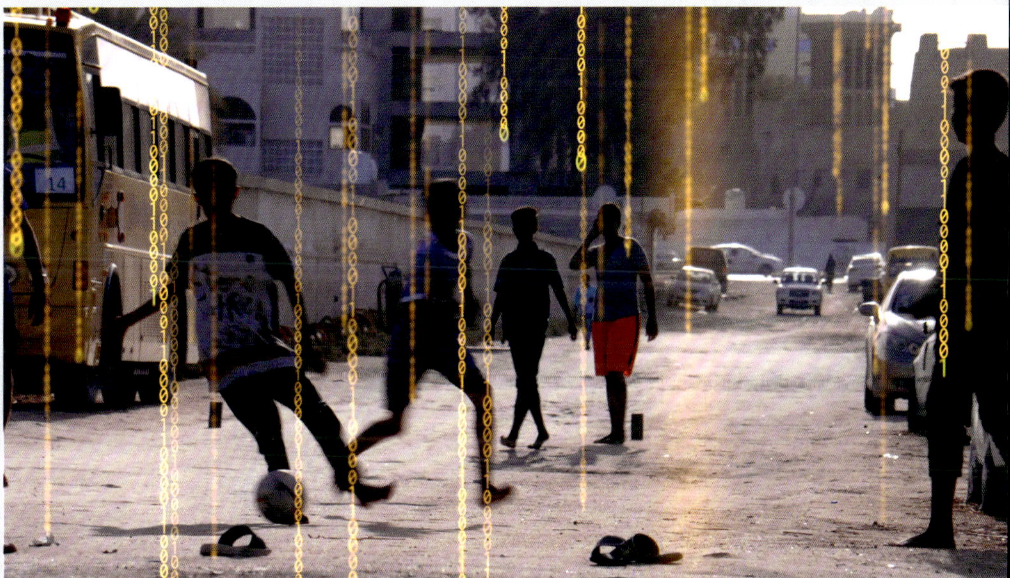
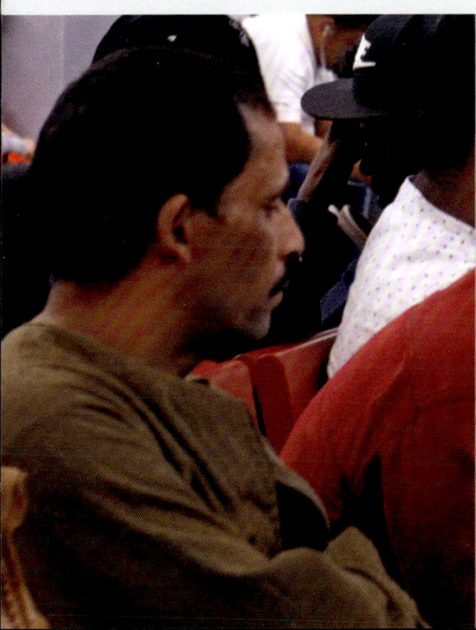
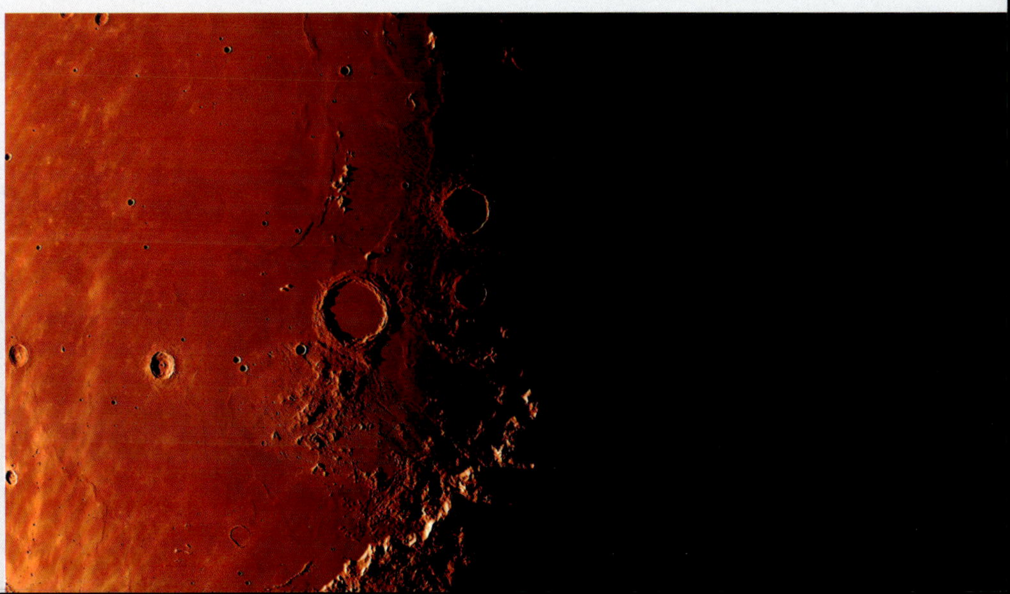

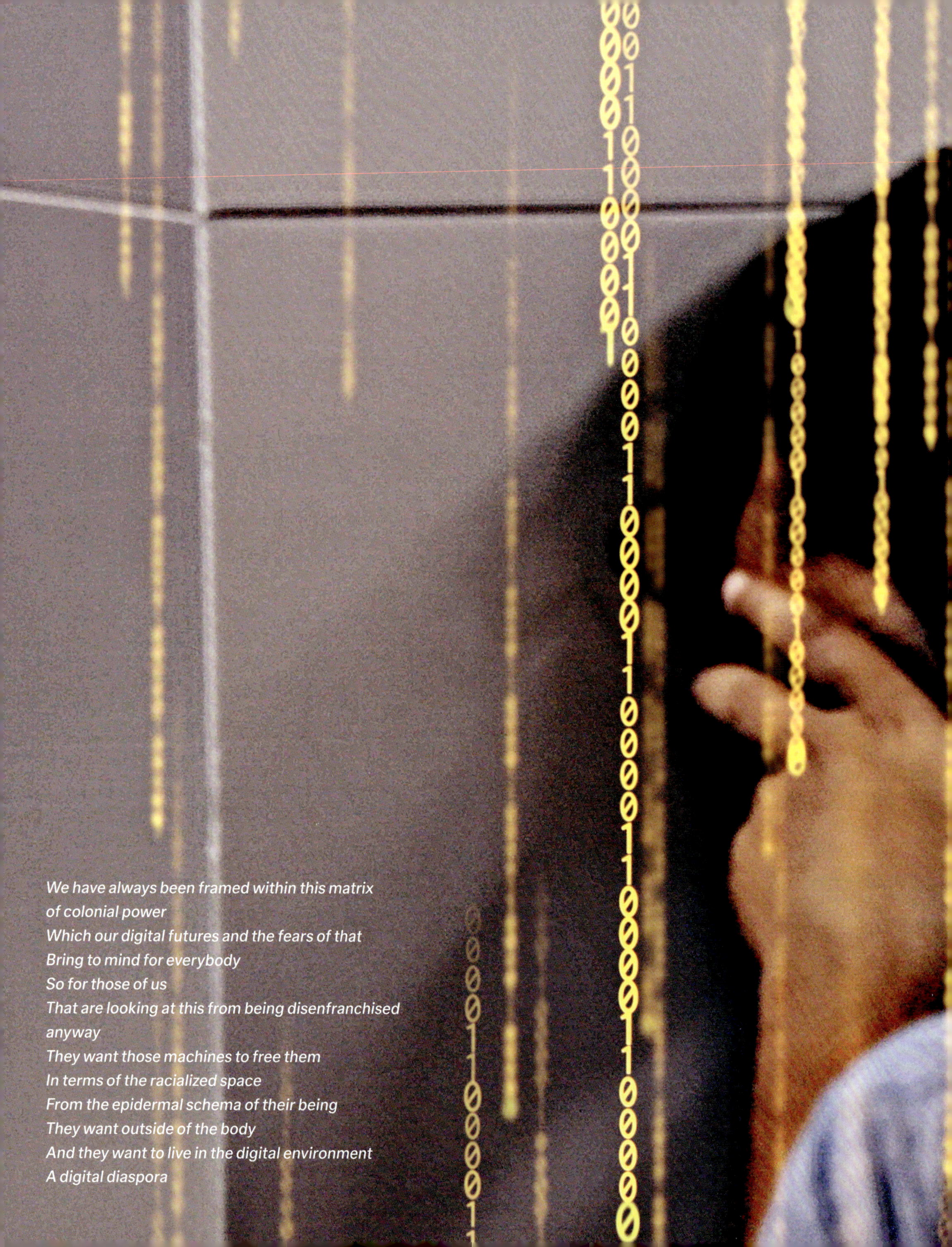

We have always been framed within this matrix
of colonial power
Which our digital futures and the fears of that
Bring to mind for everybody
So for those of us
That are looking at this from being disenfranchised
anyway
They want those machines to free them
In terms of the racialized space
From the epidermal schema of their being
They want outside of the body
And they want to live in the digital environment
A digital diaspora

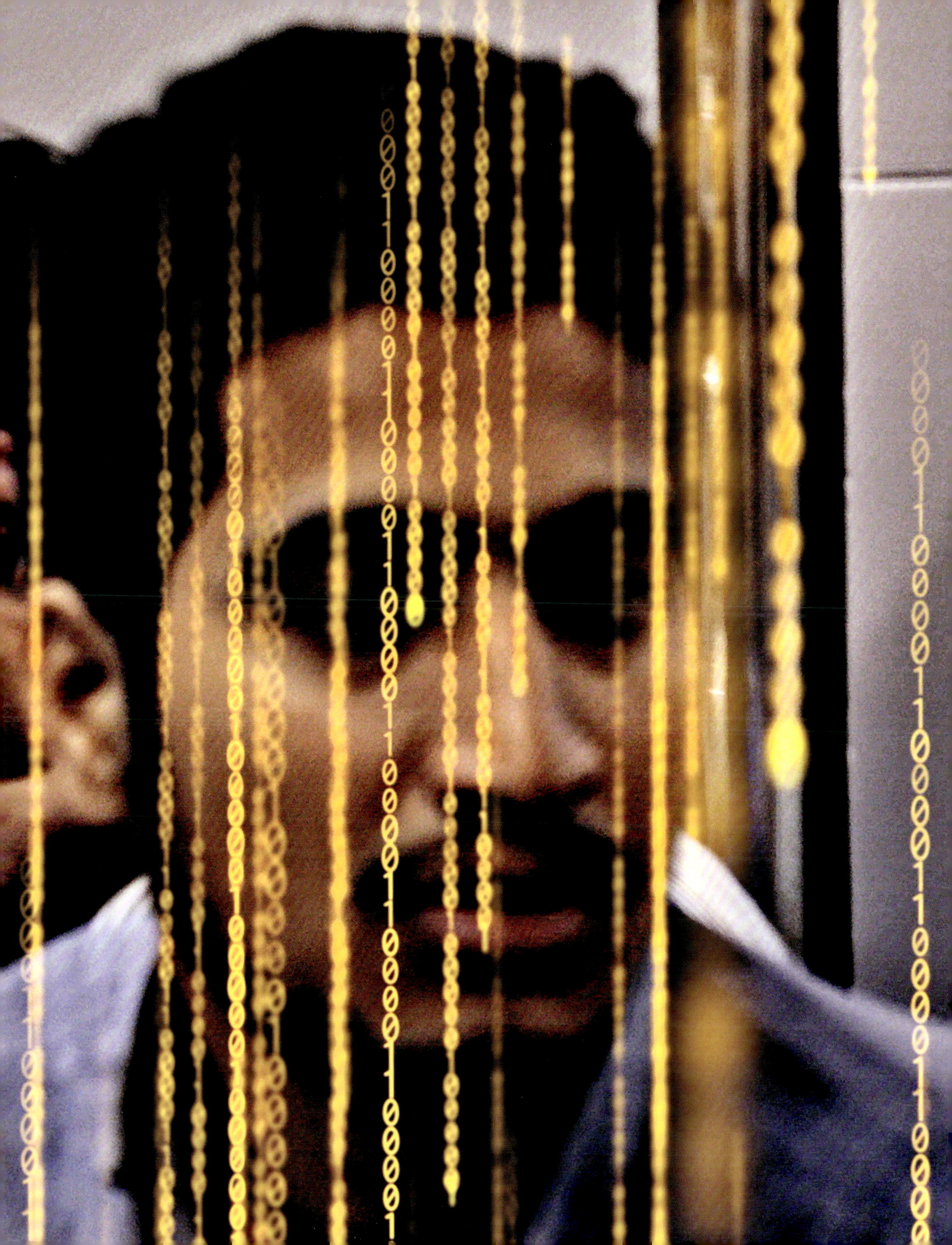

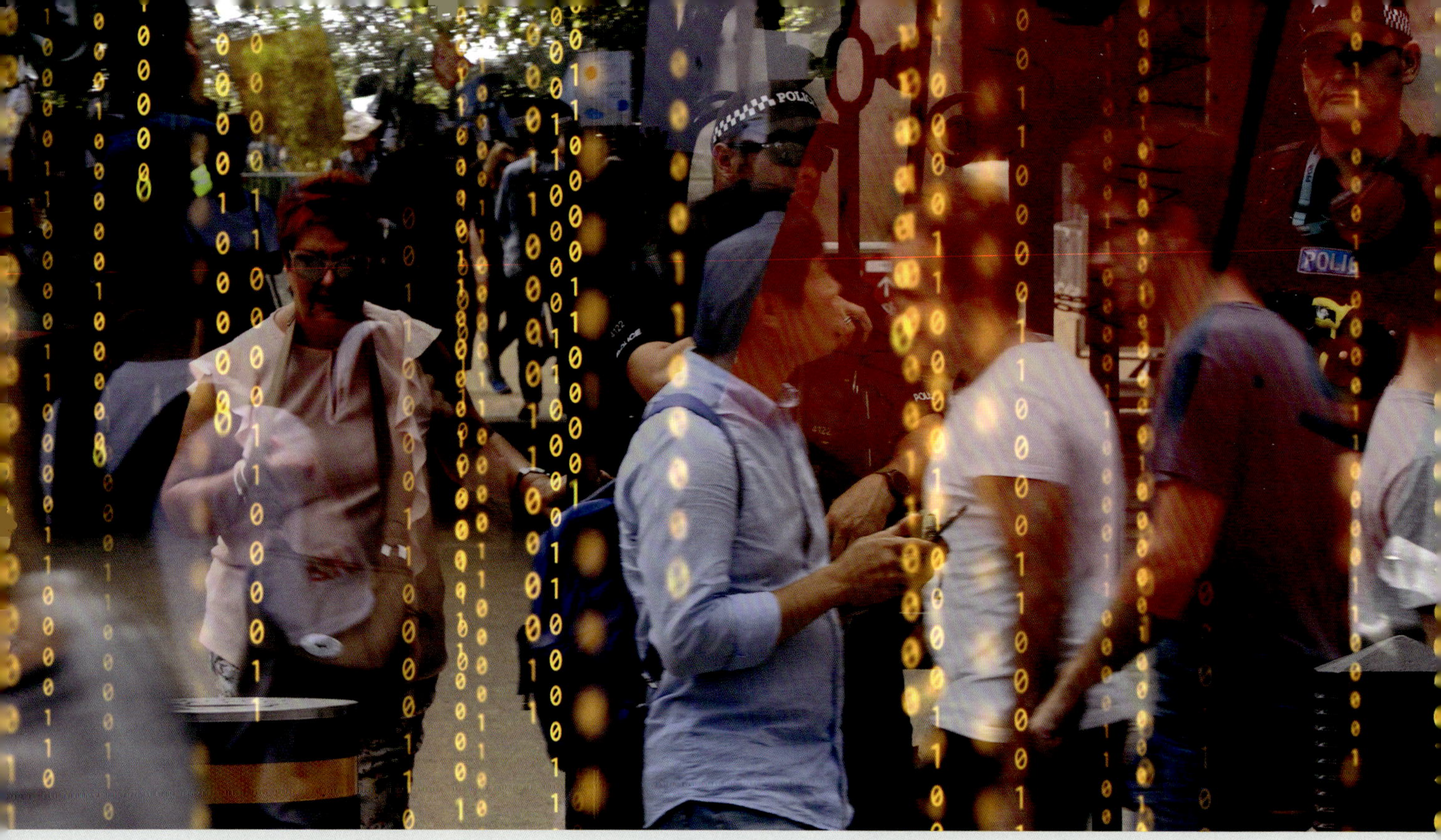

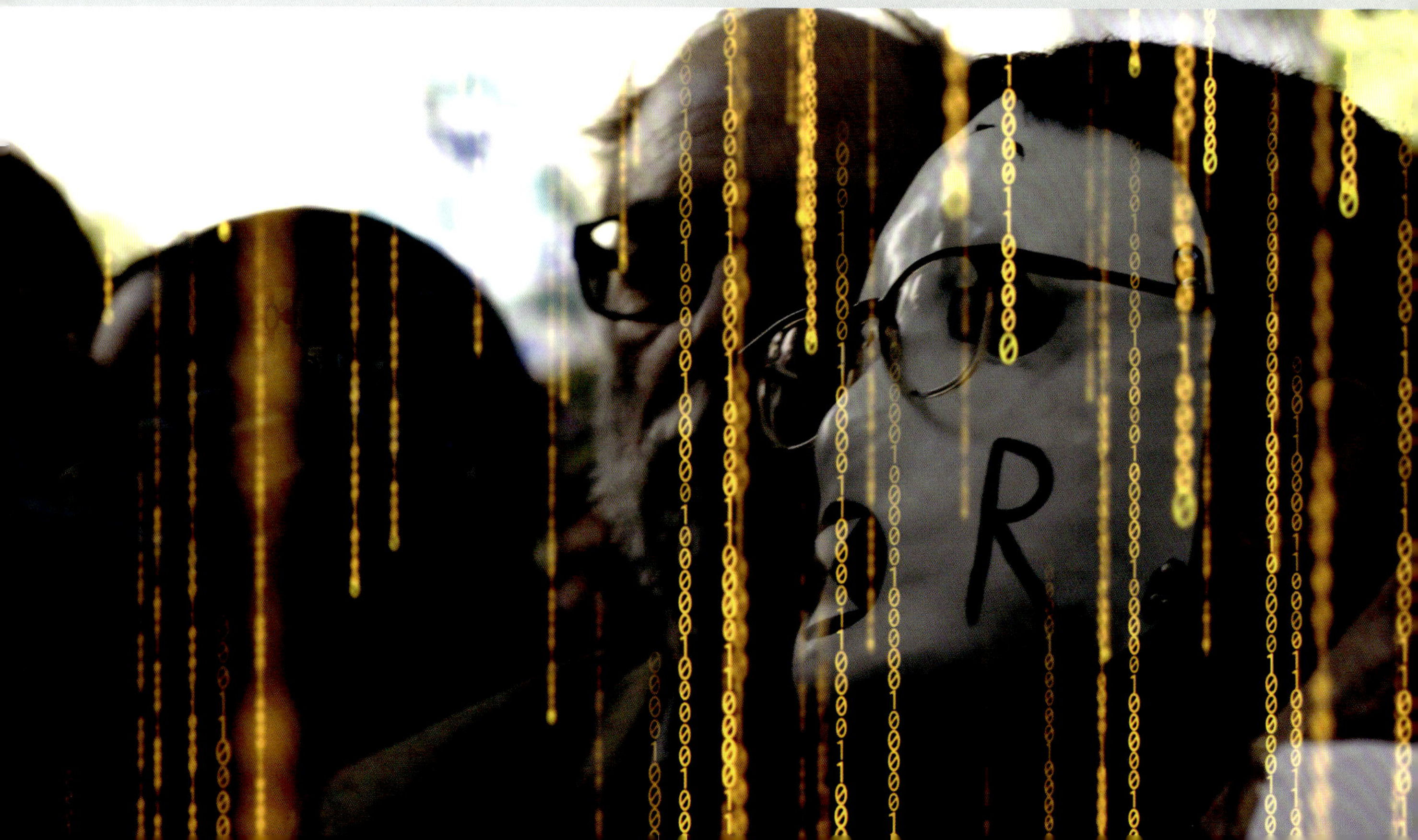

Humans need protecting
We've got an air gap
We've always lived with an air gap
Which is simply the unconnected world
The ability to exist, to breathe the air, to live
To conduct your activities of any kind
In any way you want
Without any form of connectivity, surveillance,
or control

The miniaturization especially of robotic technology
The miniaturization of drone systems
The rise of commercial drones, which are now
relatively cheap
Improvements in camera systems
Improvements in machine-learning algorithms
Developments in robotics
The move toward swarm robotics
Improvements in connectivity
Improvements in databases
All of this is currently happening
Which means that we can inevitably
See that the system of surveillance,
As it exists as a pretty hideous experimental laboratory,
Is only at an early stage of where we're going to go

And the notion of the air gap
Is something that actually we need to cling onto
Because it's going to be eradicated
Far more effectively
Than I think we ever, ever anticipated

I'm not even sure that science fiction even came close
To the reality of what we've got coming

This is finding paradoxically
The unknown individual
Targets of drone strikes do not have to be known by name
But instead in terms of a pattern-of-life activity
In other words metadata, movements, networks,
contacts, and mobile phone use

Attacks on the basis of what are known as signature
strikes
Based upon the signature of metadata
And the pattern of life

Geolocation features are pervasive in smart phones
And increased search engine power is sifting and
mapping
Geotagged photographs
All inscribed ever deeper and detailed patterns of life
A sudden mass vulnerability
An exposure that seems impossible to contain

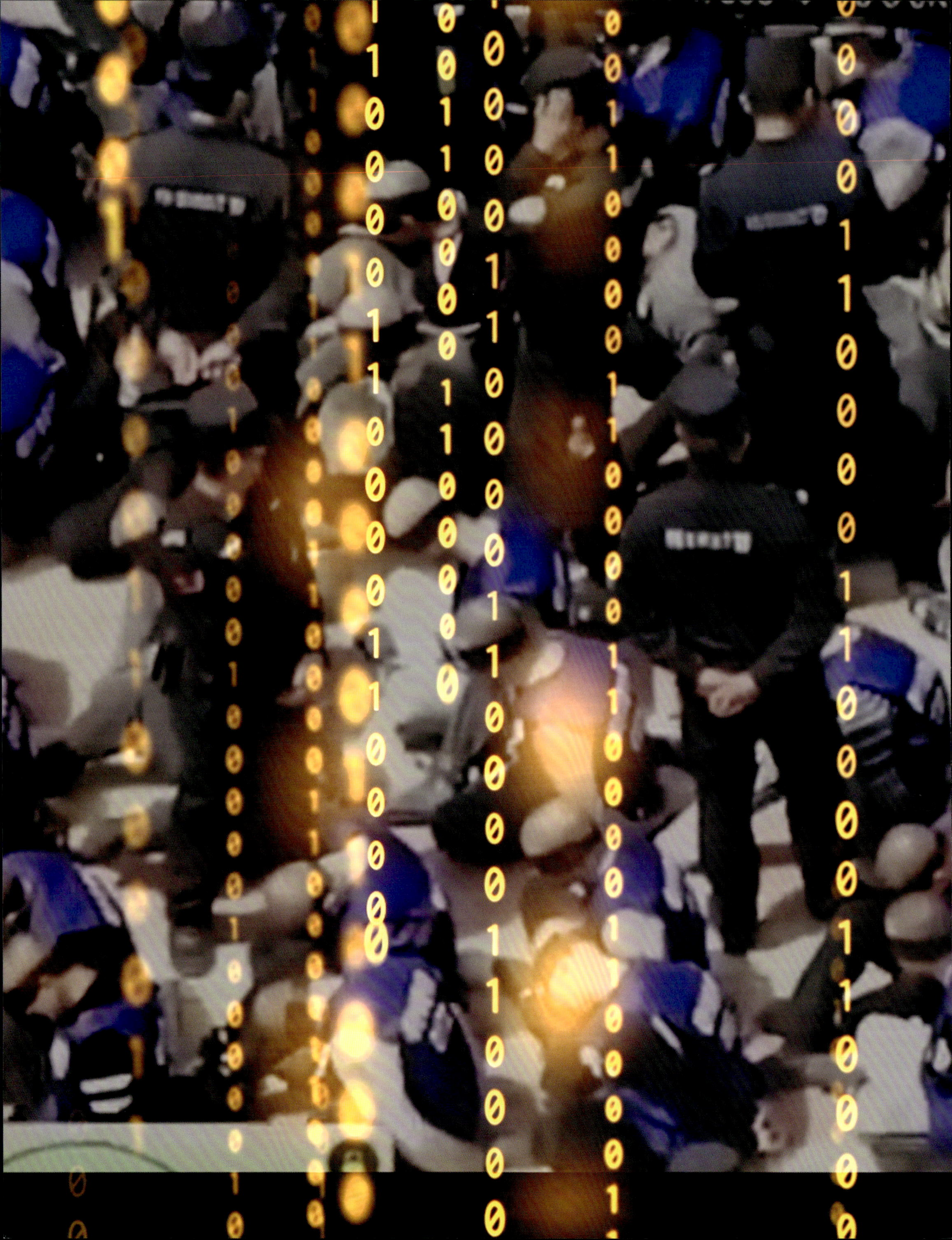

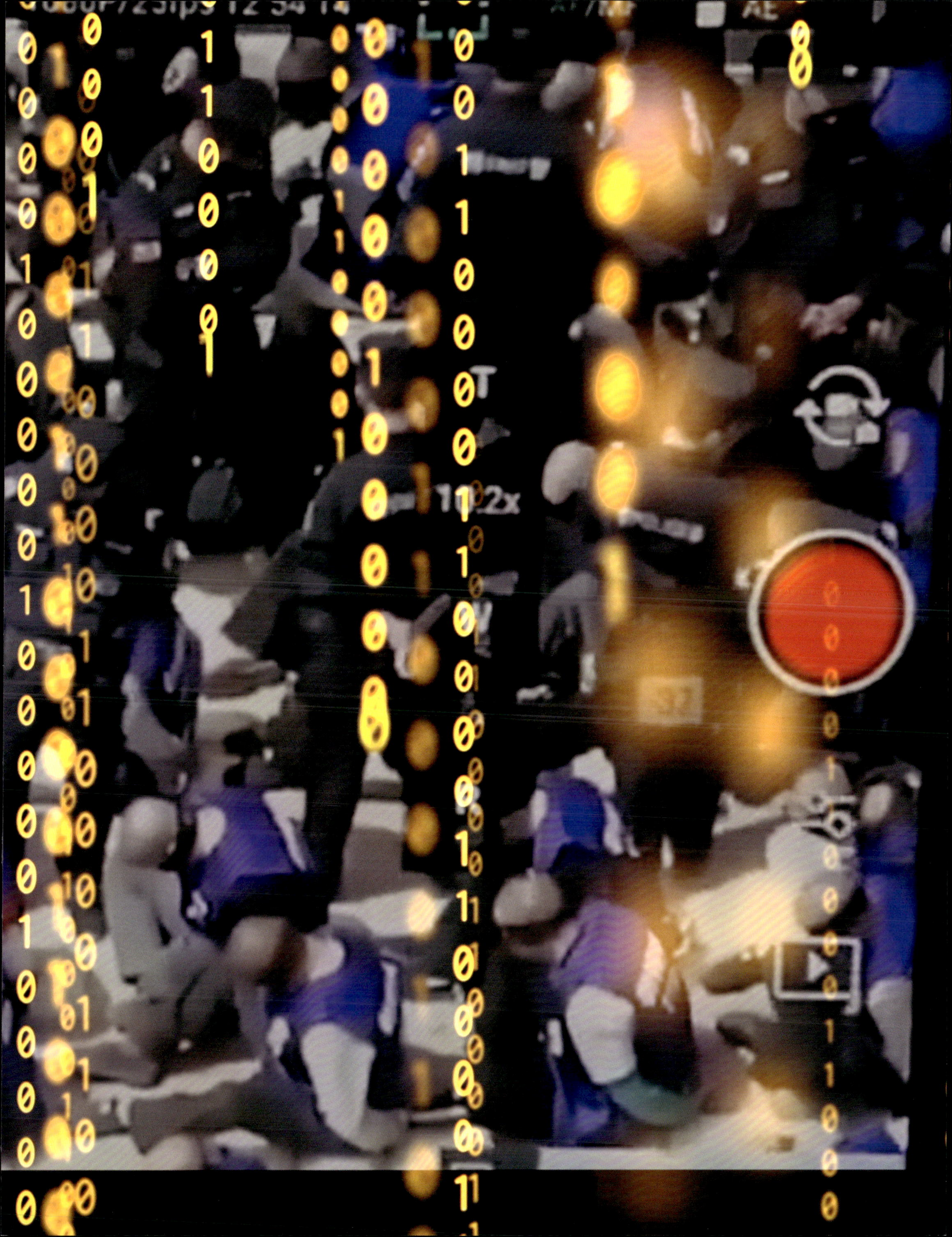

The digital self is the most surveilled and known about in history
Geolocation technologies are one mode of pattern-of-life data
That pours out of those seemingly mundane acts and devices

And this contributes for me
To an excess of available data
That encourages or necessitates or legitimizes
Pushing humans out of the analysis of that data

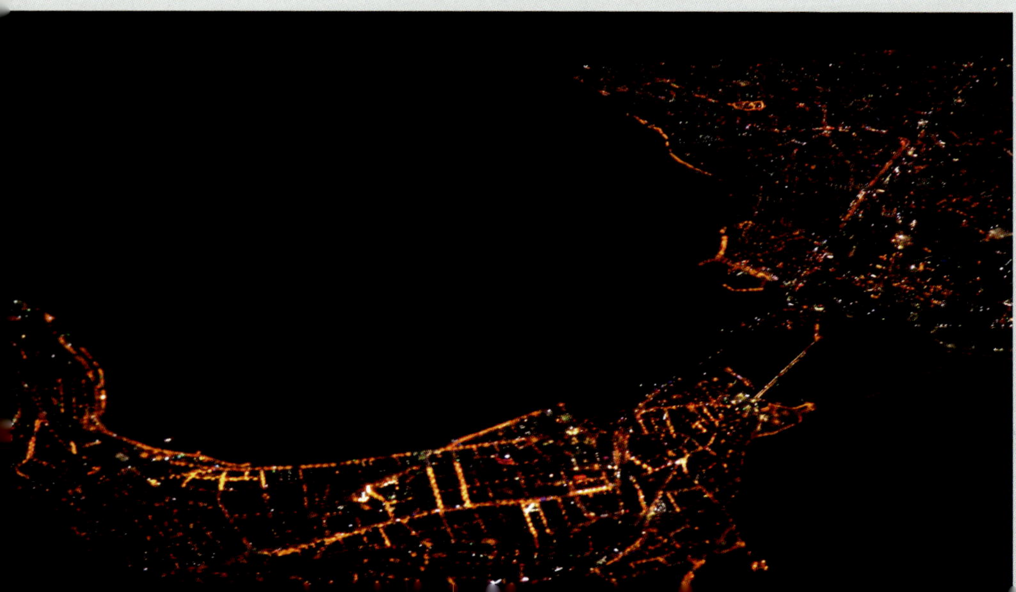

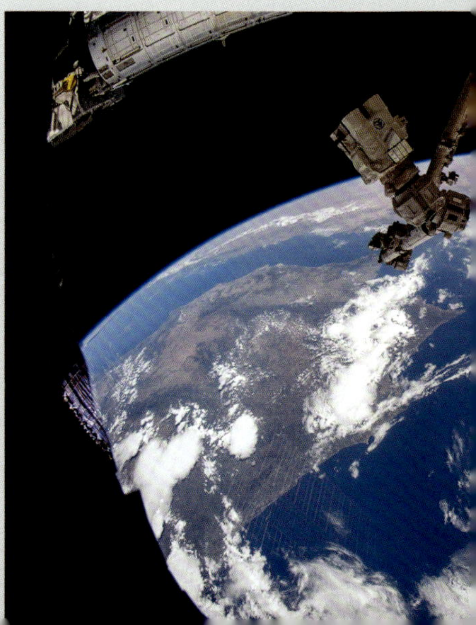

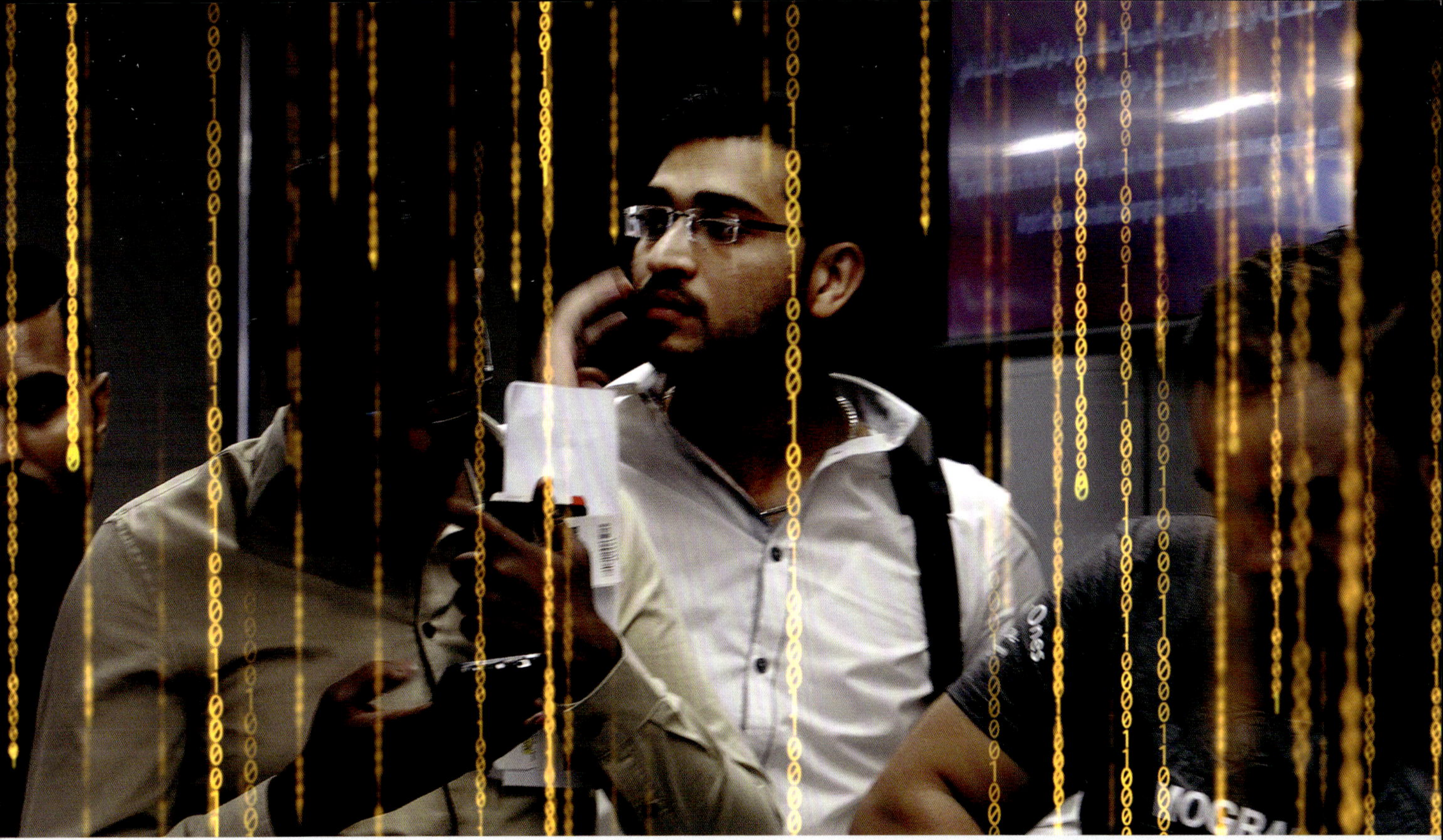

Then they enter the Shaman's universe
The knowledge enters their minds
The knowledge of the earth, water, sky, thunder, moon, stars
It shows us everything
The earth speaks to the Shamans
It says "protect me"
"don't let me die"

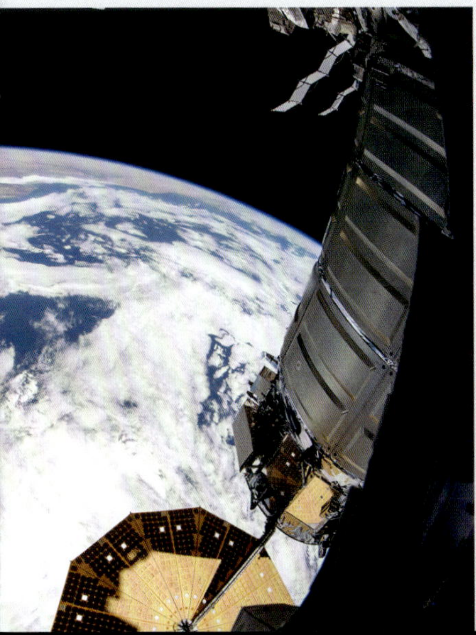

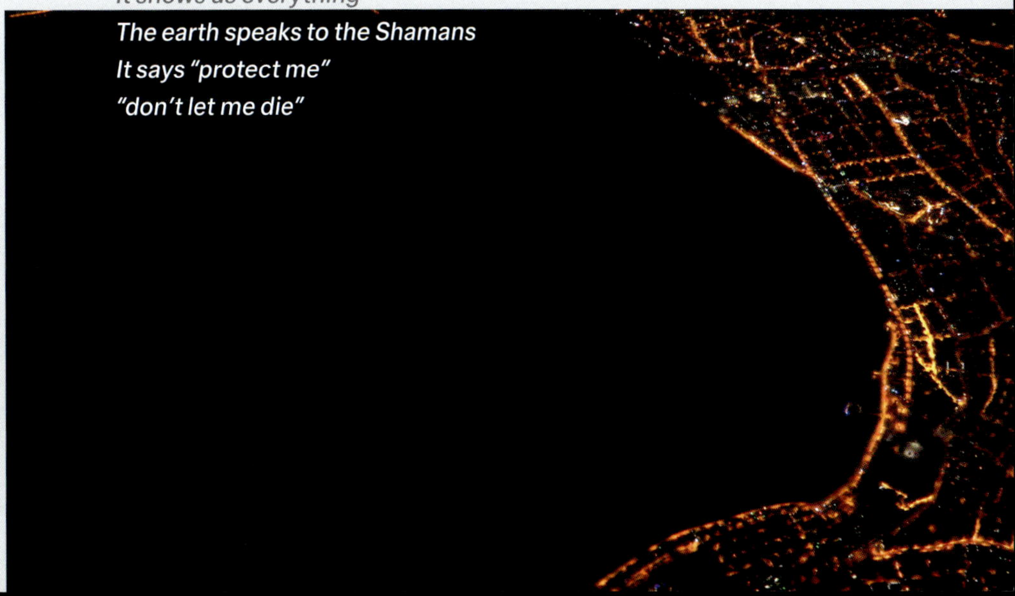

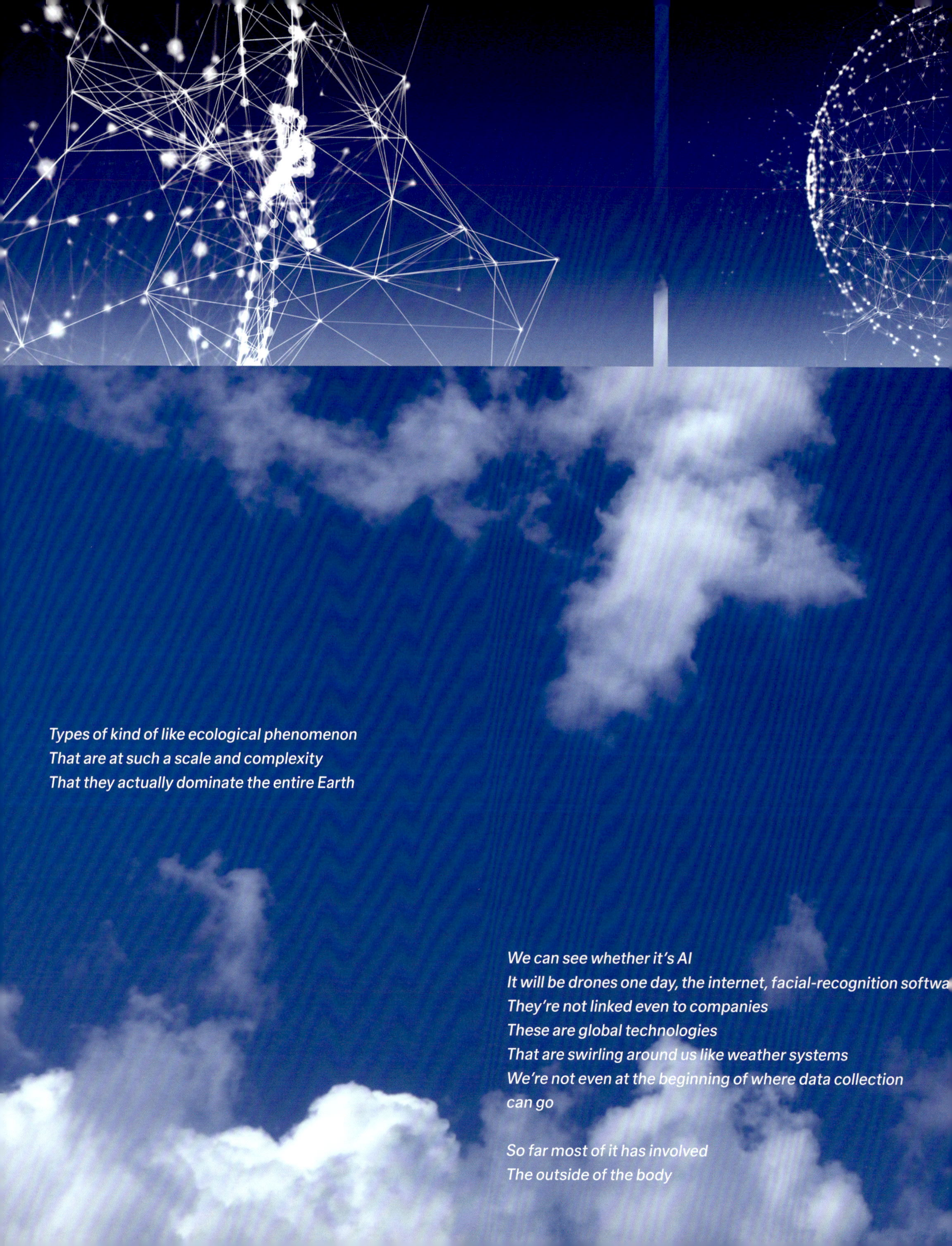

Types of kind of like ecological phenomenon
That are at such a scale and complexity
That they actually dominate the entire Earth

We can see whether it's AI
It will be drones one day, the internet, facial-recognition softwa
They're not linked even to companies
These are global technologies
That are swirling around us like weather systems
We're not even at the beginning of where data collection
can go

So far most of it has involved
The outside of the body

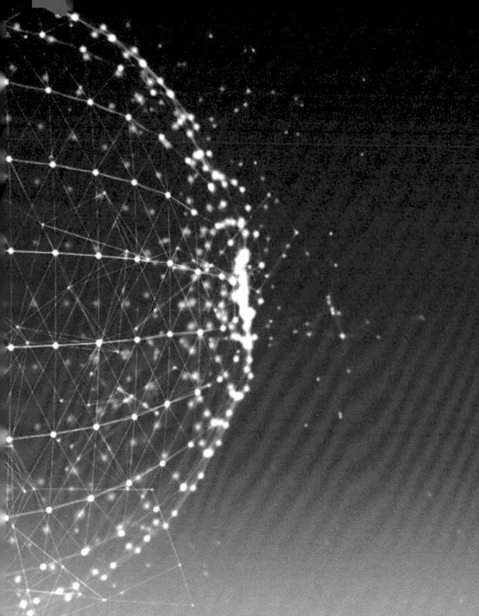
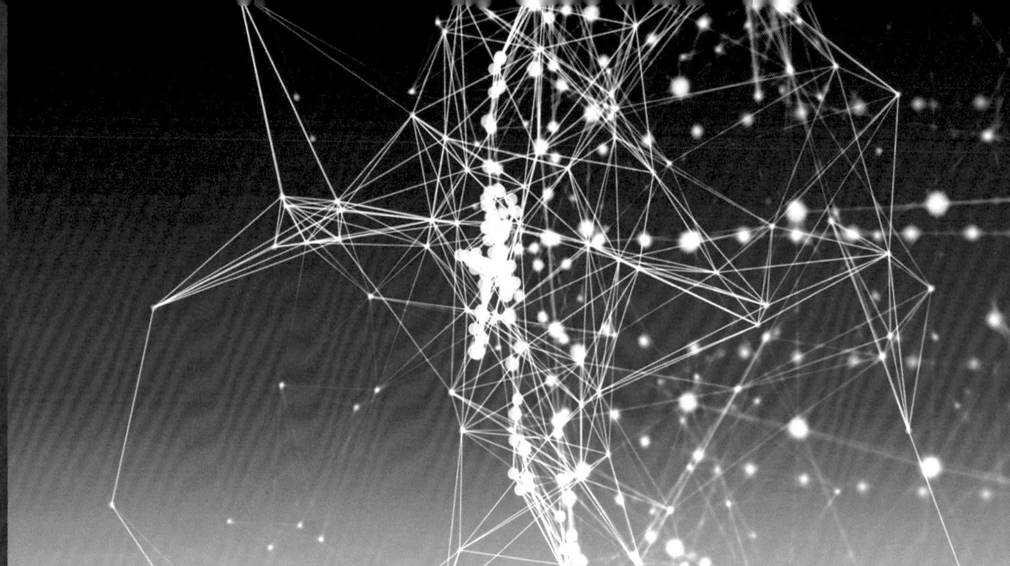
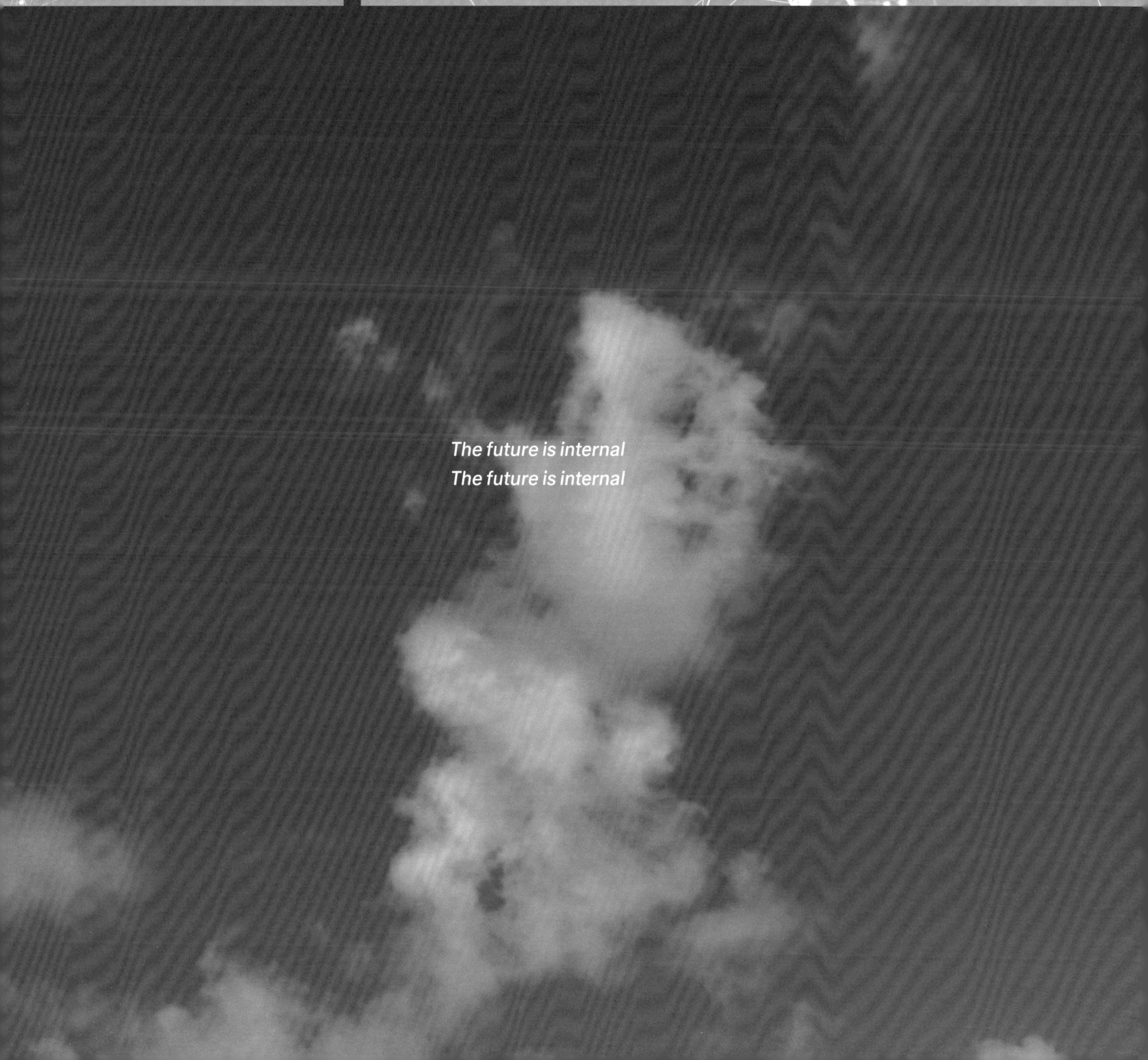

The future is internal
The future is internal

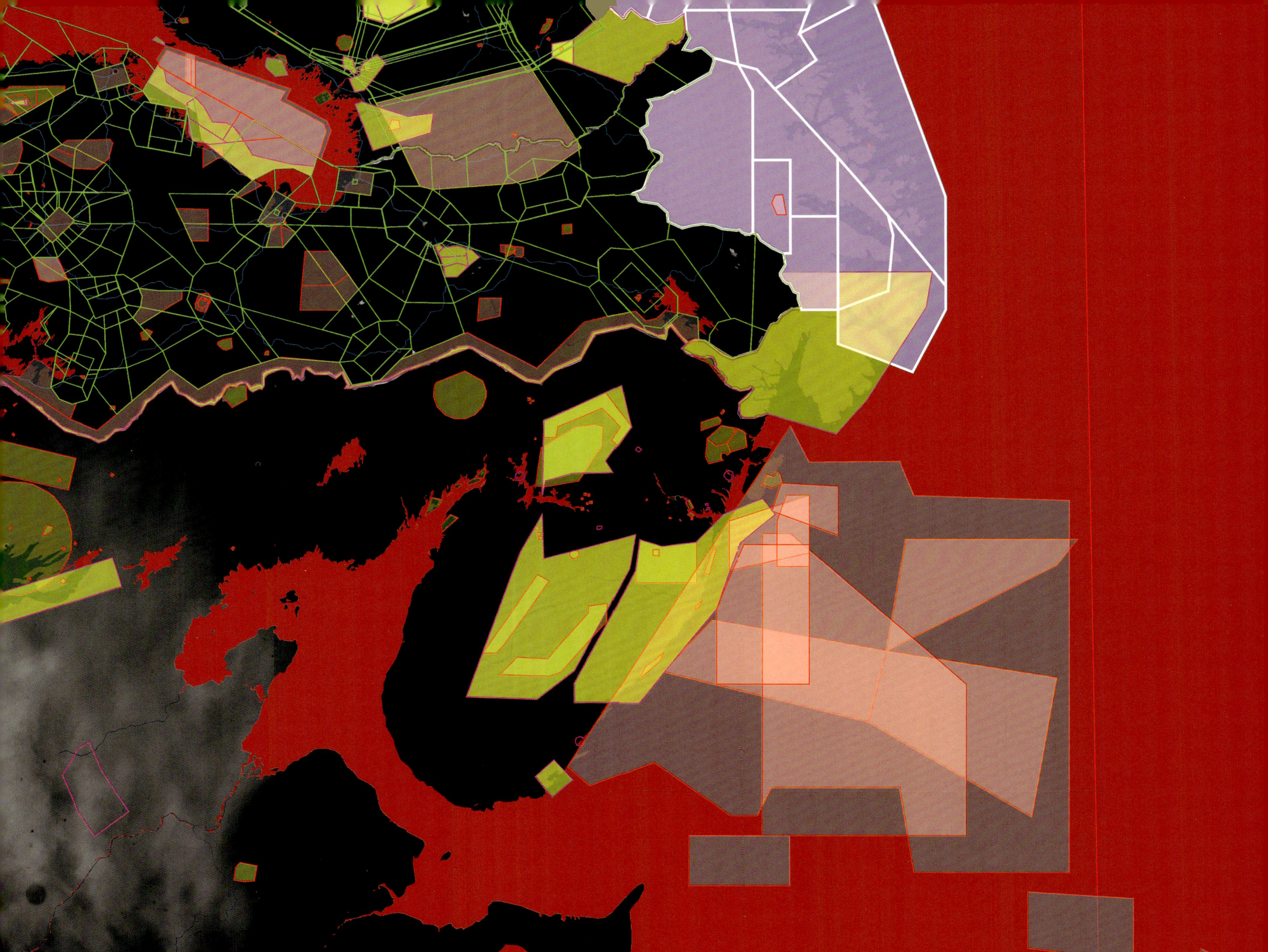

Shona Illingworth, *Restricted Airspace*, 2021. (Detail). Ongoing photograph series of archival giclee prints. Dimensions 672 × 1011 mm.

Caterina Albano

TOPOLOGIES OF AIR: SHONA ILLINGWORTH'S ART PRACTICE AND THE ETHICS OF AIR

"Away and away the aeroplane shot, till it was nothing but a bright spark; an aspiration; a concentration; a symbol": with these words, Virginia Woolf described an airplane flying over London in 1925.[1] Her words capture the awe and potential with which airspace was endowed at the beginning of the twentieth century. Woolf's description still resonates today. However, its associations are now tinged with nostalgia, as our relationship with the skies has substantially changed. Pollution has altered the atmosphere with dramatic ecological effects that endanger living environments and human health. Air bombing has imbued it with apprehension; nuclear explosions and radioactive spillage have produced long-lasting contamination. What, in 1925, stood as a new frontier of expansion has turned, for many, into a site of concern, repression, and surveillance, if not oppressive fear. For us, in the 2020s, the skies have become precarious, an intricate web of unstable gaseous locations traversed by contrasting discourses, hegemonies, and an ever-impending sense of foreboding. The mapping of these diverse airspaces, their discursive articulations, and the forms of dominance that regulate them is the subject of Shona Illingworth's immersive multi-screen video and sound installation, *Topologies of Air* (2021).

Illingworth is not new to an exploration of atmospheric environments. Indeed, the environment as an aggregate that "encompasses both the physical and the atmospheric"[2] underpins much of her research practice, which focuses on a multidisciplinary analysis of how events and their affective resonances define the environments in which we live. In *Topologies of Air*, Illingworth does not engage with the atmosphere of a specific place but rather with the very notion of airspace and its topological subdivisions by examining their conditions and the discourses predicated on them. In mathematics, the term "topology" refers to the study of the spatial properties and relations of geometrical figures as they undergo continuous deformation. By extension, it also refers to the study of a locality and to how the constituent parts of a network are connected or arranged.[3] Because topology, as Steven Connor observes, is concerned with spatial relations (i.e., continuity, "insideness," "outsideness," disjunction, and connection), "with what remains invariant as a result of transformation, it may be thought as geometry plus time, geometry given body by motion."[4] The relational inseparability of space-time-motion resonates with a consideration of airspaces, of their connectedness and malleability, their physical and affective morphologies, their historical and contemporary significances—when, in other words, we question the *topoi* and *logoi* of air.

In what follows, I shall examine the formal and thematic development of *Topologies of Air* in relation to Illingworth's art practice. In particular, I shall outline an internal research trajectory whereby *Topologies of Air* emerges from Illingworth's critical engagement with the atmosphere as a site of ethical concern and of physical and emotional immersion. Accordingly, the aim put forward in the Airspace Tribunal (2018–ongoing), part of the research development of this work, to establish a new human right to protect from threats from the air and outer space, is rooted in Illingworth's extensive investigation of airspaces. In this sense, *Topologies of*

1 Virginia Woolf, *Mrs. Dalloway* (London: Penguin, 1996), 57.

2 Jill Bennett, "Atmospheric Affects: Past Events and Present Feeling," in Shona Illingworth, *The Watch Man/Balnakiel* (London: Film and Video Umbrella, 2011), 159.

3 "Topology," OED Online, Oxford University Press, https://www.oed.com/view/Entry/203426?redirectedFrom=topology#eid.

4 Steven Connor, "Topologies: Michel Serres and the Shape of Thought," *Anglistik*, no. 15 (2004): 106.

5 Shona Illingworth, *Topologies of Air*, video and sound installation (2021), voiceover transcript.

Air and the Airspace Tribunal continue Illingworth's art research practice and its critique of hegemonies.

Topologies of Air: A Video and Sound Installation

Topologies of Air opens with images of soft cloud formations in a blue sky as they pass through the three screens of the installation. Dissonant, abrasive notes mix with the sound of air currents, upsetting the expansive depth of these images. A digital rendering of the earth's electromagnetic fields emerges from behind one of the cloud formations in the central screen and floats in space. At the same time, we hear the words of astrophysicist Ilias Fernini:

> The sun
>
> Sends this solar wind
>
> A huge amount of these highly charged particles
>
> And they may disturb
>
> This upper atmosphere
>
> So if you send a signal through this upper atmosphere
>
> The signals cannot pass through
>
> Or it can be absorbed
>
> Or it can be refracted
>
> That's why our atmosphere
>
> Is not stable.[5]

This initial sequence well exemplifies the seamless relation of the three screens and the ways in which the voiceover interacts with the visual and acoustic components of *Topologies of Air*. Neither the images nor the voiceover, mostly from contributors to the Airspace Tribunal's hearings, are illustrative of one another; rather, they are adjoining and intersecting texts that associatively interweave with each other. Through such a palimpsestic structure of images, sound, and voices, Illingworth examines diverse topologies of air in different historical periods and locations, across shifting scales and critical perspectives. The video unfolds thematically on issues concerning ecology, airspace and outer space surveillance and their economic as well as military exploitation, and air violence. Throughout, the kinetic qualities of images (speed, internal shifts of scale and focal points) together with the ways in which sounds interplay with them intensify the feeling of being drawn into the "airspace" of the work itself.

Images of flickering leaves filmed from the ground alternate with aerial views of cityscapes and brightly lit urban skylines, satellite images of the earth and the atmosphere, and images taken by drones. Shifts of scale and viewpoint are congruent with how airspaces are subdivided in the troposphere (the part of the atmosphere closer to earth), the stratosphere, and outer space, and with the forms of access, hegemony, and knowledge production that characterize each of them, including their different gaseous formations and strategic and economic relevance.

Myths and stories are also ways of understanding the skies across cultures and epochs, suggesting other ways of perceiving the immersive space that surrounds us. Historically, the skies have been a referent for our own positioning on earth and for grappling with questions about the existence of life on this planet. Today, as tree physiologist Sebastian Pfautsch observes, access to airspaces affords us the collection of ecological and other data:

Climate change, sea level rise

Absolutely rely on access
from above and the view from above

All these processes we are
documenting from above

At different spatial and also
temporal scales

Related to deforestation, illegal
mining, agricultural activities,
soil, coastal erosion, human
trafficking

But also urban planning,
infrastructure assessments

That we actually use aerial
technology now for

Terrestrial mapping of various
manmade and natural ecosystems

All rely on access from above[6]

At the same time, according to Sophie Dyer, airspaces are also indicative of the inequalities and supremacy that underpin air violence:

In terms of the kind of optical
regime Where there's a kind of
asymmetry of power

And an asymmetry of access to
satellite information

That's intelligence, surveillance
and reconnaissance,

Which is absolutely integral
To contemporary air dominated
campaigns

That kind of intelligence

That is gathered through drone
feeds and satellite imagery
Is what will then determine

If the strike takes place or not

So that kind of asymmetry of
power Is shifting even further

Towards governments and for
profit companies

Being those who have the commanding
aerial perspective[7]

Throughout *Topologies of Air*, Illingworth engages with the complexities and contradictions that denote today's perception and understanding of airspaces to convey a multilayered picture of consequential effects and affects.

The feelings of elation about the development of aviation in the first decades of the twentieth century, rendered through the inclusion of archival film footage of crowds cheering, are contrasted with the impending and ever-expanding threats posed by the economic and military exploitation of the atmosphere. We are reminded of the original "aspiration" that accompanied the first flights as a "step into a new element."[8] In this new element, bodies could "move free in three dimensions" in what was deemed "the beginning of a new aerial age" that would bring a "new way of life" characterized by the promise of "democracy, equality, and freedom."[9] "Flight," as Peter Adey puts it, "would elicit a new way to express our relation with air. It could liquefy the solid footing of the ground, yet somehow make the air that bit more tangible, that bit more 'there.'"[10]

Air, however, also made itself felt. War images of parachutists drifting in midair before landing on enemy soil and of air-raids allude to the military deployment of aviation and the fear with which the air began to be imbued.[11] Illingworth colors these archival images purple-red; thus, intimating their emotional charge as a new kind of pollution that is affective rather than environmental. *Topologies of Air* then shifts to archival film footage of

6 Sebastian Pfautsch, quoted in Illingworth, *Topologies of Air*, voiceover transcript.

7 Sophie Dyer, quoted in Illingworth, *Topologies of Air*, voiceover transcript.

8 Sven Lindqvist, quoted in Illingworth, *Topologies of Air*, voiceover transcript.

9 Lindqvist, *Topologies of Air*, voiceover transcript.

10 Peter Adey, *Air: Nature and Culture* (London: Reaktion Books, 2014), 55.

11 See Peter Sloterdijk, *Terror from the Air*, trans. Amy Patton and Steve Corcoran (Los Angeles: Semiotext(e), 2009), 22–28.

12 Tim Ingold, "The Atmosphere," *Chiasmi International*, no. 14 (2012): 76.

13 Conor Gearty, quoted in Illingworth, *Topologies of Air*, voiceover transcript.

14 Svetlana Alexievich, quoted in Illingworth, *Topologies of Air*, voiceover transcript.

the NASA Voyager program in the 1970s and the European Space Agency, suggesting the postwar international race for the colonization of outer space. These images are juxtaposed with ones taken by drones and satellites: a reference to the complex economic, military, and governmental matrixes of power and control that dominate today's airspaces, from the troposphere to outer space.

Within this layering of historical and contemporary outlooks on the skies, Illingworth examines how our existential connection to airspaces has been altered by technological advancements and what can be regarded as diverse forms of pollution—environmental, emotional, and informational. We see images of an oil field in Bahrain as we hear geologist Giusi Maggi describing her fascination with the atmosphere's make-up. This sequence is juxtaposed with satellite views of the earth and images of gas flares being burnt off in the oil field, alluding to the release of toxic gases. The focus shifts to slow-motion images of two children leaping in the air on a purple-red background. The slow speed of the frames heightens the lightness of their bodies, dark ghostly shadows suspended in midair.

As in the historical footage on the beginnings of aviation, the tinted images are suggestive of contamination; specifically, the high levels of monoxide and toxic gasses polluting the atmosphere worldwide. The internal movement of these images reminds us of Tim Ingold's description of the pattern of the weather as one "that is continually being woven in the multiple rhythmic alternations of the environment—of day and night, sun and moon, winds and tides, vegetative growth and decay, and the comings and goings of migratory animals."[12] Ingold underlines the continuity between soil, sea, and air, the terrestrial and the atmospheric. Airspaces are inseparable from life on earth. However, they are also the sites of contested practices, raising the question of how to adequately address the complex patterns of economic and political control that put them at risk. As human rights expert Conor Gearty comments,

> We are at the moment being poisoned
> on a daily basis
>
> There is maybe some connection
> to be made
>
> Between the atmosphere up here
> as it were
>
> From which things can fall on us
> as it were
>
> And the atmosphere around us
>
> That can infiltrate and destroy us[13]

Cosmic dust, the curved skyline at the arctic, and the image of an atomic explosion introduce a reflection on radioactive contamination. Radioactivity, with its long decay, is emblematic of atmospheric annihilation or what Svetlana Alexievich refers to as "a catastrophe of time."[14] Purple-red-colored and slow-motion images of children in uniform that Illingworth filmed in Peace Square in Hiroshima traverse the screens. The children appear as ghostly silhouettes, while the voiceover (in Japanese with subtitles) includes excerpts of conversations that Illingworth conducted with survivors of the nuclear bombing in August 1945 about their personal memories. We hear an elderly man recollecting when, as a child, he was begged to share the small peach he was holding by people burnt by the heat of the atomic explosion; we hear of a woman who waited her entire life for the return of her disappeared daughter, never locking her front door for fear that she might not be able to enter the house.

The internal connections across the three screens remind us of the associative interaction of memories, while interference and repetition suggest the rupture that trauma causes to remembering with its insidious recurrence. Illingworth intersects the close-up of a girl walking toward the camera with images of the closing doors of a tram and the leaping children. The slow fading of the frames creates a feeling of estrangement while shadowy silhouettes linger as afterimages. The intensified color of the footage filmed in Hiroshima alongside the recollections of survivors of the atomic bombing creates an indefinite and liminal vision where past and present overlay, and the future alluded to by the children is already compromised by an ongoing catastrophe of which we are amnesic.

In this indeterminate temporality, images and sounds of burning intersect street shots of Hiroshima. It is as if fire were consuming the video footage itself, while low, pulsating, metallic frequencies cut through Illingworth's repetition of frames. Gabriele Schwab refers to the notion of "nuclear necropolitics" to explain the type of violence and long-lasting contamination of nuclear armaments. Necropolitics describes the relationships between sovereignty and the power to rule on life and death; nuclear weapons, as Schwab argues, add "a new and sinister dimension to this power. The power of nuclear weapons can now be used to dictate not only who may live and who must die from a nuclear attack but also how some people must live with and die a slow death from the lingering effects of nuclear contamination."[15] This results in the control of bodies and minds exercised by what can be regarded as a new, pervasive form of colonialism and its related politics of fear.[16] The dark silhouettes of children in *Topologies of Air* are the ghosts of our own present. As Schwab observes,"The waves of invisible radiation that had infiltrated the survivors' bodies continue the warfare indefinitely and out of sight, so to speak. Beyond its immediate annihilating destruction, the atomic work of death continues to operate as a form of slow violence inside the bodies of victims [...] and as a spectral haunting from both the past and the future."[17] This haunting alludes to both the past of nuclear contamination or the contingent threats of climate change and contemporary chemical wars. The sequence concludes with bright fluorescent lights among tree branches, which refer to the phosphorous blue lights of decaying bodies that filled the air of Hiroshima and were seen as if they were floating spirits.

In *Topologies of Air*, Illingworth encompasses scientific and animistic understandings of the atmosphere through the plurality of voices included in the voiceover and by creating changing visual "paths of movement,"[18] to use Ingold's phrase, to articulate what Toral Gajarawala refers to in the voiceover as "a decolonial cosmology." This encompasses different belief systems and forms of knowledge about the skies to unlearn,

> A certain hubris
>
> That says one specific version of
> the cosmos
>
> Is universal[19]

The constant changes of scale, from ground to aerial views, and the internal movement of the images themselves contrast the scopic paradigms typical of universalizing visions from above. Understanding emerges, instead, through movement and an awareness of the shifting sensations that the immersive space of *Topologies of Air* creates.

Within this changing affective environment, we hear the call of shaman and spokesperson for the Yanomami people in Brazil, Davi Kopenawa Yanomami, who voices the cry of the earth asking for protection. The images on-screen show people moving in an urban environment, on whom Illingworth superimposes a rain of digital codes to address today's instability of airspaces as sites of surveillance and economic and military control, ruled by the collection of metadata produced by mobile technologies and used to map the increasingly detailed life patterns of millions of individuals.

15 Gabriele Schwab, *Radioactive Ghosts* (Minneapolis: University of Minnesota Press, 2020), 18

16 See Schwab, *Radioactive Ghosts*, 18–19.

17 Schwab, *Radioactive Ghosts*, 192–93.

18 Ingold, "The Atmosphere," 82.

19 Toral Gajarawala, quoted in Illingworth, *Topologies of Air*, voiceover transcript.

20 These include *The Watch Man* (2007), *Balnakiel* (2009), *216 Westbound* (2014), *Lesions in the Landscape* (2015), and *Time Present* (2016).

21 I follow the spelling derived from the original Gaelic name for the location. See Shona Illingworth and Martin A.Conway, "Balnakiel Survey," in *The Watch Man/ Balnakiel*, 73.

These digital traces swirl around the earth like a weather formation. The initial digital renderings of the globe return as information systems and machine-to-machine communication assemblages. We are reminded of the potentials of technological connectivity but also of the erosion of privacy effected through digital surveillance and the disappearance of the last remaining spaces of unsupervised freedom. *Topologies of Air* concludes with the words, "the future is internal," as the digital rendering of the electromagnetic fields of the globe dissolves into images of the sky accompanied by the chirping of birds.

Atmospheres: Illingworth's Immersive Art Practice

To stay with this concluding sequence as the complex fabric of images, words, and sounds that Illingworth has unfolded still swirls and envelops us means to stay in the space that *Topologies of Air* has generated and with the questions that the work has raised as we make them our own. For those familiar with Illingworth's practice, this is not unusual. *Topologies of Air* has created its own distinctive atmosphere while critically engaging with what makes atmospheres themselves. In this particular case, one is asked to unpack the intricate relations of place, time, and discourse that characterize the vast gaseous wrap that we call the skies. The themes Illingworth deals with in *Topologies of Air* are enormous. They are massive in scale and complexity because their globality and temporal span encompass both past and future with the magnitude of their potential impact—be it ecological consequences on ecosystems, military, political, and economic control, or the effects of the dominance of airspaces on our individual lives and emotional well-being.

The engagement with such themes is not new for Illingworth, for it has developed out of her extensive research and interdisciplinary collaborations informing her art practice. Hence, *Topologies of Air* is the result of an artistic trajectory that investigates airspaces across a number of works.[20] Here, I shall focus specifically on two video and sound installations, *Balnakiel* (2009) and *Lesions in the Landscape* (2015), by considering the role of collaboration, the notion of atmosphere as a thematic thread, and the formal relations of image, sound, and movement in the two works. These are not distinct aspects but rather interrelated facets of Illingworth's practice.

Both *Balnakiel* and *Lesions in the Landscape* well exemplify Illingworth's collaborative methodological approach, whereby the research process underpinning the creative process develops in dialogue with experts in diverse fields over extended periods of time. Hence, Illingworth's examination of memory, particularly in relation to trauma and amnesia—subjects that are critical to the Airspace Tribunal itself—is grounded in her long-term collaboration with cognitive neuro-psychologist Martin Conway in *Balnakiel* and, more recently, with neuropsychologist Catherine Loveday in *Lesions in the Landscape*.

Balnakiel examines the affective geography and spatial politics of Balnakiel,[21] a former military camp near the village of Durness in the north of Scotland, whose strategic position has been geopolitically key during World War II, the Cold War in the 1950s, and the War on Terror in the 2010s. The area, which is considered especially advantageous as it enables a 360-degree live range of control, is used for the training of British, NATO, and allied forces to be deployed in conflict zones across the world. In *Balnakiel*, Illingworth explores the historical legacies of the nineteenth-century Clearances, the tense relationships between the local inhabitants and those who moved to the region in the 1960s, and the military through the affective landscape of the place.

22 See Caterina Albano, *Memory, Forgetting and the Moving Image* (London: Palgrave Macmillan, 2016), 101–9.

23 See Illingworth and Conway, "Balnakiel Survey," 73–107.

24 The first three Airspace Tribunal hearings were held between 2017 and 2020 in London, Sydney, and Toronto. Related events included the Sky Forums that Illingworth organized during two residencies at, respectively, the Sharjah Art Foundation in the United Arab Emirates and the Bahrain National Museum.

Throughout, Illingworth references a spatial understanding of memory that is volumetrically layered and continually changing to map the intersecting of past and present, local and global dynamics of influence and control, and internal and external points of view.[22] The dialogues with Conway grew around and took the form of a series of drawings that delineate how memory, in its different articulations for both the individuals and groups who live in the area, defines their relationships with the surrounding environment. These drawings, together with others that chart the military use of the airspace and the simulation of training operations, underpin the conceptual development of *Balnakiel*. Illingworth layers these diverse kinds of mental maps, whose coordinates are emotional and sensorial as well as cognitive, onto time-based (filmic and photographic) documentation of the region to create the associative structure of the work. Illingworth's collaboration with Conway is, thus, dialogically embedded within the artistic investigation and formal development of the final work.[23]

Such a methodology is also recognizable in *Lesions in the Landscape*, a three-channel video and sound installation in which the geological, sociocultural, and political history of St Kilda, a volcanic archipelago west of the Outer Hebrides in the North Atlantic, and its erasure at the beginning of the twentieth century is intersected with an individual's experience of amnesia. For this work, Illingworth collaborated with both Conway and Loveday and with Claire—a woman suffering from retrograde amnesia (the inability to remember the past), anterograde amnesia (the inability to form new memories), and prosopagnosia (the inability to recognize faces). This core collaboration was further expanded to include experts in disciplines as diverse as archaeology, geology, genetics, military strategy, and media studies. Contributions were mapped across a series of five forums that addressed embodied experience through different forms of practices (clinical, scientific, and artistic), consolidating the decentering approach that is at the core of the Airspace Tribunal.

Topologies of Air was, in fact, first conceived as part of an artist research residency in the Outer Hebrides in 2012, at the same time of *Lesions in the Landscape*, and developed as a series of blueprints that led to extensive research and the collaboration with human rights expert Nick Grief. For the Airspace Tribunal, Illingworth chose the overtly performative format of legal hearings, which is congruent with the aim of this project, and an understanding of human rights as a living instrument.[24] The hearings build an interdisciplinary body of evidence and first-person testimonies from those who experience violations of airspaces, which is further captured by the voiceover of *Topologies of Air*—whose short extracts retain the vividness of the hearings' presentations, enlivening the ideas put forward with warmth and passion. Through this multiplicity of voices, Illingworth's project further unravels the complexity and interrelationship of the issues presented, not from singular disciplinary standpoints but rather from diverse and even divergent positions capable of encompassing multiple perspectives, manifold forms of knowledge, and cultural interpretations. In this sense, through her collaborative research practice, Illingworth develops a decentering approach that strives toward a "decolonial cosmology" as methodologically built within the work itself.

In *Topologies of Air*, the formal features of viewpoint, scale, and movement are integral to the articulation of such methodology in ways that are already evident in *Balnakiel* and *Lesions in the Landscape*. Both works testify to Illingworth's extensive investigations of airspaces, especially in terms of their diverse constructions and forms of dominance, and of the types of approaches

25 See Caterina Albano, "In the Spaces of Memory," in *The Watch Man/Balnakiel*, 108–19. See also "At the Edge: Balnakiel a Video and Sound Installation by Artist Shona Illingworth," *Memory Studies* 6, no. 4 (2013): 404–17.

26 Majid Rabet, quoted in Illingworth, *Topologies of Air*, voiceover transcript.

27 Email communication with the artist, January 4, 2021.

she has developed to deal with air as a filmic subject. In *Balnakiel*, the shift of planes and viewpoints is indicative of how Illingworth harnesses the physical features of the landscape as a medium in which the environment actively interacts with the social, economic, and cultural components that characterize this place and its contested appropriations. This is matched by the use of sound and movement, as evinced in a sequence in which the camera follows the movement of a girl spinning with a rope on the flat roof of one of the barracks that testify to the militarization of the region. The intermittent horizontal sound of the rope slicing through the air mixes with the deafening downward thrust of a helicopter engine and a series of rising sound frequencies. The viewpoint of the girl spinning interweaves with that of an external observer as color and black-and-white images seamlessly intercut, producing a visual and acoustic vortex for the viewer while low-frequency sounds compress the installation space itself. The effect is a physical sense of oppression.[25]

In *Topologies of Air*, the militarization of air and its latent foreboding continue as important themes in Illingworth's investigation of airspaces, encompassing both the local and global interface of contemporary geopolitics—whereby the effects of events in one location reverberate across atmospheric planes as well as longitudes. Hence, images of a blue sky and the sound of a jet taking off slowly change to those of clouds that morph onto eroded ground and then further shift to a landscape at dawn on which a horizontal line of fog lingers as the camera focuses on a desiccated tree. Over the background sound of one repeated cutting note, we hear the voice of a former Iranian conscript and now artist, Majid Rabet, recounting the effects of a chemical attack:

> It's out of imagination
>
> Nothing alive
>
> Nothing
>
> Animals, sheep, cows, kids,
> women, men
>
> All bleeding from mouth and nose
>
> You can feel how they died
>
> From pain
>
> Our imagination is about the
> bombing, and bullet
>
> But that was chemical weapons
>
> And that's nothing alive there
>
> Nothing
>
> It's I think stuck in my memory
>
> I never can forget it[26]

The images of dawn morph again onto close-ups of dry, cracked earth that gradually shift to those of a dense, low cloud, then to high aerial views and a sequence shot in the departure lounge of Sharjah airport. Illingworth links these images to video footage of GR4 Tornado jets bombing Garve Island in the Cape Wrath Range close to Balnakiel, as a pilot reports back to the Control Tower,[27] and intersects them with footage of a US Predix drone swarm coordinating a simulated hunting operation. The deafening, terrifying noise of this machine-led operation connects the preponderance of air control examined in *Balnakiel* with the dehumanized violence of the current militarization of air and ecological damage of chemical contamination.

Here is also evidence of how Illingworth harnesses movement—as both what we see on-screen and the internal flow within a frame—to deal with atmospheric

28 Email communication with the artist, January 4, 2021.

disturbance and render the dynamic volumes typical of air topologies. The repeated sequence in *Topologies of Air* of two children leaping is comparable to that of the girl spinning with a rope in *Balnakiel*. In both instances, Illingworth focuses on the kinetic force of these buoyant activities, whose playfulness seems at odds with the contexts in which they are presented. Both movements have a propelling force that Illingworth uses to generate disturbance through the manipulation of the images themselves (shifts of color/black-and-white in the first case, and different gradations of color and alteration of the image speed in the second). This intensifies the sensations, respectively, of rotation and of upward thrust and the momentous suspension of the bodies in midair. Although, as a viewer, one feels the energetic pull of the leap or rotation, the effect is one of vertigo and compression. Oppression is felt as an impending presence. Illingworth refers to them as "liminal images" to stress their intentional indeterminacy, impasse, and disturbance.[28]

Liminality is an important feature in *Topologies of Air*, especially in relation to the palpable rendering of air itself, conveyed through the internal speed and flow of images. Illingworth modulates the single frames by layering them on specific sounds that are removed in the final work, but that, nonetheless, affect them by shaping the quality of the movement of images on-screen. Hence, the impression of being drawn into the boundlessness of air through the uplifting movement of aerial views is contrasted with the warping of this movement within and across the screens, whether through the impending condensing of air into matter or through shifts of scale and approximation. As a result, movement itself acts as latency within the images and across the three screens. The "radioactive signature in the geological record," referring to the radioactive nuclides found in the Antarctic ice, figuratively corresponds to the emotional signature of fear and trauma in the atmospheric layers that have been increasingly occupied, exploited, and contaminated with pollution and violence. The dynamic expanding and folding of images, thus, embody the multidimensionality and intersecting temporalities underscoring the discursive understandings of airspaces.

In *Topologies of Air*, Illingworth also continues an exploration started in *Lesions in the Landscape* of shifting scales, from the magnitude afforded by satellite images to the ground detections of GPS systems, from the local parameters of a place, event, or experience to their global resonances, implications, or impact. Evacuated in the 1930s and a UNESCO heritage site, St Kilda is, today, a key military outpost as a satellite-controlled area and military testing zone for new generations of weapons—the archipelago and surroundings are a silent airspace area extending for thirty thousand square kilometers. Such strategic importance dates back to 1959, when the area became key to Britain's nuclear program. St Kilda is also an archaeological site, and the local Soay sheep are studied for their genetic profile in research on the effects of climate change on bio-systems. Illingworth includes references to the military telemetry tracking weapon testing, to exchanges between American and Russian operatives who cooperatively guide a supply ship docking onto the International Space Station, and to the ground mapping of St Kilda's archaeological traces through GPS. An amalgam of inputs, whose varying degree of accuracy is relative to the level of approximation that can be technically achieved, the signal data define the virtual and shifting parameters of specialized knowledge and the different "vision" that they afford: the scale of military testing and the airspace program suggest interchangeable, if not conflicting, geopolitical alliances and an evolving picture of power relations across the globe while the micro-scale introduces indeterminism and uncertainty.

These spatial scales further intersect different forms of duration and temporal constructions that relate to Illingworth's exploration of memory. Duration as the extended timeline of the geological formation of the island is rendered through a recurring sequence that shows a slow-motion filmed sequence of crumbling rocks cascading into the sea, suggesting a petrification of time and further relating to views of the archaeological remains that date back four thousand years—testifying to the cultural erasure of the people who lived in St Kilda. By contrast, the collecting of micro-data on military testing is situated in the infinitesimal contingency of constant obsolescence while its relevance is projected in the near future of potential military operations. Petrification and cultural erasure, thus, act as signs of the amnesia denoting this supposedly remote and yet strategically critical place. Within these diametrical perspectives, St Kilda is suspended in the indeterminacy of the isolation that characterizes the immobility of its cultural construction as a heritage site and of the related idealized presentation of its past.[29]

This seamless integration of and shift across different spatial and temporal scales also underscores *Topologies of Air* where it is amplified in both range and span to render the granular effects of climate change and environmental pollution as well as the increasingly dense mass of metadata swirling around the globe. The short obsolescence of such metadata contrasts with the duration of radioactive, chemical, and emotional contamination that reaches from past events into the future. As suggested for *Lesions in the Landscape*, the visual and sonic interweaving of macro- and micro-data tracking defines the parameters of diverse constructions of airspaces and their meanings, both past and present. The cross-cultural conception of the skies as limitless and liminal to our existence on earth has been replaced, as archaeologist Steffen Terp Laursen observes in *Topologies of Air*'s voiceover, by "a more manifest sense of the sky above us" afforded by technological and scientific advancements.

At the same time, as Schwab argues, the atmosphere is increasingly imbued with ontological, epistemological, and psychological fears, as it bears the mark of latent events whose vastness contends with the immanence of space and history and with the boundaries of knowability and representability.[30] As digital media expert William Merrin comments, artificial intelligence and surveillance data collection have also become phenomena comparable to climate change for their complexity and impinging presence. Such technologies, according to media sociologist Andrew Hoskins, are increasingly dehumanized and deindividualized, generating "a sudden mass vulnerability, an exposure that seems impossible to contain."[31] The interface that today happens with "the outside of the body" could shift within the body itself, merging inner and outer information as Merrin's concluding claim, "the future is internal," seems to imply.[32]

Rather than the empty openness and awe with which the skies have been traditionally endowed, we are confronted with the saturation of information that characterizes the contemporary perception of the atmosphere. Airspaces are thickening on us as sites of alienation and otherness, as ecosystems are put at risk by atmospheric changes and by the insidious contamination of matter and affect. What ensues is a feeling of foreclosure. The appearance and fading of fluorescent flakes, of a vaporous lingering line of fog on the horizon, or the overlaying of a digital rain of data are visual signifiers of such insidious presence that Illingworth renders more acutely unsettling and liminal by the ways in which sounds distort the immersive atmosphere of the work. The spatial compression and subliminal disturbance that acoustic interference causes—a characteristic in Illingworth's practice—counteracts the views from above and the

29 See Albano, *Memory, Forgetting and the Moving Image*, 109–21. Sounds also reference the macro-micro, including the buzzing sound of an energy generator on the island and the sonification of an electroencephalogram of Claire.

30 Author's notes from Gabriele Schwab's comments at the Airspace Tribunal, The Power Plant, Toronto, November 4, 2020, https://www.thepowerplant.org/ProgramsEvents/Programs/Other-Programs/Airspace-Tribunal-(1).aspx.

31 Andrew Hoskins, quoted in Illingworth, *Topologies of Air*, voiceover transcript.

32 William Merrin, quoted in Illingworth, *Topologies of Air*, voiceover transcript.

hegemonic perspective that typifies them. While, within the context of the work, individuals increasingly disappear in the trace of metadata that they leave behind, we, as viewers, are swathed by the affective textures of these topologies of air as they evaporate from the screens in the *unheimlich* view of a blue sky.

An Ethics of Air

"There is something very special about having the freedom to look up at the sky without feeling threatened," writes Nick Grief about the proposed human right to live without physical or psychological threat from above.[33] Such a right, as Grief explains, "would be a qualified right, not an absolute one," meant to strengthen international humanitarian laws by regulating airspaces.[34] This raises the question of the critical, rather than legal, significance of such a proposition in relation to *Topologies of Air*. As Conor Gearty maintains,

> The language of human rights
>
> Is among the very last of the languages available to us
>
> To fill a gap in our understanding of the world
>
> Which is rooted in equality, esteem and empathy[35]

I would add that art practices are another of those languages. In *Topologies of Air*, Illingworth generates new understandings by integrating a plurality of voices, viewpoints, and experiences across diverse epistemologies, scales, and timeframes. The topologies of air that emerge are like volumes in motion whose spatial and temporal coordinations intersect affectively and discursively, though they remain unfixed in the circulation of meanings that association and emotional resonance generate.

Topologies of Air, as suggested, decenters hegemonic visions through shifts of scale, movement, and acoustic disturbance, thus deconsolidating single or exclusive forms of knowledge production by inflecting multiple ways of experiencing and comprehending the skies—encompassing understandings that would otherwise remain marginal, as shamanic insight or indigenous rituals. Such an approach resonates with Maria Puig de la Bellacasa's argument regarding the necessity to consider soil through practices of care that involve different scales and timeframes.[36] In a time when the erosion of commons and liberties by governments and corporations restricts what Jacques Rancière refers to as the "distribution and redistribution of places and identities, [...] of the visible and invisible,"[37] both *Topologies of Air* and the Airspace Tribunal create what Gearty describes in terms of human rights language as "a momentum for change without necessarily, in singular acts, achieving change."[38] While the body of evidence gathered through the Airspace Tribunal can be used to achieve legal change, the immersive space of *Topologies of Air* dynamically holds the multiplicity and plurality on which intimate connections and empathic responses can ensue as viewers engage with the complexities of today's topologies of air.

Puig de la Bellacasa writes about soil: "Modes of soil care and soil ontologies are entangled: what soil is thought to be affects the ways in which we care for it, and vice versa."[39] The same could be argued for airspaces as their ontologies, epistemologies, and ethics cannot be separated nor considered within limiting approaches. "The freedom to look up at the sky without feeling threatened" calls for ways of talking about and looking at the skies that "are rooted in equality, esteem, and empathy." *Topologies of Air* creates a space for empathic understandings of the skies and a recognition of responsibility as a "relation always already integral to

33 Nick Grief, "The Airspace Tribunal and the Case for a New Human Right to Protect the Freedom to Live without Physical or Psychological Threat from Above," *Journal of Digital War*, no. 1 (2020): 58–64, https://doi.org/10.1057/s42984-020-00023-w.

34 Grief, "The Airspace Tribunal."

35 Gearty, *Topologies of Air*, voiceover transcript.

36 See Maria Puig de la Bellacasa, *Matters of Care: Speculative Ethics in More than Human Worlds* (Minneapolis: Minnesota University Press, 2017), 9–17

37 Jacques Rancière, *Aesthetics and Its Discontents*, trans. Steven Corcoran (Cambridge, UK: Polity Press, 2009), 24.

38 Conor Gearty, quoted in Grief, "The Airspace Tribunal."

39 Puig de la Bellacasa, *Matters of Care*, 692.

the world's ongoing inter-active becoming and not-becoming."[40] It is in such a space that the possibility of a human right to protect the freedom to live without physical or psychological threat from above is a vision for an ethical reconfiguration of our immersive relations with airspaces, a way for reimagining the contemporary topologies of air.

40 Karen Barad, "Quantum Entanglements and Hauntological Relations of Inheritance: Dis/continuities, SpaceTime Enfoldings, and Justice-to-Come," *Derrida Today* 3, no. 2 (2010): 265.

Caterina Albano is a Reader in Visual Culture and Science at Central Saint Martins, University of the Arts London. She is the author of *Breath and the Vulnerability of Air* (University of Minnesota Press, 2021), *Memory, Forgetting and the Moving Image* (Palgrave MacMillan, 2016), and *Fear and Art in the Contemporary World* (Reaktion Books, 2012), as well as journal articles and essays on emotion and affect, the politics of memory, and curating. These include: "*Balnakiel*: In the Spaces of Memory," in Shona Illingworth, *The Watch Man/Balnakiel* (Video and Film Umbrella, 2011); "At the Edge: Balnakiel a Video and Sound Installation by Artist Shona Illingworth," *Memory Studies* 6, no. 4 (October 2013); "Forgotten Images and the Geopolitics of Memory: The Italo-Ethiopian War (1935–36)," *Cultural History* 9, no. 1 (April 2020); and "Moving Emotions: Affect, the Archive and the Moving Image," *Cultural History* 7, no. 2 (October 2018).

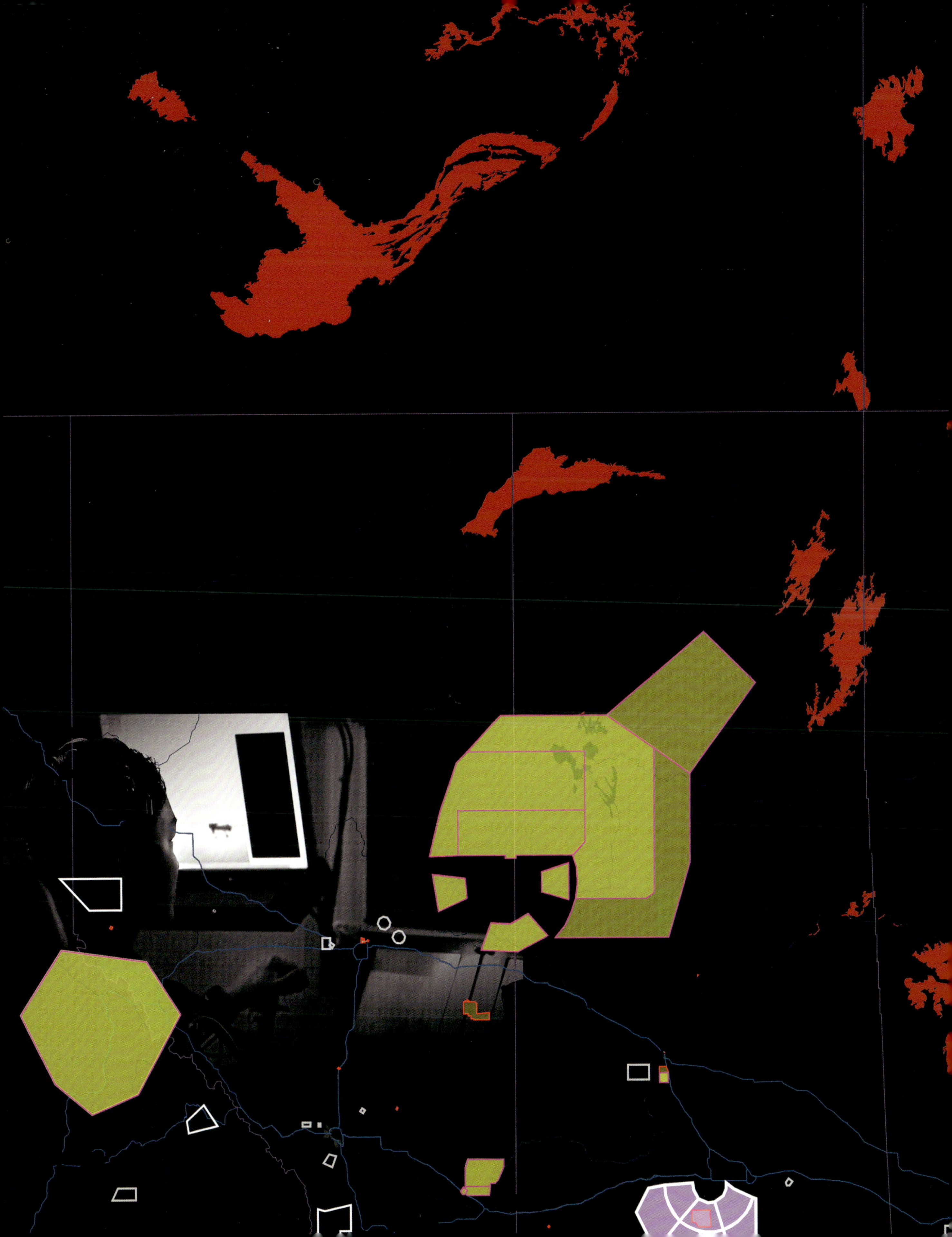

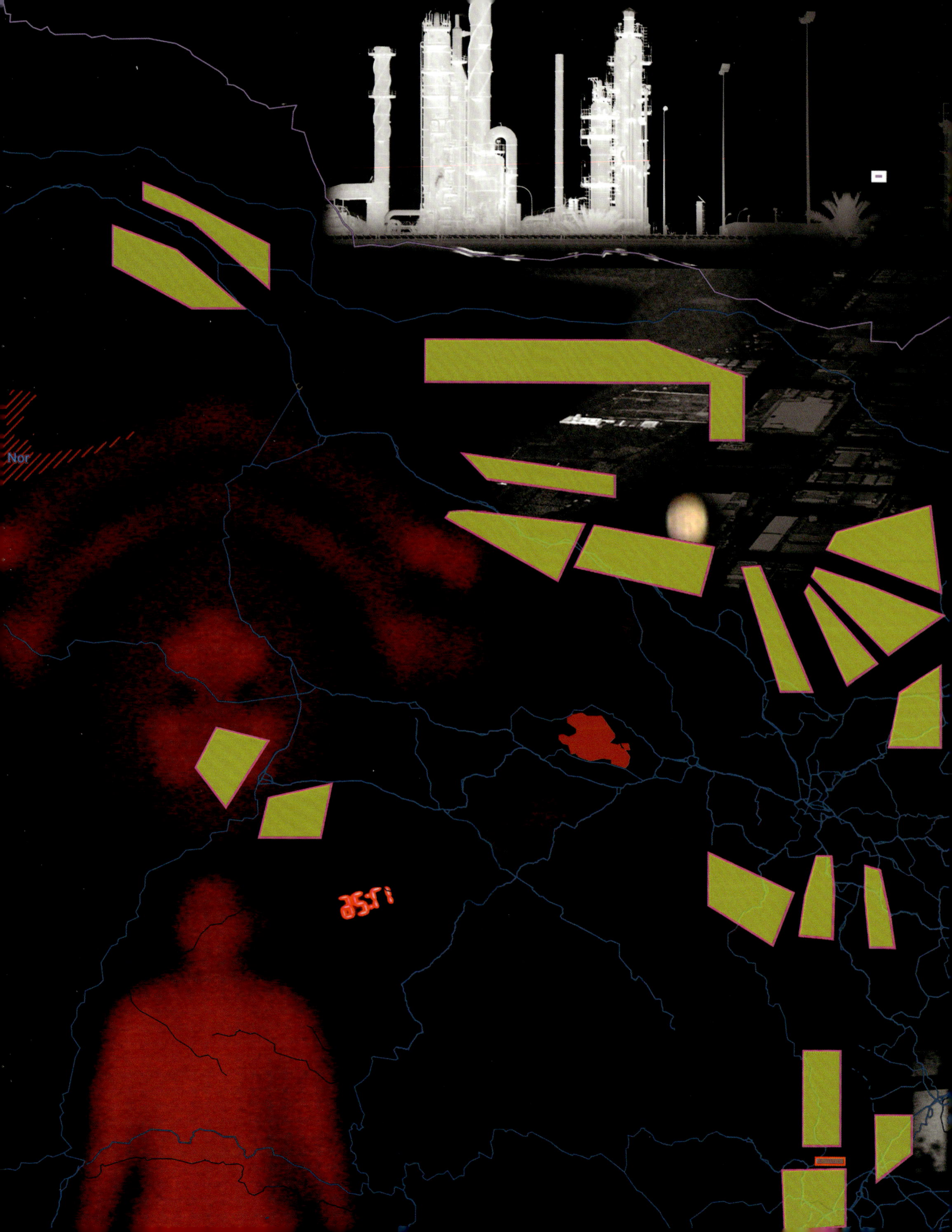
Nor

Giuliana Bruno
IN THE AIR: ATMOSPHERIC THINKING

“All living things require an atmosphere around them, a mysterious misty vapour.”
—Friedrich Nietzsche[1]

“Atmosphere is […] the air and the aroma that pervade every work of art, and that lend distinctiveness to a medium and a world.”
—Béla Balázs[2]

What is an atmosphere? How can we define it as a concept and an aesthetic practice? Is atmosphere the “climate” of a place? Is it, in the largest sense, its “air”? Is it an affect that affects us? These questions arise as we approach the work of Shona Illingworth, who asks us to examine atmosphere and the “character” of site. This is an artist profoundly interested in airspace, landscape, ambiance, affective geographies, and media ecologies. In her creative universe, these sites are thoroughly investigated in moving-image installation art. Never pictured marginally as mere context or background, atmosphere is especially featured as a central object of the work. Foregrounded in different ways, it is always conceived as an actual environment. It is a dynamic space in which temporal and spatial dimensions develop in unison, through interactions of human and nonhuman inhabitants.

Consider Illingworth’s 2015 three-screen video installation *Lesions in the Landscape*, in which the artist investigates the relationship between the formation of landscape, the construction of temporality, and the loss of memory. What is particularly affecting about this work, from an atmospheric point of view, is how the artist establishes this connection from the very beginning of the projection. We are presented with the mountain peaks of an island, a landscape clouded by fog, and we watch and hear birds flying around up there in the air. This cloudy “air” is a central character of the installation, for it can also be read as the cloudy mental landscape of Claire, the featured character of the work, a woman who suffers from amnesia and struggles to form memories. As her condition is revealed over the course of the work, it is closely aligned with the ambiance of this island. This, we learn, is an atmosphere dense with the faded memory of its disappeared population and redolent of its traces. The atmosphere of the place and the woman’s mental space then continue to be developed in conjunction with a series of hazy bird’s-eye views traveling through misty seascapes and clouded skies. These moving atmospheric formations are the external “elemental” matters that link inner landscapes together in the minds of the viewers. We can fully grasp the “air” of the site, its fading mnemonic character, as if with our hands, while exploring it from the air. Finally, the sky of this abandoned island becomes a quiet, ethereal site, even a sanitized airspace, for it, too, devoid of memory, is Claire’s own inner space.

These aerial images that survey the island, exploring the insular site of Claire’s mind, stay with us. They transmigrate and return—displaced, transposed, just as memories would be—in *Time Present* (2016), a two-screen video installation in which Illingworth continues to investigate ambiance. The ethereal, insular universe reappears now as we follow Claire in her monumental effort to structure her life and maintain her connection to her environment, her past, and her sense of self, in the absence of memories. As the petrified stones of the island appear to turn into objects of her

1 Friedrich Nietzsche, “On the Uses and Disadvantages of History for Life,” in *Nietzsche: Untimely Meditations*, ed. Daniel Breazeale, trans. R. J. Hollingdale (Cambridge, UK: Cambridge University Press, 1997), 97.

2 Béla Balázs, *Early Film Theory: “Visible Man” and “The Spirit of Film,”* ed. Erica Carter, trans. Rodney Livingstone (Oxford: Berghahn Books, 2010), 22.

memory, so do the island's breezy nebular formations and passing waves. At times, in superimposition, Claire even appears to reach out for that windy, misty sky, full of birds flying like fleeting memories, in an effort to touch it. The more these aerial shots of the deserted island mnemonically recur, the more the affect that is "an air" materializes. These medial techniques representing the air end up giving full access to this woman's subjective landscape as well as to the social landscape of cultural amnesia. As in *Lesions in the Landscape*, here, too, the bird's-eye views not only survey these two sites in combination but work at mapping a relational landscape. The tangible construction of the aerial positions, and their haptic movements, finally enable the viewer to feel a sense of empathy. Here, we can sense a life, a moving inner life—that is, we can breathe an "air."

Thinking Atmospherically

As these moving-image installations demonstrate, Illingworth is an artist who thinks atmospherically. Her work asks us to excavate the very "elemental" meaning of atmosphere, digging up the elements that materially constitute an ambiance. She foregrounds ambient spatiality in a way that also investigates the conceptual construction and interdisciplinary articulation of this space. In the effort to explicate her vision of mapping airspace in such a way, in this essay, I will contribute a reflection on the epistemic mode I, elsewhere, term "atmospheric thinking," exploring this vital conceptual modality and the different disciplinary histories that subtend it.[3] As we delve into the inner workings of atmosphere, through her work, we will touch upon what is profoundly meant by this matter of "air."

A reflection on etymology can help us define the conceptual space that Illingworth mobilizes and that this text will flesh out. The root of "atmosphere" is composed of two elements: *atmos*, meaning "vapor," and *sphaire*, or "sphere." This, elementally speaking, is a medium of life. Atmosphere, that is, is the vaporous material base, the condition, the enveloping substance—the "air"—that makes life itself possible. It is a vital, transient milieu that, according to the philosopher Emanuele Coccia, is indeterminate in the sense that it is fluid and mixed.[4] And, as Illingworth makes clear in her work, this milieu has a medial nature that is not only elemental but also cultural and social.

Atmosphere, a positively vague and cloudy concept, can also be understood, in these social and cultural terms, as an affect or mood. That is to say that atmosphere, as I claimed in a previous study, is the material constituent of an affective geography.[5] In the words of the philosopher Gernot Böhme, it is "an indeterminate spatially extended quality of feeling."[6] As *Lesions in the Landscape* and *Time Present* show, this is, indeed, an ambiance of spatially discharged sentiments or perceptions, resulting from the material assemblage of different organisms and from the intermixing of forces in space. Constituted as a live medium of spatialized affects, memories, and sensations, it provides the very basis for sentient mixture and connection between diverse beings.

In fact, as the "atmospherology" of philosopher Tonino Griffero explains, an atmosphere is always "'an in-between,' made possible by the (corporeal but also social and symbolic) co-presence of subject and object."[7] Neither a discrete element nor an entity, it is ungraspable in singular or individual form. This is an in-between that is also in balance between presence and absence, the definite and the indefinite. That is to say, to dwell in an atmosphere is to interact with life forms of various kinds and to be affected by this varied ambiance. To sense an atmosphere is to grasp a volatile feeling in the surrounding space—an "air"—and

3 For further articulation of "atmospheric thinking," see Giuliana Bruno, *Atmospheres of Projection: Environmentality in Art and Screen Media* (Chicago: University of Chicago Press, forthcoming 2022). This essay expands on the path of research undertaken in *Atmospheres of Projection*, which is aimed at defining "atmospheric thinking" and reconfiguring "the projective imagination" as an atmosphere of mediality and relationality while considering the art of projection, understood as an environment, both in history and in contemporary art.

4 See Emanuele Coccia, *The Life of Plants: A Metaphysics of Mixture*, trans. Dylan J. Montanari (Cambridge, UK: Polity Press, 2019).

5 On this subject, see Giuliana Bruno, *Atlas of Emotion: Journeys in Art, Architecture, and Film* (London: Verso, 2002); Kathleen Stewart, "Atmospheric Attunements," *Rubric*, no. 1 (2010): 1–14; and Ben Anderson, "Affective Atmospheres," *Emotion, Space, and Society*, no. 2 (2009): 77–81.

6 Gernot Böhme, "Atmosphere as the Fundamental Concept of a New Aesthetics," *Thesis Eleven* 36, no. 1 (1993): 118 and 122. The essay is reprinted in Böhme, *The Aesthetics of Atmospheres*, ed. Jean-Paul Thibaud (New York: Routledge, 2017), 11–24.

7 Tonino Griffero, *Atmospheres: Aesthetics of Emotional Spaces*, trans. Sarah De Sanctis (London: Routledge, 2014), 121.

to perceive a situational mix of living matters that is subject to change. As a microclimate, an atmosphere evolves continually and even dissolves: it is a force field of energies in a constant state of becoming. And in this ambient midst, subjects are corporeally involved in their sentient relation to space. In other words, to experience an atmosphere, as Illingworth shows, one ultimately must be open to and in resonance with the phenomenic character and lived quality of our ever-shifting surroundings.

An Atmospheric History

Atmosphere, then, defines a condition that is fundamentally experiential. To better understand the nature of this experiential environment that is central to the experience itself of Illingworth's atmospheric installations, it is therefore helpful to trace the historical appearance of this idea of atmosphere, understood as such a surrounding, vital, and fluid ambiance. As we follow the course of the subtle shifts of conceptual meanings that occurred over the course of time and in various fields, a history of the cultural experience of the sense of ambiance that shapes Illingworth's atmospherics will take form.

The term "ambiance," established as a noun, appeared in French dictionaries in 1896. Before the noun, the adjective *ambiant* was used in mostly scientific contexts to mean "what goes around" in space, having developed from the Latin verb *ambire*, which defined ambulatory activities as well as the kind of encircling that is proper to an atmospheric embrace. The modern term "ambiance" was used predominantly in relation to artistic matters but also in philosophical, sociopolitical, and anthropological discourse, in part as a synonym for the more positivist notion of "milieu." But it also came to carry different, multiple inferences and associations, referring, as one critic recaps, "to light, brightness, air, limpidity, mixed with the dynamic sense of a fluid matter enveloping and embracing people and things."[8]

Milieu maintained more empirical connotations; it developed, as the philosopher of science Georges Canguilhem explains, from the mechanics of physics, moved to biology as a behavioral notion, and ended up encompassing sociological implications in defining an anthropological and geographic setting or surrounding.[9] Ambiance would expand the meaning of milieu, understood as a mid-place, medium, or in-between, as well as its connotation of environment or *Umwelt*, as developed by Jakob von Uexküll.[10] His Umwelt defines the character of the world surrounding organisms as being subjective as well as objective, with correspondences between the two. Uexküll even sought to expose the more subjective environment that encompasses every living form and being. This expanded notion of surroundings builds on the idea of the existence of an ambient element first formulated by the ancient Greeks and subsequently reprised by modern science to define "what goes around." Such motility refers, in particular, to the (im)material consistencies of fluids or air, that is, to the space surrounding and encircling living bodies and the bodies of things.

Ambiance, then, develops as a notion of "ambient medium," as the literary critic Leo Spitzer shows in his seminal text "Milieu and Ambiance," first published in 1942.[11] Spitzer proposes that the link between medium and ambient space goes way back in history to an orbit of relations that, with Lucretius, almost becomes a form of embrace when the Roman philosopher establishes the "caressing" quality of space with respect to surrounding objects.[12] Spitzer, then, via Newton, defines ambiance as a field of forces, connoting the fluid movement of the sensible world. And so it goes that, by the end of the nineteenth century, the connotations of ambiance shift from the biosociological sphere to a realm closer to that of atmosphere, with its affecting elements,

8 Francesco Guzzetti, "The *Ambiance* of Medardo Rosso: Impressions, Critics and Patrons," in *Medardo Rosso: Two Rare Waxes* (London: Amedeo Porro Fine Arts and Peter Freeman, 2016), 27.

9 For a useful history of the notion of milieu, see Georges Canguilhem, "The Living and Its Milieu," trans. John Savage, *Grey Room*, no. 3 (Spring 2001): 7–31.

10 For a reconsideration of the notion of milieu and its relevance in contemporary theory, see Victor Petit, "Le désir du milieu (dans la philosophie française)," *La Deleuziana*, no. 6 (2017): 10–25; and Giovanni Carrozzini, "Sulla nozione di atopia a partire da Socrate. Ripensare l'ambiente-mondo," *La Deleuziana*, no. 6 (2017): 26–39, http://www.ladeleuziana.org/2017/12/31/6-milieux-of-desire/.

11 Leo Spitzer, "Milieu and Ambiance" (1942), in *Essays in Historical Semantics* (New York: Russell & Russell, 1948), 179–225.

12 Spitzer, "Milieu and Ambiance," 190.

or to "climate," arriving finally to be understood as "an air," even in the spiritual sense.[13]

In other words, with modernity, ambiance itself becomes more atmospheric. It does so in the era in which the technical reproducibility of media creates the medium of film, with its particularly "moving" ambiance—the atmosphere of projection. It is at this time that ambiance takes on the character that Illingworth dwells upon in her work—that of a more elemental, ecological, evanescent, and affective technical "medium." Tracing this atmospheric history of the terms "ambient" and "ambiance" in relation to the history of ideas, then, highlights the technological factor that this artist is invested in, for "the history of this word cannot be separated from that of medium = milieu."[14]

As for the term "atmosphere" as understood in the scientific realm as a medium, it, too, emerged at a particular historical moment.[15] Combining the ancient Greek words for "vapor" and "sphere," the idea of atmosphere made its appearance in early modernity, at the beginning of the seventeenth century. A concept of natural philosophy, it spread rapidly from astronomy and mathematics to multiple areas of research, ranging from meteorology to cosmology, medicine to botany. Discussions arose in various fields about the aerial region—the *pneuma* or vapor—surrounding the earth, and especially about the composition of the substances that permeate the earth's surface and extend all the way to the stars, often described as blankets of air, effluvia, exhalations, or emanations. In the eighteenth and early nineteenth centuries, even climates were widely spoken of as *circumfusa*, that which sheathes and flows around organisms. A particular conception that is generative for Illingworth thus developed at this point, as atmosphere became articulated as a modality of envelopment, and airspace came to be seen as a medium. The idea was to grasp an ethereal form of circumnavigation that, as Eva Horn puts it, "engulfs and transports the bodies of living beings, be they plants, animals, or human beings, in an ever-moving, ever-changing *medium*."[16]

As for the sciences proper, these discussions also involved light, an element that Illingworth also creatively deploys when she depicts her enveloping atmospheres and the "air" of a site. As historian Craig Martin recounts in his study of "the invention of atmosphere," the quality of twilight and the refraction of sunlight were especially investigated.[17] Because luminous refraction requires light to pass through an airy substance, atmosphere was engaged, analyzed, and mathematically measured. Interestingly, it did not emerge as ethereal, nor as pure air, diaphanous or transparent. It was rather assigned, as Illingworth herself does, degrees of limpidity and deemed opaque, turbid, or even gloomy, in more moody or affective terms.

And, with this material consistency, in the middle of the seventeenth century, the concept of atmosphere changed in scientific circles in even more fluid ways with the advent of the pneumatic experiments of Pierre Gassendi, Walter Charleton, and Robert Boyle. The atmosphere of the mathematicians was transformed, with added characteristics not only of weight and gravity but also pliability and fluidity. The nature of vacuity and the possibility of assigning weight to air or its particles created disputes about the borders and extent of the atmosphere and its capability for expansion, seen as curling in waves. Its density and rarity, qualities employed in its capacity to refract light, suggested a morphing matter of condensed air or gases.

By the rise of modernity, then, the earth was seen to possess an encompassing, layered atmosphere, which surrounded and moved around everything, including flora and fauna, other planets, and everything solid. The concept resulted in the idea of an elastic medium: a blanket, a pliant, "fluid substance made of corpuscles and effluvia."[18] Thus, comprised of fluid bodies

13 On this subject, and in view of Spitzer, see, among others, Emily Apter, "*The Hatred of Democracy* and 'The Democratic Torrent': Rancière's Micropolitics," in *Understanding Rancière, Understanding Modernism*, ed. Patrick M. Bray (London: Bloomsbury Academic, 2017), 11–32. In the field of architecture, Michael Hensel also acknowledges Spitzer's contribution in his book *Performance-Oriented Architecture: Rethinking Architectural Design and the Built Environment* (Chichester, UK: Wiley, 2013).

14 Spitzer, "Milieu and Ambiance," 180.

15 See Katherine Park, "Observation in the Margins, 500–1500," in *Histories of Scientific Observation*, ed. Lorraine Daston and Elizabeth Lunbeck (Chicago: University of Chicago Press, 2011), 15–44.

16 Eva Horn, "Air as Medium," *Grey Room*, no. 73 (Fall 2018): 18 (emphasis mine).

17 Craig Martin, "The Invention of Atmosphere," *Studies in History and Philosophy of Science*, no. 52 (2015): 44–54.

18 Martin, "The Invention of Atmosphere," 52.

and layers that are not fixed but rather unstable, atmosphere became defined by flux and movement. In such a way, it became more closely connected to ambiance—the space in which we breathe and move.

The Materiality of Air: Atmosphere as Mixed Medium

"Atmosphere is a metaphysical space in which everything depends on everything else, […] a space in which each person's life is mixed with the life of others. […] It is the absolute medium, […] the principle through which the world makes itself inhabitable. […] One is always, in the matter of the atmosphere itself, *in* the world, because the world exists as atmosphere."
—Emanuele Coccia[19]

As a space in which we breathe, move, and mix with the life of others, atmosphere can, thus, be truly understood, theoretically and historically, in the way Illingworth creatively conceives it experientially—as an "air." Atmosphere is the air that generates and vibrates in all forms of life. And, as such, it does not simply "go around" but creates a mixture of elements, forms, and species. This is essentially a vast, immersive climate of transformative fluidity. In this sense, atmosphere can also be said to create a climate. In fact, conceived in a broad sense, climate can be understood as the "air" of a place. And this kind of "air" is culturally, socially, and psychically constructed, in a sense that both encompasses and surpasses some of the scientific notions we have touched upon.

This sense or rather sensing of air is a crucial factor in the development of Illingworth's work. One can experience this matter taking shape in the very construction of her *Topologies of Air* (2021). This interestingly titled three-screen video installation continues the atmospheric line of thinking presented in *Lesions in the Landscape* and *Time Present* but expands its range. As the artist herself explains, the conceptual construction of this work "extends into the air, or becomes 'airborne.'"[20] The projection begins again with a familiar landscape: a returning, yet more expansive, cloudy sky. It then progresses with the aim of exploring the actual materiality of air as well as the psychic matter that constitutes an "air." Extending the spatiotemporal and emotional dimensions of ambiance and its mnemonic substance explored in the previous works, here Illingworth analyzes the airy matter of atmosphere itself.

Moving across the three screens, and immersed in surround sound, we navigate an ethereal space that is dense with complex relational fragments and reciprocal interactions. This atmosphere is live. It is alive with an intermix of physical conditions, neurological networks, flying objects, information technologies, communication techniques, and modes of projection. This air is full of passages and transportation modes, ranging from balloons to airplanes, satellites to rockets, filmed as they "go around."[21] It is traversed by all kinds of communicative signals and virtual flights. Here, digital diaspora meets ghostly migration and even spirit communication. In this air, there are transfers of particulate matters, spreading of aerosols, metabolic digestions of nutrients, and transits of dust clouds. Signals are also passed, absorbed, or refracted in this atmospheric world that is never stable. Light particles themselves travel in this sensitive airspace. Sensorially traversed by wireless networks of sensors, this atmosphere is never devoid of interferences. A material space of motion, such aerial topology is full of emotion. Human beings and machines, as well as all kinds of other nonhuman agents, not only actively connect but also intersect through this ethereal yet material topology. A space of mixture and communicative exchange between the very substance of beings, this airy atmosphere is the ultimate medium.

19 Coccia, *The Life of Plants*, 48–49.

20 Cited from email conversations conducted in July 2020 with the artist, whom I thank for graciously sharing work in progress and notes about her work.

21 For a history of atmosphere as imagined and experienced through experiments with air ballooning, see Derek P. McCormack, *Atmospheric Things: On the Allure of Elemental Envelopment* (Durham, NC: Duke University Press, 2018).

A real form of "atmospheric thinking" thus takes shape in *Topologies of Air*. The work goes to the heart of this matter because it makes audible as well as visible the invisible vitality and mediatic materiality of an atmosphere. Here, one can even "sound" the medium of air's inner vibrations. The perceptual auditory mode gives viewers the intimate experience of immersion into an ecosystem of information collection and transfer, a vibrant space of energy transmission and "transport." In other words, here, we can experience atmosphere as a transitive and hybrid mediatic ecology.

It is important to note the intense sensorial quality of this experiential exploration of atmospheric mediality. While navigating this composite aerial topology, mostly with aerial views, the pure optical and omniscient qualities of this visual technique dissolvc, giving way to a haptic sensory approach. Through carefully choreographed haptic cinematic motion, one is able to sense the movement of this mixed medium—the unstable substance and morphing blend that makes up an air. As if actually moving through the resounding medium of air, the viewer tactilely perceives its composite strata and layers and can even feel the various electromagnetic frequencies that traverse it internally.

As it explores from the air the mediatic power of such transfers of energies, *Topologies of Air* aims at producing a climate, while questioning its meaning. Multiple voices from across a variety of expertise, convened from the Airspace Tribunal (2018–ongoing), ask us to reflect on the substances and properties of air as they challenge its proprietary areas.[22] They urge us, from different corners of the world, to consider how airspace, infringed upon, is rapidly changing and to feel the impact of climate, and climate change, on life on the earth. In the end, we are presented with the mapping of a densely enveloping substance to which we need to pay close attention, hold on to, and take care of if we wish to avoid the destruction of our planet and continue to breathe.

What is particularly interesting, in this atmospheric respect, is the feeling of density, opacity, and even murkiness assigned to air. As she gives weight to this matter, Illingworth emphasizes the inner material intensity and internal complexity of this apparently ethereal subject or evanescent sphere. This is not a vision of clean air. It is rather a view of its cloudy, hazy, and even dirty inner workings, for, as we are told, "The future is internal." With her ecological emphasis on the inner materiality of aerial surfaces, the artist counters as well the idea of the "cleaned out," purified air that is the effect of surveillance and control. In such a way, she produces a polyphonic vision of climate that is not sanitized.

With *Topologies of Air*, we thus experience the particular shades of air's materiality that pertain, in the largest sense, to climate, understood as well as meteorology. At times, the installation's cinematic rendition of climate, and of its shifting, hazy formations, even appears to swirl around the three screens as if it were itself an atmospheric weather system. This meteorological constituent of atmosphere is not simply formally represented in the installation but becomes generative for the conceptualization of airspace. To better grasp the conceptual range of action of this aspect of "atmospheric thinking" evoked by Illingworth, we thus need to reflect further on the meteorological materiality of air and take a step back to see how it emerged in history as a material space.

Though it took millions of years for atmosphere to be formed around the earth, embracing us like a blanket, it was not until the nineteenth century that the elements of air became a more specific topological focus of inquiry. This period saw a rapid development in the atmospheric research that is relevant for Illingworth and that formed the meteorological sciences. As literary scholar Steven

22 An integral element of how the politics of air is constructed and conducted in *Topologies of Air* comes from the Airspace Tribunal, an innovative international public forum conceived by Shona Illingworth with Nick Grief to create this work. It brings together individuals, organizations, and groups located at different sites around the world, representing a wide range of disciplines and experiences. Working with multiple voices here, as is her practice, Illingworth convenes this forum to discuss transformations in the atmosphere and to consider the case for new human rights regarding airspace. On this subject, see http://airspacetribunal.org/.

Connor explains, writing on "the matter of air": "Around the turn of the twentieth century, the air acquired a new accent."[23] Most important, for our purposes, is the fact that when it culturally emerged in modern times as a sphere of interest, atmosphere signaled a shift in the concept of spatial corporeality. Atmospherics became "the sphere in which a new conception of mixed and mutually pervasive bodies was worked out."[24] In other words, the idea of a mixed and pervasive atmospheric corporeality is a modern idea, and so is thinking atmospherically.

Such a modern approach to the surface and matter of air is politically important, for it enables us to conceive of overcoming divisions and divides in favor of hybridity and mixture. Atmospherics is the sphere in which boundaries between bodies, and distinctions between bodies and matters, human and nonhuman, can be negotiated and crossed. As one imagines the possibility of "mixed and mutually pervasive bodies," a different conceptual universe becomes possible. Synthetically, then, we can fully recognize that atmosphere, to borrow Connor's words, "is the ultimate 'mixed body,' made up of distribution, communication and interferences," and that "in betweenness becomes the normative condition of the atmospheric."[25]

Understanding atmosphere as such an "air" in this sense, which is conceptually at work in Illingworth's corpus, also requires broadening our notion of climate beyond the literal meaning. In the words of Emanuele Coccia, climate "is not the collection of the gases that envelop the terrestrial globe. It is the essence of cosmic fluidity"; in other words, it is "the infinite mixture of all things, present, past, and future."[26] It does not simply produce this mixing but is the actual name, definition, and metaphysical structure of a mixture. In the mix of atmospheric encounters of the kind Illingworth strives to produce, topological exchanges become possible. As we can see in both *Lesions in the Landscape* and *Topologies of Air*, the medium of ambiance becomes subject, and the subject, in turn, becomes ambient.

Finally, then, this "weathered" form of mixing, proper to atmospheric currents and creative artistic paths, leads to a form of thinking that is not socially divisive. "Atmospheric thinking," to my mind, is fundamentally a relational modality—a hybrid, "moving" form of interaction that is opposed to the enclosed nature of human individuality and self-sufficiency. The topological exchange in question is diffused in, by, and through all living forms that inhabit the atmosphere. This kind of immersive fluidity, which Illingworth practices in her installations, constitutes a materially relational mode of living. Her version of "atmospheric thinking" ultimately dissolves the idea of a border between the body and air and dissipates the secure boundaries between the different bodies that dwell in the atmosphere.

This kind of atmospheric mutability that populates her artistic universe incorporates a particular kind of meteorology: an affective climate. It does not simply describe an aggregate state of matter but rather defines the constitution itself of lived space and social milieu. Here, to live in a society is to take part in constructing an atmosphere, in creating "the air" of a place. It also means taking responsibility for this climate: for the air that we breathe in and out and breathe within. If taken in this relational sense, then, meteorology can become a positive force. Such a form of atmospheric awareness can affirm the social value of porosity and hybrid contact and assert the power of transitivity, encouraging receptive relationality and reciprocal interaction.

The Atmosphere of Projection

It is also important to emphasize, in this relational sense, that atmosphere developed as a concept in the midst, and as an agent, of a major paradigm shift that

23 Steven Connor, "On Nebular Modernism" (paper presented at "Modernism and Beyond: Interdisciplinary Seminar in Art Theory and Literary Theory," Trinity College, Oxford, May 12, 2006), http://stevenconnor.com/haze.html.

24 Steven Connor, *The Matter of Air: Science and Art of the Ethereal* (Chicago: University of Chicago Press, 2010), 194.

25 Connor, *The Matter of Air*, 191.

26 Coccia, *The Life of Plants*, 27.

ended up recognizing different techniques of porous admixture and hybridity in ambiance and creating technologies of mediality. Ultimately, as such a modern concept, atmosphere can be fully recognized to be itself a site of mediation. In acknowledging this open, processual form of mixed (im)materiality in the formation of ambiance, then, it is important to continue to stress the role of atmosphere as medium. This not only is but also *acts as* a mediatic sphere. This specific mediatic aspect, as I have shown, is crucial for an artist such as Illingworth, who works with ambiance and atmosphere through the medium of film and employs not only digital video but also sound as a medium to produce resonant projections of moving images. This is why I wish to finally address the relational genealogy that links "atmospheric thinking" to "the projective imagination," and end by reflecting on a particular kind of ambiance: the atmosphere of projection.

When atmosphere becomes represented as a mixture or in mixed mediatic form, as I have argued is the case for Illingworth, it brings up the issue of its own conceptualization as a medial space of becoming admixture. In this sense, we should not forget that, as "ambiance" developed in this mediatic way as a term in modernity, joining the fluid strata of atmospheric research, so did the ambiance of projection. Film, sporting its own mediatic atmosphere, was invented, just as atmosphere itself was, as a modern "cultural technique."[27] Most importantly, the transitive qualities of transmission and relationality we described as belonging to the conceptual milieu of an ambient body are also active elements in the experience of mediums such as film, with its spatial, ambient projection of moving images.

As Illingworth ultimately shows, the projection of moving images is an atmospheric affair. "What goes around" in the art of projection is, precisely, the atmosphere of light and sound passing through air, circling and embracing things and people as they view moving pictures projected onto screen fabrics. Hence, as far as ambiance is concerned, "what goes around" describes not only the medium of diffused and refracted light but also the different forms of sonorous movement that occur on screen surfaces and resonate in the luminiferous ambiance of projection. This tangible environment includes the perambulatory activity of spectatorship, that imaginative going around—the "architectural promenade"—that constitutes filmic viewership, reprised today in the path of mobile reception of moving images in art galleries.[28]

Ambiance, which at its root is an *ambulatory* concept, then, in turn, becomes generative of various other nuanced forms of atmospheric perambulations of the kind Illingworth practices.[29] It is in this spirit that I insist on connecting the conception of ambiance as fluid energy to the fluid energy expressed in the art of projection, making a theoretically ambulatory move. This transitive gesture that conceives of ambiance as a mediatic passage points to a relation between air and light. It rests on the idea that a light medium is an element moving through air, as sound itself does, with its own capacity for reverberation. The atmosphere of projection is itself such a transitive, energetic ambiance. The ambiance of projection is, indeed, itself a vital matter that is as electrically charged as atmosphere.

Light, in particular, transmits through space an attractive, iridescent, haptic lure as it radiates and irradiates in the atmosphere—"in the air"—of the technical media of projection. This substance can be considered a "vibrant matter," that is, a component of the "vital materiality" that runs through and across the body of things as well as people.[30] What I therefore mean to emphasize here is air (or light) considered not as an element, or entity, as environmental philosophy might have it, but rather as an agent of ambiance—of that active, *conductive* force that affects perception.[31]

27 On the notion of "cultural technique," see Bernhard Siegert, *Cultural Techniques: Grids, Filters, Doors, and Other Articulations of the Real*, trans. Geoffrey Winthrop-Young (New York: Fordham University Press, 2015).

28 For further articulation of the ambiance created by screens of projection, see Giuliana Bruno, *Surface: Matters of Aesthetics, Materiality, and Media* (Chicago: University of Chicago Press, 2014); and *Atmospheres of Projection*.

29 The literary theorist Karen Pinkus also interestingly elaborates on the etymology of "ambiance," recognizing the implications of Spitzer's text, in her essay "Ambiguity, Ambience, Ambivalence, and the Environment," *Common Knowledge* 19, no. 1 (Winter 2013): 88–95. She points out that the Latin prefix *amb(i)* is inscribed in ambiance as it is in ambivalence and ambiguity. While I find this reading intriguing, for the purpose of my environmental argument, I prefer to focus on the Latin root *ambire* to emphasize the ambulatory side of ambiance.

30 For an articulation of this notion, see Jane Bennett, *Vibrant Matter: A Political Ecology of Things* (Durham, NC: Duke University Press, 2010).

31 See David Macauley, *Elemental Philosophy: Earth, Air, Fire, and Water as Environmental Ideas* (Albany: State University of New York Press, 2010). For a different reading of ambiance and environment, see Timothy Morton, *Ecology without Nature: Rethinking Environmental Aesthetics* (Cambridge, MA: Harvard University Press, 2007). For a discussion of the implication of an "ecological turn" in media theory for contemporary art, see Eric C. H. De Bruyn, "A Proposal: Must We Ecologize?," *Grey Room*, no. 77 (Fall 2019): 58–65.

32 See Gernot Böhme, "Seeing Light" and "The Phenomenology of Light," in Böhme, *The Aesthetics of Atmospheres*, 193–211.

Wary of the positing of a primordial existence for elements or claims for their stability, I am interested in environmental substances such as air and light in the way Illingworth presents them, as they shift, mix, and move—that is, because they "go around" and can embrace people and things.

Since the time of Aristotle, we have come to understand that visual perception depends on *media diaphana*, or translucent media. In *De Anima*, the philosopher sheds light on the role played by diaphanous substances such as air, clouds, smoke, water, glass, and crystal in configuring—with their different consistencies and degrees of transparency—the environment in which our sensory experience takes place. Light passing through air is a state of excitation in space that is shared by persons and objects.[32] It makes for the ever-changing quality of surfaces as it reflects and transforms all superficial matters, from skin to screens to sites. An energy space per se, it is able to make space energetically shift as well. To recognize this is to acknowledge the force that light moving through air exerts in the world, not only in terms of speed but also in the way in which it can displace objects in its path as well as accrue residues, deposit sediments, and leave mnemonic traces.

Moreover, this is a vibrant substance that not only moves but also morphs and mutates in time, as part of an environment of "temporal" change. As light morphs into darkness with the cycle of the day, it creates a different "air." This makes us perceive space differently and also perceive different aspects of a space. As things appear in different airs, literally and metaphorically, diverse views can emerge. So, finally, to sense light passing through air as an energy, in life as in the art of projection, is to be tuned to the moving materiality of the energy that surrounds us. As Illingworth knows, it is to be attuned to the many forms of mutability of an atmosphere, vigilant of the subtle changes that occur in the environment, and ready to reflect on how they are not only registered but also *transmitted* in the visual arts, especially on the surface of screens in the ambiance of projection, which is itself a relational atmosphere.

Giuliana Bruno is Emmet Blakeney Gleason Professor of Visual and Environmental Studies at Harvard University. Internationally known for her interdisciplinary research on visual arts, architecture, and media, she is the author of several award-winning books, including: *Atlas of Emotion: Journeys in Art, Architecture and Film* (Verso, 2002), winner of a Kraszna-Krausz Book Award for best moving-image book in the world; *Streetwalking on a Ruined Map* (Princeton University Press, 1993), winner of a Society for Cinema and Media Studies Book Award; *Public Intimacy: Architecture and the Visual Arts* (MIT Press, 2007); and *Surface: Matters of Aesthetics, Materiality, and Media* (University of Chicago Press, 2014). Her new book, *Atmospheres of Projection: Environmentality in Art and Screen Media* (University of Chicago Press, forthcoming), traces the histories of atmosphere and projection in visual art and culture, advocating for "environmentality" as an ecology of interrelationality.

AIRSPACE TRIBUNAL

The right to live without physical or psychological threat from above

Established by Shona Illingworth and Nick Grief in 2018, the Airspace Tribunal involves an international series of hearings that examine the case for and against the recognition of a new human right to protect the freedom to live without physical or psychological threat from above. The inaugural hearing at Doughty Street Chambers, London, was followed by hearings in Sydney, Toronto, and Berlin and included representations from a wide range of expertise and lived experience from around the world.

The hearings consider the perception and significance of airspace and outer space in the light of rapidly developing military, commercial, technological, and environmental change. Challenging the traditional state-centric view of how international law is created, the Tribunal's members ("judges") are an invited cross-section of the general public who are involved as participants. The process is led by Counsel to the Tribunal, who questions each of the experts after they deliver their statements and then opens the floor to questions from invited participants and the wider audience. The hearings are recorded and transcribed to document the drafting history of this proposed new human right and, in turn, support a people-focused proposal to present to the United Nations and other international bodies.

The Airspace Tribunal forms an integral part of the development and production of *Topologies of Air* (2021).

Nick Grief

THE AIRSPACE TRIBUNAL: DEVELOPING THE HUMAN RIGHTS DIMENSION OF AIRSPACE AND OUTER SPACE

On March 1, 1954, the United States carried out a thermonuclear weapon test, codenamed Castle Bravo, on Bikini Atoll in the Marshall Islands. It was one thousand times more powerful than the bomb that destroyed Hiroshima. Some sixty-two years later, on March 8, 2016, in his opening statement to the International Court of Justice in the case between the Marshall Islands and Pakistan, Tony de Brum, the Marshall Islands' co-agent, recalled how, as a nine-year-old boy, he had seen children playing in the radioactive dust that had fallen from the skies:

> Yesterday was a beautiful morning here in The Hague that featured a picture-perfect snowfall. As a tropical state, the Marshall Islands has experienced "snow" on one memorable and devastating occasion, the 1954 Bravo test of a thermonuclear bomb that was one thousand times the strength of the Hiroshima bomb. When that explosion occurred, there were many people, including children, who were a far distance from the bomb, on our atolls which, according to leading scientists and assurances, were predicted to be entirely safe. In reality, within five hours of the explosion, it began to rain radioactive fallout on Rongelap. Within hours, the atoll was covered with a fine, white, powdered-like substance. No one knew it was radioactive fallout. The children thought it was snow. And the children played in the snow. And the children ate the snow. So one can understand that snow, while beautiful, has a tragic and dark history in the Marshall Islands.[1]

Those words were a key catalyst and inspiration for the establishment of the Airspace Tribunal with its task of examining the case for and against a proposed new human right to live without physical or psychological threat from above. One of the things the Marshallese lost as the "snow" fell was the freedom to look up at the sky and not feel threatened.

The Legal Status of Airspace

The legal status of airspace has been settled for over a hundred years. In October 1919, the Convention Relating to the Regulation of Aerial Navigation was concluded in Paris. For the first time, a treaty proclaimed that every state has complete and exclusive sovereignty over the airspace above its territory. Twenty-five years later, that principle was confirmed and restated in a new treaty. The Chicago Convention on International Civil Aviation 1944 is still in force and, with 193 states parties, has virtually universal adherence. The fundamental principle of treaty law is expressed in a Latin maxim, *pacta sunt servanda*: "Every treaty in force is binding upon the parties to it and must be performed by them in good faith."[2] Those treaty provisions recognizing that every state enjoys complete and exclusive sovereignty over the airspace above its territory also represent "firmly established and longstanding tenets of customary international law", a separate source of international law evidenced by the general practice of states accepted as law.[3] So the sovereignty principle is expressed in two distinct but equally state-centric sources, which, according to a positivist understanding of international law, are both underpinned by consent, which is

1 Obligations concerning Negotiations relating to Cessation of the Nuclear Arms Race and to Nuclear Disarmament (Marshall Islands v. Pakistan), International Court of Justice, Oral Proceedings, March 8, 2016, Opening Statement, para. 2, https://www.icj-cij.org/public/files/case-related/159/159-20160308-ORA-01-00-BI.pdf.

2 Vienna Convention on the Law of Treaties 1969, Article 26.

3 Case concerning Military and Paramilitary Activities In and Against Nicaragua (Nicaragua v. United States of America), Merits, ICJ Reports 1986, 14, para. 212.

the basis of international law as a legal system. Not surprisingly, as we shall see, there is a tension between that understanding and the "inherent dignity" of all human beings and their "inalienable" human rights.

The horizontal limit of a coastal state's sovereignty over the airspace above its territory usually extends to the outer limit of its territorial sea, up to twelve nautical miles from the coast. Beyond that, the freedom of overflight generally prevails, both in the exclusive economic zone, extending up to two hundred nautical miles from the coast, and beyond that, above the high seas.[4] Like most freedoms, however, the freedom of overflight in international airspace must be regulated so that it can be safely exercised by all.

The Legal Status of Outer Space

The key legal principles governing outer space crystallized as customary international law soon after space flight started in 1957. They were then codified in the Outer Space Treaty 1967, which today has 110 states parties. It declares that the exploration and use of outer space shall be the province of all humankind and that, unlike the airspace above a state's territory, outer space is not subject to national appropriation by claim of sovereignty, by means of use or occupation, or by any other means.[5] Even the airspace of the high seas, an international area where the freedom of overflight generally applies, is legally distinct from outer space.

Although there is no national sovereignty in outer space, the boundary between airspace and outer space is not defined in the Outer Space Treaty and has not yet been agreed. Various approaches to delimitation have been proposed, one of the most popular theories being that the boundary lies a hundred kilometers (62 miles) above mean sea level. This is known as the Kármán Jurisdictional Line after the Hungarian-American scientist who first calculated the altitude "where aerodynamics stops and astronautics begins".[6] A functional approach has also been suggested, whereby activities would be "regulated according to their objectives and missions rather than according to the space where these activities are carried out".[7]

But how significant is the distinction between airspace and outer space as far as the human rights of individuals on the ground are concerned? In one sense, it does not seem to matter that airspace and outer space are subject to different legal regimes, or where the boundary between airspace and outer space is, or even whether there *is* a boundary. Our human rights may be violated by harmful activity in outer space, high up in airspace, or immediately over our heads.

The Human Rights Dimension of Airspace and Outer Space

After the atrocities of World War II, the adoption of the UN Charter (1945), the Universal Declaration of Human Rights (1948), and the European Convention on Human Rights (1950) marked the inception of modern international human rights law, which constrains the exercise of state sovereignty. Described as "a landmark of incalculable importance in the struggle for human decency and mutual respect",[8] the Universal Declaration begins by recognizing that "the inherent dignity and [...] the equal and inalienable rights of all members of the human family are the foundation of freedom, justice and peace in the world".[9]

Although the Universal Declaration is not a treaty, the rights proclaimed in it are recognized in two treaties that were concluded in 1966 and entered into force ten years later. Under one of those treaties, the International Covenant on Civil and Political Rights (ICCPR), each of the 173 states parties has a duty to respect the rights recognized in it and

4 UN Convention on the Law of the Sea 1982, Articles 58(1) and 87(1)(b).

5 Outer Space Treaty 1967, Articles I and II.

6 Theodore von Kármán with Lee Edson, *The Wind and Beyond: Theodore von Kármán, Pioneer in Aviation and Pathfinder in Space* (Boston: Little, Brown, and Company, 1967), 343.

7 *Max Planck Encyclopedia of Public International Law*, s.v. "Outer Space", C13.

8 Brian Urquhart, *A Life in Peace and War* (New York: Harper & Row, 1987), 117.

9 Universal Declaration of Human Rights, Preamble, first recital.

ensure those rights "to all individuals within its territory and subject to its jurisdiction".[10] The words "within its territory and subject to its jurisdiction" are interpreted disjunctively, meaning that states parties must ensure the rights laid down in the Covenant to anyone within their power or effective control, even if not located within their territory.[11]

Similarly, under the European Convention on Human Rights, the obligation to secure the Convention rights and freedoms is owed by each of the High Contracting Parties "to everyone within their jurisdiction".[12] A state's jurisdictional competence is mainly limited to its own territory, but the European Court of Human Rights has recognized that, exceptionally, acts performed or producing effects outside a state's territory can constitute an exercise of jurisdiction; in particular, where the state has effective control over an area, or there is state agent authority and control over individuals.[13]

A person's human rights can clearly be engaged as a result of acts performed in airspace, therefore, whether by the territorial sovereign or by another state. What about outer space? According to Article III of the Outer Space Treaty, states parties shall carry on activities in the exploration and use of outer space in accordance with international law, including the Charter of the United Nations. Although the UN Charter was signed twelve years before the launch of *Sputnik I*, the first artificial earth satellite, it applies in outer space no less than on earth, under the sea, and in airspace.

We rightly emphasize the Charter's prohibition of the threat or use of force in international relations and its affirmation of the inherent right of self-defense. But we should also note its emphasis on "the dignity and worth of the human person"[14] and that the purposes of the UN include "promoting and encouraging respect for human rights and for fundamental freedoms for all without distinction."[15] Whenever humans journey into outer space, therefore, they carry human rights protection with them. Similarly, all activities in space, whether involving states or corporations, humans or machines, entail human rights obligations too.

Today, space activity is not confined to states. In 2019, commercial space revenue represented about 80 percent of the global space economy.[16] Not surprisingly given its age, however, the Outer Space Treaty focuses mainly on the rights and duties of states that send objects and astronauts into space. It does not address private space companies like SpaceX, which in May 2020 became the first private company to send people into space, ferrying two NASA astronauts on a test mission to the International Space Station. In the twenty-first century, it is essential for human rights to be properly protected in the context of all space activity, including by non-state actors. For example, by making states responsible for ensuring that companies within their jurisdiction respect human rights throughout their operations no matter where they are conducted.[17]

The human rights dimension of airspace and outer space is still relatively unexplored, despite the fact that individuals are increasingly vulnerable to threats such as surveillance, location tracking, and predictive targeting. We need to reimagine what it means to call outer space "the province of humankind" and how states exercise sovereignty over the airspace above their territory, with a renewed emphasis on human rights protection. As Richard Falk has observed, "Sovereignty based on territorial boundaries and international recognition [...] tends to override human rights concerns whenever the two sources of rights clash."[18] But human rights can also be vulnerable as a result of activities in space where there is no sovereignty. To sum up, airspace sovereignty and outer space freedoms must be exercised with greater regard for human rights. In

10 International Covenant on Civil and Political Rights 1966, Article 2(1).

11 UN Human Rights Committee, General Comment No 31 [80] (2004), para. 10.

12 European Convention on Human Rights, Article 1.

13 European Court of Human Rights, "Guide on Article 1 of the European Convention on Human Rights". updated December 31, 2020, https://www.echr.coe.int/documents/guide_art_1_eng.pdf. However, the Court recently held that alleged violations of the right to life during the "active hostilities" phase of military operations by Russian forces in South Ossetia and undisputed Georgian territory did not fall within Russia's jurisdiction for the purposes of Article 1 ECHR. It attached "decisive weight to the fact that the very reality of armed confrontation and fighting between enemy military forces seeking to establish control over an area in a context of chaos not only means that there is no 'effective control' over an area [...], but also excludes any form of 'State agent authority and control' over individuals." See Georgia v. Russia (No 2), Grand Chamber, January 21, 2021, paras. 113–44, especially para. 137. For a critique of the judgment, see Marko Milanovic, "Georgia v. Russia No. 2: The European Court's Resurrection of Bankovic in the Context of Chaos," EJIL:Talk! Blog, *European Journal of International Law*, January 25, 2021, https://www.ejiltalk.org/georgia-v-russia-no-2-the-european-courts-resurrection-of-bankovic-in-the-contexts-of-chaos/.

14 UN Charter, preamble, second recital.

15 UN Charter, Article 1(3).

16 Global Space, "'The Space Report' Finds Commercial Space Revenue Climbs to $336.89 Billion in 2019", Space Foundation, October 13, 2020, https://www.spacefoundation.org/2020/10/13/the-space-report-finds-commercial-space-revenue-climbs-to-336-89-billion-in-2019/.

particular, all people everywhere should have the right to live without physical or psychological threat from above.

Why We Need a Specific Right to Live without Physical or Psychological Threat from Above

Lived experience helps us to understand why threats from above us should be taken much more seriously than they are. We know, for example, that drones cause civilians living in war zones to suffer "anticipatory anxiety" as they are reminded of deaths in previous strikes.[19] When a threat is unseen, its psychological impact is worse because the lack of control and predictability are greater. As Catherine Loveday explained at the London hearing of the Airspace Tribunal in 2018, children are especially vulnerable in this regard.[20] This was confirmed by speakers at the Sydney and Toronto hearings. From personal experience, they explained how aerial attack causes greater anxiety and trauma because it is unexpected and how traumatic experiences become encoded in memory and haunt the future, passing down through the generations.

Existing human rights such as the right to respect for one's private life do not adequately address this increasingly sinister threat from above. Although the notion of "private life" includes the protection of physical and psychological integrity,[21] stand-alone recognition of the right to live without physical or psychological threat from above is needed to highlight the particular gravity of such threats and their insidious contribution to human fear and anxiety in the context of ongoing, rapid technological change. Such recognition would set an appropriate standard of conduct, fulfill an important educational role (by ensuring that the human rights dimension was more fully understood), and hopefully, in time, promote a culture of compliance.

There is precedent for specific rights being carved out of more general ones as technology advances (such as the right to the protection of personal data, derived from the right to respect for private life) or in light of lived experience. The right not to be subjected to enforced disappearance, specifically recognized in a UN treaty in 2006, emerged as a result of several decades of lived experience, even though such treatment was a flagrant breach of multiple existing human rights of victims and their families.

A Qualified Right—And Non-derogable?

The proposed new right to live without physical or psychological threat from above would be qualified, not absolute. Restrictions would be permitted if they were "prescribed by law" and no greater than "necessary" to achieve a legitimate aim such as public safety or crime prevention. For example, aerial surveillance is not always harmful. It is helping to identify environmental destruction and human rights abuses. In September 2020, for the first time, drone footage helped to convict a human trafficker moving defenseless people across the English Channel from France to the UK.

More difficult is the question of whether the proposed right should be subject to derogation "in time of war or other public emergency threatening the life of the nation".[22] Derogation from human rights obligations is permitted "to the extent strictly required by the exigencies of the situation, provided that such measures are not inconsistent with [the derogating state's] other obligations under international law."[23] However, certain human rights are considered so fundamental that they are non-derogable, i.e., they cannot be suspended by a state under any circumstances. For example, the European Convention and the International Covenant both include the right to life

17 See Office of the High Commissioner for Human Rights, "Guiding Principles on Business and Human Rights", United Nations OHCHR, 2011, 3–4, I.A.2, https://www.ohchr.org/Documents/Publications/GuidingPrinciplesBusinessHR_EN.pdf.

18 C. J. Polychroniou, "Human Rights, State Sovereignty, and International Law: An Interview with Richard Falk", *Global Policy Opinion*, September 11, 2018, https://www.globalpolicyjournal.com/blog/11/09/2018/human-rights-state-sovereignty-and-international-law-interview-richard-falk.

19 International Human Rights and Conflict Resolution Clinic and Global Justice Clinic, "Living under Drones: Death, Injury, and Trauma to Civilians from US Drone Practices in Pakistan", IHRCRC, Stanford Law School, and GJC, NYU School of Law, September 2012, 81–82, https://www-cdn.law.stanford.edu/wp-content/uploads/2015/07/Stanford-NYU-Living-Under-Drones.pdf.

20 Catherine Loveday (University of Westminster), London hearing of the Airspace Tribunal, Doughty Street Chambers, September 21, 2018.

21 Tănase v. Romania, European Court of Human Rights, Grand Chamber, June 25, 2019, para. 126.

22 ECHR, Article 15; cf. ICCPR, Article 4.

23 ECHR, Article 15(1); cf. ICCPR, Article 4(1).

and freedom from torture and from inhuman or degrading treatment or punishment in their lists of non-derogable rights.[24]

Should the proposed right to live without physical or psychological threat from above also be non-derogable? If we compare it with the right to respect for private life on the basis that "private life" includes a person's physical and psychological integrity, the answer is probably no, since the right to respect for private life is not one of the few non-derogable rights. In view of the potentially long-lasting, traumatically intrusive, trans-generational impact of threats from above, however, a better comparison may be with the right to freedom from ill-treatment, in which case, there are stronger grounds for non-derogability.

Implications for International Humanitarian Law

If the proposed new human right existed, it would not prevent a state from using armed force in accordance with the UN Charter, i.e., in self-defense or with the authority of the UN Security Council. Indeed, if the freedom to look up and not feel threatened were specifically recognized in International Human Rights Law (IHRL), this could enhance protection under International Humanitarian Law (IHL), designed to spare civilians and other non-combatants from the effects of hostilities. In particular, it could help to ensure recognition of the psychological harm caused by aerial threats, especially harm over time.

During armed conflict, the protection offered by IHRL continues to apply alongside IHL, except by the operation of a formal derogation, where permitted. While rules of IHL may be relevant to the interpretation and application of IHRL, the reverse is also true: rules of IHRL can influence the interpretation and application of IHL. This is reflected in Article 21(3) of the Rome Statute of the International Criminal Court, which states that the Court's application of the Statute and of the principles and rules of international law, including the established principles of IHL, "must be consistent with internationally recognized human rights".[25] This applies to every article of the Statute.[26] IHL includes the rule of proportionality prohibiting attacks that may be expected to cause excessive incidental injury, i.e., incidental injury to civilians that would be excessive compared to the anticipated military advantage—a war crime under Article 8(2)(b)(iv) of the Rome Statute. A Chatham House research paper found that while there is no reason, in principle, to exclude mental harm from that proportionality assessment, most of the state practice considered did not take such harm into account. It was unclear whether that was because states did not consider that they were legally obliged to do so or because of perceived difficulties in identifying and quantifying the mental harm expected from an attack.[27] By removing any doubt that mental harm must be taken into account as part of the proportionality assessment, recognition of the proposed new human right to live without physical or psychological threat from above would help to stimulate a better understanding of the psychological effects of attacks and incentivize belligerents to develop more appropriate ways of assessing proportionality in relation to mental harm, including harm over time.

Conclusion

Consistent with the aim of giving individuals greater agency in the international legal order, the Airspace Tribunal is a people's tribunal. It is challenging the state-centric nature of international law and the dominance of powerful military and commercial interests by giving people around the world, including the Global South, the

24 ECHR, Article 15(2); ICCPR, Article 4(2). However, the former permits derogation from the right to life "in respect of deaths resulting from lawful acts of war."

25 In paragraph three of his Separate Opinion in Prosecutor v. Lubanga, International Criminal Court Appeals Chamber, Decision on the Prosecutor's Application for Leave to Reply to "Conclusions de la défense en réponse au mémoire d'appel du Procureur", September 12, 2006, Judge Pikis opined that "Internationally recognised may be regarded those human rights acknowledged by customary international law and international treaties and conventions", https://www.icc-cpi.int/CourtRecords/CR2006_03055.PDF. See also Article 31(3)(c) of the Vienna Convention on the Law of Treaties, which provides that when interpreting a treaty, "There shall be taken into account [...] any relevant rules of international law applicable in the relations between the parties."

26 Situation in the Democratic Republic of the Congo, International Criminal Court Appeals Chamber, Judgment on the Prosecutor's Application for Extraordinary Review of Pre-Trial Chamber I's March 31, 2006, Decision Denying Leave to Appeal, July 13, 2006, para. 38, https://www.legal-tools.org/doc/a60023/pdf.

27 Emanuela-Chiara Gillard, "Proportionality in the Conduct of Hostilities: The Incidental Harm Side of the Assessment", Chatham House, December 10, 2018, para. 115, https://www.chathamhouse.org/2018/12/proportionality-conduct-hostilities-incidental-harm-side-assessment.

right to be heard at its hearings and by respecting the conclusions they reach as its judges. Their views are captured in the hearing transcripts that will form part of the proposed new right's drafting history, along with expert and lived experience testimony and the submissions of Counsel to the Tribunal.

Realistically, if the proposed right is to be formally added to the catalog of human rights set out in global and regional treaties, it will need to be championed by states in the UN, the Council of Europe, or other organizations. But in the ongoing struggle for human decency and mutual respect, authentic and diverse voices and experience are being recognized and valued. Meanwhile, lawyers can use the Airspace Tribunal transcripts to argue that the proposed right should be recognized through a creative interpretation of existing rights, when arguing cases before national courts or representing people in international bodies like the UN Human Rights Committee (which supervises the implementation of the ICCPR through, *inter alia*, its consideration of individual complaints[28]) or the European Court of Human Rights.

28 Where the state party in question is also a party to the First Optional Protocol on individual complaints. See further OHCHR, "Civil and Political Rights: The Human Rights Committee", Fact Sheet No. 15 (Rev.1), https://www.ohchr.org/Documents/Publications/FactSheet15rev.1en.pdf.

Nick Grief is Emeritus Professor of Law at the University of Kent and a barrister practicing from Doughty Street Chambers, London, where he is an Associate Tenant. He is also a member of the Center of Theological Inquiry, Princeton. He specializes in public international law and human rights and has a particular interest in air and space law. A Kent graduate with a PhD on public international law in the airspace of the high seas, he taught at the University of Exeter and Bournemouth University before returning to Kent in 2010. In 2016, he was a member of the legal team that represented the Marshall Islands in the International Court of Justice (ICJ) in cases against India, Pakistan, and the UK concerning the obligation to negotiate in good faith toward nuclear disarmament. The team was nominated for the Nobel Peace Prize for its work in the ICJ. In 2018, he and Shona Illingworth established the Airspace Tribunal to examine the case for and against a proposed new human right to live without physical or psychological threat from above.

Opposite: Airspace Tribunal hearing, Doughty Street Chambers, London, September 21, 2018; Airspace Tribunal hearing, Ethics Centre, Sydney, October 14, 2019.
Overleaf: Airspace Tribunal hearing, The Power Plant, Toronto (online), November 1, 4, 7 and 14, 2020; Airspace Tribunal hearing, The European Center for Constitutional and Human Rights (ECCHR), Berlin (online), June 9 and 11, 2021.

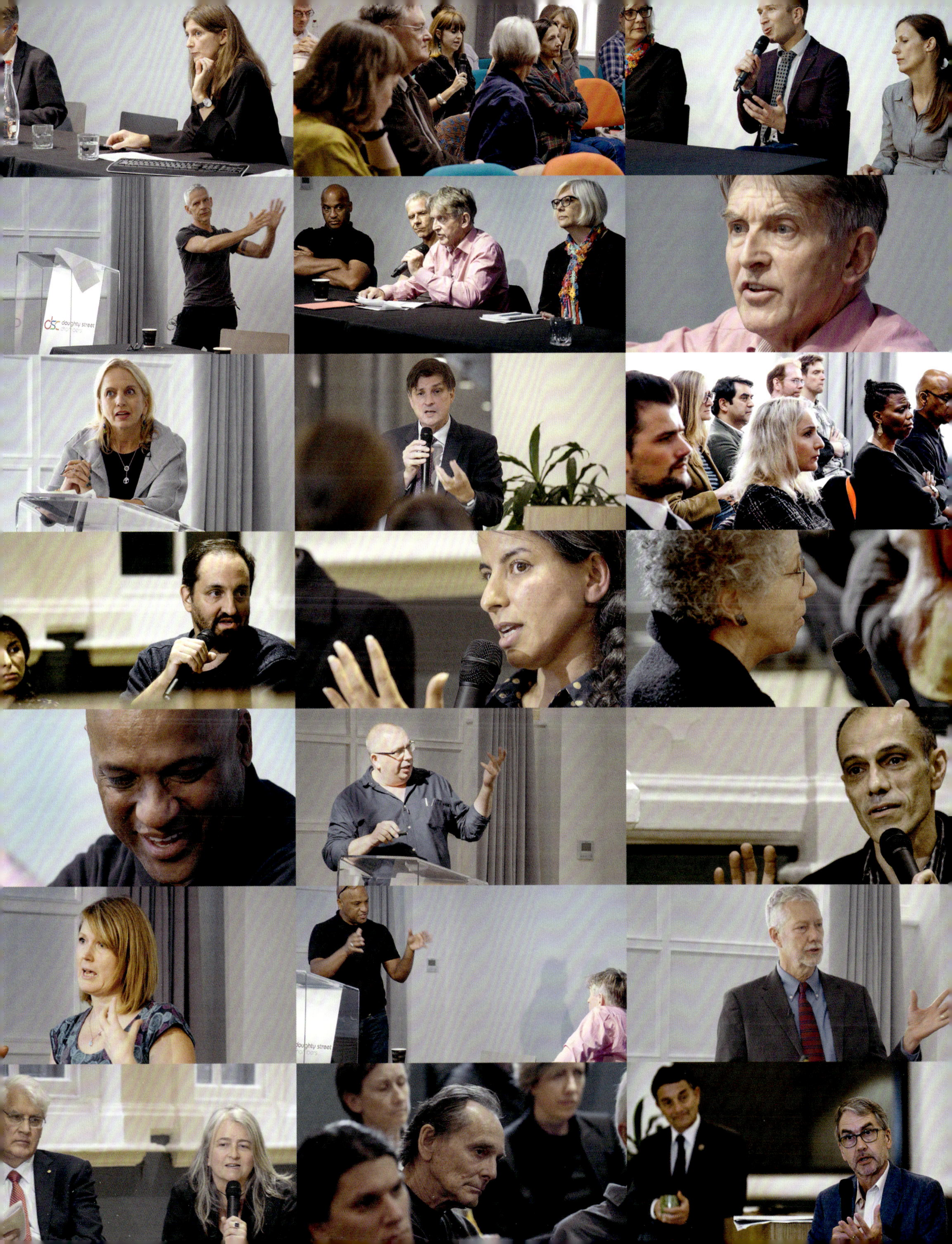
doughty street
doughty street

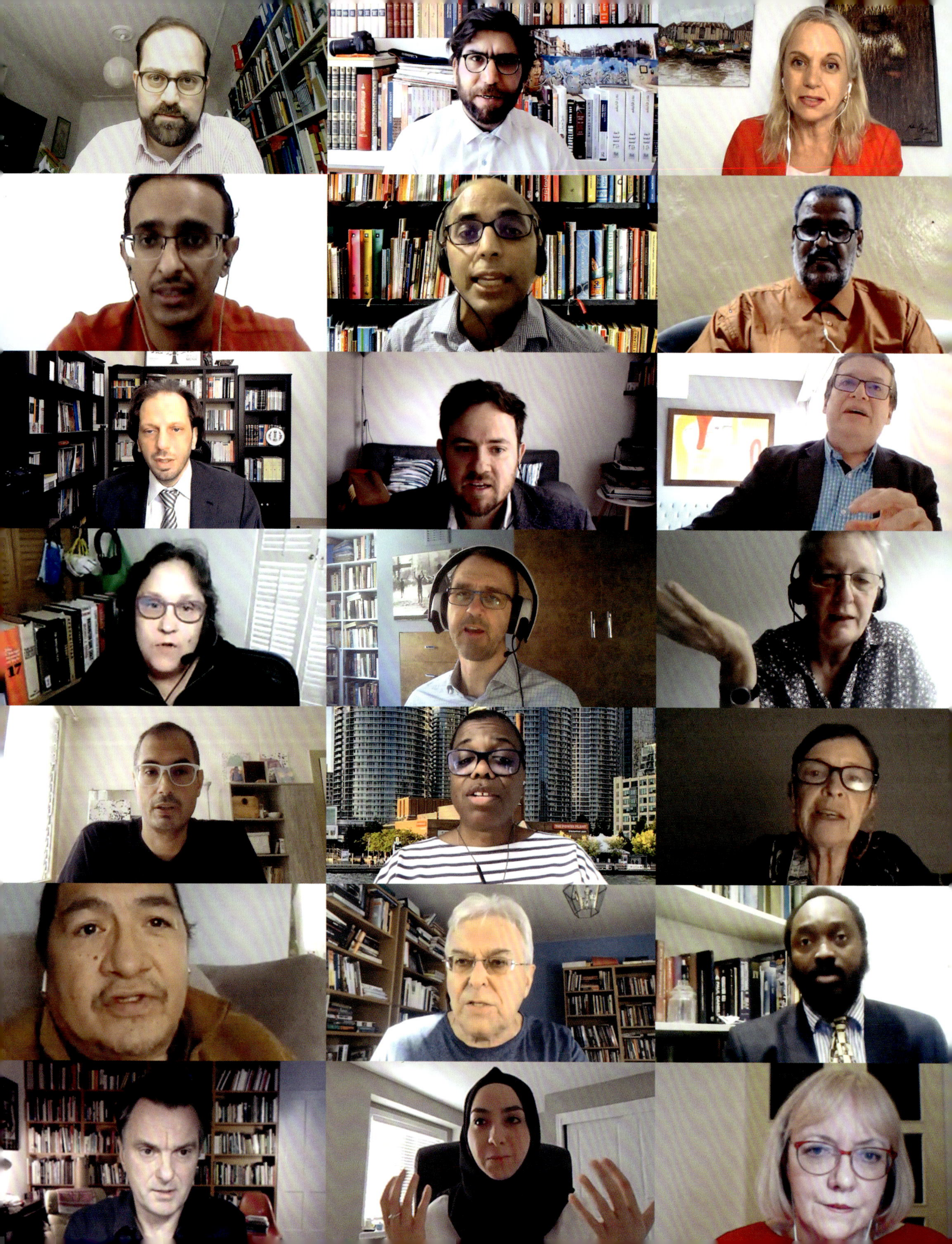

Conor Gearty

IMAGINING HUMAN RIGHTS FOR THE FUTURE: THE POWER OF POSSIBILITY

A world without human rights would be ethically shapeless. They are the way that we force ourselves—individuals, families, communities—into conversations about the future, which might otherwise be too preoccupied (by technology, utility, wealth, and power) to care. Asserting that each and every one of us has *rights* reminds us that we are *entitled* to be at the center of these discussions: our (mere, glorious) humanity is our entry ticket. And with us, we can bring concerns for our fellow species, for the world around us, welcoming advocacy of the indispensability of our natural world. Human rights are the agents of radical change, but their ever-present concern for the individual protects them from revolutionary over-reach. They keep our body politic safe from the ambitious poison of indifference to suffering. Human rights offer a roadmap to a better world without multiple "necessary" casualties along the way.

Framing Our World

There was a time when we looked to wise chieftains to shape our ethic and embed it in our communal common sense. Then came the moral demands of our great global religions, brilliantly framed by an appeal to a supernatural enforcer, demanding of us what we knew was right. Every faith has its codes of good behavior, indistinguishable from human rights charters, except that "human rights," as such, are never mentioned. They have also often been good on the world around us, on respecting the natural habitats we share. Such ruses have thrown down centuries of good practice, from which we still draw. But we have not been able to avoid getting to know our world and ourselves better, and this has made reliance on the wisdom of a chief or the dictates of a church seem passé to many.

The ethic of good behavior has risen to this challenge of threatened redundancy: it has forsaken the charismatic and the celestial in favor of a human-centered journey toward truth. We value each other as individuals; we each enjoy equality of esteem—this is right because each of us enjoys a dignity that is ineradicable, that flows out of the fact of our humanity. And this insight also drives us to see the indispensability of the world around us—the animals with which we share the planet, the air we breathe, the waters we rely on, the land that feeds us—as part of our human story. It is not only in our vital interest but also for the good of our planet that rights must reside in us and (possibly also) in themselves.

How do rights force themselves into the foreground of public truth? Early starters, backed by successful revolution and international politics, have been civil, political, economic, and social rights. Large international agreements pay testimony to their success, as do later triumphs of asserted visibility—the rights of women, children, persons with disabilities. Recently, our planet has shouted for attention via a growing understanding of the rights of Indigenous peoples and the value of their coexistence with the land.

Despite what many learned professors tell us, there is no canon of human rights. The content of our moral obligations ebbs and flows with our collective understanding of what is essential. This is shaped by power and partisan self-interest, of course, but in open societies, discourse and demonstration can also connect emerging facts about our world to how we ought to act—and in this language of human rights, we find the necessary bridge between aspiration (what we ought to be) and action (how to get there). To be clear: there is nothing culturally specific about any of this. It is true that human rights have been harnessed to the service of imperial power in the past (and even today). All emancipatory insights risk this kind of degradation. But deployed as a force for future good in the way suggested here, human rights transcend all cultures in their search for answers to immediate global questions. Ambitious—perhaps eccentric, today—such rights can soon come to be seen as the clearest common sense, joining the dots in the danger around us and giving us a set of words with which to galvanize ourselves into action.

Claiming New Rights

Our species' calamitous ransacking of the world, above and below, for short-term advantage demands a fresh language of rights to resist further destruction. How best to put words to this? Perhaps, a right to live in a clean, healthy environment, within which we could embrace a right to atmospheric integrity and freedom from overhead harm, or (to put it more ambitiously) the freedom to exist without physical or psychological threat from above. Much of the world lives under the shadow of such threats, rendering their well-established rights (free speech, liberty, and so on) neither here nor there in their daily lives. Even the affluent, lucky few moving house try to establish whether their new street will kill their children: privileged communities may keep out the poor but cannot fully protect from poison in the air or risk of nuclear immolation. Human rights can be a galvanizing tool of solidarity against the risk that our current practices will kill us all—a way of removing the veil of normalcy around polluting and war-enhancing actions and showing them for the dangerous idiocies they are.

Law is the engine that allows human rights to keep moving in the direction of new consensuses about truth. Old charters can be deployed by the creative use of litigation in innovative directions. In recent years, there have been many successes in the environmental sphere with traditional legal tools, such as the rights to life, fair procedures, and respect for privacy before national and regional courts.[1] Judgment has been very positive in a dramatic UK Supreme Court case addressing whether (and, if so, in what circumstances) a UK-domiciled parent company of a multinational group owes a common law duty of care to individuals who are said to have suffered serious harm as a result of the alleged systemic health, safety, and environmental failings of one of its overseas subsidiaries.[2] There were no fewer than 42,500 appellants in this case, all living in Nigeria, and their target was Shell. A Supreme Court decision from the year before had pointed toward potential culpability, and it proved to be the case.[3] In September 2020, a Polish court ordered the accelerated closure of a giant, polluting coal plant.[4] There have been further advances in continental Europe, and, further afield, my London School of Economics colleague Joana Setzer has recently presented arguments about the climate emergency in a two-day public hearing before the Brazilian Supreme Court.[5]

Are these traditional legal tools enough for us to get by without the need for framing new, more explicit rights? The answer is an unequivocal no. Traditional approaches are constrained by the hesitancy of courts to intrude into the "policy" sector and by their long-entrenched habit of throwing some slack to government in fields not historically within their zones of expertise. Overhead noise pollution from aircraft was briefly constrained by the European Court of Human Rights in Hatton v. The United Kingdom,[6] but the victory did not last long, and the

1 Ole W. Pedersen, "The European Convention of Human Rights and Climate Change—Finally!," EJIL: Talk! Blog, *European Journal of International Law*, September 22, 2020, https://www.ejiltalk.org/the-european-convention-of-human-rights-and-climate-change-finally/.

2 Okpabi and Others (Appellants) v. Royal Dutch Shell Plc and Another (Respondents), [2018] EWCA Civ 191, [2021] UKSC 3, https://www.supremecourt.uk/cases/uksc-2018-0068.html.

3 Vedanta Resources PLC and Another (Appellants) v. Lungowe and Others (Respondents), [2019] UKSC 20, https://www.supremecourt.uk/cases/uksc-2017-0185.html.

4 "Huge Coal Win as Judge Orders Europe's Largest Power Plant to Work with ClientEarth to Close," ClientEarth Communications, September 22, 2020, https://www.clientearth.org/latest/latest-updates/news/huge-coal-win-as-judge-orders-europe-s-largest-power-plant-to-work-with-clientearth-to-close/.

5 Caio Borges (@caiosborges), "On the 2nd day of hearings held by Brazil's Supreme Court in its 1st climate case, scientists, scholars and business reps will speak," Twitter, September 22, 2020, 11:20 a.m., https://twitter.com/caiosborges/status/1308350525486837761.

6 Case of Hatton and Others v. The United Kingdom, ECHR:2001:1002JUD003602297, October 2, 2001, https://hudoc.echr.coe.int/eng#{%22appno%22:[%2236022/97%22],%22itemid%22:[%22001-59686%22]}.

decision was overturned on appeal to the same court's Grand Chamber.[7]

An effort to use privacy law indirectly to tackle the dusk imposed on London's inhabitants by nearby high-rise buildings was unsuccessful in early 2020.[8] These innovative proceedings and occasional big wins are better viewed as efforts to push current frameworks to their absolute limits in the name of something vital rather than as substitutes for clearer legal codes. Judges are not legislators, nor can they claim in any relevant legal sense to represent "the people." Our destiny depends, in the end, on all of us.

Making Our Future

A new human rights strategy should be twin-tracked, deploying established human rights agreements to do the work they can while also pushing for sharper, more specific expressions of these new human rights challenges on the world stage—growing hard law out of soft declarations, as communities of activists have previously done in other fields. There is also value in a third track, driving change forward within national entities, particularly those sovereign states whose constitutional make-up is ostensibly (or perhaps even genuinely) democratic. The more specific the right pushed for, the more "ordinary" domestic legislation might be the appropriate place for it. The beauty of the language of human rights has been that it is pitched at a sufficient level of generality to be able to move with the times and give birth to moment-specific interventions designed to deal with specific problems.

Human rights have an added advantage here as well. Wearing their "traditional civil libertarian" clothes, they can protect the demonstrations and protests often needed to change opinion from the disproportionately aggressive attentions of hostile state actors: the right of freedom of expression is about as entrenched as can be imagined. And putting on yet another set of clothes, they can appeal to corporates as an important part of their social agenda, which is itself, of course, not morality in action but rather a business response to consumer, citizen (and, indeed, employee) pressure. In its protean character lies the true genius of the idea of human rights.

Wherever we locate our new human rights in the legal spectrum, whether international, regional, or local, it will require an independent entity capable of overseeing their proper enforcement. There needs to be a tribunal to complain to and credible remedies that are binding on states. Law is, once again, in the vanguard of progress here, taking government declarations at their word and forcing follow-up of promises when those making them were merely trying to get through their day. The power of litigation, where controls on who can access the courts have been relaxed (as in many democratic states), is that it releases mini-armies of committed activists to fight for the planet's survival by holding government to account before independent bodies. Reliance on "the rule of law" used to be greeted with a wry smile by progressives used to its emptiness. Now, it is key to the realizability of many of their ambitions.

Whichever route we go down in our search for a human rights future that saves us from a disastrous decline in our life chances, there is no alternative to robust, consistent activism. Nor should climate success come at the expense of justice, forsaking the poor to accommodate the scruples of the rich. Once again, the focus of human rights on each and every one of us is valuable here. Necessary activism can be focused on our species, but it also should not run from the world we seek to protect. A law of Mother Nature may be something to think of here (Bolivia has already asserted this), cutting out our species and going straight to nature's own rights. This may require some plausible yet incredible cases about how, for example, trees respond to imminent damage and

7 Case of Hatton and Others v. The United Kingdom, ECHR:2003:0708JUD003602297, July 8, 2003, https://hudoc.echr.coe.int/fre#{%22itemid%22:[%22001-61188%22]}.

8 Fearn and Others (Appellants) v. The Board of Trustees of the Tate Gallery (Respondent), [2020] EWCA Civ 104, February 12, 2020, https://www.judiciary.uk/wp-content/uploads/2020/02/fearn-v-tate-judgment.pdf.

appear to communicate. Are we going to learn that trees talk in the same way that dolphins do? Human rights should be an imaginative discourse that anticipates the future, or else it is nothing.

Conor Gearty is Professor of Human Rights Law at the London School of Economics and is also a barrister in practice at Matrix Chambers. His PhD was in environmental pollution law, though his academic work has mainly centered on terrorism, human rights, and civil liberties. Gearty's most recent book is *On Fantasy Island: Britain, Strasbourg and Human Rights* (Oxford University Press, 2016), and in early 2021, he published a long study on the role of the British judges in securing accountability for those engaged in or supporting torture: "British Torture, Then and Now: The Role of the Judges," *Modern Law Review* 84, no. 1 (2021): 118–54. He is currently working on the suffragettes and on political protest generally in twentieth-century Britain.

Andrew Hoskins and Shona Illingworth

WAR AS CONSTANT COMPETITION: THE WEAPONIZED FUTURE AND THE FANTASY OF TOTAL CONTROL[1]

Betawar and the Foreclosure of the Future

Air "thick" with data, signals, chemicals, electromagnetic frequencies, particles, microbes, radionuclides, pollutants, smart dust,[2] sonic interference, and encrypted machine-to-machine communications.

The sky, so profoundly connected to life and being across diverse cosmologies and shared cultural imaginaries, or conceived as an open and boundless space for imaginative projection and wonder, is rapidly becoming a source of existential threat, anxiety, and increased hyper-vigilance. Driven by a militarized imaginary of the fantasy of total control, the colonization of airspace and outer space is accelerating through the expansion of digital technologies and the algorithmic creep into weaponized spaces of surveillance and never-ending war.

In digital media ecologies, there are two principal means through which war is being made increasingly inaccessible to human perception and intelligibility. The first is the digital volume and flux of images, information, and disinformation that afford the impression of a chaotic battlefield, in which all sides are fighting with the new tools of participation, seemingly in full view. In this environment, overload is a key weapon in hampering understanding. There is little time for pause and critical reflection when in a state of constant connectivity with a relentless flow of images and information that are increasingly weaponized. The second mechanism rendering war inaccessible is the comparatively silent revolution in military and militarized data and AI, through which surveillance has massively expanded, so that civilians are increasingly subject to accelerating commercial and military exploitation of technology in airspace and outer space.

These two challenges to human perception and understanding have in common an orientation toward what the British military calls the "era of constant competition." This is not just a matter of what some have called perpetual or "forever" war, but also warfare that is driven through constant surveillance in pursuit of the next advantage and anticipation of the next threat. It is this surveillance as a default condition that drives militarization deeper and wider into all areas of human and planetary life, now extending inside the human body and into outer space. In turn, the production of a surfeit of data requires more automation to enable some kind of meaning to emerge. In the military context, meaning is derived from the automated or semiautomated identification of targets from the dehumanizing abstraction of so-called "patterns of life." This spiral of increasingly automated surveillance, analysis, and targeting obscures its origins—there is an algorithmic amnesia built into all digital archives. In military terms, this is not so much a forever war, but rather a "betawar"[3]—war in a rapid and permanent state of datafied, experimental, and archival evolution.

The accumulation, aggregation, and mining of data do not produce some kind of separable digital entity of the past but rather an interface through which memory is weaponized. And the same developments support narratives of progress driven by the narratives of colonization. These feed belief in technological supremacy and fantasies of total control, another spiral inflected with memory instrumentalized in

1 This paper is developed from Andrew Hoskins and Shona Illingworth, "Inaccessible War: Media, Memory, Trauma and the Blueprint," *Journal of Digital War* 1–3 (2020): 74–82, https://doi.org/10.1057/s42984-020-00025-8.

2 Developments in smart dust, tiny wireless microelectromechanical sensors designed to float through the air and gather and transmit data in real time, are now being oriented toward sensing neural networks in the brain. "Neural dust," dust-sized ultrasonic neural sensors, is one of the human brain/cloud interface technologies currently in development. See Ryan M. Neely, et al., "Recent Advances in Neural Dust: Towards a Neural Interface Platform," *Current Opinion in Neurobiology* 50 (June 2018): 64–71.

3 Andrew Hoskins giving evidence to the Airspace Tribunal London Hearing, Doughty Street Chambers, September 21, 2018, http://airspacetribunal.org/about/london-hearing/.

the bid to occupy or control the future. But the relationship between the past, present, and the future of warfare, so often understood in terms of traumatic memory, honoring the dead, learning lessons, and attempts to remember and forget (including to oppose or legitimize military in/action), is upended with betawar, that is war as constant competition. Here, the narratives of progress[4] as a well-established tool of colonization have been expanded through the identification of evermore territories of vulnerability and advantage driving an ever-expanding weaponization of everything and everywhere on the premise of maintaining security. This now incorporates the imaginary of the real-time, all-time adversary, which is used to legitimize the weapons of constant surveillance and of pre-emption.

A key consequence of this is a shift in the trauma of civilians from a memory of the past to include perpetual anticipation of threat in the future, subjecting increasing numbers of people to unending physical and psychological incarceration in a traumatizing present. This results in very real, long-term, physical, physiological, and psychological consequences for present and future generations of target populations. The new state of betawar is war as experimentation, not to secure advantage in the future but rather to command the present through hyper-vigilance, a kind of total surveillance.

The narrative of technological progress that has underpinned investment today in the weapons for tomorrow has looped back in on itself. In this present of never-ending threat, suspicion and the long-established narratives that perpetuate regimes of exploitation and racialized violence, and assume the moral dereliction of the adversary, drive the military imaginary, fueling the race to anticipate and weaponize territories that expand in all directions. Growing anxiety over ontological security feeds collusion with these narratives of threat and conflict, thus, narrowing the space for alternative imaginaries or horizons built on different perceptions of, or narratives for, the past.

For powerful states, the future is no longer imagined as a time and place of security achieved through military superiority or even deterrence.[5] Rather, the digital fantasy of what William Merrin calls "technological totalitarianism"[6] colludes with the imaginary of the archival pre-emption of threats to identify the human as potentially the most fertile site for the development of weapons, thus, mining ever more deeply into human and ecological tissues of life itself. This includes the weaponization of genetic data as its collection and use become commonplace, with DNA attractive for its immutability, uniqueness, and information richness.[7] All of this reflects the growing significance of AI and especially machine learning; that is, the learning from data to the auto-imagining, weaponizing of threats.

The pursuit of technological totalitarianism also seems consistent with the investment in integrating autonomous weapons systems at a new scale as part of the US Joint All-Domain Command-and-Control (JADC2). Thus, as Michael Klare observes, "Every component of a modern general staff—including battle planning, intelligence-gathering, logistics, communications, and decision-making—is, according to the Pentagon's latest plans, to be turned over to complex arrangements of sensors, computers, and software."[8] The combination of time compression of warfare and the huge growth in sensor data renders battlefield developments almost beyond the capacity of humans to keep track of.[9]

This, in turn, requires further automation, including even that of senior military leadership decision-making, in order that combat decisions keep pace. Applying this logic to the US nuclear command, control, and communications (NC3) system—many components of which were designed during the far less time-

4 Kaplan warns of the continuing risk of "remythologising and promoting the narratives generated by colonial occupations and asymmetrical warfare" when considering visuality in relation to military technologies. Caren Kaplan, *Aerial Aftermaths: Wartime from Above* (Durham, NC: Duke University Press, 2018), 210.

5 This is exemplified by the US's and Russia's recent orientation toward the deployment of "tactical" nuclear weapons. See Ryan Browne, Barbara Starr, and Zachary Cohen, "US Military Deploys New Type of Nuclear Weapon Seen as Key to Countering Russia," *CNN*, February 4, 2020, https://edition.cnn.com/2020/02/04/politics/us-nuclear-weapon-submarine/index.html. As Rob van Reit has stated, the use of terminology such as "deterrent" to describe nuclear weapons "is a sly way to shape people's thinking on the utility, legality and acceptability of such a system," in "How Terminology Skews the Nuclear Disarmament Debate," World Future Council, July 19, 2016, https://www.worldfuturecouncil.org/terminology-skewed-trident-debate/.

6 William Merrin giving evidence to the Airspace Tribunal London Hearing, Doughty Street Chambers, September 21, 2018, http://airspacetribunal.org/about/london-hearing/.

7 Sterling Sawaya, et al., "Artificial Intelligence and the Weaponization of Genetic Data," SSRN, April 24, 2020, http://dx.doi.org/10.2139/ssrn.3635050.

8 Michael T. Klare, "The Pentagon's Next Project: Automated War," *Nation*, August 27, 2020, https://www.thenation.com/article/world/trump-pentagon-jadc2/.

9 Klare, "The Pentagon's Next Project."

compressed conditions of the Cold War—suggests that what will be required is an AI-based system "with predetermined response decisions, that detects, decides, and directs strategic forces with such speed that the attack-time compression challenge does not place the United States in an impossible position."[10] When aligned with the shift from nuclear weapons as deterrent to smaller "tactical" nuclear weapons deployed as part of a strategic arsenal, and the anticipation of nuclear weapons in outer space, this signifies dramatic shifts in the narratives of war and peace.

The future, then, as a time of increasingly automated military decision-making systems, is already programmed, imagined, and simultaneously occupied—it is datafied and premediated.[11] The bandwidth for military thinking outside of the growing integration of a "system of systems" such as JADC2 is rapidly shrinking. This is an extension of the internal, institutionalized logic of doctrine, which underpins the corporate body of the military. Adherence to this logic delimits analysis of the wider human and environmental consequences of actions and the re-evaluation of previously constructed histories from multiple perspectives. And, ultimately, doctrine becomes dysfunctional, if only because it cannot keep pace with real-world actions and events.

Often, debates on machine and automated decision-making are couched in terms of humans being "in the loop," or otherwise. However, it is important to note that in addition to AI algorithms premised on reductionist, often highly inaccurate, and inherently prejudicial processes for identifying and differentiating humans, it is both military and civilians on the ground in warfare that are erased. Rather than viewing this principally as a consequence of automation, a greater focus is needed on the processes of erasure of the capacity for human agency, reflection, or action. This new state of paradoxically permanent beta warfare dehumanizes the military kill chain and the future by denying any prospect for human response or for an end—as it is already conceived as fully occupied and foretold.

Surveillance

The acceleration of militarized data and aerial surveillance and the targeting of individuals are intensifying with artificial intelligence advances in directed intelligibility and layers of air now "thick" with data. Rather than a single technology or information source, "layered sensing" of a larger surveillance apparatus (by the rapidly merging military and commercial domains) combines data: "This diversity of eyes in the sky enables a truly unblinking view of the ground."[12] But the psychological and existential impact of the very real fear of this kind of hostile surveillance and of attack from above, across whole populations, is not yet adequately understood.[13] This includes automated differentiation between categories of person underpinned by long-established, prejudicially constructed hierarchies and the imposition of cultural norms. Automation thus intensifies and granularizes dehumanizing processes of othering in the escalation of geopolitical violence from above.

In this increasingly polarized world, whilst much has been written on the possible effects of the overload of images of war on the attention and action of remote news publics,[14] the overload of attention by way of hyper-vigilance experienced by those surveilled on the ground is a very different dispersion of war. While audiences in the modern era are said to be caught in a mediated experience of warfare, which disrupts the resolutions and temporal horizons (beginnings and endings) associated with much of a Western history of conflict, surveilled populations increasingly experience perpetual trauma of enforced containment with the future already occupied.

10 Adam Lowther and Curtis McGiffin, "America Needs a 'Dead Hand,'" War on the Rocks, August 16, 2019, https://warontherocks.com/2019/08/america-needs-a-dead-hand/.

11 Astrid Erll defines "premediation" as "the cultural practices of looking, naming, and narrating." Astrid Erll, "Literature, Film, and the Mediality of Cultural Memory," in *Cultural Memory Studies: An International and Interdisciplinary Handbook*, ed. Astrid Erll and Ansgar Nünning, with Sara B. Young (Berlin: De Gruyter, 2008), 393.

12 Arthur Holland Michel, *Eyes in the Sky: The Secret Rise of Gorgon Stare and How It Will Watch Us All* (New York: Houghton Mifflin Harcourt, 2019), 157.

13 Nick Grief, et al., "The Airspace Tribunal: Towards a New Human Right to Protect the Freedom to Exist without a Physical or Psychological Threat from Above," *European Human Rights Law Review* 3 (2018): 201–7. Nick Grief, "The Airspace Tribunal and the Case for a New Human Right to Protect the Freedom to Live without Physical or Psychological Threat from Above," *Journal of Digital War* 1 (October 2020): 58–64, https://doi.org/10.1057/s42984-020-00023-w.

14 For a critical view, see Andrew Hoskins, "Media and Compassion after Digital War: Why Digital Media Haven't Transformed Responses to Human Suffering in Contemporary Conflict," *International Review of the Red Cross*, no. 913 (March 2021), https://international-review.icrc.org/articles/media-compassion-digital-war-human-suffering-contemporary-conflict-913.

The use of surveillance from above and predictive technologies creates an environment of hyper-vigilance to potential attack for those on the ground—further compounding this traumatic incarceration in the "survival space" of a locked-off present into an escalating state of vulnerability to long-term psychological and physiological harm:

> We have to consider [that] trauma doesn't have a reliable or linear half-life. [...] It changes how people thrive. It changes how we experience other events. In fact, they can come to be the very structure of experience itself.[15]

Furthermore, surveilled populations (the majority currently with a median age of between twenty-two and twenty-five)[16] include a high proportion of children and young people, who are particularly vulnerable given their predisposition to encode trauma rapidly and permanently. Here, a sense of a foreclosed future endlessly occupied by hostile forces (perpetrated by AI) is particularly damaging, especially when the threat is unseen, unpredictable, and unrelenting. This militarized occupation of the future overwhelms the dynamic between memory, perception, and imagination—vital both for a living self and the complex cultural and environmental ecologies within which individuals, communities, and societies are able to thrive.

Thus, generations of children are encoding traumatic memory of the experience of incessant threat before being able to create any narrative of the past or to imagine a future. This condition of inaccessible war, of an overburdened and impenetrable present, does not allow time for the working through of traumatic memory—in the sense of looking back at a threat that has ended—inasmuch as there is no ending and no way of knowing when this time might arrive. In this way, the future is also being made inaccessible through the blockage of the present and the past in a state of perpetual anxiety, and through being occupied by the predictive targeting of AI.

If we accept that "human memory evolved not only to allow us to remember but also to allow us to imagine what might happen in the future,"[17] the inaccessibility of, or inability to construct, memory denies the capacity to imagine what the future or futures could be. The trauma of war is often conceived of in relation to the memory of war; that is, as a past experience that needs to be confronted and worked through or, alternatively, forgotten.[18] Remembering and forgetting war are seen in the context of learning lessons, preventing repetition, honoring the victims, assuaging trauma, and feeding the sometimes incompatible pursuits of reconciliation, justice, and reparation. War as a form of hunting defined by pursuit, rather than as a form of combat,[19] shifts trauma from the memory of the past to anticipation of the threat of the future.

Inhibiting the dynamic of an accessible and usable memory in the now has significant negative impacts for individual and social agency in imagining or planning for a future. For many traumatized populations, this involves a numbing through the reality of war as a survival strategy, as Abrar Mechmechia recounts through her experience of living in Syria:

> The tragic reality of war became normalized not because we wanted to, but because we had to. It was the only way we could keep living. It was the only way we could keep living, even though there was not much life, when the sky is not safe, no other place can be safe, even if you can escape or perhaps one day the crisis would end the trauma can follow you for the rest of your life.[20]

Enduring never-ending occupation of the future and the associated traumatic imaginings affords a continual state of preparedness with profound physiological

15 Jairus Grove, giving evidence to the Airspace Tribunal Toronto Hearing, The Power Plant Contemporary Art Gallery, November 7, 2020, http://airspacetribunal.org/toronto-hearing/.

16 United Nations, Population Division, Department of Economic and Social Affairs, World Population Prospects 2019, File POP/5: Median age by region, subregion, and country, 1950–2100 (years), Estimates, 1950–2020.

17 Daniel L. Schacter and Michael Welker, "Memory and Connection: Remembering the Past and Imagining the Future in Individuals, Groups, and Cultures," *Memory Studies* 9, no. 3 (2016): 242.

18 David Rieff, *In Praise of Forgetting: Historical Memory and Its Ironies* (New Haven: Yale University Press, 2016).

19 Grégoire Chamayou, *Drone Theory* (London: Penguin, 2015), 52.

20 Abrar Mechmechia giving evidence to the Airspace Tribunal Toronto Hearing, The Power Plant Contemporary Art Gallery, November 7, 2020, http://airspacetribunal.org/toronto-hearing/.

21 Martin A. Conway, et al., "The Remembering-Imagining System," *Memory Studies* 9, no. 3 (2016): 256–65.

and psychological consequences. Mechmechia's words are even more resonant when considering that if we cannot access memory, we cannot imagine the future. Thus, Conway, Loveday, and Cole argue that our individual memories shape what we consider could happen in the future as part of a "remembering-imagining" system.[21]

The Blueprint

We have suggested that there are two dominant, distinct, yet connected regimes in the technological overloading of perceptions and experience of war. The first is the new mainstream of war and media in which participation in the digital volume and flux of the media content of war paradoxically obscures intelligibility. The second is the algorithmic creep of war through a massive accumulation of data and metadata, which serves to encourage and legitimize pushing humans out of the loop of decision-making, introducing a further layer of abstraction in identifying targets. This feeds an intensifying militarized and aerial media of hostile and dehumanizing surveillance over perpetually traumatized populations on the ground. This loss of human connectedness between the invisible and invasive processes of perpetual violence and the consequent threat, fear, and anxiety borne by civilians diminishes the prospects of the understanding and perspectives required for the formation of accessible and useable memories of war. The alignment of the narratives of progress, threat, and security promotes the military imaginary of constant competition, driving the violent continuities of expansionist colonial ambitions through technological development and potential, new, ever-widening, and invasive territories of war that are closing in and imploding in the present.

How, then, can we begin to materialize and see the multiple, simultaneous features and consequences of war that are so obscured through the media ecologies that we ourselves participate in and are constitutive of? We use these conceptualizing visual practices as a process for thought and discussion, to navigate and hold these dynamics in view. Rather than being constrained by the linear progression of written language, the "Blueprint" series enables the dynamics between simultaneous elements brought into a field of perception and new conversations to emerge. Our aim is to ground a layered materiality into the subject of immateriality that characterizes much of warfare today, in terms of remote targeting and killing and how citizens are threatened in new ways from physical and psychological threats from above. The notion of "precision targeting" has long informed an illusion of contained and containable violence, yet war and its consequences have spread everywhere.

Our blueprint layers how war today needs to be navigated and anchored in time and space, so that its human and environmental consequences are not overlooked. Specifically, this occurs through the ephemeral and invisible, but also through the overload and continuousness of information about war, flowing through social and mainstream medias, and the illusion of immateriality of the infrastructure that supports digital war. It can be said, then, that there is a new form of short-term forgetting of inaccessible war. This is not just a matter of rapid informational displacement in accelerated news feeds, but rather a kind of déjà vu, where the images and the reporting of civilian suffering are familiar, and the same familiarity feeds a stasis of response. The images of traumatized, wounded, and dead civilians in this century's Syrian civil war enter into and disappear from Western mainstream media frames in a series of short loops. And whereas repetition and rehearsal are said to be key in reinforcing individual remembering, amongst digitally connected news publics,

22 Juhani Pallasmaa, "Space, Place and Atmosphere: Emotion and Peripheral Perception in Architectural Experience," *Lebenswelt* 4 (2014): 230–46.

the forewarning of catastrophe and its repeated occurrence seem to have the opposite effects. Namely, as wars and their human and environmental consequences increasingly appear in plain sight, they become diminished rather than foregrounded in social or collective memory.

The rapid expansion in the increased asymmetries of power is seen in the mass protests on the streets of Myanmar, against the removal of the democratic government in a military coup, on February 1, 2021, seemingly playing out like previous demonstrations for democracy. However, the Myanmar military now employs a sophisticated digital arsenal against the civilian population, amassed on the pretext of modernizing law enforcement in the six years it shared power with the civilian government. There is an increasing convergence between the digital technologies that open up previously colonized, isolated, and militarily repressed places such as Myanmar to democratizing influences and those used against their own populations. In one space sits the language of ethics, freedom, and sacrifice—and in the other, population control. More broadly, the distinction between the sophisticated surveillance technologies of law enforcement and those used for military purposes is increasingly blurred.

Finally, the drone-targeting interface highlights a human disconnectedness to the consequences of warfare that, while appearing to be increasingly fought remotely and invisibly, instead intervenes in and scrutinizes the most intimate human and social interactions on the ground. AI predictive targeting technologies demand conformity to an imposed set of cultural and social registers. These reductive and prejudicially constructed levels of differentiation combined with the shift to hyper-vigilant surveillance technologies oriented to identifying "potential" threats, subject people on the ground to unending anxiety of inadvertent exposure as targets and the anticipatory trauma of a future over which they have little direct agency and of which they have little pre-warning.

The Weaponization of the Archive and the Language of Human Rights

In sum, we aim to capture and critically connect the multiple coexistences and contradictions of inaccessible war: layered, stacked, interwoven, simultaneously mainstream and periphery, old and new mainstreams, coexisting and colliding, visceral yet hidden, remembered yet forgotten, embodied and remote. Ultimately, for all the attention afforded to the traumatic memory of war, we are asking: How can we shift perspective to represent the multiple and simultaneous features of contemporary conflict? And how can we challenge assumptions that appear to place the very real human and environmental consequences of contemporary war in our view whilst simultaneously obscuring them? How can we challenge the narratives that underpin the new imaginaries of constant competition and the weaponization of everything—everywhere—that have commandeered ideas of progress at the expense of life and the future in the fantasy of total control?

How can we reclaim the spaces for multisensory and embodied knowledges and perception so vital to our existence, survival, and emotional lives,[22] yet so eroded by the abstracting, dehumanizing algorithmic warfare decimating the present? How can we reclaim the spaces of memory, creativity, and imagination—vital to the ever-changing dynamic between peoples and the cultural, social, and environmental ecologies they inhabit—and enable different knowledges, cultures, and cosmologies to open up the potential for other shared futures to be imagined? Without this, how can we even begin to imagine a world in which we can address the complex existential challenges of climate change, catastrophic loss of biodiversity, and extractive capitalism and bring to an end the relentless cycle of colonialities, political violence, and perpetual conflict that drives them?

In the midst of inaccessible war and the reductive military imaginaries that drive militarization ever more deeply into all aspects of planetary life, it is the language of human rights that, as Conor Gearty argues, can be:

> deployed to fill a gap in our understanding of the world which is rooted in changing observations about what equality entails, about what esteem and empathy entail. […] With the collapse of convincing socialist alternatives to capitalism, and with the complete loss of confidence in what liberalism entailed […] the language of human rights is among the very last of the languages available to us to capture that empathy.[23]

In this hyper-militarized present, people are increasingly subject to expanding commercial and military exploitation of technology in airspace and outer space and to the consequences of environmental change.[24] This poses significant challenges for the protection of human rights and the life of the planet itself. The further development of human rights as a living instrument,[25] expanding beyond the individual to include communities, ecologies, and environments, is urgently needed to address these existential threats and the widening disparity in the global landscape of power.

The Airspace Tribunal seeks to develop the human rights dimension of airspace and outer space by examining a proposed new human right to protect the freedom to live without physical or psychological threat from above.[26] Through creative cultural and interdisciplinary praxis, lived experience, and communal action, it is working to widen public debate about and participation in the development of international law. This can align with critical interventions in and reworking of the weaponized archives of war through civil society, social justice, and rights; interrogation and intervention into the underlying architecture and processes of digital technologies and their reorientation toward new forms of intelligibility, perception, and examination of complex, accelerating threats and their consequences; and global networks of creative and collective activism that challenge hierarchies of knowledge and open up new cultural, social, and environmental imaginaries for a future premised on life rather than foreclosed by the rapidly contracting spaces of never-ending, everywhere war.

The overabundance or over-presence of warfare of very different kinds shapes the conditions of hyper-attention and hyper-vigilance turning inward on the present. Military advances in surveillance, "pattern-of-life" models of targeting individuals, and, by extension, communities, by aggregating available data about them and pre-empting their potential as a threat, accumulate an archive without limits, which is waging metadata war.[27] At the same time, without critical new approaches, the optimistic promise of the digital values of openness and "participative war"[28] does not translate into any kind of usable future memory.

The two regimes in the technological overloading of perceptions and experience of war both create a kind of futureless archive. In the first regime, immersion in the digital volume and flux of the media content of war affords the impression of individual participation and influence, and yet the digital multitude provides chaotic cover for the trolls of war to thrive. The resulting connective glut of images, information, and disinformation is wrought through with the contradictory digital vulnerabilities of contagion and erasure. What, then, are the prospects of a usable memory of war ever being discerned or disentangled amidst this disorientating

23 Conor Gearty, giving evidence to the Airspace Tribunal London Hearing, Doughty Street Chambers, September 21, 2018, http://airspacetribunal.org/about/london-hearing/.

24 Grief, et al., "The Airspace Tribunal," 201–7.

25 The first explicit reference to the European Convention on Human Rights as "a living instrument which […] must be interpreted in the light of present-day conditions" was in the European Court's judgment in Tyrer v. United Kingdom, April 25, 1978, Series A, no 26, para. 31. See European Court of Human Rights, Judicial Seminar 2020, "The Convention as a Living Instrument at 70," Background Document, 3, https://www.echr.coe.int/Documents/Seminar_background_paper_2020_ENG.pdf.

26 The Airspace Tribunal was conceived and established by Nick Grief and Shona Illingworth. The inaugural hearing was at Doughty Street Chambers, London, on September 21, 2018.

27 Andrew Hoskins giving evidence to the Airspace Tribunal London Hearing, Doughty Street Chambers, September 21, 2018, http://airspacetribunal.org/about/london-hearing/. Hannah Beech, "Myanmar's Military Deploys Digital Arsenal of Repression in Crackdown," *New York Times*, March 1, 2021, https://www.nytimes.com/2021/03/01/world/asia/myanmar-coup-military-surveillance.html.

28 William Merrin, *Digital War: A Critical Introduction* (London: Routledge, 2018).

chaos, in which legitimacy, truth, facts, and trust are all rapidly undone?

Meanwhile, in the second regime, the algorithmic creep of the vast accumulation and aggregation of data used for surveillance and targeting hints at a state of betawar—war in a rapid and permanent state of evolution, especially from the air, with increasingly dire consequences for civilians on the ground. The intensifying militarized and aerial media of surveillance over perpetually traumatized populations is accumulating the most powerful archives in history. And yet, as Peter Pomerantsev suggests, of all the digital content of atrocities being collected by NGOs and an array of organizations pursuing justice and accountability, "it is as much archive as we have ever had relating to torture, mass murder and war crimes. And it sits there, waiting for facts to be given meaning."[29] The astonishing volume and availability of digital content prohibit a meaningful memory of warfare from coming into being.

For us, then, inaccessible war is the digital's foreclosing of the future, overrun by the weaponized archive. This weaponization of the archive contrasts with the sheer volume of images and information holding evidence of war crimes yet to be made sense of or prosecuted, but which are rendered unintelligible due to lack of resources, technological capacity, or political will in the new regimes of inaccessible war. Under the conditions of the weaponized archive, is any other memory possible? There is much work to be done. Without collective, creative, critical intervention and the forging of new imaginaries for the future, we risk losing the ability to imagine a world without the numbing trauma of never-ending and inescapable war.

29 Peter Pomerantsev, *This Is NOT Propaganda: Adventures in the War Against Reality* (London: Faber & Faber, 2019), 179.

Andrew Hoskins is Interdisciplinary Professor in Global Security at the College of Social Sciences, University of Glasgow. His research sits at the intersection of memory, war, and media. He is Founding Coeditor-in-Chief of the Cambridge journal *Memory, Mind and Media*, Founding Coeditor-in-Chief of *Journal of Digital War*, Founding Editor-in-Chief of *Memory Studies*, and Founding Coeditor of the Palgrave Memory Studies book series. His books include *Risk and Hyperconnectivity: Media and Memories of Neoliberalism* (Oxford University Press, 2016; with Tulloch) and *Digital Memory Studies: Media Pasts in Transition* (Routledge, 2018; editor). His latest book, *Radical War: Data, Attention and Control in the Twenty-First Century* (with Ford), is forthcoming in 2022 with Hurst/Oxford University Press. Twitter: @andrewhoskins.

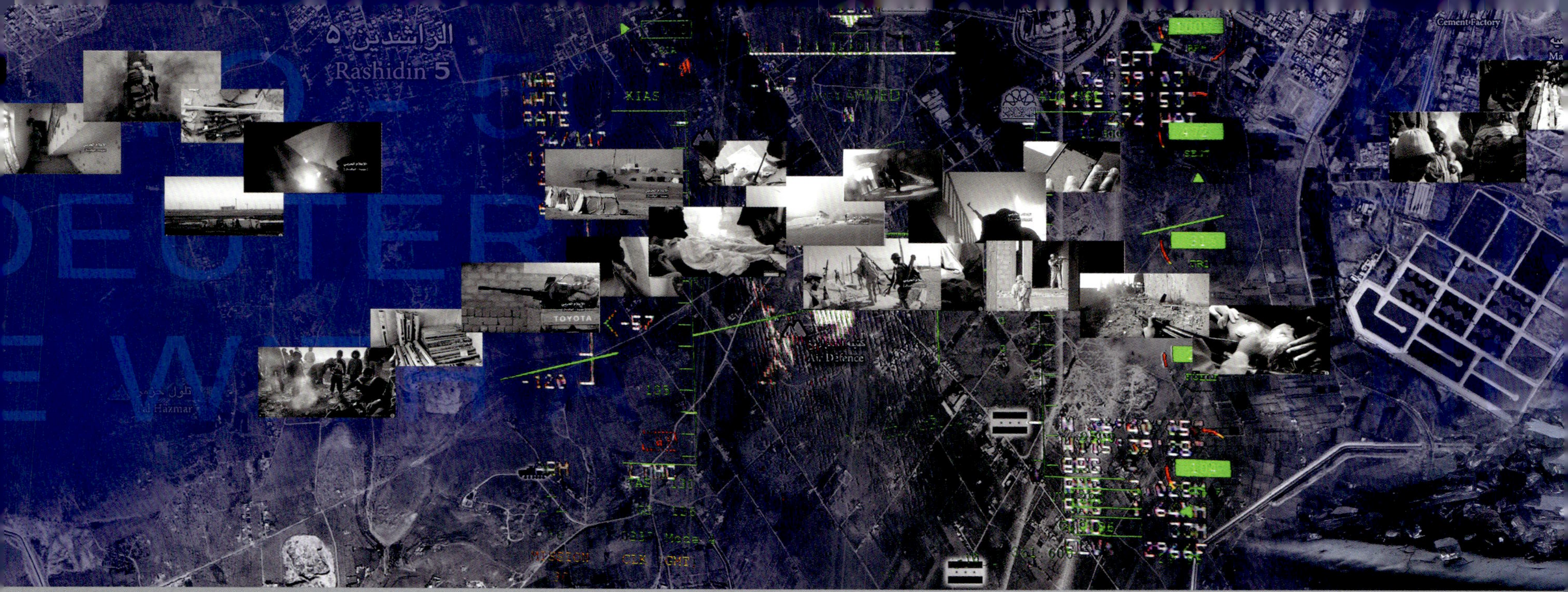

Shona Illingworth in conversation with Andrew Hoskins, *Blueprint #5*, 2018. Archival pigment print, photograph, text, and map collage. 820 × 200 mm.

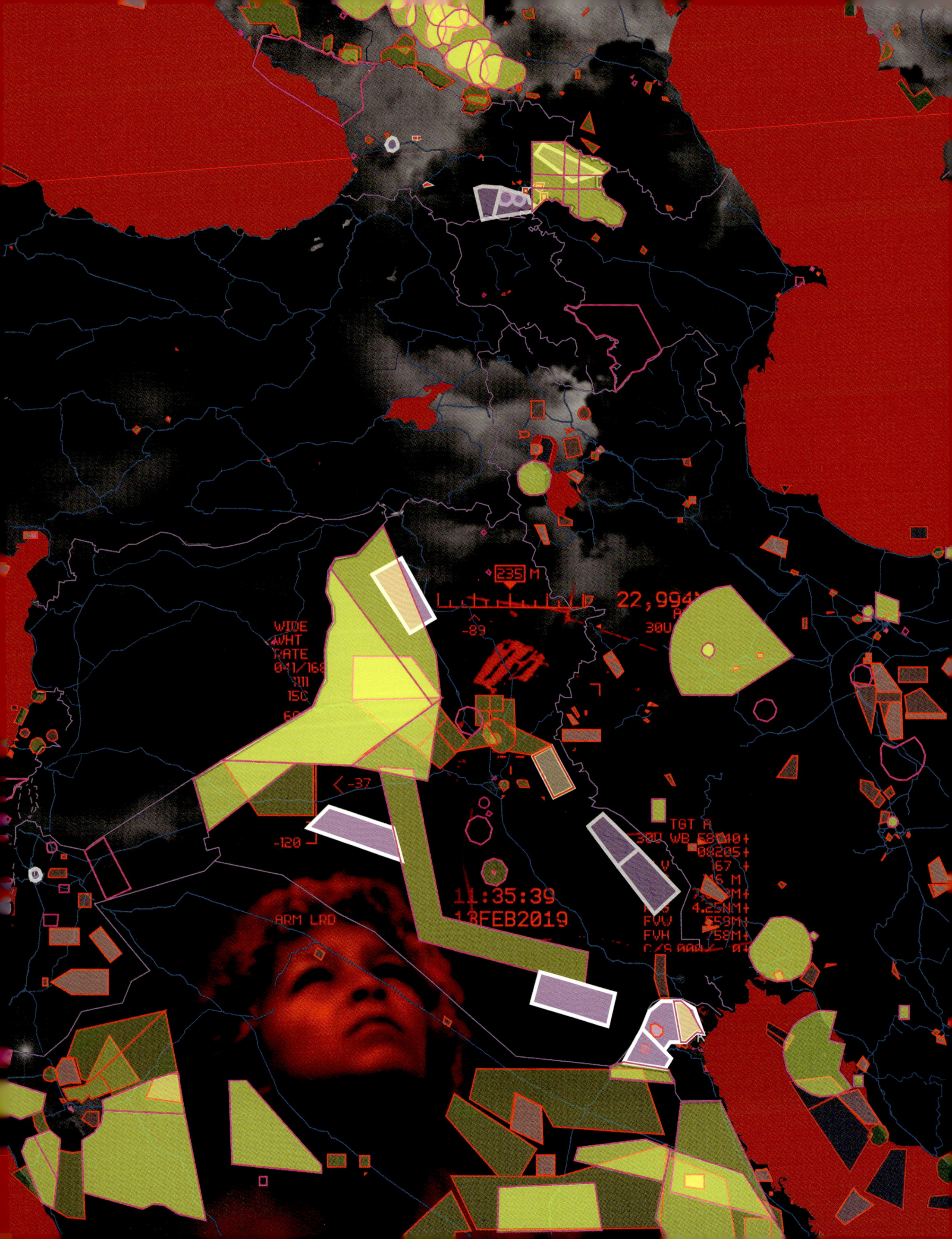
235 M
22,994
WIDE
WHT
RATE
-89
30U
-37
-120
TGT A
11:35:39
13FEB2019
ARM LRD

Catherine Loveday

FROM THE AIR: HOW TRAUMA AND THREAT HIJACK OUR MEMORY SYSTEM

Our memory system is amazing: we can time travel. We can flip back in time; we can flip forward in time. This is something we do far more than we realize, sometimes consciously but often unconsciously. The capacity to inhabit the future as well as the past is a really important part of what makes us human, and under normal circumstances, this is helpful, adaptive behavior. Thinking about the past allows us to reflect on where we have been and what we have done. This, in turn, defines who we are and enables us to nurture connections and relationships with other people. Projecting ourselves into the future prepares us for what is to come—we build expectations and create goals.

But there are consequences when this system goes wrong or gets hijacked by trauma. We are innately primed to create particularly strong memories of unusual, difficult, challenging, or painful events. When something really traumatic happens, it makes a very rapid imprint on the brain. This makes sense from an evolutionary point of view because we want to avoid being in those situations in the future. The cost, though, is that traumatic memories can be very vivid, very emotional, very powerful, and very long-lasting.

Traumatic memories can also be very easily and quickly cued by any sights, smells, feelings, or sounds that were present during the original event. The brain creates complex memory traces—patterns of neural activity—that are automatically reactivated when we re-encounter any small component of the original experience; for example, a flash of light or whiff of a pungent aroma. In these situations, the rememberer is often an unwitting time-traveler, momentarily and unavoidably cast back to a previous experience with many of the thoughts, feelings, and sensations that accompanied the original event.

Sound can be a particularly powerful cue for memories, as anyone who loves music can testify. Sound is one of the earliest and most fundamental ways that we communicate emotions. We are quick to learn that some pitches and timbres convey love and contentment, while others signal fear and distress. And this starts early: experiments show that babies can hear and respond to important sounds just twenty weeks into gestation. Research also shows that babies are born with a memory of what they heard while in the womb. Newborns will show changes in heart rate and behavior in response to songs or sounds that were played to them during gestation.

Importantly, babies are entirely capable of learning to associate particular sounds with a mother's state of mind—if the sound of an aircraft, for example, is perceived by the mother to be a stressful event, they will release stress chemicals such as adrenaline and cortisol, which will also enter the baby's bloodstream. This means that the baby is born with a conditioned association between this sound and a physiological marker of stress, which, among other things, will accelerate the heart, affect breathing rate, and alter levels of glucose.

This simple physiological mechanism means that traumatic experiences can be inadvertently passed on from mother to child. Arguably, this is evolution at its best—preparing a baby to recognize potential dangers before it is even born—but this has very physical and psychological consequences for children born into a world full of these threats but unable to take action to avoid them. Of course, transmission of traumatic memories doesn't stop there—stories are told, behaviors observed, habits absorbed—and the spread extends to whole families and communities and across generations. Collective memory is a natural, pervasive, and highly adaptive human instinct. We learn not just from our own experiences but also from those around us and those who have gone before.

While traumatic memories are very powerful, traumatic imaginings can be equally intense. Just as we can very powerfully call to mind something that has happened to us in the past, we can step into the future and vividly imagine things that might occur. The ability to project ourselves forward uses the same brain networks as those that enable us to inhabit the past and carries the same qualities of being "experience-near." People who are anticipating a fearful event, trauma, violence, or any kind of threat are not just idly picturing it; they are, to some extent, living that experience. So, if you are someone living with threat, it is not that you are simply thinking about something that might happen to you; the conscious output of our episodic memory system makes it feel as though you are almost experiencing it. This has significant psychological and physiological consequences.

One of the key features of mental time travel is that much of it is automatic and compulsive. It happens whenever the brain is not focused on a specific task thanks to a network of structures called the Default Mode Network. On the whole, this is useful. It is the memory system's way of allowing us to anticipate and prepare for what is going to come. But this mechanism is also responsible for fear; when an inhabited future is one that is full of potential threats, the body and mind are in a perpetual state of "fight or flight." Being relentlessly prepared for an imminent danger that may or may not come is a dominating and fully embodied experience.

Recent research shows that this can be particularly damaging if the danger never materializes. Mark Wetherell and his team at Northumbria University carried out a series of overnight lab studies where all participants were told that they would be undertaking a stressful task the next day. In fact, this was only true for half of them; the next day, the other half were told that it was not happening after all and they could relax. While stress hormones quickly returned to normal in those who carried out the stressful task, the levels remained unhealthily high in those where the task was canceled. Paradoxically, being relieved of the challenge did not make the body relax but led to a prolonged physical effect on the body and mind.

Living in constant fear, therefore, has very real, long-term consequences for the body and for the mind, but this is potentially even worse when the threat is uncertain and unseen. When the threat comes from above, nowhere feels safe; thus, the body and mind are on full-time alert. There is also a high likelihood that individuals develop "learned helplessness," a state where people who have faced repeated stress in situations outside their control ultimately give up trying even if circumstances improve. It has long been recognized that learned helplessness can lead to clinical depression and other problems with mental and physical health. Children and teenagers are particularly vulnerable to the impact of continued threat: it is widely recognized that the brain continues to develop and grow throughout this period and that it is heavily shaped by the world we live in and the challenges we face.

Given the significant and widespread impact of perpetual unseen threat on the brain and body, and the particular effects on the developing brain, we urgently need recognition of the proposed new human right: to protect the freedom to live without physical or psychological threat from above. Whatever form that threat takes—warfare, surveillance, noise, toxic air—the simple fact that it can come at any time, from a place that cannot be seen, in a way that cannot be controlled, means that it can hijack the body's natural evolutionary defense mechanisms and lead to long-term changes in physiology and psychology. The potentially devastating impact of this can no longer be downplayed or ignored.

Catherine Loveday is a Professor of Neuropsychology at the University of Westminster, London. She began her career with a PhD in the neuropsychology of memory and aging and continues to focus on the nature of normal and impaired memory. Much of her research is focused on the neuropsychology of autobiographical memory, but she has also worked on projects that explore stress and well-being, with a particular emphasis on developmental changes in hormones and other biological markers of stress. Loveday has engaged in a number of interdisciplinary collaborations with artists and has worked on Wellcome Trust–funded projects with Shona Illingworth and Martin Conway to explore the lived experience of memory loss. Loveday is passionate about public engagement with science and regularly appears as an expert psychologist on BBC radio and television.

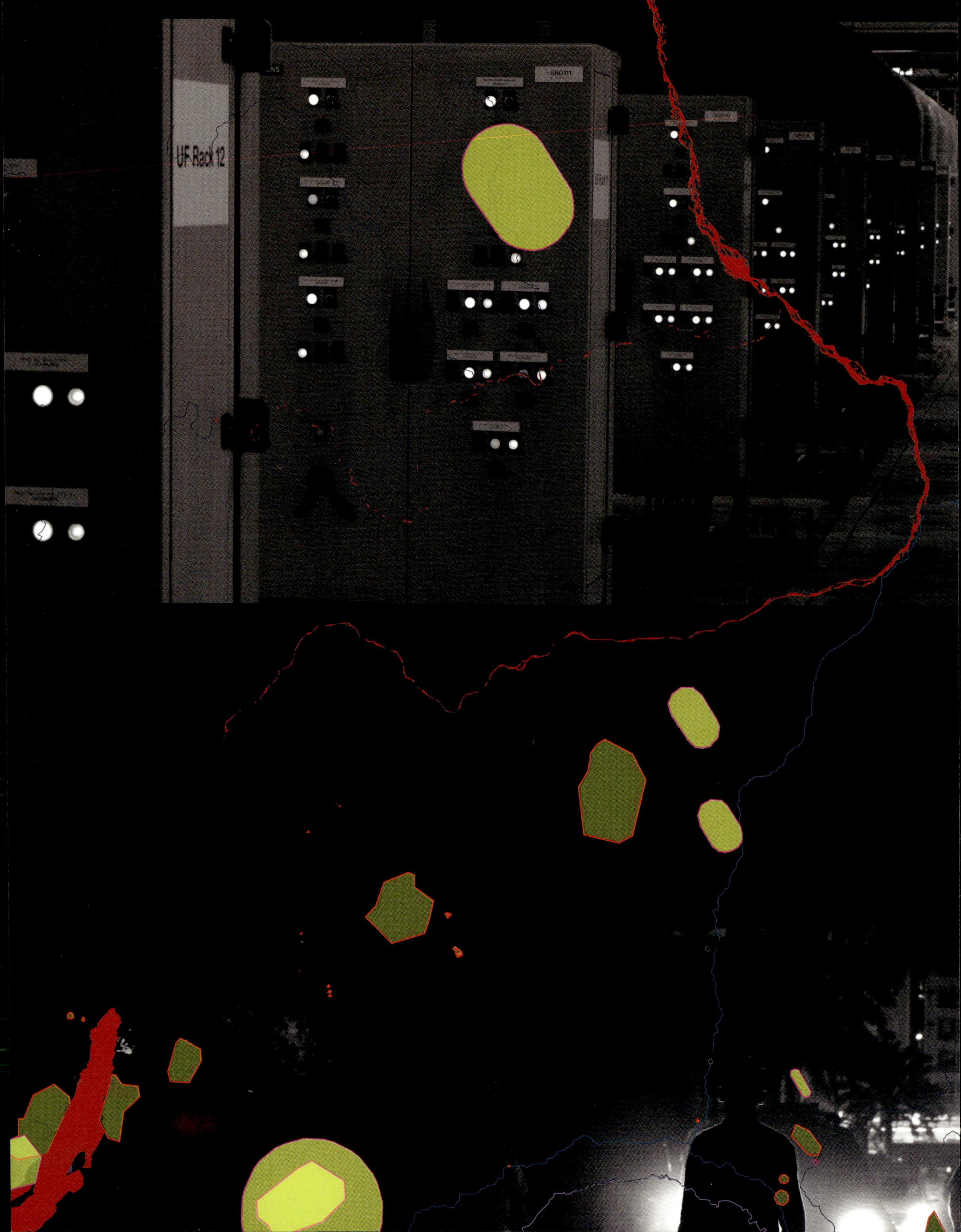
UF Rack 12
•SB0111

William Merrin

THE END OF THE AIR GAP: UIGHUR SURVEILLANCE AND INFORMATIONAL TOTALITARIANISM

Xinjiang is an autonomous region in northwestern China, bordered by eight countries. Though brought under Chinese Qing Dynasty control in the eighteenth century, the region remains contested. Following a brief period of independence in the 1940s, Communist China reasserted control in 1949, and since then, it has overseen considerable development and Han migration into the area. The reason for this is the value of Xinjiang's natural resources—oil and gas—and its central role in the Belt and Road trade-route initiative unveiled by President Xi Jinping in 2013. It is also the home of the Turkic-speaking, Muslim Uighur people.

After decades of immigration, the Uighurs are now a minority, with a 2015 estimation suggesting they constitute just under 46 percent of the 23.6-million population. The Uighurs are also victims of a systematic governmental campaign of cultural repression aimed at destroying—at "Sinecising"[1]—their culture, language, and religious practice. This has taken many forms, including limits on beard lengths and baby names, forcing restaurants to open during Ramadan, forcing mosques to remove Islamic decoration and fly the Chinese flag, and, in recent years, the wholesale physical destruction of Uighur mosques and cemeteries.[2] As a result, anti-Han sentiment and ethnic conflict have grown since the 1990s, and a Uighur separatist movement has often flared into violence, most notably in riots in Urumqi in 2009 and a series of knife and vehicle attacks in 2013–14. China condemns this violence as Islamist terrorism and, since May 2014, has responded to the "three forces" of "separatism, terrorism, and extremism" with a "Strike Hard campaign against violent activities and terrorism."[3] This expanded significantly from August 2016, when Xinjiang came under the control of Communist Party Secretary Chen Quanguo, previously Party Secretary of the Tibetan Autonomous Region (TAR). Brought in to apply the same measures of securitization that had proven successful in TAR, he oversaw the creation in Xinjiang of the most complete, integrated—and racially targeted—system of governmental surveillance ever seen on the planet. The most obvious parts of this system are physical and repressive, including the armored cars and tanks on the city streets, the huge numbers of heavily armed police, and the building of around 380 concentration camps[4]—euphemistically titled "re-education" centers by the Chinese government—where over a million Uighurs[5] have been detained for minor offenses or Islamic observance, and where reports have emerged of forced labor, medical neglect, medical experimentation and torture, the systematic gang-rape of women, and forced sterilization and abortions.[6] This physical repression goes hand-in-hand with the use of digital technologies to identify and pursue each individual.

"Convenience police stations," set out on a "grid management system," not only closely police the area but also contain night vision–enabled CCTV cameras with facial and license-plate recognition to track people, using AI to analyze suspicious behaviors or issue an alert if someone on a watchlist strays more than three hundred meters from their designated "safe areas." A government spyware app is compulsory on phones, identifying individuals, tracking their movements and phone use, blocking certain sites, searching the phone's storage for "illegal" images, copying chat records and Wi-Fi logins, and sending these records to a

1 Staff and Agencies, "'Sinicisation' of Muslims in Xinjiang Must Go on, Says Chinese Official," *Guardian*, October 14, 2018, https://www.theguardian.com/world/2018/oct/14/sinicisation-of-muslims-in-xinjiang-must-go-on-says-chinese-official.

2 AFP, "Satellite Images Reveal China Has Demolished Dozens of Mosques in Its Muslim Region since 2017 as Beijing Ramps up Control on Islamic Traditions," *Daily Mail*, June 5, 2019, https://www.dailymail.co.uk/news/article-7106855/Wrecked-mosques-police-watch-A-tense-Ramadan-Xinjiang.html; CNES/Airbus DS/Earthrise/AFP, "Then and Now: China's Destruction of Uighur Burial Grounds," *Guardian*, 2019, https://www.theguardian.com/world/2019/oct/09/chinas-destruction-of-uighur-burial-grounds-then-and-now.

3 Maya Wang, "'Eradicating Ideological Viruses': China's Campaign of Repression Against Xinjiang's Muslims," Human Rights Watch, September 9, 2018, https://www.hrw.org/report/2018/09/09/eradicating-ideological-viruses/chinas-campaign-repression-against-xinjiangs.

4 Emma Graham-Harrison, "China Has Built 380 Internment Camps in Xinjiang, Study Finds," *Guardian*, September 24, 2020, https://www.theguardian.com/world/2020/sep/24/china-has-built-380-internment-camps-in-xinjiang-study-finds.

government server. Public “Wi-Fi sniffers” also collect and track unique identificatory addresses of all passing networked devices, with all of this phone data fed into the government’s big data analytics program, the Integrated Joint Operations Platform (IJOP), which uses machine learning to analyze the combined data from phones, cameras, checkpoints, government records, and even utility usage to draw up lists of suspects for surveillance or detention.

Public security checkpoints at hotels, banks, malls, and transport links, etc., check people every day, analyzing personal data on ID cards, using biometric systems such as facial and iris recognition to confirm identities, and full body scanners and wands for security. Given the use of vehicles for attacks, cars are especially watched, with only the registered user allowed to drive them, regular checkpoints where police scanners check each individual’s phone for illegal content or activities, license plate–recognition cameras and compulsory GPS tracking devices to follow movements, and ID and facial recognition confirmation for petrol purchases.

Biometric data is collected from everyone aged twelve to sixty-five, with blood type, DNA, voice samples, 3-D portraits, iris, fingerprint, and facial data, and people’s gait being recorded in government health programs and when they apply for ID—all being fed into the individual’s file in the IJOP database. To cope with knife attacks, any purchase requires an ID-card check, with the ID card being scanned and turned into a QR code that is laser-etched into the blade so the owner can be traced. The Uighur’s home life is also controlled, with officials compiling dossiers of information about residents and their behavior and inputting data into an app connected to the IJOP system. Questionnaires are fed into a social-credit scoring system, ranking safety and worthiness, whilst QR codes have been installed on Uighur homes, which can be scanned by officials for information about those inside. In the “Becoming Kin” policy, Uighur families are even forced to “adopt” a Han official who may live with the family, checking their adherence to the rules more closely.[7] In 2019, it was reported that Uighurs were subjected to a two-year iOS malware attack by the Chinese state and that tourists to the region were having government spyware forcibly installed on their phones.[8]

In computing, an “air gap” is a security measure where a device is physically separated from all network connections to protect it. Today, our own physical air gap—that portion of our lives in which we are not digitally connected, datified, identifiable, and trackable—is vanishing. Broadband, public and domestic Wi-Fi, the Web 2.0, and post-2007 smartphone revolutions first turned digital signals into a near-continuous, personally connected stream, and all developments since then have moved us toward a total capture of life. Today, our private spaces have become recording and signaling environments with the penetration of the home by “smart” devices, meters, assistants, and cameras; “wearables” capture our intimate bodily data and rhythms; whilst, outside the home, the “internet of things” is increasingly connecting cars, streets, streetlights, and any public space with sensors, computers, cameras, and modes of public, personal identification. Indeed, as China’s use of EEG “mind-reading” helmets to surveil key workers reveals,[9] there is little, in theory, that can escape data capture.

What is important, however, is not simply the use of these technologies, but two key phenomena: firstly, the *integration* of these technologies—the combination of all these phone, internet, camera, and sensor data, the databases, machine-learning AI, big data analysis, and identificatory processes in one connected system—and, secondly, the employment of this entire system to identify, track, and analyze each individual. Hence, the

5 David Stavrou, “A Million People Are Jailed at China’s Gulags. I Managed to Escape. Here’s What Really Goes on Inside,” *Haaretz*, October 17, 2019, https://www.haaretz.com/amp/world-news/.premium.MAGAZINE-a-million-people-are-jailed-at-china-s-gulags-i-escaped-here-s-what-goes-on-inside-1.7994216?__twitter_impression=true&fbclid=IwAR25zSBGwz7pVERs1k1jR4hdHmkFhUXXpzZ5UwijFvU9luuRLRloX9msdBo.

6 Helen Davidson, “Xinjiang: More Than Half a Million Forced to Pick Cotton, Report Suggests,” *Guardian*, December 15, 2020, https://www.theguardian.com/world/2020/dec/15/xinjiang-china-more-than-half-a-million-forced-to-pick-cotton-report-finds; Sam Hancock, “Gang Raped, Shackled and Broken Students: Inside China’s ‘Horrific’ Uighur Detention Camps,” *Independent*, February 20, 2021, https://www.independent.co.uk/news/world/asia/china-uighur-detention-camps-eyewitness-b1804804.html#r3z-addoor; Emma Graham-Harrison and Lily Kuo, “Uighur Muslim Teacher Tells of Forced Sterilisation in Xinjiang,” *Guardian*, September 4, 2020, https://www.theguardian.com/world/2020/sep/04/muslim-minority-teacher-50-tells-of-forced-sterilisation-in-xinjiang-china; James Gant and Billie Thomson, “Chinese Muslims Reveal Rapes, Abortions and Forced Sterilisations ‘Using Chilli Paste’ at ‘Concentration Camps’ as Shocking Footage Emerges of Hundreds of Shackled and Blindfolded Prisoners,” *Daily Mail*, October 7, 2019, https://www.dailymail.co.uk/news/article-7546833/Chinese-muslims-reveal-rapes-abortions-forced-sterilisations-concentration-camps.html.

Uighur's surveillance is a model that prefigures all our futures. Because what we are seeing across the world is the passage of all political systems to *informational totalitarianism*.

We remain too bewitched by twentieth-century totalitarianism—distracted by the uniforms, the spectacle, the symbolism, the public terror, and the hyper-visible, aesthetically organized regimes that tried to abolish the separation of public and private to achieve Mussolini's goal of "totalitario": "All within the state, nothing outside the state, none against the state." Now, at a historical distance, we can see the essence of totalitarianism is the informational right to penetrate and oversee every aspect of private life. Today's totalitarianism fulfills itself as an ideal of digital transparency employed across all political systems, including Western liberal democracies. Freed from political theatrics, the burden of terror, and cost of costumery, it reverses from spectacle to secrecy and from public to private, as a project aiming at the oversight, monitoring, capture, and evaluation of every aspect of external human behavior and personal interiority. Today, connectivity equals capture, which equals identification, analysis, personal accountability, and behavioral change. Because the sole aim of this *digital behaviorism*, whether enacted by authoritarian or democratic governments or private, commercial organizations, is *to know, in order to predict, in order to control*.

Beyond the physical climate crisis that the world suffers from today, there is the other, overlooked, climate crisis: our loss of free, open air to the global system of digital connectivity, oversight, and capture. And this spatial freedom will only diminish further with developments in AI identification systems, cameras, sensors, and drones. Years ago, *2000AD*'s "Judge Dredd" comic strip presented a future "megacity" where individuals were followed and surveilled by miniature police camera-drones called "the spy in the sky." This is no longer science fiction: police forces regularly use drone cameras to film the public. The US military has obviously gone even further, not only in creating armed drones but also, in its recent "Project Maven," in developing an AI that can analyze drone intelligence, surveillance, and reconnaissance imagery for real-time target identification. Add individual, biometric, and data identification to this, and we have a clear vision of our future. This is a future of *mass individual surveillance*, of the further miniaturization and refinement of surveillance technologies, of the massive expansion, improvement, and integration of all these tracking and identificatory systems, of our own personally targeted swarms of nano-drones, and of our subjection to ubiquitous, continuous, algorithmic oversight, evaluation, and judgment.

It is a future where our liberties and even our very right to exist—to continue to stand there in a place, to enjoy that sensation and breathe in the open air—will be decided by digital systems watching us from above and from everywhere.

William Merrin is Associate Professor in Media Studies at Swansea University, specializing in media philosophy, digital media, digital warfare, and media law. He is the author of *Digital War* (Routledge, 2018), *Media Studies 2.0* (Routledge, 2014), and *Baudrillard and the Media* (Polity, 2005), and coeditor of *Trump's War on the Media* (Palgrave, 2018) and *Jean Baudrillard: Fatal Theories* (Routledge, 2009). He is on the editorial board of the *International Journal of Baudrillard Studies*, served on the board of *Media War and Conflict*, and is Coeditor and Cofounder of *Journal of Digital War*.

7 All of the above examples are discussed across numerous reports and stories, including: "Life inside China's Total Surveillance State," *Wall Street Journal* Youtube Channel, published on December 20, 2017, https://www.youtube.com/watch?v=0Q5LnY21Hgc; Darren Byler, "China's Hi-Tech War on Its Muslim Minority," *Guardian*, April 11, 2019, https://www.theguardian.com/news/2019/apr/11/china-hi-tech-war-on-muslim-minority-xinjiang-uighurs-surveillance-face-recognition; Tom Phillips, "China Testing Facial-Recognition Surveillance System in Xinjiang—Report," *Guardian*, January 18, 2018, https://www.theguardian.com/world/2018/jan/18/china-testing-facial-recognition-surveillance-system-in-xinjiang-report; Chris Buckley and Paul Mozur, "How China Uses High-Tech Surveillance to Subdue Minorities," *New York Times*, May 22, 2019, https://www.nytimes.com/2019/05/22/world/asia/china-surveillance-xinjiang.html.

8 Alex Hern, "Uighurs in China Were Target of Two-Year iOS Malware Attack—Reports," *Guardian*, September 2, 2019, https://www.theguardian.com/world/2019/sep/02/uighurs-china-target-two-year-ios-malware-attack-reports; Hilary Osborne and Sam Cutler, "Chinese Border Guards Put Secret Surveillance App on Tourists' Phones," *Guardian*, July 2, 2019, https://www.theguardian.com/world/2019/jul/02/chinese-border-guards-surveillance-app-tourists-phones.

9 Jamie Fullerton, "Chinese Firms Use 'Mind-Reading' Devices to Monitor Workers' Emotions," *Sydney Morning Herald*, May 1, 2018, https://www.smh.com.au/world/asia/chinese-firms-use-mind-reading-devices-to-monitor-workers-emotions-20180501-p4zck8.html.

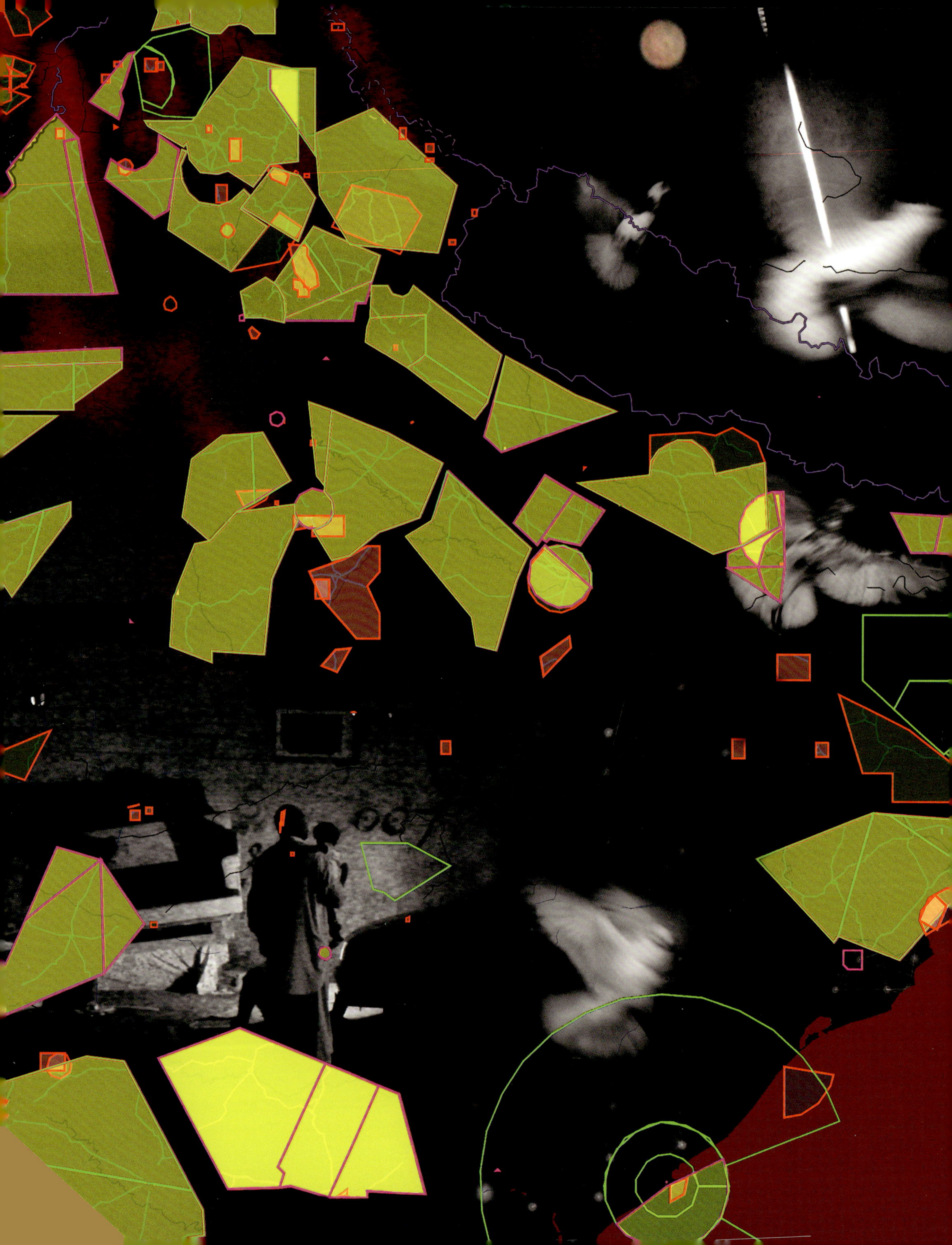

Amin Alsaden
FUELING GLOBAL CONFLICTS

On a luminous winter day in late January 1991, I had a casual encounter with the most technologically sophisticated military conflict in the world's history, one that was fought predominantly in the air.[1] I was living in Baghdad, still a boy, during what came to be known as the Gulf War. That morning, I spotted a Tomahawk cruise missile gliding noiselessly above; its slick white form sharply silhouetted by the brilliant blue sky. It was clearly on its way to hit another target, not far from where my family had been displaced due to the unprecedented aerial attack on the city.

That memory contrasts sharply with another, only a few weeks later, when apocalyptic dark clouds loomed over the city's skies. Smoke reportedly reached as far as Bulgaria to the west and Pakistan to the east after Iraqi troops, in their retreat, burned nearly six hundred Kuwaiti oil wells; they also released an estimated two to three million barrels of oil into the Gulf by the time the US-led forces launched their campaign in the region.[2] The rain left a layer of black residue across Baghdad, marking rooflines with a craggy contour of soot. The following morning, we noticed earthworms emerging aboveground in nearby parks—a mass extermination brought about by the acidic water saturating the earth.

Such recollections may amplify the representational fatigue associated with the Arab world, depicted as a land of perpetual turmoil, constantly relapsing into a nonstop chain of conflicts, ranging from organized warfare to petty strife. However, aside from underlining my personal connection to the region, to share these stories is to emphasize how no one is left unharmed by war—mentally, physically, economically, socially, or environmentally. To overlook these memories is to dismiss the fact that militarization and organized violence are the primary causes of global environmental degradation today.

In his book *Savage Ecology*, Jairus Victor Grove argues that Euro-American politics has, for centuries, been developing techniques that are fundamentally antithetical to humanity's survival. He writes about the state of affairs yielded by this enterprise today: "Geopolitics, enacted through global war [...] pursues a savage ecology, radically antagonistic to survival as a collective rather than discriminatory goal. Geopolitics [...] has as its enemy the very pursuit of what the scientists see as a commonsense, pragmatically just planet."[3] Grove emphasizes that contemporary warfare is not an anomalous or occasional event, but routine practice, a way of life for the global political order.

To disregard personal memories of war is to also deny a pivotal yet often suppressed dimension of our collective existence: the war enterprise, rooted in the history of colonialism, slavery, and genocide, and sustained by extractive capitalism, is a force that has structured and continues to shape much of the world. Achille Mbembe suggests that global democracy is increasingly embracing its double or nocturnal side, which manifests the same violent impulses that propelled colonialism. Based on a spirit of enmity that desires the annihilation of the "Other," democracies today rely on war as a survival strategy, which is paradoxically bringing about a global exit from democracy. Mbembe writes: "The hitherto more or less hidden violence of democracies is rising to the surface, producing a lethal circle that grips the

1 John A. Warden III, a colonel in the US military known as the architect of Instant Thunder (the US airstrike during the Gulf War), believed that the air campaign of 1991 was a watershed moment in the history of war, one that provided a model for aerial combat well into the twenty-first century. See John A. Warden III, "Employing Air Power in the Twenty-first Century," in *The Future of Air Power in the Aftermath of the Gulf War*, ed. Richard H. Shultz, Jr., and Robert L. Pfaltzgraff, Jr. (Maxwell Air Force Base, AL: Air University Press, 1992), 57–82; 81–82.

2 The apparent purpose was to create a smokescreen that would hinder ground advancement of allied forces and thwart airstrikes by obscuring Iraqi targets. See Marc A. Ross, "Environmental Warfare and the Persian Gulf War: Possible Remedies to Combat Intentional Destruction of the Environment," *Penn State International Law Review* 10, no. 3 (1992): 515–39.

3 Jairus Victor Grove, *Savage Ecology: War and Geopolitics at the End of the World* (Durham, NC: Duke University Press, 2019), 4.

4 Achille Mbembe, *Necropolitics*, trans. Steven Corcoran (Durham, NC: Duke University Press, 2019), 6–7.

5 Mbembe, *Necropolitics*, 23.

6 These definitions are essential to how the "environment" is actually described by the Oxford English Dictionary. See "environment, n.," OED Online, September 2020, Oxford University Press, accessed October 21, 2020, https://www-oed-com.myaccess.library.utoronto.ca/view/Entry/63089?redirectedFrom=environment.

imagination and is increasingly difficult to escape. Nearly everywhere the political order is reconstituting itself as a form of organization for death."[4]

While warfare affects the entire globe, what I would like to touch upon here is what conflict in the Arab world, and Iraq in particular, can say about the environment. I examine the work of Shona Illingworth as paradigmatic of art practices that unveil the global impact of military conflict today and how such practices can begin to unmask the complex realities of these geographies. I am interested in exploring not only how the artist's work suggests a broader understanding of the environment, cutting across the conventional focus on the climate or natural habitat, but also how she reveals hidden dimensions of the wars that rage in the Arab world, or the region stretching from Southwest Asia to North Africa. Specifically, I focus on how Illingworth's work speaks to humanity's insatiable appetite for oil, fueling its activities on earth and in the sky—an appetite that has yielded deeply problematic engagements with the Arab world, entanglements that leave an environmental footprint far beyond this region.

Whereas some Arab countries are usually reduced in the media to a volatile zone, warfare in this part of the world tends to manifest the imperial dreams of dominant powers. Therefore, the region should be seen as a microcosm of global ideological rivalries and fierce competition for resources. Mbembe writes: "Democracy, the plantation, and the colonial empire are objectively all part of the same historical matrix. This originary and structuring fact lies at the heart of every historical understanding of the violence of the contemporary global order."[5] In other words, wars that rage in the region—along with their historical roots and contemporary causes—are inextricably linked to global politics.

Indeed, instability in the region encapsulates global conflicts, capturing the dynamics of the world as they collide and erupt in episodes of environmental catastrophes and mass violence. Viewed holistically, as the world in which we collectively dwell, with all its layers, interconnections, and unfathomable complexities, the environment can be seen through the lens of the Arab world—as the region gauges the impact of warfare on the environment in ways that transcend the customary emphasis on the climate or natural habitat. What I would like to propose here is a definition of the environment that emphasizes the conditions or surroundings in which humanity dwells, as well as the social, cultural, and political circumstances of this planetary context and how these impact lives and attitudes within various communities globally.[6]

Much of the Arab world has been at the center of prolonged conflicts and frequent international interventions, largely motivated by a desire to control fossil fuels—not to mention the containment of political Islam. Iraq, for instance, became a battleground for the US administration's "global war on terror," articulated as a form of retaliation for the September 11 attacks. While I am highlighting Iraq, the country's calamities should not overshadow what is happening in the rest of the region. From regular testing of new intelligent weapons and frequent deployment of lethal drones to armed factions waging guerrilla attacks on governments and civilians alike, violence in all of its contemporary manifestations devastates large swathes of the region. However, if the Arab world can be seen as the furnace where the fires of global conflicts rage, Iraq is its crucible.

Iraq has become synonymous with warfare, chronic unrest, displacement, international sanctions, and the general collapse of state sovereignty since the 2003 US-led invasion. Although this invasion has become iconic in recent history—partly due to strong opposition internationally and partly because of the horrific consequences on the country and region—it must be remembered that the US had been leading an offensive in Iraq for over three decades.[7] Iraq's occupation has, likewise, sent shockwaves the world over.[8] Even though metropolitan centers in the West remain relatively safe and apparently distant from geographies afflicted with unrest, warfare has had a global footprint: fluctuations in oil supplies, ecological catastrophes, lost agricultural harvests, economic failures, solidarity between extremists everywhere, and the rise of far-right and xenophobic political parties that feed on popular resentment of an influx of immigrants from the region. These are only some of the spillovers outside conflict zones—war is fundamentally global in scope, with indisputable worldwide consequences. Mbembe elegantly articulates the planetary nature of war and levels a critique against the notion that battles can be fought elsewhere: "Owing to this structural proximity [of the 'Other'], there is no longer any 'outside' that might be opposed to an 'inside.' [...] One cannot 'sanctuarize' one's own home by fomenting chaos and death far away, in the homes of others. Sooner or later, one will reap at home what one has sown abroad."[9]

Although not confined to the Arab world, or Iraq specifically, Illingworth's work examines, amongst other subjects, the complex role of oil in conflict and the relationship of warfare to events on the ground and, crucially, in the airspace above. In *Topologies of Air* (2021), viewers enter a dark room with deep-blue tones seeping in from the surrounding walls and find themselves enveloped with sound and facing a three-channel video projection. Addressing an epic array of subjects, the ambitious work presents the sky as a densely colonized space, where environmental issues intersect with technological developments and emerging power structures. It probes how airspace today remains largely unregulated and, thus, ripe for exploitation, particularly in terms of information collection.

The world's connection to the sky above—historically the source of wisdom and celestial symbolism—has been severed due to air pollution and the densification of cities, not to mention heavy surveillance and colonization of the atmosphere. Illingworth points to this new relationship with airspace (or the lack thereof): throughout *Topologies of Air*, viewers witness how the sky has become central to contemporary global domination by powers with access to and control over its domain—suggesting novel, and often invisible, modes of colonization. The extensive monitoring of the skies also reveals a further potential source of the planet's destruction if we consider the unprecedented threat of autonomous combat technologies, which disproportionately affect Southwest Asia.[10]

In conjunction with Illingworth's own research-based observations, the work engages numerous voices: testimonials of victims who witnessed historic attacks from air and recordings of experts' views conveyed through the Airspace Tribunal hearings, organized by the artist in several cities. And *Topologies of Air* engages with many of the issues that impact the airspace above Iraq today. One person heard in the voiceover accompanying the installation refers to enormous sandstorms laden with radioactive particles in a war-ravaged land, while another, a witness, discusses an attack that decimated all forms of life, evoking the chemical weapons used by Saddam Hussein's regime against Iran as well as the Kurdish regions in northern Iraq in the 1980s and nineties. The generic yet all-too-familiar footage of a fighter jet taxiing on tarmac—in this case, a British RAF aircraft—recalls widely circulated imagery from the 1991 Gulf War and subsequent 2003 invasion of Iraq.

Some of the artist's footage is shot in the Gulf, and woven throughout the work are images depicting the oil industry, further highlighting the insidious role played by fossil fuels in processes of global domination. Through shots of pump

7 Writing following the invasion, Richard McCutcheon argued that the US was engaged in a continuous war with Iraq since 1991, through different kinds of violence: physical, economic, and cultural. Theoretically informed, his analysis is also refreshingly attentive to the lived experience of people on the ground (rather than focusing on political science, media coverage, or official statements). See Richard McCutcheon, "Rethinking the War against Iraq," *Anthropologica* 48, no. 1 (2006): 11–28.

8 Several observers have written about the implications of the 2003 invasion. See, for example, Howard LaFranchi, "How the Iraq War Has Changed America," *Christian Science Monitor*, December 10, 2011, https://www.csmonitor.com/layout/set/amphtml/USA/Foreign-Policy/2011/1210/How-the-Iraq-war-has-changed-America; Ian Black, "Iraq War Still Casts a Long Shadow over a Dangerous and Deeply Unstable Region," *Guardian*, July 7, 2016, https://amp.theguardian.com/uk-news/2016/jul/07/iraq-war-still-casts-a-long-shadow-over-a-dangerous-and-deeply-unstable-region; and Tallha Abdulrazaq, "Invasion of Iraq: The Original Sin of the 21st Century," *Al Jazeera*, March 20, 2018, https://www.aljazeera.com/amp/opinions/2018/3/20/invasion-of-iraq-the-original-sin-of-the-21st-century/.

9 Mbembe, *Necropolitics*, 40.

10 I have been fortunate to follow the development of this work as the curator of Illingworth's exhibition at The Power Plant Contemporary Art Gallery, Toronto. I am also thankful for several conversations with the artist, which afforded me a better understanding of the multiple layers embedded in this complex work.

jacks forcing oil out of ground wells and refineries churning out oil products day and night, the work reminds us that airspace is tethered to the ground and that warfare and extractive capitalism, anchored in the Arab world, are inseparable. The violence of extraction, whether bound to the ground or aerial, is a tool of empire that threatens not just regional but also global stability, be it in terms of climate change or the geopolitics of conflict. Nowhere is this violence more evident than in Iraq and the Arab world.

The attacks Iraq has endured to date continue to have a pernicious impact on the region's ecology. War has not only deliberately destroyed Iraq's infrastructure and, thus, the country's ability to address environmental damage but has also had largely under-researched ramifications on its airspace. Dust storms have increased after years of warfare, partly because of the decimation of the country's green cover as a result of bombardment. In addition to the respiratory problems these dust storms can cause, their sand particles have also been found to contain traces of depleted uranium, which has, in turn, been linked to a surge in cancer patients and birth defects.[11] The sources of such pollutants are said to vary, from attacks on the Tuwaitha Nuclear Research Center (by Israel in the early 1980s and the US and allies in the 1991 Gulf War), the looting of radioactive material after the 2003 invasion, and the enormous quantities of munitions utilizing depleted uranium dropped by US and British forces throughout Iraq in the 1991 and 2003 offensives.[12]

Aside from dust storms, studies have found that the country's air is laden with heavy metals like lead and aluminum, as well as lung-damaging fine particles that can increase asthma alongside other respiratory and cardiovascular diseases. In several samples, concentrations of heavy metals were found to be multiple times that of acceptable US standards—such studies have traditionally focused on the adverse effects of polluted air on US soldiers deployed in Iraq, who have reportedly experienced more respiratory problems than in other locations.[13] Furthermore, the unprecedented rise in record-breaking temperatures is not only making living in the country untenable, especially given the collapse of basic services such as electricity since 2003, but it is also ruining crops and vegetation, which are left to wither under the unmerciful sun. This environmental impact will no doubt set a precedent for a planet where climate change is already a serious threat.[14]

Local consensus, accounted for by foreign and independent observers on rare occasions, claims that rising temperatures are due to the eradication of the green lands at the center of the country—destroyed by American and Iraqi forces to prevent insurgents from hiding in the undergrowth—while uncontrolled urban sprawl has added insult to injury.[15] In recent years, droughts have reduced cultivable land in the country to half and livestock by around a third, partly due to the heat and also because Iran and Turkey, where much of Iraq's rivers originate, have been rerouting their water resources.[16] The reverberations of Iraq's changing climate are expected to intensify in years to come; temperatures are set to soar, droughts to worsen, and more water shortages—along with higher salinity and pollution in the country's water bodies—are on the horizon.[17]

Illingworth's work suggests that ongoing warfare obscures more than its impact on airspace. It certainly obfuscates pressing issues facing the natural environment and the region's populations alike, as well as exacerbating existing economic disparities and other sociopolitical predicaments that have plagued the region for decades. Such concerns include widespread poverty, unprecedented civil and social polarization, pervasive corruption, human rights violations, a decline in gender equality, dire conditions for minorities, the collapse of educational

11 Some research about the environmental and health impacts of war in Iraq has been conducted by Iraqi scholars and summarized in: Ahmed Majeed Al-Shammari, "Environmental Pollutions Associated to Conflicts in Iraq and Related Health Problems," *Reviews on Environmental Health* 31, no. 2 (2016): 245–50, https://doi.org/10.1515/reveh-2015-0024.

12 It is reported that 320 tons of depleted uranium munitions were used in the Gulf War, while nearly two thousand tons were deployed in the 2003 invasion. See Owen Dyer, "WHO Suppressed Evidence on Effects of Depleted Uranium, Expert Says," *BMJ (Clinical research ed.)* 333, no. 7576 (November 11, 2006): 990.

13 See Rachel Ehrenberg, "Not Even Breathing Is Safe in Iraq," *Wired*, March 31, 2011, https://www.wired.com/2011/03/dust-iraq/.

14 See Falih Hassan and Elian Peltier, "Scorching Temperatures Bake Middle East Amid Eid al-Adha Celebrations," *New York Times*, July 31, 2020, https://www.nytimes.com/2020/07/31/world/middleeast/Middle-East-heat-wave.html.

15 See Louisa Loveluck and Chris Mooney, "Baghdad's Record Heat Offers Glimpse of World's Climate Change Future," *Washington Post*, August 12, 2020, https://www.washingtonpost.com/world/2020/08/12/baghdad-iraq-heat-climate-change/?arc404=true.

16 See Agence France-Presse, "Iraq's Cultivated Areas Reduced by Half as Drought Tightens Grip," *National*, August 5, 2018, https://www.thenationalnews.com/world/mena/iraq-s-cultivated-areas-reduced-by-half-as-drought-tightens-grip-1.756996.

infrastructure, and the overall lack of social security. And this is despite the fact that several countries in the region—Iraq being the most pertinent example—are enormously rich in oil reserves, if not current production capacity.

Interest in oil, to which Illingworth perceptively alludes in her work, is one of the most critical dimensions concealed by contemporary warfare, which is significant for obvious reasons: oil is the most vital resource supplying much of the energy needs of the entire globe. Indeed, while oil and the Arab world often appear to be synonymous, oil is a global commodity—modern societies everywhere, along with their political structures, have come into existence through the processes of extracting and consuming oil. Timothy Mitchell argues that fossil fuels, especially oil, have created the conditions for the emergence of modern democracy, but have also delineated its limits. He contends that Iraq, specifically, has been the most critical site for an important historical development of modern democracy, when Western societies attempted imperial control of raw materials needed for the prosperity of their own democracies.[18] So it is not surprising that oil was one of the central reasons for the 2003 invasion of Iraq.

The occupation made the country's oil available for international firms (including Halliburton, headed by Dick Cheney prior to becoming one of the staunchest advocates of war on Iraq), increasing production capacity by almost half, while many Iraqis now live in abject poverty, and the majority struggle to find oil-based products locally. Companies like BP, Shell, and ExxonMobil are now taking advantage of long-term contracts, which only became possible after the invasion and the favorable conditions imposed by the US on Iraqi authorities (prior to that, the nationalization of Iraq's oil since the 1970s ensured that all revenues were controlled by the local government).[19] Even in the rare cases when attending to the environment appeared to be a priority after 2003—such as restoring the delicate ecology of southern Iraq's marshes, which were severely damaged by the Saddam Hussein regime in the 1990s to suppress Kurdish dissent—the rehabilitation of these wetlands became a political tool for the US and local governments to further open the door to war-profiteering by international corporations keen on gaining access to oil. The project was mobilized by American and Iraqi politicians to showcase positive developments in the post-2003 era and resulted in major contracts won by foreign consultants and corporations to secure access to oil, water, and other natural resources.[20]

Illingworth points to deep traumas, the staggering weight of contemporary warfare the world over, and how we are all complicit—through our collective reliance on fossil fuels, for example, or oblivion to how the sky is occupied—in the devastation being wrought on the environment today. Her work makes us realize that by continuing our engagement with the environment solely through the myopic lens of climate change (focusing only on gas emissions from cars and factories or putting the burden on our own individual shoulders), we are making a glaring omission. Grove argues that the customary emphasis on climate change only contributes to erasing the current role and culpability of the US, and formerly Europe, in creating the current world order, including vast environmental degradation everywhere.[21]

I believe that Illingworth's practice equally compels us to understand how delusional it is to imagine that bombs falling on the homeland of a little boy in some faraway geography do not concern the environment or affect the rest of the globe. Through her work, we come to understand that the Arab world is at the nexus of a planetary dependence on oil, which fuels not only civil needs but also militarization and global conflicts, fought on the ground as well as in the

17 In a report by the United Nations Office for Disaster Risk Reduction (UNDRR), water flow in many rivers in Iraq is said to have dwindled to about 40 percent, and Iraq is now facing one of the direst shortages in decades. See Kieran Cooke, "Iraq's Climate Stresses Are Set to Worsen," UNDRR: PreventionWeb, November 12, 2018, https://www.preventionweb.net/news/view/61850.

18 See Timothy Mitchell, *Carbon Democracy: Political Power in the Age of Oil* (London: Verso, 2013).

19 For an overview of how the invasion yielded this outcome, see Antonia Juhasz, "Why the War in Iraq Was Fought for Big Oil," *CNN*, April 15, 2013, https://www.cnn.com/2013/03/19/opinion/iraq-war-oil-juhasz/index.html.

20 See Bridget Guarasci, "Environmental Rehabilitation and Global Profiteering in Wartime Iraq," Costs of War project, Watson Institute, Brown University, April 23, 2017, https://watson.brown.edu/costsofwar/papers/2018/environmental-rehabilitation-and-global-profiteering-wartime-iraq.

21 See Grove, *Savage Ecology*.

airspace above. The artist helps us comprehend that to account for the environment in a more holistic sense, and to admit the global impact of warfare, is to acknowledge our interconnectedness and interdependence everywhere, to become cognizant of the links between our lives and the lands and skies we collectively inhabit.

Amin Alsaden is a curator, scholar, and educator whose work focuses on transnational exchanges of ideas and expertise across cultural boundaries. His curatorial practice is committed to advancing social justice through the arts and to the dissemination of inclusive narratives that expand existing canons and challenge hegemonic epistemological and power structures. Alsaden is particularly interested in how artists and architects ponder collective experiences in the public realm, level political and institutional critique, and envision novel spatial responses to questions of belonging, displacement, and exile. His research explores modern and contemporary art and architecture in the Global South and often involves documenting endangered heritage and examining how precarious archives and scarce resources shape lopsided global narratives. Alsaden holds graduate degrees from Harvard and Princeton and has published and lectured widely.

Derek Gregory
SEEING IN THE DARKNESS

1 Giulio Douhet, *The Command of the Air*, trans. Dino Ferrari (Maxwell Air Force Base, AL: Air University Press, 1998), 9; Thomas Hippler, *Bombing the People: Giulio Douhet and the Foundations of Air-Power Strategy, 1884–1939* (Cambridge, UK: Cambridge University Press, 2013). Douhet thought that the erasure of any distinction between combatants and civilians—and the risk to nominally defenseless civilians—suggested that "the safest place may be in the trenches."

2 Derek Gregory, "'In Another Time-zone, the Bombs Fall Unsafely…': Targets, Civilians and Later Modern War," *Arab World Geographer* 9, no. 2 (2006): 88–111; Priya Satia, "The Defense of Inhumanity: Air Control and the British Idea of Arabia," *American Historical Review* 111, no. 1 (2006): 16–51. To be clear: racism was routinely used to deny civilian status to nonwhite populations. For example, in 1932, the British High Commissioner in Iraq insisted that "the term 'civilian population' has a very different meaning in Iraq from what it has in Europe." Consequently, European sensibilities about civilian casualties there were literally misplaced: "The whole of its male population are potential fighters," he explained, "as the tribes are heavily armed." The same grotesque rationale was still in action seventy-odd years later during Israel's assaults on Gaza and the US-led wars in Afghanistan and Iraq.

"What I give form to in daylight is only one per cent of what I have seen in darkness."
—M. C. Escher, *The Graphic Work of M. C. Escher*, 1975

Remote Warfare and Risk-transfer Warfare

There is nothing new about the principle of remote warfare: sending arrows or shells in deadly arcs or releasing toxic clouds of gas, armies have long sought to attack their enemies from a safe distance by weaponizing the air itself. But the use of aircraft radically transformed the martial calculus because it transformed its target. Airpower changed its disposition—zones of military violence were no longer bounded "battlefields"—and it changed its composition to bring civilian populations within the direct sphere of military violence.

These twin transformations were already in motion in World War I. On the Western Front, aircraft was initially used purely for reconnaissance over no-man's-land and immediately behind enemy lines. Although Orville Wright insisted that "scouting" would always be their primary role, by May 1915, airships and later giant bombers were putting at risk civilian populations in cities like London and Paris, far from the battlefield. "By virtue of this new weapon," Giulio Douhet wrote in 1922, "there will be no distinction any longer between soldiers and civilians."[1] His prediction has been cited many times, but it conceals as much as it reveals.

The very idea of a civilian is complicated and contested. In most of its incarnations, it has been marked by gender and age ("women and children"), which has its own deficiencies, but throughout the history of aerial violence, the civilians subject to its assaults have also been marked by race (between the World Wars, bombing became a vital modality of colonial power)[2] and by class (many air raids on cities in World War II did deliberate and disproportionate damage to working-class districts).[3] What Douhet clearly anticipated, nevertheless, was *risk-transfer war*, in which the burden of military violence is shifted to the most vulnerable and whose depredations take full advantage of those transformations in remote targeting.

Targeting

We do not inhabit a world of targets; they have to be produced through what is presented as a scientific process that is also a profoundly bureaucratized one. After World War II, Freeman Dyson confessed that he was sickened by his role in RAF Bomber Command, sitting at a desk and "carefully calculating how to murder most economically another hundred thousand people."[4] Henry Nash described his similar postwar work for the US Air Force's Bombing Encyclopedia as "the bureaucratization of homicide." "Our office behavior was no different from that of men and women who might work for a bank or insurance company," he wrote, and "the relationship between cause and effect was obscured."[5] That was no doubt the intention. Subdividing the targeting process, reducing it to tabulations and calculations, at once dispersed responsibility and heightened abstraction. It still does, and through the expansion and integration of the military-industrial complex, advanced militaries have adopted the corporate practices, production schedules, and vocabularies of "enterprise culture" and just-in-time execution metrics for their own operations.[6]

This is about more than efficiency or "productivity"); more, even, than rendering targeting as a purely technical achievement. It constructs targeting as a nominally objective process in a double sense: not only a managerial-scientific practice, routinized and standardized but also one that produces "the target" as an *object-space*, not a subject-space. This confers what *Life* magazine described in 1943 as "the aviator's sense of remoteness from his target": a sense shared by many others in the kill-chain, the vast bombing apparatus of which the bomb or missile is only the tip of the spear, and who are even more removed from the terror below.[7] It was (and remains) a multidimensional affair.

During the strategic bombing offensive in World War II, cities were reduced to grid coordinates, captured as indistinct outlines on H2S screens, and represented on target maps as gray, white, and purple shapes that resembled "a badly bruised torso."[8] But make no mistake: real bodies were erased from view. The pre-strike process of abstraction (which was also one of interpellation) continued to exert its power even as aircraft bucked and weaved during their bombing runs, and aircrews experienced a violent, visceral sense of their own, intensely corporeal vulnerability.

To one member of a bomber command crew, German cities burning at night "looked like sparkling diamonds on a black satin background. [...] They weren't people to me, just the target. It's the distance and the blindness which enabled you to do these things." Another explained how the sight of the city seemed unreal "because we could not hear it or feel its breath. [...] Perhaps if we had seen the white, upturned faces of people," he continued, as they did when they returned over the English coast at dawn, "our hearts would have rebelled. But we never did."[9] As Jörg Friedrich observed, the bombers "dropped their load into this abstraction."[10]

The corrosive effects of abstraction extended into public administration and the public sphere. One air-raid warden, who worked in the Directorate of Bombing Operations by day, wondered how the British government came to settle on the term "incident" to describe "what happens when a bomb falls on a street":

> "Incident" cannot be held to convey very graphically the consequences of a bomb. Just the contrary. The word is wonderfully colourless, dry and remote: it touches nothing which it does not minimise. And this, it may be supposed, was what recommended it conclusively to the authorities. It formed an important part of their policy of reassurance. For while anyone might be frightened of a bomb, who could be frightened of an incident?[11]

Sixty years on, little had changed. For weeks before the US-led invasion of Iraq in 2003, which opened with a sustained bombing campaign, Baghdad was presented online and across print media as an array of targets, each one an impending "incident" (though so much more than that to those who lived there). Only after Saddam's statue had been toppled did other maps appear showing the city as a series of neighborhoods inhabited not by tyrants, terrorists, and torturers but by ordinary men, women, and children.[12]

It is sometimes claimed that the "remote-split" operations carried out by military drones—with their capacity to relay full-motion video feeds in near real time to aircrews thousands of miles away—have dispelled both "the distance and the blindness" and transformed the situation into something closer to those fuller, fleshier maps of Baghdad. But this is a complicated issue for three reasons. First, today's drones can only be used in uncontested airspace (they are relatively easy to shoot down), which is why they are typically deployed in the global borderlands against non-state actors.[13]

3 "It is important to recognize that the emphasis on killing German workers and destroying their milieu was deliberate," writes Richard Overy, the greatest British historian of the air war. "The idea of collateral damage had been turned on its head: instead of the death of workers and the destruction of their housing being a side-effect of hitting factories, damage of factories was a collateral effect of destroying working-class neighborhoods." Richard Overy, *The Bombing War: Europe 1939–1945* (London: Allen Lane, 2013), 258–9; see, more generally, Thomas Hippler, *Governing from the Skies: A Global History of Aerial Bombing* (London: Verso, 2017).

4 Freeman Dyson, *Weapons and Hope* (New York: Harper and Row, 1954), 120.

5 Henry T. Nash, "The Bureaucratization of Homicide," *Bulletin of the Atomic Scientists* 36, no. 4 (April 1980): 22–27. The US Air Force started work in January 1946 on an inventory of potential targets in the Soviet Union; the database became global and was eventually renamed the Basic Encyclopedia. See Derek Gregory, "The Bombing Encyclopedia of the World," Geographical Imaginations, August 3, 2012, https://geographicalimaginations.com/2012/08/03/bombing-encyclopedia-of-the-world.

6 Richard Adams and Chris Barrie, "The Bureaucratization of War," *Ethics and Global Politics* 6 (2013): 245–60; Astrid Nordin and Dan Öberg, "Targeting the Ontology of War: From Clausewitz to Baudrillard," *Millennium* 43, no. 2 (2015): 392–410. As in the corporate world, military lawyers are now extensively involved in the process, see Craig Jones, *The War Lawyers: The United States, Israel and Juridical Warfare* (Oxford: Oxford University Press, 2020).

7 "Saturation of Hamburg," *Life*, December 27, 1943.

8 The phrase is Len Deighton's in his novel *Bomber* (London: Pan, 1970), 383.

Even in Afghanistan, the epicenter of drone warfare, most airstrikes were carried out by conventional strike aircraft (though drones were often involved in orchestrating those attacks). In 2020, the US Air Force's inventory of remote platforms plateaued at 6 percent of its total aircraft capacity, as attention was redirected toward conflict against China and Russia.[14]

Second, drone crews often claim an unprecedented intimacy with the battlespace, but this is thoroughly conditional. When they are providing close air support to troops on the ground, crews become so immersed in what is unfolding on their screens that they insist they are not seven thousand miles but just eighteen inches away: the distance from eye to screen. The video feed from a drone may well bring the aircrew closer to the action, but the feed is silent, and their sonic landscape is composed of whatever they can hear through their headphones—the voice of a Joint Terminal Attack Controller, the ambient noise of other troops on the ground, the sound of explosions—and this fosters an identification with their own troops.[15] "Just by flying this platform and what we see," one Predator pilot testified, "I do experience stuff along with the guys on the ground. I definitely care about them. [...] I would say I am in that situation with them, just trying to support them the best I can."[16]

This intimacy is cultivated within a culturally divided field, a different sort of remote split, in which crews are interpellated to identify so closely with their comrades-in-arms that they are predisposed to interpret every other action—every Other action—as hostile.[17] Their presumptive closeness to their own troops becomes counterposed to a remoteness from the alien Other. But the execution of aerial violence cannot be reduced to an optical-visual field. In later modern war, military operations depend on radio communications and text messages.

In the most detailed transcript of a later modern airstrike that we have—an attack on three vehicles traveling through Uruzgan province in Afghanistan in February 2010—a Predator crew (including the pilot I quoted) provided subtitles for what they saw on their screens. Virtually everything was interpreted as an imminent threat to US forces on the ground: the vehicles were a "convoy," their occupants were "military-age males," their early morning prayer was a Taliban signifier ("it's what they do"), turning away from the village where the counterinsurgency operation was underway became a "flanking maneuver," few weapons were detected because all the others had been concealed. The drone crew had a more extensive discussion about the makes of the three vehicles than the make-up of the passengers precisely because the vehicles were familiar to American eyes in ways that the people were not. It is hardly surprising that the list of verbal cues, interpellated from the video feed and relayed to the forces on the ground, prompted the Special Forces commander to call in a deadly airstrike by two combat helicopters on what turned out to be a group of civilians traveling together for safety as they traveled through "Taliban country."[18]

This vignette sharpens a more general point. The occupants of the vehicles were required to perform what Christiane Wilke calls "civilian-ness" in ways that would have been familiar to those unseen (and largely unknowing) American eyes. Those framed by the Predator's targeting system did not know they were under surveillance, still less that they were suspected of being Taliban. And even had they known, what could possibly have constituted an adequate performance of "civilian-ness" by those in front of the lens to those in front of the screen? It was only when they failed to scatter after Hellfire missiles and rockets slammed into their vehicles that their conduct was re-registered, only then—too late—that their now "weird" conduct was read as that of "normal civilians." It was only "weird" because it was not the usual response of

9 James Taylor and Martin Davidson, *Bomber Crew* (London: Hodder & Stoughton, 2004), 283, 447; Don Charlwood, *No Moon Tonight* (Manchester: Crécy, 2000), 131; see also Derek Gregory, "Lines of Descent," in *From Above: War, Violence and Verticality*, ed. Peter Adey, Mark Whitehead, and Alison Williams (London: Hurst, 2013), 41–70.

10 Jörg Friedrich, *The Fire*, trans. Allison Brown (New York: Columbia University Press, 2006), 25; see also Derek Gregory, "Doors into Nowhere: Dead Cities and the Natural History of Destruction," in *Cultural Memories*, ed. Peter Meusburger, Michael Heffernan, and Edgar Wunder (Dordrecht: Springer, 2011), 266–71.

11 John Strachey, *Post D: Some Experiences of an Air Raid Warden* (London: Gollancz, 1941), 14–15.

12 Derek Gregory, *The Colonial Present: Afghanistan, Palestine, Iraq* (Oxford: Blackwell, 2004), 205–6, 213–14.

13 The war between two state actors, Armenia and Azerbaijan, over Nagorno-Karabakh in 2020 widened the scope of drone operations but did not fundamentally challenge this claim. The Azeri use of "loitering munitions," swarms of small, expendable drones that flew into their targets and exploded, and "sub-Reaper" drones, supplied by Israel and Turkey, overwhelmed Armenian ground defense systems, but they did so as much for tactical as technological reasons.

14 Mark Cancian, *US Military Forces in FY2020* (Washington, DC: Center for Strategic and International Studies, 2019), 8–9.

15 Nasser Hussain, "The Sound of Terror: Phenomenology of a Drone Strike," *Boston Review*, October 16, 2013.

16 Derek Gregory, "Under Afghan Skies," in *Reach from the Sky: Aerial Violence and the Everywhere War* (forthcoming).

the Taliban to an attack. But since the occupants of the vehicles were all "normal civilians," what could they possibly have done *differently* during the previous three hours that would have spared them from being attacked?[19]

There is a third reason for qualifying those claims to intimacy. Where drones are used to execute a targeted killing against a known, named individual, any presumption of innocence has already been adjudicated by those higher in the kill-chain. Where they are used to conduct a "signature strike" against an unknown, anonymous individual who is deemed to exhibit a suspicious "pattern of life," all those contested assumptions about what constitutes normal conduct remain in play. But both missions often rely on the *technical* production of the targeted individual(s) as an artifact of digital intelligence, and when he or she finally appears in the crosshairs, they are apprehended as a sensor signature, a mobile phone intercept, a network trace. In short, they are what Grégoire Chamayou calls "schematic bodies": individuals in a calculative rather than a corporeal sense. And at the explosive end of their day, when they are described as "squirters," "jackpots," or "bugsplat," when the drone remains on station to carry out an inventory of body parts, anything other than a voyeuristic, predatory intimacy vanishes.[20]

Slow Violence

Yet, to make all these—necessary—qualifications is still misleading. For the intensive, irruptive violence of death or injury from the air neither begins nor ends with the sound of bombs, missiles, and explosions, and we need to understand the inherently *slow violence* of bombing.[21] In war zones, the anticipation of aerial violence brings apprehension: or what Paul Saint-Amour calls "traumatic earliness."[22] In Britain, in the weeks and month leading up to World War II, the air-raid drills, the provision of shelters, the imposition of blackouts, and the installation of air-defense systems all increased a palpable fear that, as Stanley Baldwin had warned in 1932, "the bomber will always get through."[23] And once the bombs began to fall, familiarity did not breed content.

In her novel *Day*, A. L. Kennedy captured how that sense of foreboding intensified for survivors moving through the moonscape of a bombed city:

> Walk anywhere and you'll catch yourself calculating out from where the first cookie [blockbuster bomb] would fall and blast the buildings open, let the incendiaries in to lodge and play. And so you see targets beside targets: nothing but targets and ghost craters looping up from the earth, shock waves of dust and smoke ringing, crossing. You feel the aerial photograph staring down at you where you stand, waiting to wipe you away.[24]

Again, sixty years on, little had changed. Here is a young Iraqi architect describing the anxious nightly wait for airstrikes to resume on his beleaguered capital in March 2003:

> We start counting the hours from the moment one of the news channels report that the B52s have left their airfield [in Britain]. It takes them around six hours to get to Iraq. On the first day of the bombing, it worked precisely. Yesterday we were a bit surprised that after six hours bombs didn't start falling. [...] We found out today in the news that the city of Tikrit got the hell bombed out of it. Today the B52s took off at 3pm, [in] half an hour we will know whether it is Baghdad tonight or another city.[25]

London in 1941 and Baghdad in 2003 at least *had* air-raid warning systems, air defenses, and air-raid shelters. However

17 This propensity may be exacerbated by the recognition that troops on the ground are in harm's way, unlike those in the Ground Control Station: a radical asymmetry that conceivably enhances the impulse to identify with those for whom the crews are providing air support.

18 Gregory, "Under Afghan Skies."

19 Christiane Wilke, "Seeing and Unmaking Civilians in Afghanistan: Visual Technologies and Contested Professional Visions," *Science, Technology and Human Values* 42, no. 60 (2017): 1031–60; "High Altitude Legality: Visuality and Jurisdiction in the Adjudication of NATO Air Strikes," *Canadian Journal of Law and Society* 34, no. 2 (2019): 261–80.

20 Derek Gregory, "The Territory of the Screen," *Mediatropes* 6, no. 2 (2016): 126–47.

21 Slow violence "occurs gradually and out of sight, a violence of [anticipated and] delayed destruction that is dispersed across time and space." Rob Nixon, *Slow Violence and the Environmentalism of the Poor* (Cambridge, MA: Harvard University Press, 2011), 2.

22 "It is time to take seriously [Lewis] Mumford's suggestion that a collective syndrome might be instigated by expectation—that is, by the *eventuality* of a future-conditional war or attack as much as by the actual *event* of violence." Paul Saint-Amour, "Bombing and the Symptom: Traumatic Earliness and the Nuclear Uncanny," *Diacritics* 30, no. 4 (Winter 2000): 59–82; *Tense Future: Modernism, Total War, Encyclopedic Form* (New York: Oxford University Press, 2015).

23 Stanley Baldwin, Hansard International Affairs Official Report, col. 632, vol. 270 (November 10, 1932), http://hansard.millbanksystems.com/commons/1932/nov/10/international-affairs#column_632.

imperfect those turned out to be, they are all much more limited for those who live in the world's borderlands and continue to be haunted by the specter of death from the sky.

Traumatic earliness is a *collective*, not a singular affliction. Some commentators have identified the "individualization of warfare" as one of the key modalities of later modern war, where the digitization of intelligence and the precision of "smart bombs" allow for targeted killing in which, as Chamayou put it, "the body becomes the battlefield," through what the USAF proclaims as its ability to put "warheads on foreheads."[26] But this is short-sighted. Not only because the accuracy of those "surgical strikes" is far from self-evident but also because, even in its seemingly most individualized forms—the so-called "manhunting" that Chamayou despises—aerial violence *also always targets the social*. It haunts people's everyday lives, hollows them out, makes them wary of the most casual or ordinary social encounters, and constricts the intrinsic liveliness of the social.[27] "The drones have been hovering over Waziristan for several years," one resident testified, continuing:

> Their presence has been a constant element of our lives. [...] I am neither a Taliban nor an al-Qaeda. But I fear becoming part of the "collateral damage" when missiles from the drones hit a car in the bazaar, a mosque or a school. I don't want to be at the wrong place at the wrong time or find myself with the wrong people. What if I am standing near a car with tinted glass in the bazaar on my way to the shop and a missile hits the occupants of the car with some target inside?[28]

Slow violence continues after an airstrike, as its effects snake out to envelop the population at large. I'm thinking not only of the dangers of rescue (the risk from damaged buildings and fractured power lines, and the threat of a "double-tap" strike in which first responders are deliberately targeted) and of the challenge of providing medical care to the survivors, many of whom will have suffered life-changing injuries (all the more difficult where hospitals have been deliberately and systematically targeted) but also even of the difficulty of rehousing and feeding homeless, hungry, and traumatized people. For, as Samuel Weber reminded us, "every target is inscribed in a network or chain of events that inevitably exceeds the opportunity that can be seized or the horizon that can be seen."[29]

It is true that "smart bombs" and laser-guided missiles have allowed more accurate targeting since World War II and especially since Vietnam—assuming the target has been correctly identified in the first place[30]—but these refinements have also enhanced the capacity to target the social: not indiscriminately (the area bombing of World War II, the carpet bombing of Vietnam), but systematically. Shock waves ripple out through infrastructural networks, extending the envelope of destruction in space and time. It becomes possible to strike a power plant with precision—and even to take it out in the early hours of the morning when only a caretaker and a skeleton staff are at work. The claim will be that this was done to minimize casualties on-site.

Yet, as power is cut, so desalination plants are forced offline, water-pumping stations and sewage-treatment plants fail, hospitals are without light and power for their medical equipment, air conditioning, and filtering, and fridges shut off and food perishes. And a wider population has been invisibly targeted, countless lives knowingly and purposefully put at risk.[31] These effects, displaced from the original site and dispersed in time and space, might be marginalized or even legitimized by militaries as "collateral damage"—yet, they are hardly accidental or incidental: they are the very effects that "effects-based

24 A. L. Kennedy, *Day* (London: Jonathan Cape, 2007), 202–3.

25 Salam Pax [Salam Abdulmunem], *The Baghdad Blogger* (London: Guardian Books, 2003), March 23, 2003, 131.

26 Paul Kahn, "Imagining Warfare," *European Journal of International Law* 24, no. 1 (2013): 199–216; Samuel Issacharoff and Richard Pildes, "Drones and the Dilemma of Modern Warfare," in *Drone Wars: Transforming Conflict, Law and Policy*, ed. Peter Bergen and Daniel Rothenberg (Cambridge, UK: Cambridge University Press, 2015), 388–420; Grégoire Chamayou, *A Theory of the Drone*, trans. Janet Lloyd (New York: New Press, 2015), 56. "Individualization" materially affects the legal armature that permits aerial violence; as Kahn notes, "The criminal is always an individual" (which invokes international human rights law), whereas "the enemy is not" (which activates different, more permissive provisions of international humanitarian law).

27 Neal Curtis, "The Explication of the Social: Algorithms, Drones and (Counter-) Terror," *Journal of Sociology* 52, no. 3 (2016): 522–36.

28 Adam Khan, "No One Feels Safe," in *Drone Wars*, 345. Another resident testified that: "No matter what we are doing, that fear is always inculcated in us. Because whether we are driving a car, or we are working on a farm, or we are sitting home playing [...] cards—no matter what we are doing, we are always thinking the drone will strike us. So we are scared to do anything, no matter what." International Human Rights and Conflict Resolution Clinic, *Living under Drones: Death, Injury and Trauma to Civilians from US Drone Practices in Pakistan* (Stanford: Stanford Law School and Global Justice Clinic, NYU School of Law, 2012), 96.

operations" are designed to produce. Aerial violence is one of the most powerful, incendiary ways of producing them, yet the syntax of targeting—with its implication of isolating an *object*-ive—artfully distracts attention from the cascade of destruction deliberately set in motion.

Topologies of Aerial Violence

I hope it will be clear from these observations how aerial violence torques time and space and how its execution produces and depends on those torsions. Its history is one of rupture and return, of continuity and discontinuity: the temporal lines of descent, from the bombers of the two World Wars to today's Reapers, are contorted and convoluted.[32] And the infliction of aerial violence is never a linear passage from pre-strike to post-strike, punctuated only by the staccato, episodic rhythm of each strike; its slow violence depends on multiple temporalities reinforcing one another, a constellation in which, and through which, its effects are dispersed and reinforced.

Aerial violence is also a process in which distance is never fixed and frozen, a physical absolute, but is instead produced and performed. As aircrews flew over their target cities in World War II, ensnared by the probing fingers of searchlights and rocked by anti-aircraft fire, they also possessed (and in an important sense were sustained by) a startling sense of remoteness from the catastrophic effects they were producing below. When aircrews were removed from aircraft and installed in Ground Control Stations thousands of miles from their Predators and Reapers circling in the skies over Afghanistan, Iraq, or Syria, tethered only by satellite links and fiber-optic cables, they experienced at once a remarkable closeness to their comrades-in-arms on the ground and, often as not, a radical distance from others (Others) in their fields of view. In short, aerial violence does not tack through Euclidean space or even shatter it into fragments; it depends on, produces, and performs a dynamic, dialectical, and constantly shifting ensemble of spatialities.
And so, to render its inconstant, volatile geometries, we need, like Escher, to peer deep into its darkness.

Derek Gregory is the Peter Wall Distinguished Professor (2011–21) and Professor of Geography at the University of British Columbia, Vancouver. His research addresses the ways in which war has (and has not) changed over the last hundred years, and he is currently writing three books. The first, *Reach from the Sky*, is a critical investigation of bombing from before World War I through to the contemporary use of drones in the world's borderlands as a central vector of later modern war. The second, *Woundscapes*, focuses on casualty evacuation (military and civilian) from war zones—one of its primary concerns is the figuration of the wounded body and its multiple apprehensions as it moves through the evacuation chain. The two projects converge in a third book, *The Death of the Clinic*, which explores the bombing of hospitals and medical facilities from World War I to the wars in Afghanistan, Syria, and beyond.

29 Samuel Weber, *Targets of Opportunity: On the Militarization of Thinking* (New York: Fordham University Press, 2005), 18.

30 The accuracy and precision of digital intelligence should not be taken for granted. To cite just one example from many: in Pakistan's borderlands, Reprieve reported that one "known" Taliban leader, Baitullah Mehsud, was "directly targeted potentially as many as seven times, during the course of which 164 people were killed, including 11 children. His area was targeted at least a further nine times, resulting in the deaths of 123 additional people." *You Never Die Twice: Multiple Kills in the US Drone Program* (London: Reprieve, 2014), 7.

31 This example is based on US and British airstrikes on power plants in Iraq and on Israeli airstrikes on Gaza's only power plant; similarly, in Syria, the Russian and Syrian Arab Air Forces have systematically targeted hospitals for the same reasons.

32 Gregory, "Lines of Descent"; Derek Gregory, "Little Boys and Blue Skies: Drones through Post-atomic Eyes," in *Through Post-atomic Eyes*, ed. Claudette Lauzon and John O'Brian (Montreal: McGill-Queen's University Press, 2020), 152–92.

Anthony Downey

THE ALGORITHMIC APPARATUS OF NEOCOLONIALISM: COUNTER-OPERATIONAL PRACTICES AND THE FUTURE OF AERIAL SURVEILLANCE

"Human beings must learn anew to recognize the pattern of the earth from the perspective of the air."
—Harun Farocki, *Images of the World and the Inscription of War*, 1988

I

What forms of aerial threat do communities across the globe endure today, and how do they differ from previous levels of exposure? If we consider the apparently unstoppable ascendancy of drone reconnaissance and satellite surveillance, then it is evident that we are undergoing an epoch-defining evolution in the deployment of aerial technologies.[1] The multiple concerns raised by civilian, civil rights, humanitarian, and military agencies in relation to autonomous systems of warfare would suggest that such operations have likewise realigned the relationship between the material (physical, environmental, legal) and immaterial (psychological, ethical, and existential) impact of these technologies.[2] In conjunction with the enhancements afforded by Artificial Intelligence (AI), algorithms, and machine learning, autonomous systems of surveillance and warfare also engender less immediately visible forms of trauma. Ranging as they do from psychological trauma to the toxic contamination of habitats, not to mention the chronic threat associated with unexploded ordnance, the concern here becomes not so much whether consequences of these technologies have changed over time, but how we critically engage with the immaterial and nonphysical repercussions of such systems.

To these already imminent concerns, we could go further and observe that the technologies that commandeer and exploit airspace are not *only* detrimental to those who are subject to their ubiquitous apparatuses, the logistics of their deployment are also prosecuted through narrow national preoccupations of states who are party to developing the legislation that governs their use. Given the relatively inaccessible and occluded disposition of AI systems, the continued levels of secrecy and defensive concealment raise further questions: How, for one, do we conceptualize the threat associated with both the opacity of "black-box" systems and the all-too-real impact of air-bound technologies that, to a large extent, remain beyond the purview and control of the vast majority of the world's population? All of which begs another, admittedly more capacious, question: How do we effectively engage with these largely classified, off-the-record, clandestine processes? We might, thereafter, want to probe further and inquire into whether the moment of visualizing these activities effects a form of engagement that can reconceptualize the military-industrial-corporate entanglements of airspace and, in so doing, productively hold such technologies to account. Can the *mise-en-abyme* of black-box-like technologies be negotiated with or, indeed, modulated by methods of envisioning their operative logic—and, if so, how might this be achieved?

It is with these questions in mind, amongst others, that Shona Illingworth's practice methodically pursues—through interdisciplinary partnerships and research networks—a series of investigations that coalesce around two interlinked projects: the three-screen video and sound installation *Topologies of Air* (2021) and the Airspace Tribunal (2018–ongoing), the latter being a series

1 See, for example, Derek Gregory, "From a View to a Kill: Drones and Late Modern War," *Theory, Culture & Society* 28, nos. 7–8 (2011): 188–215; Medea Benjamin, *Drone Warfare: Killing by Remote Control* (London: Verso, 2013); John Kaag and Sarah Kreps, *Drone Warfare* (Cambridge, UK: Polity Press, 2014); Grégoire Chamayou, *Drone Theory* (New York: Random House, 2015); Hugh Gusterson, *Drone: Remote Control Warfare* (Cambridge, MA: MIT Press, 2016); Ian G. R. Shaw, *Predator Empire: Drone Warfare and Full Spectrum Dominance* (Minneapolis: University of Minnesota Press, 2016); Lisa Parks and Caren Kaplan, eds., *Life in the Age Of Drone Warfare* (Durham, NC: Duke University Press, 2017); Atef Abu Saif, *The Drone Eats with Me* (Manchester: Comma Press, 2015); and Rebecca A. Adelman and David Kieran, eds., *Remote Warfare: New Cultures of Violence* (Minneapolis: Minnesota University Press, 2020).

2 See Michael J. Boyle, "The Legal and Ethical Implications of Drone Warfare," *International Journal of Human Rights* 19, no. 2 (2015): 105–26.

of in-progress "people's tribunals." Operating as a mutually supportive visual platform and legislative forum for exploring how air-bound technologies adversely affect communities, both projects prompt an expanded horizon upon which to understand the complexities—political, legal, historical, and cultural—of visualizing air- and outer-space. These strategic approaches to the question of air- and outer-space evoke pressing existential concerns that include, but are not limited to, the weaponization of non-terrestrial environments, climate change, environmental destruction, biodiversity loss, ontological insecurity, nuclear threat, and the corrosive forms of disparity that define the global landscapes of political power and corporate proprietorship.

To observe as much is to note that the research-based activities that we associate with practices from within the field of contemporary visual arts—including Illingworth's and others—have historically inquired into the technologies of image production, reception, and dissemination.[3] In their use of speculative, qualitative forms of visual inquiry, we may want to examine how such practices produce quantitative or evidentiary methods for understanding the impact of these technologies on life patterns and the lives lived in their shadow. Can, we need to ask, the interpretive and heuristic context of art practice, operating as it does from within the methodological framework of visual cultures, identify and distinguish the ramifications of satellite surveillance and drone reconnaissance on the realities of life and, increasingly, death?

In what follows, I will propose that any answer to this question, however approximate it may be, needs to consider the sinuous, utilitarian, extractive technologies of colonization and, successively, the neocolonial annexation of present-day and future realities. It is there that we can register and critically evaluate the degree to which the history of drone reconnaissance and satellite surveillance is irrefutably imbricated within colonial practices, nowhere more so than when we consider the latter's reductive determinations of life and death and the callous calculations that inform the neocolonial will to actuate ascendant forms of biopolitical control.

II

Activities from the realm of extraterrestrial space not only map but also strive to predict future terrestrial movement, be it of troops, weather patterns, urban development, or population flows. Drone- and satellite-based forms of surveillance, powered by the predictive function of algorithms, seek to determine inextricably convoluted patterns of force and counterforce. To fully understand this ecosystem, and to deconstruct its amalgamations, we need to think from *within* these integrated exercises of command and power rather than merely commenting upon them—how exactly do they operate and relate to one another? In certain key images, some of which recur throughout *Topologies of Air*, we are invited to consider a drone view of the world below, from verdant rainforests to postindustrial landscapes. In one section, we vertiginously descend into a Dilmun burial mound in Bahrain from hundreds of feet above, our infernal descent sentried by images of environmental devastation.[4] This is not merely the act of representing the innards of an extended necropolis, alongside images of despoliation; it is also an invitation to occupy a privileged viewing position that draws attention to how power operates vertically in our age of perpetual surveillance and indefatigable scrutiny. To be afforded this view is to become an appurtenance or supplement to the power wielded. Involved as we are in the so-called bird's-eye or god-like view, we are entangled within the paraphernalia of the scopic regime associated with aerial technologies and

3 I would note here, albeit in passing, the work of Heba Y. Amin, Helene Kazan, Forensic Architecture, Trevor Paglen, and, of course, Harun Farocki. The latter being the filmmaker and theorist often credited with forging the original inquiry into the economy of image production—and the emergence of "operational images"—in a postindustrial age through films as varied as *Images-War* (1987), *Images of the World and the Inscription of War* (1988), *Eye/Machine I, II, III* (2001, 2002, and 2003), and *War at a Distance* (2003).

4 These burial mounds are protected as part of a UNESCO World Heritage Site in the north of the island of Bahrain. They are evidence of the early Dilmun civilization, which prospered around the second millennium BCE, when the island was a trading hub for the region.

the imperial ambition of the god-like, disembodied gaze.[5]

Such consideration moves us away from formal questions—*how do we represent aerial activities that are often designed to evade detection?*—to concerns about agency: What positions can we adopt and adapt in relation to the activity of aerial surveillance? To raise these reservations is to more fully consider the overarching operational logic of the apparatuses that produce present-day realities—be they cartographic, photographic, or digital—and how they found their organizational structures and conceptual footing in racially deterministic colonial discourses that strove to "fix" the other as an objectified, calculable entity. This other, which was often seen to possess the ontic, quantifiable character of the real, rather than inhabiting a phenomenal existence (that is, living a form of life that was commensurate with Western-centric definitions of humanness), was rarely viewed as an ontological subject capable of *being* in the world. This calculable, measurable, knowable other is, as we will see, foundational to the historical shift that we associate with the reinscription of the "imaginative command" of colonial discourse into the algorithmic calculations that we now associate with the mechanisms and contrivances of neocolonization.[6]

When we consider our responsiveness to and responsibility for interpreting activities that are intentionally rendered distant—often by virtue of literal remoteness—and opaque by the "black-box" logic of computational decision-making processes, the demand for legibility becomes a political act in itself; one that prefaces, or at least frames, an injunction toward further formal inquiries. What are the implications of exerting command, be it imaginative or algorithmic, over a people or terrain? Often used to describe the operational logic of drone and satellite surveillance technologies, the phraseology surrounding so-called "black-box" systems would appear to repudiate precisely such a question, or at least discourage or suppress scrutiny of its operative logic. When we consider the degree to which the programmatic processes associated with AI and algorithms exclude, if not prohibit, human input and cognitive interpretation, we find further evidence of a series of recursive and occluded procedures over which we have no means to exercise effective oversight, be it legal or otherwise.

This indecipherability is central to the functioning of drones and satellite systems, which often operate in an autonomous or semiautonomous continuum. It is this secured functioning that has increasingly produced a conspicuous level of individual and collective detachment, whereby the stimulus of human decision-making in the operating procedures of autonomous weapons systems is, at best, moot and, more often than not, relegated to the role of either pre-programming or calibrating systems over which operators have less and less competency. As a result, we would appear to be witnessing a widespread moral, social, political, and cultural renunciation of responsibility when it comes to the fatal use of aerial surveillance and targeting.[7] This specific point has been addressed by Illingworth and Andrew Hoskins in their jointly authored essay, "Inaccessible War: Media, Memory, Trauma and the Blueprint," published in 2020.[8] Proposing that the "comparatively silent revolution in military and militarized data and AI" submits civilian populations to newer, emerging forms of trauma, the authors focus on the psychological and neuropsychological impact of unrelenting surveillance. Trauma, they argue, has shifted "from a memory of the past to include a perpetual anticipation of the threat of the future, subjecting increasing numbers of people to unending physical and psychological incarceration in a traumatizing present."[9]

The potential of practice-based research, such as Illingworth's, lies precisely in its ability to provide

5 See Kathrin Maurer, "Visual Power: The Scopic Regime of Military Drone Operations," *Media, War & Conflict* 10, no. 2 (2017): 2.

6 I borrow this phrase from Elleke Boehmer, who writes that "to assume control over a territory or a nation was not only to exert political or economic power, it was also to have imaginative command." See Elleke Boehmer, *Colonial and Postcolonial Literature* (Oxford: Oxford University Press, 2005), 5.

7 See Jeremy Packer and Joshua Reeves, *Killer Apps: War, Media, Machine* (Durham, NC: Duke University Press, 2020). See also, Peter M. Asaro, "The Labor of Surveillance and Bureaucratized Killing: New Subjectivities of Military Drone Operators," *Social Semiotics* 23, no. 2 (2013): 196–224.

8 Andrew Hoskins and Shona Illingworth, "Inaccessible War: Media, Memory, Trauma and the Blueprint," *Journal of Digital War* 1 (2020): 74–82.

9 Hoskins and Illingworth, "Inaccessible War," 74.

discursive and visual methods—for legal and scholarly frames of reference—to detail the changing nature of the psychological impact of such technologies. It is through the interdisciplinary approaches that are applied to the visualization and conceptualization of airspace, in both *Topologies of Air* and the Airspace Tribunal, that we see how evidentiary practices (in the context of the visual) and legal debates (that is to say, the realm of legislation) can produce a critical dialogue about the epistemological "value" attached to the data harvested by surveillance systems and, thereafter, applied to predict, if not predetermine, future patterns of life and death.

How "evidence" is understood and verified in a court of law, or considered within legal processes such as those governing the use of weapons, becomes a further issue of concern here. By inquiring into how data (information) is given an epistemological value through systems that remain largely withdrawn from legal oversight, Illingworth's installation and tribunal-based platform make transparent an operational logic that has long been structured around opaque processes. In focusing interdisciplinary activities and legal testimony on a formal, fact-based presentation of evidence and peer-reviewed research, Illingworth sets about detailing the substance of the present-day and future-oriented threat that communities and individuals experience from airspace. To this end, *Topologies of Air* and the Airspace Tribunal jointly propose a structured case for pursuing new legislation from *within* an understanding of human rights as a "living instrument" and *through* an expanded notion of what we mean when we refer to air- and outer-space.[10] Practice-based research, in sum, both aggregates and proposes a formal methodological approach *toward* the promulgation of a new human right in the face of unaccountable forms of "black-box" technology.

III

The algorithmic rationalization of data harvesting and storage remains a contingent process whereby we can witness an "input" and an "output" and yet remain unaware of the internal machinations by which "raw" data becomes material evidence of, for example, nefarious activities or wrong-doing. This structure needs to be declared tangible if we are to critically address its systematic application to, for example, a zone of conflict. We need, in sum, to think from *within* the occluded interiors of these operations.[11] As part of this process, we could begin by questioning the very idea of "raw" data—in its capacity as "input"—and observe that any decision, algorithmic or otherwise, to harvest or extract information presupposes a highly defined (ideological, political, national, monetary, and strategic) prior interest in the epistemological value of such information.

The future of war, that is to observe, has been categorically programmed into algorithms. The supposed epistemological opacity of algorithmic operations, cultivated by military-industrial and commercial interests, strategically disavows this fact alongside the extent to which such systems are demonstrably produced from within societal orders. Trained on patterns of data harvested from online user behavior, algorithms are essentially social constructs powered by Big Data. Given the foundational, if not collective, nature of their constitution, there is an urgent need to deconstruct the "black-box" rhetoric that surrounds these apparatuses. A crucial element here, in relation to terrestrial and extraterrestrial "black-box" surveillance systems (the realms that form the conceptual keystones for both *Topologies of Air* and the Airspace Tribunal), is how we can make direct connections between the extraction of data—through, for example, surveillance technologies—and its alignment with the

10 The phrase "living instrument" has been used elsewhere in this volume by Hoskins and Illingworth in reference to the 2020 European Court of Human Rights Judicial Seminar. See "The Convention as a Living Instrument at 70," Background Document, 3: https://www.echr.coe.int/Documents/Seminar_background_paper_2020_ENG.pdf.

11 See, for example, Cynthia Rudin and Joanna Radin, "Why Are We Using Black Box Models in AI When We Don't Need To? A Lesson from an Explainable AI Competition," *Harvard Data Science Review* 1, no. 2 (2019). See also Cynthia Rudin, "Stop Explaining Black Box Machine Learning Models for High Stakes Decisions and Use Interpretable Models Instead," *Nature Machine Intelligence* 1 (2019): 206–15.

national, military, and commercial interests of Western nations and others such as China and Russia.

These questions are further convoluted if we consider how sovereign (national) and military-industrial interests are entangled with those of privately owned companies that were originally endorsed by venture capital models of investment.[12] In this scenario, private money demands, at the behest of shareholders, ever more perilous means of extracting—through remote technologies such as drones—information that refines and trains the targeting systems of military weapons *and* the proprietary concerns of privately owned companies.[13] As a direct result of this secretive, difficult-to-access, recalcitrant regime of data extraction and application, communities and individuals on the receiving end of such technologies live in states of hyper-alertness, always on the lookout—or, more likely, given the remoteness of such technologies, listening out—for an imminent assault or an act of irrevocable violence.

IV

From the early stages of *Topologies of Air*, there is an explicit focus on non-Western geographies that are, for the most part, the object of a Western-centric optical regime—based on the selective concentration and application of knowledge—that has been effectively resuscitated by the (neo)colonial operations of drone reconnaissance and satellite technologies. In one telling image, depicting a satellite surveying a tract of the Arabian Peninsula, Iran, and the Horn of Africa, we see a panorama of a region—the so-called "Middle East"—that has long been subject to increasingly complex systems of surveillance.[14] These aerial shots of a satellite graphically reproduce an encounter that suggests, as noted above, a distinctly vertical relationship between the viewing (sovereign) subject and the perceived (targeted) object. It is with these and other points in mind that *Topologies of Air* plots the operational modifications and technical variations of the one-time imperial and now neo-imperial ambition to maintain an "imaginative command" over its self-appointed dominions.

In an observation by Edward Said, writing in 1995, the degree to which geography is always already "the art of war" neatly sums up a historical fact: cartographic mapping, in imperial and colonial contexts, was both a predictive activity (foreshadowing as it did the region in question) and a prioritized means of substantiating (in the establishment of so-called boundaries) and maintaining dominance and control.[15] Surveillance and remote forms of mapping, which remained impenetrable to those who were subject to their sphere of influence and applied forms of power, were evident in the first triangulation-based map of Egypt, Syria, and Palestine. Published between 1809 and 1829, and comprised of 885 plates, a three-sheet geographic map, and a forty-seven-sheet topographic map of Egypt, the latter triangulation-based maps were produced by Napoleon as part of his monumental *Description de l'Égypte*. These maps were to become the basis for further cartographic surveys throughout the nineteenth century and, in testament to their enduring use and application, were only superseded by photographs produced by cameras mounted to airplanes during World War I.

The photographic images taken from aerial perspectives were, to begin with at least, concerned with the professed purpose of mapping archaeological sites, antiquities, and monuments (a historical fact noted throughout *Topologies of Air*), with hundreds of thousands of aerial photographs produced under the pretext of "preservation."[16] In the intermediate decade or so of this timeline, encompassing as it does triangulated mapping in the late eighteenth century and the development of aerial photographs in the early part of

12 For an insightful account of how military, industrial, and entertainment interests coalesce, see James Der Derian, *Virtuous Warfare: Mapping the Military-Industrial-Media-Entertainment Network* (Boulder: Westview Press Inc., 2001). See also Paul Virilio, *War and Cinema* (London: Verso, 1989).

13 For a review of Google's involvement in drone technology, see Lee Fang, "Google Hired Gig Economy Workers to Improve Artificial Intelligence in Controversial Drone-Targeting Project," *Intercept*, March 6, 2018, https://theintercept.com/2019/02/04/google-ai-project-maven-figure-eight/.

14 See Anthony Downey, "There's Always Someone Looking at You: Performative Research and the Techno-Aesthetics of Drone Surveillance," in *Heba Y. Amin: The General's Stork*, ed. Anthony Downey (Berlin: Sternberg Press, 2020), 8–30.

15 Edward Said, "Facts, Facts, and More Facts," in *Peace and Its Discontents: Essays on Palestine in the Middle East Peace Process* (New York: Vintage, 1995), 26–31, 27.

16 See Robert Bewley and David Kennedy, "Historical Aerial Imagery in Jordan and the Wider Middle East," in *Archaeology from Historical Aerial and Satellite Archives*, ed. William Hanson and Ioana Oltean (New York: Springer, 2013).

the twentieth century, another innovation was to have a profound impact upon these remote technologies of erasure and legibility—namely, the invention of photogrammetry by the Prussian architect Albrecht Meydenbauer.

First coined by Meydenbauer in 1867, the concept of photogrammetry was simple enough: rather than measure a building by "hand" and in close personal proximity to it (an activity that often courted peril), measurements could be taken directly from multiple photographs of the same building taken from different angles.[17] These indirect, remote forms of measuring from a distance introduced an automated model of vision that displaced, or separated, the human eye from the object under consideration and, thereafter, replaced it with an activity that takes place from *within* the virtual, codified space of a photograph rather than *in direct relation* to an actual object or building under consideration. This apparent simplicity of method was to have lasting connotations when we consider how, through aerial photography in particular, photogrammetry promoted a process of disembodied, automated sight that usurped accepted ontologies of envisioning realities.

The move toward the automation of sight and the ensuing questioning of its role in producing realities, evident in the 1798 topographical surveys of Egypt, Syria, and Palestine, can be seen in how the maps in question were projected from ground positions to produce aerial overviews. This would suggest, *prima facie*, that the disincarnated, projected gaze was promoted from *within* the technology of mapping.[18] And central to these technologies, we find the instrumentalizing gaze of the cartographer, the all-seeing eye who commands an ethereal view of the terrain below (from a projected vantage point) and reproduces it through the determinants, or data points, we associate with the mapping (numeric and symbolic fixing) of people and places.

Returning to our earlier discussion of implied epistemological value, this emphasis on the "instrumentality of knowledge" has been noted by Anne Godlewska, who, writing of Napoleon's cartographic ambitions, observed "how cartography as mapping assigns a position to all places and objects. *That position can be expressed numerically*."[19] Continuing this critique of the computational logic underwriting cartographic practice, Godlewska further proposes: "Maps allowed a coordination and concentration of intrusion that was relatively covert, thanks to the inherently elite and secretive nature of the cartography of this period and to the centralized coordination that maps permitted and perhaps encourage. It was, then, an extremely *effective instrument* of imperialism, and powerful consonance with the ideals of the Enlightenment."[20]

The Cartesian calibration of space through the human eye, the extraction of information based on the fixed position of the subject in relation to an object, not only anticipates technologies of automated measuring—photogrammetry, for example—but also predicts the formal components of autonomous surveillance and weapons systems today.[21] To the extent that this computational logic adumbrates the present-day ascendancy of autonomous drone-based surveillance systems, it leads us back to our earlier question: How do we think from *within* this operational logic rather than merely comment on it? To do so, we need to more fully consider *how* a photograph instrumentalizes or programs our sight from within the codified space of the photographic apparatus, as is the case with photogrammetry. This is to encourage a range of inquiry into the operational "how" rather than the conceptualized "what" of image production. It is to entertain a discussion of so-called "operational images"—images that are made by machines for machines—and how the technologies of our contemporary neocolonial image regime do not necessarily involve images that are visible to the human eye.

17 For a fuller account, see Jörg Albertz, "Albrecht Meydenbauer: Pioneer of Photogrammetric Documentation of the Cultural Heritage," *Proceedings 18 International Symposium CIPA* (Potsdam, Germany, September 18–21, 2001).

18 Writing in 1941, Frederick Stansbury Haydon observed that the French Balloon Corps, effectively the first air force in the world, did accompany Napoleon on his campaign to Egypt in 1798 but with mixed results. See Frederick Stansbury Haydon, *Military Ballooning during the Early Civil War* (Baltimore, MD: John Hopkins University Press, 2000), 13–15.

19 See Anne Godlewska, "Map, Text and Image. The Mentality of Enlightened Conquerors: A New Look at the *Description de l'Egypte*," *Transactions of the Institute of British Geographers* 20, no. 1 (1995): 5–28, 6 (emphasis added). See also, Anders Engberg-Pedersen, *Empire of Chance: The Napoleonic Wars and the Disorder of Things* (Harvard: Harvard University Press, 2015), 147–56.

20 Godlewska, "Map, Text and Image," 18 (emphasis added).

21 For a fuller account of these correspondences between Cartesianism and the modern technologies of warfare, see Antoine Bousquet, *The Eye of War: Military Perception from the Telescope to the Drone* (Minneapolis: University of Minnesota Press, 2018), passim.

22 Farocki used the phrase "operational images" to describe images made by machines for machines, the full implications of which he explored throughout his three-part film *Eye/Machine I, II, III* (2000–3).

23 Anticipating "operational images" in all but name, Paul Virilio predicted the use of "vision machines" in the context of military robotics as an inevitable outcome of such technologies, driven as they are by conflict. See Paul Virilio, *The Vision Machine*, trans. Julie Rose (London: British Film Institute, 1994), 59.

24 See Trevor Paglen, "Operational Images," *e-flux Journal*, no. 59 (November 2014), http://worker01.e-flux.com/pdf/article_8990555.pdf.

25 "The operational image emulates the look and feel of traditional images, but on closer inspection, this turns out to be a secondary function, almost a gesture or courtesy extended by the machines. The computer does not need the image." Volker Pantenburg, "Working Images: Harun Farocki and the Operational Image," in *Image Operations: Visual Media and Political Conflict*, ed. Jens Eder and Charlotte Klonk (Manchester: Manchester University Press, 2017), 49–62, 49.

Referring to a term popularized by the filmmaker and theorist Harun Farocki, "operational images" are produced by machines for machines.[22] These images, therefore, remain "unseen" by and inaccessible to the human eye. This presents us with an ontological dilemma: How do we, thereafter, conceptualize our responsibility for and responsiveness to images we cannot access nor perceive? If, thereafter, Bishop Berkeley's adage—"Esse est percipi"; or, to be (*esse*) is to be perceived (*percipi*)—is to remain apt in our post-digital age, then we must ask a further question: What forms of *being*, sovereign or otherwise, are brought forth into our contemporary world if the act of "perception," if not the formal actualization of humanness (*being*), is performed by a machine? If we accept that established ontological frames of reference—which have, to date, substantiated human rights legislation and international laws—are being surreptitiously usurped by statements of autonomously calculated fact, then the over-arching challenge here becomes one of how we can, if at all, productively interject—legally, philosophically, creatively, and politically—into the contemporary rationalizations of life and death brought about by the affordances of drone and surveillance technologies.

Photogrammetry, like cartography before it, expressed the world numerically and at one remove from the actual; however, this move toward the industrialization of automated image production, through remote technologies, necessitates the production of an industrial, mechanized, and programmable means to survey and interpret images. For Farocki, the "operational image" answers to this demand through superseding the function of the human eye.[23] Insofar as they are part of a machine-based operative logic, images made by machines for machines are effectively void of an aesthetic context—they do not, as Farocki proposes in *Eye/Machine I, II, III* (2000–3), "portray a process but are themselves part of a process." This practical functioning means that images are not only voided of social or aesthetic intent, they also anticipate the formal obsolescence of the human eye. Structurally defined by the operation in question, "operational images" are not propaganda (they do not try to convince), nor do they instruct (they are not interested in directing our attention), nor are they content-based (they exist as abstract binary data coding, rather than pictograms). Given that they are part of an operation, any manifestation of the image through the disincarnated modus operandi of "operational images" is, therefore, merely an anachronistic concession to the human eye.[24]

If "operational images" are wholly disinterested in human input, apart from initial programming and our occasional calibration of their operational apparatus, then our agency in these forms of image production and their impact (consider how drones use algorithmically trained operational images to target and eliminate subjects) remain circumstantial at best. Computers, whether engaged in cartographic processes or the targeting of "combatants," do not use images, nor do "operational images" function in this sense.[25] Arguably, the contemporary image of conflict is indeed a compromise of sorts, an anthropological sop produced by machines to make us feel more comfortable and familiar with the operational logic and real-world impact of "vision machines." Have we, as a result, disavowed our responsibility for such calculations precisely on the grounds that the affordances of aerial surveillance and drone warfare profoundly distance us—physically, psychologically, and psychically—and in that process attempt to circumvent political and legal oversight? And, if so, how can we deploy creative practices and their interdisciplinary processes to critically address the fatal global interlocking of surveillance technologies, territorial plotting, imperialist expansionism, and drone warfare? These questions are, needless to say, the explicit domain of human rights legislation (as noted throughout the Airspace Tribunal), but they also raise a series of concerns about how we determine the epistemological value and agency, not to mention epistemic violence, of "operational images"—the very same "immaterial," digital images that can impact everyday realities with often devastating, if not deadly, results.

V

I earlier quoted Said's assertion that geography is "the art of war"; it might be, therefore, incumbent upon me to continue his thoughts on the matter and draw attention to the fact that he also proposed that geography can be the "art of resistance if there is a counter-map and a counter-strategy."[26] This recalibrates our original question from an inquiry into what forms of trauma and imminent aerial threat communities across the globe endure today, to what counterstrategies are available to us in order to address this state of affairs. On one level, this is, dare I say, relatively straightforward: in drawing attention to the ideological, national, corporate, historical, and proprietorial intent inherent within the apparent objectivity of a map, we readily if not critically engage—through the form of *Topologies of Air* and the forum of the Airspace Tribunal—with its assumptions and framing of reality. To this, we must add a further, admittedly more speculative, question: Given that opaque systems tend to disavow critical analysis—by way of legal and political inquiry, for example—can we understand this design logic as a conscious byproduct of the neocolonial ambition to appropriate knowledge without having to necessarily account for the responsibilities involved in archiving, quantifying, and applying it to real-world environments?

In outlining the extent to which colonial discourse laid the groundwork for the development and application of the apparatus of global surveillance technologies and other forms of technical representation, we can go some way to observing what a counterstrategy could look like, albeit with a significant caveat: the logic of colonial discourse was developed in corporeal terms (it was the human, fleshy eye that viewed, dissected, and reproduced the discursive realities of the non-Western world through representation). Today, in our post-digital age, that eye has given way to the political economy of the remote machine eye and the recursive abstractions of "operational images." This development necessarily reframes how we can interrogate the applications of surveillance technology and what form the development of fit-for-purpose legislative action would subsequently assume in the context of human rights. Can we, that is to ask, prosecute an autonomous weapons system?[27] Working from within these implacable optical regimes, we might also want to ask whether we can frame a counterstrategy, or counter-operational-image, that would effect a transformation, legislative or otherwise, in the functioning of these systems?[28]

To investigate the potential to formulate a legally binding international human right in relation to airspace (and, perhaps more crucially, who exactly would be protected by such a right), projects such as *Topologies of Air* and the Airspace Tribunal not only concentrate a range of activities and inquiries but also formally inquire into how we can effectively pose these questions and, momentously, through what means. How do we legislate for the production, dissemination, and reception of an epistemological apparatus—a system that produces knowledge and applies it—based on opaque "operational images" and a regime of "vision machines" that increasingly exist independent of human agency? How, that is to ask, do we witness the impact and effect of neocolonial technologies when they are deployed not only to target communities on the ground, so to speak, but also to elide any notion of a witness to both the execution and the event of violence?

26 Edward Said, "Facts, Facts, and More Facts," 27.

27 For a fuller discussion of the distinction between semi- and fully-automated weapons, see Paul Scharre, *Army of None: Autonomous Weapons and the Future of War* (New York: W. W. Norton and Company, 2019).

28 For a fuller discussion of what a counter-operational strategy could potentially entail in relation to the data sets used to train algorithms, see Trevor Paglen and Anthony Downey, "Algorithmic Anxieties," *Journal of Digital War* 1 (2020): 18–28.

29 See Aimé Césaire, *Discourse on Colonialism* (New York: Monthly Review Press, 2000), 42–43.

If we recall here, finally, Aimé Césaire's all-too-memorable phrase, "colonization = thingification," we can pinpoint the inherent processes of dehumanization practiced by colonial powers and how this, in turn, produced the docile and productive—that is, monetized and commodifiable—body of the colonized as a means to extract further "value" in the name of "progress" (the latter being a barely coded term for Western interests). As befits his time, Césaire understood these processes primarily in terms of wealth extraction (raw materials) and the exploitation of physical, indentured labor: "My turn to state an equation: colonization ='thingification.' [...] I am talking about societies drained of their essence, cultures trampled underfoot, institutions undermined, lands confiscated, religions smashed, magnificent artistic creations destroyed, extraordinary possibilities wiped out."[29]

Whereas colonization was, first and foremost, preoccupied with wealth and labor extraction through occupation, neo-colonization, while furthering such ambitions, is indelibly implicated within an apparatus of data extraction that seeks to establish and predetermine, if not occupy, the future. Both effect an epistemological and actual violence on communities and individuals, and both reveal the extractive technologies of imperialism. The line connecting the two involves the violence of knowledge and applied data. The exploitation of raw materials, labor, and people, effected through the violent proficiencies of Western power, was a process, as Césaire perspicaciously noted, of dehumanization that deferred, if not truncated, the quantum possibilities of future realities. And it is to those futures that the gaze of drones and satellite surveillance systems are being increasingly directed today. It is that gaze that will determine not only who occupies those horizons but also the ontological distinction between life and death.

ARTIST'S ACKNOWLEDGMENTS

The production of this book has been a collaborative process. I would particularly like to thank Anthony Downey for his editorial acuity, sensitivity, and rigor, Elisa Adami for her elegant, careful attention to every detail, Wayne Daly for his beautiful and elegant design, Thomas Kohn at Printmanagement Plitt for his fine work on the image reproduction, and Sternberg Press, particularly Caroline Schneider and Tatjana Günthner. I am also hugely thankful to Caterina Albano, Amin Alsaden, Jill Bennett, Giuliana Bruno, Martin A. Conway, Anthony Downey, Conor Gearty, Derek Gregory, Nick Grief, Andrew Hoskins, Catherine Loveday, William Merrin, Issie McPhail, Renata Salecl, and Gabriele Schwab for their insightful, thought-provoking, and inspiring contributions to this book, and to Sarah Stephenson for her meticulous copyediting. I am especially thankful to Gaëtane Verna for her commitment to art as a space for critical conversation, her insightful interview, and invaluable support in realizing this publication, new work, and exhibition. I am also very thankful to Amin Alsaden for his thoughtful consideration and care in curating the exhibition, Jacqueline Kok for her detailed curatorial work and all of their colleagues at The Power Plant.

Thank you to the many individuals and organizations that have collaborated, supported, and worked with me on the journey to realize these projects. For *Lesions in the Landscape*, a very special thank you to Claire for her insight, creativity, and being a wonderful traveling companion, Martin A. Conway for his intellectual generosity, conceptual thinking, and support over many years, Catherine Loveday for her clarity, knowledge, and brilliant advice, and for ideas explored with Jill Bennett, Issie MacPhail, and Caterina Albano, all of which have shaped this body of work. Thank you to Bevis Bowden for his creativity and resourcefulness, Carolyn Bonnyman, Besa Berberi, Angela MacLean, Charlie Fleming, Stefan Kazassoglou, and Jeff Knowler for amazing journeys in sound. Ron Henoqc, Roger McKinley, Mike Stubbs, and Andy McKinnon for their early support for the project. Thank you to Angus Smith and the *Elinca* crew, Alasdair Maceachen, Nickolai Globe, Beka Globe, Susan Bain, Paul Sharman, Kevin Grant, Gina Prior, Jacky Olsen, Kevin Dawe, Paul Fretwell, Tim Meacham, Lesley Taker, Lol Baker, Judith Carlton, Vivien Harland, David Allen, Felicity Fenner, Gareth Evans, David Cahill Roots, Jenny Paton, Meroe Candy, Kate Forde, Emily Sargent, Ken Arnold, James Peto, Ross Macfarlane, all the participants of the Amnesia Forums, Amnesia Lab and Symposia, FACT, Southwark Park Galleries, UNSW Galleries, Taigh Chearsabhagh Museum and Arts Centre, Whitechapel Gallery, The Wellcome Trust, University of Kent, National Trust Scotland, and Scottish Screen Archives.

For *Topologies of Air*, I am especially thankful to Marta Michalowska, Thomas Zanon-Larcher, Josh Wright, and The Wapping Project for their commitment, enthusiasm, and support in realizing this work and to the British Council, University of Kent, and Arts Council England. I am very grateful to Sheikh Khalifa bin Ahmed Al Khalifa for his generous hospitality, Alyazeya Abdulmalek, Khalil Ebrahim Ahmed Ali Ajhaddad, and all at Bahrain Authority for Culture and Antiquities, and Sheikha Hoor Al Qasimi, Judith Greer, Reem Shadid, Momen Al Ajouz, Jinan Coulter, Alia Almari, and all at Sharjah Art Foundation for transformative artist residencies and invaluable support. Thank you also to Akbar Zaib, Manoj Nair, Aju Sebastian, Sunil Kumar, Marwan Shwaiki, Meher, Rene, Terry, and the many people I met and worked with. Thank you to Abdulaziz Mohammed, Ali Karimi, Balqees Fakhro, Giuse Maggi, Hasan Hujairi, Mahmood Al Shargawi, Mayasa Al Sowaidi,

Mohammed bin Nasser Al Khalifa, Steffen Laursen, Azhar Kubba, Hoda A. Alkhzaimi, Sheikh Majid Al Qassimi, James Lockhart, Toral Gajarawala, Mashhoor Ahmad Al-Wardat, Nada Raza, Ilias Fernini, Abdulaziz Abdulrahman Almusallam, Elham Seyedsayamdost, Riad Al Ajlani, and Khalifa Alhemeiri for their wonderful contributions to the Sky Forums and to this project. Thank you also to Matt Lee, Rebecca Newell, Claire Dixon, and Harriet Bowers at Imperial War Museum, London, Davi Kopenawa, Fiona Watson and Survival International, Luciano Zubillaga, Sophie Dyer, Campbell Munro, Jamie Wylde, Patrick Wright, Motitz Cheung, Sanna Moore, Noriyuki Kawano, the Centre for Peace, Hiroshima University, Hiroshi Harada, Keisuke Imanaka, Motoo Nakagawa, and especially Luli Van Der Does for ongoing collaborations. Thank you to Carolyn Bonnyman, Jeff Knowler, Tal Hendrikse, Peter Knight, and Bevis Bowden for your brilliant work on voice, sound, animation, and post-production, and to Philippe Frau-Nadal, Xan Márquez Caneda, and Hugh Clark. Thank you to Andy McKinnon, Ruth Little, and Taigh Chearsabhagh Museum and Arts Centre for your early support for this project.

For the Airspace Tribunal, a very special thank you to Nick Grief for his friendship, clarity of vision, rigour, and for being a wonderful collaborator, Kirsty Brimelow QC for her brilliant work as Counsel to the Tribunal, Andrew Byrnes for being an excellent Counsel to the Tribunal in Sydney, and to the speakers: Abrar Mechmechia, Adel Al Manthari, Alirio Uribe Munõz, Andreas Schüller, Andrew Hoskins, Anson Mackay, Anthony Downey, Baraa Shiban, Brett Biddington, Catherine Loveday, Chris Woods, Conor Gearty, Derek Gregory, Fadel Abdul Ghany, Felicity Ruby, Gabriele Schwab, Gbenga Oduntan, Jairus Grove, Jack Penashue, Jutta Weber, Kevin Bales CMG, Lisa Ling, Majid Rabet, Mark Sealy, Melanie Klinkner, Omar Mohammed, Pratap Chatterjee, Renata Salecl, Safdar Ahmed, Sara Mir, Sebastián Escobar Uribe, Sebastian Pfautsch, Steven Freeland, William Merrin, and Zrinka Bralo for the expertise, perspectives, and experience that they have brought to these discussions, and participating audiences (the judges). Thank you also to Steven Powles QC, Jonathan Cooper OBE, and all at Doughty Street Chambers for their early support. Thank you to Jill Bennett, Jackie Dent, Andrea Durbach, Melissa Neidorf, the Big Anxiety Festival, Simon Longstaff, the Ethics Centre, Sydney, Gaëtane Verna, Josh Hueman, and all at The Power Plant, Charles Stankievech and the Daniels Faculty, University of Toronto, Wolfgang Kaleck, Andreas Schüller, Kitty Austin, and all at the European Center for Constitutional and Human Rights, University of Kent, and *Journal of Digital War*. Very many thanks to Andrew Hoskins and Martin A. Conway for our collaborations and critical discussions over many years, and to Renata Salecl and Anthony Downey for inspiring conversations that are continuing to expand and develop this work.

Thank you always to Noo Philipson and Teri Harris, and to Kevin Caulfield, Hylton Murray Philipson, and Anson Mackay. A huge thank you to my family, Mark Sealy, my partner in life, time, and ideas, for his humor, critical thinking, and encouragement, my children Alina Sealy and Sonny (Antony) Sealy for their inspiration, energy, and love, my father, Dave Illingworth, and my mother, artist Lotte Glob, for always supporting creativity and for my growing up in a weather-world. They have all made this work possible.

FILM CREDITS

Lesions in the Landscape (2015)

Shona Illingworth
Three-screen video and multichannel sound installation
35 mins

Produced by FACT in association with CGP London and Dilston Grove, UNSW Galleries, and Taigh Chearsabhagh Museum and Art Centre. Supported by the Wellcome Trust, with additional support from the University of Kent.

Voices (in order of appearance):
Carolyn Bonnyman, Claire, Issie MacPhail, Martin A. Conway, Angela Maclean
Conceived, directed, and edited by: Shona Illingworth
Cinematography: Bevis Bowden
Sound recording and mixing: Charlie Fleming
Additional sound mixing: Jeff Knowler
Additional sound recording: Iain Copeland
Custom software design and technical installation (audio): Stefan Kazassoglou (Kinicho)
Video synchronization software design: Adrian Riffo
Research support, St Kilda: Issie MacPhail

Music:
"Salm Volume 1: Stornoway," Psalm 133. Courtesy of Bethesda Care Home and Hospice
"7 Ninulla Dite Te Javes," Besa Berberi

Archive film:
Courtesy the Scottish Screen Archive, NLS

Additional texts:
Martin Martin, "A Description of the Western Isles of Scotland," 1703
Issie MacPhail, "Beyond Euclidian Convenience: Notes on the Paper Artifice of St Kilda," 2015
François Rabelais, "Pantagruel: Le Quatre Livre," 1552
Peter Davidson, "The Idea of North," 2007

Time Present (2016)

Shona Illingworth
Two-screen video installation
35 mins
Voices in order of appearance:
Claire, Carolyn Bonnyman, Martin A. Conway, Issie MacPhail
Conceived, filmed, directed, and edited by: Shona Illingworth
Additional camera: Bevis Bowden
Sound mix: Jeff Knowler

Time Present was developed in creative dialogue with Claire and neuropsychologists Martin A. Conway and Catherine Loveday.

Topologies of Air (2021)

Shona Illingworth
Three-channel digital video, multichannel sound
45 mins

Topologies of Air was commissioned and funded by The Wapping Project. The production was supported by Bahrain Authority for Culture and Antiquities, Sharjah Art Foundation, and the British Council, DCMS, and GREAT through the UK-Gulf Exhibition Program, as well as a travel grant from Arts Council England.

Voices (in order of appearance):
Ilias Fernini, Kevin Bales, Sebastian Pfautsch, Sophie Dyer, Kirsty Brimelow QC, Carolyn Bonnyman, Abdulaziz Mohammed, Giuse Maggi, Abdulaziz Abdulrahman Almusallam, Conor Gearty, Anson Mackay, Hiroshi Harada, Luli Van Der Does, Keisuke Imanaka, Majid Rabet, Lola Young, Steffen Laursen, Steven Freeland, Toral Gajarawala, Mark Sealy, William Merrin, Andrew Hoskins, Davi Kopanawa

Additional text: Sven Lindqvist, "A History of Bombing," 2001
Additional music: Tal Hendrikse, Jeff Knowler, and Azhar Kubba

Archive film: Courtesy the Imperial War Museum, London, NASA, and ESA.

Conceived, filmed, directed, and edited by: Shona Illingworth
Additional sound recording: Philippe Frau-Nadal, Xan Márquez Caneda, Khalil Ebrahim Ahmed Ali Ajhaddad, Akbar Zaib
Final image grade: Bevis Bowden
Sound mix: Jeff Knowler
Sound design: Tal Hendrikse
Animation: Peter Knight

Airspace Tribunal

The Airspace Tribunal hearings formed an integral part of the content and production of *Topologies of Air* and a large body of associated artworks. They were supported in London 2018 by The Wapping Project, University of Kent, and Doughty Street Chambers; in Sydney 2019 by the Big Anxiety Festival, The Wapping Project, Arts Council England, and the Ethics Centre; in Toronto 2020 by The Power Plant; and in Berlin 2021 by the European Centre for Constitutional and Human Rights. Travel to Hiroshima was supported by Arts Council England and the Centre for Peace, Hiroshima University.